ORGANIZATIONAL BEHAVIOR: THE ESSENTIALS

ORGANIZATIONAL BEHAVIOR:
THE ESSENTIALS

DEBRA L. NELSON
Oklahoma State University

JAMES CAMPBELL QUICK
University of Texas at Arlington

WEST PUBLISHING COMPANY
Minneapolis/Saint Paul   New York   Los Angeles   San Francisco

PRODUCTION CREDITS
Text Design: Roslyn M. Stendehl, Dapper Design
Copyediting: Cathy Taylor
Composition: Carlisle Communications, Ltd.
Illustrations: Randy Miyake

WEST'S COMMITMENT TO THE ENVIRONMENT
In 1906, West Publishing Company began recycling materials left
over from the production of books. This began a tradition of
efficient and responsible use of resources. Today, up to 95
percent of our legal books and 70 percent of our college and school
texts are printed on recycled, acid-free stock. West also recycles
nearly 22 million pounds of scrap paper annually-the equivalent of
181,717 trees. Since the 1960s, West has devised ways to capture
and recycle waste inks, solvents, oils, and vapors created in the
printing process. We also recycle plastics of all kinds, wood, glass,
corrugated cardboard, and batteries, and have eliminated the use
of Styrofoam book packaging. We at West are proud of the longev-
ity and the scope of our commitment to the environment.

Production, Prepress, Printing and Binding by West Publishing Company.

 TEXT IS PRINTED ON 10% POST CONSUMER RECYCLED PAPER

British Library Cataloguing-in-Publication Data. A catalogue
record for this book is available from the British Library.

Library of Congress Cataloging-in-Publication Data

Nelson, Debra L., 1956-
     Organizational behavior : the essentials / Debra L. Nelson, James
Campbell Quick.
          p.   cm.
     Includes bibliographical references and index.
     ISBN 0-314-06436-2 (soft : alk. paper)
     1. Organizational behavior.   I. Quick, James C.   II. Title.
HD58.7.N443   1996
658.3—dc20
                                                    95-23788
                                                        CIP

To our students, who challenge us to be better than we are, who keep us in touch with reality, and who are the foundation of our careers.

CONTENTS

Chapter Two

Organizations 2001 and Managerial Challenges   18

Chapter Six

Learning and Performance Management   88

Chapter Nine

Chapter Ten

Chapter Twelve

Leadership and Followership   186

Chapter Sixteen

Organizational Culture 255

Chapter Seventeen

Career Management   273

Chapter Eighteen

Managing Change 289

PREFACE

The world of organizations is changing, and so is the way we teach organizational behavior. *Organizational Behavior: The Essentials* was developed to meet the needs expressed by many of our colleagues. Some of you are moving away from the traditional three-hour course that demands a 600-page, full-service textbook. OB is being taught in one or two-hour modules, as an alternative to principles of management, as part of larger, integrated courses, and in hundreds of other ways. *Organizational Behavior: The Essentials* is designed to offer the flexibility you need in these changing times.

Scholarly content is the hallmark of organizational behavior, the *OB: The Essentials* delivers the classic theories and research in a way that your students will enjoy. We've included contemporary, on-target examples throughout the text that reflect the application of OB issues in today's organizations. Specifically, we have keyed in on the tough challenges that managers face: product and service quality, globalization, diversity, technology, and ethics. *Essentials* is a streamlined book that combines scholarly content and managerial application to deliver a consistent message to students: knowledge of organizational behavior is essential for managers who want to succeed in a world of competitive challenges.

You will find that the pedagogy in *Essential Concepts* includes only the indispensable elements. We've included learning objectives at the outset of each chapter to provide a road map for students, and managerial implications, a chapter summary, and review questions at the close of each chapter. This provides you with the flexibility to use cases, experiential exercises, skill development activities, readings, or other pedagogical tools as you wish. You may have a favorite companion book that contains such tools, or you may have developed your own experiential exercises. *Essentials* is the perfect complement to these teaching aids, and allows you to tailor your organizational behavior course to achieve your objectives.

Debra L. Nelson
Stillwater, OK

James Campbell Quick
Arlington, TX

PART I
INTRODUCTION

CHAPTER 1
ORGANIZATIONAL BEHAVIOR
IN THE 1990s

LEARNING OBJECTIVES

After reading this chapter, you should be able to do the following:

- Define organizational behavior.
- Identify the important system components, as well as the formal and informal elements, of an organization.
- Briefly describe one hundred years of progress in the study of organizational behavior.
- Describe the important aspects of the Hawthorne Studies.
- Identify six interdisciplinary contributions to the study of organizational behavior.
- Recognize the importance of competition and quality in organizational behavior.
- Demonstrate the importance of objective knowledge and skill development in the study of organizational behavior.
- Understand the difference between manufacturing and service organizations in the economy, as illustrated in the six example companies described.

■ HUMAN BEHAVIOR IN ORGANIZATIONS

Organizational behavior is individual behavior and group dynamics in organizations. The study of organizational behavior is primarily concerned with the psychosocial, interpersonal, and behavioral dynamics in organizations. However, organizational variables that affect human behavior at work are also relevant to the study of organizational behavior. These organizational variables include jobs, the design of work, communication, performance appraisal, organizational design, and organizational structure. Therefore, although individual behavior and group dynamics are the primary concerns in the study of organizational behavior, organizational variables are important as the context in which human behavior occurs.

This chapter presents an introduction to organizational behavior. The first section provides an overview of human behavior in organizations. The second section includes a brief historical and interdisciplinary perspective on the field. The third section highlights the importance of competition and quality for organizational behavior in the 1990s. The fourth section addresses the application of knowledge and skill development when studying organizational behavior. The final section of the chapter briefly introduces six example companies used in the book.

Human behavior in organizations is complex and often difficult to understand. Organizations have been described as clockworks in which human behavior is logical and rational, but they often seem like snake pits to those who work in them.[1] The clockwork metaphor reflects an orderly, idealized view of organizational behavior devoid of conflict or dilemma because all the working parts (the people) mesh smoothly together. The snake pit metaphor conveys the daily conflict, distress, and struggle in organizations. Each metaphor reflects reality from a different point of view—the organization's versus the individual's point of view.

This section will briefly contrast two perspectives for understanding human behavior, the external and the internal perspectives. It will then discuss two important ways of describing organizations as systems: as open systems and as formal/informal systems. The study of organizational behavior requires an analysis of both the individual and the organization. Therefore, knowing about individual behavior and about organizations is important for mastering subsequent chapters.

■ Understanding Human Behavior

Most theories and models of human behavior fall into one of two basic categories: one has an internal perspective and the other an external perspective. The internal perspective considers factors inside the person to understand behavior. This view is psychodynamically oriented. People who subscribe to this view understand human behavior in terms of the thoughts, feelings, past experiences and needs of the individual. The internal perspective explains people's actions and behavior in terms of their history

and personal value systems. The internal processes of thinking, feeling, perceiving, and judging lead people to act in specific ways. The internal perspective has given rise to a wide range of motivational and leadership theories. This perspective implies that people are best understood from the inside and that people's behavior is best interpreted after understanding their thoughts and feelings.

The other category of theories and models of human behavior takes an external perspective. This perspective focuses on factors outside the person to understand behavior. People who subscribe to this view understand human behavior in terms of external events, consequences of behavior, and the environmental forces to which a person is subject. From the external perspective, a person's history, feelings, thoughts, and personal value systems are not very important in interpreting actions and behavior. This perspective has given rise to an alternative set of motivational and leadership theories. The external perspective implies that a person's behavior is best understood by examining the surrounding external events and environmental forces.

The internal and external perspectives offer alternative explanations for human behavior. For example, the internal perspective might say Mary is an outstanding employee because she has a high need for achievement, whereas the external perspective might say Mary is an outstanding employee because she is paid extremely well for her work. Kurt Lewin captured both perspectives in saying that behavior is a function of both the person and the environment.[2]

■ Organizations As Systems

Just as two different perspectives offer complementary explanations for human behavior, two other perspectives provide complementary explanations of organizations. Organizations are systems of interacting components: people, tasks, technology, and structure. These internal components also interact with components in the organization's task environment. Open systems are those which interact dynamically with their environments. Organizations as open systems have people, technology, structure, and purpose, which interact with elements in the organization's environment.

What, exactly, is an organization? The corporation is the dominant organizational form for much of the twentieth-century Western world, but other organizational forms have dominated other times and societies. Some societies have been dominated by religious organizations, such as the temple corporations of ancient Mesopotamia and the churches in colonial America.[3] Other societies have been dominated by military organizations, such as the clans of the Scottish Highlands and the regional armies of the People's Republic of China.[4,5] All these societies are woven together by family organizations, which themselves may vary from nuclear and extended families to small, collective communities.[6] The purpose and structure of the religious, military, and family organizational forms may vary, but people's behavior in these organizations may be very similar. In fact, early discoveries about power and leadership in work organizations were remarkably similar to findings about power and leadership within families.[7]

Organizations may manufacture products, such as aircraft components or steel, or deliver services, such as managing money or providing insurance protection. To understand how organizations do these things requires an understanding of the open system components of the organization and the components of its task environment.

Leavitt sets out a basic framework for understanding organizations, emphasizing four major internal components: task, people, technology, and structure.[8] These four components, along with the organization's inputs, outputs, and key elements in the task environment, are depicted in Figure 1.1. The task of the organization is its mission, purpose, or goal for existing. The people are the human resources of the organization. The technology is the wide range of tools, knowledge, and/or techniques used to transform the inputs into outputs. The structure is the way work is designed at the micro level, as well as the way departments, divisions, and the overall organization are designed at the macro level.

■ **FIGURE 1.1**
A Systems View of Organization

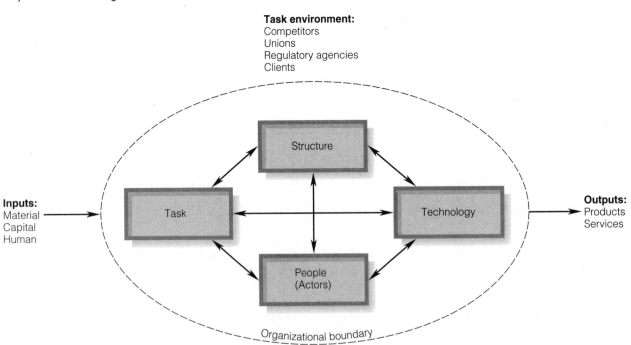

Source: A Framework for Viewing Organizational Health. Based on Harold Leavitt, "Applied Organizational Change in Industry: Structural, Technological, and Humanistic Approaches," in J. G. March (ed.), *Handbook of Organizations*, Rand McNally, Chicago, 1965, p. 1145.

In addition to these major internal components of the organization as a system, there is the organization's external task environment. The task environment is composed of different constituents, such as suppliers, customers, and federal regulators. Thompson describes the task environment as that element of the environment related to the organization's degree of goal attainment; that is, the task environment is composed of those elements of the environment related to the organization's basic task. For example, when steel was a major component in the production of cars, U.S. Steel was a major supplier for General Motors and Ford Motor Company—U.S. Steel was a major component of their task environments. As less steel and more aluminum was used to make cars, U.S. Steel became a less important supplier for General Motors and Ford—it was no longer a major component in their task environments.

The organization system works by taking inputs, converting them into throughputs, and delivering outputs to its task environment. Inputs consist of the human, informational, material, and financial resources used by the organization. Throughputs are the materials and resources as they are transformed by the organization's technology component. Once the transformation is complete, they become outputs for customers, consumers, and clients. The actions of suppliers, customers, regulators, and other elements of the task environment affect the organization and the behavior of people at work. For example, Onsite Engineering and Management, Inc., of Norcross, Georgia, experienced a threat to its survival in the mid-1980s by being totally dependent on one large utility for its outputs. By broadening its client base and improving the quality of its services (that is, its outputs) over the next several years, Onsite became a healthier, more successful small company. Transforming inputs into high-quality outputs is critical to an organization's success.

The Formal/Informal Organization Perspective

The "system" view of organization may lead one to see the design of an organization as a clockwork with a neat, precise, interrelated functioning. The formal organization is the part of the system that has legitimacy and official recognition. The snake pit

organizational metaphor mentioned earlier has its roots in the study and examination of the informal organization, which is the unofficial part of the system. The informal organization was first fully appreciated as a result of the Hawthorne Studies (which we will discuss in the next section) conducted during the 1920s and 1930s. The formal and informal elements of the organization are depicted in Figure 1.2.

Potential conflict between the formal and informal elements of the organization makes an understanding of both important. Conflicts between these two elements erupted in many organizations during the early years of this century and were embodied in the union-management strife of that era. The conflicts escalated into violence in a number of cases. For example, every supervisor in the Homestead Works of U.S. Steel was issued a pistol and a box of ammunition during the 1920s "just in case" it was necessary to shoot an unruly, dangerous steelworker. Not all organizations are characterized by such potential formal-informal, management-labor conflict. During the same era, Eastman Kodak was very progressive. The company helped with financial backing for employees' neighborhood communities, such as Meadowbrook in Rochester, New York. Kodak's concern for employees and attention to informal issues made unions unnecessary within the company.

The informal organization is a frequent point of diagnostic and intervention activities in organization development.[9] The informal organization is important because people's feelings, thoughts, and attitudes about their work do make a difference in their behavior and performance. Individual behavior plays out in the context of the formal and informal elements of the system, becoming organizational behavior. The existence of the informal organization was one of the major discoveries of the Hawthorne Studies, a landmark in the study of organizational behavior.

A BRIEF HISTORICAL PERSPECTIVE

Organizational behavior may be traced back thousands of years, as noted in Sterba's analysis of the ancient Mesopotamian temple corporations. However, we will focus on the modern history of organi-

■ **FIGURE 1.2**
Formal and Informal
Elements of Organizations

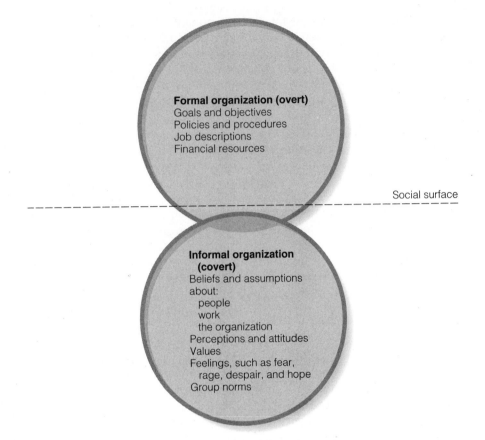

Formal organization (overt)
Goals and objectives
Policies and procedures
Job descriptions
Financial resources

Social surface

**Informal organization
(covert)**
Beliefs and assumptions
about:
 people
 work
 the organization
Perceptions and attitudes
Values
Feelings, such as fear,
 rage, despair, and hope
Group norms

zational behavior, which dates to the late nineteenth century. One of the more important series of studies conducted during this period was the Hawthorne Studies. As these and other studies have unfolded, a number of disciplines have contributed to the advancement of organizational behavior. After an overview of the progress during the past century, we will discuss the Hawthorne Studies and the influence of the various disciplines on the current study of organizational behavior.

■ One Hundred Years of Progress

Progress in any discipline, practice, or field of study is measured by significant events, discoveries, and contributions over time. The history of organizational behavior begins with the work of Frederick Taylor in scientific management at Midvale Steel Company, Bethlehem Steel Company, and elsewhere.[10] Taylor applied engineering principles to the

study of people and their behavior at work. He pioneered the use of performance standards for workers, set up differential piece-rate systems of pay, and argued for the scientific selection of employees. His ultimate hope was for an improvement in labor-management relationships in American industry. Taylor's lasting contributions include organizational goal-setting programs, incentive pay systems, and modern employee selection techniques.

Table 1.1 is a brief time line beginning in the 1890s. It notes major events in the evolving study of human behavior in organizations. The late nineteenth century saw the United States make the transition from an agricultural to an industrial society. The twentieth century has seen many important discoveries and advances. Walter Cannon's discovery of the stress response around 1915 laid a foundation for psychosomatic medicine, industrial hygiene, and an understanding of the emotional components of health at work and play.[11] The Haw-

■ **TABLE 1.1**
One Hundred Years of Progress in Organizational Behavior

1890s	Frederick Taylor's development of scientific management
1900s	Max Weber's concept of bureaucracy and the Protestant Ethic
1910s	Walter Cannon's discovery of the "emergency (stress) response"
1920s	Elton Mayo's illumination studies in the textile industry
	The Hawthorne Studies at Western Electric Company
1930s	Kurt Lewin's, Ronald Lippitt's, and Ralph White's early leadership studies
1940s	Abraham Maslow's need hierarchy theory of motivation
	B. F. Skinner's formulation of the behavioral approach
	Charles Walker's and Robert Guest's studies of routine work
1950s	Ralph Stogdill's Ohio State leadership studies
	Norman Maier's psychological approach to industrial organization
	Douglas McGregor's examination of the human side of enterprise
	Frederick Herzberg's two-factor theory of motivation and job enrichment
1960s	Arthur Turner's & Paul Lawrence's studies of diverse industrial jobs
	Robert Blake's and Jane Mouton's managerial grid
	Patricia Cain Smith's studies of satisfaction in work and retirement
	Fred Fiedler's contingency theory of leadership
1970s	J. Richard Hackman's and Greg Oldham's job characteristics theory
	Edward Lawler's approach to pay and organizational effectiveness
	Robert House's path-goal and charismatic theories of leadership
	Chris Arygsis' theory of organizational learning
1980s	Peter Block's political skills for empowered managers
	Edgar Schein's approach to leadership and organizational culture
1990s	Peter Senge's Fifth Discipline approach to the learning organization

thorne Studies, discussed in the next section of the chapter, formed the major research advancement in understanding people at work during the 1920s and 1930s.[12] Beginning at the end of the 1930s, a series of motivational theories were proposed over several decades to explain human behavior.[13-15] During the same time period, a series of leadership studies unfolded whose intent was to explain the power and influence dynamics of leader-follower relationships.[16,17] Other research during the century has attempted to explain small group behavior,[18] the design of work,[19] job satisfaction,[20] and a psychological approach to industrial problems.[21]

■ **The Hawthorne Studies**

Initiated in 1925 with a grant from Western Electric, the Hawthorne Studies were among the most significant advances in the understanding of organizational behavior during the past century. They were preceded by a series of studies of illumination conducted by Elton Mayo in the textile industry of Philadelphia. The research at the Hawthorne Works (an industrial manufacturing facility in Cicero, Illinois) was directed by Fritz Roethlisberger and consisted of four separate studies over a seven-year period.[22] These studies included (1) experiments in illumination, (2) the relay assembly test room study, (3) experiments in interviewing workers, and (4) the bank wiring room study. We will briefly examine this research program.

Experiments in Illumination. As a direct follow-up of Mayo's earlier work in the textile industry, illumination experiments were conducted at Hawthorne. They consisted of a series of studies of test groups, in which the researchers varied illumination levels, and control groups, in which conditions were held constant. The purpose was to examine the relation of the quality and quantity of illumination to the efficiency of industrial workers. The experiments began in 1925 and extended over several years.

The researchers were surprised to discover that productivity increased to roughly the same rate in both test and control groups. It was only in the final experiment, where they decreased illumination levels to 0.06 footcandle (roughly moonlight intensity), that an appreciable decline in output occurred. The anticipated finding of a positive, linear relationship between illumination and industrial efficiency was simply not found. The researchers concluded that the results were "screwy" in the absence of this simple, direct cause-and-effect relationship.

It is from these first experiments that the term Hawthorne Effect was coined, referring to the fact that people behave differently when they are being studied than they might otherwise behave. The researchers concluded that human motivation played a role for which they had not accounted in the research design.

Relay Assembly Test Room Study. The researchers next set out to study workers segregated according to a range of working condition variables, such as work room temperature and humidity, work schedule, rest breaks, and food consumption. The researchers chose five women in the relay assembly test room and kept careful records of the predictor variables, as well as output (measuring the time it took each woman to assemble a telephone relay of approximately forty parts).

Again, there was little the researchers were able to conclude from the actual data in this study in terms of a relationship between the predictor variables and industrial efficiency. However, they began to suspect that employee attitudes and sentiments were critically important variables not previously accounted for. Therefore, the researchers underwent a radical change of thought.

Experiments in Interviewing Workers. In 1928, a number of the researchers went into the work force, without their normal tools and equipment, for the purpose of getting the workers to talk about what was important to them. Nearly 20,000 workers were interviewed over a period of two years, and in this interviewing process a major breakthrough occurred. The interview study was a form of research in which the investigators did not have a set of preconceptions concerning what they would find, as was the case in the two earlier phases of research. Rather, they set out to listen, sympathetically and skillfully, to what each worker was saying. As the interviewing progressed, the researchers discovered that the workers would open up and talk freely about what were the most important, and at times

problematic, issues on their minds. The researchers discovered a rich and intriguing world previously unexamined within the Hawthorne Works.

Ultimately, Roethlisberger and his colleagues formulated guidelines for the conduct of interviews, and these guidelines became the basis for contemporary interviewing and active listening skills.[23] The discovery of the informal organization and its relationship to the formal organization, as was shown in Figure 1.2, began during the interview study. This led to a richer understanding of the social, interpersonal dynamics of people at work.

The Bank Wiring Room Study. The concluding study at Hawthorne was significant because it confirmed the importance of one aspect of the informal organization on worker productivity. Specifically, the researchers studied workers in the bank wiring room and found that the behavioral norms set by the work group had a powerful influence over the productivity of the group. The higher the norms, the greater the productivity. The lower the norms, the lower the productivity. The power of the peer group and the importance of group influence on individual behavior and productivity were confirmed in the bank wiring room.

The Hawthorne Studies laid a foundation for understanding people's social and psychological behavior in the workplace. Some of the methods used at Hawthorne, such as the experimental design methods and the interviewing technique, are used today for research in organizations. However, the discipline of organizational behavior is more than the psychology of people at work and more than the sociology of their behavior in organizations. Organizational behavior emerges from a wide range of interdisciplinary influences.

■ Interdisciplinary Influences

Organizational behavior is a blended discipline that has grown out of contributions from numerous earlier fields of study. These interdisciplinary influences are the roots for what is increasingly recognized as the independent discipline of organizational behavior. The sciences of psychology, sociology, engineering, anthropology, management, and medicine are the primary fields of study out of which organizational behavior has grown. Each of these sciences has had its own important and unique influence on the discipline of organizational behavior.

Psychology, the science of human behavior, dates back to the closing decades of the nineteenth century. Psychology traces its own origins to philosophy and the science of physiology. One of the most prominent early psychologists, William James, actually held a degree in medicine (M.D.). Since its origin, psychology has itself become differentiated into a number of specialized fields, such as clinical, experimental, military, organizational, and social psychology. The topics in organizational psychology—including work teams, work motivation, training and development, power and leadership, human resource planning, and workplace wellness-are very similar to the topics covered by organizational behavior.[24]

Robert Yerkes was an early leader in the field of psychology. His research efforts for the American military during World War I had implications later for sophisticated personnel selection methods used by corporations such as Johnson & Johnson, Valero Energy, and Chaparral Steel.[25]

Sociology, the science of society, has made important contributions to knowledge about group and intergroup dynamics in the study of organizational behavior. Because sociology takes the society rather than the individual as its point of departure, the sociologist is concerned with the variety of roles within a society or culture, the norms and standards of behavior that emerge within societies and groups, and the examination of the consequences of compliant and deviant behavior within social groups. For example, Robert Merton's concept of role set was a key contribution to role theory.[26] The role set consisted of a person in a social role and all others who had expectations of the person. A team of Harvard educators used the concept to study the school superintendent role in Massachusetts.[27] These sociological contributions were the basis for subsequent studies of role conflict and ambiguity in companies such as Tenneco, Purex, and The Western Company of North America.

Engineering, the applied science of energy and matter, has made important contributions to our understanding of the design of work. By taking basic engineering ideas and applying them to human behavior in work organizations, Frederick Tay-

lor had a profound influence on the early years of the study of organizational behavior. Taylor's engineering background led him to place special emphasis on human productivity and efficiency in work behavior. His notions of performance standards and differential piece-rate systems contributed to a congressional investigation into scientific management at the behest of organized labor.[28] Taylor was ahead of his times in many ways, and his ideas were often controversial during his lifetime. However, the application of his original ideas is embedded in organizational goal-setting programs, such as at Black & Decker, IBM, and Weyerhaeuser. Even the notions of stress and strain have their origins in the lexicon of engineering.

Anthropology, the science of human learned behavior, is especially important to understanding organizational culture. Cultural anthropology focuses on the origins of culture and the patterns of behavior that develop as culture is communicated symbolically. Current research in this tradition has examined the effects of efficient cultures on organization performance and how pathological personalities may lead to dysfunctional organizational cultures.[29] Schwartz used a psychodynamic, anthropological mode of inquiry in exploring the corporate decay in General Motors and NASA during the 1980s.[30]

Management, originally called administrative science, is a discipline concerned with the study of overseeing activities and supervising people in organizations. It emphasizes the design, implementation, and management of various administrative and organizational systems. March and Simon take the human organization as their point of departure and concern themselves with the administrative practices that will enhance the effectiveness of the system.[31] Management is the first discipline to take the modern corporation as the unit of analysis, and this viewpoint distinguishes the discipline's contribution to the study of organizational behavior.

Medicine is the applied science of healing or treatment of diseases to enhance an individual's health and well-being. Medicine embraces concern for both physical and psychological health, with the concern for industrial mental health which dates back at least sixty years.[32] More recently, as the war against acute diseases is being won, medical attention has shifted from these diseases, such as influenza, to the more chronic, such as hypertension.[33] Individual behavior and lifestyle patterns play a more important role in treating chronic diseases than in treating acute diseases. These trends have contributed to the growth of wellness programs in the context of corporate medicine, such as Johnson & Johnson's "Live for Life" program and Control Data Corporation's STAYWELL program. These programs have led to the increasing attention to medicine in organizational behavior. The surge in health care costs through the past two decades has increased organizational concern with medicine and health care in the workplace.[34]

■ COMPETITION AND QUALITY IN THE 1990s

Historically, organizations in the United States did not face the competition they do today. Competition in the U.S. and world economies has increased significantly during the past couple of decades, especially in industries such as banking, finance, and air transportation. For example, Motorola became concerned in the early 1980s about its competitive edge as an organization. Corporate competition creates performance and cost pressures for management, which has a ripple effect on people and their behavior at work. U.S. corporations anticipate continuing competitive pressure through the 1990s. This pressure has implications for motivation, leadership, followership, and other aspects of people's behavior at work. Scientech, a small power and energy company headquartered in Idaho Falls, Idaho, found it had to enhance its managerial talent and service quality to meet the challenges of growth and big-company competitors. Product and service quality is one of the leading-edge issues that distinguish the winners from the losers in a competitive environment. Problem-solving skills used by IBM, CDC, Northwest Airlines and Northwestern National Life help achieve high-quality products and services. Quality is the overarching theme for people preparing for work in the 1990s.

■ International Competition in Business

Organizations in the U.S. are changing radically in response to increased international competition. Ac-

cording to noted economist Lester Thurow, the next several decades in business will be characterized by intense competition between the U.S., Japan, and Europe in core industries.[35] Economic competition will place pressure on all categories of employees to be productive and to add value to the firm. The uncertainty of unemployment resulting from corporate warfare and competition is an ongoing feature of organizational life for people in companies or industries that pursue cost-cutting strategies to achieve economic success. The international competition in the automotive industry between the Japanese, U.S., and European car companies embodies the intensity that can be expected in other industries in the future.

Some people feel that the future must be the focus in coming to grips with this international competition, whereas others believe we can deal with the future only by studying the past. Global, economic, and organizational changes will have dramatic effects on the study and management of organizational behavior.

Success in international competition requires organizations to be more responsive to ethnic, religious, and gender diversity in the work force. Work force demographic change will be a critical challenge in itself for the study and management of organizational behavior.[36] The theories of motivation, leadership, and group behavior based on research in a work force of one composition may not be applicable in a work force of a very different composition. This may be especially problematic if ethnic, gender, and/or religious differences lead to conflict between leaders and followers in organizations. For example, the former Soviet Union's military establishment found ethnic and religious conflicts between the officers and enlisted corps a real impediment to unit cohesion and performance during the 1980s.

■ Quality: The Competitive Cutting Edge

Quality has the potential to give organizations in viable industries the competitive edge in meeting international competition. Quality has become a rubric for products and services that are of high status. Total quality has been defined in many ways. We define total quality management (TQM) as the total dedication to continuous improvement and to customers, so that the customers' needs are met and their expectations exceeded. Quality is a customer-oriented philosophy of management with important implications for virtually all aspects of organizational behavior. Quality cannot be optimized, because customer needs and expectations are always changing. Quality is a cultural value embedded in highly successful organizations. Ford Motor Company's dramatic metamorphosis during the 1980s is attributable to the decision to "make quality Job One" in all aspects of the design and manufacture of cars, and AT&T uses total quality management to tackle environmental challenges, such as office pollution. AT&T also established a corporate TQM team to reduce excess paper utilization.

The pursuit of total quality improves the probability of organizational success in increasingly competitive industries. Quality is more than a fad; it is an enduring feature of an organization's culture and of the economic competition we face in the 1990s. Quality is not an end in itself. It leads to competitive advantage through customer responsiveness, results acceleration, and resource effectiveness.[37] The three key questions in evaluating quality-improvement ideas for people at work are these: (1) Does the idea improve customer response? (2) Does the idea accelerate results? and (3) Does the idea raise the effectiveness of resources? A "yes" answer to any or all of these questions means the idea should be implemented to improve total quality. Total quality is also dependent upon the ways people behave at work.

■ Behavior and Quality at Work

Whereas total quality may draw upon reliability engineering or just-in-time management, total quality improvement can be successful only when employees have the skills and authority to respond to customer needs. Total quality has direct and important effects on the behavior of employees at all levels in the organization, not just on employees working directly with customers. Chief executives can advance total quality by engaging in participative management, being willing to change everything, focusing quality efforts on customer service (not cost cutting), including quality as a criterion in reward systems, improving the flow of information regarding quality improvement successes or failures, and being actively and personally involved in quality efforts. George Fisher, while Chairman at Motorola,

considered behavioral attributes such as leadership, cooperation, communication and participation to be very important elements for an effective total quality system[38].

Quality has become so important to our future competitiveness that the U.S. Department of Commerce now sponsors an annual award in the name of Malcolm Baldrige, former secretary of commerce in the Reagan administration, to recognize companies excelling in total quality management. The Malcolm Baldrige National Quality Award examination evaluates an organization on seven categories: leadership, information and analysis, strategic quality planning, human resource utilization, quality assurance of products and services, quality results, and customer satisfaction.

According to former president George Bush, "Quality management is not just a strategy. It must be a new style of working, even a new style of thinking. A dedication to quality and excellence is more than good business. It is a way of life, giving something back to society, offering your best to others."

Quality is the watchword for competitive success during the 1990s and beyond[39]. Organizations that do not respond to customer needs will find their customers choosing alternative product and service suppliers who are willing to exceed customer expectations. With this said, you should not conclude that total quality is a panacea for all organizations or that total quality guarantees unqualified success.

■ Managing Organizational Behavior in the 1990s

Over and above the challenge of enhancing quality to meet international competition, managing organizational behavior during the 1990s will be challenging for at least four reasons: (1) the increasing globalization of organizations' operating territory, (2) the increasing diversity of organizational work forces, (3) continuing technological innovation with its companion need for skill enhancement, and (4) the continuing demand for higher levels of moral and ethical behavior at work. These will be the issues managers need to address in managing people at work.

Each of these four issues will be explored in detail in Chapter 2 and highlighted throughout the text, because they are intertwined in the contemporary practice of organizational behavior. For example, the issue of women in the workplace concerns work force diversity while at the same time overlapping the globalization issue. Gender roles are often defined differently in various cultures and societies. In addition, sexual harassment is a frequent ethical problem for organizations as more women enter the work force. The student of organizational behavior must appreciate and understand the importance of these issues.

■ APPLYING ORGANIZATIONAL BEHAVIOR

Organizational behavior is neither a purely scientific area of inquiry nor a strictly intellectual endeavor. It involves the study of abstract ideas, such as valence and expectancy in motivation, as well as the study of concrete matters, such as observable behaviors and physiological symptoms of distress at work. Therefore, applying organizational behavior study is a three-step process, as shown in Figure 1.3. First, it requires the mastery of a certain body of objective knowledge, which results from research and scholarly activities. Second, the study of organizational behavior requires skill development and the mastery of abilities essential to successful functioning in organizations. Third, it requires the integration of objective knowledge and skill development in order to apply both appropriately in specific organizational settings.

■ Objective Knowledge

Objective knowledge in any field of study is developed through basic and applied research. Research in organizational behavior has continued since Frederick Taylor's early research on scientific manage-

ment. Acquiring objective knowledge requires the cognitive mastery of theories, conceptual models, and research findings. The objective knowledge in each chapter is reflected in the notes used to support the text material. Mastering the concepts and ideas in these notes enables you to discuss motivation and performance, leadership, executive stress and similar topics intelligently.

We encourage instructors and students of organizational behavior to think critically about the objective knowledge in this field. Only by engaging in critical thinking can one question or challenge the results of specific research and responsibly consider how to apply research results in a particular work setting. Rote memorization will not enable the student to appreciate the complexity of specific theories or the interrelationships among concepts, ideas, and topics. Good critical thinking, in contrast, enables the student to identify inconsistencies and limitations in the current body of objective knowledge.

Critical thinking, based on knowledge and understanding of basic ideas, leads to inquisitive exploration. A questioning, probing attitude is at the core of critical thinking. The student should evolve into a critical consumer of knowledge related to organizational behavior—one who is able to question the latest research results intelligently and distinguish plausible, sound new approaches from fads that lack substance or adequate foundation. Ideally, the student of organizational behavior will become a scientific professional manager, knowledgeable in the art and science of organizational behavior.

■ Skill Development

Learning about organizational behavior requires doing, as well as knowing. The development of skills and abilities requires that students be challenged, by

■ FIGURE 1.3
Learning about Organizational Behavior

the instructor or by themselves. Skill development is a very active component of the learning process.

The U.S. Department of Labor is concerned that people achieve the necessary skills to be successful in the workplace.[40] The department identifies these skills as essential: (1) resource management skills, such as time management; (2) information management skills, such as data interpretation; (3) personal interaction skills, such as teamwork; (4) systems behavior and performance skills, such as cause-effect relationships; and (5) technology-utilization skills, such as troubleshooting. Many of these skills, such as decision making and information management, are directly related to the study of organizational behavior.

Developing skills is different from acquiring objective knowledge because it requires structured practice and feedback. A key function of experiential learning is to engage the student in individual or group activities that are systematically reviewed, leading to new skills and understanding. Objective knowledge acquisition and skill development are interrelated. The student engages in an individual or group structured activity and systematically reviews that activity, which leads to new or modified knowledge and skills. If skill development and structured learning occur in this way, there should be an inherently self-correcting element to learning because of the modification of the student's knowledge and skills over time. To ensure that skill development does occur and that the learning is self-correcting as it occurs, three basic assumptions must underlie this approach to learning.

First, each student must accept responsibility for his or her own behavior, actions, and learning. A group cannot learn for its members. Each member must accept responsibility for what he or she does and learns. Denial of responsibility helps no one, least of all the learner.

Second, each student must participate actively in the individual or group structured learning activity. Structured learning is not passive; it is active. In group activities, everyone suffers if just one person adopts a passive attitude.

Third, each student must be open to new information, new skills, new ideas, and experimentation–not indiscriminately, but with a nondefensive, open attitude so that change is possible through the learning process.

■ Application of Knowledge and Skills

One of the advantages of structured, experiential learning is that a person can explore new behaviors and skills in a comparatively safe environment. Losing your temper in a classroom activity and learning about the potential adverse impact on other people will probably have dramatically different consequences from losing your temper with an important customer in a tense work situation. The ultimate objective of skill development and experiential learning is to transfer the learning process from structured activities in the classroom to unstructured opportunities in the workplace.

Although organizational behavior is an applied discipline, a student is not "trained" in organizational behavior. Rather, one is "educated" in organizational behavior. The distinction between these two modes of learning is found in the degree of direct and immediate applicability of either knowledge or skills. As an activity, training more nearly ties direct objective knowledge or skill development to specific applications. By contrast, education enhances a person's residual pool of objective knowledge and skills that may then be selectively applied later— sometimes significantly later—when the opportunity presents itself.

■ SIX EXAMPLE COMPANIES

Organizational behavior always occurs in the context of a specific organizational setting. Most attempts at explaining or predicting organizational behavior rely heavily on factors within the organization and give less weight to external environmental considerations. We think it is important for students to be sensitive to the industrial context of organizations and to develop an appreciation for an organization as a whole. In this vein, we have drawn very brief profiles of six prominent companies within the U.S. economy.

The U.S. economy is the largest in the world, with gross domestic purchases at nearly $5 trillion in 1991. The major sectors of the economy are: service (37 percent) and product manufacture for nondurable goods (21 percent) and durable goods (9 percent). Taken together, the production of products and the delivery of services account for 67 percent of the U.S. economy. Government and fixed investments account for the remaining 33 percent. Large and small organizations operate in each sector of the economy.

Our primary, but not exclusive, focus is on the private sectors of the economy. The manufacturing sector includes the production of basic materials, such as steel, and the production of finished products, such as automobiles and electronic equipment. The service sector of the economy includes transportation, financial services, insurance, and retail sales. We have chosen three manufacturing and three service organizations to describe briefly here, and to use examples from throughout the text. The three manufacturing organizations are Chaparral Steel Company, Ford Motor Company, and Motorola. The three service organizations are Federal Express, NWNL Companies, and Southwest Airlines.

These six organizations, like hundreds of others they represent, make important and unique contributions to the manufacturing and service sectors of the national economy. These companies are joined by hundreds of other small, medium, and large organizations which make valuable and significant contributions to the economic health of the U.S. We use brief examples from these six and many other organizations throughout the book. We hope that by better understanding these organizations, you have a greater appreciation for your own organization and others in the diverse world of private business enterprises.

■ Chaparral Steel Company

Chaparral Steel Company produces bar and medium-sized structural steel products from scrap steel. Much of its scrap steel comes from used cars. Chaparral can shred a car in eighteen seconds and begin steel production with the results. The company owns and operates a technologically advanced steel mill located in Midlothian, Texas. Chaparral Steel is a small- to medium-sized manufacturing company with fewer than 1,000 employees. The officers of the company describe themselves as refugees from the large, bureaucratic steel companies, which they found inhibiting. Gordon Forward, the president and chief executive officer, is an interna-

tionally recognized metallurgist and steel industry leader.[41] Chaparral Steel outperforms all other domestic and foreign steel companies in the amount of steel produced per person each year. The company is recognized around the world for its excellence and high-quality steel products, as indicated by its recognition with the Japanese Industrial Standard (JIS) certification.

■ Ford Motor Company

Ford Motor Company is the world's second largest industrial corporation, serving the automobile, agricultural, financial, and communications industries through three operating groups. Ford is probably best known for the cars and trucks that its Automotive Group manufactures, assembles, and sells. Ford has tens of thousands of employees, billions of dollars in sales each year, and operating locations all over the world. At the end of the 1970s, Ford committed itself to "making quality Job One" in the production of its cars and trucks. The 1980s saw an internal revolution within Ford Motor Company, resulting in a dramatic improvement in its financial health and the quality of its cars and trucks.[42] With continuing quality pressure from the Japanese and domestic pressure for safer and more fuel efficient cars, Ford faces challenges through the 1990s and the early twenty-first century.

■ Motorola

Motorola provides electronics equipment, system components, and services for markets throughout the world. Motorola is a large manufacturing organization that has been recognized for excellence with the Malcolm Baldrige National Quality Award. The company is headquartered near Chicago and has operating locations throughout the U.S. and the world. Motorola has a long history of, and takes great pride in, the ability to create world-class products.[43] Therefore, the company invests heavily in research and development activities. Less than 10 percent of its revenues and profits come from service activities, and the chairman of the board does not expect that to change. Like Chaparral Steel and Ford, Motorola has worldwide recognition and reach.

■ Federal Express

Federal Express is an internationally recognized service company specializing in the transportation and distribution of priority goods and documents throughout the world. Like Motorola, Federal Express has been honored with a Malcolm Baldrige National Quality Award for service. The company uses a systematic goal-setting program to achieve high levels of performance throughout the organization. Federal Express is a medium- to large-sized organization headquartered in Memphis. In 1989, Federal Express acquired Tiger International and positioned itself for international service. It currently serves 119 countries through 167 airports. Federal Express has created a "people-first" work environment that emphasizes a nonhierarchical structure and, in some cases, an inverted hierarchical structure.[44]

■ NWNL Companies

NWNL Companies, a holding company headquartered in Minneapolis, is one of the fifty largest of over 2,000 companies in the insurance industry. NWNL is composed of three main operating companies. These are Northern Life Insurance Company, of Seattle; Northwestern National Life Insurance Company, of Minneapolis; and Northern Atlantic Life Insurance Company, of New York State. NWNL delivers a variety of individual and group insurance products, as well as providing reinsurance services. The company has several thousand employees. NWNL's medical department is unique in the industry for its leading role in national health care issues for over fifty years, beginning with the idea of mainstreaming disabled people in 1930.[45]

■ Southwest Airlines

Southwest Airlines is an air transportation service company providing single-class, high-frequency service to thirty-seven cities in the midwestern, southwestern, and western U.S. Southwest is a medium-sized service organization based on number of employees, yet it is the seventh largest airline based on number of passengers carried in 1992. The company is headquartered in Dallas. It has been recognized with numerous Triple Crown Awards. South-west has an informal organizational culture.[46] In 1991, the company celebrated its twentieth anniversary of incorporation. Southwest emphasizes high aircraft utilization and high employee productivity. It has created a unique niche in the air transportation industry because it competes against ground and rail transportation systems, not against the major airlines.

■ MANAGERIAL IMPLICATIONS: FOUNDATIONS FOR THE FUTURE

Managers must consider personal and environmental factors to understand fully how people behave in organizations. Human behavior is complex and at times confusing. Characteristics of the organizational system and formal-informal dynamics at work are important environmental factors that influence people's behavior. Managers should look for similarities and differences in manufacturing, service-oriented, nonprofit, and governmental organizations.

Research over the past one hundred years has shown how complex human behavior can be. The Hawthorne Studies were a testing ground for modern research methods and resulted in the discovery of the informal organization. Research during the past century has also provided a wealth of knowledge about the selection, placement, and management of people in organizations. A well-trained manager needs some grasp of psychology, sociology, engineering, anthropology, and medicine as well as management.

The primary concern for managers over the next decade or two will be achieving high-quality outputs to meet the international competition. Organizations making a commitment to total quality will be more likely to succeed in the face of the competition. Another aspect of meeting the competition will be learning. Managers must continually upgrade their knowledge about all aspects of their businesses. They also must hone their technical and interpersonal skills.

■ CHAPTER SUMMARY

- ■ Organizational behavior is individual behavior and group dynamics in organizations.

- Organizations are systems composed of people, structure, and technology committed to a task. They have formal and informal components.
- The Hawthorne Studies are among the most prominent pioneering programs of research, practice, and scholarship of the one hundred years of modern organizational behavior.
- The disciplines of psychology, sociology, engineering, anthropology, management, and medicine have contributed to the development of the discipline of organizational behavior.
- Organizations in the U.S. are in an era of intense international competition, and total quality is at the cutting edge of success in meeting the competition.
- Learning about organizational behavior requires mastery of objective knowledge and specific skill development.
- Manufacturing organizations (such as Chaparral Steel, Ford, and Motorola) and service organizations (such as Federal Express, NWNL Companies, and Southwest Airlines) constitute 67 percent of the U.S. economy based on gross domestic purchases.

■ REVIEW QUESTIONS

1. Define organizational behavior.
2. What are the four components of all organizational systems? Give examples of formal and informal components.
3. Suppose you would be able to beat the competition if you presented a prospective customer with negative information about the competition's quality program. Should you provide the information? Further assume that the information relates to safety. Would that make a difference in whether you told the customer?
4. Briefly describe the four studies conducted at the Hawthorne Works of Western Electric Company.
5. Identify the contributions of six disciplines to the development of organizational behavior.
6. Which disciplines are important in understanding moral and ethical rules for organizations and management?
7. Describe how competition and total quality are related to the study of organizational behavior.

8. What are the most sensitive ethical issues in your business today?

■ REFERENCES

1. H. Schwartz, "The Clockwork or the Snakepit: An Essay on the Meaning of Teaching Organizational Behavior," *Organizational Behavior Teaching Review* 11, No. 2 (1987): 19–26.
2. K. Lewin, *Field Theory in Social Science,* selected theoretical papers, Dorin Cartwright, ed. (New York: Harper, 1951).
3. R. L. A. Sterba, "The Organization and Management of the Temple Corporations in Ancient Mesopotamia," *Academy of Management Review* 1 (1976): 16–26; S. P. Dorsey, *Early English Churches in America* (New York: Oxford University Press, 1952).
4. Sir I. Moncreiffe of That Ilk, *The Highland Clans: The Dynastic Origins, Chiefs, and Background of the Clans and of Some Other Families Connected to Highland History,* rev. ed. (New York: C. N. Potter, 1982).
5. D. Shambaugh, "The Soldier and the State in China: The Political Work System in the People's Liberation Army," *Chinese Quarterly* 127 (1991): 527–568.
6. L. L'Abate, ed., *Handbook of Developmental Family Psychology and Psychopathology* (New York: Wiley, 1993).
7. J. M. Lewis, "The Family System and Physical Illness" in *No Single Thread: Psychological Health in Family Systems* (New York: Brunner/Mazel, 1976).
8. H. J. Leavitt, "Applied Organizational Change in Industry: Structural, Technological, and Humanistic Approaches," in J. G. March, ed., *Handbook of Organizations* (Chicago: Rand McNally, 1965), 1144–1170.
9. W. L. French and C. H. Bell, *Organization Development,* 4th ed. (Englewood Cliffs, N.J.: Prentice-Hall, 1990).
10. F. W. Taylor, *The Principles of Scientific Management* (New York: Norton, 1911).
11. W. B. Cannon, *Bodily Changes in Pain, Hunger, Fear, and Rage* (New York: Appleton, 1915).
12. F. J. Roethlisberger and W. J. Dickson, *Management and the Worker* (Cambridge, Mass.: Harvard University Press, 1939).
13. A. H. Maslow, *Motivation and Personality* (New York: Harper & Row, 1954).
14. F. Herzberg, B. Mausner, and B. Snyderman, *The Motivation to Work,* 2d ed. (New York: Wiley, 1959).
15. E. A. Locke, "Toward a Theory of Task Motivation and Incentives," *Organizational Behavior and Human Performance* 3 (1968): 157–189.
16. R. M. Stogdill, *Handbook of Leadership: A Survey of Theory and Research* (New York: Free Press, 1974).
17. G. A. Yukl, *Leadership in Organizations,* 2d ed. (Englewood Cliffs, N.J.: Prentice-Hall, 1989).
18. G. C. Homans, *The Human Group* (New York: Harcourt Brace Jovanovich, 1950).

19. J. R. Hackman and G. Oldham, *Work Redesign* (Reading, Mass.: Addison-Wesley, 1980).

20. P. C. Smith, L. M. Kendall, and C. L. Hulin, *The Measurement of Satisfaction in Work and Retirement* (Chicago: Rand McNally 1969).

21. N. R. F. Maier, *Psychology in Industry: A Psychological Approach to Industrial Problems, 2d* Ed. (Boston: Houghton Mifflin, 1955).

22. F. J. Roethlisberger, *Management and Morale* (Cambridge, Mass.: Harvard University Press, 1941) and F. J. Roethlisberger, W. J. Dickson, and H. A. Wright, *Management and the Worker: An Account of a Research Program Conducted by the Western Electric Company, Hawthorne Works, Chicago* (Cambridge, Mass.: Harvard University Press, 1950).

23. A. G. Athos and J. J. Gabarro, *Interpersonal Behavior: Communication and Understanding in Relationships* (Englewood Cliffs, N.J.: Prentice-Hall, 1978).

24. L. R. Offermann and M. K. Gowing, guest eds., "Special Issue: Organizational Psychology," *American Psychologist* 45 (1990): 95–283.

25. R. M. Yerkes, "The Relation of Psychology to Military Activities," *Mental Hygiene* 1 (1917): 371–376.

26. R. K. Merton, "The Role Set," *British Journal of Sociology* 8 (1957): 106–120.

27. N. Gross, W. Mason, and A. McEachen, *Explorations in Role Analysis: Studies of the School Superintendency Role* (New York: Wiley, 1958).

28. Hearings before Special Committee of the House of Representatives to Investigate the Taylor and Other Systems of Shop Management under Authority of House Resolution 90; Vol. 3: 1377-1508 contains Dr. Taylor's testimony before the committee from Thursday, January 25, through Tuesday, January 30, 1912.

29. A. L. Wilkins and W. G. Ouchi, "Efficient Cultures: Exploring the Relationship between Culture and Organizational Performance," *Administrative Science Quarterly* 28 (1983): 468-481 and M. F. R. Kets de Vries and D. Miller, "Personality, Culture, and Organization," *Academy of Management Review* 11 (1986): 266–279.

30. H. Schwartz, *Narcissistic Process and Corporate Decay: The Theory of the Organizational Ideal* (New York: NYU Press, 1990).

31. J. G. March and H. A. Simon, *Organizations* (New York: Wiley, 1958).

32. H. B. Elkind, *Preventive Management: Mental Hygiene in Industry* (New York: B. C. Forbes, 1931).

33. L. Foss and K. Rothenberg, *The Second Medical Revolution: From Biomedical to Infomedical* (Boston: New Science Library, 1987).

34. D. R. Ilgen, "Health Issues at Work," *American Psychologist* 45 (1990): 273–283.

35. L. E. Thurow, *Head to Head: The Coming Economic Battle among Japan, Europe, and America* (New York: William Morrow, 1992).

36. R. S. Fosler, W. Alonso, J. A. Meyer, and R. Kern, *Demographic Change and the American Future* (Pittsburgh, Pa.: University of Pittsburgh Press, 1990).

37. P. M. Thomas, L. J. Gallace, and K. R. Martin, *Quality Alone Is Not Enough* (New York: American Management Association, 1992).

38. G. M. C. Fisher, *The Dimensions of Quality* (Arlington, Tex.: University of Texas at Arlington, 1990).

39. L. L. Berry, A. Parasoraman and V. A. Zeithaml, "Improving Service Quality in America: Lessons Learned," *Academy of Management Executive* 8 (1994): 32–52.

40. D. L. Whetzel, "The Department of Labor Identifies Workplace Skills," *Industrial/Organizational Psychologist* 29 (1991): 89–90.

41. G. J. McManus, "Beaming with Pride: Steelmaker of the Year," *Iron Age,* August 1992, 14–21.

42. R. L. Shook, *Turn Around: The New Ford Motor Company* (New York: Prentice-Hall, 1990).

43. H. M Petrakis, *The Founder's Touch: The Life of Paul Galvin of Motorola* (New York: McGraw-Hill, 1965).

44. American Management Association, *Blueprints for Service Quality: The Federal Express Approach* (New York: American Management Association, 1991).

45. S. R. Kaufman, ed., *100 Years: Northwestern National Life Insurance Company, 1885–1985* (Minneapolis: NWNL Companies, 1985).

46. J. C. Quick, "Crafting an Organizational Culture: Herb's Hand at Southwest Airlines," *Organizational Dynamics* 21 (1992): 45–56.

CHAPTER 2
ORGANIZATIONS 2001 AND MANAGERIAL CHALLENGES

LEARNING OBJECTIVES

After reading this chapter, you should be able to do the following:

- Describe the dimensions of cultural differences that affect work-related attitudes and behavior.
- Explain the social and demographic changes that produce diversity in organizations.
- Describe actions managers can take to help employees value diversity.
- Understand the technological changes that will affect organizations most dramatically by the year 2000.
- Explain the ways managers can help employees adjust to technological change.
- Discuss the assumptions of consequential, rule-based, and cultural ethical theories.
- Explain eight issues that pose ethical dilemmas for managers.

■ COMPETITION: THE CHALLENGES MANAGERS FACE

The vast majority of U.S. executives believe U.S. firms are encountering unprecedented global competition.[1] Many organizations have undertaken bold initiatives to improve product and service quality. Federal Express, Rubbermaid, and Hewlett-Packard are companies at the forefront of the quality movement. With competition increasing both at home and abroad, managers must find new and creative ways to deal with the competitive challenges they face.

What are the major challenges? Chief executive officers of U.S. corporations of all sizes responded to a survey that asked them to identify the greatest challenges they face in the 1990s and beyond.[2] The top three responses were global competition and globalizing the firm's operations, making sure the human side of the enterprise works at all levels, and keeping up with technology and implementing it in the workplace. Complementing these is the challenge of managing ethical behavior. Internal abuses of trust are serious threats to organizations today.

This chapter introduces these four specific challenges for managers and describes the ways some organizations are tackling them. First, the challenge of globalization is discussed. Rapid political and social changes have broken down national barriers, and the drive for global expansion has become a reality in many organizations.

Second, the challenge of work force diversity is presented. The human side of the enterprise is more diverse than ever before. When managers try to unite employees of different backgrounds, they face the challenge of varied communication styles, insensitivity, and ignorance of others' motivations and cultures.

Third, the challenge of technological change is explored. Organizations must take advantage of technology as a key to strategic competitiveness. Technological change is complex, because it often necessitates changes in individual and group behavior, information flows, work design, social interactions, and organizational structure.

Finally, the challenge of managing ethical behavior is discussed. With recent insider trading scandals, junk bond proliferation, savings and loan crises, contract frauds, check-kiting practices, and influence peddling, ethical behavior has come to the forefront of public consciousness. These four challenges are the engines that drive organizations in their push to remain competitive.

■ MANAGING IN A GLOBAL ENVIRONMENT

Only a few years ago, business conducted across national borders was referred to as "international" activity. The word "international" shows that the individual's or the organization's nationality is held strongly in consciousness. "Globalization," in contrast, implies that this is really a borderless world free from national boundaries.[3] U.S. workers are now competing with workers in other countries. Organizations from other countries, such as Honda and Mazda, are locating subsidiaries in the U.S.

Similarly, organizations that were once called multinational (doing business in several countries)

are now referred to as transnational. In transnational organizations, the global viewpoint supersedes national issues.[4] Transnational organizations operate over large global distances and are multicultural in terms of the people they employ. 3M and Dow Chemical are transnational organizations. CNN showed that it is a transnational organization in its coverage of the Persian Gulf War. Correspondents from a host of different cultures reported on the war from locations around the world.

■ Changes in the Global Marketplace

Social and political upheavals have led organizations to change the way they conduct business and to encourage their members to think globally. The collapse of Eastern Europe was followed quickly by the demise of the Berlin Wall. East and West Germany were united into a single country. In the Soviet Union, *perestroika* led to the liberation of the satellite countries and the breaking away of the Soviet Union's member nations. *Perestroika* also brought about many opportunities for U.S. businesses, as witnessed by the press photos showing extremely long waiting lines at Moscow's first McDonald's restaurant.

Ventures in China have become increasingly attractive to U.S. businesses. One challenge to U.S. managers is attempting to understand the Chinese way of doing business. Chinese managers' practices have been shaped by the Communist party, socialism, feudalistic values, and *guanxi* (a system of influence peddling through the back door).[5] In China, the family is regarded as being responsible for a worker's productivity, and in turn, the company is responsible for the worker's family. Because of socialism, Chinese managers have very little experience with rewards and punishments, and are reluctant to use them in the workplace. To work with Chinese managers, Americans can learn to build their own *guanxi*; understand the Chinese chain of command; and negotiate slow, general agreements in order to interact effectively. Using the foreign government as the local franchisee may be effective in China. For example, Kentucky Fried Chicken's operation in China is a joint venture between KFC (60 percent) and two Chinese government bodies (40 percent).

The European Union was designed to integrate twelve nations into a single market by removing trade barriers. The member nations of the European Union (EU) are Belgium, Denmark, France, Germany, Greece, Ireland, Italy, Luxembourg, the Netherlands, Portugal, Spain, and the United Kingdom, with others to follow. The integration of Europe provides many opportunities for U.S. organizations, including 350 million potential customers. Companies like Ford Motor Company and IBM, which entered the market early with wholly owned subsidiaries, will have a head start on these opportunities. However, competition within the EU will increase, as will competition from Japan and the former Soviet nations.

All of these changes have brought about the need to think globally. Given the domestic economic problems in the U.S., a global focus provides a way to maintain profitability. To benefit from global thinking, managers will also need to take a long-term view. Entry into global markets is a long-term proposition, and it requires long-term strategies. Ford has taken a long-term view in its global operations. It hopes to move beyond exporting to Europe soon and to expand its production of "world cars" that satisfy customer needs on several continents.

■ Understanding Cultural Differences

One of the keys for any company competing in the global marketplace is to understand the diverse cultures of the individuals involved. Whether managing culturally diverse employees within a single location or managing individuals at remote locations around the globe, an appreciation of the differences among cultures is crucial.

Do cultural differences translate into differences in work-related attitudes? The pioneering work of Dutch researcher Geert Hofstede has focused on this question. He and his colleagues surveyed 160,000 managers and employees of IBM in sixty countries.[6] In this way, the researchers were able to study individuals from the same company in the same jobs, but working in different countries. Hofstede's work is important, because his studies showed that national culture explains more differences in work-related attitudes than do age, gender, profession, or position within the organization. Thus, cultural differences do affect individuals' work-related attitudes. Hofstede found five dimensions of cultural differences that formed the basis for work-related attitudes. These dimensions are shown in Figure 2.1.

Individualism Versus Collectivism. In cultures where individualism predominates, people belong to loose social frameworks, and their primary concern is for themselves and their families. People are responsible for taking care of their own interests. They believe that individuals should make decisions. Cultures characterized by collectivism are tightly knit social frameworks in which individual members depend strongly on extended families or clans. Group decisions are valued and accepted.

The North American culture is individualistic in orientation. It is a "can-do" culture that values individual freedom and responsibility. In contrast,

■ FIGURE 2.1
Hofstede's Dimensions of Cultural Differences

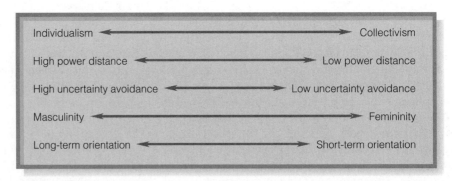

Source: G. Hofstede, "Cultural Constraints in Management Theories," *Academy of Management Executive 7* (1993): 81-94. Reprinted with permission.

collectivist cultures emphasize group welfare and harmony. Israeli kibbutzim and the Japanese culture are examples of societies in which group loyalty and unity are paramount. Organization charts show these orientations. In Canada and the U.S., which are individualistic cultures, organization charts show individual positions. In Malaysia, which is a collectivist culture, organization charts show only sections or departments.

This dimension of cultural differences has other workplace implications. Individualistic managers, as found in Great Britain and the Netherlands, emphasize and encourage individual achievement. In contrast, collectivistic managers, such as in Japan and Colombia, seek to fit harmoniously within the group. They also encourage these behaviors among their employees.

Power Distance. The second dimension of cultural differences examines the acceptance of unequal distribution of power. In countries with a high power distance, bosses are afforded more power simply because they are the bosses. Titles are used, formality is the rule, and bypassing authority is seldom seen. Power holders are entitled to their privileges, and managers and employees see one another as fundamentally different kinds of people. India is a country with a high power distance, as are Venezuela and Mexico.

In countries with a low power distance, people believe that inequality in society should be minimized. People at various power levels are less threatened by, and more willing to trust, one another. Managers and employees see one another as similar. Managers are given power only if they have expertise. Employees frequently bypass the boss in order to get work done in countries with a low power distance, such as Denmark and Australia.

Uncertainty Avoidance. Some cultures are quite comfortable with ambiguity and uncertainty, whereas others do not tolerate these conditions as well. Cultures with high uncertainty avoidance are concerned with security and tend to avoid conflict. People have a need for consensus. The inherent uncertainty in life is a threat against which people in such cultures constantly struggle.

Cultures with low uncertainty avoidance are more tolerant of ambiguity. People are more willing to take risks and more tolerant of individual differences. Conflict is seen as constructive, and people accept dissenting viewpoints. Norway and Australia are characterized by low uncertainty avoidance, and this trait is seen in the value placed on job mobility. Japan and Italy are characterized by high uncertainty avoidance, so career stability is emphasized.

Masculinity Versus Femininity. In cultures that are characterized by masculinity, assertiveness and materialism are valued. Men should be assertive, and women should be nurturing. Money and possessions are important, and performance is what counts. Achievement is admired. Cultures that are characterized by femininity emphasize relationships and concern for others. Men and women are expected to assume both assertive and nurturing roles. Quality of life is important, and people and the environment are emphasized.

Masculine societies, such as in Austria and Venezuela, define gender roles strictly. Feminine societies, in contrast, tend to blur gender roles. Women may be the providers, and men may stay home with the children. The Scandinavian countries of Norway, Sweden, and Denmark exemplify the feminine orientation.

Time Orientation. Cultures also differ in time orientation; that is, whether the culture's values are oriented toward the future (long-term orientation) or toward the past and present (short-term orientation).[7] In China, a culture with a long-term orientation, values such as thrift and persistence, which focus on the future, are emphasized. In Russia, the orientation is short-term. Values such as respect for tradition (past) and meeting social obligations (present) are emphasized.

U.S. Culture. The position of the U.S. on these five dimensions is interesting. Hofstede found the U.S. to be the most individualistic country of all those studied. On the power distance dimension, the U.S. ranked among the countries with weak power distance. Its rank on uncertainty avoidance indicated a tolerance of uncertainty. The U.S. also ranked as a masculine culture with a short-term orientation. These values have shaped U.S. management theory, and Hofstede's work casts doubt on the universal applicability of U.S. management theories. Because cultures differ so widely on these dimensions, management practices should be adjusted to account for cultural differences. Managers in transnational organizations must learn as much as they can about other cultures in order to lead their culturally diverse organizations effectively.

Careers in management have taken on a global dimension. Working in transnational organizations is likely to give managers the opportunity to work in other countries. Expatriate managers, those who work outside their home country, should know as much as possible about cultural differences. Because many future managers will have global work experience, it is never too early to begin planning for this aspect of your career.

Understanding cultural differences becomes especially important for companies that are considering opening foreign offices, because workplace customs can vary widely from one country to another. Carefully searching out this information in advance can help companies manage foreign operations successfully. Consulate offices and companies operating within the foreign country are excellent sources of information about national customs and legal requirements.

Another reality that can affect global business practices is the cost of layoffs in other countries. The practice of "rightsizing" is not unique to the U.S. Dismissing a forty-five year-old middle manager with twenty years of service and a $50,000 annual salary can vary in cost from a low of $13,000 in Ireland to a high of $130,000 in Italy.[8] The cost of laying off this manager in the U.S. would be approximately $19,000. The wide variability in costs stems from the various legal protections that certain countries give workers. In Italy, laid-off employees must receive a "notice period" payment (one year's pay if they have nine or more years of service) plus a severance payment (based on pay and years of service). U.S. companies operating overseas often adopt the European tradition of spending more time training and retraining workers to avoid overstaffing and potential layoffs. An appreciation of the customs and rules for doing business in another country is essential if a company wants to go global.

■ Developing Cross-Cultural Sensitivity

As organizations compete in the global marketplace, employees must learn to deal with individuals from diverse cultural backgrounds. Stereotypes may pervade employees' perceptions of other cultures. In addition, employees may be unaware of others' perceptions of the employees' national culture. A potentially valuable exercise is to ask members from various cultures to describe one another's cultures. This provides a lesson on the misinterpretation of culture.

Cultural sensitivity training is a popular method for helping employees recognize and appreciate cultural differences. Northern Telecom, for example, conducts a sixteen-hour training program to help employees modify negative attitudes toward individuals from different cultures.

Another way of developing sensitivity is to use cross-cultural task forces or teams. The Milwaukee-based GE Medical Systems Group (GEMS) has 7,000 of its 15,000 employees working outside the U.S. GEMS has developed a vehicle for bringing managers from each of its three regions (the Americas, Europe, and Asia) together to work on a variety of business projects. The plan is called the Global Leadership Program, and several work groups made up of managers from various regions of the world are formed in the program. The teams work on important projects, such as worldwide employee integration to increase the employees' sense of belonging throughout the GEMS international organization.[9]

The globalization of business affects all parts of the organization, and human resource management is affected in particular. Companies have employees around the world, and human resource managers face the daunting task of effectively supporting a culturally diverse work force. Human resource managers must adopt a global view of all functions, including human resource planning, recruitment and selection, compensation, and training and development. They must have a working knowledge of the legal systems in various countries, as well as of global economics, culture, and customs. Human resource managers must not only prepare U.S. workers to become expatriates but also help foreign employees interact with U.S. culture. Global human resource management is a complex endeavor, but it is critical to the success of organizations in the global marketplace.

Globalization is one challenge managers must face in order to remain competitive in the changing world. Related to globalization is the challenge of managing an increasingly diverse work force. Cultural differences contribute a great deal to the diversity of the work force, but there are other forms of diversity as well.

◼ Managing Work Force Diversity

Work force diversity has always been an important issue for organizations. The U.S., as a melting pot nation, has always had a mix of individuals in its work force. We once sought to be all alike, as in the melting pot. However, we now recognize and try to appreciate individual differences. Diversity encompasses all forms of differences among individuals, including culture, gender, age, ability, religious affiliation, personality, economic class, social status, military attachment, and sexual orientation. Attention to diversity has increased in recent years, particularly because of the changing demographics of the working population.

Dealing with diversity successfully is an issue of paramount concern in organizations. Managers may lack the knowledge of how to motivate diverse work groups. In addition, managers may be unsure how to communicate effectively with employees who have different values and language skills.

Several demographic trends, in particular, will be forced upon organizations in the coming years. By the year 2000, the work force is predicted to be more culturally diverse, more female, and older than ever.[10] In addition, new legislation and new technologies will bring more disabled workers into the work force.

◼ Cultural Diversity

Cultural diversity in the workplace is growing due to the globalization of business, as we discussed earlier. People of diverse national origins—Koreans, Bolivians, Pakistanis, Vietnamese, Swedes, Australians, and others—will find themselves cooperating in teams to perform the work of the organization. In addition, changing demographics within the U.S. will significantly affect the cultural diversity in organizations. Over the next ten years, only 58 percent of the new entrants to the labor force will be white Americans ("majority" workers). The participation rates of African-Americans and Hispanic-Americans in the labor force have increased dramatically in recent years. African-American women are predicted to make up the largest share of the increase in the minority labor force, and they are expected to outnumber the African-American men in the work force by the year 2000.

These trends have important implications for organizations. African-Americans and Hispanic-Americans are overrepresented in declining occupations, thus limiting their opportunities. Further, African-Americans and Hispanic-Americans tend to live in a small number of large cities which are facing severe economic difficulties and high crime rates. Because of these factors, minority workers are likely to be at a disadvantage within organizations.

The jobs available in the future will require more skills than has been the case in the past. Often, minority workers have not had opportunities to develop their skills. Minority skills deficits are large, and the proportions of African-Americans and Hispanic-Americans who are qualified for higher-level jobs are often much lower than the proportions of qualified whites and Asian-Americans.[11] Minority workers are less likely to be prepared because they are less likely to have had satisfactory schooling and on-the-job training. Educational systems within the workplace are needed to supply minority workers with the skills necessary for success. Companies such as Motorola are already recognizing and meeting this need by focusing on basic skills training.

The globalization of business and changing demographic trends will present organizations with a tremendously diverse work force. This represents both a challenge and a risk. The challenge is to harness the wealth of differences that cultural diversity provides. The risk is that prejudices and stereotypes will prevent managers and employees from developing a synergy that can benefit the organization.

Most large organizations in the U.S. today are plural organizations; that is, they have a heterogeneous membership and have taken steps to be more inclusive of members from minority-group cultures. Plural organizations contain many different cultural groups, and the focus in plural organizations is on assimilation of these cultural groups. Many organizations, however, are moving toward becoming multicultural organizations. The focus in multicultural organizations is on fully integrating diverse cultures into the organization. Multicultural organizations are also characterized by an absence of prejudice and discrimination, and low levels of intergroup conflict. The difference between plural and multicultural organizations is thus the difference between containing diversity and valuing diversity.[12]

■ Gender Diversity

The feminization of the work force has increased substantially. The number of women in the labor force increased from 31.5 million in 1970 to 58.5 million in 1993.[13] This increase accounts for almost 60 percent of the overall expansion of the entire labor force in the United States for this time period. In 1989, women made up almost 40 percent of the labor force, and by the year 2000, the labor force is predicted to be balanced with respect to gender. Women are also better prepared to contribute in organizations than ever before. Women earned 31 percent of the master of business administration (MBA) degrees, 39 percent of the law degrees, 13 percent of the engineering degrees, and half of all undergraduate degrees awarded in 1990. Thus, women are better educated, and more are electing to work: in 1989, 58 percent of U.S. women were employed.

Women's participation in the work force is increasing, but their share of the rewards of participation is not increasing commensurately. In 1990, less than 0.5 percent of all top-level jobs in major organizations were held by women. Salaries for women persist at a level of 60 percent of their male counterparts' earnings.[14] Furthermore, because benefits are tied to compensation, women also face lower levels of benefits.

In addition to lower earnings, women face other obstacles at work. The glass ceiling is a transparent barrier that keeps women from rising above a certain level in organizations. In the U.S., it is rare to find women in positions above middle management in corporations. The glass ceiling is not based on women's lack of ability to handle upper-level management positions. Instead, the barrier keeps women from advancing higher in an organization because they are women.

Removing the glass ceiling and other obstacles to women's success represents a major challenge to organizations. Policies that promote equity in pay and benefits, encourage benefit programs of special interest to women, and provide equal starting salaries for jobs of equal value are needed in organizations.

Although women in our society have adopted provider roles, men have not been as quick to share domestic responsibilities. Managing the home and arranging for child care are still seen as the woman's domain. In addition, working women often find themselves in the position of caretaker for their elderly parents. Because of their multiple roles, women are more likely than men to experience conflicts between work and home. Organizations can offer incentives such as flexible work schedules, child care, elder care, and work site health promotion programs to assist working women in managing the stress of their lives.

More women in the work force means that organizations must help them achieve their potential. To do less would be to underutilize the talents of half of the U.S. work force.

■ Age Diversity

The graying of the U.S. work force is another source of diversity in organizations. Aging baby boomers (those individuals born from 1946 through 1964) will contribute to the rise of the median age in the U.S. to thirty-six by the year 2000—six years older than at any earlier time in history. This means also that the number of middle-aged Americans will rise dramatically. In the work force, the number of younger workers will decline, as will the number of older workers (over age sixty-five). The net result will be a gain in workers aged thirty-five to fifty-four.[15]

This change in worker profile has profound implications for organizations. The job crunch among middle-aged workers will become more intense as companies seek flatter organizations and the elimination of middle-management jobs. Older workers are often higher paid, and companies that employ large numbers of aging baby boomers may find these pay scales a handicap to competitiveness. However, a more experienced, stable, reliable, and healthy work force can pay dividends to companies. The baby boomers are well trained and educated, and their knowledge can be a definite asset to organizations.

Another effect of the aging work force is greater intergenerational contact in the workplace.[16] As organizations grow flatter, workers who were traditionally segregated by old corporate hierarchies (with older workers at the top and younger workers at the bottom) will be working together. Four generations will be cooperating: the swing generation (those born from 1910 through 1929), who lived through the Great Depression and World War II and are now in their sixties to eighties; the silent generation (people born from 1930 through 1945), a small group that includes most organizations' top managers; the baby boomers, whose substantial numbers give them a strong influence; and the baby bust generation (those born from 1965 through 1976). Although there is certainly diversity within each generation, each generation differs in general ways from other generations.

The differences in attitudes and values among these four generations can be substantial, and managers face the challenge of integrating these individuals into a cohesive group. Currently, as already noted, most positions of leadership are held by members of the silent generation. Baby boomers regard the silent generation as complacent and as having done little to reduce social inequities. Baby boomers strive for moral rights in the workplace and take a more activist position regarding employee rights. The baby busters, new to the workplace, are impatient, want short-term gratification, and believe that family should come before work. They scorn the achievement orientation and materialism of the baby boomers. Managing such diverse perspectives is a challenge that must be addressed.

One company that is succeeding in accommodating the baby busters is Patagonia, a manufacturer of products for outdoor enthusiasts. While the company does not actively recruit 20-year-olds, approximately 20 percent of Patagonia's workers are in this age group because they are attracted to its products. To retain baby busters, the company offers several options, one of which is flextime. Employees can arrive at work as early as 6 a.m., and work as late as 6 p.m., as long as they work the core hours between 9 a.m. and 3 p.m. Workers also have the option of working at the office for five hours a day and at home for three hours.

Personal leaves of absence are also offered, generally unpaid, for as much as four months per year. This allows employees to take an extended summer break and prevents job burnout. Patagonia has taken into consideration the baby busters' desires for more time for personal concerns and has incorporated these desires into the company.[17]

Younger workers may have false impressions of older workers, viewing them as resistant to change, unable to learn new work methods, less physically capable, and less creative than younger employees.[18] Research indicates, however, that older employees are more satisfied with their jobs, are more committed to the organization, and possess more internal work motivation than their younger cohorts.[19] Motivating the aging work force and helping them maintain high levels of contribution to the organization will be a key task for managers.

■ Ability Diversity

The work force is full of individuals with different abilities, which presents another form of diversity. Individuals with disabilities are an underutilized human resource. An estimated 43 million disabled individuals live in the U.S., and their unemployment rate is estimated to exceed 60 percent.[20] The representation of disabled individuals in the work force is expected to increase dramatically because of the Americans with Disabilities Act, which went into effect in the summer of 1992. Under this law, employers are required to make reasonable accommodations to permit workers with disabilities to perform jobs. The act defines a disabled person as "anyone possessing a physical or mental impairment that substantially limits one or more major life activities." It protects individuals with temporary, as well as permanent, disabilities. A broad range of illnesses that produce disabilities are included in the act's protection. Among these are acquired immune deficiency syndrome (AIDS), cancer, hypertension, anxiety disorders, dyslexia, blindness, and cerebral palsy, to name only a few.

Some companies recognized the value of employing disabled workers long before the legislation. Pizza Hut employs 3,000 disabled workers and plans to hire more. The turnover rates for disabled Pizza Hut workers is only one-fifth of the normal turnover rate.[21]

McDonald's created McJobs, a program that has trained and hired over 9,000 mentally and physically challenged individuals since 1981. McJobs is a corporate plan to recruit, train, and retain disabled individuals. Its participants include workers with visual, hearing, or orthopedic impairments; learning disabilities; and mental retardation. Through classroom and on-site training, the McJobs program prepares disabled individuals for the work environment. Before McJobs workers go on-site, sensitivity training sessions are held with store managers and crew members. These sessions help nondisabled workers understand what it means to be a worker with a disabling condition. Most McJobs workers start part-time and advance according to their own abilities and the opportunities available. Some visually impaired McJobs workers prefer to work on the back line, whereas others who are wheelchair users can work the drive-through window.

Companies like Pizza Hut and McDonald's have led the way in hiring disabled individuals. One key to the success of these firms is helping able-bodied employees understand how disabled workers can contribute to the organization. In this way, ability diversity becomes an asset and helps the organizations meet the challenge of unleashing the talents of disabled workers.

■ Differences as Assets

Diversity involves much more than culture, gender, age, ability, or personality. It also encompasses religious affiliation, economic class, social status, military attachment, and sexual orientation. The scope of diversity is broad and inclusive. All these types of diversity lend heterogeneity to the work force.

Diversity is advantageous to the organization. Some organizations have recognized the potential benefits of aggressively working to increase the diversity of their work forces. Pepsico's Kentucky Fried Chicken (KFC) has a goal of attracting and retaining female and minority-group executives. Honeywell has a director of workforce diversity, and Avon Products has a director of multicultural planning and design.

Digital Equipment Corporation (DEC) faced a challenge in managing diversity in its Springfield, Massachusetts plant, which employed predominantly African-American workers. The task was to overcome the perception that the plant was separate from, different from, and not as good as DEC's predominantly white plants. DEC's Springfield employees succeeded in tackling the issue by stressing empowerment (sharing power throughout the organization) and pushing for high-technology products that would give it a solid identity. The model used by the plant, called Valuing Differences, was based on two key ideas. First, people work best when they are valued and when diversity is taken into account. Second, when people feel valued, they build relationships and work together as a team.[22]

Achieving diversity at management and executive levels requires that organizational practices reinforce the idea of differences as assets. Including diversity goals in performance evaluations and incorporating competence in managing diversity into promotion decisions are two such practices. Succession planning should include explicit consideration of candidates with diverse backgrounds. These actions, along with top management support, can help increase diversity at the managerial and executive levels of organizations.[23]

Managing diversity is one way a company can become more competitive. It is more than simply being a good corporate citizen or complying with affirmative action. It is also more than assimilating women and minorities into a dominant male culture. Instead, managing diversity involves creating an overall, dominant, single heterogeneous culture. In addition, managing diversity may involve a painful examination of hidden assumptions that employees hold. Biases and prejudices about people's differences must be uncovered and dealt with so that differences can be celebrated and exploited to their full advantage.

Managing diversity also involves helping employees understand their own cultures. Whites of European heritage do not think of themselves as having a culture—they often believe culture is something that only minorities have. Whereas the struggle for equal employment opportunity is a battle against racism and prejudice, managing diversity is a battle to value the differences that individuals bring to the workplace. Organizations that manage diversity effectively can reap the rewards of increased productivity and improved organizational health.

■ MANAGING TECHNOLOGICAL INNOVATION

Another challenge that managers face is managing technological innovation effectively. Technology consists of the intellectual and mechanical processes used by an organization to transform inputs into products or services that meet organizational goals. Managers must cope with rapidly changing technology and the need to put the technology to optimum use in organizations. The inability of managers to incorporate new technologies into their organizations successfully is a major factor that has limited economic growth in the U.S. Although the U.S. still leads the way in developing new technologies, it lags behind in making productive use of these new technologies in workplace settings.[24]

Any change that affects the way work is performed is a technological change. One such change is telecommuting, transmitting work from a home computer to the office using a modem. IBM, for example, was one of the first companies to experiment with the notion of installing computer terminals at employees' homes and having employees work at home. By telecommuting, employees gain flexibility, save the commute to work, and enjoy the comforts of being at home. There are disadvantages of telecommuting as well. Distractions, lack of opportunities to socialize with other workers, lack of interaction with supervisors, and decreased identification with the organization are a few.

Another technological change involves expert systems, computer-based applications that use a representation of human expertise in a specialized field of knowledge to solve problems. Expert systems can be used in many ways, including providing advice to nonexperts, assisting experts, replacing experts, and serving as a training and development tools in organizations. Examples of expert systems include PROSPECTOR, which isolates promising locations for mineral exploration, and MYCIN, a medically oriented expert system that diagnoses diseases and recommends treatment. One organization currently using an expert system is Anheuser Busch. The company uses an expert system to assist managers in ensuring that personnel decisions comply with antidiscrimination laws.

Robots, which make up another technological innovation, were invented in the U.S., and advanced research on robotics is still conducted here. However, Japan leads the world in the use of robotics in organizations.[25] The U.S. now has fewer robots in organizations than were added in Japan in 1989 alone in Japan. At Japan Airlines (JAL), robots weigh and identify turbine blades for jet engines. Robots also refinish cracks in compressor and turbine disks. At JAL, the use of robotics has improved the quality of repair and maintenance work.[26] The main reason for the reluctance of U.S. organizations to use robots is their slow payout. Robotics represents a big investment that does not pay off in the short term. Japanese managers are more willing to use a long-term horizon to evaluate the effectiveness of robotics technology. Labor unions may also resist robotics because of the fear that robots will replace employees.

Some U.S. companies that experimented with robotics had bad experiences. John Deere and Company originally used robots to paint its tractors, but the company scrapped them because the robots took too long to program for the multitude of types of paint used. Now Deere uses robots to torque cap screws on tractors, a repetitive job that once had a high degree of human error.

■ Technologies of the Future

The technological innovations already described may seem like dramatic examples, but they are realities in many organizations. The challenge to managers is putting advanced technologies into productive use by employees. What can be expected in terms of technological changes managers will need to apply between now and the year 2000?

New technologies, as well as exploitations of older technologies, continue to reshape jobs and organizations. Five technologies in particular are predicted to have the greatest impact from now until the year 2000. These technologies are information storage and processing, communications, advanced materials, biotechnologies, and superconductivity.[27]

Information Storage and Processing. Continuing improvements in information storage and processing will ensure that by the year 2000, desktop computing capability will be measured by gigabytes (billion words) and terabytes (trillion words) instead of the megabytes (million words) that are used today. Improvements in the price/performance ratios of equipment will mean that it will be very inexpensive to apply machine intelligence to jobs currently performed by humans.

Communications. By the year 2000, the U.S. will have a digital telecommunications network made possible by fiber optics technology. This innovation will mean that most homes will use a computer terminal as much or more than they use the telephone to access systems for home shopping, banking, and entertainment. Print media such as newspapers and magazines will fade in use in favor of electronic media.

Advanced Materials. Improvements in the traditional materials used in industry will mean declines in jobs that produce raw materials by the year 2000. Coatings such as ceramics and reinforced plastics will extend the life of manufactured products. Because of this increase in durability, fewer raw materials will be used.

Biotechnologies. By the year 2000, agriculture and health care will be dramatically affected by advances in biotechnology, especially by the increased ability to manipulate life forms at the cellular and subcellular levels. New plant varieties that can withstand extreme environmental conditions will be introduced. Pork with less cholesterol is being produced, as are cows that produce better milk. These innovations will create an abundance of farm produce.

The impacts of biotechnologies on health care will be delayed by extensive testing and licensing re-quirements. Although AIDS may not be cured by the year 2000, the knowledge gained about the immune system will lead to vastly improved treatments for a host of diseases. Mapping the human genetic system will make it possible to predict and treat birth defects and other diseases.

Superconductivity. The development of superconductive materials (those that carry electric current without energy loss) is predicted to be the technology that has the most rapid impact on industry. The efficiency of electric motors of all kinds will be improved. Electric cars could become commonplace.

These five areas of technological change are only a few that affect organizations. Workers also face changes in the way their work is performed on a daily basis, and these range from the relatively minor to major effects on the worker and the job. As mentioned, technological changes bring a host of changes in the way managerial work is performed.

The Changing Nature of Managerial Work. Technological innovation affects the very nature of the management job. Managers who once had to coax workers back to their desks from coffee breaks now find that they need to encourage workers mesmerized by new technology to take more frequent breaks.[28] Working with a computer can be stressful, both physically and psychologically. Eye strain, neck and back strain, and headaches can result from sitting at a computer terminal too long. In addition, workers can become accustomed to the fast response time of the computer and expect the same from their co-workers. When co-workers do not respond with the speed and accuracy of the computer, they may receive a harsh retort.[29]

Computerized monitoring provides managers with a wealth of information about employee performance, but it also holds great potential for misuse. The telecommunications, airline, and mail-order merchandise industries make wide use of systems that secretly monitor employees' interactions with customers. Employers praise such systems, saying that they improve customer service. Workers, however, are not so positive; they react with higher levels of depression, anxiety, and exhaustion from working under such secret scrutiny. At Bell Canada, operators were evaluated on a system that tabulated average working time with customers. Operators found the practice highly stressful, and they sabotaged the system by giving callers wrong directory assistance numbers rather than taking the time to look up the correct ones. As a result, Bell Canada now uses average working time scores for entire offices rather than for individuals.[30]

New technologies and rapid innovation place a premium on a manager's technical skills. Early management theories rated technical skills as less important than human and conceptual skills, but this has become wisdom of the past. Managers today must develop technical competence in order to gain workers' respect, which does not come automatically. Computer-integrated manufacturing systems, for example, have been shown to require managers to use participative management styles, open communication, and greater technical expertise in order to be effective.[31]

In a world of rapid technological innovation, managers must focus more carefully on helping workers manage the stress of their work. They must also take advantage of the wealth of information at their disposal to motivate, coach, and counsel workers rather than try to control them more stringently or police them. In addition, managers will need to develop their technical competence in order to gain workers' respect.

Technological change occurs so rapidly that turbulence characterizes most organizations. Workers must constantly learn and adapt to changing technology so that organizations can remain competitive. Managers must help workers adapt and make effective use of new technologies.

■ Helping Employees Adjust to Technological Change

Most workers are well aware of the benefits of modern technologies. The availability of skilled jobs and improved working conditions has been the by-product of innovation in many organizations. Technology is also bringing disadvantaged individuals into the work force. Microchips have dramatically increased opportunities for visually impaired workers. Information can be decoded into speech using a speech synthesizer, into braille using a hard-copy printer, or into enlarged print visible on a computer monitor. Visually impaired workers are no longer dependent on sighted persons to translate printed information for them, and this has opened new doors of opportunity.[32] Engineers at Carnegie-Mellon University have developed PizzaBot, a robot that disabled individuals can operate using a voice-recognition system. Despite knowledge of these and other benefits of new technology in the workplace, however, employees may still resist change.

Technological innovations bring about changes in employees' work environments, and change has been described as the ultimate stressor. Many workers react negatively to change that they perceive will threaten their work situation. Many of their fears center around loss—of freedom, of control, of the things they like about their jobs. Employees may fear that their quality of work life will deteriorate and that pressure at work will increase. Further, they may fear being replaced by technology or being displaced into jobs of lower skill levels.

Managers can take several actions to help employees adjust to changing technology. The workers' participation in early phases of the decision-making process regarding technological changes is important. Individuals who help plan for the implementation of new technology gain important information about the potential changes in their jobs; therefore, they are less resistant to the change. Workers are the users of the new technology. Their inputs in early stages can lead to a smoother transition into the new ways of performing work.

Managers can also keep in mind the effects that new technology will have on the skill requirements of workers. Many employees support changes that increase the skill requirements of their jobs.[33] Increased skill requirements often lead to increases in job autonomy, responsibility, and potential pay increases, all of which are received positively by employees. Whenever possible, managers should select technology that increases workers' skill requirements.

Effective training about ways to use the new technology also is essential. Training helps employees perceive that they control the technology rather than being controlled by it. The training should be designed to match workers' needs, and it should increase the workers' sense of mastery of the new technology.

Forming support groups within the organization is another way of helping employees adjust to technological change. Technological change is stressful, and support groups are important emotional outlets for workers. Support groups can also function as information exchanges so that workers can share advice on using the technology. The sense of communion provided helps workers feel less alone with the problem through the knowledge that other workers share their frustration.

A related challenge is to encourage workers to invent new uses for technology already in place. Reinvention is the term for applying new technology creatively.[34] Innovators should be rewarded for their efforts. Individuals who explore the boundaries of a new technology can personalize the technology and adapt it to their own job needs, as well as share this information with others in the work group. In one large public utility, service representatives (without their supervisor's knowledge) developed a personal note-passing system that later became the basis of a formal communication system that improved the efficiency of their work group.

Managers face a substantial challenge in leading organizations to adopt new technologies more humanely and effectively. Technological changes are essential for earnings growth and for expanded employment opportunities. The adoption of new technologies is a critical determinant of U.S. competitiveness in the global marketplace.

■ MANAGING ETHICAL ISSUES AT WORK

In addition to the challenges of globalization, work force diversity, and technology, managers must confront the ethical questions encountered in organizations. Some organizations manage ethical issues well. Johnson & Johnson employees operate under an organizational credo that spells out the company's ethical principles. Along with Corning and Rubbermaid, Johnson & Johnson is admired for its community and environmental responsibility.[35]

Despite the positive ways some organizations handle ethical issues, however, there is plenty of evidence that unethical conduct does occur in other organizations. Foodmaker Inc. faced several lawsuits after two children were killed and over 300 people became ill from eating bacteria-tainted hamburgers at its Jack-in-the-Box restaurants. Washington state rules require hamburger to be cooked to a certain temperature that kills the bacteria, but employees followed the restaurant chain's rules. The lower temperature standards failed to kill the bacteria, and the deadly outbreak followed.[36]

How can managers in organizations think through decisions carefully so that they make ethical choices? Ethical theories give us a basis for understanding, evaluating, and classifying moral arguments, and then defending conclusions about what is right and wrong. Ethical theories can be classified as consequential, rule-based, or cultural.

Consequential theories of ethics emphasize the consequences or results of behavior. John Stuart Mill's utilitarianism, a well-known consequential theory, suggests that right and wrong is determined by the consequences of the action.[37] "Good" is the ultimate moral value, and we should seek the most good for the greatest number of people. But do good ethics make for good business? Right actions do not always produce good consequences, and good consequences do not always follow right actions. And how do we determine the greatest good—in short-term or long-term consequences? Using the "greatest number" criterion can imply that minorities (less than 50 percent) might be excluded in evaluating the morality of actions. An issue that may be important for a minority but unimportant for the majority might be ignored. These are but a few of the dilemmas raised by utilitarianism.

In contrast, rule-based theories of ethics emphasize the character of the act itself, not its effects, in arriving at universal moral rights and wrongs. Moral rights, the basis for legal rights, are associated with such theories. In a theological context, the Bible, the Talmud, and the Koran are rule-based guides to ethical behavior. Immanuel Kant worked toward the ultimate moral principle in formulating his categorical imperative, a universal standard of behavior.[38] Kant argued that individuals should be treated with respect and dignity, and that they should not be used as a means to an end. He argued that we should put ourselves in the other person's position and ask if we would make the same decision if we were in the other person's situation.

Corporations and business enterprises are more prone to subscribe to consequential ethics than rule-based ethics, in part due to the persuasive arguments of the Scottish political economist and moral philosopher Adam Smith.[39] He believed that the self-interest of human beings is God's providence, not the government's. Smith set forth a doctrine of natural liberty, presenting the classical argument for open market competition and free trade. Within this framework, people should be allowed to pursue what is in their economic self-interest, and the natural efficiency of the marketplace would serve the well-being of society.

Cultural theories form a third type of ethical theory.[40] Cultural relativism contends that there are no universal ethical principles and that people should not impose their own ethical standards on others. Local standards should be the guides for ethical behavior. Cultural theories encourage individuals to operate under the old adage, "When in Rome, do as the Romans do." Strict adherence to cultural relativism can lead individuals to deny their accountability for their own decisions and to avoid difficult ethical dilemmas.

People need ethical theories to help them think through confusing, complex, difficult moral choices and ethical decisions. In contemporary organizations, people face ethical and moral dilemmas in many diverse areas. The key areas we will address are white-collar crime, computer use, employee rights, sexual harassment, romantic involvements, organizational justice, whistle-blowing, and social responsibility. We conclude with a discussion of professionalism and codes of ethics.

■ White-Collar Crime

Corporate criminal behaviors have resulted in tough new sentencing guidelines for corporate crimes and in the trend in corporate America to teach employees about ethics. In addition, corporations set up ethics committees or appointed ethics officers. However, such practices do not always work. For example, Dow Corning had an ethics program for eighteen years before its breast-implant scandal, in which the implants were found to leak and cause several health problems. No questions of safety or of testing the implants were ever given to the ethics committee. Since the savings and loan scandals of the late 1980s, the U.S. Justice Department has been keener on catching and punishing white-collar criminals such as Charles Keating. In April 1992, prosecutors ended some of the biggest 1980s financial scandals, as previously discussed.

White-collar crime may occur in more subtle forms as well. Using work hours for conducting personal business, sending out personal mail using the company postage meter, and padding an expense account are all examples of practices some individuals would consider unethical. Whether the impact is large or small, white-collar crimes are important issues in organizations.

■ Computer Use

Computers are among the core technologies of our times and give rise to various ethical dilemmas for computer professionals and users. People in organizations face a wide range of ethical questions and dilemmas with regard to the use and abuse of computerized information. What constitutes a computer crime? Software theft? Invasion of privacy?

As organizations computerize the workplace, what are the responsibilities of the corporation for the stress and health risks posed by computers? To what extent should the organization be allowed to secure itself against hackers and computer viruses? What are the moral, ethical, and legal obligations of designers and producers of unreliable computers? Who accepts moral, ethical, and legal liability for expert systems that go wrong?

■ Employee Rights

Managing the rights of employees at work creates many ethical dilemmas in organizations. Some of these dilemmas are privacy issues related to technology. Computerized monitoring, as we discussed earlier in the chapter, constitutes an invasion of privacy in the minds of some individuals. The use of employee data from computerized information systems presents many ethical concerns. Safeguarding the employee's right to privacy while preserving access to the data for those who need it requires the manager to balance competing interests.

Drug testing, free speech, downsizing and layoffs, and due process are but a few of the employee rights concerns with which managers must deal. Perhaps no other issue generates as much need for managers to balance the interests of employees and the interests of the organization as the reality of AIDS in the workplace. New drugs have shown the promise of extended lives for people with human immunodeficiency virus (HIV), and this means that HIV-infected individuals can remain in the work force and stay productive. Managers will be caught in the middle of a conflict between the rights of HIV-infected workers and the rights of their co-workers who feel threatened.

Laws exist that protect HIV-infected workers. As stated earlier, the Americans with Disabilities Act requires employees to treat HIV-infected workers as disabled individuals and to make reasonable accommodations for them. However, the ethical dilemmas involved with this situation go far beyond the legal issues. How does a manager protect the dignity of the person with AIDS and preserve the morale and productivity of the work group when so much prejudice and ignorance surround this disease? Many organizations, such as Wells Fargo, believe the answer is education. Many of us do not know as much about AIDS as we should, and many of our fears arise because of a lack of knowledge. Wells Fargo has a written AIDS policy because of the special issues associated with the disease—such as confidentiality, employee socialization, co-worker education, and counseling—that must be addressed. Polaroid corporation has a comprehensive AIDS education and prevention plan that provides HIV-infected employees the full range of benefits and guarantees them continued employment. Managers at Polaroid say that the cost of their HIV/AIDS program is one-fifth the cost of treating a single AIDS victim.[41]

■ Sexual Harassment

Anita Hill's sexual harassment charges against Associate Supreme Court Justice Clarence Thomas during his senate confirmation hearings generated a tremendous national controversy. According to the Equal Employment Opportunity Commission, sexual harassment is unwelcome sexual attention, whether verbal or physical, that affects an employee's job conditions or creates a hostile working environment. Recent court rulings, too, have broadened the definition of sexual harassment beyond job-related abuse to include acts that create a hostile work environment. More than 90 percent of Fortune 500 companies, such as Digital Equipment Corporation, reported that they offer employees special training about sexual harassment.[42] Some of the best training programs use role-playing, videotapes, and group discussions of real cases to help supervisors recognize unlawful sexual harassment and investigate complaints properly.

■ Romantic Involvements

Hugging, sexual innuendos, and repeated requests for dates may constitute sexual harassment for some, but they are a prelude to romance for others. This situation carries with it a different set of ethical dilemmas for organizations.

The office romance between William Agee, at the time chairman of Bendix Corporation, and Mary Cunningham, a corporate vice-president at Bendix, was one of the first cases to bring the ethical dilemmas of office romance to the fore. Their much-publicized liaison exemplified the conflicts that occur within an organization when romantic involvements at work become disruptive. Both Agee and Cunningham ultimately left Bendix and went on to a long-term marital and family relationship. Unfortunately, many office romances do not lead to such positive outcomes.

Eliza Collins examines a set of six case studies in thinking through the moral and ethical dilemmas posed by office romance for the organization and its employees.[43] She concludes that romantic relationships in the workplace create a basic conflict of interest for the two parties involved. Without moralizing, she presents a helpful approach for executives and romantic partners to use in working through the conflict to resolution. Unfortunately, the woman is too often treated as the scapegoat in such office romances and pays the dearest price if the situation blows up. Collins contends that ignoring office romances is not the answer. Clear-cut company policies are needed that spell out the potential conflicts of interest and consequences of office romance.

Organizational Justice

Another area in which moral and ethical dilemmas may arise for people at work concerns organizational justice, both distributive and procedural. Distributive justice concerns the fairness of outcomes individuals receive. For example, the salaries and bonuses for U.S. corporate executives became a central issue with Japanese executives during President George Bush's 1992 visit to Japan with accompanying American CEOs in key industries. The Japanese CEOs questioned the distributive justice in the American CEOs' salaries at a time when so many companies were in difficulty and laying off workers.

Procedural justice concerns the fairness of the process by which outcomes are allocated.[44] The ethical questions here do not concern the just or unjust distribution of organizational resources. Rather, the ethical questions in procedural justice concern the process. Has the organization used the correct procedures in allocating resources? Have the right considerations, such as competence and skill, been brought to bear in the decision process? And have the wrong considerations, such as race and gender, been excluded from the decision process?

Whistle-Blowing

Whistle-blowers are employees who inform authorities of wrongdoings of their companies or co-workers. Whistle-blowers can be perceived as either heroes or "vile wretches" depending on the circumstances of the situation. For a whistle-blower to be considered a public hero, the gravity of the situation that the whistle-blower reports to authorities must be of such magnitude and quality as to be perceived as abhorrent by others. In contrast, the whistle-blower is considered a vile wretch if the act of whistle-blowing is seen by others as more offensive than the situation the whistle-blower reports to authorities.

Whistle-blowing is important in the U.S. because committed organization members sometimes engage in unethical behavior in an intense desire to succeed. Many examples of whistle-blowing can be found in corporate America. For example, in 1984, a laboratory technician employed at a General Electric Company nuclear fuels production facility complained to management that fellow workers were failing to clean up radioactive spills. Although the spills were eventually cleaned up, the complaining employee was laid off later.[45] Laws are now in place to provide remedy for workers who suffer employment discrimination in retaliation for whistle-blowing.

Organizations can manage whistle-blowing by communicating the conditions that are appropriate for the disclosure of wrongdoing.[46] Clearly delineating wrongful behavior and the appropriate ways to respond are important organizational actions.

Social Responsibility

Corporate social responsibility is the obligation of an organization to behave in ethical ways in the social environment in which it operates. Ethical conduct at the individual level can translate into social responsibility at the organizational level. Johnson & Johnson, for example, acted in a socially responsible fashion in 1984 and 1985 when it was discovered that some bottles of Tylenol had been tampered with and poisoned. Managers moved quickly to remove Tylenol from the retailers and held press conferences to warn the public about the situation. The company had encouraged ethical behavior among employees for years, and thus employees knew how to respond to the crisis.

Socially responsible actions are expected of organizations. Current concerns include protecting the environment, promoting worker safety, supporting social issues, and investing in the community, among others. Some organizations, like IBM, loan executives to inner-city schools to teach science and math. Managers must encourage both individual ethical behavior and organizational social responsibility.

Codes of Ethics

One of the characteristics of mature professions is the existence of a code of ethics to which the practitioners adhere in their actions and behavior. Such is the case with the Hippocratic oath in medicine. Although some of the individual differences we will address in Chapter 4 produce ethical or unethical orientations in specific people, a profession's code of ethics becomes a standard against which members can measure themselves in the absence of internalized standards.

No universal code of ethics or oath exists for business as it does for medicine. However, Paul Harris and four business colleagues, who founded Rotary International in 1904, made an effort to address ethical and moral behavior right from the beginning. They developed the Four-Way Test, which is now used in over 180 nations throughout the world by the nearly 2 million Rotarians in 25,000 Rotary clubs. The four questions in the Four-Way test are (1) Is it the truth? (2) Is it fair to all concerned? (3) Will it build goodwill and better friendships? and (4) Will it be beneficial to all concerned?

Beyond the individual and profession level, corporate culture is another excellent starting point for addressing ethics and morality. In Chapter 16 we will examine the way corporate culture and leader behavior trickles down the company, setting a standard for all below. In some cases, the corporate ethics may be captured in a regulation. For example, Air Force Regulation 30-30 (Codes of Conduct) specifies the ethical and moral standards to which all U.S. Air Force personnel are to adhere. In other cases, the corporate ethics may be in the form of a credo. Johnson & Johnson's credo helped hundreds of employees address the criminal tampering with Tylenol products already mentioned. In the 1986 centennial annual report, J & J attributed its success in this crisis, as well as its long-term business growth (a compound sales rate of 11.6 percent for 100 years), to "our unique form of decentralized management, our adherence to the ethical principles embodied in our credo, and our emphasis on managing the business for the long term."

Individual codes of ethics, professional oaths, and organizational credos all must be anchored in a moral, ethical framework. They are always open to question and continuous improvement using ethical theories as a tool for reexamining the soundness of the current standard. Although a universal right and wrong may exist, it would be hard to argue that there is only one code of ethics to which all individuals, professions, and organizations can subscribe.

■ MANAGERIAL IMPLICATIONS: FACING THE CHALLENGES

Globalization, work force diversity, emerging technologies, and ethical dilemmas are challenges to managers in all organizations during the next decade. If organizations are to gain competitive advantage, they must meet these challenges head-on, as well as in a proactive manner. You will find the challenges addressed in each chapter as you continue through this textbook.

Managers take on ethical and diversity challenges when they make employee selection decisions and complete performance evaluations. Technology challenges come when managers learn new methods and take advantage of new tools for performing their jobs, as well as when they help implement technological innovation throughout their organizations. Managers work through global competition issues when their industries are challenged by foreign competition. They encounter diversity challenges when they work side by side with people who are ethnically, sexually, or in any other way different from them. The success of organizations during the next decade will be dependent upon managers' success in addressing these four challenges.

■ CHAPTER SUMMARY

- To ensure that their organizations meet the competition, managers must tackle four important challenges: globalization, work force diversity, technological change, and ethical behavior at work.
- The five cultural differences that affect work-related attitudes are individualism versus collectivism, power distance, uncertainty avoidance, masculinity versus femininity, and time orientation.
- Diversity encompasses gender, culture, personality, sexual orientation, religion, military affiliation, ability, economic class, social status, and a host of other differences.
- Managers must take a proactive approach to managing diversity so that differences are valued and capitalized upon.

- Technological changes will have dramatic effects on organizations by the year 2000. Through supportive relationships and training, managers can help employees adjust to technological change.
- Three types of ethical theories include consequential theories, rule-based theories, and cultural theories.
- Ethical dilemmas emerge for people at work in the areas of white-collar crime, computer use, employee rights, sexual harassment, romantic involvements, organizational justice, whistle-blowing, and social responsibility.

■ REVIEW QUESTIONS

1. What are Hofstede's five dimensions of cultural differences that affect work attitudes? Using these dimensions, describe the U.S.
2. What are the primary sources of diversity in the U.S. work force?
3. What specific actions can managers take to manage a diverse work force?
4. Discuss five areas of rapid technological advancement that will affect organizations by the year 2000.
5. Explain four ways managers can help employees adjust to technology.
6. Describe three types of ethical theories and their assumptions.
7. Discuss the ethical dilemmas people face at work concerning crime, computer use, employee rights, sexual harassment, romantic involvements, organizational justice, whistle-blowing, and social responsibility.
8. Some companies have a policy that employees should not become romantically involved with each other. Is this ethical?
9. What are some of the concerns that a person with AIDS would have about his or her job? What are some of the fears that co-workers would have? How can a manager balance these two sets of concerns?

■ REFERENCES

1. M. A. Hitt, R. E. Hoskisson, and J. S. Harrison, "Strategic Competitiveness in the 1990s: Challenges and Opportunities for U.S. Executives," *Academy of Management Executive* 5 (1991): 7–22.
2. S. C. Harper, "The Challenges Facing CEOs: Past, Present, and Future," *Academy of Management Executive* 6 (1992): 7–25.
3. K. Ohmae, *Borderless World: Power and Strategies in the Interlinked Economy* (New York: Harper & Row, 1990).
4. C. A. Bartlett and S. Ghoshal, *Managing across Borders: The Transnational Solution* (Boston: Harvard Business School Press, 1989).
5. J. A. Wall, Jr., "Managers in the People's Republic of China," *Academy of Management Executive* 4 (1990): 19–32.
6. G. Hofstede, *Culture's Consequences: International Differences in Work-related Values* (Beverly Hills, Calif.: Sage Publications, 1980).
7. G. Hofstede, "Cultural Constraints in Management Theories," *Academy of Management Executive* 7 (1993): 81–94.
8. A. J. Michel, "Goodbyes Can Cost Plenty in Europe," *Fortune*, 6 April 1992, 16.
9. E. Brandt, "Global HR," *Personnel Journal* 70 (1991): 38–44.
10. W. B. Johnston and E. A. Packer, *Workforce 2000: Work and Workers for the 21st Century* (Indianapolis: Hudson Institute, 1987).
11. L. S. Gottfredson, "Dilemmas in Developing Diversity Programs," in S. E. Jackson, ed., *Diversity in the Workplace: Human Resources Initiatives* (New York: Guilford Press, 1992), 279–305.
12. T. Cox, Jr. "The Multicultural Organization," *Academy of Management Executive* 5 (1991): 34–47.
13. U.S. Dept. of Labor, Bureau of Labor Statistics, *Employment and Earnings* (Washington, D.C.: Government Printing Office, January 1993).
14. D. L. Nelson and M. A. Hitt, "Employed Women and Stress: Implications for Enhancing Women's Mental Health in the Workplace," in J. C. Quick, L. R. Murphy, and J. J. Hurrell, Jr., eds., *Stress and Well-Being at Work* (Washington, D.C.: American Psychological Association, 1992), 164–177.
15. Johnston and Packer, *Workforce 2000*.
16. S. E. Jackson and E. B. Alvarez, "Working through Diversity as a Strategic Imperative," in S. E. Jackson, ed., *Diversity in the Workplace: Human Resources Initiatives* (New York: Guilford Press, 1992), 13–36.
17. C. M. Solomon, "Managing the Baby Busters," *Personnel Journal* (March 1992): 52–59.
18. B. Rosen and T. Jerdee, "The Influence of Age Stereotypes on Managerial Decisions," *Journal of Applied Psychology* 61 (1976): 428–432.
19. S. R. Rhodes, "Age-related Differences in Work Attitudes and Behavior: A Review and Conceptual Analysis," *Psychological Bulletin* 93 (1983): 338–367.
20. J. J. Laabs, "The Golden Arches Provide Golden Opportunities," *Personnel Journal* (July 1991): 52–57.
21. J. Waldrop, "The Cost of Hiring the Disabled," *American Demographics*, March 1991, 12.
22. P. A. Galagan, "Tapping the Power of a Diverse Workforce," *Training and Development Journal* 26 (1991): 38–44.

23. C. T. Schreiber, K. F. Price, and A. Morrison, "Workforce Diversity and the Glass Ceiling: Practices, Barriers, Possibilities," *Human Resource Planning* 16 (1993): 51–69.

24. C. H. Ferguson, "Computers and the Coming of the U.S. Keiretsu," *Harvard Business Review* 68 (1990): 55–70.

25. A. Tanzer and R. Simon, "Why Japan Loves Robots and We Don't," *Forbes,* 16 April 1990, 148–153.

26. P. Proctor and E. Sekigawa, "Japan Focusing on Robotics, Automation to Improve Quality, Meet Demand," *Aviation Week and Space Technology* 135 (1991): 67–68.

27. Johnston and Packer, *Workforce 2000.*

28. D. L. Nelson, "Individual Adjustment to Information-driven Technologies: A Critical Review," *MIS Quarterly* 14 (1990): 79–98.

29. C. Brod, *Technostress* (Reading, Mass.: Addison-Wesley, 1984).

30. M. Allen, "Legislation Could Restrict Bosses from Snooping on Their Workers," *Wall Street Journal,* 24 September 1991, B1–B8.

31. K. D. Hill and S. Kerr, "The Impact of Computer-integrated Manufacturing Systems on the First Line Supervisor," *Journal of Organizational Behavior Management* 6 (1984): 81–87.

32. J. Anderson, "How Technology Brings Blind People into the Workplace," *Harvard Business Review* 67 (1989): 36–39.

33. B. Bemmels and Y. Reshef, "Manufacturing Employees and Technological Change," *Journal of Labor Research* 12 (1991): 231–246.

34. D. Mankin, T. Bikson, B. Gutek, and C. Stasz, "Managing Technological Change: The Process Is the Key," *Datamation* 34 (1988), 69–80.

35. T. Welsh, "Best and Worst Corporate Reputation," *Fortune,* 7 February 1994, 58–66.

36. J. Tannenbaum, "Focus on Franchising: Franchises Learn from a Death, Seek U.S. Pre-Emption," *Wall Street Journal,* 5 February 1993: B2–B3.

37. J. S. Mill, *Utilitarianism, Liberty, and Representative Government* (London: Dent, 1910).

38. I. Kant, *Groundwork of the Metaphysics of Morals,* trans. H. J. Paton (New York: Harper & Row, 1964).

39. A. Smith, *An Inquiry into the Nature and Causes of the Wealth of Nations,* vol. 10 of *The Harvard Classics,* ed. C. J. Bullock (New York: P. F. Collier & Son, 1909).

40. H. W. Lane and J. J. DiStefano, *International Management Behavior,* 2d ed. (Boston: PWS-Kent, 1992).

41. R. A. Stone, "AIDS in the Workplace: An Executive Update," *Academy of Management Executive* 8 (1994): 52–62.

42. J. S. Lublin, "Sexual Harassment Is Topping Agenda in Many Executive Education Programs," *Wall Street Journal,* 2 December 1991, B1, B6.

43. E. C. G. Collins, "Managers and Lovers," *Harvard Business Review* 61 (1983): 142–153.

44. J. Greenberg and R. Folger, "Procedural Justice, Participation, and the Fair Process Effect in Groups and Organizations," in P. B. Paulus, ed., *Basic Group Processes* (New York: Springer-Verlag, 1983), 235–256.

45. C. Hukill, "Whistleblowers," *Monthly Labor Review* (October 1990): 41.

46. M. P. Miceli and J. P. Near, "Whistle Blowing: Reaping the Benefits," *Academy of Management Executive* 8 (1994): 65–72.

PART II
INDIVIDUAL PROCESSES
AND BEHAVIOR

CHAPTER 3
PERSONALITY, PERCEPTION, AND ATTRIBUTION

LEARNING OBJECTIVES

After reading this chapter, you should be able to do the following:

- Describe individual differences and their importance in understanding behavior.
- Define personality.
- Explain four theories of personality.
- Identify several personality characteristics and their influences on behavior in organizations.
- Explain how personality is measured.
- Define social perception and explain how characteristics of the perceiver, the target, and the situation affect it.
- Identify five common barriers to social perception.
- Explain the attribution process and how attributions affect managerial behavior.

■ INDIVIDUAL DIFFERENCES AND ORGANIZATIONAL BEHAVIOR

In this chapter and continuing in Chapter 4, we explore the concept of individual differences. Individuals are unique in terms of their skills, abilities, personalities, perceptions, attitudes, values, and ethics. These are just a few of the ways individuals may be similar to or different from one another. Individual differences represent the essence of the chal-lenge of management, because no two individuals are completely alike. At Southwest Airlines, individual differences are celebrated. Employees are encouraged to be themselves and to find creative ways to deliver "Positively Outrageous Service." By hiring people who break the mold, Southwest is able to break records in delivering high quality customer service.

Managers face the challenge of working with people who possess a multitude of individual char-

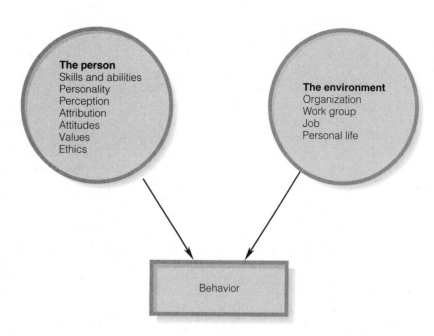

■ **FIGURE 3.1**
Variables Influencing
Individual Behavior

acteristics, so the more managers understand individual differences, the better they can work with others. Figure 3.1 illustrates how individual differences affect human behavior.

The basis for understanding individual differences stems from Lewin's early contention that behavior is a function of the person and the environment.[1] Lewin expressed this idea in an equation: B = f (P, E), where B = behavior, P = person, and E = environment. This idea has been carried through by the interactional psychology approach. Basically, this approach says that in order to understand human behavior, we must know something about the person and something about the situation. There are four basic propositions of interactional psychology:

1. Behavior is a function of a continuous, multidirectional interaction between the person and the situation.
2. The person is active in this process and both is changed by situations *and* changes situations.
3. People vary in many characteristics, including cognitive, affective, motivational, and ability factors.
4. Two interpretations of situations are important: the objective situation and the person's subjective view of the situation.[2]

The interactional psychology approach points out the need to study both persons and situations. We will focus on personal and situational factors throughout the text. The person consists of individual differences such as those we emphasize in this chapter and Chapter 4: personality, perception, attribution, attitudes, values, and ethics. The situation consists of the environment the person operates in, and it can include things like the organization, work group, personal life situation, job characteristics, and many other environmental influences. One important and fascinating individual difference is personality.

■ **PERSONALITY**

What makes an individual behave in consistent ways in a variety of situations? Personality is an individual difference that lends consistency to a person's behavior. Personality is defined as a relatively stable set of characteristics that influence an individual's behavior. Although there is debate about the determinants of personality, we conclude that there are several origins. One determinant is heredity, and some interesting studies have supported this position. Identical twins who are separated at birth and raised apart in very different situations have been found to share personality traits and job preferences. For example, about half of the variation in traits like extraversion, impulsiveness, and flexibility was found to be genetically determined; that is, identical twins who grew up in different environments shared these traits. In addition, the twins held similar jobs.[3] Thus, there does appear to be a genetic influence on personality.

Another determinant of personality is the environment to which a person is exposed. Family, cultural, and educational influences and other environmental forces shape personality. Therefore, personality is shaped by both heredity and environment.

■ Personality Theories

Four major theories of personality are the trait theory, psychodynamic theory, humanistic theory, and the integrative approach. Each theory has influenced the study of personality in organizations.

Trait Theory.   Some early personality researchers believed that to understand individuals, we must break down behavior patterns into a series of observable traits. According to trait theory, these traits combined into a group form an individual's personality. Gordon Allport, a leading trait theorist, saw traits as broad, general guides that lend consistency to behavior.[4] Thousands of traits have been identified over the years. Raymond Cattell, another prominent trait theorist, identified sixteen traits that formed the basis for differences in individual behavior. He described traits in bipolar adjective combinations such as self-assured/apprehensive, reserved/outgoing, and submissive/dominant.[5]

More recently, researchers have argued that all traits can be reduced to five basic factors. The "big five" traits include extraversion, agreeableness, will to achieve, emotional stability, and openness to experience.[6] Although there is evidence to support the existence of the big five traits, research is needed to see whether these five traits actually predict behavior.

The trait approach has been the subject of considerable criticism. Some theorists argue that simply identifying traits is not enough; instead, personality is dynamic and not completely stable. Further, trait theorists tended to ignore the influence of situations. Other researchers believe that behavior is not consistent; rather, it varies as a function of situational factors.

Psychodynamic Theory.   Based on the work of Sigmund Freud, psychodynamic theory emphasizes the unconscious determinants of behavior.[7] Freud saw personality as the interaction between three elements of personality: the id, ego, and superego. The id is the most primitive element, the source of drives and impulses, and operates in an uncensored manner. The superego, similar to what we know as conscience, contains values and the "shoulds and should nots" of the personality. There is an ongoing conflict between the id and the superego. The ego serves to manage the conflict between the id and the superego. In this role, the ego compromises, and the result is the individual's use of defense mechanisms such as denial of reality. The contribution of psychodynamic theory to our understanding of personality is its focus on unconscious influences on behavior.

Humanistic Theory.   Carl Rogers believed that all people have a basic drive toward self-actualization, which is the quest to be all you can be.[8] The humanistic theory focuses on individual growth and improvement. It is distinctly people-centered, and also emphasizes the individual's view of the world. The humanistic approach contributes an understanding of the self to personality theory and contends that the self-concept is the most important part of an individual's personality.

Integrative Approach.   Recently, researchers have taken a broader, more integrative approach to the study of personality.[9] To capture its influence on behavior, personality is described as a composite of the individual's psychological processes. Personality dispositions include emotions, cognitions, attitudes, expectancies, and fantasies. "Dispositions," in this approach, simply means the tendencies of individuals to respond to situations in consistent ways. Influenced by both genetics and experiences, dispositions can be modified. The integrative approach focuses on both person (dispositions) and situational variables as combined predictors of behavior.

■ Personality Characteristics in Organizations

Hundreds of personality characteristics have been identified. We have selected five because of their particular influences on individual behavior in organizations. Managers should learn as much as possible about personality in order to understand their employees. Personality conflicts occur frequently in organizations and a working knowledge of personality helps managers deal with the conflicts that may arise. We will focus on several personality characteristics, including locus of control, self-esteem, self-efficacy, self-monitoring, and positive/negative affect.

Locus of Control. An individual's generalized belief about internal (self) versus external (situation or others) control is called locus of control. People who believe they control what happens to them are said to have an internal locus of control, whereas people who believe that circumstances or other people control their fate have an external locus of control. Research on locus of control has strong implications for organizations. Internals (those with an internal locus of control) have been found to have higher job satisfaction, to be more likely to assume managerial positions, and to prefer participative management styles. In addition, internals have been shown to display higher work motivation, hold stronger beliefs that effort leads to performance, receive higher salaries, and display less anxiety than externals (those with an external locus of control).[10]

Knowing about locus of control can prove valuable to managers. Because internals believe they control what happens to them, they will want to exercise control in their work environment. Allowing internals considerable voice in the way work is performed is important. Internals will not react well to being closely supervised. Externals, in contrast, may prefer a more structured work setting, and they may be more reluctant to participate in decision making.

Self-Esteem. Self-esteem is an individual's general feeling of self-worth. Individuals with high self-esteem have positive feelings about themselves, perceive themselves to have strengths as well as weaknesses, and believe their strengths are more important than their weaknesses. Individuals with low self-esteem view themselves negatively. They are more strongly affected by what other people think of them, and they compliment individuals who give them positive feedback while cutting down people who give them negative feedback.

A person's self-esteem affects a host of other attitudes and has important implications for behavior in organizations. People with high self-esteem perform better and are more satisfied with their jobs. When they are involved in a job search, they seek out higher-status jobs. A work team made up of individuals with high self-esteem is more likely to be successful than a team with lower average self-esteem.[11]

Very high self-esteem may be too much of a good thing. When people with high self-esteem find themselves in stressful situations, they may brag inappropriately.[12] This may be viewed negatively by others, who see spontaneous boasting as egotistical.

Self-esteem may be strongly affected by situations. Success tends to raise self-esteem, whereas failure tends to lower it. Given that high self-esteem is generally a positive characteristic, managers should encourage employees to raise their self-esteem by giving them appropriate challenges and opportunities for success.

Self-Efficacy. An individual's beliefs and expectancies about his or her ability to accomplish a specific task effectively is known as self-efficacy. Individuals with high self-efficacy believe that they have the ability to get things done, that they are capable of putting forth the effort to accomplish the task, and that they can overcome any obstacles to their success. There are four sources of self-efficacy: prior experiences, behavior models (witnessing the success of others), persuasion from other people, and assessment of current physical and emotional capabilities.[13] Believing in one's own capability to get something done is an important facilitator of success. There is strong evidence that self-efficacy leads to high performance on a wide variety of physical and mental tasks.[14] High self-efficacy has also led to success in breaking addictions, increasing pain tolerance, and recovering from illnesses.

Managers can help employees develop their self-efficacy. This can be done by providing job challenges, coaching and counseling for improved performance, and rewarding employees' achievements. Empowerment, or sharing power with employees, can be accomplished by interventions that help employees increase their self-esteem and self-efficacy. Given the increasing diversity of the work force, managers may want to target their efforts toward women and minorities in particular. Research has indicated that women and minorities tend to have lower than average self-efficacy.[15]

Self-Monitoring. A characteristic with great potential for affecting behavior in organizations is self-monitoring—the extent to which people base their behavior on cues from people and situations.[16] High self-monitors pay attention to what is appropriate in particular situations and to the behavior of other people, and they behave accordingly. Low self-monitors, in contrast, are not as vigilant for situational cues and act from internal states rather than paying attention to the situation. As a result, the behavior of low self-monitors is consistent across situations. High self-monitors, because their behavior varies with the situation, appear to be more unpredictable and less consistent. Although research on self-monitoring in organizations is in its early stages, we can speculate that high self-monitors respond more readily to work group norms, organizational culture, and supervisory feedback than do low self-monitors, who adhere more to internal guidelines for behavior ("I am who I am"). In addition, high self-monitors may be enthusiastic participants in the trend toward work teams because of their ability to assume flexible roles. The chameleon-like flexibility may pay off, too. A study that tracked MBA graduates for five years showed that high self-monitors were more likely to change employers, work in more locations, and achieve cross-company promotions. High self-monitors who did not change employers obtained more internal promotions than low self-monitors. The ability to adapt their behavior to different circumstances and readiness to follow opportunities helped the high self-monitors get ahead.[17]

Positive/Negative Affect. Recently, researchers have explored the effects of persistent mood dispositions at work. Individuals who focus on the positive aspects of themselves, other people, and the world in general are said to have positive affect.[18] In contrast, those who accentuate the negative in themselves, others, and the world are said to possess negative affect (also referred to as negative affectivity). Interviewers who exhibit positive affect evaluate job candidates more favorably than do interviewers whose affect is neutral.[19] Employees with positive affect are absent from work less often. Individuals with negative affect report more work stress.[20] Individual affect also influences the work group. Negative individual affect produces negative group affect, and this leads to less cooperative behavior in the work group.[21]

Positive affect is a definite asset in work settings. Managers can do several things to promote positive affect, including the use of participative decision making and the provision of pleasant working conditions. We need to know more about inducing positive affect in the workplace.

The characteristics previously described are but a few of the personality characteristics that affect behavior in organizations. Can managers predict the behavior of their employees by knowing their personalities? Not completely. You may recall that the interactional psychology model (Figure 3.1) requires both person and situation variables to predict behavior. Another idea to remember in predicting behavior is the strength of situational influences. Some situations are strong situations in that they overwhelm the effects of individual personalities. These situations are interpreted in the same way by different individuals, evoke agreement on the appropriate behavior in the situation, and provide cues to appropriate behavior. A performance appraisal session is an example of a strong situation. Employees know to listen to their boss and to contribute when asked to do so.

A weak situation, in contrast, is one that is open to many interpretations. It provides few cues to appropriate behavior and no obvious rewards for one behavior over another. Thus, individual personalities have a stronger influence in weak situations than in strong situations. An informal meeting without an agenda can be seen as a weak situation.

Organizations present combinations of strong and weak situations; therefore, personality has a stronger effect on behavior in some situations than in others.

■ Measuring Personality

Several methods can be used to assess personality. These include projective tests, behavioral measures, and self-report questionnaires.

The projective test is one method used to measure personality. In these tests, individuals are shown a picture, abstract image, or photo and are asked to describe what they see or to tell a story about what they see. The rationale behind projective tests is that each individual responds to the stimulus in a way that reflects his or her unique personality. The Rorschach ink blot test is a projective test commonly used to assess personality.[22] Like other projective tests, however, it has low reliability.

There are behavioral measures of personality as well. Measuring behavior involves observing an individual's behavior in a controlled situation. We might assess a person's sociability, for example, by counting the number of times he or she approaches strangers at a party. The behavior is scored in some manner to produce an index of personality.

The most common method of assessing personality is the self-report questionnaire. Individuals respond to a series of questions, usually in an agree/disagree or true/false format. One of the more widely recognized questionnaires is the Minnesota Multiphasic Personality Inventory (MMPI). The MMPI is comprehensive and assesses a variety of traits, as well as various neurotic or psychotic disorders. Used extensively in psychological counseling to identify disorders, the MMPI is a long questionnaire. The big five traits we discussed earlier are measured by another self-report questionnaire, the NEO Personality Inventory.

Another popular self-report questionnaire is the Myers-Briggs Type Indicator (MBTI). The Myers-Briggs Type Indicator is an instrument that has been developed to measure Carl Jung's ideas about individual differences. Swiss psychiatrist Carl Jung built his work upon the notion that people are fundamentally different, but also fundamentally alike. His classic treatise *Psychological Types* proposed that the population was made up of two basic types—extraverted and introverted.[23] He went on to identify two types of perception (sensing and intuiting) and two types of judgment (thinking and feeling). Perception (how we gather information) and judgment (how we make decisions) represent the basic mental functions that everyone uses.

Jung suggested that human similarities and differences could be understood by combining preferences. We prefer and choose one way of doing things over another. We are not exclusively one way or another; rather, we have a preference for extraversion or introversion, just as we have a preference for right-handedness or left-handedness. We may use each hand equally well, but when a ball is thrown at us by surprise, we will reach to catch it with our preferred hand. Jung's type theory argues that no preferences are better than others. Differences are to be understood, celebrated, and appreciated.

During the 1940s, a mother-daughter team became fascinated with individual differences among people and with the work of Carl Jung. Katharine Briggs and her daughter, Isabel Briggs Myers, developed the Myers-Briggs Type Indicator to put Jung's type theory into practical use. The MBTI is used extensively in organizations as a basis for understanding individual differences. It has been used in career counseling, team building, conflict management, and understanding management styles.

We turn now to another psychological process that forms the basis for individual differences. Perception shapes the way we view the world, and it varies greatly among individuals.

■ SOCIAL PERCEPTION

Perception involves the way we view the world around us. It adds meaning to information gathered via the five senses of touch, smell, hearing, vision, and taste. Perception is the primary vehicle through which we come to understand ourselves and our surroundings. Social perception is the process of interpreting information about another person. Virtually all management activities rely on perception. In appraising performance, managers use their perceptions of an employee's behavior as a basis for the evaluation.

One work situation that highlights the importance of perception is the selection interview. The consequences of a bad match between an individual and the organization are devastating for both parties, so it is essential that the data gathered be accurate.

■ **FIGURE 3.2**
A Model of Social
Perception

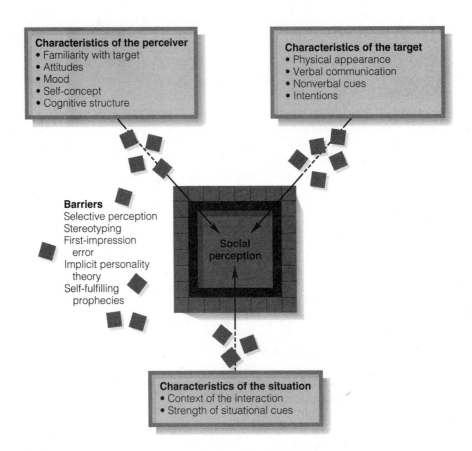

Characteristics of the perceiver
• Familiarity with target
• Attitudes
• Mood
• Self-concept
• Cognitive structure

Characteristics of the target
• Physical appearance
• Verbal communication
• Nonverbal cues
• Intentions

Barriers
Selective perception
Stereotyping
First-impression
  error
Implicit personality
  theory
Self-fulfilling
  prophecies

Social
perception

Characteristics of the situation
• Context of the interaction
• Strength of situational cues

Typical first interviews are brief, and the candidate is usually one of many seen by an interviewer during a day. How long does it take for the interviewer to reach a decision about a candidate? In the first four to five minutes, the interviewer has often made an accept or reject decision based on his or her perception of the candidate.[24]

Valuing diversity, including cultural diversity, is the key to international competitiveness.[25] This challenge and others make social perception skills essential to managerial success. Marilyn Gowing, assistant director for personnel research and development at the U.S. Office of Personnel Management, has extensive experience in human resource management. In her view, social perception skills have become even more important in perceiving employees' capabilities, recognizing customers' needs, and providing top quality service in a world of global competition.

Three major categories of factors influence our perception of another person: characteristics of ourselves, as perceivers; characteristics of the target person we are perceiving; and characteristics of the situation in which the interaction takes place. Figure 3.2 shows a model of social perception.

■ Characteristics of the Perceiver

Several characteristics of the perceiver can affect social perception. One such characteristic is familiarity with the target (the person being perceived). When we are familiar with a person, we have multiple observations upon which to base our impression of him or her. If the information we have gathered during these observations is accurate, we may have an accurate perception of the other person. Familiarity does not always mean accuracy, however. Sometimes, when we know a person well, we tend to screen out information that is inconsistent with what we believe the person is like. This is a particular danger in performance appraisals where the rater is familiar with the person being rated.

The perceivers' attitudes also affect social perception. Suppose you are interviewing candidates for a very important position in your organization—a position that requires negotiating contracts with suppliers, most of whom are male. You may feel that women are not capable of holding their own in tough negotiations. This attitude will doubtless affect your perceptions of the female candidates you interview.

Mood can have a strong influence on the way we perceive someone.[26] We think differently when we are happy than we do when we are depressed. In addition, we remember information that is consistent with our mood state better than information that is inconsistent with it. When in a positive mood, we form more positive impressions of others. When in a negative mood, we tend to evaluate others unfavorably.

Another factor that can affect social perception is the perceiver's self-concept. An individual with a positive self-concept tends to notice positive attributes in another person. In contrast, a negative self-concept can lead a perceiver to pick out negative traits in another person. Greater understanding of self allows us to have more accurate perceptions of others.

Cognitive structure, an individual's pattern of thinking, also affects social perception. Some people have a tendency to perceive physical traits, such as height, weight, and appearance, more readily. Others tend to focus more on central traits, or personality dispositions. Cognitive complexity allows a person to perceive multiple characteristics of another person rather than attending to just a few traits.

■ Characteristics of the Target

Characteristics of the target, who is the person being perceived, influence social perception. Physical appearance plays a big role in our perception of others. The perceiver will notice the target's physical features such as height, weight, estimated age, race, and gender. Clothing says a great deal about a person. Blue pin-striped suits, for example, are decoded to mean banking or Wall Street. Perceivers tend to notice physical appearance characteristics that contrast with the norm, that are intense, or that are new or unusual. A loud person, one who dresses outlandishly, a very tall

person, or a hyperactive child will be noticed because he or she provides a contrast to what is commonly encountered. In addition, people who are novel can attract attention. Newcomers or minorities in the organization are examples of novel individuals.

Physical attractiveness often colors our entire impression of another person. Interviewers rate attractive candidates more favorably, and attractive candidates are awarded higher starting salaries.[27] People who are perceived as physically attractive face stereotypes as well. We will discuss these and other stereotypes later in this chapter.

Verbal communication from targets also affects our perception of them. We listen to the topics they speak about, their voice tone, and their accent and make judgments based on this input.

Nonverbal communication conveys a great deal of information about the target. Eye contact, facial expressions, body movements, and posture all are deciphered by the perceiver in an attempt to form an impression of the target. It is interesting that some nonverbal signals mean very different things in different cultures. The "okay" sign in the U.S. (forming a circle with the thumb and forefinger) is an insult in South America. Facial expressions, however, seem to have universal meanings. Individuals from different cultures are able to recognize and decipher expressions the same way.[28]

The intentions of the target are inferred by the perceiver, who observes the target's behavior. We may see our boss appear in our office doorway and think, "Oh no! She's going to give me more work to do." Or we may perceive that her intention is to congratulate us on a recent success. In any case, the perceiver's interpretation of the target's intentions affects the way the perceiver views the target.

■ Characteristics of the Situation

The situation in which the interaction between the perceiver and the target takes place has an influence on the perceiver's impression of the target. The social context of the interaction is a major influence. Meeting a professor in his or her office affects your impression in a certain way that may contrast with the impression you would form had you met the professor in a local restaurant. In Japan, social context is very important. Business conversations after working hours or at lunch are taboo. If you try to talk business during these times, you may be perceived as rude.[29]

The strength of situational cues also affects social perception. As we discussed earlier in the chapter, some situations provide strong cues as to appropriate behavior. In these situations, we assume that the individual's behavior can be accounted for by the situation, and that it may not reflect the individual's disposition. This is the discounting principle in social perception. For example, you may encounter an automobile salesperson who has a warm and personable manner, asks about your work and hobbies, and seems genuinely interested in your taste in cars. Can you assume that this behavior reflects the salesperson's personality? You probably cannot, because of the influence of the situation. This person is trying to sell you a car, and in this particular situation he or she probably treats all customers in this manner.

You can see that characteristics of the perceiver, the target, and the situation all affect social perception. It would be wonderful if all of us had accurate social perception skills. Unfortunately, barriers often prevent us from perceiving another person accurately.

■ Barriers to Social Perception

Several factors lead us to form inaccurate impressions of others. Five of these barriers to social perception are selective perception, stereotyping, first-impression error, implicit personality theories, and self-fulfilling prophecies.

We receive a vast amount of information. Selective perception is our tendency to choose information that supports our viewpoints. Individuals often ignore information that makes them feel uncomfortable or threatens their viewpoints. Suppose, for example, that a sales manager is evaluating the performance of his employees. One employee does not get along well with colleagues and rarely completes sales reports on time. This employee, however, generates the most new sales contracts in the office. The sales manager may ignore the negative information, choosing to evaluate the salesperson only on contracts generated. The manager is exercising selective perception.

A stereotype is a generalization about a group of people. Stereotypes reduce information about other people to a workable level, and they are efficient for compiling and using information. Stereotypes can be accurate, and when they are accurate, they can be useful perceptual guidelines. Most of the time, however, stereotypes are inaccurate. They harm individuals when inaccurate impressions of them are inferred and are never tested or changed. Thus, stereotypes may not be effective if they are too rigid or based on false information. At Hoechst Celanese, the top 26 executives are required to join two organizations in which they are a minority. This has proved to be a powerful way of changing perceptions. Many executives at the giant chemical company find the experience more valuable than diversity training.[30]

Suppose that a white male manager passes the coffee area and notices two African-American men talking there. He becomes irritated at them for wasting time. Later in the day, he sees two women talking in the coffee area. He thinks they should do their gossiping on their own time. The next morning, the same manager sees two white men talking in the coffee area. He thinks nothing of it; he is sure they are discussing business. The manager may hold a stereotype that women and minorities do not work hard unless closely supervised.

In multicultural work teams, members often stereotype foreign co-workers rather than getting to know them before forming an impression. Team members from less developed countries are often assumed to have less knowledge simply because their homeland is economically or technologically less developed. Stereotypes like these can deflate the productivity of the work team, as well as create low morale.

Attractiveness is a powerful stereotype. We assume that attractive individuals are also warm, kind, sensitive, poised, sociable, outgoing, independent, and strong. Are attractive people really like this? Certainly all of them are not. A recent study of romantic relationships showed that most attractive individuals do not fit the stereotype, except for possessing good social skills and being popular.[31]

Some individuals may seem to us to fit the stereotype of attractiveness because our behavior elicits behavior that confirms the stereotype from them.

Consider, for example, a situation in which you meet an attractive fellow student. Chances are that you respond positively to this person, because you assume he or she is warm, sociable, and so on. Even though the person may not possess these traits, your positive response may bring out these behaviors in the person. The interaction between the two of you may be channeled such that the stereotype confirms itself.[32]

First impressions are lasting impressions, so the saying goes. Individuals place a good deal of importance on first impressions, and for good reason. We tend to remember what we perceive first about a person, and sometimes we are quite reluctant to change our initial impressions. First-impression error means that we observe a very brief bit of a person's behavior in our first encounter and infer that this behavior reflects what the person is really like. Primacy effects can be particularly dangerous in interviews, given that we form first impressions quickly and that these impressions may be the basis for long-term employment relationships.

Implicit personality theories can also lead to inaccurate perceptions. We tend to have our own mini-theories about how people look and behave. These theories help us organize our perceptions and take shortcuts instead of integrating new information all the time. We are cognitive misers. Because the world is complex and ambiguous and we have a limited mental capacity, we try to expend the least effort possible in attempting to make sense of the world.[33] We group traits and appearances into clusters that seem to go together. For example, you may believe that introverted people are also worriers and intellectuals, or that fashionable dressers are also up on current events and like modern music. These implicit personality theories are barriers, because they limit our ability to take in new information when it is available.

Self-fulfilling prophecies are also barriers to social perception. Sometimes our expectations affect the way we interact with others such that we get what we wish for. Self-fulfilling prophecy is also known as the Pygmalion effect, named for the sculptor in Greek mythology who carved a statue of a woman that came to life when he prayed for this wish and it was granted.

Early studies of self-fulfilling prophecy were conducted in elementary school classrooms. Teachers were given bogus information that some of their pupils had high intellectual potential. These pupils were chosen randomly; there were really no differences among the students. Eight months later, the "gifted" pupils scored significantly higher on an IQ test. The teachers' expectations had elicited growth from these students, and teachers had given them tougher assignments and more feedback on their performance.

The Pygmalion effect has been observed in work organizations as well. A manager's expectations of an individual affect both the manager's behavior toward the individual and the individual's response. For example, suppose you have an initial impression of an employee as having the potential to move up within the organization. Chances are you will spend a great deal of time coaching and counseling the employee, providing challenging assignments, and grooming the individual for success.

Can managers harness the power of the Pygmalion effect to improve productivity in the organization? It appears that high expectations of individuals come true. Can a manager extend these high expectations to an entire group and have similar positive results? A study of military platoons in the Israeli Defense Forces indicated that platoons whose leaders had high expectations of them out-performed the other platoons.[34] It appears that when a manager expects positive things from a group, the group delivers.

■ Impression Management

Most people want to make favorable impressions on others. This is particularly true in organizations, where individuals compete for jobs, favorable performance evaluations, and salary increases. The process by which individuals try to control the impressions others have of them is called impression management. Individuals use several techniques to control others' impressions of them.

Some impression management techniques are self-enhancing. These techniques focus on enhancing others' impressions of the person using the technique. Name-dropping, which involves mentioning an association with important people in the hopes of improving one's image, is often used. Managing one's appearance is another technique for impression management. Individuals dress carefully for interviews because they want to "look the part" in order to get the job. Self-descriptions, or statements about one's characteristics, are used to manage impressions as well.

Another group of impression management techniques are other-enhancing. The aim of these techniques is to focus on the individual whose impression is to be managed. Flattery is a common other-enhancing technique whereby compliments are given to an individual in order to win his or her approval. Favors are also used to gain the approval of others. Agreement with someone's opinion is a technique often used to gain a positive impression.

Are impression management techniques effective? Most of the research has focused on employment interviews, and the results indicate that candidates who engage in impression management perform better in interviews and are more likely to get hired.[35] In addition, employees who engage in impression management are rated more favorably in performance appraisals than those who do not.[36]

Impression management seems to have an impact on others' impressions. As long as the impressions conveyed are accurate, this process can be a beneficial one in organizations. If the impressions are found to be false, however, a strongly negative overall impression may result. Furthermore, excessive impression management can lead to the perception that the user is manipulative or insincere.

We have discussed the influences on social perception, the potential barriers to perceiving another person, and impression management. Another psychological process that managers should understand is attribution.

ATTRIBUTION IN ORGANIZATIONS

As human beings, we are innately curious. We are not content merely to observe the behavior of others; rather, we want to know why they behave the way they do. We also seek to understand and explain our own behavior. Attribution theory explains how we pinpoint the causes of our own behavior and that of other people.

The attributions, or inferred causes, we provide for behavior have important implications in organizations. In explaining the causes of employee perfor-

mance, good or bad, we are asked to explain the behavior that was the basis for the performance. We explore Harold Kelley's attribution model, which is based on the pioneering work of Fritz Heider, the founder of attribution theory.[37]

■ Internal and External Attributions

Attributions can be made to an internal source of responsibility (something within the individual's control) or an external source (something outside the individual's control). Suppose you perform well on an exam in this course. You might say you aced the test because you are smart, or because you studied hard. If you attribute your success to ability or effort, you are citing an internal source.

Alternatively, you might cite external sources for your performance. You might say it was an easy test (you would attribute your success to degree of task difficulty) or that you had good luck. In this case, you are attributing your performance to sources beyond your control, or external attributions. You can see that internal attributions include such causes as ability and effort, whereas external attributions include causes like task difficulty or luck.

Attribution patterns differ among individuals. Achievement-oriented individuals attribute their success to ability and their failures to lack of effort, both internal causes. Failure-oriented individuals attribute their failures to lack of ability, and they may develop feelings of incompetence as a result of their attributional pattern. Evidence indicates that this attributional pattern also leads to depression.

■ Kelley's Attribution Theory

Attribution is a perceptual process. The way we explain success or failure—whether our own or that of another person—affects our feelings and our subsequent behavior. Harold Kelley extended attribution theory by trying to identify the antecedents of internal and external attributions. Kelley proposed that individuals make attributions based on information gathered in the form of three informational cues: consensus, distinctiveness, and consistency.[38] We observe an individual's behavior and then seek out information in the form of these three cues. Consensus is the extent to which peers in the same situation behave the same way. Distinctiveness is the degree to which the person behaves the same way in other situations. Consistency refers to the frequency of a particular behavior over time.

We form attributions based on whether these cues are low or high. Figure 3.3 shows how the combination of these cues helps us form internal or external attributions. Suppose you have received several complaints from customers regarding one of your customer service representatives, John. You have not received complaints about your other service representatives (low consensus). Upon reviewing John's records, you note that he also received customer

complaints during his previous job as a sales clerk (low distinctiveness). The complaints have been coming in steadily for about three months (high consistency). In this case, you would most likely make an internal attribution and conclude that the complaints must stem from John's behavior. The combination of low consensus, low distinctiveness, and high consistency leads to internal attributions.

Other combinations of these cues, however, produce external attributions. High consensus, high distinctiveness, and low consistency, for example, produce external attributions. Suppose one of your employees, Mary, is performing poorly on collecting

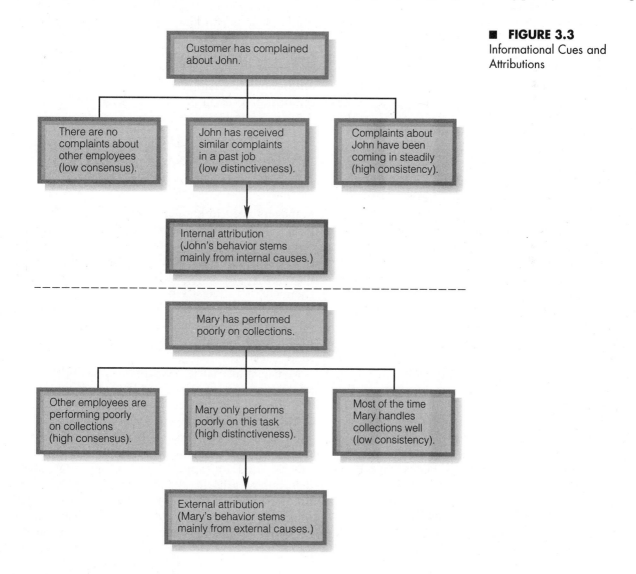

■ **FIGURE 3.3**
Informational Cues and Attributions

overdue accounts. You find that the behavior is widespread within your work team (high consensus), that Mary is performing poorly only on this aspect of the job (high distinctiveness), and that most of the time she handles this aspect of the job well (low consistency). You will probably decide that something about the work situation caused the poor performance—perhaps work overload or an unfair deadline.

Consensus, distinctiveness, and consistency are the cues used to determine whether the cause of behavior is internal or external. The process of determining the cause of a behavior may not be simple and clear-cut, however, due to some biases that occur in forming attributions.

■ Attributional Biases

The attribution process may be affected by two very common errors: the fundamental attribution error and the self-serving bias. The tendency to make attributions to internal causes when focusing on someone else's behavior is known as the fundamental attribution error.[39] The other error, self-serving bias, occurs when focusing on one's own behavior. Individuals tend to make internal attributions for their own successes and external attributions for their own failures.[40] In other words, when we succeed, we take credit for it; when we fail, we blame the situation or other people.

Both of these biases were illustrated in a study of health care managers who were asked to cite the causes of their employees' poor performance.[41] The managers claimed that internal causes (their employees' lack of effort or lack of ability) were the bases for their employees' poor performance. This is an example of the fundamental attribution error. When the employees were asked to pinpoint the cause of their own performance problems, they blamed a lack of support from the managers (an external cause), which illustrates self-serving bias.

There probably are cultural differences in these two attribution errors. As these biases have been described above, they apply to people from the United States. In cultures that are more fatalistic, as is India, people tend to believe that fate is responsible for much that happens. People in such cultures tend to emphasize external causes of behavior.[42]

The way individuals interpret the events around them has a strong influence on their behavior. People try to understand the causes of behavior in order to gain predictability and control over future behavior. Managers use attributions in all aspects of their jobs. In evaluating performance and rewarding employees, managers must determine the causes of behavior and a perceived source of responsibility. Attribution theory can explain how performance evaluation judgments can lead to differential rewards. A supervisor attributing an employee's good performance to internal causes, such as effort or ability, may give a larger raise than a supervisor attributing the good performance to external causes, such as help from others or good training. Managers are often called upon to explain their own actions as well, and in doing so they make attributions about the causes of their own behavior. We continue our discussion of attributions in Chapter 6 in terms of the ways attributions are used in managing performance.

■ MANAGERIAL IMPLICATIONS: USING PERSONALITY, PERCEPTION, AND ATTRIBUTION AT WORK

Managers need to know as much as possible about individual differences in order to understand themselves and those with whom they work. An understanding of personality characteristics can help a manager appreciate differences in employees. With the increased diversity of the work force, tools like the MBTI can be used to help employees see someone else's point of view. These tools also can help make communication among diverse employees more effective.

Managers use social perception constantly on the job. Knowledge of the forces that affect perception and the barriers to accuracy can help the manager form more accurate impressions of others.

Determining the causes of job performance is a major task for the manager, and attribution theory can be used to explain how managers go about determining causality. In addition, knowledge of the fundamental attribution error and self-serving bias can help a manager guard against these biases in the processes of looking for causes of behavior on the job.

In this chapter, we have explored the psychological processes of personality, perception, and attribution as individual differences. In the following chapter, we will continue our discussion of individual differences in terms of attitudes, values and ethics.

■ CHAPTER SUMMARY

- Individual differences are factors that make individuals unique. They include personalities, perceptions, skills and abilities, attitudes, values, and ethics.
- The trait theory, psychodynamic theory, humanistic theory, and integrative approach are all personality theories.
- Managers should understand personality because of its effect on behavior. Several characteristics affect behavior in organizations, including locus of control, self-esteem, self-efficacy, self-monitoring, and positive/negative affect.
- Personality has a stronger influence in weak situations, where there are few cues to guide behavior.
- Social perception is the process of interpreting information about another person. It is influenced by characteristics of the perceiver, the target, and the situation.
- Barriers to social perception include selective perception, stereotyping, first-impression error, implicit personality theories, and self-fulfilling prophecies.
- Impression management techniques such as name-dropping, managing one's appearance, self-descriptions, flattery, favors, and agreement are used by individuals to control others' impressions of them.
- Attribution is the process of determining the cause of behavior. It is used extensively by managers, especially in evaluating performance.

■ REVIEW QUESTIONS

1. What are individual differences, and why should managers understand them?
2. Define personality, and describe its origins.
3. Describe four theories of personality and what each contributes to our knowledge of personality.
4. What factors influence social perception? What are the barriers to social perception?
5. What are the three types of informational cues used to make attributions? Describe each one.
6. Describe the errors that affect the attribution process.
7. What are the ethical uses of personality tests? What are the unethical uses?
8. Suppose a manager makes a misattribution of an employee's poor performance. What are the ethical consequences of this?

■ REFERENCES

1. K. Lewin, "Formalization and Progress in Psychology," in D. Cartwright, ed., *Field Theory in Social Science* (New York: Harper, 1951).
2. J. R. Terborg, "Interactional Psychology and Research on Human Behavior in Organizations," *Academy of Management Review* 6 (1981): 561–576.
3. R. D. Arvey, T. J. Bouchard, Jr., N. L. Segal, and L. M. Abraham, "Job Satisfaction: Environmental and Genetic Components," *Journal of Applied Psychology* 74 (1989): 235–248.
4. G. Allport, *Pattern and Growth in Personality* (New York: Holt, 1961).
5. R. B. Cattell, *Personality and Mood by Questionnaire* (San Francisco: Jossey-Bass, 1973).
6. R. R. McCrae, "Why I Advocate the Five-Factor Model: Joint Factor Analyses of the NEO-PI with Other Instruments," in D. M. Buss and N. Cantor, eds., *Personality Psychology: Recent Trends and Emerging Directions* (New York: Springer-Verlag, 1989), 237–345.
7. S. Freud, *An Outline of Psychoanalysis* (New York: Norton, 1949).
8. C. Rogers, *On Becoming a Person: A Therapist's View of Psychotherapy*, 2d ed. (Boston: Houghton Mifflin, 1970).
9. D. D. Clark and R. Hoyle, "A Theoretical Solution to the Problem of Personality-Situational Interaction," *Personality and Individual Differences* 9 (1988): 133–138.
10. P. Spector, "Behavior in Organizations as a Function of Locus of Control," *Psychological Bulletin* 93 (1982): 482–497.
11. J. Brockner and T. Hess, "Self-Esteem and Task Performance in Quality Circles," *Academy of Management Journal* 29 (1986): 617–623.
12. B. R. Schlenker, M. F. Weingold, and J. R. Hallam, "Self-Serving Attributions in Social Context: Effects of Self-Esteem and Social Pressure," *Journal of Personality and Social Psychology* 57 (1990): 855–863.

13. A. Bandura, "Regulation of Cognitive Processes Through Perceived Self-Efficacy," *Developmental Psychology* (September 1989): 729–735.

14. H. Garland, R. Weinberg, L. Bruya, and A. Jackson, "Self-Efficacy and Endurance Performance: A Longitudinal Field Test of Cognitive Mediation Theory," *Applied Psychology: An International Review* 37 (1988): 381–394.

15. V. Gecas, "The Social Psychology of Self-efficacy," *Annual Review of Sociology* 15 (1989): 291–316.

16. M. Snyder and S. Gangestad, "On the Nature of Self-monitoring: Matters of Assessment, Matters of Validity," *Journal of Personality and Social Psychology* 51 (1986): 123–139.

17. M. Kilduff and D.V. Day, "Do Chameleons Get Ahead? The Effects of Self-Monitoring on Managerial Careers," *Academy of Management Journal* 37 (1994): 1047–1060.

18. A. M. Isen and R. A. Baron, "Positive Affect and Organizational Behavior," in B. M. Staw and L. L. Cummings, eds., *Research in Organizational Behavior*, vol. 12 (Greenwich, Conn.: JAI Press, 1990).

19. R. A. Baron, "Interviewer's Moods and Reactions to Job Applicants: The Influence of Affective States on Applied Social Judgments," *Journal of Applied Social Psychology* 16 (1987): 16–28.

20. A. P. Brief, M. J. Burke, J. M. George, B. S. Robinson, and J. Webster, "Should Negative Affectivity Remain an Unmeasured Variable in the Study of Job Stress?" *Journal of Applied Psychology* 73 (1988): 193–198.

21. J. M. George, "Personality, Affect, and Behavior in Groups," *Journal of Applied Psychology* 75 (1990): 107–116.

22. H. Rorschach, *Psychodiagnostics* (Bern: Hans Huber, 1921).

23. C. G. Jung, *Psychological Types* (New York: Harcourt & Brace, 1923).

24. E. C. Webster, *The Employment Interview: A Social Judgment Process* (Schomberg, Canada: SIP, 1982).

25. L. R. Offerman and M. K. Gowing, "Personnel Selection in the Future: The Impact of Changing Demographics and the Nature of Work," in Schmitt, Borman & Associates, eds., *Personnel Selection in Organizations* (San Francisco: Jossey-Bass, 1993).

26. J. P. Forgas and G. H. Bower, "Mood Effects on Person-Perception Judgments," *Journal of Personality and Social Psychology* 53 (1987): 53–60.

27. I. H. Frieze, J. E. Olson, and J. Russell, "Attractiveness and Income for Men and Women in Management," *Journal of Applied Social Psychology* 21 (1991): 1039–1057.

28. P. Ekman and W. Friesen, *Unmasking the Face* (Englewood Cliffs, N.J.: Prentice-Hall, 1975).

29. J. E. Rehfeld, "What Working for a Japanese Company Taught Me," *Harvard Business Review* (November-December 1990): 167–176.

30. R. Rice, "How to Make Diversity Pay," *Fortune*, 8 August 1994, 78–86.

31. A. Feingold, "Gender Differences in Effects of Physical Attractiveness on Romantic Attraction: A Comparison across Five Research Paradigms," *Journal of Personality and Social Psychology* 59 (1990): 981–993.

32. M. Snyder, "When Belief Creates Reality," *Advances in Experimental Social Psychology* 18 (1984): 247–305.

33. S. T. Fiske and S. E. Taylor, *Social Cognition* (Reading, Mass.: Addison-Wesley, 1984).

34. D. Eden, "Pygmalion Without Interpersonal Contrast Effects: White Groups Gain from Raising Manager Expectations," *Journal of Applied Psychology* 75 (1990): 394–398.

35. D. C. Gilmore and G. R. Ferris, "The Effects of Applicant Impression Management Tactics on Interviewer Judgments," *Journal of Management* (December 1989): 557–564.

36. S. J. Wayne and K. M. Kacmar, "The Effects of Impression Management on the Performance Appraisal Process," *Organizational Behavior and Human Decision Processes* 48 (1991): 70–88.

37. F. Heider, *Psychology of Interpersonal Relations* (New York: Wiley, 1958).

38. H. H. Kelley, "The Processes of Causal Attribution," *American Psychologist* (February 1973): 107–128.

39. L. Ross, "The Intuitive Psychologist and His Shortcomings: Distortions in the Attribution Process," in L. Berkowitz, ed., *Advances in Experimental Social Psychology* (New York: Academic Press, 1977).

40. D. T. Miller and M. Ross, "Self-serving Biases in the Attribution of Causality: Fact or Fiction?" *Psychological Bulletin* 82 (1975): 313–325.

41. J. R. Schermerhorn, Jr., "Team Development for High-Performance Management," *Training and Development Journal* 40 (1986): 38–41.

42. J. G. Miller, "Culture and the Development of Everyday Causal Explanation," *Journal of Personality and Social Psychology* 46 (1984): 961–978.

CHAPTER 4
ATTITUDES, VALUES, AND ETHICS

LEARNING OBJECTIVES

After reading this chapter, you should be able to do the following:

- Explain the ABC model of an attitude.
- Describe how attitudes are formed.
- Define job satisfaction and organizational commitment and discuss the importance of these two work attitudes.
- Identify the characteristics of the source, target, and message that affect persuasion.
- Distinguish between instrumental and terminal values.
- Explain how managers can deal with the diverse value systems that characterize the global environment.
- Describe a model of individual and organizational influences on ethical behavior.
- Discuss how value systems, locus of control, Machiavellianism, and cognitive moral development affect ethical behavior.

In this chapter, we continue the discussion of individual differences we began in Chapter 3 with personality, perception, and attribution. Persons and situations are joint influences on behavior, and individual differences help us to better understand the influence of the person. Our focus now is on three other individual difference factors: attitudes, values, and ethics.

■ ATTITUDES

Attitudes are individuals' general affective, cognitive, and intentional responses toward objects, other people, themselves, or social issues.[1] As individuals, we respond favorably or unfavorably toward many things: animals, co-workers, our own appearance, politics. The importance of attitudes lies in their link to behavior. For example, some people prefer either cats or dogs. Individuals who prefer cats may be friendly to cats but hesitate in approaching dogs.

Attitudes are an integral part of the world of work. Managers speak of workers who have "bad attitudes" and conduct "attitude adjustment" talks with employees. Often, poor performance attributed to bad attitudes really stems from lack of motivation, minimal feedback, lack of trust in management, or other problems. These are areas that managers must explore.

One company that believes employee attitudes are important is Northwestern National Life Insurance (NWNL). The company surveys employee attitudes extensively on a broad range of issues. Managers, for example, wanted to know employees' attitudes toward NWNL's quality process, and they needed feedback on what was working and what wasn't. The attitude survey revealed that employees had a strong commitment to customer service. It also showed two impediments to quality: conflicting priorities, and lack of cooperation between departments. The barriers were removed quickly by teams who developed action plans. NWNL believes employee attitudes are key components in delivering quality services to customers.

You can see that it is important for managers to understand the antecedents to attitudes as well as their consequences. Managers also need to understand the different components of attitudes, how attitudes are formed, the major ones that affect work behavior, and how to use persuasion to change them.

■ The ABC Model

We tend to associate attitudes with surveys; therefore, we believe that to find out how a person feels about an issue, we simply ask him or her. This method is incomplete, however. To understand the complexity of an attitude, we can break it down into three components, as depicted in Table 4.1.

These components—affect, behavioral intentions, and cognition—compose what we call the ABC model of an attitude. Affect is the emotional component of an attitude. It refers to an individual's feeling about something or someone. Statements such as "I like this," or "I prefer that," reflect the affective component of an attitude. Affect is measured by physiological indicators such as galvanic skin re-

■ **TABLE 4.1**
The ABC Model of an Attitude

COMPONENT	MEASURED BY
A Affect	Physiological indicators Verbal statements about feelings
B Behavioral intentions	Observed behavior Verbal statements about intentions
C Cognition	Attitude scales Verbal statements about beliefs

SOURCE: Adapted from M. J. Rosenberg and C. I. Hovland, "Cognitive, Affective, and Behavioral Components of Attitude," in M. J. Rosenberg, C. I. Hovland, W. J. McGuire, R. P. Abelson, and J. H. Brehm, *Attitude Organization and Change* (New Haven: Yale University Press, 1960). Copyright 1960 Yale University Press. Used with permission.

sponse (changes in electrical resistance of skin which indicate emotional arousal) and blood pressure. These indicators show changes in emotions by measuring physiological arousal. If an individual is trying to hide his or her feelings, this might be shown by a change in arousal.

The second component is the intention to behave in a certain way toward an object or person. Our attitudes toward women in management, for example, may be inferred from an observation of the way we behave toward a female supervisor. We may be supportive, passive, or hostile, depending on our attitude. The behavioral component of an attitude is measured by observing behavior or by asking a person about behavior or intentions. The statement, "If I were asked to speak at commencement, I'd be willing to try to do so, even though I'd be nervous," reflects a behavioral intention.

The third component of an attitude, cognition (thought), reflects a person's perceptions or beliefs. Cognitive elements are evaluative beliefs and are measured by attitude scales or by asking about thoughts. The statement, "I believe Japanese workers are industrious," reflects the cognitive component of an attitude.

The ABC model shows that to understand an attitude thoroughly, we must assess all three components. Suppose, for example, you want to evaluate your employees' attitudes toward flextime (flexible work scheduling). You would want to determine how they feel about flextime (affect), whether they would use flextime (behavioral intention), and what they think about the policy (cognition). The most common method of attitude measurement, the attitude scale, measures only the cognitive component.

As rational beings, individuals try to be consistent in everything they believe in and do. They prefer consistency (consonance) between their attitudes and behavior. Anything that disrupts this consistency causes tension (dissonance), which motivates individuals to change either their attitudes or their behavior to return to a state of consistency. The tension produced when there is a conflict between attitudes and behavior is cognitive dissonance.[2]

Suppose, for example, a salesperson is required to sell damaged televisions for the full retail price, without revealing the damage to customers. She believes, however, that doing so constitutes unethical behavior. This creates a conflict between her attitude (concealing information from customers is unethical) and her behavior (selling defective TVs without informing customers about the damage).

The salesperson, experiencing the discomfort from dissonance, will try to resolve the conflict. She might change her behavior by refusing to sell the defective TV sets. Alternatively, she might rationalize that the defects are minor and that the customers will not be harmed by their lack of awareness of them. These are attempts by the salesperson to restore equilibrium between her attitudes and behavior, thereby eliminating the tension from cognitive dissonance.

Managers need to understand cognitive dissonance because employees often find themselves in situations in which their attitudes conflict with their behavior. They manage the tension by changing their attitudes or behavior. Employees who display sudden shifts in behavior may be attempting to reduce dissonance. Some employees find the conflicts between strongly held attitudes and required work behavior so uncomfortable that they leave the organization to escape the dissonance.

■ Attitude Formation

Attitudes are learned. Our responses to people and issues evolve over time. Two major influences on attitudes are direct experience and social learning.

Direct experience with an object or person is a powerful influence on attitudes. How do you know that you like biology or dislike math? You have probably formed these attitudes from experience in studying the subjects. Attitudes that are derived from direct experience are stronger, are held more confidently, and are more resistant to change than are attitudes formed through indirect experience. One reason attitudes derived from direct experience are so powerful is their availability. This means that the attitudes are easily accessed and are active in our cognitive processes. When attitudes are available, we can call them into consciousness quickly. Attitudes that are not learned from direct experience are not as available, and therefore we do not recall them as easily.

Through social learning, the family, peer groups, religious organizations, and culture shape an individual's attitudes in an indirect manner. Children learn to adopt certain attitudes by the reinforcement they are given by their parents when they display behaviors that reflect an appropriate attitude. This is evident when very young children express political preferences similar to their parents'. Peer pressure molds attitudes through group acceptance of individuals who express popular attitudes and through sanctions, such as exclusion from the group, placed on individuals who espouse unpopular attitudes.

Substantial social learning occurs through modeling, in which individuals acquire attitudes by merely observing others. The observer overhears other individuals expressing an opinion or watches them engaging in a behavior that reflects an attitude, and this attitude is adopted by the observer.

For an individual to learn from observing a model, four processes must take place:

1. The learner must focus attention on the model.
2. The learner must retain what was observed from the model. Retention is accomplished in two basic ways. One way is for the learner to "stamp in" what was observed by forming a verbal code for it. The other way is through symbolic rehearsal, by which the learner forms a mental image of himself or herself behaving like the model.
3. Behavioral reproduction must occur; that is, the learner must practice the behavior.

4. The learner must be motivated to learn from the model.

Culture also plays a definitive role in attitude development. Consider, for example, the contrast in the North American and European attitudes toward vacation and leisure. The typical vacation in the United States is two weeks, and some workers do not use all of their vacation time. In Europe, the norm is longer vacations; and in some countries, holiday means everyone taking a month off. The European attitude is that an investment in longer vacations is important to health and performance.

■ Attitudes and Behavior

If you have a favorable attitude toward participative management, will your management style be participative? As managers, if we know an employee's attitude, to what extent can we predict the person's behavior? These questions illustrate the fundamental issue of attitude-behavior correspondence; that is, the degree to which an attitude predicts behavior.

This correspondence has concerned organizational behaviorists and social psychologists for quite some time. Some studies suggested that attitudes and behavior are closely linked, while others found no relationship at all or a weak relationship at best. Attention then became focused on when attitudes predict behavior and when they do not. Attitude-behavior correspondence depends on five things: attitude specificity, attitude relevance, timing of measurement, personality factors, and social constraints.

Individuals possess both general and specific attitudes. You may favor women's right to reproductive freedom (a general attitude) and prefer pro-choice political candidates (a specific attitude). However, you may not attend pro-choice rallies or send money to Planned Parenthood. The fact that you don't perform these behaviors may make the link between your attitude and behavior on this issue seem rather weak. However, given a choice between a pro-choice and an anti-abortion political candidate you will probably vote for the pro-choice candidate. In this case, your attitude seems quite predictive of your behavior. The point is that the greater the attitude specificity, the stronger its link to behavior.[3]

Another factor that affects the attitude-behavior link is relevance.[4] Attitudes that address an issue in which we have some self-interest are more relevant for us, and our subsequent behavior is consistent with our expressed attitude. Suppose there is a proposal to raise income taxes on those who earn $150,000 or more. If you are a student, you may not find the issue of great personal relevance. Individuals in that income bracket, however, might find it highly relevant; and their attitude toward the issue would be strongly predictive of whether they would vote for the tax increase.

The timing of the measurement also affects attitude-behavior correspondence. The shorter the time between the attitude measurement and the observed behavior, the stronger the relationship. For example, voter preference polls taken close to an election are more accurate than earlier polls are.

Personality factors also influence the attitude-behavior link. One personality disposition that affects the consistency between attitudes and behavior is self-monitoring. Recall from Chapter 3 that low self-monitors rely on their internal states when making decisions about behavior, while high self-monitors are more responsive to situational cues. Low self-monitors therefore display greater correspondence between their attitudes and behaviors.[5] High self-monitors display little correspondence between the two because they behave according to signals from others and from the environment.

Finally, social constraints affect the relationship between attitudes and behavior. The social context provides information about acceptable attitudes and behaviors.[6] New employees in an organization, for example, are exposed to the attitudes of their work group. Suppose a newcomer from Afghanistan holds a negative attitude toward women in management because in his country the prevailing attitude is that women should not be in positions of power. He sees, however, that his work group members respond positively to their female supervisor. His own behavior may therefore be compliant because of social constraints. This behavior is inconsistent with his attitude and cultural belief system.

■ Work Attitudes

Attitudes at work are important because, directly or indirectly, they affect work behavior. This was dramatically illustrated in a comparison of product quality among air conditioners manufactured in the

U.S. versus those made in Japan.[7] In general, there is a perception that Japanese products are of higher quality. The product quality of air conditioners from nine U.S. plants and seven Japanese plants was compared, and the results were bad news for the U.S. plants. The Japanese products had significantly fewer defects than the U.S. products.

The researchers continued their study by asking managers in both countries' plants about their attitudes toward various goals. Japanese supervisors reported that their companies had strong attitudes favoring high-quality products, while U.S. supervisors reported quality goals to be less important. U.S. supervisors reported strong attitudes favoring the achievement of production scheduling goals, while Japanese supervisors indicated that schedules were less important. The researchers' conclusion was that the attitudes of U.S. managers toward quality were at least partly responsible for lower-quality products.

While many work attitudes are important, two attitudes in particular have been emphasized. Job satisfaction and organizational commitment are key attitudes of interest to managers and researchers.

Job Satisfaction. Most of us believe that work should be a positive experience. Job satisfaction is a pleasurable or positive emotional state resulting from the appraisal of one's job or job experiences.[8] It has been treated both as a general attitude and as satisfaction with five specific dimensions of the job: pay, the work itself, promotion opportunities, supervision, and co-workers.

An individual may hold different attitudes toward various aspects of the job. For example, an employee may like her job responsibilities but be dissatisfied with the opportunities for promotion. Characteristics of individuals also affect job satisfaction. Those with high negative affectivity are more likely to be dissatisfied with their jobs. Challenging work, valued rewards, opportunities for advancement, competent supervision, and supportive co-workers are dimensions of the job that can lead to satisfaction.

There are several measures of job satisfaction. One of the most widely used measures comes from the Job Descriptive Index (JDI). This index measures the specific facets of satisfaction by asking employees to respond "yes," "no," or "cannot decide" to a series of statements describing their jobs. Another popular

measure is the Minnesota Satisfaction Questionnaire (MSQ). This survey also asks employees to respond to statements about their jobs, using a five-point scale that ranges from "very dissatisfied" to "very satisfied." Figure 4.1 presents some sample items from each questionnaire.

Are satisfied workers more productive? Or, are more productive workers more satisfied? The link between satisfaction and performance has been widely explored. One view holds that satisfaction causes good performance. If this were true, then the manager's job would simply be to keep workers happy. While this may be the case for certain individuals, job satisfaction for most people is one of several causes of good performance.

Another view holds that good performance causes satisfaction. If this were true, managers would need to help employees perform well, and satisfaction would follow. However, some employees who are high performers are not satisfied with their jobs.

The research shows weak support for both views, but no simple, direct relationship between satisfaction and performance has been found.[9] One reason for these results may be the difficulty of demonstrating the attitude-behavior links we described earlier in this chapter. Future studies using specific, relevant attitudes and measuring personality variables and behavioral intentions may be able to demonstrate a link between job satisfaction and performance.

Another reason for the lack of a clear relationship between satisfaction and performance is the intervening role of rewards. Employees who receive valued rewards are more satisfied. In addition, employees who receive rewards that are contingent on performance (the higher the performance, the larger the reward) tend to perform better. Rewards thus influence both satisfaction and performance. The key to influencing both satisfaction and performance through rewards is that the rewards are valued by employees and are tied directly to performance.

Job satisfaction has been shown to be related to many other important personal and organizational outcomes. People who are dissatisfied with their jobs are absent more frequently, are more likely to quit, and report more psychological and medical problems than do satisfied employees.[10] In addition, job satisfaction may be related to organizational citizenship behavior—behavior that facilitates coop-

Job Descriptive Index

Think of the work you do at present. How well does each of the following words or phrases describe your work? In the blank beside each word given below, write

__Y__ for "Yes" if it describes your work

__N__ for "No" if it does NOT describe it

__?__ If you cannot decide

WORK ON YOUR PRESENT JOB:

_____ Routine

_____ Satisfying

_____ Good

Think of the majority of the people that you work with now or the people you meet in connection with your work. How well does each of the following words or phrases describe these people? In the blank beside each word, write

__Y__ for "Yes" if it describes the people you work with

__N__ for "No" if it does NOT describe them

__?__ if you cannot decide

CO-WORKERS (PEOPLE):

_____ Boring

_____ Responsible

_____ Intelligent

Minnesota Satisfaction Questionnaire

1 = Very dissatisfied

2 = Dissatisfied

3 = I can't decide whether I am satisfied or not

4 = Satisfied

5 = Very satisfied

On my present job, this is how I feel about:

_____ The chance to work alone on the job (independence)

_____ My changes for advancement on this job (Advancement)

_____ The chance to tell people what to do (Authority)

_____ The praise I get for a good job (Recognition)

_____ My pay and the amount of work I do (Compensation)

SOURCE: The Job Descriptive Index is copyrighted by Bowling Green State University. The complete forms, scoring key, instructions, and norms can be obtained from Dr. Patricia C. Smith, Department of Psychology, Bowling Green State University, Bowling Green, OH 43403. Minnesota Satisfaction Questionnaire from D. J. Weiss, R. V. Davis, G. W. England, and L. H. Lofquist, *Manual for the Minnesota Satisfaction Questionnaire* (University of Minnesota Industrial Relations Center, 1967).

eration and supportive relationships at work. Satisfied employees are more likely to help their co-workers, make positive comments about the company, and refrain from complaining when things at work do not go well.

Like all attitudes, job satisfaction is influenced by culture. One study found that Japanese workers reported significantly lower job satisfaction than did U.S. workers.[11] Interestingly, the study showed that job satisfaction in both Japan and the U.S. could be improved by participative techniques such as quality circles and social activities sponsored by the company. Research also has shown that executives in less industrialized countries have lower levels of job satisfaction.[12]

Culture may also affect the factors that lead to job satisfaction. In a comparison of employees in the U.S. and India, the factors differed substantially. Leadership style, pay, and security influenced job satisfaction for the Americans. For the employees in India, however, recognition, innovation, and the absence of conflict led to job satisfaction.[13]

Because organizations face the challenge of operating in the global environment, managers must understand that job satisfaction is significantly affected by culture. Employees from different cultures may have differing expectations of their jobs; thus, there may be no single prescription for increasing the job satisfaction of a multicultural work force.

Organizational Commitment. The strength of an individual's identification with an organization is known as organizational commitment. There are two kinds of organizational commitment: affective and continuance.[14] Affective commitment is an employee's intention to remain in an organization because of a strong desire to do so. It consists of three factors:

- A belief in the goals and values of the organization.
- A willingness to put forth effort on behalf of the organization.
- A desire to remain a member of the organization.[15]

Affective commitment encompasses loyalty, but it is also a deep concern for the organization's welfare.

Continuance commitment is an employee's tendency to remain in an organization because the person cannot afford to leave. Sometimes, employees believe that if they leave, they will lose a great deal of their investments in time, effort, and benefits and that they cannot replace these investments.

Certain organizational conditions encourage affective commitment. Participation in decision making and job security are two such conditions. Certain job characteristics also influence commitment positively. These include autonomy, responsibility, and interesting work.

Organizational commitment is related to lower rates of absenteeism, higher quality of work, and increased productivity. Managers should be concerned about organizational commitment because committed individuals expend more task-related effort and are less likely than others to leave the organization.

There has been a decline in commitment to U.S. organizations over the past few years. The old "deal" between employees and organizations that traded loyalty for job security is no longer possible. Instead, some companies are taking an honest approach that promises interesting work, freedom, fair pay, and training in return for an employee's promise to add value to the organization continually. Chevron, for example, works hard to develop organizational commitment by taking a painfully honest approach, holding meetings to explain how business is changing and how the volatile environment affects employees' careers and advancement potential.[16]

Recent research on organizational commitment has been conducted in different countries. One study of workers in Saudi Arabia found that Asians working there were more committed to the organization than were Westerners and Arab workers.[17] Another study revealed that American workers displayed higher affective commitment than did Korean and Japanese workers.[18] The reasons for these differences need to be explored in further research.

Job satisfaction and organizational commitment are two important work attitudes that managers can strive to improve among their employees. To begin with, managers can use attitude surveys to reveal employees' satisfaction or dissatisfaction with specific facets of their jobs. Then they can take action to make the deficient aspects of the job more satisfying.

Participative management has been shown to increase both satisfaction and commitment. Managers can give employees opportunities to participate in decision making to help improve these attitudes.

■ Persuasion and Attitude Change

To understand how attitudes can change, it is necessary to understand the process of persuasion. Through persuasion, one individual (the source) tries to change the attitude of another person (the target). Certain characteristics of the source, the target, and the message affect the persuasion process. There are also two cognitive routes to persuasion.

Source Characteristics.   Three major characteristics of the source affect persuasion: expertise, trustworthiness, and attractiveness.[19] A source who is perceived as an expert is particularly persuasive. Arnold Schwarzenegger, for example, would be a persuasive force for changing our attitude toward fitness because of his expertise. Trustworthiness is also important. Dr. C. Everett Koop, the former surgeon general, engendered a great deal of trust through his many public appearances and open style of communication. He consequently was credited with helping change Americans' attitudes toward smoking. Finally, attractiveness and likability play a role in persuasion. Attractive communicators have long been used in advertising to persuade consumers to buy certain products. As a source of persuasion, managers who are perceived as being experts, who are trustworthy, or who are attractive or likable will have an edge in changing employee attitudes.

Target Characteristics.   Some people are more easily persuaded than others. Individuals with low self-esteem are more likely to change their attitudes in response to persuasion than are individuals with high self-esteem. Individuals who hold very extreme attitudes are more resistant to persuasion, and people who are in a good mood are easier to persuade.[20] Undoubtedly, individuals differ widely in their susceptibility to persuasion. Managers must recognize these differences and realize that their attempts to change attitudes may not receive universal acceptance.

Message Characteristics.   Suppose you must implement an unpopular policy at work. You want to persuade your employees that the policy is a positive change. Should you present one side of the issue or both sides? Given that your employees are already negatively inclined toward the policy, you will have more success in changing their attitudes if you present both sides. This shows support for one side of the issue while acknowledging that another side does exist. Moreover, refuting the other side makes it more difficult for the targets to hang on to their negative attitudes.

Messages that are obviously designed to change the target's attitude may be met with considerable negative reaction. In fact, undisguised deliberate attempts at changing attitudes may cause attitude change in the opposite direction! This is most likely to occur when the target of the persuasive communication feels her or his freedom is threatened.[21] Less threatening approaches are less likely to elicit negative reactions.

Cognitive Routes to Persuasion.   When are message characteristics more important, and when are other characteristics more important in persuasion? The elaboration likelihood model of persuasion, presented in Figure 4.2, proposes that persuasion occurs over one of two routes: the central route and the peripheral route.[22] The routes are differentiated by the amount of elaboration, or scrutiny, the target is motivated to give the message.

The central route to persuasion involves direct cognitive processing of the message's content. When an issue is personally relevant, the individual is motivated to think carefully about it. In the central route, the content of the message is very important. If the arguments presented are logical and convincing, attitude change will follow.

In the peripheral route to persuasion, the individual is not motivated to pay much attention to the message's content. The message may not be perceived as personally relevant, or the individual may be distracted. In this route, the individual is persuaded by characteristics of the persuader—for example, expertise, trustworthiness, and attractiveness. In addition, the individual may be persuaded by statistics, the number of arguments presented, or the method of presentation—all of which are nonsubstantial aspects of the message.

■ **FIGURE 4.2**

The Elaboration Likelihood Model of Persuasion

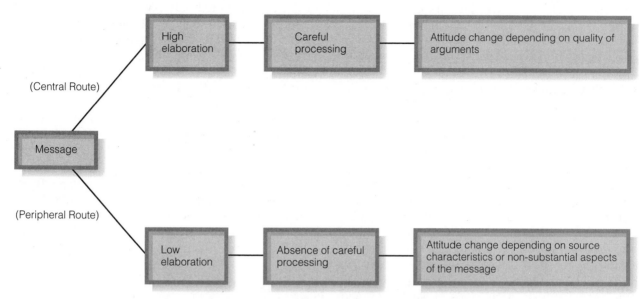

SOURCE: Adapted from R. E. Perry and J. T. Cacioppo, "The Elaboration Likelihood Model of Persuasion," in L. Berkowitz, ed., *Advances in Experimental Social Psychology,* vol. 19 (New York: Academic Press, 1986), 123-205.

The elaboration likelihood model shows that the target's level of involvement with the issue is important. That involvement also determines which route to persuasion will be more effective. We have seen that the process of persuading individuals to change their attitudes is affected by the source, the target, the message, and the route. When all is said and done, however, managers are merely catalysts for encouraging attitude change.

■ VALUES

Another source of individual differences is values. Values exist at a deeper level than attitudes and are more general and basic in nature. We use them to evaluate our own behavior and that of others. As such, they vary widely among individuals. Values are enduring beliefs that a specific mode of conduct or end state of existence is personally or socially preferable to an opposite or converse mode of conduct or end state of existence. This definition was proposed by Rokeach, an early scholar of human values. Values give us a sense of right and wrong, good and bad.

Values are learned by individuals as they grow and mature. They may change over the life span as an individual develops a sense of self. Cultures, societies, and organizations shape values. Parents and others who are respected by the individual play crucial roles in value development by providing guidance about what is right and wrong. Adolescence is a time when values come to the forefront of an individual's development, and many individuals stabilize their value systems during this life stage.

Businesses have shown increasing interest in values over recent years. This interest goes along with the emphasis on ethics in organizations that we described in Chapter 2. Because values are general beliefs about right and wrong, they form the basis for ethical behavior. Tandem Computers hires individuals who share the company's values of personal growth and freedom. Six-week sabbaticals every four years allow Tandem employees to pursue personal growth in areas as diverse as climbing the mountains of Nepal and studying at a world-renowned cooking school. We will focus on the importance of shared values in the organization in Chapter 16. Our emphasis in this chapter is on values as sources of variation among individuals.

■ Instrumental and Terminal Values

Rokeach distinguished between two types of values: instrumental and terminal. Instrumental values reflect the means to achieving goals; that is, they represent the acceptable behaviors to be used in achieving some end state. Instrumental values identified by Rokeach include ambition, honesty, self-sufficiency, and courageousness. Terminal values, in contrast, represent the goals to be achieved, or the end states of existence. Rokeach identified happiness, love, pleasure, self-respect, and freedom among the terminal values. A complete list of instrumental and terminal values is presented in Table 4.2. Instrumental and terminal values work in concert to provide individuals with goals to strive for and acceptable ways to achieve the goals.

Americans' rankings of instrumental and terminal values have shown remarkable stability over time.[23] Rokeach studied their rankings in four national samples from 1968, 1971, 1974, and 1981. There was considerable stability in the rankings across the studies, which spanned a thirteen-year period. Most of the values shifted only one position in the rankings over this time span. The highest-ranked instrumental values were honesty, ambition, responsibility, forgiving nature, open-mindedness, and courage. The highest-ranked terminal values were world peace, family security, freedom, happiness, self-respect, and wisdom.

Although the values of Americans as a group have been stable, individuals vary widely in their value systems. For example, social respect is one terminal value that people differ on. Some people desire respect from others and work diligently to achieve it, and other people place little importance on what others think of them. Individuals may agree that achievement is an important terminal value but may disagree on how to attain that goal.

■ Work Values

Work values are important because they affect how individuals behave on their jobs in terms of what is right and wrong. The work values most relevant to individuals are achievement, concern for others, honesty, and fairness. Achievement is a concern for

■ TABLE 4.2
Instrumental and Terminal Values

INSTRUMENTAL VALUES		
Honesty	Ambition	Responsibility
Forgiving nature	Open-mindedness	Courage
Helpfulness	Cleanliness	Competence
Self-control	Affection/love	Cheerfulness
Independence	Politeness	Intelligence
Obedience	Rationality	Imagination
TERMINAL VALUES		
World peace	Family security	Freedom
Happiness	Self-respect	Wisdom
Equality	Salvation	Prosperity
Achievement	Friendship	National security
Inner peace	Mature love	Social respect
Beauty in art and nature	Pleasure	Exciting, active life

SOURCE: Adapted with the permission of The Free Press, a Division of Simon and Schuster from *The Nature of Human Values*, by Milton Rokeach. Copyright © 1973 by The Free Press.

the advancement of one's career. This is shown in such behavior as working hard and seeking opportunities to develop new skills. Concern for others reflects caring, compassionate behaviors such as encouraging other employees or helping others work on difficult tasks. These behaviors constitute organizational citizenship, as we discussed earlier. Honesty is accurately providing information and refusing to mislead others for personal gain. Fairness emphasizes impartiality and recognizes different points of view. Individuals can rank-order these values in terms of their importance in their work lives.[24]

Although individuals vary in their value systems, when they share similar values at work, the results are positive. Employees who share their supervisor's values are more satisfied with their jobs and more committed to the organization.[25] Values also have profound effects on the choice of jobs. Traditionally, pay and advancement potential have been the strongest influences on job choice decisions. However, a recent study found that three other work values—achievement, concern for others, and fairness—exerted more influence on job choice decisions than did pay and promotion opportunities.[26]

This means that organizations recruiting job candidates should pay careful attention to individuals' values and to the messages that organizations send about company values. At Prudential Insurance, the key value is integrity; it is Prudential's "rock" in guiding relationships among employees, customers, and regulatory agencies. At Southwest Airlines, pilots are often seen helping clean the planes, a behavior that reflects the value of teamwork.

■ Cultural Differences in Values

As organizations face the challenges of an increasingly diverse work force and a global marketplace, it becomes more important than ever for them to understand the influence of culture on values. Doing business in a global marketplace often means that managers encounter a clash of values between different cultures. Take the value of loyalty, for example. Japanese workers are completely loyal to their companies; corporate loyalty is more important than even family loyalty and political loyalty.[27] In contrast, Koreans value loyalty to the person for whom one works.[28] In the U.S., family and other

personal loyalties are more highly valued than is loyalty to the company or one's supervisor.

Doing business in the new Russia has its challenges in terms of value differences. Cargill, a Minnesota company that is trying to establish a foodprocessing plant in Russia, faces many challenges. Among them is dealing with the country's nonconvertible currency. But the toughest challenge, according to Jules Carson, who heads the project, centers around value differences. "The main obstacle is getting the people to adopt a business attitude and business ethics," he said. "I don't know any short way to solve that. It will take persistence and coaching."[29]

Values also affect individuals' views of what constitutes authority. French managers value authority as a right of office and rank. Their behavior reflects this value, as they tend to use power based on their position in the organization. In contrast, managers from the Netherlands and Scandinavia value group inputs to decisions and expect their decisions to be challenged and discussed by employees.[30]

Conducting business on a global scale often presents managers with dilemmas that call their own value systems into question. The solicitation or exchange of gifts among business people in the U.S. is frowned upon. In Asia and in some parts of Mexico, however, it is traditional to exchange gifts in business relationships. These gifts begin a cycle of future favors to be exchanged between the parties. What American managers may consider payoffs and bribes may be considered legitimate ways of doing business in other countries.

Value differences between cultures must be acknowledged in today's global economy. We may be prone to judging the value systems of others, but we should resist the temptation to do so. Tolerating diversity in values can help us understand other cultures.

Values are important because they provide guidance for behavior. They are intertwined with the concept of ethics, the next dimension of individual differences to be examined.

■ ETHICAL BEHAVIOR

Ethics is the study of moral values and moral behavior. Ethical behavior is acting in ways consistent with one's personal values and the commonly held values of the organization and society. As we saw in Chapter 2, ethical issues are a major concern in organizations. There is evidence that paying attention to ethical issues pays off for companies. James Burke, CEO of Johnson & Johnson, put together a list of companies that devoted a great deal of attention to ethics. The group included Johnson & Johnson, Coca-Cola, Gerber, Kodak, 3M, and Pitney Bowes, among others. From 1950 to 1990, the market value of these organizations grew at an annual rate of 11.3 percent, as compared to 6.2 percent for the Dow Jones industrials as a whole.[31] Doing the right thing can positively affect an organization's performance.

Unethical behavior by employees can affect individuals, work teams, and even the organization. Organizations thus depend on individuals to act ethically. One company recognized for its comprehensive efforts to encourage ethical behavior is General Dynamics. Several years ago, the company launched a program to integrate its ethical standards into everyday business conduct.[32] It developed a booklet of ethical standards, distributed it to all employees, and undertook a massive training effort to express to all employees the importance of ethical behavior. The company also appointed employees throughout the corporation to serve as ethics directors. The directors answer employees' questions about ethical problems and screen allegations about potential violations of General Dynamics' code of conduct. Many of the directors maintain hotlines for employees to use.

Since the hotlines were established in 1985, General Dynamics employees have contacted ethics directors over 30,000 times. While most employee calls are requests for information or advice, some calls have been of a more serious nature. Ethics contacts have resulted in 1,400 sanctions, the most common being warnings. Violations of time reporting, in which employees overstate the number of hours they work, are the most frequent reasons for warnings.

Managers must examine the messages that they send through their own behavior. When managers preach one doctrine and practice another, their behavior sends a signal that ethics aren't important. Some managers, while reengineering and cutting budgets, raise their own salaries and perks. Giving lip service to teamwork and then rewarding individual stars is another form of managerial hypocrisy.[33]

The ethical issues that individuals face at work are complex. A review of articles appearing in the Wall Street Journal during just one week in 1991 revealed over sixty articles dealing with ethical issues in business. As Table 4.3 shows, the themes appearing

■ **TABLE 4.3**
Ethical Issues from One Week in the *Wall Street Journal*

1. **Stealing:** Taking things that don't belong to you.
2. **Lying:** Saying things you know aren't true.
3. **Fraud and deceit:** Creating or perpetuating false impressions.
4. **Conflict of interest and influence buying:** Bribes, payoffs, and kickbacks.
5. **Hiding versus divulging information:** Concealing information that another party has a right to know, or failing to protect personal or proprietary information.
6. **Cheating:** Taking unfair advantage of a situation.
7. **Personal decadence:** Aiming below excellence in terms of work performance (e.g., careless or sloppy work).
8. **Interpersonal abuse:** Behaviors that are abusive of others (e.g., sexism, racism, emotional abuse).
9. **Organizational abuse:** Organizational practices that abuse members (e.g., inequitable compensation, misuses of power).
10. **Rule violations:** Breaking organizational rules.
11. **Accessory to unethical acts:** Knowing about unethical behavior and failing to report it.
12. **Ethical dilemmas:** Choosing between two equally desirable or undesirable options.

Source: Adapted from J. O. Cherrington and D. J. Cherrington, "A Menu of Moral Issues: One Week in the Life of the *Wall Street Journal*," *Journal of Business Ethics* 11 (1992): 255–265. Reprinted by permission of Kluwer Academic Publishers.

■ **FIGURE 4.3**
Individual/Organizational
Model of Ethical Behavior

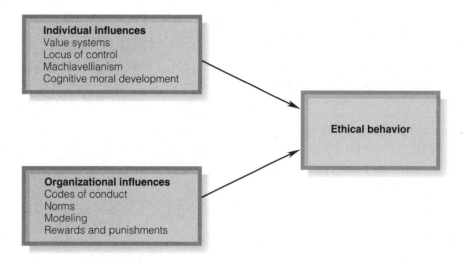

throughout the articles were distilled into twelve major ethical issues. You can see that few of these issues are clear-cut. All of them depend on the specifics of the situation, and their interpretation depends on the characteristics of the individuals examining them. For example, look at issue number 2: lying. We all know that "white lies" are told in business. Is this acceptable? The answer to this question varies from person to person. Thus, the perception of what constitutes ethical versus unethical behavior in organizations varies among individuals.

Ethical behavior is influenced by two major categories of factors: individual characteristics and organizational factors.[34] Our purpose in this section is to look at the individual influences on ethical behavior. We examine organizational influences throughout the remainder of the book—particularly in Chapter 16, where we focus on creating an organizational culture that reinforces ethical behavior.

The model that guides our discussion of individual influences on ethical behavior is presented in Figure 4.3. It shows both individual and organizational influences.

Making ethical decisions is part of each manager's job. It has been suggested that ethical decision making requires three qualities of individuals:[35]

1. The competence to identify ethical issues and evaluate the consequences of alternative courses of action.

2. The self-confidence to seek out different opinions about the issue and decide what is right in terms of a particular situation.

3. Toughmindedness—the willingness to make decisions when all that needs to be known cannot be known and when the ethical issue has no established, unambiguous solution.

What are the individual characteristics that lead to these qualities? Our model presents four major individual differences that affect ethical behavior: value systems, locus of control, Machiavellianism, and cognitive moral development.

■ **Value Systems**

Values are systems of beliefs that affect what the individual defines as right, good, and fair. Ethics reflect the way the values are acted out. Ethical behavior, as noted earlier, is acting in ways consistent with one's personal values and the commonly held values of the organization and society.

Employees are exposed to multiple value systems: their own, their supervisor's, the company's, the customers', and others'. In most cases, the individual's greatest allegiance will be to personal values. When the value system conflicts with the behavior the person feels must be exhibited, the person experiences a value conflict. Suppose, for example, that an individual believes honesty is important in all endeavors. Yet, this individual sees that those who get ahead in business fudge their numbers and deceive other people. Why should the individual be honest if honesty doesn't pay? It is the individual's values, a basic sense of what is right and wrong, that override the temptation to be dishonest.[36]

One person who believes that good values make good business is Kim Dawson, founder of the internationally known Kim Dawson Agency. Values such as insisting on total honesty and promoting long-term development of people have shaped her approach to the modeling and talent industries. In industries that sell image, the Kim Dawson Agency successfully handled ethical dilemmas by operating within its values.

■ Locus of Control

Another individual influence on ethical behavior is locus of control. In Chapter 3, we introduced locus of control as a personality variable that affects individual behavior. Recall that individuals with an internal locus of control believe that they control events in their lives and that they are responsible for what happens to them. In contrast, individuals with an external locus of control believe that outside forces such as fate, chance, or other people control what happens to them.

Internals are more likely than externals to take personal responsibility for the consequences of their ethical or unethical behavior. Externals are more apt to believe that external forces caused their ethical or unethical behavior. Research has shown that internals make more ethical decisions than do externals.[37] Internals also are more resistant to social pressure and are less willing to hurt another person, even if ordered to do so by an authority figure.[38]

■ Machiavellianism

Another individual difference that affects ethical behavior is Machiavellianism. Niccolo Machiavelli was an Italian statesman during the sixteenth century. He wrote *The Prince*, a guide for acquiring and using power.[39] The primary method he suggested for achieving power was manipulation of others. Machiavellianism, then, is a personality characteristic indicating one's willingness to do whatever it takes to get one's own way.

A high-Mach individual behaves in accordance with Machiavelli's ideas, which include the notion that it is better to be feared than loved. High-Machs tend to use deceit in relationships, have a cynical view of human nature, and have little concern for conventional notions of right and wrong.[40] They are skilled manipulators of other people, relying on their persuasive abilities. Low-Machs, in contrast, value loyalty and relationships. They are less willing to manipulate others for personal gain and are concerned with others' opinions.

High-Machs believe that any means justify the desired ends. They believe that manipulation of others is fine if it helps achieve a goal. Thus, high-Machs are likely to justify their manipulative behavior as ethical. They are emotionally detached from other people and are oriented toward objective aspects of situations. And high-Machs are more likely than low-Machs to engage in behavior that is ethically questionable.[41] Employees can counter Machiavellian individuals by focusing on teamwork instead of on one-on-one relationships, where high-Machs have the upper hand. It is also beneficial to make interpersonal agreements public and thus less susceptible to manipulation by high-Machs.

■ Cognitive Moral Development

An individual's level of cognitive moral development also affects ethical behavior. Psychologist Lawrence Kohlberg proposed that as individuals mature, they move through a series of six stages of moral development.[42] With each successive stage, they become less dependent on other people's opinions of right and wrong and less self-centered (acting in one's own interest). At higher levels of moral development, individuals are concerned with broad principles of justice and with their self-chosen ethical principles. Kohlberg's model focuses on the decision-making process and on the ways individuals justify ethical decisions. His model is a cognitive developmental theory about the ways people think about what is right and wrong and how the decision-making process changes through interaction with peers and the environment.

Cognitive moral development occurs at three levels, and each level consists of two stages. In Level I, called the premoral level, the person's ethical decisions are based on rewards, punishments, and self-interest. In Stage 1, the individual obeys rules to avoid punishment. In Stage 2, the individual follows the rules only if it is in his or her immediate interest to do so.

In Level II, the conventional level, the focus is on the expectations of others (parents, peers) or society. In Stage 3, individuals try to live up to the expectations of people close to them. In Stage 4, they broaden their perspective to include the laws of the larger society. They fulfill duties and obligations and want to contribute to society.

In Level III, the principled level, what is "right" is determined by universal values. The individual sees beyond laws, rules, and the expectations of other people. In Stage 5, individuals are aware that people have diverse value systems. They uphold their own values despite what others think. For a person to be classified as being in Stage 5, decisions must be based on principles of justice and rights. For example, a person who decides to picket an abortion clinic just because his religion says abortion is wrong is not a Stage 5 individual. A person who arrived at the same decision through a complex decision process based on justice and rights may be a Stage 5 individual. The key is the process rather than the decision itself. In Stage 6, the individual follows self-selected ethical principles. If there is a conflict between a law and a self-selected ethical principle, the individual acts according to the principle.

As individuals mature, their moral development passes through these stages in an irreversible sequence. Research suggests that most adults are in Stage 3 or 4. Most adults thus never reach the principled level of development (Stages 5 and 6).

Since it was proposed, over twenty years ago, Kohlberg's model of cognitive moral development has received a great deal of research support. Individuals at higher stages of development are more likely to engage in whistle-blowing,[43] and more likely to make ethical business decisions.[44]

Kohlberg's model has also been criticized. Gilligan, for example, has argued that the model does not take gender differences into account. Kohlberg's model was developed from a twenty-year study of eighty-four boys.[45] Gilligan contends that women's moral development follows a different pattern—one that is based not on individual rights and rules but

on responsibility and relationships. Women and men face the same moral dilemmas but approach them from different perspectives—men from the perspective of equal respect and women from the perspective of compassion and care. More research is needed on gender differences in cognitive moral development.

Individual differences in values, locus of control, Machiavellianism, and cognitive moral development are important influences on ethical behavior in organizations. Given that these influences vary widely from person to person, how can organizations use this knowledge to improve ethical behavior? One action would be to hire individuals who share the organization's values. Another would be to hire only internals, low-Machs, and individuals at higher stages of cognitive moral development. This strategy obviously presents practical and legal problems.

There is evidence that cognitive moral development can be increased through training.[46] Organizations could help individuals move to higher stages of moral development by providing educational seminars. However, values, locus of control, Machiavellianism, and cognitive moral development are fairly stable in adults.

The best way to use the knowledge of individual differences may be to recognize that they help explain why ethical behavior differs among individuals, and to focus managerial efforts on creating a work situation that supports ethical behavior.

Most adults are susceptible to external influences; they do not act as independent ethical agents. Instead, they look to others and to the organization for guidance. Managers can offer such guidance by providing encouragement of ethical behavior through codes of conduct, norms, modeling, and rewards and punishments, as is shown in Figure 4.3. We discuss these areas further in Chapter 16.

■ MANAGERIAL IMPLICATIONS: ATTITUDES, VALUES, AND ETHICS AT WORK

Managers must understand attitudes because of their effects on work behavior. By understanding how attitudes are formed and how they can be changed, managers can shape employee attitudes. Attitudes are learned through observation of other employees and by the way they are reinforced. Job satisfaction and organizational commitment are important attitudes to encourage among employees, and participative management is an excellent tool for doing so.

Values affect work behavior because they affect employees' views of what constitutes right and wrong. The diversity of the work force makes it imperative that managers understand differences in value systems. Shared values within an organization can provide the foundation for cooperative efforts toward achieving organizational goals.

Ethical behavior at work is affected by individual and organizational influences. A knowledge of individual differences in value systems, locus of control, Machiavellianism, and cognitive moral development helps managers understand why individuals have diverse views about what constitutes ethical behavior.

This chapter concludes our discussion of individual differences that affect behavior in organizations. Attitudes, values, and ethics combine with personality, perception, and attribution to make individuals unique. Individual uniqueness is a major managerial challenge, and it is one reason there is no single best way to manage people.

■ CHAPTER SUMMARY

- The ABC model of an attitude contends that there are three components in an attitude: affect, behavioral intentions, and cognition. Cognitive dissonance is the tension produced by a conflict between attitudes and behavior.
- Attitudes are formed through direct experience and social learning. Direct experience creates strong attitudes because the attitudes are easily accessed and active in cognitive processes.
- Attitude-behavior correspondence depends on attitude specificity, attitude relevance, timing of measurement, personality factors, and social constraints.
- Two important work attitudes are job satisfaction and organizational commitment. There are cultural differences in these attitudes, and both

attitudes can be improved by providing employees with opportunities for participation in decision making.

- A manager's ability to persuade employees to change their attitudes depends on characteristics of the manager (expertise, trustworthiness, and attractiveness), the employees (self-esteem, original attitude, and mood), the message (one-sided versus two-sided), and the route (central versus peripheral).
- Values are enduring beliefs and are strongly influenced by cultures, societies, and organizations.
- Instrumental values reflect the means to achieving goals; terminal values represent the goals to be achieved.
- Ethical behavior is influenced by the individual's value system, locus of control, Machiavellianism, and cognitive moral development.

■ REVIEW QUESTIONS

1. Describe the ABC model of an attitude. How should each component be measured?
2. How are attitudes formed? Which source is stronger?
3. Discuss cultural differences in job satisfaction and organizational commitment.
4. What are the major influences on attitude-behavior correspondence? Why do some individuals seem to exhibit behavior that is inconsistent with their attitudes?
5. What should managers know about the persuasion process?
6. Define values. Distinguish between instrumental values and terminal values. Are these values generally stable, or do they change over time?
7. What is the relationship between values and ethics?
8. How does locus of control affect ethical behavior?
9. What is Machiavellianism, and how does it relate to ethical behavior?
10. Describe the stages of cognitive moral development. How does this concept affect ethical behavior in organizations?

■ REFERENCES

1. R. E. Petty and J. T. Cacioppo, *Attitudes and Persuasion: Classic and Contemporary Approaches* (Dubuque, Iowa: Wm. C. Brown, 1981).

2. L. Festinger, *A Theory of Cognitive Dissonance* (Evanston, Ill.: Row, Peterson, 1957).

3. I. Ajzen and M. Fishbein, "Attitude-Behavior Relations: A Theoretical Analysis and Review of Empirical Research," *Psychological Bulletin* 84 (1977): 888–918.

4. B. T. Johnson and A. H. Eagly, "Effects of Involvement on Persuasion: A Meta-Analysis," *Psychological Bulletin* 106 (1989): 290–314.

5. M. Snyder and W. B. Swann, "When Actions Reflect Attitudes: The Politics of Impression Management," *Journal of Personality and Social Psychology* 34 (1976): 1034–1042.

6. I. Ajzen, "From Intentions to Action: A Theory of Planned Behavior," in J. Kuhl and J. Beckmann, eds., *Action-Control: From Cognition to Behavior* (Heidelberg: Springer, 1985).

7. D. A. Garvin, "Quality Problems, Policies, and Attitudes in the United States and Japan: An Exploratory Study," *Academy of Management Journal* 29 (1986): 653–673.

8. E. A. Locke, "The Nature and Causes of Job Satisfaction," in M. Dunnette, ed., *Handbook of Industrial and Organizational Psychology* (Chicago: Rand McNally, 1976).

9. M. T. Iaffaldano and P. M. Muchinsky, "Job Satisfaction and Job Performance: A Meta-Analysis," *Psychological Bulletin* 97 (1985): 251–273.

10. R. Griffin and T. Bateman, "Job Satisfaction and Organizational Commitment," in C. Cooper and I. Robertson, eds., *International Review of Industrial and Organizational Psychology* (New York: Wiley, 1986).

11. J. R. Lincoln, "Employee Work Attitudes and Management Practice in the U.S. and Japan: Evidence from a Large Comparative Survey," *California Management Review* (Fall 1989): 89–106.

12. I. A. McCormick and C. L. Cooper, "Executive Stress: Extending the International Comparison," *Human Relations* 41 (1988): 65–72.

13. A. Krishnan and R. Krishnan, "Organizational Variables and Job Satisfaction," *Psychological Research Journal* 8 (1984): 1–11.

14. J. P. Meyer, N. J. Allen, and I. R. Gellatly, "Affective and Continuance Commitment to Organizations: Evaluation of Measures and Analysis of Concurrent and Time-Lagged Relations," *Journal of Applied Psychology* 75 (1990): 710–720.

15. R. T. Mowday, L. W. Porter, and R. M. Steers, *Employee-Organization Linkages: The Psychology of Commitment* (New York: Academic Press, 1982).

16. B. O'Reilly, "The New Deal: What Companies and Employees Owe One Another," *Fortune,* 13 June 1994, 44–52.

17. A. al-Meer, "Organizational Commitment: A Comparison of Westerners, Asians, and Saudis," *International Studies of Management and Organization* 19 (1989): 74–84.

18. F. Luthans, H. S. McCaul, and N. C. Dodd, "Organizational Commitment: A Comparison of American, Japanese, and Korean Employees," *Academy of Management Journal* 28 (1985): 213–219.

19. J. Cooper and R. T. Croyle, "Attitudes and Attitude Change," *Annual Review of Psychology* 35 (1984): 395–426.

20. D. M. Mackie and L. T. Worth, "Processing Deficits and the Mediation of Positive Affect in Persuasion," *Journal of Personality and Social Psychology* 57 (1989): 27–40.

21. J. W. Brehm, *Responses to Loss of Freedom: A Theory of Psychological Reactance* (New York: General Learning Press, 1972).

22. R. E. Petty and J. T. Cacioppo, *Communication and Persuasion: Central and Peripheral Routes to Attitude Change* (New York: Springer-Verlag, 1985).

23. M. Rokeach and S. J. Ball-Rokeach. "Stability and Change in American Value Priorities, 1968–1981," *American Psychologist* 44 (1989): 775–784.

24. E. C. Ravlin and B. M. Meglino, "The Transitivity of Work Values: Hierarchical Preference Ordering of Socially Desirable Stimuli," *Organizational Behavior and Human Decision Processes* 44 (1989): 494–508.

25. B. M. Meglino, E. C. Ravlin, and C. L. Adkins, "A Work Values Approach to Corporate Culture: A Field Test of the Value Congruence Process and Its Relationship to Individual Outcomes," *Journal of Applied Psychology* 74 (1989): 424–432.

26. T. A. Judge and R. D. Bretz, Jr., "Effects of Work Values on Job Choice Decisions," *Journal of Applied Psychology* 77 (1992): 261–271.

27. R. H. Doktor, "Asian and American CEOs: A Comparative Study," *Organizational Dynamics* 18 (1990): 46–56.

28. R. L. Tung, "Handshakes Across the Sea: Cross-cultural Negotiating for Business Success," *Organizational Dynamics* (Winter 1991): 30–40.

29. S. E. Peterson, "3M Company Announces the Establishment of Wholly Owned Subsidiary in Moscow," *Minneapolis Star Tribune,* 30 January 1992, 1–2.

30. R. Neale and R. Mindel, "Rigging Up Multicultural Teamworking," *Personnel Management* (January 1992): 27–30.

31. K. Labich, "The New Crisis in Business Ethics," *Fortune,* 20 April 1992, 167–176.

32. W. H. Wagel, "A New Focus on Business Ethics at General Dynamics," *Personnel* (August 1987): 4–8.

33. K. Labich, "Why Companies Fail," *Fortune,* 14 November 1994, 52–68.

34. L. K. Trevino, "Ethical Decision Making in Organizations: A Person-Situation Interactionist Model," *Academy of Management Review* 11 (1986): 601–617.

35. K. R. Andrews, "Ethics in Practice," *Harvard Business Review* (September-October 1989): 99–104.

36. A. Bhide and H. H. Stevens, "Why Be Honest if Honesty Doesn't Pay?" *Harvard Business Review* (September-October 1990): 121–129.

37. L. K. Trevino and S. A. Youngblood, "Bad Apples in Bad Barrels: A Causal Analysis of Ethical Decision-Making Behavior," *Journal of Applied Psychology* 75 (1990): 378–385.

38. H. M. Lefcourt, *Locus of Control: Current Trends in Theory and Research*, 2d ed. (Hillsdale, N.J.: Erlbaum, 1982).

39. N. Machiavelli, *The Prince*, trans. George Bull (Middlesex, England: Penguin Books, 1961).

40. R. Christie and F. L. Geis, *Studies in Machiavellianism* (New York: Academic Press, 1970).

41. S. B. Knouse and R. A. Giacalone, "Ethical Decision-Making in Business: Behavioral Issues and Concerns," *Journal of Business Ethics* 11 (1992): 369–377.

42. L. Kohlberg, "Stage and Sequence: The Cognitive-Developmental Approach to Socialization," in D. A. Goslin, ed., *Handbook of Socialization Theory and Research* (Chicago: Rand McNally, 1969), 347–480.

43. M. Brabeck, "Ethical Characteristics of Whistleblowers," *Journal of Research In Personality* 18 (1984): 41–53.

44. W. Y. Penn and B. D. Collier, "Current Research in Moral Development as a Decision Support System," *Journal of Business Ethics* 4 (1985): 131–136.

45. C. Gilligan, *In a Different Voice: Psychological Theory and Women's Development* (Cambridge: Harvard University Press, 1982).

46. S. A. Goldman and J. Arbuthnot, "Teaching Medical Ethics: The Cognitive-Developmental Approach," *Journal of Medical Ethics* 5 (1979): 171–181.

Chapter 5
Motivation in Organizations

LEARNING OBJECTIVES

After reading this chapter, you should be able to do the following:

- Define motivation.
- Explain how McGregor's Theory X and Theory Y assumptions relate to Maslow's hierarchy of needs.
- Describe Herzberg's two-factor theory of motivation.
- Discuss the needs for achievement, power, and affiliation.
- Describe how inequity is determined in individual-organizational exchange relationships.
- Explain seven different strategies for resolving inequity.
- Describe the expectancy theory of motivation.
- Describe cultural differences in motivation.

This is the first of two chapters about motivation, behavior, and performance in work organizations. These chapters examine factors that explain behavior: Chapter 5 emphasizes factors within the person; Chapter 6, factors outside the person. In this chapter, the early sections examine needs and motives in several content theories of motivation, beginning with the early work of Abraham Maslow and Douglas McGregor. Frederick Herzberg's two-factor theory and David McClelland's need theory are then addressed in some detail. Next, the discussion turns to Adams' theory of inequity, a process theory of motivation, in the context of a contractual exchange relationship between an individual and an organization. The last section addresses expectancy theory, another process theory of motivation.

■ WORK, NEEDS, MOTIVES, AND BEHAVIOR

Motivation, the process of arousing and sustaining goal-directed behavior, is one of the more complex topics in organizational behavior. The word "motivation" comes from the Latin root word *movere*, which means, "to move."

Motivation theories attempt to explain and predict observable behavior. Some motivation theories emphasize factors external to the person, or exogenous causes, in attempting to explain and predict the person's behavior. Other theories emphasize internal attributes and characteristics of the person, or endogenous processes, to do the same thing.[1] Exogenous theories include reinforcement theory and goal setting, whereas endogenous theories include need theories of motivation, equity theory, and expectancy theory. This chapter focuses on the endogenous theories.

Even within these two classes of theoretical perspectives, there are substantial numbers of specific motivation theories. This is attributable to two factors. The first is the diversity of basic assumptions and beliefs about human nature. There are both philosophical and theological differences in perspective that have important implications for theories of motivation. Second, any single motivation theory explains only a small proportion of the variance in human behavior. Therefore, alternative theories have developed over time in an effort to account for the unexplained portions of the variance in behavior. In an effort to account for the variety of endogenous attributes and processes that influence human behavior, motivation theories have examined the depth and the breadth of internal needs and motives.

■ The Depth of Internal Needs

Philosophers and scholars have theorized for centuries about internal needs and motives. Over the past century, attention has narrowed to understanding motivation in businesses and other organizations. Max Weber, an early German organizational scholar, argued that the meaning of work lay not in the work itself but in its deeper potential for contributing to a person's ultimate salvation.[2] From this Calvinistic perspective, the Protestant Ethic was the fuel for human industriousness. The Protestant Ethic said a person should work hard because a person who prospered at work was more likely to find a place in heaven. A significantly deeper and more complex motivation theory was proposed by Sigmund Freud. He argued that a person's organizational life was founded on the compulsion to work and the power

of love.[3] For Freud, much of human motivation had a sexual and unconscious basis. Psychoanalysis was Freud's method for delving into the unconscious mind to better understand a person's motives and needs. Freud's psychodynamic theory offers explanations for irrational and self-destructive behavior, such as the behavior manifested by the postal worker in Oklahoma who gunned down several co-workers in the late 1980s. The motives underlying such traumatic work events can be understood by analyzing a person's unconscious needs and motives. Freud's theorizing is important as the basis for subsequent need theories of motivation.

■ The Breadth of Internal Needs

Whereas Freud's research focused on the depth of human nature, later research with people in industrial settings focused on a greater breadth of internal needs and motives. Early organizational scholars made economic assumptions about human motivation and developed corresponding differential piece rate systems of pay.[4] These organizational scholars assumed that people were motivated by self-interest for economic gain. The Hawthorne Studies found social and interpersonal motives in behavior to be important while also confirming the beneficial effects of pay incentives on productivity.[5]

Each motivation theory makes assumptions about human nature and offers explanations for behavior. However, no one motivation theory or set of theories has been found universally superior. For this reason, it is important to appreciate the diversity of motivation theories. One or another may be useful in specific organizational contexts, with specific individuals or groups, or at particular times. For example, money was a strong motivator for Ford employees in the early days, but survival was an even more intense motivator during Ford's period of crisis.

■ EARLY THEORIES OF MOTIVATION

The earliest theories for explaining human behavior and motivation to work made the assumption that people act out of self-interest for the purpose of economic and material gain. Early proponents of

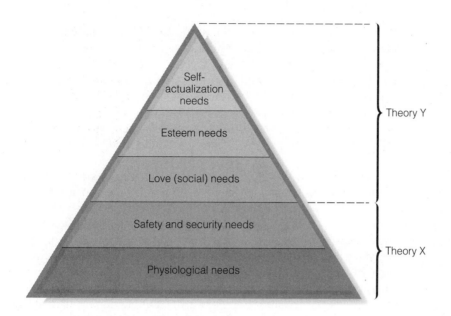

this perspective were Adam Smith and Frederick Taylor. Adam Smith was a Scottish political economist and moral philosopher who argued that a person's self-interest was God's providence, not the government's.[6] Gordon E. Forward, President and CEO of Chaparral Steel Company, subscribes to many of Smith's ideas and believes people are motivated by "enlightened" self-interest. Self-interest is what is in the best interest and benefit to the individual; enlightened self-interest additionally recognizes the self-interest of other people. The implication of this approach is that financial and economic incentives to work are the most important considerations in understanding human behavior. Further, employees are most productive when motivated by self-interest. Further, technology is an important concept in Smith's view, because it multiplies the productivity of labor in the creation of products or the delivery of services.

Frederick Taylor, the founder of scientific management, was a scholar also concerned with labor efficiency and effectiveness.[7] The central concern in scientific management was with the reformation of the relationship between management and labor so that they would cooperate to enlarge the total profits of the firm. These earliest motivational approaches stand in contrast to the more psychological theories

of motivation embodied in the works of Abraham Maslow, Douglas McGregor, and Clayton Alderfer.

■ Abraham Maslow, Douglas McGregor and Clayton Alderfer

Abraham Maslow was a psychologist who proposed a theory of human motivation for understanding behavior based primarily upon a hierarchy of five need categories.[8] He recognized that there were factors other than one's needs (for example, culture) that were determinants of behavior. However, he focused his theoretical attention on specifying people's internal needs. Maslow labeled the five hierarchical categories as physiological needs, safety and security needs, love (social) needs, esteem needs, and the need for self-actualization. Maslow's need hierarchy is depicted in Figure 5.1, also showing how the needs relate to Douglas McGregor's assumptions about people, which will be discussed next.

Maslow conceptually derived the five need categories from the early thoughts of William James[9] and John Dewey,[10] coupled with the psychodynamic thinking of the psychoanalysts. Maslow's need theory was later tested in research with working populations. For example, one study reported that middle managers and lower-level managers had different perceptions of their need deficiencies and the importance of their needs.[11] One distinguishing feature of Maslow's need hierarchy is the following progression hypothesis. Although some research has challenged the assumption, the theory says that only ungratified needs motivate behavior. Further, ungratified needs on the lowest level in the hierarchy are the ones that motivate behavior. As a lower level of need is met, a person progresses to the next higher level of need as a source of motivation. Hence, people progress up the hierarchy as they gratify each level of need in succession. For example, an employee may satisfy security needs by obtaining two big promotions and then be motivated by developing good working relationships with co-workers. The problem with the progression hypothesis is that it leaves no way to move down the hierarchy, which could occur, for example, if a person at the esteem level lost a job and was now worried about security.

One important organizational implication of the need hierarchy concerns how to manage people at work (see Figure 5.1). Douglas McGregor understood people's motivation using Maslow's need theory. He grouped the physiological and safety needs as "lower-order" needs and the social, esteem, and self-actualization needs as "upper-order" needs. McGregor proposed two alternative sets of assumptions about people at work based upon which sets of needs were the motivators. He labeled these sets of assumptions Theory X and Theory Y. Theory X assumed people were indolent, self-centered, gullible, resistant to change and lacking in ambition and the desire to be responsible. Theory Y assumed people are motivated, capable of responsibility and development, and ready to direct behavior to organizational goals given proper management. Regardless of people's motivation to work, McGregor saw the responsibility of management as being the same. Specifically, "management is responsible for organizing the elements of productive enterprise-money, materials, equipment, people-in the interest of economic ends."[12]

According to McGregor, people should be treated differently according to whether they are motivated by lower-order or higher-order needs. Specifically, McGregor believed that Theory X assumptions are appropriate for employees motivated by lower-order needs. Theory Y assumptions, in contrast, are appropriate for employees motivated by higher-order needs, and Theory X assumptions are then inappropriate. In addition, McGregor believed that in the 1950s, when he was writing, the majority of American workers had satisfied their lower-order needs and were therefore motivated by higher-order needs.

Employee participation programs are among the consequences of McGregor's Theory Y assumptions. Ford Motor Company's first step in revitalizing its work force through an employee involvement (EI) program is based on Theory Y assumptions about human nature.[13] However, some companies, such as Lincoln Electric, use money as the chief source of employee motivation.

Gordon E. Forward, CEO of Chaparral Steel Company, has applied Maslow's hierarchy and McGregor's assumptions about people in leading and managing Chaparral people.[14] He views employees as resources to be developed, not labor costs to be charged off. A future-thinking, enlightened executive, Forward has fun at work and at play. Chaparral Steel has cultivated and developed a productive, loyal work force by focusing on Maslow's higher-order needs and Theory Y assumptions about people.

Clayton Alderfer and ERG Theory, while recognizing the value of Maslow's contribution to understanding motivation, believed that the original need hierarchy was not quite accurate in identifying and categorizing human needs.[15] As an evolutionary development of the need hierarchy, Alderfer proposed the ERG theory of motivation, which grouped human needs into only three basic categories: existence, relatedness, and growth. Alderfer classified Maslow's physiological and physical safety needs in the existence need category; Maslow's interpersonal safety, love, and interpersonal esteem needs as relatedness needs; and Maslow's self-actualization and self-esteem needs as growth needs. In addition to the differences in categorization of human needs, ERG theory added a regression hypothesis to go along with the progression hypothesis originally proposed by Maslow. Alderfer's regression hypothesis helped explain people's behavior when frustrated in trying to meet needs at the next higher level in the hierarchy. Specifically, the regression hypothesis states that people regress to the next lower category of needs and intensify their desire to gratify these needs. Hence, ERG theory explains both progressive need and gratification up the hierarchy and regression when people are faced with frustration.

■ HERZBERG'S TWO-FACTOR THEORY

Frederick Herzberg departed from the need hierarchy approach to motivation and examined the experiences that satisfied or dissatisfied people's needs at work. This need motivation theory became known as the two-factor theory.[16] Herzberg's original study included 200 engineers and accountants in western Pennsylvania during the 1950s. Herzberg asked these people to describe two important incidents at their jobs: one that was very satisfying and made them feel exceptionally good at work, and another that was very dissatisfying and made them feel exceptionally bad at work.

Herzberg and his colleagues believed that people had two sets of needs--one related to the animalistic avoidance of pain and one related to the humanistic desire for psychological growth. Conditions in the work environment would affect one or the other of these needs. Work conditions related to satisfaction of the need for psychological growth were labeled motivation factors. Work conditions related to dissatisfaction caused by discomfort or pain were labeled hygiene factors. Each set of factors related to one aspect of what Herzberg identified as the human being's dual nature regarding the work environment. Thus, motivation factors relate to job satisfaction, and hygiene factors relate to job dissatisfaction. These two independent factors are depicted in Figure 5.2 (page 76).

■ Motivation Factors

Job satisfaction is produced by building motivation factors into a job, according to Herzberg. This process is known as job enrichment. In the original research, the motivation factors were identified as responsibility, achievement, recognition, advancement, and the work itself. These factors relate to the content of the job and what the employee actually does on the job. When these factors are present, they lead to superior performance and effort on the part of job incumbents. These factors directly influence the way people feel about their work. Motivation factors lead to positive mental health and challenge people to grow, contribute to the work environment, and invest themselves in the organization. Recognition as an important motivation factor is used at Perpetual Financial Corporation who hosts a company-wide "Salute to Associates" to thank employees. However, recognition programs like Perpetual's require constant supervision and do not eliminate the need for other rewards.

According to the theory and Herzberg's original results, the absence of these factors does not lead to dissatisfaction. Rather, it leads to the lack of satisfaction. The motivation factors are the more important of the two sets of factors, because they directly affect a person's motivational drive to do a good job. When they are absent, the person will be demotivated to perform well and achieve excellence. The hygiene factors are a completely distinct set of factors unrelated to the motivation to achieve and do excellent work.

■ Hygiene Factors

Job dissatisfaction occurs when the hygiene factors are either not present or not good enough. In the original research, the hygiene factors were company policy and administration, technical supervision,, interpersonal relations with one's supervisor, working conditions, salary, status, and security. These factors relate to the context of the job and may be considered support factors. They do not directly affect a person's motivation to work, but influence the extent of the person's discontent. These factors cannot stimulate psychological growth or human development. They may be thought of as maintenance factors, because they contribute to an individual's basic needs. When hygiene factors are excellent, employees are not dissatisfied, and complaints about these contextual considerations are reduced.

When these hygiene factors are poor or absent, the person complains about "poor supervision," "poor medical benefits," or whatever the hygiene factor is that is poor. Employees experience a deficit and are

■ FIGURE 5.2

The Motivation-Hygiene Theory of Motivation

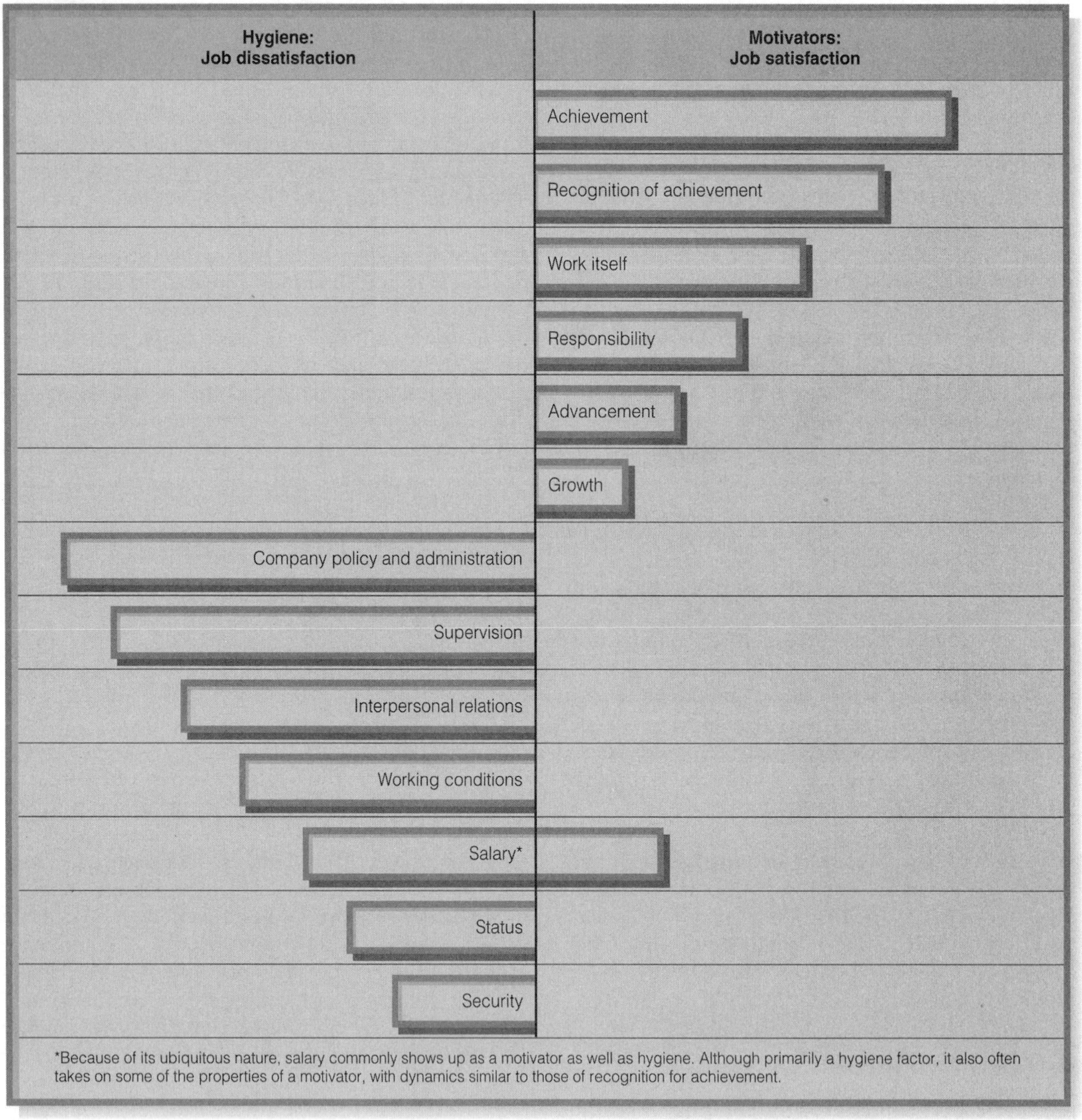

Hygiene: Job dissatisfaction	Motivators: Job satisfaction
	Achievement
	Recognition of achievement
	Work itself
	Responsibility
	Advancement
	Growth
Company policy and administration	
Supervision	
Interpersonal relations	
Working conditions	
Salary*	
Status	
Security	

*Because of its ubiquitous nature, salary commonly shows up as a motivator as well as hygiene. Although primarily a hygiene factor, it also often takes on some of the properties of a motivator, with dynamics similar to those of recognition for achievement.

SOURCE: Reprinted from Frederick Herzberg, *The Managerial Choice: To Be Efficient or to Be Human* (Salt Lake City: Olympus, 1982). Used with permission.

dissatisfied when the hygiene factors are not present. Employees may still be very motivated to perform their jobs well if the motivation factors are present, even in the absence of good hygiene factors. Although this may appear to be a paradox, it is not, because the motivation and hygiene factors are independent of each other.

The combination of motivation and hygiene factors can result in one of four possible job conditions. First, a job high in both motivation and hygiene factors leads to high motivation and few complaints among employees. In this job condition, employees are motivated to perform well and are contented with the conditions of their work environment. Second, a job low in both factors leads to low motivation and many complaints among employees. Under such conditions, employees are not only demotivated to perform well but are also discontented with the conditions of their work environment. Third, a job high in motivation factors and low in hygiene factors leads to high employee motivation to perform, coupled with complaints about aspects of the work environment. Discontented employees may still be able to do an excellent job if they take pride in the product or service. Fourth, a job low in motivation factors and high in hygiene factors leads to low employee motivation to excel, but few complaints about the work environment. These complacent employees have little motivation to do an outstanding job.

Two conclusions may be drawn at this point. First, hygiene factors are of some importance up to a threshold level, and beyond the threshold there is little value in improving the hygiene factors. Second, the presence of motivation factors is essential to enhancing employee motivation to excel at work.

Criticisms have been made of Herzberg's two-factor theory. One criticism concerns the classification of motivation and hygiene factors. Data have not shown a clear dichotomization of incidents into hygiene and motivator factors. For example, pay is classified by employees almost equally as a hygiene factor and a motivation factor. A second criticism is the absence of individual differences in the theory. Specifically, individual differences such as age, sex, social status, education, or occupational level may influence the classification of factors as motivation or hygiene. A third criticism is that intrinsic job factors, such as the work flow process, may be more important in determining satisfaction or dissatisfaction on the job.[17] Finally, almost all of the supporting data for the theory come from Herzberg and his students using his peculiar type of critical-incident storytelling technique. These criticisms challenge and qualify, yet do not invalidate, the theory. Herzberg's two-factor theory has important implications for job enrichment and the design of work, as discussed in Chapter 14.

◼ MCCLELLAND'S NEED THEORY

The final need theory of motivation we consider focuses on personality, as opposed to satisfaction-dissatisfaction or a hierarchy of needs. Henry Murray developed a long list of motives and manifest needs in his early studies of personality, and David McClelland was one psychologist inspired by this early work.[18] McClelland identified three learned or acquired needs he called manifest needs. These were for achievement, for power, and for affiliation. Individuals and national cultures differ in their levels of these needs. Some individuals have a high need for achievement, whereas others have a moderate or low need for achievement. The same is true for the other two needs. Each need has quite different implications for people's behavior. The Murray Thematic Apperception Test (TAT) was used as an early measure of the achievement motive and was further developed, both qualitatively and quantitatively, by McClelland and his associates.[19] The TAT is a projective test, as was discussed in Chapter 3.

◼ Need for Achievement

The need for achievement concerns issues of excellence, competition, challenging goals, persistence, and overcoming difficulties.[20] A person with a high need for achievement is one who seeks excellence in performance, enjoys difficult and challenging goals, and is persevering and competitive in work activities. Questions that address the need for achievement include: Do you enjoy difficult, challenging work activities? Do you strive to exceed your performance objectives? Do you seek out new ways to overcome difficulties?

McClelland found that people with a high need for achievement perform better than those with a moderate or low need for achievement, and he has noted national differences in achievement motivation. Individuals with a high need for achievement have three unique characteristics. First, they set moderately difficult, yet achievable, goals because they want both challenge and a good chance for success. Second, they like to receive feedback on their progress toward these goals. Because success is important to them, they like to know how they are doing. Third, they do not like having external events or other people interfere with their progress toward the goals. They are most comfortable working on individual tasks and activities that they control.

High achievers often hope and plan for success. They may be quite content to work alone or with other people--whichever is most appropriate to their task. High achievers like being very good at what they do, and they establish expertise and competence in their chosen endeavors. An example of a person with a high need for achievement is an information systems engineer who declines supervisory or managerial responsibility and devotes her energy to being the very best information systems engineer she can be.

People with moderate and low needs for achievement will be satisfied with less challenging goals, lower levels of excellence, and less persistence in the face of difficulty. However, these same people may have high needs for power or affiliation.

■ Need for Power

The need for power is concerned with making an impact on others, the desire to influence others, the urge to change people or events, and the desire to make a difference in life.[21] The need for power is interpersonal, because it involves influence attempts directed at other people. People with a high need for power like to be in control of people and events. McClelland makes an important distinction between socialized power, used for the social benefit of many, and personalized power, used for the personal gain of the individual. The former is a constructive force in organizations, whereas the latter may be a very disruptive, destructive force in organizations.

A high need for power was one distinguishing characteristic of managers rated the "best" in McClelland's research. Specifically, the best managers had a very high need for socialized power, used for the collective well-being of the group, as opposed to personalized power. These managers are concerned for others; have an interest in the organization's larger goals; and have a desire to be useful to the larger group, organization, and society.

Social and hierarchical status are important considerations for people with a high need for power. The more they are able to rise to the top of their organizations, the greater is their ability to exercise power, influence, and control so as to make an impact. Successful managers have the greatest upward velocity in an organization; they rise to higher managerial levels more quickly than their contemporaries.[22] These successful managers benefit their organizations most if they have a high socialized power need. The need for power is discussed further in Chapter 11, on power and politics.

■ Need for Affiliation

The need for affiliation is concerned with establishing and maintaining warm, close, intimate relationships with other people.[23] People with a high need for affiliation are motivated to express their emotions and feelings to others while expecting other people to do the same in return. They find conflicts and complications in their relationships disturbing and are strongly motivated to work through any such barriers to closeness. The relationships they have with others are therefore close and personal, emphasizing friendship and companionship.

People who have moderate to low needs for affiliation are more likely to feel comfortable working alone for extended periods of time. Modest or low levels of interaction with others are likely to satisfy these people's affiliation needs, allowing them to focus their attention on other needs and activities. People with a high need for affiliation, in contrast, always hope to be included in a range of interpersonal activities, in or away from work. They may play important integrative roles in group or intergroup activities because they work to achieve harmony and closeness in all relationships.

■ FIGURE 5.3
Four Need Theories of Motivation

		Maslow	Alderfer		Herzberg	McClelland
Higher order needs		Self-actualization	Growth	**Motivational factors**	The work itself: • Responsibility • Advancement • Growth	Need for achievement
		Esteem			Achievement	
		Belongingness (social and love)	Relatedness		Recognition	Need for power
					Quality of interpersonal working relationships	Need for affiliation
					Job security	
Lower order needs		Safety and security		**Hygiene factors**	Working conditions	
		Physiological	Existence		Salary	

Over and above these three needs, Murray's manifest needs theory included the need for autonomy.[24] This is the desire for independence and freedom from any constraints. People with a high need for autonomy like to work alone and to control the pace of their work. They dislike bureaucratic rules, regulations, and procedures. Figure 5.3 is a summary chart of the four need theories of motivation just discussed; it shows the parallel relationships between the needs in each of the theories. Where Maslow and Alderfer would refer to higher- and lower-order needs, Herzberg would refer to motivation and hygiene factors.

■ INDIVIDUAL-ORGANIZATIONAL EXCHANGES

Each need theory we have examined focuses on the internal human needs that motivate behavior. We now turn our attention to the social processes that influence motivation and behavior. For example, Peter Blau's examination of social life suggested that power and exchange are important considerations in

understanding human behavior.[25] In the same vein, Amitai Etzioni developed three categories of exchange relationships or involvements people have with organizations: committed, calculated, and alienated involvements.[26] The implications of these involvements for power are discussed in detail in Chapter 11. Etzioni characterized committed involvements as moral relationships of high positive intensity, calculated involvements as those of low positive or low negative intensity, and alienated involvements as those of high negative intensity. Committed involvements may characterize a person's relationship with a religious group; alienated involvements, a relationship with a prison system. Calculated involvements and Blau's ideas about power in social exchange are the best frameworks for understanding a person's relationship with a work organization.

■ Demands and Contributions

Calculated involvements are based on the notion of social exchange, in which each party in the relationship demands certain things of the other and contributes accordingly to the exchange. Business partnerships and commercial deals are excellent examples of calculated involvements. When they work well and both parties to the exchange benefit, the relationship has a positive orientation. When losses occur or conflicts arise, the relationship has a negative orientation. To examine calculated exchange relationships, it is necessary to consider the demands each party makes on the relationship as well as the contribution each makes.

Demands.   Each party to the exchange makes demands on the other. These demands express the expectations that each party has of the other in the relationship. The organization expresses its demands on the individual in the form of goal or mission statements, job expectations, performance objectives, and performance feedback. These are among the primary and formal mechanisms through which people learn about the organization's demands and expectations of them.

The organization is not alone in making demands of the relationship. The individual has needs to be satisfied as well, as we have previously discussed. These needs form the basis for the expectations or demands placed on the organization by the individual. These needs may be conceptualized from the perspective of Maslow, Alderfer, Herzberg, or McClelland. Different individuals have different needs.

Contributions.   Whereas each party to the exchange makes demands upon the other, each also has contributions to make to the relationship. These contributions are the basis for satisfying the demands expressed by the other party in the relationship. The processes of person-organization fit in this regard, and of reciprocity, are discussed in Chapter 17. Employees are able to satisfy organizational demands through a range of contributions. These contributions include their skills, abilities, knowledge, energy, professional contacts, and native talents. As people grow and develop over time, they are *more* able to satisfy the range of demands and expectations placed upon them by the organization.

In a similar fashion, organizations have a range of contributions available to the exchange relationship to meet individual needs. These contributions include salary, benefits, advancement opportunities, security, status, and social affiliation. Some organizations are richer in resources and better able to meet employee needs, whereas other organizations have fewer resources available to meet employee needs. Thus, one of the concerns that individuals and organizations alike have is whether the relationship is a fair deal or an equitable arrangement for both members of the relationship.

■ Adams' Theory of Inequity

Blau's and Etzioni's ideas about social exchange and relationship provide a context for understanding fairness, equity, and inequity in work relationships. Stacy Adams explicitly developed the issue of inequity in the social exchange process.[27] Adams' theory of inequity suggests that people are motivated when they find themselves in situations of inequity or unfairness.[28] Inequity is when a person receives more, or less, than the person believes is deserved for effort and/or contribution. Inequity leads to the experience of tension, and tension motivates a person to act in a manner to resolve the inequity.

When does a person know that the situation is inequitable or unfair? Adams suggests that people examine the contribution portion of the exchange relationship just discussed. Specifically, people consider their inputs (their own contributions to the relationship) and their outcomes (the organization's contributions to the relationship). People then calculate an input/outcome ratio, which they compare with that of a generalized or comparison other. An inequitable situation is depicted in Figure 5.4. In the example, the comparison other is making $11,000 more per year than the person while all other input and outcome considerations are the same. This underpayment condition motivates the person to resolve the inequity, according to Adams.

Although not illustrated in the example, nontangible inputs, like emotional investment, and nontangible outcomes, like job satisfaction, may well enter into a person's equity equation. With regard to pay inequity, this has been a particularly thorny issue for women in some professions and companies. Eastman Kodak and other companies have made real progress in addressing this inequity through pay equity.[29] As organizations become increasingly international, it may be difficult to determine pay and benefit equity/inequity across national borders.

■ FIGURE 5.4
Inequity in the Work
Environment

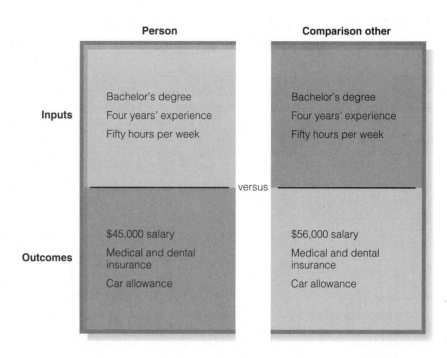

Person		Comparison other
Inputs	Bachelor's degree	Bachelor's degree
	Four years' experience	Four years' experience
	Fifty hours per week	Fifty hours per week
	versus	
Outcomes	$45,000 salary	$56,000 salary
	Medical and dental insurance	Medical and dental insurance
	Car allowance	Car allowance

Adams would consider the inequity in Figure 5.4 to be on the first level of inequity. A more severe, second level of inequity would occur if the comparison other's inputs were lower than the person's. This would occur, for example, if the comparison other worked only thirty-five hours a week or had only two years of experience. Inequalities in one (inputs or outcomes) coupled with equality in the other (inputs or outcomes) is experienced as a less severe inequity than inequalities in both inputs and outcomes. Adams' theory, however, does not provide a way of determining if some inputs (such as effort or experience) or some outcomes are more important or weighted more than others, such as a degree or certification.

■ The Resolution of Inequity

Once a person establishes the existence of an inequity, a number of strategies can be used to restore equity to the situation. Adams' theory provides seven basic strategies to restore equity for the person. These strategies are (1) to alter the person's outcomes, (2) to alter the person's inputs, (3) to alter the comparison other's outcomes, (4) to alter the comparison other's inputs, (5) to use a different person as a comparison other, (6) to rationalize the inequity, and (7) to leave the organizational situation.

Within each of the first four strategies, a wide variety of tactics can be employed. For example, if the strategy in the example shown in Figure 5.4 is to increase the person's outcomes by $11,000 per year, the tactic would be a meeting between the person and the manager concerning the issue of salary equity. The person would present relevant data on the issue. Another tactic would be for the person to work with the company's compensation specialists. A third would be for the person to bring the matter before an equity committee in the company. A fourth would be for the person to seek advice from the legal department.

The selection of a strategy and a set of tactics is a sensitive issue with possible long-term consequences. In this example, a strategy aimed at reducing the comparison other's outcomes may have the desired short-term effect of restoring equity while having adverse long-term consequences in terms of morale and productivity. Similarly, the choice of legal tactics may result in equity but have the long-term consequence of damaged relationships in the workplace. Therefore, as a person formulates the strategy and tactics to restore equity, the range of consequences of alternative actions must be taken into account. Hence, not all strategies or tactics are equally preferred. The equity theory does not include a hierarchy predicting which inequity reduction strategy a person will or should choose.

Field studies on equity theory suggest that it may help explain important organizational behaviors. For example, one study found that workers who perceived compensation decisions as equitable displayed greater job satisfaction and organizational commitment.[30] In addition, equity theory may play an important role in labor-management relationships with regard to union-negotiated benefits.

■ New Perspectives on Equity Theory

Since the original formulation of the theory of inequity, now usually referred to as equity theory, a number of revisions have been made in light of new theories and research. One important theoretical revision proposes three types of individuals based on preferences for equity.[31] Equity sensitives prefer equity based on the originally formed theory. Benevolents are comfortable with an equity ratio less than that of their comparison others, as exhibited in the Calvinistic heritage of the Dutch. These people may be thought of as givers. Entitleds are comfortable with an equity ratio greater than that of their comparison others, as exhibited by some offspring of the affluent who want and expect more.[32] These people may be thought of as takers.

Recent research found that a person's organizational position influences self-imposed performance expectations.[33] Specifically, a two-level move up in an organization with no additional pay creates a higher self-imposed performance expectation than a one-level move up with modest additional pay. Similarly, a two-level move down in an organization with no reduction in pay creates a lower self-imposed performance expectation than a one-level move down with a modest decrease in pay. This suggests that organizational position may be more important than pay in determining the level of a person's performance expectations. Some limitations of equity theory include its heavy emphasis on pay as an outcome, the difficulty in controlling the choices of a comparison other, and the difficulty the theory has had in explaining the overpayment condition.

Most studies of equity theory take a short-term perspective.[34] However, equity comparisons over the long term should be considered as well. Increasing, decreasing, or constant experiences of inequity over time may have very different consequences for people.[35] For example, do increasing experiences of inequity have a debilitating effect on people? In addition, equity theory may help companies implement two-tiered wage structures, such as those at American Airlines. In a two-tiered system, one group of employees receives different pay and benefits from those of another group of employees. A study of 1,935 rank-and-file members in one retail chain using a two-tiered wage structure confirmed the predictions of equity theory.[36] The researchers suggest that unions and management may want to consider work location and employment status (part-time versus full-time) prior to the implementation of a two-tiered system.

■ EXPECTANCY THEORY OF MOTIVATION

Whereas Adams' theory of inequity focuses on a social process, Vroom's expectancy theory of motivation focuses on personal perceptions. His theory is founded on the basic notions that people desire certain outcomes of behavior, which may be thought of as rewards or consequences of behavior, and that they believe there are relationships between the effort they put forth, the performance they achieve, and the outcomes they receive. Expectancy theory is a cognitive, process theory of motivation.

The key constructs in the expectancy theory of motivation are the valence of an outcome, expectancy, and instrumentality.[37] Valence is the value or importance one places on a particular reward. Expectancy is the belief that effort leads to performance (for example, "If I try harder, I can do better"). Instrumentality is the belief that performance is related to the rewards (for example, "If I perform better, I will get more pay"). A model for the expectancy theory notions of effort, performance, and rewards is depicted in Figure 5.5.

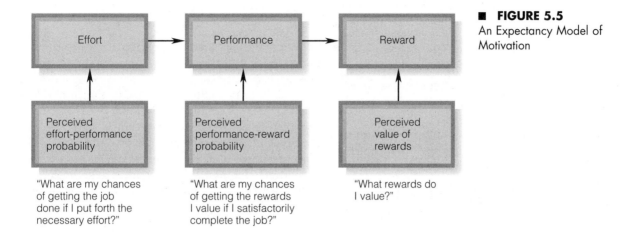

■ FIGURE 5.5
An Expectancy Model of Motivation

Valence, expectancy, and instrumentality are all important to a person's motivation. Expectancy and instrumentality concern a person's beliefs about how effort, performance, and rewards are related. For example, a person may firmly believe that an increase in effort has a direct, positive effect on improved performance and that reduced effort results in a commensurate reduction in performance. Another person may have a very different set of beliefs about the effort-performance link. The person might believe that regardless of the amount of additional effort put forth, no improvement in performance is possible. Therefore, the perceived relationship between effort and performance varies from person to person and from activity to activity.

In a similar fashion, people's beliefs about the performance-reward link vary. One person may believe that an improvement in performance has a direct, positive effect on the rewards received, another may believe that an improvement in performance has no effect on the rewards received. Again, the perceived relationship between performance and rewards varies from person to person and from situation to situation. From a motivation perspective, it is the person's belief about the relationships between these constructs that is important, not the actual nature of the relationship.

Expectancy theory has been used by managers and companies to design motivation programs, such as Tenneco's PP&E (Performance Planning and Evaluation) system.[38] In Tenneco's case, the PP&E system was designed to enhance a person's belief

that effort would lead to better performance and that better performance would lead to merit pay increases and other rewards. Valence and expectancy are particularly important in establishing priorities for people pursuing multiple goals.[39] For example, Washburn International, famous for its acoustic guitars, changed its goals and incentive system to solve a sales problem. By implementing a 1% sales incentive "override" for meeting quotas in six product lines, Washburn found 75 percent of its reps earning the override within one year.

A person's motivation increases along with his or her belief that effort leads to performance and that performance leads to rewards, assuming the person wants the rewards. This is the third key idea within the expectancy theory of motivation. It is the idea that the valence, or value, that people place on various rewards varies. One person prefers salary to benefits, whereas another person prefers just the reverse. All people do not place the same value on each reward.

■ Motivational Problems

Motivational problems stem from three basic causes within the expectancy theory framework. These causes are: disbelief in a relationship between effort and performance, disbelief in a relationship between performance and rewards, and lack of desire for the rewards offered.

If the motivational problem is related to the person's belief that effort will not result in performance, the solution lies in altering this belief. The person can be shown how an increase in effort or an alteration in the kind of effort put forth can be converted into improved performance. For example, the textbook salesperson who does not believe more calls (effort) will result in greater sales (performance) might be shown how to distinguish departments with high-probability sales opportunities from those with low-probability sales opportunities. Hence, more calls (effort) can be converted into greater sales (performance).

If the motivational problem is related to the person's belief that performance will not result in rewards, the solution lies in altering this belief. The person can be shown how an increase in performance or a somewhat altered form of performance will be converted into rewards. For example, the textbook salesperson who does not believe greater sales (performance) will result in overall higher commissions (rewards) might be shown computationally or graphically that a direct relationship does exist. Hence, greater sales (performance) are directly converted into higher commissions (rewards).

If the motivational problem is related to the value placed on, or the preference for, certain rewards, the solution lies in influencing the value placed on the rewards or altering the rewards themselves. For example, the textbook salesperson may not particularly want higher commissions, given the small incremental gain to the salesperson at his tax level. In this case, the company might establish a mechanism for sheltering commissions from being taxed or alternative mechanisms for deferred compensation.

Research results on expectancy theory have been mixed.[40] The theory has been shown to predict job satisfaction accurately.[41] However, the theory's complexity makes it difficult to test the full model, and the measures of instrumentality, valence, and expectancy have only weak validity.[42] In addition, it is time-consuming to measure the expectancy constructs, and the values for each construct change over time for an individual. Finally, a theory assumes the individual is totally rational and acts as a minicomputer, calculating probabilities and values. In reality, the theory may be more complex than people as they typically function.

■ Motivation and Moral Maturity

Expectancy theory would predict that people work to maximize their personal outcomes. This is consistent with Adam Smith's ideas of working in one's own self-interest. Ultimately, Adam Smith and expectancy theorists show a belief that people work to benefit themselves alone. Expectancy theory would not explain altruistic behavior for the benefit of others. Therefore, it may be necessary to consider an individual's moral maturity in order to better understand altruistic, fair, and equitable behavior. Cognitive moral development was discussed in Chapter 4. Moral maturity is the measure of a person's cognitive moral development. Morally mature people act and behave based on universal ethical principles, whereas morally immature people act and behave based on egocentric motivations.[43] While principled people are the most mature and premoral people the least mature, the conventional people constitute the norm in their moral development.

■ Cultural Differences in Motivation

Most motivation theories in use today have been developed by Americans in the United States and are about Americans.[44] Recent efforts have examined the universality of these theories and cultural differences have been found to exist, at least with regard to Maslow's, McClelland's, Herzberg's, and Vroom's theories. For example, while self-actualization may be the pinnacle need for Americans in Maslow's need hierarchy, security may be the most important need for people in cultures such as Greece and Japan who have a high need to avoid uncertainty.[45] While achievement is an important need for Americans, other cultures do not value achievement as much as Americans do.

Herzberg's theory has been tested in other countries as well. Results in New Zealand did not replicate the results found in the U.S. Supervision and interpersonal relationships were important motivators in New Zealand, rather than hygienic factors as in America.[46] Finally, expectancy theory may hold up very nicely in cultures that value individualism while breaking down in more collectivist cultures that value cooperative efforts. In collectivist cultures, rewards are more closely tied to group and team efforts, thus obviating the utility of expectancy theory.

MANAGERIAL IMPLICATIONS: THE MANY METHODS TO MOTIVATE PEOPLE

Managers must realize that all motivation theories are not equally good or equally useful. The later motivation theories, such as the equity and expectancy theories, may be more scientifically sound than earlier theories, such as the two-factor theory. However, the older theories of motivation have conceptual value, show us the importance of human needs, and provide a basis for the later theories. Many motivation theories are less than perfect. Each has faults, as well as strengths, and none works all of the time for all people.

Managers cannot assume they understand employees' needs. They should recognize the variety of needs that motivate employee behavior and solicit input from employees to better understand their needs. Individual employees differ in their needs, and managers should be sensitive to ethnic, national, gender, and age differences in this regard. Employees with high needs for power must be given opportunities to exercise influence, and employees with high needs for achievement must be allowed to excel at work.

Managers can increase employee motivation by training (increased perceptions of success because of increased ability), coaching (increased confidence), and task assignments (increased perceptions of success because of more experience). Managers should ensure that rewards are contingent on good performance and that valued rewards, such as time off or flexible work schedules, are available. Managers must understand what their employees want.

Finally, managers should be aware that morally mature employees are more likely to be sensitive to inequities at work. At the same time, these employees are less likely to be selfish or self-centered and more likely to be concerned about equity issues for all employees. Morally mature employees will act ethically for the common good of all employees and the organization.

CHAPTER SUMMARY

- Early economic theories of motivation emphasized self-interest as the basis for motivation and technology as a force with great impact.
- Early psychological theories of motivation emphasized internal needs but did not take into account individual diversity in these needs.
- Maslow's hierarchy of needs theory of motivation was the basis for McGregor's assumptions about the ways people should be treated at work.
- Herzberg found that the presence of motivation factors led to job satisfaction, and the presence of hygiene factors prevented job dissatisfaction.
- According to McClelland, the needs for achievement, power, and affiliation are learned needs that differ among cultures.
- Social exchange theory holds that people form calculated working relationships and expect fair, equitable, ethical treatment.
- Expectancy theory says that effort is the basis for motivation and that people want their effort to lead to performance and rewards.
- Theories of motivation are culturally bound and differences occur between nations.

REVIEW QUESTIONS

1. Define the terms *motivation, needs,* and *equity.*
2. Is it ethical for you to pursue your self-interest at work? Are the thoughts and feelings of other people at work important? (ethics questions)
3. What are the five categories of motivational needs described by Maslow? Give an example of how each can be satisfied.
4. What are the Theory X and Theory Y assumptions about human nature proposed by McGregor? How do they relate to Maslow's needs?
5. What three manifest needs does McClelland identify?
6. How is inequity determined by a person in an organization? How can inequity be resolved if it exists?
7. What are the key concepts in the expectancy theory of motivation?

8. Suppose your company has an employee who has been with the company for a long time and now has health problems that prevent him or her from being fully productive for at least a year. Should the company attempt to carry this person? Or, reduce the person's pay and benefits according to performance?

■ REFERENCES

1. R. A. Katzell and D. E. Thompson, "Work Motivation: Theory and Practice," *American Psychologist* 45 (1990): 144–153.

2. M. Weber, *The Protestant Ethic and the Spirit of Capitalism* (London: Talcott Parson, tr., 1930).

3. S. Freud, *Civilization and Its Discontents,* trans. and ed. J. Strachey (New York: Norton, 1961).

4. F. W. Taylor, "Shop Management" (Paper presented at the national meeting of the American Society of Mechanical Engineers, Sarasota, New York, 1903).

5. F. J. Roethlisberger, *Management and Morale* (Cambridge, Mass.: Harvard University Press, 1941).

6. A. Smith, *An Inquiry into the Nature and Causes of the Wealth of Nations,* vol. 10 of The Harvard Classics, ed. C. J. Bullock (New York: Collier, 1909).

7. F. W. Taylor, *The Principles of Scientific Management* (New York: Norton, 1911).

8. A. H. Maslow, "A Theory of Human Motivation," *Psychological Review* 50 (1943): 370–396.

9. W. James, *The Principles of Psychology* (New York: H. Holt & Co., 1890; Cambridge, Mass.: Harvard University Press, 1983).

10. J. Dewey, *Human Nature and Conduct: An Introduction to Social Psychology* (New York: Holt, 1922).

11. L. W. Porter, "A Study of Perceived Need Satisfactions in Bottom and Middle Management Jobs," *Journal of Applied Psychology* 45 (1961): 1–10.

12. D. M. McGregor, "The Human Side of Enterprise," *Management Review* (November 1957): 22–28, 88–92.

13. D. E. Petersen and J. Hillkirk, *A Better Idea: Redefining the Way Americans Work* (Boston: Houghton Mifflin, 1991).

14. G. E. Forward, D. E. Beach, D. A. Gray, and J. C. Quick, "Mentofacturing: A Vision for American Industrial Excellence," *Academy of Management Executive* 5 (1991): 32–44.

15. C. P. Alderfer, *Human Needs in Organizational Settings* (New York: Free Press, 1972).

16. F. Herzberg, B. Mausner, and B. Snyderman, *The Motivation to Work* (New York: Wiley, 1959).

17. R. J. House and L. Wigdor, "Herzberg's Dual-Factor Theory of Job Satisfaction and Motivation: A Review of the Evidence and a Criticism," *Personnel Psychology* 20 (1967): 369–389.

18. D. C. McClelland, *Motivational Trends in Society* (Morristown, N.J.: General Learning Press, 1971).

19. J. P. Chaplin and T. S. Krawiec, *Systems and Theories of Psychology* (New York: Holt, Rinehart & Winston, 1960).

20. D. C. McClelland, "Achievement Motivation Can Be Learned," *Harvard Business Review* 43 (1965): 6–24.

21. D. C. McClelland and D. Burnham, "Power Is the Great Motivator," *Harvard Business Review* 54 (1976): 100–111.

22. F. Luthans, "Successful vs. Effective Real Managers," *Academy of Management Executive* 2 (1988): 127–131.

23. S. Schachter, *The Psychology of Affiliation* (Stanford, Calif.: Stanford University Press, 1959).

24. R. M. Steers, "Murray's Manifest Needs Theory," in R. M. Steers and L. W. Porter, eds., *Motivation and Work Behavior,* 3d ed. (New York: McGraw-Hill, 1983): 42–50.

25. P. M. Blau, *Exchange and Power in Social Life* (New York: Wiley, 1964).

26. A. Etzioni, "A Basis for Comparative Analysis of Complex Organizations," in A. Etzioni, ed., *A Sociological Reader on Complex Organizations,* 2d ed., (New York: Holt, Rinehart & Winston, 1969), 59–76.

27. J. S. Adams, "Inequity in Social Exchange," in L. Berkowitz, ed., *Advances in Experimental Social Psychology,* vol. 2 (New York: Academic Press, 1965), 267–299.

28. J. S. Adams, "Toward an Understanding of Inequity," *Journal of Abnormal and Social Psychology* 67 (1963): 422–436.

29. J. Nelson-Horchler, "The Best Man for the Job Is a Man," *Industry Week,* 7 January 1991, 50–52.

30. P. D. Sweeney, D. B. McFarlin, and E. J. Inderrieden, "Using Relative Deprivation Theory to Explain Satisfaction with Income and Pay Level: A Multistudy Examination," *Academy of Management Journal* 33 (1990): 423–436.

31. R. C. Huseman, J. D. Hatfield, and E. A. Miles, "A New Perspective on Equity Theory: The Equity Sensitivity Construct," *Academy of Management Review* 12 (1987): 222–234.

32. R. Coles, *Privileged Ones* (Boston: Little, Brown, 1977).

33. J. Greenberg, "Equity and Workplace Status: A Field Experiment," *Journal of Applied Psychology* 73 (1988): 606–613.

34. R. Vecchio, "Predicting Worker Performance in Inequitable Settings," *Academy of Management Review* 7 (1982): 103–110.

35. R. A. Cosier and D. R. Dalton, "Equity Theory and Time: A Reformulation," *Academy of Management Review* 8 (1983): 311–319.

36. J. E. Martin and M. W. Peterson, "Two-Tier Wage Structures: Implications for Equity Theory," *Academy of Management Journal* 30 (1987): 297–315.

37. V. H. Vroom, *Work and Motivation* (New York: Wiley, 1964/1970).

38. M. F. Fadden and B. L. Smith, *High Performance Flying* (Houston: Tenneco Chemicals, 1976).

39. M. C. Kernan and R. G. Lord, "Effects of Valence, Expectancies, and Goal-Performance Discrepancies in Single and Multiple Goal Environments," *Journal of Applied Psychology* 75 (1990): 194–203.

40. T. R. Mitchell, "Expectancy Models of Job Satisfaction, Occupational Preference and Effort: A Theoretical, Methodological, and Empirical Appraisal," *Psychological Bulletin* 81 (1974): 1053–1077.

41. E. D. Pulakos and N. Schmitt, "A Longitudinal Study of a Valence Model Approach for the Prediction of Job Satisfaction of New Employees," *Journal of Applied Psychology* 68 (1983): 307–312.

42. F. J. Landy and W. S. Becker, "Motivation Theory Reconsidered," in L. L. Cummings and B. M. Staw, eds., *Research in Organizational Behavior* 9 (Greenwich, Conn.: JAI Press, 1987), 1–38.

43. L. Kohlberg, "The Cognitive-Developmental Approach to Socialization," in D. A. Goslin, ed., *Handbook of Socialization Theory and Research* (Chicago: Rand McNally, 1969).

44. N. J. Adler, *International Dimensions of Organizational Behavior* (Boston: PWS-KENT, 1991).

45. G. Hofstede, "Motivation, Leadership, and Organization: Do American Theories Apply Abroad?" *Organizational Dynamics* 9 (1980): 42–63.

46. G. H. Hines, "Cross-Cultural Differences in Two-Factor Theory," *Journal of Applied Psychology* 58 (1981): 313–317.

CHAPTER 6
LEARNING AND PERFORMANCE MANAGEMENT

LEARNING OBJECTIVES

After reading this chapter, you should be able to do the following:

- Define learning, reinforcement, punishment, extinction, and goal setting.
- Distinguish between classical and operant conditioning.
- Explain the strategies of reinforcement and punishment using positive and negative consequences of behavior.
- Identify the purposes of goal setting and the five characteristics of effective goals.
- Describe effective strategies for giving and receiving performance feedback.
- Compare individual and team-oriented reward systems.
- Describe strategies for correcting poor performance.

This is the second of two chapters addressing motivation and behavior. Chapter 5 took an endogenous (internal), content-oriented approach to human motivation. This chapter focuses primarily on exogenous (external) causes of behavior. The first section addresses learning theory and the use of reinforcement, punishment, and extinction at work. It also touches on Bandura's social learning theory and Jung's personality approach to learning. The second section presents theory, research, and practice related to goal setting in organizations. The third section addresses the definition and measurement of performance. The fourth section is concerned with rewarding performance. The fifth and concluding section addresses ways to correct poor performance.

■ LEARNING IN ORGANIZATIONS

Learning is a change in behavior acquired through experience. It is not simply the cognitive activity of developing knowledge about a subject. The behaviorist approach to learning assumes that observable behavior is a function of its consequences. Learning has its basis in classical and operant conditioning.

■ Classical Conditioning

Classical conditioning is the process of modifying behavior so that a conditioned stimulus is paired with an unconditioned stimulus and elicits an unconditioned response. It is largely the result of the research on animals (primarily dogs) by the Russian physiologist Ivan Pavlov.[1] Pavlov's professional exchanges with Walter B. Cannon and other American researchers during the early twentieth century led to the application of his ideas in the United States.[2] Classical conditioning builds on the natural consequence of an unconditioned response to an unconditioned stimulus. In dogs, this might be the natural production of saliva (unconditioned response) in response to the presentation of meat (unconditioned stimulus). By presenting a conditioned stimulus (for example, a bell) simultaneously with the unconditioned stimulus (the meat), the researcher caused the dog to develop a conditioned response (salivation in response to the bell).

Classical conditioning may occur in a similar fashion in humans. For example, a person working at a computer terminal may get lower back tension (unconditioned response) as a result of poor posture (unconditioned stimulus). If the person becomes aware of that tension only when the manager enters the work area (conditioned stimulus), then the person may develop a conditioned response (lower back tension) to the appearance of the manager.

Although this example is logical, classical conditioning has real limitations in its applicability to human behavior in organizations for at least three reasons. First, humans are more complex than dogs and less amenable to simple cause-and-effect conditioning. Second, the behavioral environments in organizations are complex and not very amenable to single stimulus-response manipulations. Third, complex human decision making makes it possible to override simple conditioning.

■ Operant Conditioning

Operant conditioning is the process of modifying behavior through the use of positive or negative consequences following specific behaviors. It is based on the notion that behavior is a function of its consequences,[3] which may be either positive or negative. The consequences of behavior are used to influence, or shape, behavior through three strategies: reinforcement, punishment, and extinction. Organizational behavior modification is a form of operant conditioning used successfully in a variety of organizations to shape behavior.[4]

■ The Strategies of Reinforcement, Punishment, and Extinction

Reinforcement is used to enhance desirable behavior, and punishment and extinction are used to diminish undesirable behavior. (The three strategies are defined and described in detail later in this section of the chapter.) Organizations, families, and other social systems define and categorize desirable and undesirable behavior. A behavior may be desirable in one context and undesirable in another. For example, a police officer's use of physical force to restrain an unruly adult might be viewed as desirable behavior while his use of the same physical force with a teenager might be viewed as undesirable behavior. Knowing what behavior is desirable and what behavior is undesirable is not always easy. A team of motivational experts was once asked by a military unit to help increase combat soldiers' desire to kill the enemy. The team declined for two reasons. First, its members were not sure they knew how to design such a program. Second, they were uncertain about the social desirability of doing it. The problem posed to the team raises an ethical question about how society should define desirable and undesirable behavior.

Reinforcement and punishment are administered through the management of positive and negative consequences of behavior. Positive consequences are the results of a person's behavior that the person finds attractive or pleasurable. They might include a pay increase, a bonus, a promotion, a transfer to a more desirable geographical location, or praise from a supervisor. Negative consequences are the results of a person's behavior that the person finds unattractive or aversive. They might include disciplinary action, an undesirable transfer, a demotion, or harsh criticism from a supervisor. Positive and negative

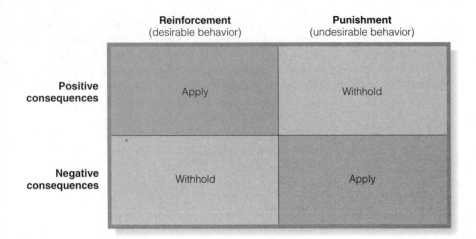

■ FIGURE 6.1
Reinforcement and Punishment Strategies

consequences must be defined for the person receiving them. Therefore, individual, gender, and cultural differences may be important in their classification.

The use of positive and negative consequences following a specific behavior either reinforces or punishes that behavior.[5] Thorndike's law of effect states that behaviors followed by positive consequences are more likely to recur and behaviors followed by negative consequences are less likely to recur.[6] Figure 6.1 shows how positive and negative consequences may be applied or withheld in the strategies of reinforcement and punishment.

Reinforcement. Reinforcement is the attempt to develop or strengthen desirable behavior by either bestowing positive consequences or withholding negative consequences. Positive reinforcement results from the application of a positive consequence following a desirable behavior. Bonuses paid at the end of successful business years are an example of positive reinforcement. Marriott Corporation provides positive reinforcement by honoring fifteen to twenty employees each year with its J. Willard Marriott Award of Excellence. Marriott Awards are presented to a cross-section of employees at banquets attended by honorees, spouses, nominees, and top executives.

Negative reinforcement results from withholding a threatened negative consequence when a desirable behavior occurs. For example, a manager who reduces an employee's pay (negative consequence) if the employee comes to work late (undesirable behavior) and refrains from doing so when the employee is on time (desirable behavior) has negatively reinforced the employee's on-time behavior. The employee avoids the negative consequence (a reduction in pay) by exhibiting the desirable behavior (being on time to work).

Either continuous or intermittent schedules of reinforcement may be used. These are described in Table 6.1.

Punishment. Punishment is the attempt to eliminate or weaken undesirable behavior. It is used in two ways. One way to punish a person is through the application of a negative consequence following an undesirable behavior. For example, a professional athlete who is excessively offensive to an official (undesirable behavior) may be ejected from a game (negative consequence). The other way is through the withholding of a positive consequence following an undesirable behavior. For example, a salesperson who makes few visits to companies (undesirable behavior) and whose sales are well below the quota (undesirable behavior) is likely to receive a very small commission check (positive consequence) at the end of the month.

One problem with punishment is that it may have unintended results. Because punishment is discomforting to the individual being punished, the experience of punishment may result in negative psychological, emotional, performance, or behavioral consequences. For example, the person being punished may become angry, hostile, depressed, or de-

■ **TABLE 6.1**
Schedules of Reinforcement

SCHEDULE	DESCRIPTION	EFFECTS ON RESPONDING
Continuous		
	Reinforcer follows every response	1. Steady high rate of performance as long as reinforcement follows every response 2. High frequency of reinforcement may lead to early satiation 3. Behavior weakens rapidly (undergoes extinction) when reinforcers are withheld 4. Appropriate for newly emitted, unstable, low-frequency responses
Intermittent		
	Reinforcer does not follow every response	1. Capable of producing high frequencies of responding 2. Low frequency or reinforcement precludes early satiation 3. Appropriate for stable or high-frequency responses
Fixed ratio	A fixed number of responses must be emitted before reinforcement occurs	1. A fixed ratio of 1:1 (reinforcement occurs after every response) is the same as a continuous schedule 2. Tends to produce a high rate of response that is vigorous and steady
Variable ratio	A varying or random number of responses must be emitted before reinforcement occurs	Capable of producing a high rate of response that is vigorous, steady, and resistant to extinction
Fixed interval	The first response after a specific period of time has elapsed is reinforced	Produces an uneven response pattern varying from a very slow, unenergetic response immediately following reinforcement to a very fast, vigorous response immediately preceding reinforcement
Variable interval	The first response after varying or random periods of time have elapsed is reinforced	Tends to produce a high rate of response that is vigorous, steady, and resistant to extinction

SOURCE: From *Organizational Behavior Modification and Beyond* by Fred Luthans and Robert Kreitner. Copyright © 1985 by Scott Foresman and Company. Reprinted by permission of Harper Collins Publishers.

spondent. From an organizational standpoint, this result becomes important when the punished person translates negative emotional and psychological responses into negative actions. A General Motors employee who had been disciplined pulled an emergency cord and shut down an entire assembly line. A hardware store owner was killed by a man he had fired for poor performance. Work slowdowns, sabotage, and subversive behavior are all unintended negative consequences of punishment.

Extinction. An alternative to punishing undesirable behavior is extinction—the attempt to weaken a behavior by attaching no consequences (either positive or negative) to it. It is equivalent to ignoring the behavior. The rationale for using extinction is that a behavior not followed by any consequence is weakened. However, some patience and time may be needed for it to be effective.

Extinction may be practiced, for example, by not responding (no consequence) to the sarcasm (behavior) of a colleague. Extinction may be most effective when used in conjunction with the positive reinforcement of desirable behaviors. Therefore, in the example, the best approach might be to compliment the sarcastic colleague for constructive comments (reinforcing desirable behavior) while ignoring the colleague's sarcastic comments (extinguishing undesirable behavior).

Extinction is not always the best strategy, however. Punishment might be preferable in cases of dangerous behavior to deliver a swift, clear lesson. It might also be preferable in cases of seriously undesirable behavior, such as employee embezzlement or other unethical behavior.

■ Bandura's Social Learning Theory

Albert Bandura, using the social learning theory perspective discussed in Chapter 4 as related to attitude formation, believes learning occurs through the observation of other people and the modeling of their behavior.[7] Executives can teach their subordinates a wide range of behaviors, such as leader-follower interactions and stress management, by exhibiting these behaviors. Since employees look to their supervisors for acceptable norms of behavior, they are likely to pattern their own responses on the supervisor's. Central to Bandura's thinking is the notion of self-efficacy, as defined and discussed in Chapter 3. People with high levels of self-efficacy are more effective at learning than are those with low levels. According to Bandura, self-efficacy expectations may be enhanced through four means: (1) performance accomplishments (just do it!), (2) vicarious experiences (watch someone else do it), (3) verbal persuasion (be convinced by someone else to do it), or (4) emotional arousal (get excited about doing it).

■ Learning and Personality Differences

Jung's theory of personality differences (discussed in Chapter 3) has two implications for learning and working relationships.[8] First, introverts and extraverts learn differently. Introverts need quiet time to study, concentrate, and reflect on what they are learning. They think best when they are alone. Extraverts need to interact with other people, learn-

■ TABLE 6.2
Personality Functions and Learning

PERSONALITY PREFERENCE	IMPLICATIONS FOR LEARNING BY INDIVIDUALS
Information Gathering	
Intuitors	Prefer theoretical frameworks. Look for the meaning in material. Attempt to understand the grand scheme. Look for possibilities and interrelations.
Sensors	Prefer specific, empirical data. Look for practical applications. Attempt to master details of a subject. Look for what is realistic and doable.
Decision Making	
Thinkers	Prefer analysis of data and information. Work to be fairminded and even-handed. Seek logical, just conclusions. Do not like to be too personally involved.
Feelers	Prefer interpersonal involvement. Work to be tenderhearted and harmonious. Seek subjective, merciful results. Do not like objective, factual analysis.

Source: Excerpted from O. Kroeger and J. M. Thuesen, *Type Talk: The 16 Personality Types that Determine How We Live, Love, and Work,* New York: Dell Publishing Co., 1988, pp. 188–190.

ing through the process of expressing and exchanging ideas with others. They think best in groups and while they are talking. Second, the personality functions of intuition, sensing, thinking, and feeling have implications for how people learn, as shown in Table 6.2. The functions of intuition and sensing determine the individual's preference for information gathering. The functions of thinking and feeling determine the way the individual evaluates and makes decisions about newly acquired information. Each person has a preferred mode of gathering information and of evaluating and making decisions about that information. For example, when considering a total quality program, an intuitive thinker may want to skim research reports about implementing total quality programs and then, working on hunches, decide how to apply the research findings to the organization. A sensing feeler may prefer to view videotaped interviews with people in companies that have implemented total quality programs, then identify people in the organization most likely to be receptive to the approaches presented.

■ Organizational Learning

Organizations do not learn. Individuals, acting on behalf of the organization, produce behavior that can lead to learning. Chris Argyris encourages individuals to engage in double-loop learning to create the most productive work environments.[9] Double-loop learning questions the underlying assumptions of, the governing variables for, and the reasoning behind the organizational system when problems or failure occur. In contrast, single-loop learning simply tries to correct the problem or failure without questioning why the failure occurred in the first place. The smartest, most successful people in organizations often have the greatest difficulty learning because they defend the organization that has led to their success.[10] The most fruitful organizational learning occurs when individuals question, rather than defend, organizational practices that have led to failure or problems in the work environment. Leaders can be especially good models of double-loop learning to overcome conflicts and create healthier approaches to threatening work situations.[11]

■ GOAL SETTING AT WORK

Goal setting is the process of establishing desired results that guide and direct behavior. In organizations, it began with Frederick Taylor's idea that performance standards would lead to higher worker performance. It is based on laboratory studies, field research experiments, and comparative investigations by Edwin Locke, Gary Latham, John M. Ivancevich and others.[12]

■ Characteristics of Effective Goals

How difficult and specific are your work or school goals? Various organizations define the characteristics of effective goals differently. For the former Sanger-Harris, a retail organization, the acronym SMART communicates the approach to effective goals. SMART stands for Specific, Measurable, Attainable, Realistic, and Time-bound. Five commonly accepted characteristics of effective goals are being specific, challenging, measurable, time-bound, and prioritized.

Specific and challenging goals serve to cue or focus the person's attention on exactly what is to be accomplished and to arouse the person to peak performance. People in a wide range of occupations who set specific, challenging goals consistently outperform people who have easy or unspecified goals.

Measurable, quantitative goals are useful as a basis for feedback about goal progress. Qualitative goals are also valuable. The Western Company of North America allowed about 15 percent of a manager's goals to be of a qualitative nature. A qualitative goal might be to improve relationships with customers. Further work might convert the qualitative goal into quantitative measures such as the number of complaints or frequency of complimentary letters. However, the qualitative goal may well be sufficient and most meaningful in this case.

Time-bound goals enhance measurability. The time limit may be implicit in the goal or it may need to be made explicit. For example, without the six-month time limit, an insurance salesperson might think the sales goal is for the whole year rather than for six months. Many organizations work on standardized cycles, such as quarters or years, where very explicit time limits are assumed. If there is any uncertainty about the time period of the goal effort, the time limit should be explicitly stated.

The priority ordering of goals allows for effective decision making about the allocation of resources.[13] As time, energy, or other resources become available, a person can move down the list of goals in descending order. The key concern is with achieving the top-priority goals. Priority helps direct a person's efforts and behavior. While these characteristics help increase motivation and performance, that is not the only function of goal setting in organizations.

Goal setting serves one or more of three functions. First, it can increase work motivation and task performance.[14] Second, it can reduce the role stress that is associated with conflicting or confusing expectations.[15] Third, it can improve the accuracy and validity of performance evaluation.[16]

■ Increasing Work Motivation and Task Performance

Goals are often used to increase employee effort and motivation, which in turn improve task performance. The higher the goal, the better the performance; that is, people work harder to reach difficult goals. "Stretch Targets" are goals that really stretch employee performance as opposed to incremental goals that add marginally to performance.[17] The positive relationship between goal difficulty and task performance is one of the best researched relationships in organizational behavior.

Three important behavioral aspects of enhancing performance motivation through goal setting are employee participation, supervisory commitment, and useful performance feedback. Employee participation in goal setting leads to goal acceptance by employees. Goal acceptance is thought to lead to goal commitment and then to goal accomplishment. Special attention has been given to factors that influence commitment to difficult goals, such as participation in the process of setting the difficult goals.[18] Even in the case of assigned goals, goal acceptance and commitment are considered essential prerequisites of goal accomplishment.

Supervisory goal commitment is a reflection of the organization's commitment to goal setting. Organizational commitment is a prerequisite for successful goal-setting programs, such as management by objectives (MBO) programs. The organization must be committed to the program, and the employee and supervisors must be committed to specific work goals as well as to the program. (MBO will be discussed in more detail later in the chapter.)

The supervisor plays a second important role by providing employees with interim performance feedback on progress toward goals. Performance feedback is most useful when the goals are specific, and specific goals improve performance most when interim feedback is given.[19] For example, assume an insurance salesperson has a goal of selling $500,000 worth of insurance in six months but has achieved sales of only $200,000 after three months. During an interim performance feedback session, the supervi-

sor may help the salesperson identify the fact that he is not focusing his calls on the likeliest prospects. This useful feedback coupled with the specific goal helps the salesperson better focus his efforts to achieve the goal. Feedback is most helpful when it is useful (helping the salesperson identify high probability prospects) and timely (halfway through the performance period).

■ Reducing Role Stress of Conflicting and Confusing Expectations

A second function of goal setting is to reduce the role stress associated with conflicting and confusing expectations. This is done by clarifying the task-role expectations communicated to employees. Supervisors, co-workers, and employees are all important sources of task-related information. A fourteen-month evaluation of goal setting in reducing role stress found that conflict, confusion, and absenteeism were all reduced through the use of goal setting.[20]

The improved role clarity resulting from goal setting may be attributable to improved communication between managers and employees. An early study of the MBO goal-setting program at Ford Motor Company found an initial 25 percent lack of agreement between managers and their bosses concerning the definition of the managers' jobs. Through effective goal-setting activities, this lack of agreement was reduced to about 5 percent.[21] At Federal Express, managers are encouraged to include communication-related targets in their annual MBO goal-setting process.

■ Improving the Accuracy and Validity of Performance Evaluation

The third major function of goal setting is improving the accuracy and validity of performance evaluation. One of the best methods of doing so is to use management by objectives (MBO)—a goal-setting program based on interaction and negotiation between employees and managers. MBO programs have been pervasive in organizations for nearly thirty years.[22]

According to Peter Drucker, who originated the concept, the objectives-setting process begins with the employee writing an "employee's letter" to the manager.[23] The letter would explain the employee's general understanding of the scope of the manager's job, an understanding of the scope of the employee's own job, and the set of specific objectives to be pursued over the next six months or year. After some discussion and negotiation, the manager and the employee would finalize these items into a performance plan.

Drucker considers MBO a participative and interactive process. This does not mean that goal setting begins at the bottom of the organization. It means that goal setting is applicable to all employees, with lower-level organizational members and professional staff having a clear influence over the goal-setting process. (The performance aspect of goal setting is discussed in the next section of the chapter.)

Goal setting programs operate under a variety of names, including goals and controls at Purex, work planning and review at Black & Decker and General Electric, and performance planning and evaluation at Tenneco and IBM. Most of these programs are designed to enhance performance.[24] Their two central ingredients are planning and evaluation.

The planning component consists of organizational and individual goal setting. Organizational goal setting is an essential prerequisite to individual goal setting; the two must be closely linked for the success of both. At Federal Express, all individual objectives must be tied to the overall corporate objectives of people, service, and profit.

In planning, discretionary control is usually given to individuals and departments to develop operational and tactical plans to support the corporate objectives. The emphasis is on formulating a clear, consistent, measurable, and ordered set of goals to articulate what to do. It is also assumed that operational support planning helps determine how to do it. Intention is a concept used to encompass both the goal (what) and the set of pathways that lead to goal attainment (how), thus recognizing the importance of both what and how.

The evaluation component consists of interim reviews by managers and employees of goal progress and of formal performance evaluation. The reviews are mid-term assessments designed to help employees take self-corrective action. They are not designed

as final or formal performance evaluations. The formal performance evaluation occurs at the close of a reporting period, usually once a year. The Tenneco program is an example of a goal-setting program that systematically incorporates planning and evaluation components.[25]

Because goal-setting programs are somewhat mechanical by nature, they are most easily implemented in stable, predictable industrial settings. While most programs allow for some flexibility and change, they are less useful in organizations where high levels of unpredictability exist, such as in basic research and development, or where the organization requires substantial adaptation or adjustment. Finally, individual, gender, and cultural differences do not appear to threaten the success of goal-setting programs. Thus, goal-setting programs may be widely applied and effective in a diverse work force.[26]

■ PERFORMANCE: A KEY CONSTRUCT

Goal setting is designed to improve work performance, an important organizational behavior directly related to the production of goods or the delivery of services. Performance is most often thought of as task accomplishment, the term task coming from Taylor's early notion of a worker's required activity.[27] Taylor considered performance standards and differential piece-rate pay key ingredients in achieving high levels of performance. Robert Yerkes found arousal and stress helpful in improving performance up to an optimum point.[28] Hence, outcomes and effort are both important for good performance. This section focuses on task-oriented performance. Federal Express is one company that elicits high levels of performance from its people, emphasizing performance feedback and performance-based rewards.

Performance appraisal is the evaluation of a person's performance. Accurate appraisals help supervisors fulfill their dual roles as evaluators and coaches. As a coach, a supervisor is responsible for encouraging employee growth and development. As an evaluator, a supervisor is responsible for making judgments that influence employees' roles in the organization.

■ FIGURE 6.2
Actual and Measured
Performance

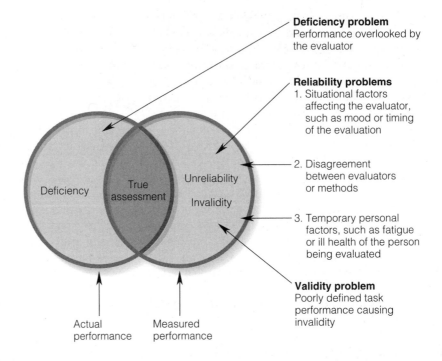

Deficiency problem
Performance overlooked by
the evaluator

Reliability problems
1. Situational factors
   affecting the evaluator,
   such as mood or timing
   of the evaluation

2. Disagreement
   between evaluators
   or methods

3. Temporary personal
   factors, such as fatigue
   or ill health of the person
   being evaluated

Validity problem
Poorly defined task
performance causing
invalidity

Deficiency   True
              assessment

Unreliability

Invalidity

Actual   Measured
performance   performance

The major functions of performance appraisals are to give employees feedback on performance, to identify the employees' developmental needs, to make promotion and reward decisions, to make demotion and termination decisions, and to develop information about the organization's selection and placement decisions. Therefore, it is important for performance appraisals to measure performance accurately.

■ Measuring Performance

Ideally, actual performance and measured performance are the same. Practically, this is seldom the case. Measuring operational performance is easier than measuring managerial performance because of the availability of quantifiable data. Measuring production performance is easier than measuring research and development performance because of the reliability of the measures.

Performance appraisal systems are intended to improve the accuracy of measured performance and increase its agreement with actual performance. The extent of agreement is called the true assessment, as Figure 6.2 shows. The figure also identifies the performance measurement problems that contribute to inaccuracy. They include deficiency, unreliability

and invalidity. Deficiency results from overlooking important aspects of a person's actual performance. Unreliability results from poor-quality performance measures. Invalidity results from inaccurate definition of the expected job performance. Early performance appraisal systems were often quite biased.

Performance monitoring systems using modern electronic technology are sometimes used to measure the performance of vehicle operators, computer technicians, and telephone operators. For example, such systems might record the rate of keystrokes or the total number of keystrokes for a computer technician. The people subject to this type of monitoring are in some cases unaware that their performance is being measured. What is appropriate performance monitoring? What constitutes inappropriate electronic spying on the employee? Are people entitled to know when their performance is being measured? The ethics of monitoring performance may differ by culture. The U.S. and Sweden, for example, respect individual freedom more than Japan and China do. The overriding issue, however, is how far organizations should go in using modern technology to measure human performance.

Goal setting and MBO are results-oriented methods of performance appraisal that do not necessarily rely on modern technology. As with performance monitoring systems, the emphasis is shifted from subjective, judgmental performance dimensions to observable, verifiable results. Goals established in the planning phase of goal setting become the standard against which to measure subsequent performance. However, rigid adherence to a results-oriented approach may risk overlooking performance opportunities.

Another method for improving the accuracy of performance appraisal is to have multiple evaluators contribute to the final appraisal. Groups of superiors, peers, employees, and clients each contribute something unique because each group has a different vantage point. Most traditional evaluations are completed by superiors. Peer and employee evaluations may add a new dimension by covering such areas as cooperation and supervisory style. For example, one mid-level executive behaved very differently in dealing with superiors, peers, and employees. With superiors, he was positive, compliant, and deferential. With peers, he was largely indifferent, often ignoring them. With employees, he was tough and demanding, bordering on being cruel and abusive. Without each of these perspectives, the executive's performance would not have been accurately assessed.

Federal Express has incorporated a novel and challenging approach to evaluation in its blueprint for service quality. All managers at Federal Express are evaluated by their employees through a survey-feedback-action system. Employees evaluate their managers using a five-point scale on twenty-nine standard statements and ten local-option statements. Low ratings suggest problem areas requiring management attention. For example, the following statement received low ratings from employees in 1990: Upper management (including directors and above) pays attention to ideas and suggestions from people at my level. CEO Fred Smith became directly involved in addressing this problem area. One of the actions he took to correct the problem was the development of a biweekly employee newsletter.

■ Performance Feedback: A Communication Challenge

Once clearly defined and accurate performance measures are developed, there is still the challenge of performance feedback. Feedback sessions are among the more stressful events for supervisors and employees. Early research at General Electric found employees responded constructively to positive feedback and were defensive over half the time in response to critical or negative feedback. Typical responses to negative feedback included shifting responsibility for the shortcoming or behavior, denying it outright, or providing a wide range of excuses for it.[29]

Both parties to a performance feedback session should try to make it a constructive learning experience, since positive and negative performance feedback has long-term implications for the employee's performance and for the working relationship. American Airlines follows three guidelines in providing evaluative feedback so the experience is constructive for supervisor and employee alike.[30] First, refer to specific, verbatim statements and specific, observable behaviors displayed by the person receiving the feedback. This enhances the acceptance of the feedback while reducing the chances of denial. Second, focus on changeable behaviors, as opposed to intrinsic or personality-based attributes. People are often more defensive about who they are than what they do. Third, plan and organize for the session ahead of time. Be sure to notify the person who will receive the feedback. Both the leader and the follower should be ready.

In addition to these ideas, Tenneco recommends beginning coaching and counseling sessions with something positive.[31] The intent is to reduce defensiveness and enhance useful communication. There is almost always at least one positive element to emphasize. Once the session is under way and rapport is established, then the evaluator can introduce more difficult and negative material. Because people are not perfect, there is always an opportunity for them to learn and to grow through performance feedback sessions. Critical feedback, the basis for improvement, is essential to a session like this.

Self-evaluations are increasingly used for performance feedback, and there is evidence they lead to more satisfying, constructive evaluation interviews and less defensiveness concerning the evaluation process.[32] In addition, self-evaluations may improve job performance through greater commitment to organizational goals. On the other hand, a key criticism of self-evaluations is their low level of agreement with supervisory evaluations.[33] However, high levels of agreement may not necessarily be desirable if what is intended through the overall evaluation process is a full picture of the person's performance.

Developing People and Enhancing Careers

A key function of a good performance appraisal system is to develop people and enhance careers. Developmentally, performance appraisals should emphasize individual growth needs and future performance. If the supervisor is to coach and develop employees effectively, there must be mutual trust. The supervisor must be vulnerable and open to challenge from the subordinate while maintaining a position of responsibility for what is in the subordinate's best interests.[34] The supervisor must also be a skilled, empathetic listener who encourages the employee to talk about hopes and aspirations.

The employee must be able to take active responsibility for future development and growth. This might mean challenging the supervisor's ideas about future development as well as expressing individual preferences and goals. Passive, compliant employees are unable to accept responsibility for themselves or to achieve full emotional development. Individual responsibility is a key characteristic of the Chaparral Steel Company's culture. The company joke is that the company manages by "adultry" (pun intended); it treats people like adults and expects adult behavior from them.

Key Characteristics of an Effective Appraisal System

An effective performance appraisal system has five key characteristics: validity, reliability, responsiveness, flexibility, and equitableness. Its validity comes from capturing multiple dimensions of a person's job performance. Its reliability comes from capturing evaluations from multiple sources and at different times over the course of the evaluation period. Its responsiveness allows the person being evaluated some input into the final outcome. Its flexibility leaves it open to modification based on new information, such as federal requirements. Its equitability results in fair evaluations against established performance criteria, regardless of individual differences.

REWARDING PERFORMANCE

One function of a performance appraisal system is to provide input for reward decisions. If an organization wants good performance, then it must reward good performance. If it does not want bad performance, then it must not reward bad performance. Although this idea is conceptually simple, it can become very complicated in practice. Reward decisions are among the most difficult and complicated decisions made in organizations. They are also among the most important decisions made in organizations.

A Key Organizational Decision Process

Reward and punishment decisions in organizations affect many people throughout the system, not just the persons being rewarded or punished. Reward allocation involves sequential decisions about which people to reward, how to reward them, and when to reward them. Taken together, these decisions shape the behavior of everyone in the organization. This is because of the vicarious learning that occurs as people watch what happens to others, especially when new programs or initiatives are implemented. People watch carefully what happens to peers who make mistakes or have problems with the new system, gauging their own behavior accordingly.

Pay: A Key Organizational Reward

Edward Lawler suggests that pay is a key organizational reward which is a source of individual motivation and has an influence on organizational effectiveness.[35] Hence, pay is an important factor in individual behavior and organizational performance. Lawler says that to design effective pay systems, organizations must first establish a set of strategic objectives for the pay system.[36] Base pay, incentive pay, merit pay, and total compensation are each important components to be considered in developing a total pay system. When the pay system is well designed, it will motivate individuals to perform at their best and will enhance the organization's effectiveness. However, not all pay and reward systems are based on individual performance.

■ Individual Versus Team Reward Systems

Individualism is a distinguishing American value. Systems that reward individuals are common in organizations in the U.S. One of their strengths is that they foster autonomous and independent behavior that may lead to creativity, to novel solutions to old problems, and to distinctive contributions to the organization. Individual reward systems directly affect individual behavior and may encourage competitive striving within a work team.

Too much competition within a work environment, however, may be dysfunctional. At the Western Company of North America, individual success in the MBO program was tied too tightly to rewards, and individual managers became divisively competitive. For example, some managers took last-minute interdepartmental financial actions in a quarter to meet their objectives, only to cause heartache for other managers whom they caused to miss their objectives. These actions raise ethical questions about how far individual managers should go in serving their own self-interest at the expense of their peers.

Team reward systems solve the problems caused by individual competitive behavior. These systems emphasize cooperation, joint efforts, and the sharing of information, knowledge, and expertise. The Japanese and Chinese cultures, with their collectivist orientations, place greater emphasis than Americans on the individual as an element of the team, not a member apart from the team. Digital Equipment Corporation has a partnership approach to performance appraisals in which work groups participate in the performance appraisal system. Self-managed work group members participate in their own appraisal process. This approach emphasizes teamwork and responsibility.

Some organizations have experimented with individual and group alternative reward systems.[37] At the individual level, these include skill-based and pay-for-knowledge systems. Each emphasizes skills or knowledge possessed by an employee over and above the requirements for the basic job. At the group level, gain-sharing plans emphasize collective cost reduction and allow workers to share in the gains achieved by reducing production or other operating costs. In such plans, everyone shares equally in the collective gain.

■ The Power of Earning

The purpose behind both individual and team reward systems is to shape productive behavior. If one wants the rewards available in the organization, then one should work to earn them. These systems assume a demonstrable connection between performance and rewards. Organizations get the performance they reward, not the performance they say they want. Further, when there is no apparent link between performance and rewards, people may begin to believe they are entitled to rewards regardless of how they perform. The concept of entitlement is very different from the concept of earning, which assumes a performance-reward link.

The notion of entitlement at work is counterproductive when taken to the extreme because it counteracts the power of earning.[38] People who believe they are entitled to rewards regardless of their behavior or performance are not motivated to behave constructively. They believe they have a right to be taken care of by someone, whether that is the organization or a specific person. Entitlement engenders passive, irresponsible behavior in people, whereas earning engenders active, responsible, adult behavior. If rewards depend on performance, then people must perform responsibly to receive them. The power of earning rests on a direct link between performance and rewards.

■ CORRECTING POOR PERFORMANCE

Often a complicated, difficult challenge for supervisors, correcting poor performance is a three-step process. First, the cause or primary responsibility for the poor performance must be identified. Second, if the primary responsibility is a person's, then the source of the personal problem must be determined. Third, a plan of action to correct the poor performance must be developed.

Poor performance may result from a variety of causes, the more important being poorly designed work systems, poor selection processes, inadequate training and skills development, lack of personal motivation, and personal problems intruding on the work environment. Not all poor performance is self-motivated; some is induced by the work system.

■ **FIGURE 6.3**
Attribution Model

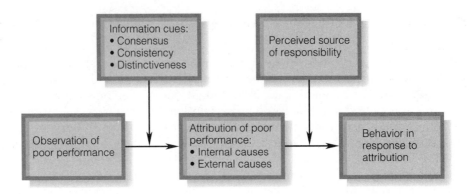

Therefore, a good diagnosis should precede corrective action. For example, it may be that an employee is subject to a work design or selection system that does not allow the person to exhibit good performance. Identifying the cause of the poor performance comes first and should be done in communication with the employee. If the problem is with the system and the supervisor can fix it, then everyone wins as a result.

If the poor performance is not attributable to work design or organizational process problems, then attention should be focused on the employee. At least three possible causes of poor performance can be attributed to the employee. The problem may lie in (1) some aspect of the person's relationship to the organization or supervisor, (2) some area of the employee's personal life, or (3) a training or developmental deficiency. In the latter two cases, poor performance may be treated as a symptom as opposed to a motivated consequence. In such cases, identifying financial problems, family difficulties, or health disorders may enable the supervisor to help the employee solve problems before they become too extensive. Employee Assistance Programs (EAPs) can be helpful to employees managing personal problems and are discussed in Chapter 7 related to managing stress.

Poor performance may also be motivated as a result of an employee's displaced anger or conflict with the organization or supervisor. In such cases, the employee may or may not be aware of the internal reactions causing the problem. In either event, sabotage, work slowdowns, work stoppages, and similar forms of poor performance are the result of such motivated behavior. The supervisor may attribute the cause of the problem to the employee, and the employee may attribute it to the supervisor or organization. To solve motivated performance problems requires treating the poor performance as a symptom with a deeper cause. Resolving the underlying anger or conflict results in the disappearance of the symptom (poor performance).

■ **Attribution and Performance Management**

According to attribution theory, as we discussed in Chapter 3, managers make attributions (inferences) concerning employees' behavior and performance.[39] The attributions may not always be accurate. For example, an executive with Capital Cities Corporation who had a very positive relationship with his boss was not held responsible for profit problems in his district. The boss attributed the problem to the economy instead.

Supervisors and employees who share perceptions and attitudes, as in the Capital Cities situation, tend to evaluate each other highly.[40] Supervisors and employees who do not share perceptions and attitudes are more likely to blame each other for performance problems.

Figure 6.3 presents an attribution model that specifically addresses *the way* supervisors respond to poor performance. A supervisor who observes poor performance seeks cues about the employee's behavior in three forms: consensus, consistency, and distinctiveness. Consensus is the extent of a behavior in an organization. Consistency is the frequency of the performance. Distinctiveness describes a performance problem: is it unique to a particular task, or does it appear in other aspects of the job? (These cues were first discussed in Chapter 3.)

On the basis of this information, the supervisor makes either an internal (personal) attribution or an external (situational) attribution. Internal attributions might include low effort, lack of commitment, or lack of ability. External attributions are outside the employee's control and might include equipment failure or unrealistic goals. The supervisor then determines the source of responsibility for the performance problem and tries to correct the problem.

Supervisors may choose from a wide range of responses. They can, for example, express personal concern, reprimand the employee, or provide training. Supervisors who attribute the cause of poor performance to a person (an internal cause) will respond more harshly than supervisors who attribute the cause to the work situation (an external cause). Supervisors should try not to make either of the two common attribution errors discussed in Chapter 3: the fundamental attribution error and the self-serving bias.

■ **Coaching, Counseling, and Mentoring**

Supervisors have important coaching, counseling, and mentoring responsibilities to their subordinates. They should maintain a helping relationship with employees.[41] This relationship may address performance-based deficiencies or personal problems that diminish employee performance, such as depression.[42] In either case, the supervisors can play a helpful role in employee problem-solving activities without accepting responsibility for the employees' problems. One important form of help is to refer the employee to trained professionals.

Coaching and counseling are among the career and psychosocial functions of a mentoring relationship.[43] Mentoring is a work relationship that encourages development and career enhancement for people moving through the career cycle. Mentor relationships typically go through four phases: initiation, cultivation, separation, and redefinition. The relationship can significantly enhance the early development of a newcomer and the mid-career development of an experienced employee, enabling employees to achieve their full potential.[44] Career development can be enhanced through peer relationships as an alternative to traditional mentoring relationships. Informational, collegial, and special peers aid the individual's development through information sharing, career strategizing, job-related feedback, emotional support, and friendship. Hence, mentors and peers may both play constructive roles in correcting an employee's poor performance and in enhancing overall career development. This mentoring process is discussed in detail in Chapter 17.

■ **MANAGERIAL IMPLICATIONS: PERFORMANCE MANAGEMENT IS A KEY TASK**

People in organizations learn from the consequences of their actions. Therefore, managers must exercise care in the application of positive and negative consequences, ensuring that they are connected to the behaviors they intend to reward or punish. Managers should also be judicious in the use of punishment and should consider extinction coupled with positive reinforcement as an alternative to punishment for shaping employee behavior. Managers can serve as positive role models for the vicarious learning of employees about ethical behavior and high-quality performance.

Goal-setting activities may be valuable to managers in bringing out the best performance from employees. Managers can use challenging, specific goals for this purpose and must be prepared to provide employees with timely, useful feedback on goal progress so employees will know how they are doing. Goal-setting activities that are misused may create dysfunctional competition in an organization and lead to lower performance.

Good performance evaluation systems are valuable tools for providing employees with clear feedback on their actions. Managers who rely on valid and reliable performance measures may use them in employee development and to correct poor performance. Managers who use high-technology performance monitoring systems must remember that employees are humans, not machines. Managers are responsible for creating a positive learning atmosphere in performance feedback sessions, and employees are responsible for learning from these sessions.

Finally, managers can use rewards as one of the most powerful positive consequences for shaping employee behavior. If rewards are to improve performance, managers must make a clear connection between specific performance and the rewards. Employees should be expected to earn the rewards they receive; they should expect rewards related to performance quality and skill development.

■ CHAPTER SUMMARY

■ Learning is a change in behavior acquired through experience. The operant conditioning approach to learning states that behavior is a function of its positive and negative consequences.

■ Reinforcement is used to develop desirable behavior; punishment and extinction are used to decrease undesirable behavior.

■ Bandura's social learning theory suggests that self-efficacy is important to effective learning.

■ Goal setting improves work motivation and task performance, reduces role stress, and improves the accuracy and validity of performance appraisal.

■ Performance appraisals help organizations develop employees and make decisions about them.

■ Problems with performance appraisals include deficiency, poor reliability, and poor validity.

■ High-quality performance should be rewarded and poor performance should be corrected.

■ Mentoring is a relationship for encouraging development and career enhancement for people moving through the career cycle.

■ REVIEW QUESTIONS

1. Define the terms *learning, reinforcement, punishment,* and *extinction.*
2. What are positive and negative consequences in shaping behavior and how should they be managed? Explain the value of extinction as a strategy.

3. How can self-efficacy be enhanced? How do introverted, extraverted, intuitive, and sensing people learn differently?
4. Referring to the case of the motivational team asked to teach soldiers to want to kill the enemy: Is this request ethical? Is it socially desirable? Should the team have accepted the assignment? Explain.
5. What are the five characteristics of well-developed goals? Why is feedback on goal progress important?
6. Suppose the organization you work for simply assigns employees their task goals without consulting them. Is there an ethical problem with this approach? Does the organization have to consult its employees?
7. What are the purposes for conducting performance appraisals? Who should appraise performance? Why?
8. What possible problems limit accurate performance appraisals? What are five characteristics of a good performance appraisal system?
9. How can supervisors best provide useful performance feedback?
10. How do mentors and peers help people develop and enhance their careers?

■ REFERENCES

1. I. P. Pavlov, *Conditioned Reflexes* (New York: Oxford University Press, 1927).
2. Bradford Cannon, "Walter B. Cannon: Reflections on the Man and His Contributions," Centennial Session, American Psychological Association Centennial Convention, Washington, D.C., 1992.
3. B. F. Skinner, *Science and Human Behavior* (New York: Free Press, 1953).
4. F. Luthans and R. Kreitner, *Organizational Behavior Modification and Beyond* (Glenview, Ill.: Scott, Foresman, 1985).
5. B. F. Skinner, *Contingencies of Reinforcement: A Theoretical Analysis* (New York: Appleton-Century-Crofts, 1969).
6. J. P. Chaplin and T. S. Krawiec, *Systems and Theories of Psychology* (New York: Holt, Rinehart & Winston, 1960).
7. A. Bandura, *Social Learning Theory* (Englewood Cliffs, N.J.: Prentice-Hall, 1977).
8. C. G. Jung, *Psychological Types,* trans. H. G. Baynes (New York: Harcourt Brace, 1923); O. Isachsen and L. V. Berens, *Working Together: A Personality Centered Approach to Management* (Coronado, Calif.: Neworld Management Press, 1988);

and O. Krueger and J. M. Thuesen, *Type Talk* (New York: Tilden Press, 1988).

9. C. Argyris, *On Organizational Learning* (Cambridge, MA: Blackwell, 1992).

10. C. Argyris, "Teaching Smart People How to Learn," *Harvard Business Review* 69 (1994): 99–109.

11. C. Argyris, "Education for Leading-Learning," *Organizational Dynamics* 21 (1993): 5–18.

12. E. A. Locke and G. P. Latham, *A Theory of Goal Setting and Task Performance* (Englewood Cliffs, N.J.: Prentice-Hall, 1990).

13. W. T. Brooks and T. W. Mullins, *High Impact Time Management* (Englewood Cliffs, N.J.: Prentice-Hall, 1989).

14. E. A. Locke, "Toward a Theory of Task Motivation and Incentives," *Organizational Behavior and Human Performance* 3 (1968): 157–189.

15. J. C. Quick, "Dyadic Goal Setting within Organizations: Role Making and Motivational Considerations," *Academy of Management Review* 4 (1979): 369–380.

16. D. McGregor, "An Uneasy Look at Performance Appraisal," *Harvard Business Review* 35 (1957): 89–94.

17. "Stretch Targets," *Fortune,* 14 November 1994, 45.

18. J. R. Hollenbeck, C. R. Williams, and H. J. Klein, "An Empirical Examination of the Antecedents of Commitment to Difficult Goals," *Journal of Applied Psychology* 74 (1989): 18–23.

19. E. A. Locke, K. N. Shaw, L. M. Saari, and G. P. Latham, "Goal Setting and Task Performance: 1969–1980," *Psychological Bulletin* 90 (1981): 125–152.

20. J. C. Quick, "Dyadic Goal Setting and Role Stress," *Academy of Management Journal* 22 (1979): 241–252.

21. G. S. Odiorne, *Management by Objectives: A System of Managerial Leadership* (New York: Pitman, 1965).

22. G. P. Latham and G. A. Yukl, "A Review of Research on the Application of Goal Setting in Organizations," *Academy of Management Journal* 18 (1975): 824–845.

23. P. F. Drucker, *The Practice of Management* (New York: Harper & Bros., 1954).

24. R. D. Prichard, P. L. Roth, S. D. Jones, P. J. Galgay, and M. D. Watson, "Designing a Goal-Setting System to Enhance Performance: A Practical Guide," *Organizational Dynamics* 17 (1988): 69–78.

25. J. M. Ivancevich, J. T. McMahon, J. W. Streidl, and A. D. Szilagyi, "Goal Setting: The Tenneco Approach to Personnel Development and Management Effectiveness," *Organizational Dynamics* 7 (1978): 58–80.

26. J. R. Hollenbeck and A. P. Brief, "The Effects of Individual Differences and Goal Origin on Goal Setting and Performance," *Organizational Behavior and Human Decision Processes* 40 (1987): 392–414.

27. E. A. Locke, "The Ideas of Frederick W. Taylor: An Evaluation," *Academy of Management Review* 7 (1982): 15–16.

28. R. M Yerkes and J. D. Dodson, "The Relation of Strength of Stimulus to Rapidity of Habit-Formation," *Journal of Comparative Neurology and Psychology* 18 (1908): 459–482.

29. H. H. Meyer, E. Kay, and J. R. P. French, "Split Roles in Performance Appraisal," *Harvard Business Review* 43 (1965): 123–129.

30. W. A. Fisher, J. C. Quick, L. L. Schkade, and G. W. Ayers, "Developing Administrative Personnel through the Assessment Center Technique," *Personnel Administrator* 25 (1980): 44–46, 62.

31. *Guidelines for Employee Coaching and Counselling* (Houston, Tex.: Tenneco, 1982).

32. M. B. DeGregorio and C. D. Fisher, "Providing Performance Feedback: Reactions to Alternative Methods," *Journal of Management* 14 (1988): 605–616.

33. G. C. Thornton, "The Relationship between Supervisory and Self-Appraisals of Executive Performance," *Personnel Psychology* 21 (1968): 441–455.

34. L. Hirschhorn, "Leaders and Followers in a Postindustrial Age: A Psychodynamic View," *Journal of Applied Behavioral Science* 26 (1990): 529–542.

35. E. E. Lawler III, *Pay and Organizational Effectiveness: A Psychological View* (New York: McGraw-Hill, 1971).

36. E. E. Lawler III, *Strategic Pay: Aligning Organizational Strategies and Pay Systems* (San Francisco: Jossey-Bass, 1990).

37. George T. Milkovich and Jerry M. Newman, *Compensation,* 4th ed. (Homewood, Ill.: Irwin, 1993).

38. J. M. Bardwick, *Danger in the Comfort Zone* (New York: American Management Association, 1991).

39. T. R. Mitchell and R. E. Wood, "An Empirical Test of an Attributional Model of Leaders' Responses to Poor Performance," in *Proceedings of the Academy of Management,* ed. R. C. Huseman (Starkville, Miss.: Academy of Management, 1979), p. 94, and M. J. Martinko and W. L. Gardner, "The Leader/Member Attributional Process," *Academy of Management Review* 12 (1987): 235–249.

40. K. N. Wexley, R. A. Alexander, J. P. Greenawalt, and M. A. Couch, "Attitudinal Congruence and Similarity as Related to Interpersonal Evaluations in Manager-Subordinate Dyads," *Academy of Management Journal* 23 (1980): 320–330.

41. A. G. Athos and J. J. Gabarro, *Interpersonal Behavior: Communication and Understanding in Relationships* (Englewood Cliffs, N.J.: Prentice-Hall, 1978).

42. K. Doherty, "The Good News about Depression," *Business and Health* 3 (1989):1–4

43. K. E. Kram, "Phases of the Mentor Relationship," *Academy of Management Journal* 26 (1983): 608–625.

44. G. F. Shea, *Mentoring: Helping Employees Reach Their Full Potential* (New York: American Management Association, 1994).

CHAPTER 7
STRESS AND
WELL-BEING AT WORK

LEARNING OBJECTIVES

After reading this chapter, you should be able to do the following:

- Define stress, distress, strain, and eustress.
- Discuss the evolution of the stress concept.
- Explain the psychophysiology of the stress response.
- Identify work and nonwork causes of stress.
- Describe the benefits of eustress and the costs of distress.
- Discuss four moderators of the stress-strain relationship.
- Distinguish the primary, secondary, and tertiary stages of preventive stress management.
- Discuss organizational and individual methods of preventive stress management.

Over the past decade, stress has become a significant topic in organizational behavior. This chapter has five major sections, each addressing one aspect of stress. The first section examines the question, "What is stress?" The discussion includes four approaches to the stress response. The second section reviews the demands and stressors that trigger the stress response at work. The third section examines the performance and health benefits of stress and the individual and organizational forms of distress. The fourth section considers individual difference factors, such as gender and personality hardiness, moderating the stress-distress relationship. The fifth section presents a framework for preventive stress management and reviews a wide range of individual and organizational stress management methods.

■ WHAT IS STRESS?

Stress is one of the most creatively ambiguous words in the English language, with as many interpretations as there are people who use the word. Even the stress experts do not agree on its definition. Stress carries a negative connotation for some people, as though it were something to be avoided. This is unfortunate, because stress is a great asset in managing legitimate emergencies and achieving peak performance. Stress, or the stress response, is the unconscious preparation to fight or flee, which a person experiences when faced with any demand.[1] A stressor, or demand, is the person or event that triggers the stress response. Distress or strain refers to the adverse psychological, physical, behavioral, and organizational consequences that may occur as a result of stressful events.

■ Evolution of the Stress Construct

The stress response was identified by Walter B. Cannon early in this century. Later researchers added to our understanding of stress. We begin with a brief discussion of Cannon's homeostatic/medical model and then examine how various psychologists have enriched our knowledge of stress. This historical perspective gives you a more complete understanding of what stress really is.

Walter B. Cannon was the medical physiologist who originally identified stress and called it "the emergency response" or "the militaristic response," arguing that it was rooted in "the fighting emotions." His early writings provide the basis for calling the stress response the fight-or-flight response. According to Cannon, stress resulted when an external, environmental demand upset the person's natural steady-state balance.[2] He referred to this steady-state balance, or equilibrium, as homeostasis. Cannon believed the body was designed with natural defense mechanisms to keep it in homeostasis. He was especially interested in the role of the sympathetic nervous system in activating a person under stressful conditions.[3]

Richard Lazarus was a psychologist interested in the mind's cognitive evaluation of and response to stressors. He emphasized the psychological-cognitive aspects of the stress response.[4] Like Cannon, Lazarus saw stress as a result of a person-environment interaction, and he emphasized the person's cognitive appraisal in classifying persons or events as stressful or not. Individuals differ in their appraisal of events and people. What is stressful for one person may not be stressful for another. Perception and cognitive appraisal are important processes in determining what is stressful, and a person's organizational position can shape such a perception. For example, an employee is more likely to be stressed by an upset supervisor than another supervisor would be. Lazarus also introduced problem-focused and emotion-focused coping. Problem-focused coping emphasizes managing the stressor, and emotion-focused coping emphasizes managing your response.

Robert Kahn was a concerned psychologist interested in understanding how a person's social roles cause stress. His approach emphasized how confusing and conflicting expectations of a person in a social role create stress for the person. He extended the approach to examine a person's fit with the environment. A good person-environment fit occurs when a person's skills and abilities match a clearly defined, consistent set of role expectations. This results in a lack of stress for the person. Stress occurs when the role expectations are confusing and/or conflicting, or when a person's skills and abilities are not able to meet the demands of the social role. After a period of this stress, the person can expect to experience strain—in the form of depression, for example.

Harry Levinson was a third psychologist who defined stress based on Freudian psychoanalytic theory.[5] Levinson believes that two elements of the personality interact to cause stress. The first element is the ego-ideal, the embodiment of a person's perfect self. The second element is the self-image—the way the person really sees himself or herself, both positively and negatively. Although not sharply defined, the ego-ideal encompasses admirable attributes of parental personalities, wished-for and/or imaginable qualities a person would like to possess, and the absence of any negative or distasteful qualities. Stress results from the discrepancy between the idealized self (ego-ideal) and the real self-image; the greater the discrepancy, the more stress a person experiences. More generally, psychoanalytic theory helps us understand the role of unconscious personality factors as causes of stress within a person.

The Stress Response

While Lazarus, Kahn, and Levinson helped us better understand the psychological aspects of stress, there is still the core sequence of predictable mind and body events that constitute the stress reponse. First, catecholamines, primarily adrenaline and noradrenaline, are released into the bloodstream. Second, these chemical messengers activate the sympathetic nervous system and the endocrine (hormone) system. Third, these two systems work together to create four mind-body changes to prepare one for fight-or-flight:

1. The redirection of the blood to the brain and large-muscle groups and away from the skin, vegetative organs, and extremities.
2. Increased alertness by way of improved vision, hearing, and other sensory processes. This occurs when the reticular activating system, a formation in the brainstem (ancient brain), is activated under stress.
3. The release of glucose (blood sugar) and fatty acids into the bloodstream to sustain the body during the stressful event.
4. Depression of the immune system, as well as restorative and emergent processes (such as digestion).

This set of four changes shifts the person from a neutral, or naturally defensive, posture to an offensive posture. The stress response can be very functional in preparing a person to deal with legitimate emergencies and to achieve peak performance. It is neither inherently bad nor necessarily destructive.

SOURCES OF STRESS AT WORK

The stress response begins when a person experiences work or nonwork demands, or sources of stress. We can organize work demands into the general categories of task demands, role demands, interpersonal demands, and physical demands. In addition, the organization needs to be sensitive to

■ TABLE 7.1
Work and Nonwork Demands

WORK DEMANDS	
Task Demands	**Role Demands**
Uncertainty	Role conflict:
Lack of control	■ Interrole
Career progress	■ Intrarole
New technologies	■ Person-role
Work overload	Role ambiguity
Interpersonal Demands	**Physical Demands**
Abrasive personalities	Extreme environments
Sexual harassment	Strenuous activities
Leadership styles	Hazardous substances
NONWORK DEMANDS	
Family Demands	**Personal Demands**
Marital expectations	Religious activities
Child-rearing/day care	Self-improvement tasks
arrangements	Traumatic events
Parental care	

nonwork stressors, such as demands from the person's family or nonwork activities. For example, child care considerations are of increasing concern to organizations as more women have gone to work and more men are the primary caregivers. Finally, global factors, such as general economic conditions within a society and the international economy, create widespread stress for individuals. Table 7.1 summarizes the specific demands that we discuss.

■ Task Demands

Uncertainty and lack of control are two of the most stressful demands people face at work.[6] Uncertainty may be created by a lack of predictability in a person's daily tasks and activities, or it may be created by job insecurity related to difficult economic times. During the 1980s, U.S. Steel had to lay off tens of thousands of workers because of the economic difficulties in the industry resulting from intense international competition. Corporate warfare led to extensive mergers, acquisitions, and downsizing during the 1980s; this resulted in significant uncertainty for thousands of employees.[7] Technology and technological innovation also create uncertainty for many employees, requiring adjustments in training, education, and skill development.

Lack of control is a second major source of stress, especially in work environments that are difficult and psychologically demanding. The lack of control may be caused by inability to influence the timing of tasks and activities, to select tools or methods for accomplishing the work, to make decisions that influence work outcomes, or to exercise direct action to affect the work outcomes. One U.S. study found heart attacks for male workers to be more common in occupations with low job autonomy (lack of control) and high job demands (heavy work loads).[8]

Concerns over career progress, new technologies, and work overload, or work underload, are three additional task demands triggering stress for the person at work. Career stress is related to the thinning of mid-managerial ranks in organizations through mergers, acquisitions, and downsizing over the past two decades, causing career gridlock for many. Thinning the organizational ranks often leaves an abundance of work for those who are still employed. Work overload was found in a national study as the leading stressor for 28 percent of those surveyed. This has become especially problematic for university presidents during the 1990s, as evident when Harvard President Neil L. Rodenstine took a stress leave.[9] New technologies also create both career stress and "technostress" for people at work who wonder if they will be replaced by "smart" machines. Although they enhance the organization's productive capacity, new technologies may be viewed as the enemy by workers who must ultimately learn to use them. This creates a real dilemma for management.

■ Role Demands

The social-psychological demands of the work environment may be every bit as stressful as task demands at work. People encounter two major categories of role stress at work: role conflict and role ambiguity.[10] Role conflict results from inconsistent or incompatible expectations communicated to a person. The conflict may be either an interrole, intrarole, or person-role conflict.

Interrole conflict is caused by conflicting expectations related to two separate roles, such as employee and parent. For example, the employee with a major sales presentation on Monday and a sick child at home Sunday night is likely to experience interrole conflict.

Intrarole conflict is caused by conflicting expectations related to a single role, such as employee. For example, the manager who presses employees for both very fast work and high-quality work may be viewed at some point as creating a conflict for employees.

Ethics violations are likely to cause person-role conflicts. Employees expected to behave in ways that violate personal values, beliefs, or principles experience conflict. The unethical acts of committed employees exemplify this problem. Organizations with high ethical standards, such as Johnson & Johnson, are less likely to create ethical conflicts for employees. Person-role conflicts and ethics violations create a sense of divided loyalty for an employee.

The second major cause of role stress is role ambiguity. Role ambiguity is the confusion a person experiences related to the expectations of others. Role ambiguity may be caused by not understanding what is expected, not knowing how to do it, or not knowing the result of failure to do it. For example, a new magazine employee asked to copyedit a manuscript for the next issue may experience confusion because of lack of familiarity with copyediting procedures and conventions for the specific magazine.

■ Interpersonal Demands

Abrasive personalities, sexual harassment, and the leadership style in the organization are interpersonal demands for people at work.[11] The abrasive person may be an able and talented employee, but one who creates emotional waves that others at work must accommodate. Abrasive personalities stand out at work, and some organizational cultures tolerate them. Organizations are increasingly less tolerant of sexual harassment, a gender-related interpersonal demand. The vast majority of sexual harassment is directed at women in the workplace, creating a stressful working environment for the person being harassed, as well as for others. Leadership styles in organizations, whether authoritarian or participative, create stress for different personality types. Employees who feel secure with firm, directive leadership may be anxious with an open, participative style. Those comfortable with participative leadership may feel restrained by a directive style.

■ Physical Demands

Extreme environments, strenuous activities, and hazardous substances create physical demands for people at work.[12] Work environments that are very hot or very cold impose differing physical demands on people and create unique risks. Dehydration is one problem of extremely hot climates, whereas frostbite is one problem of extremely cold climates. The strenuous job of a steelworker and the hazards associated with bomb disposal work are physically very demanding in different ways. The unique physical demands of work are often occupation-specific, such as the risk of gravitationally-induced loss of consciousness for pilots flying the latest generation of high-performance fighters.[13]

Office work has its physical hazards as well. Noisy, crowded offices, such as those of some stock brokerages, can prove stressful to work in. Working with a computer terminal can also be stressful, especially if the ergonomic fit between the person and machine is not correct. Eyestrain, neck stiffness, and arm and wrist problems can occur. Office designs that use partitions (cubicles) rather than full walls can create stress. These systems offer little privacy for the occupant (for example, to conduct employee counseling or performance appraisal sessions) and little protection from interruptions.

■ Nonwork Demands

Nonwork demands create stress for people, which may carry over into the work environment.[14] Not all workers are subject to family demands related to marriage, child rearing, and parental care. For those who are, these demands may create role conflicts or overloads that are difficult to manage. For example, the loss of good day care for children may be especially stressful for dual-career families. As a result of the maturing of the American population, an increasing number of people face the added demand of parental care. Even when one works to achieve an integrative social identity, integrating one's many social roles into a "whole" identity for a more stress-free balance in work and nonwork identities, the process of integration is not an easy one.[15]

In addition to family demands, people have personal demands related to nonwork organizational commitments, such as in churches, synagogues, and public service organizations. These demands become more or less stressful, depending upon their compatibility with the person's work and family life and their capacity to provide alternative satisfactions for the person. Finally, traumatic events and their aftermath are stressful for people who experience them.[16] Traumatic events need not be catastrophic in nature, although catastrophic events related to war or death of a loved one are traumatic. Job loss, examination failures, and termination of romantic attachments are all traumatic and may lead to distress if not addressed and resolved.[17]

■ THE CONSEQUENCES OF STRESS

Contrary to one report, Americans are not failing the stress test, and not all the consequences of stress are bad or destructive. The consequences of healthy, normal stress (called eustress, for "euphoria + stress") include a number of performance and health benefits to be added to the more commonly known costs of individual and organizational distress.[18] The benefits of eustress and the costs of distress are listed in Table 7.2. An organization striving for high-quality products and services needs a healthy work force to support the effort. Eustress is one characteristic of healthy people; distress is not.

■ Performance and Health Benefits of Stress

The Yerkes-Dodson law, shown in Figure 7.1, indicates that stress leads to improved performance up to an optimum point.[19] Beyond the optimum point, further stress and arousal have a detrimental effect on performance. Therefore, healthy amounts of eustress are desirable to improve performance by arousing a person to action. It is in the midrange of the curve that the greatest performance benefits from stress are achieved. Joseph McGrath has suggested that performance declines beyond the midpoint in the Yerkes-Dodson curve because of the increasing difficulty of the task to be performed. The stress response does provide momentary strength and physical force for brief periods of exertion, thus providing a basis for peak performance in athletic competition or other events.

Specific stressful activities, including aerobic exercise, weight training, and flexibility training, improve health and enhance a person's ability to manage stressful demands or situations. Cannon argued that the stress response better prepares soldiers for combat.[20] In survival or combat situations, stress provides one with the necessary energy boost to manage the situation successfully.

The stress response is not inherently bad or destructive. The various individual and organizational forms of distress often associated with the word "stress" are the result of prolonged activation of the stress response, mismanagement of the energy induced by the response, or unique vulnerabilities in a person. Next, we examine the forms of individual distress, and the forms of organizational distress.

■ Individual Distress

Individual distress usually takes one of the three basic forms shown in Table 7.2. Work-related psychological disorders are among the ten leading

■ TABLE 7.2
Benefits of Eustress and Costs of Distress

BENEFITS OF EUSTRESS	
Performance	**Health**
Increased arousal	Cardiovascular efficiency
Bursts of physical strength	Enhanced focus in an emergency
COSTS OF DISTRESS	
Individual	**Organizational**
Psychological disorders	Participation problems
Medical illnesses	Performance decrements
Behavioral problems	Compensation awards

health disorders and diseases in the U.S., according to the National Institute for Occupational Safety and Health.[21] The most common types of psychological distress are depression, burnout, and psychogenic disorders. In the early stages, depression and burnout result in a decline in efficiency; diminished interest in work; fatigue; and an exhausted, rundown feeling. Psychogenic disorders are physical disorders with a genesis, or beginning, in the psyche, or mind. For example, the intense stress of public speaking may result in a psychogenic speech disorder; that is, the person is under so much stress that the mind literally will not allow speech to occur.

A number of medical illnesses have a stress-related component.[22] The most significant medical illnesses of this form are heart disease and strokes, backaches, peptic ulcers, and headaches. Ford Motor Company found that cardiovascular diseases, the leading cause of death in the U.S. since 1910, constituted only 1.5 percent of the medical incidents among 800 salaried employees at its headquarters, but accounted for 29 percent of the reported medical costs.[23] On the positive side, premature death and disability rates have dropped 24 to 36 percent since the mid-1970s. Backache is a nonfatal medical problem to which stress contributes through the strong muscular contractions related to preparation for fight-or-flight. Headaches may be related to eyestrain or have a migraine component, but tension headaches are caused by the contraction of the head and neck muscles under stressful conditions. Finally, stress is a contributing factor to peptic ulcers. A popular comedian commented, "I don't get angry; I just grow a tumor!" While there is no clear evidence that stress is a direct causal agent in the onset of cancer, it may play an indirect role in the progression of the disease.

Behavioral problems make up the third form of individual distress. These problems include violence, substance abuse of various kinds, and accidents. Violence need not necessarily be physical to be destructive. Interpersonal conflicts can be a form of nonphysical violence. One study found that conflicts with workmates, neighbors, and other "nonintimates" account for about 80 percent of our bad moods.[24] Ethnic and cultural differences are too often a basis for interpersonal conflicts and may escalate into physical violence in the workplace. For

■ **FIGURE 7.1**
Yerkes-Dodson Law

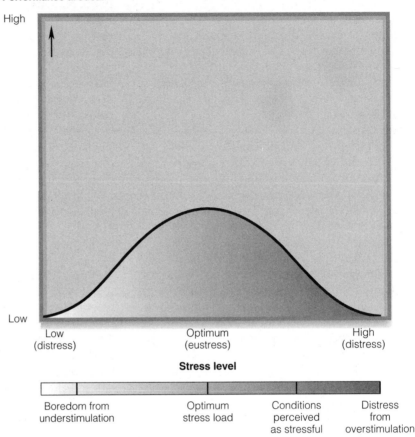

example, some U.S. employees of Arab descent experienced ethnic slurs at work during the Gulf War with Iraq, a largely Arab nation.

Substance abuse ranges from legal behaviors such as alcohol abuse, excessive smoking, and the overuse of prescription drugs, to illegal behaviors such as heroin addiction. Former Surgeon General C. Everett Koop's war on smoking, begun in the late 1980s, may be warranted from the health-risk standpoint, but it raises an ethical debate about the restriction of individual behavior. How far can the government or society go in restricting individual behavior that has adverse health consequences for many? This is even more problematic in light of recent research results showing the adverse health effects of passive smoking (that is, nonsmokers breathing smoky air).

Accidents, both on and off the job, compose another behavioral form of distress that can sometimes be traced to work-related stressors. For example, an unresolved problem at work may continue to preoccupy or distract an employee driving home and result in an automobile accident.

These three forms of individual distress—psychological disorders, medical illnesses, and behavioral problems—cause a personal burden of suffering. They also cause a collective burden of suffering reflected in organizational distress.

■ **Organizational Distress**

The University of Michigan studies on organizational stress identified a variety of indirect costs of mismanaged stress for the organization, such as low morale, dissatisfaction, breakdowns in communication, and disruption of working relationships. Subsequent research at the Survey Research Center at

Michigan established behavioral costing guidelines, which specify the direct costs of organizational distress.[25]

Participation problems are the costs associated with absenteeism, tardiness, strikes and work stoppages, and turnover. In the case of absenteeism, the organization may compensate for this participation problem by hiring temporary personnel who take the place of the absentee, thus elevating personnel costs. When considering turnover, a distinction should be made between dysfunctional and functional turnover. Dysfunctional turnover occurs when an organization loses a valuable employee. It is costly for the organization. Replacement costs, including recruiting and retraining, for the valued employee are anywhere from five to seven times the person's monthly salary. Functional turnover, in contrast, benefits the organization by creating opportunities for new members, new ideas, and fresh approaches. Functional turnover occurs when an organization loses an employee who has little or no value, or is a problem. Functional turnover is good for the organization. The "up or out" promotion policy for members of some organizations is designed to create functional turnover.

Performance decrements are the costs resulting from poor quality or low quantity of production, grievances, and unscheduled machine downtime and repair. As in the case of medical illnesses, stress is not the only causal agent in these performance decrements. Stress does play a role, however, whether the poor quality or low quantity of production is motivated by distressed employees or by an unconscious response to stress on the job. In California, some employees have the option of taking a "stress leave" rather than filing a grievance against the boss.

Compensation awards, a third type of organizational cost, result from court awards for job distress.[26] Given the case law framework for most of the nation's legal system, it takes a history of judgments to determine how far the courts will go in honoring stress-related claims. One former insurance employee in Louisiana filed a federal suit against the company, alleging it created a high-strain job for him that resulted in an incapacitating depression.[27]

INDIVIDUAL DIFFERENCES IN THE STRESS-STRAIN RELATIONSHIP

The same stressful events may lead to distress and strain for one person and to excitement and healthy results for another. Individual differences play a central role in the stress-strain relationship. The weak organ hypothesis in medicine, also known as the "Achilles heel" phenomenon, suggests that a person breaks down at his or her weakest point. Some individual differences, such as gender and Type A behavior pattern, enhance vulnerability to strain under stressful conditions. Other individual differences, such as personality hardiness and self-reliance, reduce vulnerability to strain under stressful conditions.

Gender Effects

According to Estelle Ramey, women are designed for long, miserable lives, whereas men are designed for short, violent ones.[28] The truth of this is that the life expectancy for American women is approximately seven years greater than for American men. Ramey attributes part of the increased life span to hormonal differences between the sexes.

Some literature suggests that there are differences in the stressors to which the two sexes are subject.[29] For example, sexual harassment is a gender-related source of stress for many working women. There is also substantive evidence that the important differences in the sexes are in vulnerabilities.[30] For example, males are more vulnerable at an earlier age to fatal health problems, such as cardiovascular disorders, whereas women report more nonfatal, but long-term and disabling, health problems. We can conclude that gender indeed creates a differential vulnerability between the two sexes.

Type A Behavior Pattern

Type A behavior pattern is also labeled coronary-prone behavior. Type A behavior pattern is a complex of personality and behavioral characteristics, including competitiveness, time urgency, social status insecurity, aggression, hostility, and a quest for achievements.

There are two primary hypotheses concerning the lethal part of the Type A behavior pattern. One hypothesis suggests that the problem is time urgency, whereas the other hypothesis suggests that it is the hostility and aggression. The weight of evidence suggests that hostility and aggression, not time urgency, are the lethal agents.[31]

The alternative to the Type A behavior pattern is the Type B behavior pattern. People with Type B personalities are relatively free of the Type A behaviors and characteristics. Type B people are less coronary prone, but if they do have a heart attack, they do not appear to recover as well as those with Type A personalities. Organizations can also be characterized as Type A or Type B organizations.[32] Type A individuals in Type B organizations and Type B individuals in Type A organizations experience stress related to a misfit between their personality type and the predominant type of the organization. However, preliminary evidence suggests that Type A individuals in Type A organizations are most at risk of health disorders.

Type A behavior can be modified. The first step is recognizing that an individual is prone to the Type A pattern. Another possible step in modifying Type A behavior is to spend time with Type B individuals. Type B people often recognize Type A behavior and can help Type A individuals take hassles less seriously and see the humor in situations. Type A individuals can also pace themselves, manage their time well, and try not to do multiple things at once. Focusing only on the task at hand and its completion, rather than worrying about other tasks, can help Type A individuals cope more effectively.

■ Personality Hardiness

People who have personality hardiness resist strain reactions when subjected to stressful events more effectively than do people who are not hardy.[33] The components of personality hardiness are commitment (versus alienation), control (versus powerlessness), and challenge (versus threat). Commitment is a curiosity and engagement with one's environment that leads to the experience of activities as interesting and enjoyable. Control is an ability to influence the process and outcomes of events that leads to the experience of activities as personal choices. Challenge is the viewing of change as a stimulus to personal development, which leads to the experience of activities with openness.

The hardy personality appears to use these three components actively to engage in transformational coping when faced with stressful events. Transformational coping is actively changing an event into something less subjectively stressful by viewing it in a broader life perspective, by altering the course and outcome of the event through action, and/or by achieving greater understanding of the process. The alternative to transformational coping is regressive coping, a much less healthy form of coping with stressful events, characterized by a passive avoidance of events by decreasing interaction with the environment. Regressive coping may lead to short-term stress reduction at the cost of long-term healthy life adjustment.

■ Self-Reliance

There is increasing evidence that social relationships have an important impact on health and life expectancy.[34] Self-reliance is a personality attribute related to the ways people form and maintain supportive attachments with others. Self-reliance was originally based in attachment theory, a theory about normal human development.[35] The theory identifies three distinct patterns of attachment, and new research suggests that these patterns extend into behavioral strategies during adulthood, in professional as well as personal relationships.[36] Self-reliance results in a secure pattern of attachment and interdependent behavior. Interpersonal attachment is emotional and psychological connectedness to another person. The two insecure patterns of attachment are counterdependence and overdependence.

Self-reliance is a healthy, secure, interdependent pattern of behavior. It may appear paradoxical, because a person appears independent while maintaining a host of supportive attachments.[37] Self-reliant people respond to stressful, threatening situations by reaching out to others appropriately. Self-reliance is a flexible, responsive strategy of forming and maintaining multiple, diverse relationships. Self-reliant people are confident, enthusiastic, and persistent in facing challenges.

Counterdependence is an unhealthy, insecure pattern of behavior that leads to separation in relationships with other people. Counterdependent people draw into themselves when faced with stressful and threatening situations, attempting to exhibit strength and power. Counterdependence may be characterized as a rigid, dismissing denial of the need for other people in difficult and stressful times. Counterdependent people exhibit a fearless, aggressive, and actively powerful response to challenges.

Overdependence is also an unhealthy, insecure pattern of behavior. Overdependent people respond to stressful and threatening situations by clinging to other people in any way possible. Overdependence may be characterized as a desperate, preoccupied attempt to achieve a sense of security through relationships. Overdependent people exhibit an active, but disorganized and anxious, response to challenges. Overdependence prevents a person from being able to organize and maintain healthy relationships, and thus creates much distress. It is interesting to note that both counterdependence and overdependence are exhibited by some military personnel who are experiencing adjustment difficulties during the first thirty days of basic training.[38] In particular, basic military trainees who have the most difficulty have overdependence problems and find it difficult to function on their own during the rigors of training.

■ PREVENTIVE STRESS MANAGEMENT

Stress is an inevitable feature of work and personal life. It is neither inherently bad nor destructive. Stress can be managed. The following is the central principle of preventive stress management: Individual and organizational distress are not inevitable. Preventive stress management is an organizational philosophy about people and organizations taking joint responsibility for promoting health and preventing distress and strain. Preventive stress management is rooted in the public health notions of prevention, which were first used in preventive medicine. The three stages of prevention are primary, secondary, and tertiary prevention. A framework for understanding preventive stress management is presented in Figure 7.2, which includes the three stages of prevention in a preventive medicine context, along with these stages in an organizational context.

Primary prevention is intended to reduce, modify, or eliminate the demand or stressor causing stress. The idea behind primary prevention is to eliminate or ameliorate the source of a problem. True organizational stress prevention is largely primary in nature, because it changes and shapes the demands the organization places on people at work. Secondary prevention is intended to alter or modify the individual's or the organization's response to a demand or stressor. People must learn to manage the inevitable, inalterable work stressors and demands so as to avert distress and strain while promoting health and well-being. Tertiary prevention is intended to heal individual or organizational symptoms of distress and strain. The symptoms may range from early warning signs (such as headaches or absenteeism) to more severe forms of distress (such as hypertension, work stoppages, and strikes). Tertiary prevention is therapeutic, aimed at arresting distress and healing the individual, the organization, or both. We will discuss these stages of prevention in the context of organizational prevention, individual prevention, and comprehensive health promotion.

■ Organizational Stress Prevention

Some organizations are low-stress, healthy ones, whereas other organizations are high-stress ones that may place their employees' health at risk. Organizational stress prevention focuses on people's work demands and ways to reduce distress at work. Most organizational prevention is primary prevention, including job redesign, goal setting, role negotiation, and career management. Two organizational stress prevention methods, team building and social support at work, are secondary prevention. Team building and career management are discussed extensively in Chapters 8 and 17, respectively.

Job Redesign. The job strain model presented in Figure 7.3 suggests that the combination of high job demands and restricted job decision latitude or worker control leads to a high-strain job.[39] A major concern in job redesign should be to enhance worker control, because this reduces distress and strain without necessarily reducing productivity.

Job redesign to increase worker control is one cure identified by Northwestern National Life in its stud-

■ **FIGURE 7.2**
A Framework for Preventive
Stress Management

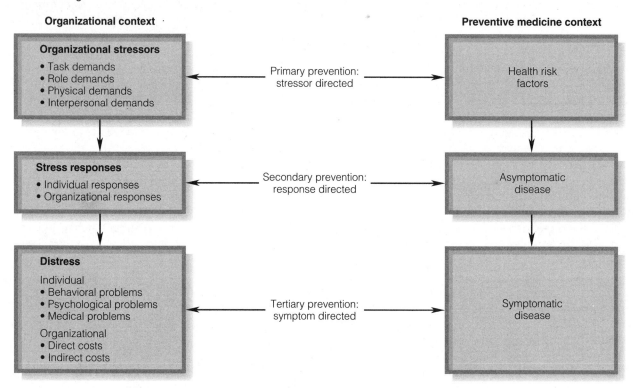

ies of workplace stress. It can be accomplished in a number of ways, the most common being to increase job decision latitude. This might include greater decision authority over the sequencing of work activities, the timing of work schedules, the selection and sequencing of work tools, or the selection of work teams. A second objective of job redesign should be to reduce uncertainty and increase predictability in the workplace. Uncertainty is a major stressor, as was the case for one Rhode Island manufacturer with 435 employees who underwent a major reorganization, with some layoffs.

Goal Setting. Organizational preventive stress management can also be achieved through goal-setting activities. These activities are designed to increase task motivation, as discussed in Chapter 6, while reducing the degree of role conflict and ambiguity to which people at work are subject. Goal

setting focuses a person's attention while directing energy in a productive channel. Implicit in much of the goal-setting literature is the assumption that people participate in, and accept, their work goals. Chapter 6 addressed goal setting in depth.

Role Negotiation. The organizational development technique of role negotiation has value as a stress management method, because it allows people to modify their work roles. Role negotiation begins with the definition of a specific role, called the focal role, within its organizational context. The person in the focal role then identifies the expectations understood for that role, and key organizational members specify their expectations of the person in the focal role. The actual negotiation follows from the comparison of the role incumbent's expectations and key members' expectations. The points of confusion and conflict are opportunities for clarification and resolu-

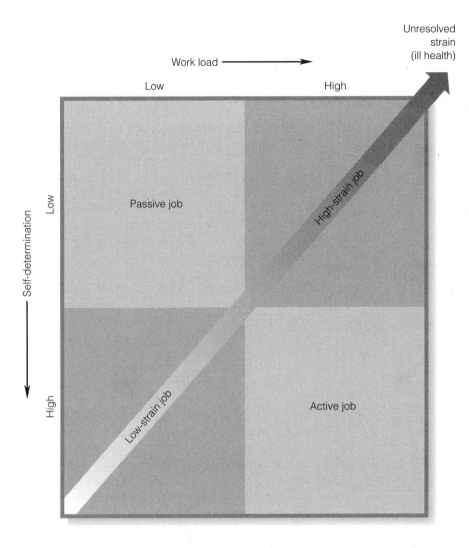

■ **FIGURE 7.3**
Job Strain Model

tion. The final result of the role negotiation process should be a clear, well-defined focal role with which the incumbent and organizational members are comfortable.

Social Support Systems.   Team building, discussed in Chapter 9, is one way to develop supportive social relationships in the workplace. However, team building is primarily task-oriented, not socioemotional, in nature. Although employees may receive much of their socioemotional support from personal relationships outside the workplace, some socioemotional support within the workplace is also necessary for psychological well-being.

Social support systems can be enhanced through the work environment in a number of ways. For example, some research has shown that psychologically intimate, cross-sex relationships in the workplace are possible and enhance social identity integration.[40] Key elements in a person's work and nonwork social support system provide emotional caring, information, evaluative feedback, modeling, and instrumental support.

■ **Individual Prevention**

Individual prevention focuses on how the person can manage stress before it becomes a problem.

■ **TABLE 7.3**
Individual Preventive Stress Management

Primary Prevention	
Learned optimism:	Alters the person's internal self-talk and reduces depression.
Time management:	Improves planning and prioritizes activities.
Leisure time activities:	Balance work and nonwork activities.

Secondary Prevention	
Physical Exercise:	Improves cardiovascular function and muscular flexibility.
Relaxation training:	Lowers all indicators of the stress response.
Diet:	Lowers the risk of cardiovascular disease and improves overall physical health.

Tertiary Prevention	
Opening up:	Releases internalized traumas and emotional tensions.
Professional help:	Provides information, emotional support, and therapeutic guidance.

Individual prevention can be of a primary, secondary, or tertiary nature. The primary prevention activities we discuss are learned optimism, time management, and leisure time activities. The secondary prevention activities we discuss are physical exercise, relaxation, and diet. The tertiary prevention activities we discuss are opening up and professional help. These eight methods and their benefits are summarized in Table 7.3.

Learned Optimism. Optimism and pessimism are two different thinking styles people use to explain the good and bad events in their lives to themselves.[41] These explanatory styles are habits of thinking learned over time, not inborn attributes. Pessimism is an explanatory style leading to depression, physical health problems, and low levels of achievement. Optimism is an alternative explanatory style that enhances physical health and achievement and averts susceptibility to depression.

Optimistic people avoid distress by understanding the bad events and difficult times in their lives as temporary, limited, and caused by something other than themselves. They face difficult times and adversity with hope. Optimists take more credit for the good events in their lives; they see these good events as more pervasive and generalized. Learned optimism begins with identifying pessimistic thoughts and then distracting oneself from these thoughts or disputing them with evidence and alternative thoughts. Learned optimism is non-negative thinking.

Time Management. Work overload, as noted earlier in the chapter, can lead to time pressure and overtime work. Time management skills can help employees make the most effective, efficient use of the time they spend at work. The good time manager is not necessarily the person who gets the most done. Rather, the good time manager is a "macro time manager" who knows the activities that contribute most to his or her long-term life development.[42] Time management enables a person to minimize the stress of work overload and to prioritize work and leisure time activities. Organizing and prioritizing may be the two most important time management skills for successful people managing very busy activity schedules.

Leisure Time Activities. Unremitted striving characterizes many people with a high need for achievement. Leisure time activities provide employees an opportunity for rest and recovery from strenuous activities either at home or at work. Many individuals, when asked what they do with their leisure time, say that they clean the house or mow the lawn. These activities are fine, as long as the individual gets the stress-reducing benefit of pleasure from these activities. Some say our work ethic is a cultural barrier to pleasure. We work longer hours, and two-income families are the norm. Leisure is increasingly a luxury among working people. The key to the effective use of leisure time is enjoyment. Leisure time can be used for spontaneity, joy, and connection with others in our lives.

Physical Exercise. Two different types of physical exercise are important secondary stress prevention activities for individuals. First, aerobic exercise improves a person's responsiveness to stressful activities. Kenneth Cooper has long advocated aerobic exercise.[43] Research at the Aerobics Center in Dallas has found that aerobically fit people (1) have lower levels of catecholamines in their blood at rest; (2) have a slower, more efficient cardiovascular system; (3) have better interactions between their sympathetic and parasympathetic nervous systems; and (4) recover from stressful events more quickly.

Second, flexibility training is important because of the muscular contractions associated with the stress response. One component of the stress response is the contraction of the flexor muscles, which prepares a person to fight or flee. Flexibility training enables a person to stretch and relax these muscles to prevent the accumulation of unnecessary muscular tension. Flexibility exercises help maintain joint mobility, increase strength, and play an important role in the prevention of injury.

Relaxation Training. Herbert Benson was one of the first people to identify the relaxation response as the natural counterresponse to the stress response.[44] In studying Western and Eastern peoples, Benson found that the Judeo-Christian people have elicited this response through their time-honored tradition of prayer, whereas the Eastern people have elicited it through meditation. The relaxation response does not require a theological or religious component. However, if you have a practice of regular prayer or meditation, you may already elicit the relaxation response regularly. Keep in mind that digestion may interfere with the elicitation of the response, so avoid practicing relaxation shortly after eating.

Diet. Diet may play an indirect role in stress and stress management. High sugar content in the diet can stimulate the stress response, and foods high in cholesterol can adversely effect blood chemistry. Good dietary practices contribute to a person's overall health, making the person less vulnerable to distress. With the use of surgery or drug therapy to treat or reverse heart disease, Dean Ornish proposes a very stringent "reversal diet" for people with identifiable blockage(s) in their arteries.[45] Ornish recommends a somewhat less stringent "prevention diet" as one of four elements for opening up the arteries. Another element in his program is being open in relationships with other people.

Opening Up. Everyone experiences a traumatic, stressful, or painful event in life at one time or another. One of the most therapeutic, curative responses to such an event is to confide in another person. Discussing difficult experiences with another person is not always easy, yet health benefits, immune system improvement, and healing accrue through self-disclosure. In one study comparing those who wrote once a week about traumatic events with those who wrote about nontraumatic events, significant health benefits and reduced absenteeism were found in the first group.[46] Confession need not be through a personal relationship with friends. It may occur through a private diary. For example, a lawyer might write each evening about all of his or her most troubling thoughts, feelings, and emotions during the course of the day. The process of opening up and confessing appears to counter the detrimental effects of stress.

Professional Help. Confession and opening up may occur through professional helping relationships. People who need healing have psychological counseling, career counseling, physical therapy, medical treatment, surgical intervention, and other therapeutic techniques available. Employee assistance programs (EAPs) may be very helpful in referring employees to the appropriate caregivers. Even combat soldiers who experience battle stress reactions severe enough to take them out of action can heal and be ready for subsequent combat duty. The early detection of distress and strain reactions, coupled with prompt professional treatment, can be instrumental in averting permanent physical and psychological damage.

■ Comprehensive Health Promotion

Whereas organizational stress prevention is aimed at eliminating health risks at work, comprehensive health promotion programs are aimed at establishing a "strong and resistent host" by building on individual prevention and life-style change. Physical fitness and exercise programs characterize corporate health promotion programs in the U.S. and Canada. A health promotion and wellness survey of the 143 accredited medical schools in the U.S., Canada, and Puerto Rico found that these programs place the most emphasis on physical well-being and the least emphasis on spiritual well-being.[47] A review of the most intensively researched programs, such as Johnson & Johnson's "Live for Life," AT&T's "TLC," Control Data's "Staywell," and the Coors wellness program, shows a strong emphasis on life-style change.[48] Unfortunately, these programs may be among those most at risk in corporate cost-cutting and downsizing programs.

Johnson & Johnson's "Live for Life" program is a comprehensive health promotion program with a significant number of educational modules for individuals and groups. Each module addresses a specific topic, such as Type A behavior, exercise, diet (through cooperative activities with the American Heart Association), and risk assessment (through regular risk assessments and health profiles for participants). Johnson & Johnson has found health improvements among even non-participating employees in their "Live for Life" program.

■ MANAGERIAL IMPLICATIONS: STRESS WITHOUT DISTRESS

Stress is an inevitable result of work and personal life. Distress is not an inevitable consequence of stressful events, however; in fact, well-managed stress can improve health and performance. Managers must learn how to create healthy stress for employees to facilitate performance and well-being without distress. Managers can help employees by adjusting work loads, avoiding ethical dilemmas, being sensitive to diversity among individuals concerning what is stressful, and being sensitive to employees' personal life demands.

New technologies create demands and stress for employees. Managers can help employees adjust to new technologies by ensuring that their design and implementation are sensitive to employees and that employee involvement is strong.

Managers can be sensitive to early signs of distress at work, such as employee fatigue or changes in work habits, in order to avoid serious forms of distress. The serious forms of distress include violent behavior, psychological depression, and cardiovascular problems. Distress is important to the organization because of the costs associated with turnover and absenteeism, as well as poor-quality production.

Managers should understand gender, personality, and behavioral differences to better manage stress in the workplace. Men and women have different vulnerabilities when it comes to distress. Men, for example, are at greater risk of fatal disorders, and women are more vulnerable to nonfatal disorders, such as depression. Personality hardiness and self-reliance are helpful in managing stressful events.

Managers can use the principles and methods of preventive stress management to create healthier work environments. They can practice several forms of individual stress prevention to create healthier life-styles for themselves, and they can encourage employees to do the same. Large organizations can create healthier work forces through the implementation of comprehensive health promotion programs. Setting an example is one of the best things a manager can do for employees when it comes to preventive stress management.

■ CHAPTER SUMMARY

- Stress is the unconscious preparation to fight or flee when faced with any demand. Distress is the adverse consequence of stress.
- The stress concept has evolved from its physiological and medical origins to a more complete understanding of the psychological dimensions of stress.
- The stress response is a natural mind-body response characterized by four basic mind-body changes.
- Employees face task, role, interpersonal, and physical demands at work, along with nonwork (extraorganizational) demands. Global competition and advanced technologies create new stresses at work.
- Nonwork stressors, such as family problems and work-home conflicts, can affect an individual's work life and home life.
- Stress has health benefits, including enhanced performance.
- Distress is costly to individuals and organizations.
- Individual diversity requires attention to gender, Type A behavior, personality hardiness, and self-

reliance in determining the links between stress and strain.

■ Preventive stress management aims to enhance health and reduce distress or strain. Primary prevention focuses on the stressor, secondary prevention focuses on the response to the stressor, and tertiary prevention focuses on symptoms of distress.

■ REVIEW QUESTIONS

1. Define stress, distress, strain, and eustress.
2. Describe four approaches to understanding stress. How does each add something new to our understanding of stress?
3. What are the four changes associated with the stress response?
4. List three demands of each type: task, role, interpersonal, and physical.
5. Describe the relationship between stress and performance.
6. What are the major medical, behavioral, and psychological consequences of distress?
7. Why should organizations be concerned about stress at work? What are the costs of distress to organizations?
8. How do gender, the Type A behavior pattern, personality hardiness, and self-reliance moderate the relationship between stress and strain?
9. Is it ethical for a company to prescribe certain healthy behaviors for all employees, such as regular exercise and the practice of relaxation?
10. Assume that a company finds that many employees have lower back problems associated with bending over work benches. In looking into the problem, the company finds that it can either raise the benches so employees bend less or send all the employees to a lower back care class. Should the most cost-efficient approach be the one the company chooses? What else should the company consider?

■ REFERENCES

1. J. C. Quick and J. D. Quick, *Organizational Stress and Preventive Management* (New York: McGraw-Hill, 1984).
2. W. B. Cannon, "Stresses and Strains of Homeostasis," *American Journal of the Medical Sciences* 189 (1935): 1–14.
3. W. B. Cannon, *The Wisdom of the Body* (New York: Norton, 1932).
4. R. S. Lazarus, *Psychological Stress and the Coping Process* (New York: McGraw-Hill, 1966).
5. H. Levinson, "A Psychoanalytic View of Occupational Stress," *Occupational Mental Health* 3 (1978): 2–13.
6. F. J. Landy, "Work Design and Stress," in G. P. Keita and S. L. Sauter, eds., *Work and Well-being: An Agenda for the 1990s* (Washington, D.C.: American Psychological Association, 1992), 119–158.
7. D. L. Nelson, J. C. Quick, and J. D. Quick, "Corporate Warfare: Preventing Combat Stress and Battle Fatigue," *Organizational Dynamics* 18 (1989): 65–79.
8. R. A. Karasek, T. Theorell, J. E. Schwartz, P. L. Schnall, C. F. Pieper, and J. L. Michela, "Job Characteristics in Relation to the Prevalence of Myocardial Infarction in the U.S. Health Examination Survey (HES) and the Health and Nutrition Examination Survey (Hanes)," *American Journal of Public Health* (1988): 910–918.
9. S. Stecklow, "Management 101," *Wall Street Journal*, 9 December 1994, A1, A10.
10. R. L. Kahn, D. M. Wolfe, R. P. Quinn, J. D. Snoek, and R. A. Rosenthal, *Organizational Stress: Studies in Role Conflict and Ambiguity* (New York: Wiley, 1964).
11. H. Levinson, "The Abrasive Personality," *Harvard Business Review* 56 (1978): 86–94; K. Lewin, R. Lippitt, and R. K. White, "Patterns of Aggressive Behavior in Experimentally Created 'Social Climates,' " *Journal of Social Psychology* 10 (1939): 271–299.
12. R. Gal and A. D. Mangelsdorff, eds., *Handbook of Military Psychology* (Chichester, England: Wiley, 1991).
13. K. K. Gillingham, "High-G Stress and Orientational Stress: Physiologic Effects of Aerial Maneuvering," *Aviation, Space, and Environmental Medicine* 59 (1988): A10–A20.
14. R. S. Bhagat, S. J. McQuaid, S. Lindholm, and J. Segovis, "Total Life Stress: A Multimethod Validation of the Construct and Its Effect on Organizationally Valued Outcomes and Withdrawal Behaviors," *Journal of Applied Psychology* 70 (1985): 202–214.
15. S. A. Lobel, "Allocation of Investment in Work and Family Roles: Alternative Theories and Implications for Research," *Academy of Management Review* 16 (1991): 507–521.
16. J. W. Pennebaker, C. F. Hughes, and R. C. O'Heeron, "The Psychophysiology of Confession: Linking Inhibitory and Psychosomatic Processes," *Journal of Personality and Social Psychology* 52 (1987): 781–793.
17. R. S. DeFrank and J. E. Pliner, "Job Security, Job Loss, and Outplacement: Implications for Stress and Stress Management," in J. C. Quick, R. S. Bhagat, J. E. Dalton, and J. D. Quick, eds., *Work Stress: Health Care Systems in the Workplace* (New York: Praeger Scientific, 1987), 195–219.
18. J. D. Quick, R. S. Horn, and J. C. Quick, "Health Consequences of Stress," *Journal of Organizational Behavior Management* 8 (1986): 19–36.
19. R. M. Yerkes and J. D. Dodson, "The Relation of Strength of Stimulus to Rapidity of Habit-Formation," *Journal of Comparative Neurology and Psychology* 18 (1908): 459–482.

20. W. B. Cannon, *Bodily Changes in Pain, Hunger, Fear, and Rage* (New York: Appleton, 1915).

21. S. Sauter, L. R. Murphy, and J. J. Hurrell, Jr., "Prevention of Work-related Psychological Distress: A National Strategy Proposed by the National Institute for Occupational Safety and Health," *American Psychologist* 45 (1990): 1146–1158.

22. H. Selye, *Stress in Health and Disease* (Boston: Butterworth, 1976).

23. B. G. Ware and D. L. Block, "Cardiovascular Risk Intervention at a Work Site: The Ford Motor Company Program," *International Journal of Mental Health* 11 (1982): 68–75.

24. N. Bolger, A. DeLongis, R. C. Kessler, and E. A. Schilling, "Effects of Daily Stress on Negative Mood," *Journal of Personality and Social Psychology* 57 (1989): 808–818.

25. B. A. Macy and P. H. Mirvis, "A Methodology for Assessment of Quality of Work Life and Organizational Effectiveness in Behavioral-Economic Terms," *Administrative Science Quarterly* 21 (1976): 212–226.

26. J. M. Ivancevich, M. T. Matteson, and E. Richards, "Who's Liable for Stress on the Job?" *Harvard Business Review* 64 (1985): 60–72.

27. Frank S. Deus v. Allstate Insurance Company, civil action no. 88–2099, U.S. District Court, Western District of Louisiana.

28. E. Ramey, "Gender Differences in Cardiac Disease: The Paradox of Heart Disease in Women" (paper delivered at the Healing the Heart Conference, Boston, 3–5 May 1990).

29. T. D. Jick and L. F. Mitz, "Sex Differences in Work Stress," *Academy of Management Review* 10 (1985): 408–420; D. L. Nelson and J. C. Quick, "Professional Women: Are Distress and Disease Inevitable?" *Academy of Management Review* 10 (1985): 206–218.

30. L. Verbrugge, "Recent, Present, and Future Health of American Adults," *Annual Review of Public Health* 10 (1989): 333–361.

31. L. Wright, "The Type A Behavior Pattern and Coronary Artery Disease," *American Psychologist* 43 (1988): 2–14.

32. J. M. Ivancevich and M. T. Matteson, "A Type A-B Person-Work Environment Interaction Model for Examining Occupational Stress and Consequences," *Human Relations* 37 (1984): 491–513.

33. S. O. C. Kobasa, "Conceptualization and Measurement of Personality in Job Stress Research," in J. J. Hurrell, Jr., L. R. Murphy, S. L. Sauter, and C. L. Cooper, eds., *Occupational Stress: Issues and Developments in Research* (New York: Taylor & Francis, 1988): 100–109.

34. J. S. House, K. R. Landis, and D. Umberson, "Social Relationships and Health," *Science* 241 (1988): 540–545.

35. J. Bowlby, *A Secure Base* (New York: Basic Books, 1988).

36. C. Hazan and P. Shaver, "Love and Work: An Attachment-Theoretical Perspective," *Journal of Personality and Social Psychology* 59 (1990): 270–280.

37. D. L. Nelson and J. C. Quick, "Social Support and Newcomer Adjustment in Organization: Attachment Theory at Work?" *Journal of Organizational Behavior* 12 (1991): 543–554; J. C. Quick, J. R. Joplin, D. L. Nelson, and J. D. Quick, "Behavioral Responses to Anxiety: Self-Reliance, Counterdependence, and Overdependence," *Anxiety, Stress, and Coping* 5 (1992): 41–54; J. C. Quick, D. L. Nelson, and J. D. Quick, *Stress and Challenge at the Top: The Paradox of the Successful Executive* (Chichester, England: Wiley, 1990).

38. J. C. Quick, J. R. Joplin, D. L. Nelson, and J. D. Quick, "Self-reliance for Stress and Combat" (Proceedings of the 8th Combat Stress Conference, U.S. Army Health Services Command, Fort Sam Houston, Texas, 23–27 September 1991): 1–5.

39. B. Gardell, "Efficiency and Health Hazards in Mechanized Work," in J. C. Quick, R. S. Bhagat, J. E. Dalton, and J. D. Quick, eds., *Work Stress: Health Care Systems in the Workplace* (New York: Praeger Scientific, 1987), 50–71.

40. S. A. Lobel and L. St. Clair, "Effects of Family Responsibilities, Gender, and Career Identity Salience on Performance Outcomes of Professionals," *Academy of Management Journal* 35 (1992): 1057–1069.

41. M. E. P. Seligman, *Learned Optimism* (New York: Knopf, 1990).

42. W. T. Brooks and T. W. Mullins, *High-Impact Time Management* (Englewood Cliffs, N.J.: Prentice-Hall, 1989).

43. K. H. Cooper, *The Aerobic Program for Total Well-being: Exercise, Diet, Emotional Balance* (New York: M. Evans, 1982).

44. H. Benson, "Your Innate Asset for Combating Stress," *Harvard Business Review* 52 (1974): 49–60.

45. D. Ornish, *Dr. Dean Ornish's Program for Reversing Cardiovascular Disease* (New York: Random House, 1990).

46. M. E. Francis and J. W. Pennebaker, "Putting Stress into Words: The Impact of Writing on Physiological, Absentee, and Self-reported Emotional Well-being Measures," *American Journal of Health Promotion* 6 (1992): 280–287.

47. T. Wolf, H. Randall, and J. Faucett, "A Survey of Health Promotion Programs in U.S. and Canadian Medical Schools," *American Journal of Health Promotion* 3 (1988): 33–36.

48. S. Weiss, J. Fielding, and A. Baum, *Health at Work* (Hillsdale, N.J.: Erlbaum, 1990).

PART III
INTERPERSONAL PROCESSES AND BEHAVIOR

CHAPTER 8
COMMUNICATION

LEARNING OBJECTIVES

After reading this chapter, you should be able to do the following:

- Understand the roles of the communicator, the receiver, perceptual screens, and the message in interpersonal communication.
- Practice good reflective listening skills.
- Describe the five communication skills of effective supervisors.
- Explain five barriers to communication and how to overcome them.
- Distinguish between defensive and nondefensive communication.
- Describe contemporary information technologies used by managers.

Chaparral Steel is just one manufacturing company that has improved communication through dramatic advances in information technology,[1] and information technology has been used in the service sector of the economy to increase productivity.[2]

However, for all of the importance of information technology in communication, the personal and interpersonal processes of reading, listening, managing and interpreting information, and of serving clients, are among the interpersonal communication skills identified by the Department of Labor as necessary for successful functioning in the workplace.[3]

This chapter addresses the interpersonal and information technology dimensions of communication in organizations. The first section presents an interpersonal communication model and a reflective listening technique intended to improve communication. The next section of the chapter addresses the five communication skills that characterize effective supervisors. The third section examines five barriers to effective communication and gives suggestions for overcoming them. The fourth section compares defensive and nondefensive communication. The fifth section discusses kinds of nonverbal communication. The final section gives an overview of the latest technologies for information managment in organizations.

■ INTERPERSONAL COMMUNICATION

Interpersonal communication is important in building and sustaining human relationships at work. It cannot be replaced by the advances in information technology and data management that have taken place over the past several decades. This section of the chapter provides a basis for understanding the key elements of interpersonal communication. These elements are the communicator, the receiver, the perceptual screens, and the message. Reflective listening, as this section shows, is a valuable tool for improving interpersonal communication.

■ An Interpersonal Communication Model

Figure 8.1 presents an interpersonal communication model as a basis for the discussion of communication. The model has four basic elements: the communicator, the receiver, perceptual screens, and the message. The communicator is the person originating the message. The receiver is the person receiving the message, who must interpret and understand it. Perceptual screens are the windows through which we interact with people in the world. The communicator's and the receiver's perceptual screens influence the quality, accuracy, and clarity of the message. The screens influence whether the message sent and the message received are the same or whether distortion occurs in the message. Perceptual screens are composed of the personal factors each person brings to interpersonal communication, such as age, gender, values, beliefs, past experiences, cultural influences, and individual needs. The extent to which these screens are open or closed significantly influences both the sent and received messages.

The message contains the thoughts and feelings that the communicator intends to evoke in the receiver. The message has two primary components. The thought or conceptual component of the message (its content) is contained in the words, ideas, symbols, and concepts chosen to relay the message. The feeling or emotional component of the message (its affect) is contained in the intensity, force, demeanor, and sometimes the gestures of the communicator. This component of the message adds to the conceptual component the emotional overtones, such as joy or anger, fear or pain. This addition often enriches and clarifies the message. The feeling component gives the message its full meaning.

The feedback loop may or may not be activated in the model. Feedback occurs when the receiver provides the communicator with a response to the message. The language of the message is increasingly important because of the multinational nature of many organizations. Language includes the words, their pronunciation, and the methods of combining them used by a community of people. Language will be addressed as a possible barrier to communication. For example, special language barriers arise for non-Japanese-speaking Americans who work with Japanese workers and for non-

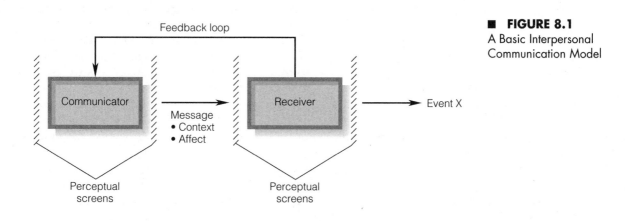

Communicator

Message
• Context
• Affect

Receiver

Event X

Feedback loop

Perceptual screens

Perceptual screens

■ **FIGURE 8.1**
A Basic Interpersonal Communication Model

■ TABLE 8.1
Communication Media: Information Richness and Data Capacity

MEDIUM	INFORMATION RICHNESS	DATA CAPACITY
Face-to-face discussion	Highest	Lowest
Telephone	High	Low
Electronic Mail	Moderate	Moderate
Individualized letter	Moderate	Moderate
Personalized note or memo	Moderate	Moderate
Formal written report	Low	High
Flyer or bulletin	Low	High
Formal numeric report	Lowest	Highest

SOURCE: Adapted by Edwin A. Gerloff from "Information Richness: A New Approach to Managerial Behavior and Organizational Design," Richard L. Daft and R. H. Lengel, in *Research in Organizational Behavior*, v.6 (Greenwich, CN: JAI Press, 1984): pp. 191-233.

Spanish-speaking Canadians who work with Spanish-speaking workers.

Data are the uninterpreted, unanalyzed elements of a message. Information is data with meaning to some person who has interpreted or analyzed it. Messages are conveyed through a medium, such as a telephone or face-to-face discussion. Messages differ in richness, the ability of the medium to convey the meaning.[4] Table 8.1 compares different media with regard to data capacity and information richness.

■ Reflective Listening

Reflective listening is the skill of carefully listening to another person and repeating back to the speaker the heard message to correct any inaccuracies or misunderstandings. This kind of listening emphasizes the role of the receiver or audience in interpersonal communication. Managers use it to understand other people and help them solve problems at work.[5] Reflective listening enables the listener to understand the communicator's meaning, reduce perceptual distortions, and overcome interpersonal barriers that lead to communication failures. Reflective listening ensures that the meanings of the sent and received messages are the same. Reflecting back the message helps the communicator clarify and sharpen the intended meaning. It is especially useful in problem solving.

Reflective listening can be characterized as personal, feeling-oriented, and responsive. First, reflective listening emphasizes the personal elements of the communication process, not the impersonal or abstract elements of the message. The reflective listener demonstrates empathy and concern for the communicator as a person, not an inanimate object. Second, reflective listening emphasizes the feelings communicated in the message. Thoughts and ideas are often the primary focus of a receiver's response, but that is not the case in reflective listening. The receiver should pay special attention to the feeling component of the message. Third, reflective listening emphasizes responding to the communicator, not leading the communicator. Receivers should distinguish their own feelings and thoughts from those of the speaker so as not to confuse the two. The focus must be on the speaker's feelings and thoughts in order to respond to them. A good reflective listener does not lead the speaker according to the listener's own thoughts and feelings.

Four levels of verbal response by the receiver are part of active reflective listening.[6] First, affirming contact occurs through simple statements such as "I see," "Uh-huh," and "Yes, I understand." Affirming contact is especially reassuring to a speaker in the early stages of expressing thoughts and feelings about a problem, especially when there may be some associated anxiety or discomfort. Second, paraphrasing expressed thoughts and feelings is useful because it reflects back to the speaker the thoughts and feelings as the receiver heard them. This verbal response encourages empathy, openness, and acceptance while ensuring the accuracy of the communication process. Third, clarifying implicit thoughts and feelings may help the communicator become more aware of that which is not clearly or fully expressed. The listener cannot assume that the implicit thoughts and feelings are within the awareness of the speaker. Fourth, reflecting "core" feelings not fully expressed is reaching beyond the immediate awareness level of the speaker to the deepest, most important ones from the speaker's perspective. Because the listener runs a risk of overreaching in reflecting core feelings, it is important to exercise caution with this level of response.

Nonverbal behaviors also are useful in reflective listening. Specifically, silence and eye contact are responses that enhance reflective listening.[7] First, silence may be useful to the speaker in moments of thought or confusion about how to express difficult ideas or feelings. Listeners can use brief periods of silence to sort out their own thoughts and feelings from those of the speaker. Second, within the American culture, moderate direct eye contact communicates openness and affirmation without causing either speaker or listener to feel intimidated. Periodic aversion of the eyes allows for a sense of privacy and control, even in intense interpersonal communication.

■ One-Way Versus Two-Way Communication

Reflective listening encourages two-way communication, an interactive form of communication featuring an exchange of thoughts, feelings, or both, and through which shared meaning often occurs. Problem-solving and decision-making are often examples of two-way communication. One-way communication occurs when a person sends a message to another person and no feedback, questions, or interactions follow. Instructions and directions are examples. One-way communication occurs whenever a person sends a one-directional message to a receiver with no reflective listening or feedback in the communication.

One-way communication is faster, although how much faster depends on the amount and complexity of information communicated and the medium chosen. Even though it is faster, one-way communication is often less accurate than two-way communication. This is especially true for complex tasks where clarifications and iterations may be required for task completion. Where time and accuracy are both important to the successful completion of a task, such as in combat or emergency situations, extensive training prior to execution enhances accuracy and efficiency of execution without two-way communication.[8] Fire fighters and military combat personnel engage extensively in such training to minimize the need for communication during emergencies. These highly trained professionals rely on fast, abbreviated, one-way communication as a shorthand for more complex information. However, this communication works only within the range of situations for which the professionals are specifically trained.

It is difficult to draw general conclusions about people's satisfaction with one-way versus two-way communication. For example, communicators who have a stronger need for feedback, or who are not uncomfortable with conflicting or confusing questions, may find two-way communication more satisfying. In contrast, receivers who believe that a message is very straightforward may be satisfied with one-way communication and dissatisfied with two-way communication because of its lengthy, drawn-out nature.

■ KEYS TO EFFECTIVE SUPERVISORY COMMUNICATION

Interpersonal communication between managers and their employees is a critical foundation for effective performance in organizations. One large study of managers in a variety of jobs and industries found that managers with the most effective work units engaged in routine communication within their units, whereas the managers with the highest promotion rates engaged in networking activities with superiors.[9] In a study of communication competence among banking managers, female managers were found to have significantly higher levels of apprehension than their male counterparts.[10] Good supervisors have different communication skills from those of their less effective counterparts.[11]

First, the better supervisors express their thoughts, ideas, and feelings and speak up in meetings. They are comfortable expressing themselves and tend toward extraversion.

Second, in addition to being expressive speakers, the better supervisors are willing, empathetic listeners who use reflective listening skills and are patient with, and responsive to, others' problems. For example, the president of a health care operating company estimated that he spends 70 percent of his interpersonal time at work listening to others.[12]

Third, the better supervisors are persuasive leaders rather than directive, autocratic ones. While there are some notable exceptions in emergency or high-crisis situations where clear authority is necessary, the better supervisors use persuasive communication when influencing others.

Fourth, the better supervisors are also sensitive to the feelings and self-images of their employees. Although the supervisor is capable of giving criticism and negative feedback to employees, he or she does it confidentially and constructively in private, reserving public settings for praise.

Finally, the better supervisors keep those who work for them well informed and are skilled at engaging in the "disseminator" role.[13] These supervisors filter large volumes of information, and then disseminate what is needed by others.

A person may become a good supervisor even in the absence of one of these communication skills. For example, a person with special talents in planning and organizing or in decision making may compensate for a shortcoming in expressiveness or sensitivity. Overall, interpersonal communication is the foundation for human relationships.

■ BARRIERS TO COMMUNICATION

Barriers to communication are factors that block or significantly distort successful communication. Effective managerial communication skills help overcome some, but not all, barriers to communication in organizations. These barriers to communication in organizations may be temporary and can be overcome. Awareness and recognition are the first steps in formulating ways to overcome the barriers. Five communication barriers are physical separation, status differences, gender differences, cultural diversity, and language. The discussion of each concludes with one or two ways to overcome the barrier.

■ Physical Separation

The physical separation of people in the work environment poses a barrier to communication. Telephones and technology, such as electronic mail, often help bridge the physical gap. We address a variety of new technologies in the closing section of the chapter. Although telephones and technology can be helpful, they are not as information-rich as face-to-face communication (see Table 8.1).

Periodic face-to-face interactions help overcome physical separation problems, because the communication is much richer, largely due to nonverbal cues. The richer the communication, the less the potential for confusion or misunderstandings. Another way to overcome the barrier of physical separation is through regularly scheduled meetings for people who are organizationally interrelated.

■ Status Differences

Status differences related to power and the organizational hierarchy pose another barrier to communication among people at work, especially within manager-employee pairs.[14] Because the employee is dependent upon the manager as the primary link to the organization, the employee is more likely to distort upward communication than either horizontal or downward communication.[15]

Effective supervisory skills, discussed at the beginning of the chapter, make the supervisor more approachable and help reduce the risk of problems related to status differences. In addition, when employees feel secure, they are more likely to be straightforward in upward communication. The absence of status, power, and hierarchical differences, however, is not a cure-all. New information technologies provide another way to overcome status-difference barriers, because they encourage the formation of nonhierarchical working relationships.[16]

■ Gender Differences

Communication barriers can be explained in part by differences in conversational styles.[17] Thus, when people of different ethnic or class backgrounds talk to one another, what the receiver understands may not be the same as what the speaker meant. In a similar way, men and women have different conversational styles, which may pose a communication barrier between those of opposite sexes.[18] For example, women prefer to converse face to face, whereas men are comfortable sitting side by side and concentrating on some focal point in front of them. Hence, conversation style differences may result in a failure to communicate between men and women. Again, what is said by one may be understood to have an entirely different meaning by the other. Male-female conversation is really cross-cultural communication.

An important first step to overcoming the gender barrier to communication is developing an awareness of gender-specific differences in conversational style. A second step is to seek clarification of the person's meaning rather than freely interpreting meaning from one's own frame of reference.

■ Cultural Diversity

Cultural values and patterns of behavior can be very confusing barriers to communication. Important international differences in work-related values exist between people in the United States, Germany, the United Kingdom, Japan, and other nations.[19] These value differences have implications for motivation, leadership, and teamwork in work organizations.[20] Habitual patterns of interaction within a culture often substitute for communication. Outsiders working in a culture foreign to them often find these habitual patterns confusing and at times bizarre. For example, the German culture places greater value on authority and hierarchical differences. It is therefore more difficult for German workers to engage in direct, open communication with their supervisors than it is for U.S. workers.[21] A first step to overcoming cultural diversity as a communication barrier is increasing awareness and sensitivity. In addition, companies can provide seminars for expatriate managers as part of their training for overseas assignments.

■ Language

Language is a central element in communication. It may pose a barrier if its use obscures meaning and distorts intent. Although English is the international language of aviation, it is not the international language of business. Where the native languages of supervisors and employees differ, the risk of barriers to communication exists. Less obvious are subtle distinctions in dialects within the same language, which may cause confusion and miscommunication. For example, the word lift means an elevator in Great Britain and a ride in the United States. In a different vein, there are language barriers created across disciplines and professional boundaries by the technical terminology. Acronyms may be very useful to those on the inside of a profession or discipline as means of shorthand communication. Technical terms can convey precise meaning between professionals. However, acronyms and technical terms may serve only to confuse, obscure, and derail any attempt at clear understanding for people unfamiliar with their meaning and usage. For example, clinical depression has meaning to a professional psychologist and may have a wide range of meanings to a layperson. Use simple, direct, declarative language. Speak in brief sentences and use terms or words you have heard from your audience. As much as possible, speak in the language of the listener. Therefore, do not use jargon or technical language except with those who clearly understand it.

■ DEFENSIVE AND NONDEFENSIVE COMMUNICATION

Defensive communication in organizations can create barriers between people, whereas nondefensive communication helps open up relationships.[22] Defensive communication includes both aggressive, attacking, angry communication and passive, withdrawing communication. Nondefensive communication, an assertive, direct, powerful form, is an alternative to defensive communication. Organizations are increasingly engaged in courtroom battles and media exchanges, which are especially fertile settings for defensive communication. For example, Catherine Crier learned to manage defensive communication as a trial lawyer and judge, later using the knowledge and skill as a reporter for ABC News on *20/20*.

Defensive communication in organizations leads to a wide range of problems, including injured feelings, communication breakdowns, alienation in working relationships, destructive and retaliatory behaviors, nonproductive efforts, and problem-solving failures. When such problems arise in organizations, everyone is prone to blame everyone else for what is not working.[23] The defensive responses of counterattack and sheepish withdrawal derail communication.

Nondefensive communication, in contrast, provides a basis for asserting and defending oneself when attacked, without being defensive. An assertive, nondefensive style restores order, balance, and effectiveness in working relationships. A discussion of nondefensive communication follows the discussion of defensive communication.

■ Defensive Communication At Work

Defensive communication often elicits defensive communication in response. The two basic patterns of defensiveness are dominant defensiveness and subordinate defensiveness. One must be able to recognize various forms of defensive communication before learning to engage in constructive, nondefensive communication.

Subordinate Defensiveness. Subordinate defensiveness is characterized by passive, submissive, withdrawing behavior. The psychological attitude of the subordinately defensive person is, "You are right, and I am wrong." People with low self-esteem may be prone to this form of defensive behavior. Sensitive and critical information for organizational performance may be lost when lower level organization members are subordinately defensive.[24] Subordinately defensive people do not adequately assert themselves in the workplace. Passive-aggressive behavior is a form of defensiveness that appears very passive but, in fact, masks underlying aggression and hostility, which are forms of dominant defensiveness.

Dominant Defensiveness. Dominant defensiveness is characterized by active, aggressive, attacking behavior. It is offensive in nature: "The best defense is a good offense." The core psychological attitude is, "I am right, and you are wrong." People who compensate for low self-esteem may exhibit this pattern of behavior. The domineering, intimidating bank chairman who browbeat his junior banking officers was exhibiting dominant defensiveness.

■ Defensive Tactics

Unfortunately, defensive tactics are all too common in work organizations. Eight major defensive tactics are summarized in Table 8.2. They might be best understood in the context of a work situation where Joe is in the process of completing a critical report for his boss, and the report's deadline is drawing near. Mary, one of Joe's peers at work, is to provide him with some input for the report, and the department secretary is to prepare a final copy of the report. Each work example in the table is related to this situation.

Until defensiveness and defensive tactics are recognized for what they are, it is difficult either to change them or to respond to them in nondefensive ways. Defensive tactics are the ways defensive communication is acted out. In many cases, such tactics raise ethical dilemmas and issues for those involved. For example, is it ethical to raise doubts about another person's values, beliefs, or sexuality? At what point does simple defensiveness become unethical behavior?

■ TABLE 8.2
Defensive Tactics

DEFENSIVE TACTIC	SPEAKER	WORK EXAMPLE
Power play	The boss	"Finish this report by month's end or lose your promotion."
Put-down	The boss	"A capable manager would already be done with this report."
Labeling	The boss	"You must be a slow learner. Your report is still not done?"
Raising doubts	The boss	"How can I trust you, Joe, if you can't finish an easy report?"
Misleading information	Joe	"Mary has not gone over with me the information I need from her for the report." (She left him a copy.)
Scapegoating	Joe	"Mary did not give me her input until just today."
Hostile jokes	Joe	"You can't be serious! The report isn't that important."
Deception	Joe	"I gave it to the secretary. Did she lose it?"

Power plays are used by people to control and manipulate others through the use of choice definition (defining the choice another person is allowed to make), either/or conditions, and overt aggression. The underlying dynamic in power plays is that of domination and control.

A put-down is an effort by the speaker to gain the upper hand in the relationship. Intentionally ignoring another person or pointing out his or her mistakes in a meeting are kinds of put-downs.

Labeling is often used to portray another person as abnormal or deficient. Psychological labels are often used out of context for this purpose, such as calling a person "paranoid," a word that has a specific, clinical meaning. Raising doubts about a person's abilities, values, preferential orientations, or other aspects of his or her life creates confusion and uncertainty. This tactic tends to lack the specificity and clarity present in labeling.

Giving misleading information is the selective presentation of information designed to leave a false and inaccurate impression in the listener's mind. It is not the same as lying or misinforming. Giving misleading information is one form of deception.

Scapegoating and its companion, buck-passing, are methods of shifting responsibility to the wrong person. Blaming other people is another form of scapegoating or buck-passing.

Hostile jokes should not be confused with good humor, which is both therapeutic and nondefensive. Jokes created at the expense of others are destructive and hostile.

Deception may occur through a variety of means, such as lying or creating an impression or image that is at variance with the truth. Deception can be very useful in military operations, but it can be a destructive force in work organizations.

■ Nondefensive Communication

Nondefensive communication is a constructive, healthy alternative to defensive communication in working relationships. The person who communicates nondefensively may be characterized as centered, assertive, controlled, informative, realistic, and honest. Nondefensive communication is powerful, because the speaker is exhibiting self-control and self-possession without rejecting the listener. Con-

verting defensive patterns of communication to nondefensive ones is not difficult. It takes the awareness and recognition that alternatives to defensiveness exist and then the desire and effort to change.

The subordinately defensive person needs to learn to be more assertive. This may be done in many ways, of which two examples follow. First, instead of asking for permission to do something, report what you intend to do, and invite confirmation. Second, instead of using self-deprecating words, such as "I'm just following orders," drop the "just," and convert the message into a self-assertive, declarative statement. Nondefensive communication should be self-affirming without being self-aggrandizing. Some people overcompensate for subordinate defensiveness and inadvertently become domineering.

The person prone to be domineering and dominantly defensive needs to learn to be less aggressive. This may be especially difficult because it requires overcoming the person's sense of "I am right." People who are working to overcome dominant defensiveness should be particularly sensitive to feedback from others about their behavior. There are many ways to change this pattern of behavior. Here are two examples. First, instead of giving and denying permission, give people free rein except in situations where permission is essential as a means of clearing approval or ensuring the security of the task. Second, instead of becoming inappropriately angry, provide information about the adverse consequences of a particular course of action.

■ NONVERBAL COMMUNICATION

Much defensive and nondefensive communication focuses on the language used. However, most of the meaning in a message (an estimated 65 to 90 percent) is conveyed through nonverbal communication.[25] Nonverbal communication includes all elements of communication, such as gestures and the use of space, that do not involve words or do not involve language.[26] The four basic kinds of nonverbal communication are proxemics, kinesics, facial and eye behavior, and paralanguage. They are important topics for managers attempting to understand the types and meanings of nonverbal signals from employees.

■ **FIGURE 8.2**
Zones of Territorial Space in
U.S. Culture

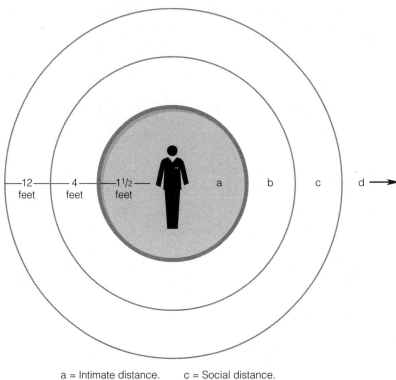

a = Intimate distance.   c = Social distance.
b = Personal distance.   d = Public distance.

Some scholars consider this area of communication to be less scientifically rigorous than other areas of communication. In any case, the interpretation of nonverbal communication is specific to the context of the interaction and the actors. That is, nonverbal cues give meaning only in the context of the situation and the interaction of the actors. It is also important to note that nonverbal behavior is culturally bound. Gestures, facial expressions, and body locations have different meanings in different cultures. The globalization of business means managers should be sensitive to the nonverbal customs of other cultures in which they do business. For example, withholding eye contact in the United States may communicate shyness or deception, while in Japan it shows deference to authority. Displaying the palm of the hand in the United States is a form of greeting (a wave or handshake), while in Greece it is an insult.

■ **Proxemics**

The study of an individual's perception and use of space, including territorial space, is called prox-

emics.[27] Territorial space refers to bands of space extending outward from the body. These bands constitute comfort zones. In each comfort zone, different cultures prefer different types of interaction with others. Figure 8.2 presents four zones of territorial space based on U.S. culture.

The first zone, intimate space, extends outward from the body to about 1 ½ feet. In this zone, we interact with spouses, significant others, family members, and others with whom we have intimate relationships. The next zone, the personal distance zone, extends from 1 ½ feet outward to 4 feet. Friends typically interact within this distance. The third zone, the social distance zone, spans the distance from 4 to 12 feet. We prefer that business associates and acquaintances interact with us in this zone. The final zone is the public distance zone, extending 12 feet from the body outward. Most of us prefer that strangers stay at least 12 feet from us, and we become uncomfortable when they move closer.

Territorial space varies greatly across cultures. People often become uncomfortable when operating in territorial spaces different from those with which they are familiar. Edward Hall, a leading proxemics researcher, says Americans working in the Middle East tend to back away to a comfortable conversation distance when interacting with Arabs. Because Arabs' comfortable conversation distance is closer than that of Americans, Arabs perceive Americans as cold and aloof. One Arab wondered, "What's the matter? Does he find me somehow offensive?"[28] Personal space tends to be larger in cultures with cool climates, such as the United States, Great Britain, and northern Europe, and smaller in cultures with warm climates, such as southern Europe, the Caribbean, India, or South America.[29]

Our relationships shape our use of territorial space. For example, we hold hands with, or put an arm around, significant others to pull them into intimate space. Conversely, the use of territorial space can shape people's interactions. A 4-foot-wide business desk pushes business interactions into the social distance zone. An exception occurred for one Southwestern Bell manager who held meetings with her seven first-line supervisors around her desk. Being elbow-to-elbow placed the supervisors in one another's intimate and personal space. They appeared to act more like friends and frequently talked about their children, favorite television shows, and other personal concerns. When the manager moved the staff meeting to a larger room and the spaces around each supervisor were in the social distance zone, the personal exchanges ceased, and they acted more like business associates again.

Seating dynamics, another aspect of proxemics, is the art of seating people in certain positions according to a person's purpose in communication. To encourage cooperation, you should seat the other party beside you, facing the same direction. To facilitate direct and open communication, seat the other party across a corner of your desk from you or in another place where you will be at right angles. This allows for more honest disclosure. To take a competitive stand with someone, position the person directly across from you. Suppose you hold a meeting around a conference table, and two of the attendees are disrupting your meeting. Where should you seat them? If you place one on each side of yourself, it should stifle the disruptions (unless one is so bold as to lean in front of you to keep chatting).

■ Kinesics

Kinesics is the study of body movements, including posture.[30] Like proxemics, kinesics is culturally bound; there is no single universal gesture. For example, the U.S. hand signal for "okay" is an insult in other countries. With this in mind, we can interpret some common U.S. gestures. Rubbing one's hands together or exhibiting a sharp intake of breath indicates anticipation. Stress is indicated by a closed hand position (that is, tight fists), hand wringing, or rubbing the temples. Nervousness may be exhibited through drumming fingers, pacing, or jingling coins in the pocket. Perhaps most fun to watch is preening behavior, seen most often in couples on a first date. Preening communicates "I want to look good for you" to the other party and consists of smoothing skirts, straightening the tie, or arranging the hair. No discussion of gestures would be complete without mention of insult gestures—some learned at an early age, much to the anxiety of parents. Sticking out one's tongue and waving fingers with one's thumbs in the ears is a childhood insult gesture.

■ Facial and Eye Behavior

The face is a rich source of nonverbal communication. Facial expression and eye behavior are used to add cues for the receiver. The face often gives unintended clues to emotions the sender is trying to hide.

Although smiles have universal meaning, frowns, raised eyebrows, and wrinkled foreheads must all be interpreted in conjunction with the actors, the situation, and the culture. One study of Japanese and U.S. students illustrates the point. The students were shown a stress-inducing film, and their facial expressions were videotaped. When alone, the students had almost identical expressions. However, the Japanese students masked their facial expressions of unpleasant feelings much better than did the American students when another person was present.[31]

As mentioned earlier, eye contact can enhance reflective listening, and it varies by culture. A direct gaze indicates honesty and forthrightness in the United States. This may not be true in other cultures. For example, Barbara Walters was uncomfortable interviewing Muammar al-Qaddafi in Libya because he did not look directly at her. However, in Libya, it is a serious offense to look directly at a woman.[32] In Asian cultures it is considered good behavior to bow the head in deference to a superior rather than to look in the supervisor's eyes.

■ Paralanguage

Paralanguage consists of variations in speech, such as pitch, loudness, tempo, tone, duration, laughing, and crying.[33] People make attributions about the sender by deciphering paralanguage cues. A high-pitched, breathy voice in a female may contribute to the stereotype of the "dumb blonde." Rapid, loud speech may be taken as a sign of nervousness or anger. Interruptions such as "mmm" and "ah-hah" may be used to speed up the speaker so that the receiver can get in a few words. Clucking of the tongue or the "tsk-tsk" sound is used to shame someone. All these cues relate to the way something is said.

■ How Accurately Do We Decode Nonverbal Cues?

People's confidence in their ability to decode non-verbal communication is greater than their accuracy in doing so. Judges with several years' experience in interviewing were asked in one study to watch videotapes of job applicants and to rate the applicants' social skills and motivation levels.[34] The judges were fairly accurate about the social skills, but not about motivation. The judges relied on smiling, gesturing, and speaking as cues to motivation, yet none of these cues are motivation indicators. Thus, incorrectly interpreting nonverbal codes leads to inaccuracy.

Studies of deception emphasize how to use nonverbal cues to interpret whether someone is lying. In one simulation study, customers were asked to detect whether or not automobile salespeople were lying. The customers' ability to detect lies in this study was no better than chance. Does this suggest that salespeople are skilled deceivers who control nonverbal behaviors to prevent detection?[35]

Paul Ekman, a psychologist who has trained judges, Secret Service agents, and polygraphers to detect lies, says that the best way is to look for inconsistencies in the nonverbal cues. Rapidly shifting facial expressions and discrepancies between the person's words and body, voice, or facial expressions are some clues.[36]

Nonverbal communication is important for managers because of its impact on the meaning of the message. However, a manager must consider the total message and all media of communication. A message can be given meaning only in context, and cues are easy to misinterpret. Table 8.3 presents common nonverbal behaviors exhibited by managers and how employees may interpret them. Nonverbal cues can give others the wrong signal.

■ COMMUNICATING THROUGH NEW TECHNOLOGIES

Nonverbal behaviors can be important in establishing trust in working relationships, but modern technologies may challenge our ability to maintain trust in relationships. New technologies are essential features of modern management. Managers in today's business world have access to more communication tools than ever before, with 73% of the CEOs in *Inc's* 500 saying they use their PCs daily.[37] An understanding of the use of these new technologies will influence effective, successful communication during the 1990s and beyond. In addition, it is important to understand how these new technologies affect others' communication and behavior.

■ Written Communication

Chaparral Steel has attempted to use new technologies to create a paperless interface with its customers. Some written communication was still required, however. Forms compose one category of written communication. Manuals make up another. Policy manuals are important in organizations, because they set out guidelines for decision making and rules of actions for organization members. Operations and procedures manuals explain how to perform various tasks and resolve problems that may occur at work. Reports make up a third category of written communication; the company's annual report is an example. Reports may summarize the results of a committee's or department's work or provide information on progress toward certain objectives.

Letters and memorandums are briefer, more frequently used categories of written communication in

■ **TABLE 8.3**
Common Nonverbal Cues from Manager to Employee

NONVERBAL COMMUNICATION	SIGNAL RECEIVED	REACTION FROM RECEIVER
Manager looks away when talking to the employee.	Divided attention.	My supervisor is too busy to listen to my problem or simply does not care.
Manager fails to acknowledge greeting from fellow employee.	Unfriendliness.	This person is unapproachable.
Manager glares ominously (i.e., gives the evil eye).	Anger.	Reciprocal anger, fear, or avoidance, depending on who is sending the signal in the organization.
Manager rolls the eyes.	Not taking person seriously.	This person thinks he or she is smarter or better than I am.
Manager sighs deeply.	Disgust or displeasure.	My opinions do not count. I must be stupid or boring to this person.
Manager uses heavy breathing (sometimes accompanied by hand waving).	Anger or heavy stress.	Avoid this person at all costs.
Manager does not maintain eye contact when communicating.	Suspicion or uncertainty.	What does this person have to hide?
Manager crosses arms and leans away.	Apathy and closed-mindedness.	This person already has made up his or her mind; my opinions are not important.
Manager peers over glasses.	Skepticism or distrust.	He or she does not believe what I am saying.
Manager continues to read a report when employee is speaking.	Lack of interest.	My opinions are not important enough to get the supervisor's undivided attention.

SOURCE: "Steps to Better Listening," by C. Hamilton and B. H. Kleiner, © February 1987. Reprinted with permission, *Personnel Journal*, all rights reserved.

organizations. Letters are formal means of communication—often with people outside the organization—and may vary substantially in length. Memorandums are also formal means of communication, often to constituencies within the organization. Memos are sometimes used to create a formal, historical record of a specific event or occurrence to which people in the organization may want to refer at some future date. Referring back to Table 8.1, we can conclude that written communication has the advantage of high to moderate data capacity and the possible disadvantage of moderate to low information richness.

■ **Communication Technologies**

Computer-mediated communication was once used only by technical specialists, but now influences virtually all managers' behavior in the work environment. Informational data bases are becoming more commonplace. These data bases provide a tremendous amount of information with the push of a button. Another example of an informational data base is the type of system used in many university libraries, in which books and journals are available through an electronic card catalog.

Electronic mail systems represent another technology; users can leave messages via the computer to be accessed at any time by the receiver. This eliminates the time delay of regular mail and allows for immediate reply. The Internet system is an information network system using telephones to link people from many organizations together.

Voicemail systems are another widely used communication mode, especially in sales jobs where people are away from the office. Some voicemail systems even allow the user to retrieve messages from remote locations. Timely retrieval of messages is important. One manager in the office furniture industry had a problem with her voicemail when first learning to use it. She would forget to check it until late in the day. Employees who called about problems early in the day felt frustrated with her slow response time. When using voicemail, it is important to remember that the receiver may not retrieve the messages in a timely manner. Urgent messages must be delivered directly.

Facsimile (fax) machine systems allow the immediate transmission of documents. This medium allows the sender to communicate facts, graphs, and illustrations very rapidly. Fax machines are used in cars, as well as offices and remote locations.

Car phones are also becoming more commonplace. These permit communication while away from the office and on the commute to and from work. They are used extensively in sales jobs involving travel. Not all reactions to car phones are positive. For example, one oil producer did not want a car phone to disturb his thinking time while driving.

■ How Do Communication Technologies Affect Behavior?

The new communication technologies provide faster, more immediate access to information than was available in the past. They provide instant exchange of information in minutes or seconds across geographic boundaries and time zones. Schedules and office hours become irrelevant. The normal considerations of time and distance become less important in the exchange. Hence, these technologies have important influences on people's behavior.

One aspect of computer-mediated communication is its impersonal nature. The sender interacts with a machine, not a person. Studies show that using these technologies results in an increase in flaming, or making rude or obscene outbursts by computer.[38] Interpersonal skills like tact and graciousness diminish, and managers are more blunt when using electronic media. People who participate in discussions quietly and politely when face to face may become impolite, more intimate, and uninhibited when they communicate using computer conferencing or electronic mail.[39]

Another effect of the new technologies is that the nonverbal cues we rely on to decipher a message are absent. Gesturing, touching, facial expressions, and eye contact are not available, so the emotional element of the message is difficult to access. In addition, clues to power, such as organizational position and department membership, may not be available, so the social context of the exchange is altered.

Communication via technologies also changes group interaction. It tends to equalize participation, because group members participate more equally, and charismatic or higher-status members may have less power.[40] Studies of groups that make decisions via computer interaction (computer-mediated groups) have shown that the computer-mediated groups took longer to reach consensus than face-to-face groups. In addition, they were more uninhibited, and there was less influence from any one dominant person. It appears that groups that communicate by computer experience a breakdown of social and organizational barriers.

The potential for overload is particularly great with the new communication technologies. Not only is information available more quickly; the sheer volume of information at the manager's fingertips also is staggering. An individual can easily become overwhelmed by information and must learn to be selective about the information accessed.

Communication technology has advantages as well as a danger. The danger is that managers cannot get away from the office as much as in the past, because they are more accessible to co-workers, subordinates, and the boss via telecommunications. Interactions are no longer confined to the 8:00 to 5:00 work hours.

In addition, the use of new technologies encourages polyphasic activity (that is, doing more than one thing at a time).[41] Managers can simultaneously make phone calls, send computer messages, and work on memos. Polyphasic activity has its advantages in terms of getting more done—but only up to a point. Paying attention to more than one task at a time splits a person's attention and may reduce effectiveness. Constantly focusing on multiple tasks can become a habit, making it psychologically difficult for a person to let go of work.

Finally, the new technologies may make people less patient with face-to-face communication. The speed advantage of the electronic media may translate into an expectation of greater speed in all forms of communication. However, individuals may miss the social interaction with others and may find their social needs unmet. Communicating via computer means an absence of small talk; people tend to get to the point right away.

With many of these technologies, the potential for immediate feedback is reduced, and the exchange can become one way. Managers can use the new technologies more effectively by keeping the following hints in mind:

1. Strive for completeness in your message.
2. Build in opportunities for feedback.
3. Do not assume you will get an immediate response.
4. Ask yourself whether the communication is really necessary.
5. "Disconnect" yourself from the technology at regular intervals.
6. Provide opportunities for social interaction at work.

■ MANAGERIAL IMPLICATIONS: COMMUNICATION WITH STRENGTH AND CLARITY

Interpersonal communication has important implications for the quality of working relationships in organizations. Managers who are sensitive and responsive in communicating with employees encourage the development of trusting, loyal relationships. Managers and employees alike benefit from secure working relations. Managers who are directive, dictatorial, or overbearing with employees are likely to find such behavior counterproductive, especially in periods of change.

Encouraging feedback and practicing reflective listening skills at work can open up communication channels in the work environment. Open communication benefits decision-making processes, because managers are better informed and more likely to base decisions on complete information. Open communication encourages nondefensive relationships, as opposed to defensive relationships, among people at work. Defensive relationships create problems because of the use of tactics that create conflict and division among people.

Managers benefit from sensitivity to employees' nonverbal behavior and territorial space, recognizing that understanding individual and cultural diversity is important in interpreting a person's nonverbal behavior. Seeking verbal clarification on nonverbal cues improves the accuracy of the communication and helps build trusting relationships. In addition, managers benefit from an awareness of their own nonverbal behaviors. Seeking employee feedback about their own nonverbal behavior helps managers provide a message consistent with their intentions.

Managers may complement good interpersonal contact with the appropriate use of new information technology. New information technologies' high data capacity is an advantage in a global workplace. The high information richness of interpersonal contacts is an advantage in a culturally diverse work force. Therefore, managers benefit from both interpersonal and technological media by treating them as complementary modes of communication, not as substitutes for each other.

Chaparral has added an automated phone system that customers can use for specialized information requests. Chaparral then faxes them a rapid response.

Chaparral is still in the early stages of the information age, and the capabilities of the technology are ahead of people's acceptance of it. Needed now are future advances in the technology, such as larger computer screens, coupled with advances in people's attitudes, such as greater trust of people and systems in the absence of a hard copy of a message. Even with advancing information technology, however, the need for interpersonal communication and personal exchange continues. The person cannot and should not be taken out of communication.

■ CHAPTER SUMMARY

- The perceptual screens of communicators and listeners either help clarify or distort a message that is sent and received. Age, gender, and culture influence the sent and received messages.
- Reflective listening involves affirming contact, paraphrasing what is expressed, clarifying the implicit, reflecting "core" feelings, and using ap-

propriate nonverbal behavior to enhance communication.

- The best supervisors talk easily with different kinds of people and listen empathetically. They are generally persuasive and not directive, are sensitive to a person's self-esteem, and are communication minded.
- Physical separation, status differences, gender differences, cultural diversity, and language are potential communication barriers that can be overcome.
- Active or passive defensive communication destroys interpersonal relationships, whereas assertive, nondefensive communication leads to clarity.
- Nonverbal communication includes the use of territorial space, seating arrangements, facial gestures, eye contact, and paralanguage. Nonverbal communication varies by nation and culture around the world.
- New communication technologies include electronic mail, voicemail, fax machines, and car phones. High-tech innovations require high-touch responses.

■ REVIEW QUESTIONS

1. What different components of a person's perceptual screens may distort communication?
2. What are the three defining features of reflective listening? The four levels of verbal response?
3. What are the five communication skills of effective supervisors?
4. Describe superior and subordinate defensive communication. Describe nondefensive communication.
5. What four kinds of nonverbal communication are important in interpersonal relationships?
6. Suppose that you have heard informally that one of your best friends at work is going to be fired. Should you tell your friend or not?
7. If you believe that someone you are working with is lying about the work and deceiving your boss, but you do not have clear proof of it, what should you do?
8. Assume you are a good, empathetic listener. Someone at work confides in you concerning wrongdoing, yet does not ask your advice about what to do. Should you tell the person what to do? Encourage the person to confess? Report the person?

■ REFERENCES

1. G. E. Forward, D. E. Beach, D. A. Gray, and J. C. Quick, "Mentofacturing: A Vision for American Industrial Excellence," *Academy of Management Executive* 5 (1991): 32–44.

2. J. B. Quinn and M. N. Baily, "Information Technology," *Academy of Management Executive* 8 (1994): 28–48.

3. D. L. Whetzel, "The Department of Labor Identifies Workplace Skills," *The Industrial/Organizational Psychologist* (July 1991): 89–90.

4. "Richness" is a term originally coined by W. D. Bodensteiner, "Information Channel Utilization Under Varying Research and Development Project Conditions" (Ph.D. diss., University of Texas at Austin, 1970).

5. A. G. Athos and J. J. Gabarro, *Interpersonal Behavior: Communication and Understanding in Relationships* (Englewood Cliffs, N.J.: Prentice-Hall, 1978); R. Reik, *Listen with the Third Ear* (New York: Pyramid, 1972).

6. Athos and Gabarro, *Interpersonal Behavior*, 432–438.

7. A. Benjamin, *The Helping Interview* (Boston: Houghton Mifflin, 1969).

8. A. D. Mangelsdorff, "Lessons Learned from the Military: Implications for Management" (Distinguished Visiting Lecture, University of Texas at Arlington, 29 January 1993).

9. F. Luthans, "Successful versus Effective Real Managers," *Academy of Management Executive* 2 (1988): 127–132.

10. L. E. Penley, E. R. Alexander, I. E. Jernigan, and C. I. Henwood, "Communication Abilities of Managers: The Relationship of Performance," *Journal of Management* 17 (1991): 57–76.

11. F. M. Jablin, "Superior-Subordinate Communication: The State of the Art," *Psychological Bulletin* 86 (1979): 1201–1222; W. C. Reddin, *Communication within the Organization: An Interpretive Review of Theory and Research* (New York: Industrial Communication Council, 1972).

12. J. C. Quick, D. L. Nelson, and J. D. Quick, *Stress and Challenge at the Top: The Paradox of the Successful Executive* (Chichester, England: Wiley, 1990).

13. H. Mintzberg, *The Nature of Managerial Work* (Englewood Cliffs, N.J.: Prentice-Hall, 1973), 71–75.

14. J. C. Wofford, E. A. Gerloff, and R. C. Cummins, *Organizational Communication: The Keystone to Managerial Effectiveness* (New York: McGraw-Hill, 1977).

15. E. A. Gerloff and J. C. Quick, "Task Role Ambiguity and Conflict in Supervision-Subordinate Relationships," *Journal of Applied Communication Research* 12 (1984): 90–102.

16. E. H. Schein, "Reassessing the 'Divine Rights' of Managers," *Sloan Management Review* 30 (1989): 63–68.

17. D. Tannen, *That's Not What I Mean! How Conversational Style Makes or Breaks Your Relations with Others* (New York: Morrow, 1986).

18. D. Tannen, *You Just Don't Understand* (New York: Ballentine, 1990).

19. G. Hofstede, *Culture's Consequences: International Differences in Work-related Values* (Beverly Hills, Calif.: Sage Publications, 1980).

20. G. Hofstede, "Motivation, Leadership, and Organization: Do American Theories Apply Abroad?" *Organizational Dynamics* 9 (1980): 42–63.

21. H. Levinson, *Executive* (Cambridge, Mass.: Harvard University Press, 1981).

22. T. Wells, *Keeping Your Cool under Fire: Communicating Nondefensively* (New York: McGraw-Hill, 1980).

23. R. D. Laing, *The Politics of the Family and Other Essays* (New York: Pantheon, 1971).

24. H. S. Schwartz, *Narcissistic Process and Corporate Decay: The Theory of the Organizational Ideal* (New York: New York University Press, 1990).

25. M. L. Knapp, *Nonverbal Communication in Human Interaction* (New York: Holt, Rinehart & Winston, 1978); J. McCroskey and L. Wheeless, *Introduction to Human Communication* (New York: Allyn & Bacon, 1976).

26. A. M. Katz and V. T. Katz, eds., *Foundations of Nonverbal Communication* (Carbondale, Ill.: Southern Illinois University Press, 1983).

27. E. T. Hall, *The Hidden Dimension* (Garden City, N.Y.: Doubleday Anchor, 1966).

28. E. T. Hall, "Proxemics," in A. M. Katz and V. T. Katz, eds., *Foundations of Nonverbal Communication* (Carbondale, Ill.: Southern Illinois University Press, 1983).

29. R. T. Barker and C. G. Pearce, "The Importance of Proxemics at Work," *Supervisory Management* 35 (1990): 10–11.

30. R. L. Birdwhistell, *Kinesics and Context* (Philadelphia: University of Pennsylvania Press, 1970).

31. P. Ekman and W. V. Friesen, "Research on Facial Expressions of Emotion," in A. M. Katz and V. T. Katz, eds., *Foundations of Nonverbal Communication* (Carbondale, Ill.: Southern Illinois University Press, 1983).

32. C. Barnum and N. Wolniansky, "Taking Cues from Body Language," *Management Review* 78 (1989): 59.

33. Katz and Katz, *Foundations of Nonverbal Communication*, 181.

34. R. Gifford, C. F. Ng, and M. Wilkinson, "Nonverbal Cues in the Employment Interview: Links between Applicant Qualities and Interviewer Judgments," *Journal of Applied Psychology* 70 (1985): 729–736.

35. P. J. DePaulo and B. M. DePaulo, "Can Deception by Salespersons and Customers Be Detected through Nonverbal Behavioral Cues?" *Journal of Applied Social Psychology* 19 (1989): 1552–1577.

36. P. Ekman, *Telling Lies* (New York: Norton, 1985); D. Goleman, "Nonverbal Cues Are Easy to Misinterpret," *New York Times*, 17 September 1991, B5.

37. "The 1991 Inc. 500 List." Reprinted with permission, *Inc.* Magazine, December 1991. Copyright 1991 Coldhirsh Group, Inc., 38 Commercial Wharf, Boston MA 02110.

38. C. Brod, *Technostress: The Human Cost of the Computer Revolution* (Reading, Mass.: Addison-Wesley, 1984).

39. S. Kiesler, "Technology and the Development of Creative Environments," in Y. Ijiri and R. L. Kuhn, eds, *New Directions in Creative and Innovative Management* (Cambridge, Mass.: Ballinger Press, 1988).

40. S. Kiesler, J. Siegel, and T. W. McGuire, "Social Psychological Aspects of Computer-mediated Communication," *American Psychologist* 39 (1984): 1123–1134.

41. B. A. Baldwin, "Managing the Stress of Technology," *CPA Journal* (October 1990): 94.

Chapter 9
Work Groups and Teams

LEARNING OBJECTIVES

After reading this chapter, you should be able to do the following:

- Define group and team.
- Explain four important aspects of group behavior.
- Describe group formation, the four stages of a group's development, and the characteristics of a mature group.
- Discuss quality circles and quality teams.
- Identify the social benefits of group and team membership.
- Explain the task and maintenance functions in teams.
- Discuss empowerment, teamwork, and self-managed teams.
- Explain the importance of upper echelons and top management teams.

Lee Iacocca received much of the credit for the design of the first Mustang in 1965, but he reported that the venture was a team effort from the beginning.[1] Thus, Ford's use of the Special Vehicle Team (SVT) 28 years later was no departure from company precedent. Indeed, it is difficult to imagine any work environment in which teams and groups do not play a vital role.

A group is two or more people having common interests or objectives.[2] Table 9.1 summarizes Douglas McGregor's characterization of a well-functioning, effective group. A team is a small number of people with complementary skills who are committed to a common mission, performance goals, and approach for which they hold themselves mutually accountable.[3] Groups emphasize individual leadership, individual accountability, and individual work products. Teams emphasize shared leadership, mutual accountability, and collective work products.

The chapter begins with a traditional discussion in the first two sections of group behavior and group development. The third section discusses teams. The final two sections explore the contemporary team issues of empowerment, self-managed teams, and upper echelon teams.

■ TABLE 9.1
Characteristics of a Well-Functioning, Effective Group

> ■ The atmosphere tends to be relaxed, comfortable, and informal.
>
> ■ The group's task is well understood and accepted by the members.
>
> ■ The members listen well to one another; most members participate in a good deal of task-relevant discussion.
>
> ■ People express both their feelings and their ideas.
>
> ■ Conflict and disagreement are present and centered around ideas or methods, not personalities or people.
>
> ■ The group is aware and conscious of its own operations and functions.
>
> ■ Decisions are usually based on consensus, not majority vote.
>
> ■ When actions are decided, clear assignments are made and accepted by members of the group.

■ GROUP BEHAVIOR

Group behavior has been a subject of interest in social psychology for a long time, and many different aspects of group behavior have been studied over the years. We now look at four topics relevant to groups functioning in organizations: norms of behavior, group cohesion, social loafing, and loss of individuality. Group behavior topics related to decision making, such as polarization and groupthink, are addressed in Chapter 10.

■ Norms of Behavior

The standards that a work group uses to evaluate the behavior of its members are its norms of behavior. These norms may be written or unwritten, verbalized or not verbalized, implicit or explicit. Well-understood and accepted norms of behavior, especially with regard to performance, characterize a mature group and are discussed later in the chapter.

Norms may exist in any aspect of work group life. They may evolve informally or unconsciously within a group, or they may arise in response to challenges, such as the norm of disciplined behavior by firefighters in responding to a three-alarm fire to

protect the group.[4] Organizational culture and corporate codes of ethics, such as Johnson & Johnson's credo (see Chapter 2), reflect behavioral norms expected within work groups.

■ Group Cohesion

The "interpersonal glue" that makes the members of a group stick together is group cohesion. Group cohesion can enhance job satisfaction for members and improve organizational productivity.[5] Highly cohesive groups at work may not have many interpersonal exchanges away from the workplace. However, they are able to control and manage their membership better than work groups low in cohesion. This is due to the strong motivation in highly cohesive groups to maintain good, close relationships with other members. We examine group cohesion in further detail, along with factors leading to high levels of group cohesion, when discussing the common characteristics of well-developed groups.

■ Social Loafing

Social loafing occurs when one or more group members rely on the efforts of other group members and fail to contribute their own time, effort, thoughts, or other resources to a group.[6] This may create a real drag on the group's efforts and achievements. Some scholars argue that social loafing, or free riding, is rational behavior from the individual's standpoint to restore an experience of inequity or when individual efforts are hard to observe. However, social loafing shortchanges the group, which loses potentially valuable resources possessed by individual members.[7] A global business environment requires attention to international culture and diversity issues in social loafing, as in other aspects of organizational behavior.[8]

A number of methods for countering social loafing exist, such as identifiable individual contributions to the group product and member self-evaluation systems. For example, if each group member is responsible for a specific input to the group, a member's failure to contribute will be noticed by everyone. If members must formally evaluate their contributions to the group, they are less likely to loaf.

■ Loss of Individuality

Social loafing may be detrimental to group achievement, but it does not have the potentially explosive effects of loss of individuality. Loss of individuality, or deindividuation, is a social process in which individual group members lose self-awareness and its accompanying sense of accountability, inhibition, and responsibility for individual behavior.[9]

When individuality is lost, people may engage in morally reprehensible acts and even violent behavior as committed members of their group or organization. For example, loss of individuality was one of several contributing factors in the violent and aggressive acts that led to the riot that ravaged Los Angeles following the Rodney King verdict in the early 1990s. However, loss of individuality is not always negative or destructive. The loosening of normal ego control mechanisms in the individual may lead to prosocial behavior and heroic acts in dangerous situations.[10] A group that successfully develops into a mature group may not encounter problems with loss of individuality.

■ GROUP FORMATION AND DEVELOPMENT

After its formation, a group goes through predictable stages of development. If successful, it emerges as a mature group. One logical group development model proposes four stages following the group's formation.[11] These stages are mutual acceptance, decision making, motivation and commitment, and control and sanctions. To become a mature group, each of the stages in development must be successfully negotiated.

Within this group development model, a group addresses three types of issues: interpersonal issues, task issues, and authority issues. The interpersonal issues include matters of trust, personal comfort, and security. The task issues include the mission or purpose of the group, the methods the group employs, and the outcomes expected of the group. The authority issues include decisions about questions like these: who is in charge, how power and influence are managed, and who has the right to tell whom to do what. This section addresses group formation, each stage of group development, and the characteristics of a mature group.

■ Group Formation

Formal and informal groups form in organizations for different reasons. Formal groups are sometimes called official or assigned groups, and informal groups may be called unofficial or emergent groups. Formal groups gather to perform various tasks and include an executive and staff, standing committees of the board of directors, project task forces, and temporary committees. An example of a formal group is the task force assembled by the Hospital Corporation of America during the mid-1980s to examine the mission of the corporation. Headed by a divisional vice-president, the task force was composed of 15 members with a wide professional and geographical diversity. The task force met approximately once a month for about nine months to complete its task.

Diversity is an important consideration in the formation of groups. For example, Monsanto Agricultural Company (MAC) created a task force titled Valuing Diversity to address subtle discrimination resulting from work force diversity.[12] The original task force was titled Eliminating Subtle Discrimination (ESD) and was composed of 15 women, minorities, and white males. Subtle discrimination might include the use of gender- or culture-specific language. The intent of MAC and the task force was to build on individual differences—whether in terms of gender, race, or culture—in developing a dominant heterogeneous culture. Education and awareness were key ingredients to an understanding that a diverse work force can be an advantage, not a liability, for a company.

Ethnic diversity has characterized many industrial work groups in the United States since the nineteenth century. This was especially true during the early years of the twentieth century, when waves of immigrant workers came to the country from Germany, Yugoslavia, Italy, Poland, Scotland, the Scandinavian countries, and many other nations.[13] Organizations were challenged to blend these culturally and linguistically diverse peoples into effective work groups.

In addition to ethnic, gender, and cultural diversity, there is interpersonal diversity. Chaparral Steel

Company has a strong, stable team of officers who achieved compatibility through interpersonal diversity. Successful interpersonal relationships are the basis of group effort, a key foundation for business success. In the case of the Chaparral Steel officers, interpersonal compatibility and complimentarity was based on the diversity of needs for inclusion, control, and affection. For example, Libor Rostik and Dennis Beach have strong needs to be included, and President Gordon Forward has a moderate need to include others in his activities. Hence, he is able to satisfy Rostik's and Beach's inclusion needs by involving them in work activities.

Informal groups evolve in the work setting to gratify a variety of member needs not met by formal groups. For example, organization members' inclusion and affection needs might be satisfied through informal athletic or interest groups. Athletic teams representing a department, unit, or company may achieve semiofficial status, such as the American Airlines long-distance running teams who use the corporate logo on their race shirts.

■ Stages of Group Development

All groups, formal and informal, go through four stages of development: mutual acceptance, decision making, motivation and commitment, and control and sanctions.

Mutual Acceptance. Mutual acceptance is the first stage in a group's development. In this stage, the focus is on the interpersonal relations among the members. Members assess one another with regard to trustworthiness, emotional comfort, and evaluative acceptance. For the Valuing Diversity task force at MAC, trust was one of the early issues to be worked through. The power, influence, and authority issues may also emerge at this point if strong personalities immediately attempt to dominate other group members or dictate the group's agenda. This authority issue is also an interpersonal issue related to trust and acceptance. Once team members establish a comfortable level of mutual trust and acceptance, they can focus their attention on the work of the group.

Decision Making. Planning and decision making occur during the second stage of a group's develop-

ment. The focus turns from interpersonal relations to decision-making activities related to the group's task accomplishment. Specifically, the group must decide what its task is and the way to accomplish that task. Wallace Company, an industrial distributor of pipes, valves, and fittings, has found employee teams particularly valuable in this aspect of work life.[14] This second stage may be thought of as the planning stage in a group's development. In addition, the issue of authority often begins to surface during this stage of development, if it did not surface during the first stage. The group addresses authority questions like these: Who is responsible for what aspects of the group's work? Does the group need one primary leader and spokesperson, or not?

Motivation and Commitment. In the third stage of development, the group has largely resolved the interpersonal and task issues. Member attention is directed to self-motivation and the motivation of other group members for task accomplishment. Some members focus on the task function of initiating activity and ensure that the work of the group really gets moving. Other members contribute to motivation and commitment within the group through maintenance functions such as supporting, encouraging, and recognizing the contributions of their teammates, or through establishing the standards that the team may use in evaluating its performance and members. For example, a 25-member leadership group monitors "the flow," Eastman Kodak's unique black-and-white film production process named for its layout design. The people who work the flow are called Zebras. With motivation, commitment, and evaluative feedback from the 25-person leadership team, the Zebras substantially enhanced productivity, profitability, and morale.

The emphasis during the motivation and commitment stage of team development is on execution and achievement, whether through a process of questioning and prodding or through facilitation and work load sharing. If key decisions or plans established in the second stage of development need to be revisited, they are. However, this is done only in the context of getting work done.

Control and Sanctions. In its final stage of development, a group has become a mature, effective, efficient, and productive unit. The group has successfully worked through necessary interpersonal, task, and authority issues. A mature group is characterized by a clear purpose or mission; a well-understood set of norms of behavior; a high level of cohesion; and a clear, but flexible, status structure of leader-follower relationships. A mature group is able to control its members through the judicious application of specific positive and negative sanctions used in response to specific member behaviors. If the group's membership changes, either through a loss of an established member or the inclusion of a newcomer, it may well engage in some activities common in earlier stages of development as it accommodates the newcomer or adjusts to the loss.

■ Characteristics of a Mature Group

The well-functioning, effective group described in Table 9.1 characterizes a mature group. Such a group has four distinguishing characteristics: a clear purpose and mission, well-understood norms and standards of conduct, a high level of group cohesion, and a flexible status structure.

Purpose and Mission.   The purpose and mission may be assigned to a group (as in the case of a Hospital Corporation of America task force, which received a charter to examine the corporate mission) or emerge from within the group (as in the case of the American Airlines long-distance running team). Even in the case of an assigned mission, the group may reexamine, modify, revise, or question the mission. It also may embrace the mission as stated. The importance of mission is exemplified in IBM's Process Quality Management, which requires that a process team of not more than 12 people develop a clear understanding of mission as the first step in the process.[15] The IBM approach demands that all members agree to go in the same direction. The mission statement is converted into a specific agenda, clear goals, and a set of critical success factors. Stating the purpose and mission in the form of specific goals enhances productivity over and above any performance benefits achieved through individual goal setting.

Behavioral Norms.   Behavioral norms, which evolve over a period of time, are well-understood standards of behavior within a group.[16] They are benchmarks against which team members are evaluated and judged by other team members. Some behavioral norms become written rules, such as an attendance policy or an ethical code for a team. Other norms remain informal, although they are no less well understood by team members. Dress codes and norms about after-hours socializing may fall in this category. Behavioral norms also evolve around performance and productivity. The group's productivity norm may or may not be consistent with, and supportive of, the organization's productivity standards. A high-performance team sets productivity standards above organizational expectations with the intent to excel. Average teams set productivity standards based upon, and consistent with, organizational expectations. Noncompliant or counterproductive teams may set productivity standards below organizational expectations with the intent of damaging the organization or creating change.

Group Cohesion.   Group cohesion was earlier described as the interpersonal attraction binding group members together. It enables a group to exercise effective control over its members in relation to its behavioral norms and standards. Goal conflict in a group, unpleasant experiences, and domination of a subgroup are among the threats to a group's cohesion. Groups with low levels of cohesion have greater difficulty exercising control over their members and enforcing their standards of behavior. A classic study of cohesiveness in 238 industrial work groups found cohesion to be an important factor influencing anxiety, tension, and productivity within the groups.[17] Specifically, work-related tension and anxiety were lower in teams high in cohesion, and they were higher in teams low in cohesion, as depicted in Figure 9.1. This suggests that cohesion has a calming effect on team members, at least concerning work-related tension and anxiety. In addition, actual productivity was found to vary significantly less in highly cohesive teams, making these teams much more predictable with regard to their productivity. The actual productivity levels were primarily determined by the productivity norms within each work group. That is, highly cohesive groups with high production standards are very productive. Similarly, highly cohesive groups with low productivity standards are unproductive. Mem-

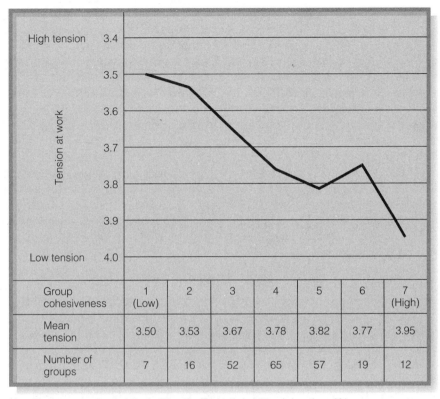

■ **FIGURE 9.1**
Cohesiveness and
Work-Related Tension*

*The measure of tension at work
is based on group mean response to the question, "Does
your work ever make you feel
'jumpy' or nervous?" A low nu-
merical score represents relatively high tension. Chaparral
Steel Officers

Group cohesiveness	1 (Low)	2	3	4	5	6	7 (High)
Mean tension	3.50	3.53	3.67	3.78	3.82	3.77	3.95
Number of groups	7	16	52	65	57	19	12

Note: Product-moment correlation is .28, and critical ratio is 4.20; p is less than .001.

SOURCE: S.E. Seashore, *Group Cohesiveness in the Industrial Work Group* (Ann Arbor, Mich.:
University of Michigan, 1954). Research conducted by Stanley E. Seashore at the Institute for Social Research, University of Michigan.

ber satisfaction, commitment, and communication are better in highly cohesive groups. Groupthink may be a problem in highly cohesive groups and is discussed in Chapter 10.

Group cohesion is influenced by a number of factors, most notably time, size, the prestige of the team, external pressure, and internal competition. Group cohesion evolves gradually over time through a group's normal development. Smaller groups—those of 5 or 7 members, for example—are more cohesive than those of over 25, although cohesion does not decline much with size after 40 or more members. Prestige or social status also influences a group's cohesion, with more prestigious groups, such as the U.S. Air Force Thunderbirds, being highly cohesive. However, even groups of very low prestige may be highly cohesive in the way they stick together. Finally, external pressure and internal competition influence group cohesion. Al-

though the mechanics union, pilots, and other internal constituencies at Eastern Airlines had various differences of opinion, they all pulled together in a cohesive fashion in resisting Frank Lorenzo when he came in to reshape the airline before its demise. Whereas external pressures tend to enhance cohesion, internal competition usually decreases cohesion within a team. This is especially true when there is competition and unresolved conflict over the issue of authority.

Status Structure.   Status structure is the set of authority and task relations among a group's members. The status structure may be hierarchical or egalitarian (i.e. democratic), depending on the group. Successful resolution of the authority issue within a team results in a well-understood status structure of leader-follower relationships. Whereas groups tend to have one leader, teams tend to share leadership. For example, one person may be the team's task master, who sets the agenda, initiates much of the work activity, and ensures that the team meets its deadlines. Another team member may take a leadership role in maintaining effective interpersonal relationships in the group. Hence, shared leadership is very feasible in teams. An effective status structure results in role interrelatedness among group members.

Diversity in a group is healthy, and members may contribute to the collective effort through one of four basic styles.[18] These are the contributor, the collaborator, the communicator, and the challenger. The contributor is data driven, supplies necessary information, and adheres to high performance standards. The collaborator sees the big picture and is able to keep a constant focus on the mission and urge other members to join efforts for mission accomplishment. The communicator listens well, facilitates the group's process, and humanizes the collective effort. The challenger is the devil's advocate who questions everything from the group's mission, purpose, and methods to its ethics. Members may exhibit one or more of these four basic styles over a period of time. In addition, an effective group must have an integrator.[19] This can be especially important in cross-functional teams, where different perspectives carry the seeds of conflict. However, cross-functional teams are not necessarily a problem. Effectively managing cross-functional teams of artists, designers, printers, and financial experts has enabled Hallmark Cards to cut its new-product development time in half.[20]

Emergent leadership in groups was studied among 62 men and 60 women.[21] Groups performed tasks not classified as either masculine or feminine, that is, "sex-neutral" tasks. Men and women both emerged as leaders and neither gender had significantly more emergent leaders. However, group members who described themselves in masculine terms were significantly more likely to emerge as leaders than group members who described themselves in feminine, androgynous (both masculine and feminine), or undifferentiated (neither masculine nor feminine) terms. Hence, gender stereotypes may play a role in emergent leadership.

■ TEAMS AT WORK

Teams are task-oriented work groups; they can be formally designated or informally evolved. Both formal and informal teams make important and valuable contributions to the organization and are important to member need satisfaction. For example, an informal Xerox team from accounting, sales, administration, and distribution saved the company $200 million in inventory costs during 1991 through innovative production and inventory planning.[22]

One classification scheme for teams uses a sports analogy. Some teams work like baseball teams with set responsibilities, others like football teams with coordinated action, and still others like doubles tennis teams with primary yet flexible responsibilities. While each type of team can be useful to the organization, the individual expert should not be overlooked.

■ Why Teams?

Teams are very useful in performing work that is complicated, complex, interrelated, and/or more voluminous than one person can handle. Harold Geneen, while chairman of ITT, said, "If I had enough arms and legs and time, I'd do it all myself." Obviously, people working in organizations cannot do everything because of the limitations of arms, legs, time, expertise, knowledge, and other resources. Individual limitations are overcome through teamwork and collaboration. For example, General Motors' NDH Bearings plant in Sandusky, Ohio, has become a world-class supplier of automotive components in terms of quality, cost, and delivery by emphasizing teamwork, open communication, and advanced technology.[23] In particular, union-management teams, such as the "bid teams," enabled NDH to make impressive gains from 1985 through 1991.

Teams make important contributions to organizations in work areas that lend themselves to teamwork. Teamwork is a core value at Hewlett-Packard, according to CEO Lew Platt. Teamwork is especially suitable for complex, interdependent work tasks and activities requiring collaboration to complete. Teams are appropriate where knowledge, talent, skills, and abilities are dispersed among organization members and require integrated effort for task accomplishment. The recent emphasis on team-oriented work environments is based on empowerment with collaboration, not on power and competition. Larry Hirschhorn labels this "the new team environment"

■   **TABLE 9.2**
A Comparison of the New Team Environment Versus the Old Work Environment

NEW TEAM ENVIRONMENT	OLD WORK ENVIRONMENT
Person comes up with initiatives.	Person follows orders.
Team has considerable authority to chart its own steps.	Team depends on the manager to chart its course.
Members form a team because people learn to collaborate in the face of their emerging right to think for themselves. People both rock the boat and work together.	Members were a team because people conformed to the direction set by the manager. No one rocked the boat.
People cooperate by using their thoughts and feelings. They link up through direct talk.	People cooperated by suppressing their thoughts and feelings. They wanted to get along.

SOURCE: Larry Hirschhorn, *Managing in the New Team Environment* (adapted from p. 13), copyright 1991 by Addison Wesley Publishing Company, Inc. Reprinted by permission.

founded on a significantly more empowered work force in the industrial sectors of the American economy. This new team environment is compared with the old work environment in Table 9.2.

That teams are necessary is a driving principle of total quality efforts in organizations. Total quality efforts often require the formation of teams—especially cross-functional teams composed of people from different functions, such as manufacturing and design, who are responsible for specific organizational processes. While CEO of Motorola, George Fisher emphasized the importance of participation and cooperation as foundations for teamwork and a total quality program. Although teams are an essential feature of a total quality work environment, there is a danger of insufficient training and direction if too many teams are formed very quickly.[24]

■   **Quality Circles and Teams**

Quality circles make up one form of team in a total quality program. Quality circles (QCs) are small groups of employees who work voluntarily on company time—typically one hour per week—to address quality-related problems such as quality control, cost reduction, production planning and techniques, and even product design. Membership in a QC is typically voluntary and fixed once a circle is formed, although some changes may occur as appropriate. QCs use various problem-solving techniques in which they receive training to address the work-related problems.

QCs were popularized as a Japanese management method when an American, W. Edward Deming, exported his thinking about QCs to Japan following World War II.[25] QCs became popular in the United States in the 1980s, when companies such as Ford, Hewlett-Packard, and Eastman Kodak implemented them. KL Spring and Stamping Corporation is an automotive industry supplier that has used quality circles and employee involvement for successful productivity improvements.

QCs must deal with substantive issues if they are to be effective; otherwise, employees begin to believe the QC effort is simply a management ploy. QCs do not necessarily require final decision authority to be effective if their recommendations are always considered seriously and implemented when appropriate. One study found QCs to be effective for a period of time, and then their contributions began to diminish.[26] This may suggest that QCs must be reinforced and periodically reenergized to maintain their effectiveness over long periods of time. Decision making in quality circles and quality teams is discussed in Chapter 10.

Quality teams are different from QCs in that they are more formal, designed and assigned by upper-level management. Quality teams are not voluntary and have more formal power than QCs. Although QCs and quality teams are not intended to provide members with social benefits, all teams in an organization have the potential to afford team members a number of social benefits.

■ Social Benefits

Two sets of social benefits are available to team or group members. One set of social benefits accrues from achieving psychological intimacy. The other comes from achieving integrated involvement.[27]

Psychological intimacy is emotional and psychological closeness to other team or group members. It results in feelings of affection and warmth, unconditional positive regard, opportunity for emotional expression, openness, security and emotional support, and giving and receiving nurturance. The failure to achieve psychological intimacy results in feelings of emotional isolation and loneliness. This may be especially problematic for chief executives who experience the loneliness at the top. Although psychological intimacy is valuable for emotional health and well-being, it need not necessarily be achieved in the work setting.

Integrated involvement is closeness achieved through tasks and activities. It results in enjoyable and involving activities, social identity and self-definition, being valued for one's skills and abilities, opportunity for power and influence, conditional positive regard, and support for one's beliefs and values. The failure to achieve integrated involvement results in social isolation. Whereas psychological intimacy is more emotion-based, integrated involvement is more behavior- and activity-based. Integrated involvement contributes to social psychological health and well-being.

Psychological intimacy and integrated involvement both contribute to overall health. It is not necessary to achieve both in the same team or group. For example, as a marathon runner while chief executive at Xerox Corporation, David Kearns found integrated involvement with his executive team and psychological intimacy with his athletic companions on long-distance runs.

Teams and groups have two sets of functions that operate to enable members to achieve psychological intimacy and integrated involvement. These are task and maintenance functions.

■ Task and Maintenance Functions

An effective team carries out various task functions to perform its work successfully and various main-

■ TABLE 9.3
Task and Maintenance Functions in Teams or Groups

TASK FUNCTIONS	MAINTENANCE FUNCTIONS
Initiating activities	Supporting others
Seeking information	Following others' leads
Giving information	Gatekeeping communication
Elaborating concepts	Setting standards
Coordinating activities	Expressing member feelings
Summarizing ideas	Testing group decisions
Testing ideas	Consensus testing
Evaluating effectiveness	Harmonizing conflict
Diagnosing problems	Reducing tension

tenance functions to ensure member satisfaction and a sense of team spirit. Teams that successfully fulfill these functions afford their members the potential for psychological intimacy and integrated involvement. Table 9.3 presents nine task and nine maintenance functions in teams or groups.

Task functions are those activities directly related to the effective completion of the team's work. For example, the task of initiating activity involves suggesting ideas, defining problems, and proposing approaches and/or solutions to problems. The task of seeking information involves asking for ideas, suggestions, information, or facts. Effective teams have members who fulfill various task functions as they are required.

Some task functions are more important at one time in the life of a group, and other functions are more important at other times. For example, during the engineering test periods for new technologies, the engineering team needs members who focus on testing the practical applications of suggestions and those who diagnose problems and suggest solutions.

The effective use of task functions leads to the success of the team, and the failure to use them may lead to disaster. For example, the successful initiation and coordination of an emergency room (ER) team's activities by the senior resident saved the life of a knife wound victim.[28] The victim was stabbed one quarter inch below the heart, and the ER team acted quickly to stem the bleeding, begin intravenous fluids, and monitor the victim's vital signs.

Maintenance functions are those activities essential to effective, satisfying interpersonal relationships within a team or group. For example, following another group member's lead may be as important as leading others. Communication gatekeepers within a group ensure balanced contributions from all members. Because task activities build tension into teams and groups working together, tension-reduction activities are important to drain off negative or destructive feelings. For example, in a study of 25 work groups over a five-year period, humor and joking behavior were found to enhance the social relationships in the groups.[29] The researchers concluded that performance improvements in the 25 groups resulted indirectly from improved relationships attributable to the humor and joking behaviors. Maintenance functions enhance togetherness, cooperation, and teamwork, enabling members to achieve psychological intimacy while furthering the success of the team. Joseph M. Grant's supportive attitude and comfortable demeanor as chief financial officer of Electronic Data Systems have enabled him to build a strong finance organization in the corporation. Grant is respected for his expertise and his ability to build relationships. Both task and maintenance functions are important for successful teams.

EMPOWERMENT AND SELF-MANAGED TEAMS

Quality circles and quality teams, as we discussed earlier, are ways to implement teamwork in organizations. Self-managed teams are broad-based work teams that deal with issues beyond quality. Decision making in self-managed teams is also discussed in Chapter 10. General Motors' NDH Bearings plant, for example, fostered teamwork by empowering employees to make important decisions at work. The company's approach was to push decision making down throughout the plant.

Empowerment may be thought of as an attribute of a person or of an organization's culture.[30] As an organizational culture attribute, empowerment encourages participation, an essential ingredient for teamwork.[31] Quality Action Teams (QATs) at Federal Express are the primary Quality Improvement Process (QIP) technique used by the company to engage management and hourly employees in four- to ten-member problem-solving teams. The teams are empowered to act and solve problems as specific as charting the best route from the Phoenix airport to the local distribution center or as global as making major software enhancements to the COSMOS IIB on-line package-tracking system.

Empowerment may give employees the power of a lightning strike, but empowered employees must be properly focused through careful planning and preparation before they use the power.[32]

Foundations for Empowerment

Organizational and individual foundations underlie empowerment that enhances task motivation and performance. The organizational foundations for empowerment include a participative, supportive organizational culture and a team-oriented work design. A participative, supportive work environment is essential because of the uncertainty that empowerment can cause within the organization. Empowerment requires that lower-level organizational members be able to make decisions and take action on those decisions. As operational employees become empowered, the process can create real fear, anxiety, or even terror among middle managers in the organization.[33] Senior leadership must create an organizational culture that is supportive and reassuring for these middle managers as the power dynamics of the system change. If not supported and reassured, the middle managers can become a restraining, disruptive force to empowerment.

A second organizational foundation for empowerment concerns the design of work. The old factory system relied on work specialization and narrow tasks with the intent of achieving routinized efficiency.[34] This approach to the design of work had some economic advantages, but it also had some distressing disadvantages leading to monotony and fatigue. The old factory approach is inconsistent with empowerment and teamwork, because it leads the individual to feel absolved of much responsibility for a whole piece of work. Team-oriented work designs are key organizational foundations for empowerment, because they lead to broader tasks and a greater sense of responsibility. For example, Volvo builds cars using a team-oriented work design in which each person does many different tasks, and each person has direct responsibility for the finished product.[35] Such work designs create a context for effective empowerment so long as the empowered individuals meet necessary individual prerequisites.

The three individual prerequisites for empowerment include (1) the capability to become psychologically involved in participative activities, (2) the motivation to act autonomously, and (3) the capacity to see the relevance of participation for one's own well-being.[36] First, people must be psychologically equipped to become involved in participative activities if they are to be empowered and become effective team members. Not all people are so predisposed. For example, Germany has an authoritarian tradition that runs counter to participation and empowerment at the individual and group level. General Motors encountered significant difficulties implementing quality circles in its German plants, because workers expected to be directed by supervisors, not to engage in participative problem solving. The German effort to establish supervisory/worker boards in corporations is an attempt to alter this authoritarian tradition.

A second individual prerequisite to empowerment and teamwork is the motivation to act autonomously. People with dependent personalities are predisposed to be told what to do and to rely on external motivation rather than internal, intrinsic motivation.[37] These dependent people are not effective team members. The prerequisite of a motivation to act autonomously creates a dynamic tension or paradox for people; they are asked to act autonomously and independently while also subordinating themselves to the team. This is the heart of the conflict between individual autonomy and group membership. Managing the conflict requires balancing the processes of developing individual identity and blending one's identity with other people.

Finally, if empowerment is to work, people must be able to see how it provides a personal benefit to them. The personal payoff for the individual need not be short-term. It may be a long-term benefit that they foresee. Thus, empowerment becomes of instrumental value to the person in achieving work satisfaction; in receiving greater rewards through enhanced organizational profitability; or in reshaping the design of work, and ultimately the organization, to a more humanistic "fit."

■ Empowerment Skills

Empowerment through employee self-management is an alternative to empowerment through teamwork.[38] Whether through self-management or teamwork, empowerment requires the development of certain skills if it is to be enacted effectively. The first skills required for empowerment are competence skills. Mastery and experience in one's chosen discipline and profession provide an essential foundation for empowerment. This means that new employees and trainees should experience only limited empowerment until they demonstrate the capacity to accept more responsibility, a key aspect of empowerment.

Empowerment also requires certain process skills. The most critical include negotiating skills, especially with allies, opponents, and adversaries.[39] Allies are the easiest people to negotiate with, because they agree with you about the team's mission, and you can trust their actions and behavior. Opponents require a different negotiating strategy; although you can predict their actions and behavior, they do not agree with your concept of the team's mission. Adversaries are dangerous, difficult people to negotiate with because you cannot predict their actions or behaviors, and they do not agree with your concept of the team's mission.

A third set of empowerment skills is the development of cooperative and helping behaviors.[40] Cooperative people are motivated to maximize the gains for everyone on the team; they engage in encouraging, helpful behavior to bring about that end. The alternatives to cooperation are competitive, individualistic, and egalitarian orientations. Competitive people are motivated to maximize their personal gains regardless of the expense to other people. This can be very counterproductive from the standpoint of the team. Individualistic people are motivated to act autonomously, though not necessarily to maximize their personal gains. They are less prone to contribute to the efforts of the team. Egalitarian people are motivated to equalize the outcomes for each team member, which may or may not be beneficial to the team's well-being.

Communication skills are the final set of essential empowerment skills. These include skills in self-expression and reflective listening. We explored these skills in detail in Chapter 8. Empowerment cannot occur in a team unless members are able to express themselves effectively, as well as listen carefully to one another.

■ Self-Managed Teams

Self-managed teams make decisions that were once reserved for managers. They are sometimes called self-directed teams or autonomous work groups. Self-managed teams form one way to implement empowerment in organizations. Self-managed teams may have a positive impact on employee attitudes, if not necessarily absenteeism or turnover. Evaluative research is helpful in achieving a better understanding of this relatively new way of approaching teamwork and the design of work. Research can help in establishing expectations for self-managed teams. For example, it is probably unreasonable to expect these teams to be fully functional and self-directed in short periods of time. It may take two or three years for new teams to be fully self-directed.

Other evaluations of self-managed teams are more positive. Southwest Industries engaged in a major reorganization based on self-managed teams to fit its high-technology production process. The results included a 30% increase in shipment, a 30% decrease in lead time, a 40% decrease in total inventory, a decrease in machine downtime, and a decrease of over 30% in production costs.

A game (Learning Teams) is available to help people create self-directed teams, learn cooperatively, and master factual information.[41] With no outside help, an engineering team in Texas Instruments' Defense Systems and Electronics Group (DSEG) developed themselves into a highly effective, productive, self-managed team. They then helped DSEG in their successful effort to win a Malcolm Baldrige National Quality Award.

■ UPPER ECHELONS: TEAMS AT THE TOP

Self-managed teams at the top of the organization—top-level executive teams—are referred to as upper echelons. Organizations are often a reflection of these upper echelons.[42] Upper echelon theory argues that the background characteristics of the top management team can predict organizational characteristics. Furthermore, the upper echelon is one key to the strategic success of the organization.[43] Thus, the teams at the top are instrumental in defining the organization over time such that the values, competence, ethics, and unique characteristics of the top management team are eventually reflected throughout the organization. This great power and influence throughout the entire organization makes the top management team a key to the organization's success.

For example, when Lee Iacocca became CEO at Chrysler Corporation, his top management team was assembled to bring about strategic realignment within the corporation by building on Chrysler's historical engineering strength. The dramatic success of Chrysler during the early 1980s was followed by struggle and accommodation during the late 1980s. This raises the question of how long a CEO and the top management team can sustain organizational success.

Hambrick and Fukutomi address this question by examining the dynamic relationship between a CEO's tenure and the success of the organization.[44] They found five seasons in a CEO's tenure: (1) response to a mandate, (2) experimentation, (3) selection of an enduring theme, (4) convergence, and (5) dysfunction. All else being equal, this seasons model has significant implications for organizational performance. Specifically, organizational performance increases with a CEO's tenure to a peak, after which performance declines. This relationship is depicted in Figure 9.2. The peak has been found to come at about seven years—somewhere in the middle of the executive's seasons. As indicated by the dotted lines in the figure, the peak may be extended, depending on several factors, such as diversity in the executive's support team.

From an organizational health standpoint, diversity and depth in the top management team enhances the CEO's well-being. From a performance standpoint, the CEO's top management team can influence the timing of the performance peak, the degree of dysfunction during the closing season of the CEO's tenure, and the rate of decline in organi-

■ **FIGURE 9.2**
Executive Tenure and
Organizational Performance

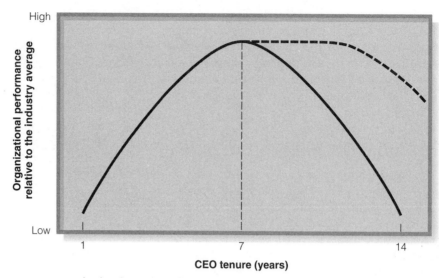

SOURCE: D. Hambrick, "The Seasons of an Executive's Tenure," keynote address, the Sixth Annual Texas Conference on Organizatins, Lago Vista, Texas, April, 1991.

zational performance. Diversity and heterogeneity in the top management team help sustain high levels of organizational performance at the peak and help maintain the CEO's vitality. The presence of a "wild turkey" in the top management team can be a particularly positive force. The wild turkey is a devil's advocate who challenges the thinking of the CEO and other top executives and provides a counterpoint during debates. If not shouted down or inhibited, the wild turkey helps the CEO and the team sustain peak performance and retard the CEO's dysfunction and decline. Roger Smith and General Motors lost a possible opportunity to change and improve the corporation's performance by silencing Ross Perot, a wild turkey, after GM's acquisition of EDS. Because Perot's ideas were never implemented at GM, we will never know if they would have been beneficial. Perot was inhibited, and GM's decline continued.

We can conclude that the leadership, composition, and dynamics of the top management team have an important influence on the organization's performance. In some cases, corporations have eliminated the single CEO. For example, in early 1992, Xerox and Microsoft announced plans for a team of executives to function in lieu of a president.[45] Walter Wriston created such a three-member team when he was chairman at Citicorp.

■ **Multicultural Teams**

The backgrounds of group members may be quite different in the global workplace. Homogeneous groups in which all members share similar backgrounds are giving way to token groups in which all but one member come from the same background, bicultural groups in which two or more members represent each of two distinct cultures, and multicultural groups in which members represent three or more ethnic backgrounds.[46] Diversity within a group may increase the uncertainty, complexity, and inherent confusion in group processes, making it more difficult for the group to achieve its full potential productivity.[47] The advantages of culturally diverse groups include the generation of more and better ideas while limiting the risk of groupthink, to be discussed in Chapter 10.

■ **MANAGERIAL IMPLICATIONS: TEAMWORK FOR PRODUCTIVITY AND QUALITY**

Work groups and teams are important vehicles through which organizations achieve high-quality performance. The current emphasis on the new team environment, shown in Table 9.2, places unique demands on managers, teams and individuals in leading, working, and managing. Managing these demands requires an understanding of individual diversity and the interrelationships of individuals, teams, and managers. Expectations associated with these three key organizational roles for people at work are different. The first role is as an individual, empowered employee. The second is as an active member of one or more teams. The third is the role of manager or formal supervisor. Earlier in the chapter, we discussed the foundations for teamwork, empowerment, and skills for working in the new team environment. Individual empowerment must be balanced with collaborative teamwork.

The manager in the triangle is responsible for creating a receptive organizational environment for work groups and teams. This requires that the manager achieve a balance between setting limits (so that individuals and teams do not go too far afield) and removing barriers (so that empowered individuals and self-managed teams can accomplish their work). In addition, the manager should establish a flexible charter for each team. Once the charter is established, the manager continues to be available to the team as a coaching resource, as necessary. The manager establishes criteria for evaluating the performance effectiveness of the team, as well as the individuals, being supervised. In an optimum environment, this involves useful and timely performance feedback to teams that carries a sense of equity and fairness with it. The manager's responsibilities are different from the team leader's.

Effective team leaders may guide a work group or share leadership responsibility with their teams, especially self-managed teams. Team leaders are active team members with responsibility for nurturing the development and performance of the team. They require skills different from those of the manager. Whereas the manager establishes the environment in which teams flourish, the team leader teaches, listens, solves problems, manages conflict, and enhances the dynamics of team functioning to ensure the team's success. It is the team leader's task to bring the team to maturity; help the team work through interpersonal, task, and authority issues; and be skilled in nurturing a cohesive, effective team. The skills a team leader requires are the hands-on skills of direct involvement and full membership in the team. Flexibility, delegation, and collaboration are characteristics of healthy teams and team leaders. Increasing globalization requires team leaders to be skilled at forging teamwork among diverse individuals, whereas managers must be skilled at forging collaboration among diverse groups.

■ CHAPTER SUMMARY

■ Groups are often composed of diverse people at work. Teams in organizations are a key to enhance quality and achieve success.

■ Important aspects of group behavior include norms of behavior, group cohesion, social loafing, and loss of individuality.

■ Once a group forms, it goes through four stages of development. If successful, the group emerges as a mature group with a purpose, clear behavioral norms, high cohesion, and a flexible status structure.

■ Quality circles, originally popularized in Japan, and quality teams contribute to solving technological and quality problems in the organization.

■ Teams provide social benefits for team members, as well as enhance organizational performance.

■ Empowerment and teamwork require specific organizational design elements and individual psychological characteristics and skills.

■ Upper echelons and top management teams are key players in determining the strategy and performance of an organization. Diversity and a devil's advocate, or "wild turkey," in the top management team enhance organizational performance.

■ Managing in the new team environment places new demands on managers, teams, and individuals. Managers must create a supportive and flexible environment for collaborative teams and empowered individuals. Team leaders must nurture the team's development.

■ REVIEW QUESTIONS

1. What is a group? A team?
2. Assume you know someone who is engaged in social loafing within a group of which you are a

member. What should you do? Is this person acting in an unethical manner?

3. Explain what happens in each of the four stages of a group's development. When does the group address interpersonal issues? Task issues? Authority issues?

4. Describe the four characteristics of mature groups.

5. Why are teams important to organizations today? How and why are teams formed?

6. What are the organizational foundations of empowerment and teamwork? The individual foundations?

7. Suppose an empowered employee makes a mistake at your place of work that damages some property but does not hurt anyone. Assuming the employee was empowered to act, should the employee be punished for the unfortunate consequences of the action? Would your answer differ according to whether the employee had or had not been properly trained and supervised before being empowered?

8. What is the role of the manager in the new team environment? What is the role of the team leader?

■ REFERENCES

1. L. Iacocca, *Iacocca: An Autobiography* (New York: Bantam Books, 1984).

2. M. E. Shaw, *Group Dynamics: The Psychology of Small Group Behavior* (New York: McGraw-Hill, 1971).

3. J. R. Katzenbach and D. K. Smith, "The Discipline of Teams," *Harvard Business Review* 71 (1993): 111–120.

4. K. L. Bettenhausen and J. K. Murnighan, "The Development and Stability of Norms in Groups Facing Interpersonal and Structural Challenge," *Administrative Science Quarterly* 36 (1991): 20–35.

5. I. Summers, T. Coffelt, and R. E. Horton, "Work-Group Cohesion," *Psychological Reports* 63 (1988): 627–636.

6. K. H. Price, "Decision Responsibility, Task Responsibility, Identifiability, and Social Loafing," *Organizational Behavior and Human Decision Processes* 40 (1987): 330–345.

7. R. Albanese and D. D. Van Fleet, "Rational Behavior in Groups: The Free-riding Tendency," *Academy of Management Review* 10 (1985): 244–255.

8. W. J. Duncan, "Why Some People Loaf in Groups while Others Loaf Alone," Research Translation, *Academy of Management Executive* 8 (1994): 79–80.

9. E. Diener, "Deindividuation, Self-awareness, and Disinhibition," *Journal of Personality and Social Psychology* 37 (1979): 1160–1171.

10. S. Prentice-Dunn and R. W. Rogers, "Deindividuation and the Self-regulation of Behavior," in P. Paulus, ed., *Psychology of Group Influence* (Hillsdale, N.J.: Erlbaum, 1989), 87–109.

11. B. M. Bass and E. C. Ryterband, *Organizational Psychology* 2d ed. (Boston: Allyn & Bacon, 1979); B. W. Tuckman, "Developmental Sequences in Small Groups," *Psychological Bulletin* 63 (1963): 384–399.

12. S. Caudron, "Monsanto Responds to Diversity," *Personnel Journal* (November 1990): 72–80.

13. W. P. Anthony, "Managing Diversity, Then and Now," *Wall Street Journal*, 3 July 1992, A8.

14. D. Nichols, "Quality Program Sparked Company Turnaround," *Personnel* (October 1991): 24. For a commentary on Wallace's hard times and subsequent emergence from Chapter 11 bankruptcy, see R. C. Hill, "When the Going Gets Tough: A Baldrige Award Winner on the Line," *Academy of Management Executive* 7 (1993): 75–79.

15. M. Hardaker and B. K. Ward, "How to Make a Team Work," *Harvard Business Review* 65 (1987): 112–120.

16. K. L. Bettenhausen and J. K. Murnighan, "The Emergence of Norms in Competitive Decision-making Groups," *Administrative Science Quarterly* 30 (1985): 350–372; K. L. Bettenhausen, "Five Years of Groups Research: What We Have Learned and What Needs to Be Addressed," *Journal of Management* 17 (1991): 345–381.

17. S. E. Seashore, *Group Cohesiveness in the Industrial Work Group* (Ann Arbor, Mich.: University of Michigan, 1954).

18. G. Parker, *Team Players and Teamwork* (San Francisco: Jossey-Bass, 1990).

19. N. R. F. Maier, "Assets and Liabilities in Group Problem Solving: The Need for an Integrative Function," *Psychological Review* 74 (1967): 239–249.

20. T. A. Stewart, "The Search for the Organization of Tomorrow," *Fortune*, 18 May 1992, 92–98.

21. J. R. Goktepe and C. E. Schneier, "Role of Sex, Gender Roles, and Attraction in Predicting Emergent Leaders," *Journal of Applied Psychology* 74 (1989): 165–167.

22. B. Dumaine, "The Bureaucracy Busters," *Fortune*, 17 June 1991, 36.

23. J. H. Sheridan, "A Star in the GM Heavens," *Industry Week*, 18 March 1991, 50–54.

24. P. McLagan, "The Dark Side of Quality," *Training*, November 1991, 13–33.

25. W. L. Mohr and H. Mohr, *Quality Circles: Changing Images of People at Work* (Reading, Mass.: Addison-Wesley, 1983).

26. R. W. Griffin, "A Longitudinal Assessment of the Consequences of Quality Circles in an Industrial Setting," *Academy of Management Journal* 31 (1988): 338–358.

27. P. Shaver and D. Buhrmester, "Loneliness, Sex-Role Orientation, and Group Life: A Social Needs Perspective," in P.

Paulus, ed., *Basic Group Processes* (New York: Springer-Verlag, 1985), 259–288.

28. J. D. Quick, G. Moorhead, J. C. Quick, E. A. Gerloff, K. L. Mattox, and C. Mullins, "Decision Making among Emergency Room Residents: Preliminary Observations and a Decision Model," *Journal of Medical Education* 58: 117–125.

29. W. J. Duncan and J. P. Feisal, "No Laughing Matter: Patterns of Humor in the Workplace," *Organizational Dynamics* 17 (1989): 18–30.

30. K. W. Thomas and B. A. Velthouse, "Cognitive Elements of Empowerment: An 'Interpretive' Model of Intrinsic Task Motivation," *Academy of Management Review* 15 (1990): 666–681.

31. R. R. Blake, J. S. Mouton, and R. L. Allen, *Spectacular Teamwork: How to Develop the Leadership Skills for Team Success* (New York: Wiley, 1987).

32. W. C. Byham, *ZAPP! The Human Lightning of Empowerment* (Pittsburgh: Developmental Dimensions, 1989).

33. T. L. Brown, "Fearful of 'Empowerment': Should Managers Be Terrified?" *Industry Week*, 18 June 1990, 12.

34. L. Hirschhorn, "Stresses and Patterns of Adjustment in the Postindustrial Factory," in G. M. Green and F. Baker, eds., *Work, Health, and Productivity* (New York: Oxford University Press, 1991), 115–126.

35. P. G. Gyllenhammar, *People at Work* (Reading, Mass.: Addison-Wesley, 1977).

36. R. Tannenbaum and F. Massarik, "Participation by Subordinates in the Managerial Decision-making Process," *Canadian Journal of Economics and Political Science* 16 (1950): 408–418.

37. H. Levinson, *Executive* (Cambridge, Mass.: Harvard University Press, 1981).

38. F. Shipper and C. C. Manz, "Employee Self-management Without Formally Designated Teams: An Alternative Road to Empowerment," *Organizational Dynamics*, (Winter 1992): 48–62.

39. P. Block, *The Empowered Manager: Positive Political Skills at Work* (San Francisco: Jossey-Bass, 1987).

40. V. J. Derlega and J. Grzelak, eds., *Cooperation and Helping Behavior: Theories and Research* (New York: Academic Press, 1982).

41. S. Thiagaraian, "A Game for Cooperative Learning," *Training and Development* (May 1992): 35–41.

42. D. C. Hambrick and P. Mason, "Upper Echelons: The Organization as a Reflection of Its Top Managers," *Academy of Management Review* 9 (1984): 193–206.

43. D. C. Hambrick, "The Top Management Team: Key to Strategic Success," *California Management Review* 30 (1987): 88–108.

44. D. C. Hambrick and G. D. S. Fukutomi, "The Seasons of a CEO's Tenure," *Academy of Management Review* 16 (1991): 719–742.

45. A. Bennett, "Firms Run by Executive Teams Can Reap Rewards, Incur Risks," *Wall Street Journal*, 5 February 1991, B1, B2.

46. N. J. Adler, *International Dimensions of Organizational Behavior* (Boston: PWS-KENT, 1991).

47. I. D. Steiner, *Group Process and Productivity* (New York: Academic Press, 1972).

CHAPTER 10
DECISION MAKING BY
INDIVIDUALS AND GROUPS

LEARNING OBJECTIVES

After reading this chapter, you should be able to do the following:

■ Explain the assumptions of bounded rationality.
■ Describe Jung's cognitive styles and how they affect managerial decision making.
■ Understand the role of creativity in decision making.
■ Identify the advantages and disadvantages of group decision making.
■ Discuss the symptoms of groupthink and ways to prevent it.
■ Evaluate the strengths and weaknesses of several group decision-making techniques.
■ Describe the effects that expert systems and group decision support systems have on decision making in organizations.
■ Utilize an "ethics check" for examining managerial decisions.

■ THE DECISION MAKING PROCESS

For managers, decision making is a critical activity. The decisions a manager faces can range from very simple, routine matters for which the manager has an established decision rule (programmed decisions) to new and complex decisions that demand creative solutions (nonprogrammed decisions).[1] Scheduling lunch hours for one's work team is a programmed decision. The manager performs the decision activity on a daily basis, using established procedures with the same clear goal in mind. An example of a non-programmed decision was Federal Express's decision to acquire Flying Tigers to expand its international operations. FedEx needed Flying Tigers' routes to Malaysia, Australia, and the Philippines. The decision to acquire the company was unique, was unstructured, and required considerable judg-

■ **FIGURE 10.1**
The Decision-Making Process

Recognize the problem and the need for a decision.

↓

Identify the objective of the decision.

↓

Gather and evaluate data and diagnose the situation.

↓

List and evaluate alternatives.

↓

Select the best course of action.

↓

Implement the decision.

↓

Gather feedback.

↓

Follow up.

ment. Regardless of the type of decision made, managers must understand as much as possible about how individuals and groups make decisions.

Decision making is a process involving a series of steps, as shown in Figure 10.1. The first step is recognition of the problem; that is, the manager realizes that a decision must be made. Identification of the real problem is important; otherwise, the manager may be reacting to symptoms and firefighting rather than dealing with the source of the problem. It is also important at this stage to identify the objective of the decision. In other words, the manager must determine what is to be accomplished by the decision.

The second step in the decision making process is gathering information relevant to the problem. The manager must pull together sufficient information about why the problem occurred. This involves conducting a thorough diagnosis of the situation and going on a fact-finding mission.

The third step is listing and evaluating alternative courses of action. During this step, a thorough "what if" analysis should also be conducted to determine the various factors that could influence the outcome of the decision. Managers must generate a wide range of options and creative solutions in order to be able to move on to the fourth step.

Next, the manager selects the alternative that best meets the decision objective. If the problem has been diagnosed correctly and sufficient alternatives have been identified, this step is much easier.

Finally, the solution is implemented. The situation must then be monitored to see whether the decision met its objective. Consistent monitoring and periodic feedback are essential elements in the follow-up process.

Decision making is often stressful. One U.S. Navy research and development (R & D) project manager described it this way: "The decision to use a particular piece of equipment at the U.S. Navy's primary ship-to-shore radio wireline interface sites was very stressful to me. The decision had an international impact, and I had to consider joint service/NATO/U.S. Navy interoperability, developmental risks, and budgetary constraints in the decision."[2] R & D project managers in the U.S. Navy are faced with large-scale technologically sophisticated projects that require nonprogrammed decisions. They must make decisions with significant risk and uncertainty, often without full information. They must trust and rely on others in arriving at their decisions, but they are ultimately responsible.

■ MODELS OF DECISION MAKING

The U.S. Navy project manager just described, like all managers, must make effective decisions. An effective decision is timely, is acceptable to the individuals affected by it, and meets the desired objective. This section describes three models of decision making: the rational model, the bounded rationality model, and the garbage can model.

■ Rational Model

Rationality refers to a logical, step-by-step approach to decision making, with a thorough analysis of alternatives and their consequences. The rational model of decision making is derived from classic economic theory and contends that the decision maker is completely rational in his or her approach. The rational model has the following important assumptions:

1. The outcome will be completely rational.
2. The decision maker has a consistent system of preferences, which is used to choose the best alternative.
3. The decision maker is aware of all the possible alternatives.
4. The decision maker can calculate the probability of success for each alternative.[3]

In the rational model, the decision maker strives to *optimize,* that is, to select the best possible alternative.

Given the assumptions of the rational model, it may seem unrealistic for the managerial job. There are time constraints and limits to human knowledge and information-processing capabilities. In addition, a manager's preferences frequently change. The rational model is thus an ideal that managers strive for in making decisions. It captures the way a decision should be made but does not reflect the reality of managerial decision making.

■ Bounded Rationality Model

Recognizing the deficiencies of the rational model, Herbert Simon suggested that there are limits upon how rational a decision maker can actually be. His decision theory, the bounded rationality model, earned a Nobel Prize in 1978.

Simon's model, also referred to as the "administrative man" theory, rests on the idea that there are constraints that force a decision maker to be less than completely rational. The bounded rationality model has four assumptions:

1. Managers select the first alternative that is satisfactory.
2. Managers recognize that their conception of the world is simple.

3. Managers are comfortable making decisions without determining all the alternatives.
4. Managers make decisions by rules of thumb or heuristics.

Bounded rationality assumes that managers *satisfice;* that is, they select the first alternative that is "good enough," because the costs of optimizing in terms of time and effort are too great. Further, the theory assumes that managers develop shortcuts, called heuristics, to make decisions in order to save mental activity. Heuristics are rules of thumb that allow managers to make decisions based on what has worked in past experiences.

Does the bounded rationality model more realistically portray the managerial decision process? Research indicates that it does.[4] One of the reasons managers face limits to their rationality is because they must make decisions under risk and time pressure. The situation they find themselves in is highly uncertain, and the probability of success is not known.

■ Garbage Can Model

Sometimes the decision–making process in organizations appears to be haphazard and unpredictable. In the garbage can model, decisions are random and unsystematic.[5] Figure 10.2 depicts the garbage can model. In this model, the organization is a garbage can in which problems, solutions, participants, and choice opportunities are floating around randomly. If the four factors happen to connect, a decision is made. The quality of the decision depends on timing. The right participants must find the right solution to the right problem at the right time.

The garbage can model illustrates the idea that not all organizational decisions are made in a step-by-step, systematic fashion. Especially under conditions of high uncertainty, the decision process may be chaotic. Some decisions appear to happen out of sheer luck.

■ DECISION MAKING AND RISK

Federal Express's management team faced many risks in their decision to acquire Flying Tiger. Would the two groups of employees mesh well? What

■ FIGURE 10.2
The Garbage Can Model

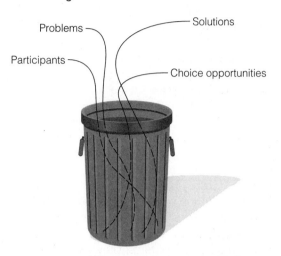

Problems —
Participants —
Solutions
Choice opportunities

SOURCE: Reprinted from "A Garbage Can Model of Organizational Choice," M. D. Cohen, J. G. March, and J. P. Olsen. Published in *Administrative Science Quarterly* 17 (March 1972) 1–25. Used with permission of *Administrative Science Quarterly*.

would be their competitors' reactions? Could Federal Express generate enough international business to make a profit, given the costliness of the acquisition? The uncertainty of these issues made it a risky decision.

Individuals differ in terms of their willingness to take risks. Some managers are risk averse. They choose options that entail fewer risks, preferring familiarity and certainty. Other managers are risk takers; that is, they accept greater potential for loss in decisions, tolerate greater uncertainty, and in general are more likely to make risky decisions.

Research indicates that women are more averse to risk taking than men and that older, more experienced managers are more risk averse than younger managers. There is also some evidence that successful managers take more risks than unsuccessful managers.[6] However, the tendency to take risks or avoid them is only part of behavior toward risk. Risk taking is influenced not only by an individual's tendency but also by the specific situation the decision maker faces.

The way managers behave in response to uncertainty and risk has important implications for organizations. Many individuals find uncertainty stressful, and one of the negative consequences of distress in organizations is faulty decision making by managers. One way to manage the decision–making behavior of employees is for managers to model effective decision making under uncertainty by displaying the desired behavior. This communicates to employees the acceptable level of risk-taking behavior in the organization.

Upper-level managers face a definite challenge in managing risk-taking behavior. By discouraging lower-level managers from taking risks, they may stifle creativity and innovation. However, if upper-level managers are going to encourage risk taking, they must allow employees to fail without fear of punishment. The key is establishing a consistent attitude toward risk within the organization.

When individuals take risks, losses may occur. Suppose an oil producer thinks there is an opportunity to uncover oil by reentering an old drilling site. She gathers a group of investors, she shows them the logs, and they contribute funds to finance the venture. The reentry is drilled to a certain depth, and nothing is found. Convinced they did not drill deep enough, the producer goes back to the investors and requests additional financial backing to continue drilling. The investors consent, and she drills deeper, only to find nothing. She approaches the investors, and after lengthy discussion, they agree to provide more money to drill deeper. Why do decision makers sometimes throw good money after bad? Why do they continue to provide resources to what looks like a losing venture?

■ Escalation of Commitment

Continuing to commit resources to a losing course of action is known as escalation of commitment. A situation often cited as an example is former president Lyndon Johnson's continued commitment of troops and money to the Vietnam War, even though many advisors had warned that U.S. involvement was a losing effort.

In situations characterized by escalation of commitment, individuals who make decisions that turn out to be poor choices tend to hold fast to those choices, even when substantial costs are incurred.[7] Why does escalation of commitment occur? One explanation is offered by cognitive dissonance theory, as we discussed in Chapter 4. This theory assumes that humans dislike inconsistency, and that when there is inconsistency among their attitudes or between their attitudes and behavior, they strive to reduce the dissonance.

Continuing to commit resources to a poor decision can be costly to organizations. Organizations can deal with escalation of commitment in several ways. One is to split the responsibility for decisions about projects. One individual can make the initial decision, and another individual can make subsequent decisions on the project. Another suggestion is to provide individuals with a graceful exit from poor decisions so that their images are not threatened. One way of accomplishing this is to reward people who admit to poor decisions before escalating their commitment to them. A recent study also suggested that having groups, rather than individuals, make an initial investment decision would reduce escalation. Support was found for this idea. Participants in group decision making may experience a diffusion of responsibility for the failed decision rather than feeling personally responsible; thus, they can pull out of a bad decision without threatening their image.[8]

We have seen that there are limits to how rational a manager can be in making decisions. Most managerial decisions involve considerable risk, and individuals react differently to risk situations.

■ JUNG'S COGNITIVE STYLES

Jungian theory is a way of understanding and appreciating differences among individuals. This theory is especially useful in pointing out that individuals have different styles of making decisions. Carl Jung's original theory identified two styles of information gathering (sensing and intuiting) and two styles of making judgments (thinking and feeling). Sensing is gathering information through the five senses of touch, sight, hearing, smell, and taste. Sensors focus on gathering practical information and the realities of decision situations. Intuiting is gathering information through a "sixth sense" and focusing on what could be rather than what actually exists. Sensing and intuiting are different styles of perceiving.

Thinking and feeling are two styles of making judgments. Thinking is making decisions in a logi-

cal, objective fashion. In contrast, feeling is making decisions in a personal, value-oriented way. Thinkers tend to analyze situations impersonally, whereas feelers base their decisions on the way people will be affected.

Jung contended that individuals prefer one style of perceiving and one style of judging.[9] The combination of a perceiving style and a judging style is called a cognitive style. There are four cognitive styles: sensing/thinking (ST), sensing/feeling (SF), intuiting/thinking (NT), and intuiting/feeling (NF). Let us analyze how each of the cognitive styles affects managerial decision making.

STs rely on facts. They conduct an impersonal analysis of the situation and then make an analytical, objective decision. The ST cognitive style is valuable in organizations because it produces a clear, simple solution. STs are masters of facts; they remember details and seldom make factual errors. Their weakness is that they may alienate others because of their tendency to ignore interpersonal aspects of decisions. In addition, they tend to avoid risks.

SFs also gather factual information, but they make judgments in terms of how they affect people. They place great importance on interpersonal relationships but also take a practical approach to gathering information for problem solving. The SFs' strength in decision making lies in their ability to handle interpersonal problems well and their ability to take calculated risks. SFs may have trouble accepting new ideas that break the rules in the organization.

NTs focus on the alternative possibilities in a situation and then evaluate the possibilities objectively and impersonally. NTs love to initiate ideas, and they like to focus on the long term. They are innovative and will take risks. Weaknesses of NTs include their tendencies to ignore arguments based on facts and to ignore the feelings of others.

NFs also search out alternative possibilities, but they evaluate the possibilities in terms of how they will affect the people involved. They enjoy participative decision making and are committed to developing their employees. However, NFs may be prone to making decisions based on personal preferences rather than on more objective data. They may also become too responsive to the needs of others.

Research tends to support the existence of these four cognitive styles. One study asked managers to

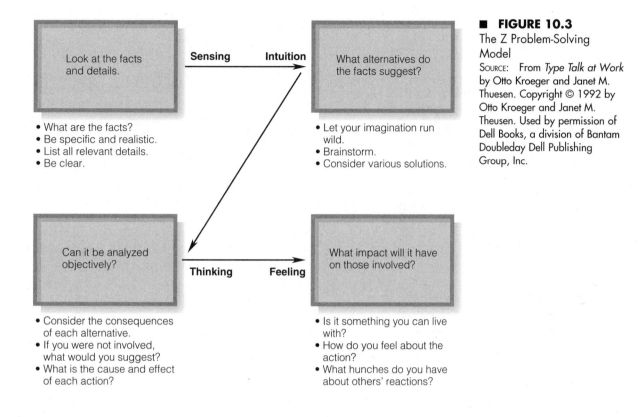

■ **FIGURE 10.3**
The Z Problem-Solving Model
SOURCE: From *Type Talk at Work* by Otto Kroeger and Janet M. Thuesen. Copyright © 1992 by Otto Kroeger and Janet M. Theusen. Used by permission of Dell Books, a division of Bantam Doubleday Dell Publishing Group, Inc.

describe their ideal organization, and researchers found strong similarities in the description of managers with the same cognitive style.[10] STs wanted an organization that relied on facts and details and that exercised impersonal methods of control. SFs focused on facts, too, but they did so in terms of the relationships within the organization. NTs emphasized broad issues and described impersonal, idealistic organizations. NFs described an organization that would serve humankind well and focused on general, humanistic values. Other studies have found that MBA students with different cognitive styles exhibited these different styles in making strategic planning decisions and production decisions in a computer-simulated manufacturing environment.[11,12]

All four cognitive styles have much to contribute to organizational decision making.[13] The Z problem-solving model, presented in Figure 10.3, capitalizes on the strengths of the four separate preferences (sensing, intuiting, thinking, and feeling). By using the Z problem-solving model, managers can use both their preferences and nonpreferences to make decisions more effectively.

According to this model, good problem solving has four steps:

1. Examine the facts and details. Use sensing to gather information about the problem.
2. Generate alternatives. Use intuiting to develop possibilities.
3. Analyze the alternatives objectively. Use thinking to determine logically the effects of each alternative.
4. Weigh the impact. Use feeling to determine how the people involved will be affected.

Using the Z model can help an individual develop his or her nonpreferences. Another way to use the Z model is to rely on others to perform the nonpreferred activities. For example, a manager who is an NF might want to turn to a trusted NT for help in analyzing alternatives objectively.

■ OTHER INDIVIDUAL INFLUENCES ON DECISION MAKING

In addition to the cognitive styles just examined, many other individual differences affect a manager's decision making. Other personality characteristics, attitudes, and values, along with all of the individual differences variables that were discussed in Chapters 3 and 4, have implications for managerial decision making. Two particular individual influences that can enhance decision–making effectiveness will be highlighted in this section: intuition and creativity.

■ The Role of Intuition

There is some evidence that managers use their intuition to make decisions. Henry Mintzberg, in his work on managerial roles, found that in many cases managers do not appear to use a systematic, step-by-step approach to decision making. Rather, Mintzberg argued, managers make judgments based on "hunches."[14] Some managers use intuition as a mechanism to evaluate decisions made more rationally. BankAmerica managers used intuition extensively to make decisions about the future direction of the company following the deregulation of the banking industry. These managers used intuition as an antidote to "analysis paralysis," or the tendency to analyze decisions rather than developing innovative solutions.[15]

Just what is intuition? In Jungian theory, intuiting is one preference used to gather data. This is only one way that the concept of intuition has been applied to managerial decision making, and it is perhaps the most widely researched form of the concept of intuition. Chester Barnard, one of the early influential management researchers, argued that intuition's main attributes were speed and the inability of the decision maker to determine how the decision was made.[16] Because intuition occurs at an unconscious level, decision makers sometimes cannot verbalize how the decision was made.

Intuition is a fast, positive force in decision making utilized at a level below consciousness that involves learned patterns of information. One question that arises is whether managers can be taught to use their intuition. Weston Agor, who has conducted workshops on developing intuitive skills in managers, has attained positive results in organizations such as Tenneco and the city of Phoenix. Agor suggests relaxation techniques, using images to guide the mind, and taking creative pauses before making a decision.[17] Although intuition itself cannot be taught, managers can be trained to rely more fully on the promptings of their intuition.

There is an interesting paradox regarding intuition. Some researchers view "rational" methods as preferable to intuition, yet satisfaction with a rational decision is usually determined by the way the decision feels intuitively. Intuition appears to have a positive effect on managerial decision making, yet researchers need to conduct additional research to increase our knowledge of the role of intuition at work and the influence of experience on our intuitive capabilities.

■ Creativity at Work

Creativity is a process, influenced by individual and organizational factors, that results in the production of novel and useful ideas, products, or both.[18] The social and technological changes that organizations face require creative decisions. Managers of the future need to develop special competencies to deal with the turbulence of change, and one of these is the ability to promote creativity in organizations.

The process of creativity is at least in part unconscious. The four stages of the creative process are preparation, incubation, illumination, and verification.[19] Preparation means seeking out new experiences and opportunities to learn, because creativity grows from a base of knowledge. Travel and educational opportunities of all kinds open the individual's mind. Incubation is a process of reflective thought and is often conducted unconsciously. During incubation, the individual engages in other pursuits while the mind considers the problem and works on it. Illumination occurs when the individual senses an insight for solving the problem. Finally, verification is conducted to determine whether the solution or idea is valid. This is accomplished by thinking through the implications of the decision, presenting the idea to another person, or trying out the decision. There are both individual and organizational influences on the creative process.

Individual Influences. Several individual variables are related to creativity. One group of factors involves the cognitive processes that creative individuals tend to use. One is divergent thinking, meaning the individual's ability to generate several potential solutions to a problem. In addition, associational abilities and the use of imagery are associated with creativity. Unconscious processes such as dreams are also essential cognitive processes related to creative thinking.

Personality factors have also been related to creativity in studies of individuals from several different occupations. These characteristics include intellectual and artistic values, breadth of interests, high energy, concern with achievement, independence of judgment, intuition, self-confidence, and a creative self-image. Tolerance of ambiguity, intrinsic motivation, risk taking, and a desire for recognition are also associated with creativity. People who are in a good mood are more creative.

Organizational Influences. Supportive supervision and support from peers also are related to creativity.[20] Flexible organizational structures and participative decision making have also been associated with creativity.

Studies of the role of organizational rewards in encouraging creativity have mixed results. Some studies have shown that monetary incentives improve creative performance, whereas others have found that material rewards do not influence innovative activity. Still other studies have indicated that explicitly contracting to obtain a reward led to lower levels of creativity when compared with contracting for no reward, being presented with just the task, or being presented with both the task and receiving the reward later.[21]

Although the role of rewards is unclear, there are other ways to encourage creative efforts among employees. Organizations can therefore enhance individuals' creative decision making by providing a supportive environment, participative decision making, and a flexible structure.

Individual/Organization Fit. Creative performance is highest when there is a match, or fit, between the individual and organizational influences on creativity. For example, when individuals who desire to be creative are matched with an organization that values creative ideas, the result is more creative performance.[22]

One mistaken assumption that many people have regarding creativity is that either you have it or you do not. Research refutes this myth and has shown that individuals can be trained to be more creative.[23] One company that has found success in this way is Frito-Lay, which offers three courses in creative problem solving and trains its own trainers to hold creativity workshops within each plant. The company saved $500 million during the first six years of its creativity training effort, and managers believe this is directly related to the employees' creative problem-solving skills.

Part of creativity training involves learning to open up mental locks that keep us from generating creative alternatives to decisions or problems. Some mental locks that diminish creativity include the fear of failure, searching for a single "right" answer, believing we are not really creative, and being afraid to look foolish.[24]

Many of these mental locks stem from values within organizations. Organizations can facilitate creative decision making in many ways. Rewarding creativity, allowing employees to fail, making work more fun, and providing creativity training are a few suggestions.

Japanese companies manage creativity in much different ways than do North American firms. Min Basadur visited several major Japanese companies, including Matsushita, Hitachi, Toyota, and others, to conduct comparative research on organizational creativity in Japan and North America. He found several differences between the two cultures. First, Japanese companies place a strong emphasis on problem finding. Companies in North America, in contrast, have a greater reluctance to identify problems, because rewards go more often to individuals who appear not to have many problems. Furthermore, Japanese companies have a structured mechanism for encouraging problem finding. Workers are given cards on which to write down problems or discontents, and these are posted on a wall. When others notice a problem that interests them, they join forces to solve it.

Another difference that Basadur found involves rewards. In North America, the motivating factor for suggestions is money. A few employees submit ideas that save a company large sums of money and reap large cash rewards. In Japan, all employees participate, and monetary rewards are small. Every suggestion gets a reward. For the Japanese, the most motivating rewards are intrinsic: accomplishment, recognition, and personal growth.[25]

Both intuition and creativity are important influences on managerial decision making. Both concepts require additional research so that managers can better understand how to use intuition and creativity, and how to encourage their employees to use them to make more effective decisions.

■ PARTICIPATION IN DECISION MAKING

We have examined several features of individual decision making. In organizations, however, not all decisions are made by individuals acting alone. For one thing, managers work with employees who may participate in decision making. This section discusses the effects of employee participation and the appropriate level of participation for given circumstances.

■ The Effects of Participation

Participative decision making occurs when individuals who are affected by decisions influence the making of those decisions.[26] Participation is associated with greater feelings of autonomy and meaningfulness of work. In addition, participative management has been found to increase employee creativity and job satisfaction. Some studies have reported a positive link between participation and productivity.[27,28]

It is also important to acknowledge that some individuals do not respond well to participative decision making. They prefer instead to have managers make the decisions.

■ The Vroom-Yetton-Jago Normative Decision Model

How does a manager know when to have employees participate in the decision making process? Victor Vroom, Phillip Yetton, and Arthur Jago developed and refined the normative decision model, which helps managers determine the appropriate decision-making strategy to use.[29] In their model, they describe five forms of decision making. Two are autocratic (AI and AII), two are consultative (CI and CII), and one is a group method (G). The five forms of decision making follow:

- The AI form. The manager makes the decision alone, using whatever information is available at the time. This is the most authoritarian method.
- The AII form. The manager seeks information from employees or peers and then makes the decision. Employees may or may not know what the problem is before providing the information to the manager.
- The CI form. The manager explains the problem to appropriate peers or employees in a one-on-one format. The manager makes the decision, which may or may not reflect the others' inputs.
- The CII form. The manager explains the problem to employees or peers as a group. The manager makes the decision, which may or may not reflect the others' inputs.
- The G form. The manager explains the problem to employees and peers as a group, and the group makes the final decision.

The key to the normative decision model is that a manager should use the decision method most appropriate for a given decision situation. The manager arrives at the proper method by working through the decision tree shown in Figure 10.4. Each node in the decision tree asks the manager to answer a question about the decision situation. The questions reflect key attributes of the decision situation: time, quality, commitment, and information. Working through the decision tree leads to a prescribed decision style at the end of the path.

This version of the normative decision model is relatively new, so it is too early to ascertain how well it is supported by research. However, studies have supported an earlier version of the model proposed in 1973. Managers who were trained to diagnose the key attributes of the decision situation were better able to select the appropriate level of participation than managers who had not received training. In addition, research has shown that selecting the cor-

■ **FIGURE 10.4**

The Vroom-Yetton-Jago Normative Decision Model

| QR | Quality requirement | How important is the technical quality of this decision? |

| CR | Commitment requirement | How important is employee commitment to the decision? |

| LI | Leader's information | Do you have sufficient information to make a high-quality decision? |

| ST | Problem structure | Is the problem well structured? |

| CP | Commitment probability | If you were to make the decision by yourself, is it reasonably certain that your employees would be commited to the decision? |

| GC | Goal congruence | Do employees share the organizational goals to be attained in solving this problem? |

| CO | Employee conflict | Is conflict among employees over preferred solutions likely? |

| SI | Employee information | Do employees have sufficient information to make a high-quality decision? |

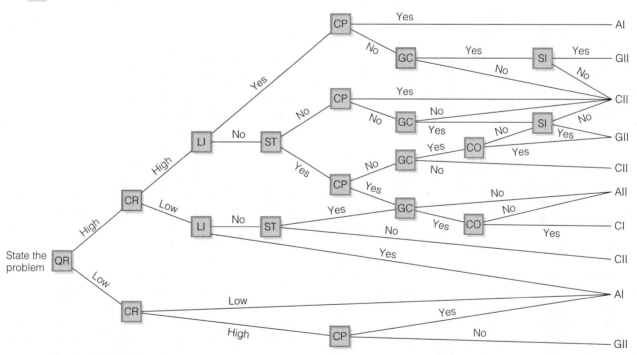

SOURCE: Reprinted from *The New Leadership: Managing Participation in Organizations* by Victor H. Vroom and Arthur G. Jago, 1988, Englewood Cliffs, NJ: Prentice-Hall. Copyright 1987 by V. H. Vroom and A. G. Jago. Used with permission of the authors.

rect level of participation increases the effectiveness of decision making.[30] A study conducted in a large department store found that managers who used a decision style prescribed by the model had higher-performing work groups.[31] Research has also indicated that the skills of the manager are important in normative decision theory. For managers with strong conflict management skills, the use of more participative methods led to higher employee performance. However, managers with weak conflict management skills who used participative styles had more poorly performing employees.

In summary, the normative decision model emphasizes the importance of choosing the level of participation in decision making most appropriate to the situation. It shows managers that they must evaluate the decision thoroughly before choosing a process for reaching a decision. Research on earlier versions of the model is positive, and the new version appears to have promise. Given that group decision making is sometimes appropriate, we now turn to an examination of the process of group decision making.

THE GROUP DECISION MAKING PROCESS

Managers use groups to make decisions for several reasons. One is for synergy; that is, group members stimulate new solutions to problems through the process of mutual influence and encouragement in the group. Another reason for using a group is to gain commitment to a decision. Groups also bring more knowledge and experience to the problem-solving situation.

Advantages and Disadvantages of Group Decision Making

Both advantages and disadvantages are associated with group decision making. The advantages include (1) more knowledge and information through the pooling of group member resources; (2) increased acceptance of, and commitment to, the decision, because the members had a voice in it; and (3) greater understanding of the decision, because members were involved in the various stages of the decision process. The disadvantages of group decision making include (1) pressure within the group to conform and fit in; (2) domination of the group by one forceful member or a dominant clique, who may ramrod the decision; and (3) the amount of time required, because a group is slower than an individual to make a decision.

Given these advantages and disadvantages, should an individual or a group make a decision? The Vroom-Yetton-Jago model is one tool for making this judgment. There is also substantial empirical research indicating that whether a group or an individual should be used depends on the type of task involved. For judgment tasks requiring an estimate or a prediction, groups are usually superior to individuals because of the breadth of experience that multiple individuals bring to the problem.[32] However, other studies have indicated that on tasks where there is a correct solution, the most competent individual outperforms the group.[33]

Many managers believe that groups produce better decisions than do individuals, yet the research evidence is mixed. More research needs to be conducted in organizational settings to help answer this question.

Two potential liabilities are found in group decision making: groupthink and group polarization. These problems are discussed in the following sections.

Groupthink

One liability of a cohesive group is its tendency to develop groupthink, a dysfunctional process. Irving Janis, the originator of the groupthink concept, describes groupthink as "a deterioration of mental efficiency, reality testing, and moral judgment" resulting from in-group pressures.[34]

Certain conditions favor the development of groupthink. One of the antecedents is high cohesiveness. Cohesive groups tend to avoid conflicts and to demand conformity. Other antecedents include directive leadership, high stress, insulation of the group, and lack of methodical procedures for developing and evaluating alternatives. These antecedents cause members to prefer concurrence in decisions and to fail to evaluate one another's suggestions critically. A group suffering from groupthink shows recognizable symptoms. Table 10.1 presents these symptoms and makes suggestions on how to avoid groupthink.

A recent incident that has been examined for these symptoms of groupthink is the Space Shuttle Challenger disaster. On January 28, 1986, seventy-three seconds into its flight, the Challenger exploded, killing all seven members of its crew. The evidence pointed toward an O-ring seal that was still cold from nighttime temperatures and failed to do its job. A presidential commission was convened, and its

■ **TABLE 10.1**
Symptoms of Groupthink and How to Prevent It

Symptoms of Groupthink

■ *Illusions of invulnerability.* Group members feel they are above criticism. This symptom leads to excessive optimism and risk taking.

■ *Illusions of group morality.* Group members feel they are moral in their actions and therefore above reproach. This symptom leads the group to ignore the ethical implications of their decisions.

■ *Illusions of unanimity.* Group members believe there is unanimous agreement on the decisions. Silence is misconstrued as consent.

■ *Rationalization.* Group members concoct explanations for their decisions to make them appear rational and correct. The results are that other alternatives are not considered, and there is an unwillingness to reconsider the group's assumptions.

■ *Stereotyping the enemy.* Competitors are stereotyped as evil or stupid. This leads the group to underestimate its opposition.

■ *Self-censorship.* Members do not express their doubts about the course of action. This prevents critical analysis of the decisions.

■ *Peer pressure.* Any member who express doubts or concerns are pressured by other group members, who question their loyalty.

■ *Mindguards.* Some members take it upon themselves to protect the group from negative feedback. Group members are thus shielded from information that might lead them to question their actions.

Guidelines for Preventing Groupthink

■ Ask each group member to assume the role of the critical evaluator who actively voices objections or doubts.

■ Have the leader avoid stating his or her position on the issue prior to the group decision.

■ Create several groups that work on the decision simultaneously.

■ Bring in outside experts to evaluate the group process.

■ Appoint a devil's advocate to question the group's course of action consistently.

■ Evaluate the competition carefully, posing as many different motivations and intentions as possible.

■ Once consensus is reached, encourage the group to rethink its position by reexamining the alternatives.

Source: Janis, Irving L., *Groupthink: Psychological Studies of Policy Decisions and Fiascoes, Second Edition.* Copyright © 1982 by Houghton Mifflin Company. Used with permission.

---

investigation cited flawed decision making as a primary cause of the accident.

An analysis of the Challenger incident indicated that the negative symptoms of groupthink increased during the twenty-four hours prior to the decision to launch the spacecraft.[35] National Aeronautics and Space Administration (NASA) management officials were warned by engineers that the launch should be canceled because the O-rings would not withstand the temperatures. The engineers were pressured by their bosses to stifle their dissent, and their opinions were devalued. Further, the decision to launch was made by polling managers—engineers were not polled. There was overconfidence among the decision makers because of the record of success at NASA. Some managers knew that the redesign of the rocket casings had been ordered, but this information was withheld from other decision makers.

Consequences of groupthink include an incomplete survey of alternatives, failure to evaluate the risks of the preferred course of action, biased information processing, and a failure to work out contingency plans. The overall result of groupthink is defective decision making. This was evident in the Challenger situation. The group considered only two alternatives: launch or no launch. They failed to consider the risks of their decision to launch the shuttle, and they did not develop any contingency plans.

Table 10.1 also presents Janis's guidelines for avoiding groupthink. Many of these suggestions center around the notion of ensuring that decisions are evaluated completely, with opportunities for discussion from all group members. This strategy helps encourage members to evaluate one another's ideas critically.

Janis has used the groupthink framework to conduct historical analyses of several political and military fiascoes, including the Bay of Pigs invasion, the Vietnam War, and Watergate. When a decision must be made quickly, there is more potential for groupthink. Leadership style can either promote groupthink (if the leader makes his or her opinion known up front) or avoid groupthink (if the leader encourages open and frank discussion).

There are few empirical studies of groupthink, and most of these involved students in a laboratory setting. More applied research may be seen in the future, however. A questionnaire has been developed to measure the constructs associated with groupthink.[36]

■ Group Polarization

Another group phenomenon was discovered by a graduate student. His study showed that groups made riskier decisions; in fact, the group and each individual accepted greater levels of risk following a group discussion of the issue. Subsequent studies uncovered another shift—toward caution. Thus, group discussion produced shifts both toward more risky positions and toward more cautious positions.[37] Further research revealed that individual group member attitudes simply became more extreme following group discussion. Individuals who were initially against an issue became more radically opposed, and individuals who were in favor of the issue became more strongly supportive following

discussion. These shifts came to be known as group polarization.[38]

The tendency toward polarization has important implications for group decision making. Groups whose initial views lean a certain way can be expected to adopt more extreme views following interaction. Group polarization leads groups to adopt extreme attitudes. In some cases, this can be disastrous. For instance, if individuals are leaning toward a dangerous decision, they are likely to support it more strongly following discussion. Both groupthink and group polarization are potential liabilities of group decision making. However, several techniques can be used to help prevent or control these two liabilities.

■ TECHNIQUES FOR GROUP DECISION MAKING

Once a manager has determined that a group decision approach should be used, he or she can determine the technique that is best suited to the decision situation. Seven techniques will be briefly summarized: brainstorming, nominal group technique, Delphi technique, devil's advocacy, dialectical inquiry, quality circles and quality teams, and self-managed teams.

■ Brainstorming

Brainstorming is a good technique for generating alternatives. The idea behind brainstorming is to generate as many ideas as possible, suspending evaluation until all of the ideas have been suggested. Participants are encouraged to build upon the suggestions of others, and imagination is emphasized. Groups that use brainstorming have been shown to produce significantly more ideas than groups that do not.[39]

■ Nominal Group Technique

A structured approach to decision making that focuses on generating alternatives and choosing one is called nominal group technique (NGT). NGT has the following discrete steps:

1. Individuals silently list their ideas.
2. Ideas are written on a chart one at a time until all ideas are listed.
3. Discussion is permitted, but only to clarify the ideas. No criticism is allowed.
4. A written vote is taken.

NGT is a good technique to use in a situation where group members fear criticism from others.

Delphi Technique

The Delphi technique originated at the Rand Corporation to gather the judgments of experts for use in decision making. Experts at remote locations respond to a questionnaire. A coordinator summarizes the responses to the questionnaire, and the summary is sent back to the experts. The experts then rate the various alternatives generated, and the coordinator tabulates the results. The Delphi technique is valuable in its ability to generate a number of independent judgments without the requirement of a face-to-face meeting.

Devil's Advocacy

In the devil's advocacy decision method, a group or individual is given the role of critic. This devil's advocate has the task of coming up with the potential problems of a proposed decision. This helps organizations avoid costly mistakes in decision making by identifying potential pitfalls in advance. As we discussed in Chapter 9, a devil's advocate who challenges the CEO and top management team can help sustain the vitality and performance of the upper echelon.

Dialectical Inquiry

Dialectical inquiry is essentially a debate between two opposing sets of recommendations. Although it sets up a conflict, it is a constructive approach, because it brings out the benefits and limitations of both sets of ideas. When using this technique, it is important to guard against a win-lose attitude and to concentrate on reaching the most effective solution for all concerned. Recent research has shown that the way a decision is framed (that is, win-win

versus win-lose) is very important. A decision's outcome could be viewed as a gain or a loss, depending on the way the decision is framed.[40]

Quality Circles and Quality Teams

As you recall from Chapter 9, quality circles are small groups that voluntarily meet to provide input for solving quality or production problems. The quality circle is also a way of extending participative decision making into teams. Managers often listen to recommendations from quality circles and implement the suggestions. The rewards for the suggestions are intrinsic—involvement in the decision making process is the primary reward.

Quality circles are often generated from the bottom up; that is, they provide advice to managers, who still retain decision making authority. As such, quality circles are not empowered to implement their own recommendations. They operate in parallel fashion to the organization's structure, and they rely on voluntary participation. In Japan, quality circles have been integrated into the organization instead of added on. This may be one reason for Japan's success with this technique.

Quality teams, in contrast, are included in total quality management and other quality improvement efforts as part of a change in the organization's structure. Quality teams are generated from the top down and are empowered to act on their own recommendations. Whereas quality circles emphasize the generation of ideas, quality teams make data-based decisions about improving product and service quality. Various decision making techniques are employed within quality teams. Brainstorming, flowcharts, and cause-and-effect diagrams help pinpoint problems that affect quality.

Because quality teams are empowered to implement their decisions, managers may resist them. At Campbell Soup Company, middle managers resisted the team efforts because the managers felt they were losing power. As a result, middle managers at Campbell Soup were given training on operating in a more hands-off fashion.

Quality circles and quality teams are methods for using groups in the decision making process. Self-managed teams take the concept of participation one step further.

■ Self-Managed Teams

Another group decision–making method is the use of self-managed teams, which we also discussed in Chapter 9. The decision–making activities of self-managed teams are more broadly focused than those of quality circles and quality teams, which usually emphasize quality and production problems. Self-managed teams make many of the decisions that were once reserved for managers, such as work scheduling, job assignments, and staffing. Unlike quality circles, whose role is an advisory one, self-managed teams are delegated authority in the organization's decision–making process.

Many organizations have claimed success with self-managed teams. At Northern Telecom, revenues rose 63 percent and sales increased 26 percent following the implementation of self-managed teams.[41] Preliminary research evidence is also encouraging. An analysis of seventy studies concluded that self-managed teams positively affected productivity and attitudes toward self-management. However, the analysis indicated no significant effects of self-managed teams on job satisfaction, absenteeism, or turnover.[42]

Before choosing a group decision–making technique, the manager should carefully evaluate the group members and the decision situation. Then the best method for accomplishing the objectives of the group decision–making process can be selected. If the goal is generating a large number of alternatives, for example, brainstorming would be a good choice. If group members are reluctant to contribute ideas, nominal group technique would be appropriate. The need for expert input would be best facilitated by the Delphi technique. To guard against groupthink, devil's advocacy or dialectical inquiry would be effective. Decisions that concern quality or production would benefit from the advice of quality circles or the empowered decisions of quality teams. Finally, a manager who wants to provide total empowerment to a group should consider self-managed teams.

■ TECHNOLOGICAL AIDS TO DECISION MAKING

Many computerized decision tools are available to managers. These systems can be used to support the decision–making process in organizations.

■ Expert Systems

Artificial intelligence is used to develop an expert system, which is a programmed decision tool. The system is set up using decision rules, and the effectiveness of the expert system is highly dependent on its design. Because expert systems are sources of knowledge and experience and not just passive software, the organization must decide who is responsible for the decisions made by expert systems. Organizations must therefore be concerned about the liability for using the recommendations of expert systems.

An expert system for use in an organization can be developed in many ways. DuPont, for example, uses a dispersed design whereby the users of the system are primarily responsible for its design. Digital Equipment Corporation, in contrast, created a separate department of specialists to develop expert systems for the company.

Expert systems hold great potential for affecting managerial decisions. Thus, managers must carefully scrutinize the expert system rather than simply accepting its decisions.

■ Group Decision Support Systems

Another tool for decision making focuses on helping groups make decisions. A group decision support system (GDSS) uses computer support and communication facilities to support group decision–making processes in either face-to-face meetings or dispersed meetings. The GDSS has been shown to affect conflict management within a group by depersonalizing the issue and by forcing the group to discuss its conflict management process.[43] Boeing is one company that has seen the benefits of GDSS (groupware). By participating in team meetings using groupware, shy group members feel less intimidated and contribute more frequently.

■ ETHICAL ISSUES IN DECISION MAKING

One criterion that should be applied to decision making is the ethical implications of the decision. Ethical decision making in organizations is influenced by many factors, including individual differences and organizational rewards and punishments.

Kenneth Blanchard and Norman Vincent Peale proposed an "ethics check" for decision makers in their book *The Power of Ethical Management.*[44] They contend that the decision maker should ponder three questions:

1. Is it legal? (Will I be violating the law or company policy?)
2. Is it balanced? (Is it fair to all concerned in the short term and long term? Does it promote win-win relationships?)
3. How will it make me feel about myself? (Will it make me proud of my actions? How will I feel when others become aware of the decision?)

Groups and teams can also make decisions that are unethical. Beech-Nut, for example, admitted selling millions of jars of "phony" apple juice that contained cheap, adulterated concentrate. Groupthink may have played a role in this unethical decision. Beech-Nut was losing money, and its managers believed that other companies were selling fake juice. They were convinced that their fake juice was safe for consumers and that no laboratory test could conclusively discriminate real juice from artificial ingredients. Normally a reputable company, Beech-Nut rejected caution and conscience in favor of bottom-line mentality, ignored dissent, and thus suffered damage to its reputation because of unethical practices.[45]

Unethical group decisions like the one at Beech-Nut can be prevented by using the techniques for overcoming groupthink. Appointing a devil's advocate who constantly questions the group's course of action can help bring ethical issues to the surface. Setting up a dialectical inquiry between two subgroups can head off unethical decisions by leading the group to question its course of action.

In summary, all decisions, whether made by individuals or by groups, must be evaluated for their ethics. Organizations should reinforce ethical decision making among employees by encouraging and rewarding it. Socialization processes should convey to newcomers the ethical standards of behavior in the organization. Groups should use devil's advocates and dialectical methods to reduce the potential for groupthink and the unethical decisions that may result. Effective and ethical decisions are not mutually exclusive.

■ MANAGERIAL IMPLICATIONS: DECISION MAKING IS A CRITICAL ACTIVITY

Decision making is important at all levels of every organization. At times managers may have the luxury of optimizing (selecting the best alternative), but more often they are forced to satisfice (select the alternative that is good enough). And, at times, the decision process can even seem unpredictable and random.

Individuals differ in their preferences for risk, as well as in their styles of information gathering and making judgments. Understanding individual differences can help managers maximize strengths in employee decision styles and build teams that capitalize on strengths. Creativity is one such strength. It can be encouraged by providing employees with a supportive environment that nourishes innovative ideas. Creativity training has been used in some organizations with positive results.

Some decisions are best made by individuals and some by teams or groups. The task of the manager is to diagnose the situation and implement the appropriate level of participation. To do this effectively, managers should know the advantages and disadvantages of various group decision–making techniques and should minimize the potential for groupthink. Finally, decisions made by individuals or groups should be analyzed to see whether or not they are ethical.

■ CHAPTER SUMMARY

- Bounded rationality assumes that there are limits to how rational managers can be.
- The garbage can model shows that under high uncertainty, decision making in organizations can be an unsystematic process.
- Jung's cognitive styles can be used to help explain individual differences in gathering information and evaluating alternatives.
- Intuition and creativity are positive influences on decision making and should be encouraged in organizations.
- Managers should carefully determine the appropriate level of participation in the decision–

making process. They can use the normative decision model to accomplish this.

- Techniques such as brainstorming, nominal group technique, Delphi technique, devil's advocacy, dialectical inquiry, quality circles and teams, and self-managed teams can help managers reap the benefits of group methods while limiting the possibilities of groupthink and group polarization.
- Technology is providing assistance to managerial decision making, especially through expert systems and group decision support systems. More research is needed to determine the effects of these technologies.
- Managers should carefully weigh the ethical issues surrounding decisions and encourage ethical decision making throughout the organization.

■ REVIEW QUESTIONS

1. Compare the garbage can model with the bounded rationality model. Compare the usefulness of these models in today's organizations.
2. List and describe Jung's four cognitive styles. How does the Z problem-solving model capitalize on the strengths of the four preferences?
3. What are the individual and organizational influences on creativity?
4. According to the normative decision model, what situational variables affect the level of participation in decision making?
5. Describe the advantages and disadvantages of group decision making.
6. Describe the symptoms of groupthink and actions that can be taken to prevent it. Describe groupthink as an ethical problem.
7. What techniques can be used to improve group decisions?

■ REFERENCES

1. H. A. Simon, *The New Science of Management Decision* (New York: Harper & Row, 1960).
2. W. D. Bodensteiner, E. A. Gerloff, and J. C. Quick, "Uncertainty and Stress in an R & D Project Environment," *R & D Management* 19 (1989): 309–323.
3. H. A. Simon, *Administrative Behavior* (New York: MacMillan, 1957).
4. R. M. Cyert and J. G. March, eds., *A Behavioral Theory of the Firm* (Englewood Cliffs, N.J.: Prentice-Hall, 1963).
5. J. G. March and J. P. Olsen, "Garbage Can Models of Decision Making in Organizations," in J. G. March and R. Weissinger-Baylon, eds., *Ambiguity and Command* (Marshfield, Mass.: Pitman, 1986), 11–53.
6. K. R. MacCrimmon and D. Wehrung, *Taking Risks* (New York: Free Press, 1986).
7. B. M. Staw and J. Ross, "Understanding Behavior in Escalation Situations," *Science* 246 (1989): 216–220.
8. G. Whyte, "Diffusion of Responsibility: Effects on the Escalation Tendency," *Journal of Applied Psychology* 76 (1991): 408–415.
9. C. G. Jung, *Psychological Types* (London: Routledge and Kegan Paul, 1923).
10. I. I. Mitroff and R. H. Kilmann, "On Organization Stories: An Approach to the Design and Analysis of Organization through Myths and Stories," in R. H. Killman, L. R. Pondy, and D. P. Slevin, eds., *The Management of Organization Design* (New York: Elsevier-North Holland, 1976).
11. B. K. Blaylock and L. P. Rees, "Cognitive Style and the Usefulness of Information," *Decision Sciences* 15 (1984): 74–91.
12. D. L. Davis, S. J. Grove, and P. A. Knowles, "An Experimental Application of Personality Type as an Analogue for Decision-making Style," *Psychological Reports* 66 (1990): 167–175.
13. I. B. Myers, *Gifts Differing* (Palo Alto, Calif.: Consulting Psychologists Press, 1980).
14. H. Mintzberg, "Planning on the Left Side and Managing on the Right," *Harvard Business Review* 54 (1976): 51–63.
15. R. N. Beck, "Visions, Values, and Strategies: Changing Attitudes and Culture," *Academy of Managment Executive* 1 (1987): 33–41.
16. C. I. Barnard, *The Functions of the Executive* (Cambridge, Mass.: Harvard University Press, 1938).
17. W. H. Agor, "How Top Executives Use Their Intuition to Make Important Decisions," *Business Horizons* 29 (1986): 49–53.
18. L. Livingstone, "Person-Environment Fit on the Dimension of Creativity: Relationships with Strain, Job Satisfaction, and Performance" (Ph.D. diss., Oklahoma State University, 1992).
19. G. Wallas, *The Art of Thought* (New York: Harcourt Brace, 1926).
20. T. M. Amabile, "Creativity Motivation in Research and Development" (Paper presented at the annual meeting of the American Psychological Association, Toronto, 1984).
21. T. M. Amabile, B. A. Hennessey, and B. S. Grossman, "Social Influences on Creativity: The Effects of Contracted-for Reward," *Journal of Personality and Social Psychology* 50 (1986): 14–23.
22. Livingstone, "Person-Environment Fit."

23. R. L. Firestein, "Effects of Creative Problem-solving Training on Communication Behaviors in Small Groups," *Small Group Research* (November 1989): 507–521.

24. R. von Oech, *A Whack on the Side of the Head* (New York: Warner, 1983).

25. M. Basadur, "Managing Creativity: A Japanese Model," *Academy of Management Executive* 6 (1992): 29–42.

26. P. E. Conner, "Decision-making Participation Patterns: The Role of Organizational Context," *Academy of Management Journal* 35 (1992): 218–231.

27. C. R. Leana, E. A. Locke, and D. M. Schweiger, "Fact and Fiction in Analyzing Research on Participative Decision Making: A Critique of Cotton, Vollrath, Froggatt, Lengnick-Hall, and Jennings," *Academy of Management Review* 15 (1990): 137–146.

28. J. L. Cotton, D. A. Vollrath, M. L. Lengnick-Hall, and K. L. Froggatt, "Fact: The Form of Participation Does Matter—A Rebuttal to Leana, Locke, and Schweiler," *Academy of Management Review* 15 (1990): 147–153.

29. V. H. Vroom and A. G. Jago, *The New Leadership: Managing Participation in Organizations* (Englewood Cliffs, N.J.: Prentice-Hall, 1988).

30. R. H. Field, "A Test of the Vroom-Yetton Normative Model of Leadership," *Journal of Applied Psychology* 67 (1982): 523–532.

31. R. J. Paul and Y. M. Ebadi, "Leadership Decision Making in a Service Organization: A Field Test of the Vroom-Yetton Model," *Journal of Occupational Psychology* 62 (1989): 201–211.

32. M. E. Shaw, *Group Dynamics: The Psychology of Small Group Behavior,* 3d ed. (New York: McGraw-Hill, 1981).

33. P. W. Yetton and P. C. Bottger, "Individual versus Group Problem Solving: An Empirical Test of a Best Member Strategy," *Organizational Behavior and Human Performance* 29 (1982): 307–321.

34. I. Janis, *Groupthink,* 2d ed. (Boston: Houghton Mifflin, 1982).

35. J. K. Esser and J. S. Lindoerfer, "Groupthink and the Space Shuttle Challenger Accident: Toward a Quantitative Case Analysis," *Journal of Behavioral Decision Making* 2 (1989): 167–177.

36. J. R. Montanari and G. Moorhead, "Development of the Groupthink Assessment Inventory," *Educational and Psychological Measurement* 49 (1989): 209–219.

37. J. A. F. Stoner, "Risky and Cautious Shifts in Group Decisions: The Influence of Widely Held Values," *Journal of Experimental Social Psychology* 4 (1968): 442–459.

38. S. Moscovici and M. Zavalloni, "The Group as a Polarizer of Attitudes," *Journal of Personality and Social Psychology* 12 (1969): 125–135.

39. T. Bouchard, "Whatever Happened to Brainstorming?" *Journal of Creative Behavior* 5 (1971): 182–189.

40. G. Whyte, "Decision Failures: Why They Occur and How to Prevent Them," *Academy of Management Executive* 5 (1991): 23–31.

41. J. Schilder, "Work Teams Boost Productivity," *Personnel Journal* 71 (1992): 67–72.

42. P. S. Goodman, R. Devadas, and T. L. Griffith-Hughson, "Groups and Productivity: Analyzing the Effectiveness of Self-managed Teams," in J. P. Campbell, R. J. Campbell, and Associates, eds., *Productivity in Organizations* (San Francisco: Jossey-Bass, 1988), 295–327.

43. M. S. Poole, M. Holmes, and G. DeSanctis, "Conflict Management in a Computer-supported Meeting Environment," *Management Science* 37 (1991): 926–953.

44. K. Blanchard and N. V. Peale, *The Power of Ethical Management* (New York: Fawcett Crest, 1988).

45. R. R. Sims, "Linking Groupthink to Unethical Behavior in Organizations," *Journal of Business Ethics* 11 (1992): 651–662.

CHAPTER 11
POWER AND POLITICAL BEHAVIOR

LEARNING OBJECTIVES

After reading this chapter, you should be able to do the following:

- Distinguish power, influence, and authority from each other.
- Describe the interpersonal and intergroup sources of power.
- Understand the ethical use of power.
- Explain Etzioni's organizational-level theory of power.
- Identify symbols of power and powerlessness in organizations.
- Define organizational politics and understand the major influence tactics used in organizations.
- Develop a plan for managing employee-boss relationships.
- Discuss the ways managers can empower others.

■ THE CONCEPT OF POWER

Power is the ability to influence someone else. As an exchange relationship, it occurs in transactions between an agent and a target. The agent is the person using the power, and the target is the recipient of the attempt to use power.[1]

Because power is an ability, individuals can learn to use it effectively. Influence is the process of affecting the thoughts, behavior, and feelings of another person. Authority is the right to influence another person. It is important to understand the subtle differences among these terms. For instance, a manager may have authority but no power. She may have the right, by virtue of her position as boss, to tell someone what to do. But she may not have the skill or ability to influence other people.

In a relationship between the agent and the target, there are many influence attempts that the target considers legitimate. Working forty hours per week, greeting customers, solving problems, and collecting bills are actions that, when requested by the manager, are considered legitimate by a customer service representative. Requests such as these fall within the employee's zone of indifference—the range in which attempts to influence the employee are perceived as legitimate and are acted on without a great deal of thought.[2] The employee accepts that the manager has the authority to request such behaviors and complies with the requests. Some requests, however, fall outside the zone of indifference, so the manager must work to enlarge the employee's zone of indifference. Enlarging the zone is accomplished with power (an ability) rather than with authority (a right).

Suppose the manager asks the employee to purchase a birthday gift for the manager's wife or to overcharge a customer for a service call. The employee may think that the manager has no right to ask these things. These requests fall outside the zone of indifference; they're viewed as extraordinary, and the manager has to operate from outside the authority base to induce the employee to fulfill them. In some cases, no power base is enough to induce the employee to comply, especially if the behaviors requested by the manager are considered unethical by the employee.

■ FORMS AND SOURCES OF POWER IN ORGANIZATIONS

Individuals have many forms of power to use in their work settings. Some of them are interpersonal—used in interactions with others. One of the earliest and most influential theories of power comes from French and Raven, who tried to determine the sources of power a manager uses to influence other people.

■ Interpersonal Forms of Power

French and Raven identified five forms of interpersonal power that managers use. They are reward, coercive, legitimate, referent, and expert power.[3,4]

Reward power is based on the agent's ability to control rewards that a target wants. For example, managers control the rewards of salary increases, bonuses, and promotions. Reward power can lead to better performance, but only as long as the employee sees a clear and strong link between performance and rewards. To use reward power effectively, then, the manager should be explicit about the behavior being rewarded and should make the connection between the behavior and the reward clear.

Coercive power is based on the agent's ability to cause the target to have an unpleasant experience. To coerce someone into doing something means to force the person to do it, often with threats of punishment. Managers using coercive power may verbally abuse employees or withhold support from them.

Legitimate power, which is similar to authority, is power that is based on position and mutual agreement. The agent and target agree that the agent has the right to influence the target. It doesn't matter that a manager thinks he has the right to influence his employees; for legitimate power to be effective, the employees must also believe the manager has the right to tell them what to do. In Native American societies, the chieftain has legitimate power; tribe members believe in his right to influence the decisions in their lives.

Referent power is an elusive power based on interpersonal attraction. The agent has referent power over the target because the target identifies with or wants to be like the agent. Charismatic individuals are often thought to have referent power. Interestingly, the agent need not be superior to the target in any way. People who use referent power well are most often individualistic and respected by the target.

Expert power exists when the agent has information or knowledge that the target needs. For expert power to work, three conditions must be in place. First, the target must trust that the information given is accurate. Second, the information involved must be relevant and useful to the target. Third, the target's perception of the agent as an expert is crucial. As a manager, you may believe you are an expert, but if your employees do not share this view, then your expert power will not be effective.

Which type of interpersonal power is most effective? This is the question that research has focused on since French and Raven introduced their five forms of power. Some of the results are surprising. Reward power and coercive power have similar effects.[5] Both lead to compliance. That is, employees will do what the manager asks them to, at least temporarily, if the manager offers a reward or threatens them with punishment. However, reliance on these sources of power is dangerous because it may require the manager to be physically present and watchful in order to apply rewards or punishment when the behavior occurs. Constant surveillance creates an uncomfortable situation for managers and employees and eventually results in a dependency relationship. Employees will not work unless the manager is present.

Legitimate power also leads to compliance. When told, "Do this because I'm your boss," most employees will comply. However, the use of legitimate power has not been linked to organizational effectiveness or to employee satisfaction.[6] In organizations where managers rely heavily on legitimate power, organizational goals are not necessarily met.

Referent power is linked with organizational effectiveness. However, it is the most dangerous power because it can be too extensive and intensive in altering the behavior of others. Charismatic leaders need an accompanying sense of responsibility for others. Magic Johnson's referent power has made him a powerful spokesman for AIDS prevention, especially among young people.

Expert power has been called the power of the future.[7,8] Of the five forms of power, it has the strongest relationship with performance and satisfaction. It is through expert power that vital skills, abilities, and knowledge are passed on within the organization. Employees internalize what they observe and learn from managers they perceive to be experts.

■ Using Power Ethically

Managers can work at developing all five of these forms of power for future use. The key to using them well is using them ethically, as Table 11.1 shows. Coercive power, for example, requires careful administration if it is to be used in an ethical manner. Employees should be informed of the rules in advance, and any punishment should be used consistently, uniformly, and privately. The key to using all five types of interpersonal power ethically is to be sensitive to employees' concerns and to communicate well.

Determining whether a power-related behavior is ethical is a complex process. Another way to look at the ethics surrounding the use of power is to ask three questions that show the criteria for examining power-related behaviors:[9]

■ TABLE 11.1
Guidelines for the Ethical Use of Power

FORM OF POWER	GUIDELINES FOR USE
Reward power	Verify compliance. Make feasible, reasonable requests. Make only ethical requests. Offer rewards desired by subordinates. Offer only credible rewards.
Coercive power	Inform subordinates of rules and penalties. Warn before punishing. Administer punishment consistently and uniformly. Understand the situation before acting. Maintain credibility. Fit punishment to the infraction. Punish in private.
Legitimate power	Be cordial and polite. Be confident. Be clear and follow up to verify understanding. Make sure request is appropriate. Explain reasons for request. Follow proper channels. Exercise power consistently. Enforce compliance. Be sensitive to subordinates' concerns.
Referent power	Treat subordinates fairly. Defend subordinates' interests. Be sensitive to subordinates' needs and feelings. Select subordinates similar to oneself. Engage in role modeling.
Expert power	Maintain credibility. Act confident and decisive. Keep informed. Recognize employee concerns. Avoid threatening subordinates' self-esteem.

SOURCE: Gary A. Yukl, *Leadership in Organizations*, Copyright 1981, pp. 44–58, adapted by permission of Prentice Hall, Englewood Cliffs, NJ.

1. Does the behavior produce a good outcome for people both inside and outside the organization? This question represents the criterion of utilitarian outcomes. The behavior should result in the greatest good for the greatest number of people. If the power-related behavior serves only the individual's self-interest and fails to help the organization reach its goals, it is considered unethical. A salesperson might be tempted to discount a product deeply in order to make a sale that would win a contest. Doing so would be in her self-interest but would not benefit the organization.

2. Does the behavior respect the rights of all parties? This question emphasizes the criterion of individual rights. Free speech, privacy, and due process are individual rights that are to be respected, and power-related behaviors that violate these rights are considered unethical.

3. Does the behavior treat all parties equitably and fairly? This question represents the criterion of distributive justice. Power-related behavior that treats one party arbitrarily or benefits one party at the expense of another is unethical. Granting a day of vacation to one employee in a busy week in which co-workers must struggle to cover for him might be considered unethical.

To be considered ethical, power-related behavior must meet all three criteria. If the behavior fails to meet the criteria, then alternate actions should be considered. Unfortunately, most power-related behaviors are not easy to analyze. Conflicts may exist among the criteria; for example, a behavior may maximize the greatest good for the greatest number of people but may not treat all parties equitably. Individual needs may need to be sacrificed for the good of the organization. A CEO may need to be removed from power for the organization to be saved. Still, these criteria can be used on a case-by-case basis to sort through the complex ethical issues surrounding the use of power.

■ McClelland's Two Faces of Power

We turn now to a theory of power that takes a strong stand on the "right" versus the "wrong" kind of power to use in organizations. David McClelland has spent a great deal of his career studying the need for power and the ways managers use power. As was discussed in Chapter 5, he believes that there are two distinct faces of power, one negative and one positive.[10] The negative face is personal power—power used for personal gain. Managers who use personal power are commonly described as "power hungry." Personal power is a win-lose form in which the manager tends to treat others as objects to be utilized to get ahead. It is based on the traditional notion of power as domination over others.

The positive face of power is social power—used to create motivation or to accomplish group goals. McClelland clearly favors the use of social power by managers. He has found that the best managers are those who have a high need for social power coupled with a relatively low need for affiliation. In addition, he has found that managers who use power successfully have four power-oriented characteristics:

1. Belief in the authority system. They believe that the institution is important and that its authority system is valid. They are comfortable influencing and being influenced. The source of their power is the authority system of which they are a part.

2. Preference for work and discipline. They like their work and are very orderly. They have a basic value preference for a strong work ethic, and believe that work is good for a person over and beyond its income-producing value.

3. Altruism. They publicly put the company and its needs before their own needs. They are able to do this because they see their own well-being as integrally tied to the corporate well-being.

4. Belief in justice. They believe justice is to be sought above all else. People should receive that to which they are entitled and that which they earn.

McClelland takes a definite stand on the proper use of power by managers. When power is used for the good of the group, rather than for individual gain, it is positive. McClelland's approach to power is basically psychological in nature, focusing on the needs and drives of the individual.

■ Intergroup Sources of Power

Groups or teams within an organization can also use power from several sources. One source of intergroup power is control of critical resources.[11] When one group controls an important resource that another group desires, the first group holds power. Controlling resources needed by another group allows the power-holding group to influence the actions of the less powerful group.

Salancik and Pfeffer, who proposed this resource dependency model, conducted a study of university budgeting decisions. Various departments within a university have power by virtue of their national ranking, their ability to win outside grant monies, and their success in attracting promising graduate students. Departments that obtain these critical outside resources are awarded more internal resources from within the university.[12] Thus, one source of group power is control over valued resources.

Groups also have power to the extent that they control strategic contingencies—activities that other groups depend on in order to complete their tasks. The dean's office, for example, may control the number of faculty positions to be filled in each department of a college. The departmental hiring plans are thus contingent on approval from the dean's office. In this case, the dean's office controls the strategic contingency of faculty hiring, and thus has power.

Three factors can give a group control over a strategic contingency.[13] One is the ability to cope with uncertainty. If a group can help another group deal with uncertainty, it has power. One organizational group that has gained power in recent years is the legal department. Faced with increasing government regulations and fears of litigation, many other departments seek guidance from the legal department.

Another factor that can give a group control power is a high degree of centrality within the organization. If a group's functioning is important to the organization's success, it has high centrality. The sales force in a computer firm, for example, has power because of its immediate effect on the firm's operations and because other groups (accounting and servicing groups for example) depend on its activities.

The third factor that can give a group power is nonsubstitutability—the extent to which a group performs a function that is indispensable to an organization. A team of computer specialists may be powerful because of its expertise with a system. It may have specialized experience that another team cannot provide.

The strategic contingencies model thus shows that groups hold power over other groups when they can reduce uncertainty, when their functioning is central to the organization's success, and when the group's activities are difficult to replace.[14]

■ Etzioni's Power Analysis

Amitai Etzioni takes a more sociological orientation to power. Etzioni has developed a theory of power analysis.[15] He says that there are three types of organizational power and three types of organizational involvement, or membership, that will lead to either congruent or incongruent uses of power. The three types of organizational power are the following:

1. Coercive power—influencing members by forcing them to do something under threat of punishment, or through fear intimidation.
2. Utilitarian power—influencing members by providing them with rewards and benefits.
3. Normative power—influencing members by using knowledge that they want very much to belong to the organization and by letting them know that what they are expected to do is the "right" thing to do.

Along with these three types of organizational power, Etzioni proposes that we can classify organizations by the type of membership they have:

1. Alienative membership. The members have hostile, negative feelings about being in the organization. They don't want to be there. Prisons are a good example of alienative memberships.
2. Calculative membership. Members weigh the benefits and limitations of belonging to the organization. Businesses are good examples of organizations with calculative memberships.

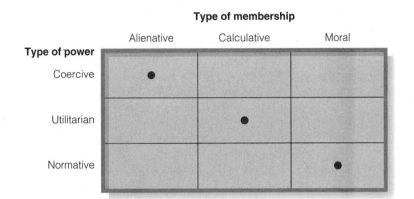

Type of membership

■ FIGURE 11.1
Etzioni's Power Analysis

3. **Moral membership.** Members have such positive feelings about organizational membership that they are willing to deny their own needs. Organizations with many volunteer workers, such as the American Heart Association, are examples of moral memberships. Religious groups are another example.

Etzioni argues that you should match the type of organizational power to the type of membership in the organization in order to achieve congruence. Figure 11.1 shows the matches in his power analysis theory.

In an alienative membership, members have hostile feelings. In prisons, for example, Etzioni would contend that coercive power is the appropriate type to use.

A calculative membership is characterized by an analysis of the goods and bads of being in the organization. In the business partnership example, each partner weighs the benefits from the partnership against the costs entailed in the contractual arrangement. Utilitarian, or reward-based, power is the most appropriate type to use.

In a moral membership, the members have strong positive feelings about the particular cause or goal of the organization. Normative power is the most appropriate to use because it capitalizes on the members' desires to belong.

Etzioni's power analysis is an organizational level theory. It emphasizes that the characteristics of an organization play a role in determining the type of power appropriate for use in the organization. Etzioni's theory is controversial in its contention that a single type of power is appropriate in any organization.

■ KANTER'S SYMBOLS OF POWER

Organization charts show who has authority, but they do not reveal much about who has power. Kanter provides several characteristics of powerful people in organizations:[16]

1. **Ability to intercede for someone in trouble.** An individual who can pull someone out of a jam has power.
2. **Ability to get placements for favored employees.** Getting a key promotion for an employee is a sign of power.
3. **Exceeding budget limitations.** A manager who can go above budget limits without being reprimanded has power.
4. **Procuring above-average raises for employees.** One faculty member reported that her department head distributed 10 percent raises to the most productive faculty members although the budget allowed for only 4 percent increases. "I don't know how he did it; he must have pull," she said.
5. **Getting items on the agenda at meetings.** If a manager can raise issues for action at meetings, it's a sign of power.
6. **Access to early information.** Having information before anyone else does is a signal that a manager is plugged in to key sources.
7. **Having top managers seek out their opinion.** When top managers have a problem, they may ask for advice from lower-level managers. The managers they turn to are the ones who have power.

A theme that runs through Kanter's list is doing things for others: for people in trouble, for employees, for bosses. There is an active, other-directed element in her symbols of power. You can use Kanter's symbols of power to identify powerful people in organizations. They can be particularly useful in finding a mentor who can use power effectively.

■ KANTER'S SYMBOLS OF POWERLESSNESS

Kanter also wrote about symptoms of powerlessness—a lack of power—in managers at different levels of the organization. First-line supervisors, for example, often display three symptoms of powerlessness: overly close supervision, inflexible adherence to the rules, and a tendency to do the job themselves rather than training their employees to do it. Staff professionals such as accountants and lawyers display different symptoms of powerlessness. When they feel powerless, they tend to resist change and try to protect their turf. Top executives can also feel powerless. They show symptoms such as focusing on budget cutting, punishing others, and using dictatorial, top-down communication. Employees at any level can feel powerless. When caught in powerless jobs, they may react passively and display overdependence on their boss.[17] In contrast, they may become frustrated and disrupt the work group.[18] The key to overcoming powerlessness is to share power and delegate tasks to employees.

■ POLITICAL BEHAVIOR IN ORGANIZATIONS

Like power, the term "politics" in organizations may conjure up a few negative images. However, organizational politics is not necessarily negative; it is the use of power and influence in organizations. As people try to acquire power and expand their power base, they use various tactics and strategies. Some are sanctioned (acceptable to the organization); others are not. Political behavior includes actions not officially sanctioned by an organization that are taken to influence others in order to meet one's personal goals.[19]

Politics is a controversial topic among managers. Some managers take a favorable view of political behavior; others see it as detrimental to the organization. In a study of managers, 53 percent reported that politics had a positive impact on the achievement of the organization's goals.[20] In contrast, 44 percent reported that politics distracted organization members from focusing on goal achievement. In a different study, managers displayed conflicting attitudes toward politics in organizations. Over 89 percent agreed that workplace politics were common in most organizations and that successful executives must be good politicians. However, 59 percent indicated that workplaces that were free of politics were more satisfying to work in.[21] Organizational politics can create stress in several ways. Politics may turn individuals and/or groups against each other. In addition, it may appear to employees that certain political behaviors are permitted which are not sanctioned by the organizations. Individuals who have a good understanding of the organizational political system experience less anxiety and distress related to office politics.[22]

Many organizational conditions encourage political activity. Among them are unclear goals, autocratic decision making, ambiguous lines of authority, scarce resources, and uncertainty.[23,24] Even supposedly objective activities may involve politics. One such activity is the performance appraisal process. A study of sixty executives who had extensive experience in employee evaluation indicated that political considerations were nearly always part of the performance appraisal process.[25]

■ Influence Tactics

Influence is the process of affecting the thoughts, behavior, or feelings of another person. That other person could be the boss (upward influence), an employee (downward influence), or a co-worker (lateral influence). There are eight basic types of influence tactics. They are listed and described in Table 11.2.[26,27,28]

Research has shown that the four tactics used most frequently are consultation, rational persua-

■ **TABLE 11.2**
Influence Tactics Used in Organizations

TACTICS	DESCRIPTION	EXAMPLES
Pressure	The person uses demands, threats, or intimidation to convince you to comply with a request or to support a proposal.	If you don't do this, you're fired. You have until 5:00 to change your mind, or I'm going without you.
Upward appeals	The person seeks to persuade you that the request is approved by higher management, or appeals to higher management for assistance in gaining your compliance with the request.	I'm reporting you to my boss. My boss supports this idea.
Exchange	The person makes an explicit or implicit promise that you will receive rewards or tangible benefits if you comply with a request or support a proposal, or reminds you of a prior favor to be reciprocated.	You owe me a favor. I'll take you to lunch if you'll support me on this.
Coalition	The person seeks the aid of others to persuade you to do something or uses the support of others as an argument for you to agree also.	All the other supervisors agree with me. I'll ask you in front of the whole committee.
Ingratiation	The person seeks to get you in a good mood or to think favorably of him or her before asking you to do something.	Only you can do this job right. I can always count on you, so I have another request.
Rational persuasion	The person uses logical arguments and factual evidence to persuade you that a proposal or request is viable and likely to result in the attainment of task objectives.	This new procedure will save us $150,000 in overhead. It makes sense to hire John; he has the most experience.
Inspirational appeals	The person makes an emotional request or proposal that arouses enthusiasm by appealing to your values and ideals, or by increasing your confidence that you can do it.	Being environmentally conscious is the right thing. Getting that account will be tough, but I know you can do it.
Consultation	The person seeks your participation in making a decision or planning how to implement a proposed policy, strategy, or change.	This new attendance plan is controversial. How can we make it more acceptable? What do you think we can do to make our workers less fearful of the new robots on the production line?

SOURCE: First two columns from G. Yukl and C. M. Falbe, "Influence Tactics and Objectives in Upward, Downward, and Lateral Influence Attempts," *Journal of Applied Psychology* 5 (1990): 132–140. Copyright 1990 by the American Psychological Association. Reprinted by permission.

sion, inspirational appeals, and ingratiation, regardless of the target of the influence attempt. Thus, individuals do not differentiate among bosses, subordinates, and peers in terms of the tactic they choose. Upward appeals and coalition tactics are used moderately. Exchange tactics are used least often.

Some of the influence tactics are used for impression management, which was described in Chapter 3. In impression management, individuals use influence tactics to control others' impressions of them. Ingratiation is an example of one tactic often used for impression management. Ingratiation can take many forms, including flattery, opinion conformity, and subservient behavior.[29] Exchange is another influence tactic that may be used for impression management. Offering to do favors for someone in an effort to create a favorable impression is an exchange tactic.

Which influence tactics are most effective? In several studies of managers from a wide variety of organizations, it was found that rational ideas based on the needs of the target were most likely to achieve the influence objective. In addition, it was found that threatening or pressure tactics led to failed influence attempts.[30] Another study found that employees tailored their upward influence tactics to the management styles of their bosses. Ingratiation and upward appeals were used with authoritarian managers, and rational persuasion was used to influence managers with participative styles.[31]

There is evidence that men and women view politics and influence attempts differently. Men tend to view political behavior more favorably than do women. When both men and women witness political behavior, they view it more positively if the agent is of their gender and the target is of the opposite gender.[32]

There is also some preliminary evidence that different cultures prefer different influence tactics at work. One study found that American managers dealing with a tardy employee tended to rely on pressure tactics such as "If you don't start reporting on time for work, I will have no choice but to start docking your pay." In contrast, Japanese managers relied on influence tactics that either appealed to the employee's sense of duty ("It is your duty as a responsible employee of this company to begin work on time,") or emphasized a consultative approach ("Is there anything I can do to help you overcome the problems that are preventing you from coming to work on time?").[33]

How can a manager use influence tactics well? First, a manager can develop and maintain open lines of communication in all directions: upward, downward, and lateral. Then, the manager can treat the targets of influence attempts—whether managers, employees, or peers—with basic respect. Finally, the manager can understand that influence relationships are reciprocal—they are two-way relationships. As long as the influence attempts are directed toward organizational goals, the process of influence can be advantageous to all involved.

■ Managing Political Behavior in Organizations

Politics cannot and should not be eliminated from organizations. Managers can, however, take a proactive stance and manage the political behavior that inevitably occurs.[34] James E. Dalton, Jr., has a simple approach to managing political behavior. As president and CEO of Quorum Health Group, the world's largest hospital management and consulting services company, he has learned how to manage political behavior to the company's advantage. Dalton notes that if a manager does not recognize the informal political network and fails to participate in it, he/she runs a risk of being vulnerable to an attack. And, he says, informal networks can be used to promote continuous improvement of quality throughout the organizations.

Open communication is one key to managing political behavior. Uncertainty is a condition that tends to increase political behavior, and communication that reduces the uncertainty is important. One form of communication that will help is to clarify the sanctioned and nonsanctioned political behaviors in the organization. For example, you may want to encourage social power as opposed to personal power.

Another key is to clarify expectations regarding performance. This can be accomplished through the use of clear, quantifiable goals and through the use of a clear connection between goal accomplishment and rewards.

Participative management is yet another key. Often, people engage in political behavior when they feel excluded from decision-making processes in the organization. By including them, you will encourage positive input and eliminate behind-the-scenes maneuvering.

Managing scarce resources well is also important. An obvious solution to the problem of scarce resources is to increase the resource pool, but few managers have this luxury. Clarifying the resource allocation process and making the connection between performance and resources explicit can help discourage dysfunctional political behavior.

■ MANAGING UP: MANAGING THE BOSS

One of the least discussed aspects of power and politics is the relationship between you and your boss. This is a crucial relationship, because your boss is your most important link with the rest of the organization.[35] The employee-boss relationship is one of mutual dependence; you depend on your boss to give you performance feedback, provide resources, and supply critical information. She depends on you for performance, information, and support. Because it's a mutual relationship, you should take an active role in managing it. Too often, the management of this relationship is left to the boss; but if the relationship doesn't meet your needs, chances are you haven't taken the responsibility to manage it proactively.

Table 11.3 shows the basic steps to take in managing your relationship with your boss. The first step is to try to understand as much as you can about

■ TABLE 11.3
Managing Your Relationship with Your Boss

Make Sure You Understand Your Boss and Her Context, Including:
Her goals and objectives.
The pressures on her.
Her strengths, weaknesses, blind spots.
Her preferred work style.
Assess Yourself and Your Needs, Including:
Your own strengths and weaknesses.
Your personal style.
Your predisposition toward dependence on authority figures.
Develop and Maintain a Relationship That:
Fits both your needs and styles.
Is characterized by mutual expectations.
Keeps your boss informed.
Is based on dependability and honesty.
Selectively uses your boss's time and resources.

SOURCE: J. J. Gabarro and J. P. Kotter, "Managing Your Boss," *Harvard Business Review* (January–February 1980): 92–100

your boss. What are the person's goals and objectives? What kind of pressures does the person face in the job? Many individuals naively expect the boss to be perfect and are disappointed when they find that this is not the case. What are the boss's strengths, weaknesses, and blind spots? Because this is an emotionally charged relationship, it is difficult to be objective; but this is a critical step in forging an effective working relationship. What is the boss's preferred work style? Does the person prefer everything in writing or hate detail? Does the boss prefer that you make appointments, or is dropping in at the boss's office acceptable? The point is to gather as much information about your boss as you can and to try to put yourself in that person's shoes.

The second step in managing this important relationship is to assess yourself and your own needs much in the same way you analyzed your boss's. What are your strengths, weaknesses, and blind spots? What is your work style? How do you normally relate to authority figures? Some of us have tendencies toward counterdependence; that is, we rebel against the boss as an authority and view the boss as a hindrance to our performance. Or, in contrast, we might take an overdependent stance, passively accepting the boss-employee relationship and treating the boss as an all-wise, protective parent. What is your tendency? Knowing how you react to authority figures can help you understand your interactions with your boss.

Once you have done a careful self-analysis and tried to understand your boss, the next step is to work to develop an effective relationship. Both parties' needs and styles must be accommodated. A fundraiser for a large volunteer organization related a story about a new boss, describing him as cold, aloof, unorganized, and inept. She made repeated attempts to meet with him and clarify expectations, and his usual reply was that he didn't have the time. Frustrated, she almost looked for a new job. "I just can't reach him!" was her refrain. Then she stepped back to consider her boss's and her own styles. Being an intuitive-feeling type of person, she prefers constant feedback and reinforcement from others. Her boss, an intuitive-thinker, works comfortably without feedback from others and has a tendency to fail to praise or reward others. She sat down with him and cautiously discussed the differences in their needs. This discussion became the basis for working out a comfortable relationship. "I still don't like him, but I understand him better," she said.

Another aspect of managing the relationship involves working out mutual expectations. One key activity is to develop a plan for work objectives and have the boss agree to it.[36] It is important to do things right, but it is also important to do the right things. Neither party to the relationship is a mind reader, and clarifying the goals is a crucial step.

Keeping the boss informed is also a priority. No one likes to be caught off guard and surprised, and there are several ways to keep the boss informed. Give the boss a weekly to-do list as a reminder of the progress towards goals. When you read something pertaining to your work, clip it out for the boss. Most busy executives appreciate being given materials they don't have time to find for themselves. Give the boss interim reports, and let the boss know if the work schedule is slipping. Don't wait until it's too late to take action.

The employee-boss relationship must be based on mutual respect and honesty. This means giving and receiving positive and negative feedback. Most of us are reluctant to give any feedback to the boss, but positive feedback is welcomed at the top. Negative feedback, while tougher to initiate, can clear the air. If given in a problem-solving format, it can even bring about a closer relationship.[37]

One university professor was constantly bombarded by the department head's requests that she serve on committees. When she complained about this to a colleague, she was told, "It's your fault; you need to learn how to say no." She went to the department head, explained that the committee work was keeping her from being an effective researcher and teacher, and asked that he reassign other faculty members to the committees. The department head was astonished that he had relied on her so heavily. "I just didn't realize that you were on so many committees already. Thanks for pointing it out. We need to spread these responsibilities around better."

Another point about negative feedback is that it is better to give it directly, rather than behind the boss's back. If the boss never gets the information, how can the problem be corrected?

Being considerate of the boss's time is important. Before running into the person's office, ask yourself if the meeting is necessary at that particular time. Does the boss need the information right now? Could you supply the information in a note? Is it a matter you could handle yourself? Another good time management technique is to submit an agenda before your meeting with the boss; that way, the boss can select an appropriate time slot and will have time to think about the items.

Finally, remember that the boss is on the same team you are. The golden rule is to make the boss look good, because you expect the boss to do the same for you.

■ SHARING POWER: EMPOWERMENT

Another positive strategy for managing political behavior is empowerment—sharing power within an organization. As modern organizations grow flatter, eliminating layers of management, empowerment becomes more and more important. Jay Conger defines empowerment as "creating conditions for heightened motivation through the development of a strong sense of personal self-efficacy."[38] This means sharing power in such a way that individuals learn to believe in their ability to do the job. The driving idea of empowerment is that the individuals closest to the work and to the customers should make the decisions and that this makes the best use of employees' skills and talents.[39] Peter Block, author of *The Empowered Manager*, describes his philosophy of empowerment this way: "If we want to empower people—to get them to take responsibility for their own actions and the success of their own units-we have to give up some control, de-emphasize the power we have over people under us, and acknowledge that while the captain may set the course, the engines drive the ship."[40]

Empowerment is easy to advocate but difficult to put into practice. Conger offers some guidelines on how leaders can empower others. First, managers should express confidence in employees and set high performance expectations. Positive expectations can go a long way toward enabling good performance, as the Pygmalion effect shows (Chapter 3).

Second, managers should create opportunities for employees to participate in decision making. This means participation in the forms of both voice and choice. Employees should not only be asked to contribute their opinions about any issue; they should also have a vote in the decision that is made. One method for increasing participation is using self-managed teams, as we discussed in Chapter 9.

Third, managers should remove bureaucratic constraints that stifle autonomy. Often, companies have antiquated rules and policies that prevent employees from managing themselves. An example is a collection agency where a manager's signature was once required to approve long-term payment arrangements for delinquent customers. Collectors, who spoke directly with customers, were the best judges of whether the payment arrangements were workable, and having to consult a manager made them feel closely supervised and powerless. The rule was dropped, and collections increased.

Fourth, managers should set inspirational or meaningful goals. When individuals feel they "own" a goal, they are more willing to take personal responsibility for it.

One organization that practices empowerment successfully is Square D Company, an electronics technology company of 20,000 employees.[41] Square D created Vision College in 1987 to focus on personal accountability for the company's vision: "Dedicated to growth, committed to quality." Vision College provides an opportunity for Square D employees to compare their current state with their vision, or desired state. All Square D employees participate in two-day Vision College sessions, in which the employees provide information about what works, what doesn't work, and what needs improvement in the company. They also discuss and define their own role in that improvement process. The establishment of Vision College to promote empowerment has moved accountability to the lowest levels of the organization.

At Oregon Cutting Systems, empowerment is a key element of the quality process. The company designs and manufactures cutting tools and holds half of the world's market in chains for saws. In this company, machine operators use statistical process control to improve product quality. Operators are empowered to gather their own data, find the causes of problems, make decisions, and act to fix the problems. Managers at Oregon Cutting Systems prefer that employees ask for forgiveness rather than permission. Empowerment is essential to an organizational culture that supports quality.

The empowerment process also carries with it a risk of failure. When you delegate responsibility and authority, you must be prepared to allow employees to fail; and failure is not something most managers tolerate well. At Levi Strauss, an employee failed to order enough fabric to meet a production run on jeans. The manager sat down with the employee and found out what had gone wrong and how to prevent that problem in the future. She did this in a nonthreatening way, without blaming or finger-pointing.[42] Coaching and counseling following a failure can turn it into a learning experience.

Empowerment is a major emphasis for all ten of *Industry Week's* "Best Plants" winners. As a key contributor to manufacturing excellence, empowerment efforts in these plants are often part of quality improvement programs. "Best Plant" winners include Exxon Chemical Company of Baytown, Texas and Unisys Government Systems of Pueblo, Colorado, among others.[43]

■ MANAGERIAL IMPLICATIONS: USING POWER EFFECTIVELY

Managers must depend on others to get things done. John Kotter argues that managers therefore need to develop power strategies to operate effectively.[44,45] Kotter offers some guidelines for managing dependence on others and for using power successfully:

■ Use power in ethical ways. People have certain assumptions about the use of power. One way of using the various forms of power ethically is by applying the criteria of utilitarian outcomes, individual rights, and distributive justice.

■ Understand and use all of the various types of power and influence. Successful managers diagnose the situation, understand the people involved, and choose a compatible influence method.

- Seek out jobs that allow you to develop your power skills. Recognize that managerial positions are dependent ones, and look for positions that allow you to focus on a critical issue or problem.
- Use power tempered by maturity and self-control. Power for its own sake should not be a goal, nor should power be used for self-aggrandizement.
- Accept that influencing people is an important part of the management job. Power means getting things accomplished; it is not a dirty word. Acquiring and using power well is a key to managerial success.

Mastering the power and politics within an organization takes respect and patience. When all people are treated as important, the total amount of power within the organization will increase.

■ CHAPTER SUMMARY

- Power is the ability to influence others. Influence is the process of affecting the thoughts, behavior, and feelings of others. Authority is the right to influence others.
- French and Raven's five forms of interpersonal power are reward, coercive, legitimate, referent, and expert power. The key to using all of these types of power well is to use them ethically.
- McClelland believes personal power is negative and social power is positive.
- Intergroup power sources include control of critical resources and strategic contingencies.
- According to Etzioni, an important factor in deciding the type of power to use is the characteristics of the organization.
- Recognizing symbols of both power and powerlessness is a key diagnostic skill for managers.
- Organizational politics is an inevitable feature of work life. Political behavior consists of actions not officially sanctioned that are taken to influence others in order to meet personal goals.*
- Managers should take a proactive role in managing politics.
- Empowerment is a positive strategy for sharing power throughout the organization.

■ REVIEW QUESTIONS

1. What are the five types of power according to French and Raven? What are the effects of these types of power?
2. What are the intergroup sources of power?
3. Distinguish between personal and social power. What are the four power-oriented characteristics of the best managers?
4. Identify Etzioni's types of power and types of membership used to achieve congruence.
5. According to Rosabeth Moss Kanter, what are the symbols of power? The symptoms of powerlessness?
6. What are some ways to empower people at work?
7. Which of French and Raven's five types of power has the most potential for abuse? How can the abuse be prevented?
8. Is it possible to have an organization where all power is equally shared, or is the unequal distribution of power a necessary evil in organizations? Explain.

■ REFERENCES

1. G. C. Homans, "Social Behavior as Exchange," *American Journal of Sociology* 63 (1958): 597–606.
2. C. Barnard, *The Functions of the Executive* (Cambridge, Mass., Harvard University Press, 1938).
3. J. R. P. French and B. Raven, "The Bases of Social Power," in D. Cartwright, ed., *Group Dynamics: Research and Theory* (Evanston, Ill.: Row, Peterson, 1962).
4. T. R. Hinkin and C. A. Schriesheim, "Development and Application of New Scales to Measure the French and Raven (1959) Bases of Social Power," *Journal of Applied Psychology* 74 (1989): 561–567.
5. P. M. Podsakoff and C. A. Schriesheim, "Field Studies of French and Raven's Bases of Power: Critique, Reanalysis, and Suggestions for Future Research," *Psychological Bulletin* 97 (1985): 387–411.
6. M. A. Rahim, "Relationships of Leader Power to Compliance and Satisfaction with Supervision: Evidence from a National Sample of Managers," *Journal of Management* 15 (1989): 545–556.
7. C. Argyris, "Management Information Systems: The Challenge to Rationality and Emotionality," *Management Science* 17 (1971): 275–292.

8. J. Naisbitt and P. Aburdene, *Megatrends 2000* (New York: Morrow, 1990).

9. M. Velasquez, D. J. Moberg, and G. F. Cavanaugh, "Organizational Statesmanship and Dirty Politics: Ethical Guidelines for the Organizational Politician," *Organizational Dynamics* 11 (1982): 65–79.

10. D. E. McClelland, *Power: The Inner Experience* (New York: Irvington, 1975).

11. J. Pfeffer and G. Salancik, *The External Control of Organizations* (New York: Harper & Row, 1978).

12. G. Salancik and J. Pfeffer, "The Bases and Uses of Power in Organizational Decision Making," *Administrative Science Quarterly* 15 (1971): 216–229.

13. D. Hickson, C. Hinings, C. Lee, R. E. Schneck, and J. M. Pennings, "A Strategic Contingencies Theory of Intraorganizational Power," *Administrative Science Quarterly* 14 (1971): 219–220.

14. C. R. Hinings, D. J. Hickson, J. M. Pennings, and R. E. Schneck, "Structural Conditions of Intraorganizational Power," *Administrative Science Quarterly* 19 (1974): 22–44.

15. A. Etzioni, *Modern Organizations* (Englewood Cliffs, N.J.: Prentice-Hall, 1964).

16. R. Kanter, "Power Failure in Management Circuits," *Harvard Business Review* (July-August 1979): 31–54.

17. L. Mainiero, "Coping with Powerlessness: The Relationship of Gender and Job Dependency to Empowerment Strategy Usage," *Administrative Science Quarterly* 31 (1986): 633–653.

18. B. E. Ashforth, "The Experience of Powerlessness in Organizations," *Organizational Behavior and Human Decision Processes* 43 (1989): 207–242.

19. B. T. Mayes and R. T. Allen, "Toward a Definition of Organizational Politics," *Academy of Management Review* 2 (1977): 672–678.

20. D. L. Madison, R. W. Allen, L. W. Porter, and B. T. Mayes, "Organizational Politics: An Exploration of Managers' Perceptions," *Human Relations* 33 (1980): 92–107.

21. J. Gandz and V. Murray, "The Experience of Workplace Politics," *Academy of Management Journal* 23 (1980): 237–251.

22. G. Ferris, D. Frink, D. Gilmore, and K. M. Kacmar, "Understanding as an Antidote for Dysfunctional Consequences of Organizational Politics as a Stressor," *Journal of Applied Social Psychology* 24 (1994): 1209–1220.

23. D. A. Ralston, "Employee Ingratiation: The Role of Management," *Academy of Management Review* 10 (1985): 477–487.

24. D. R. Beeman and T. W. Sharkey, "The Use and Abuse of Corporate Politics," *Business Horizons* (March-April 1987): 25–35.

25. C. O. Longnecker, H. P. Sims, and D. A. Gioia, "Behind the Mask: The Politics of Employee Appraisal," *Academy of Management Executive* 1 (1987): 183–193.

26. D. Kipnis, S. M. Schmidt, and I. Wilkinson, "Intraorganizational Influence Tactics: Explorations in Getting One's Way," *Journal of Applied Psychology* 65 (1980): 440–452.

27. D. Kipnis, S. Schmidt, C. Swaffin-Smith, and I. Wilkinson, "Patterns of Managerial Influence: Shotgun Managers, Tacticians, and Bystanders," *Organizational Dynamics* (Winter 1984): 60–67.

28. G. Yukl and C. M. Falbe, "Influence Tactics and Objectives in Upward, Downward, and Lateral Influence Attempts," *Journal of Applied Psychology* 2 (1990): 132–140.

29. G. R. Ferris and T. A. Judge, "Personnel/Human Resources Management: A Political Influence Perspective," *Journal of Management* 17 (1991): 447–488.

30. B. Keys and T. Case, "How To Become an Influential Manager," *Academy of Management Executive* 4 (1990): 38–51.

31. M. A. Ansari and A. Kapoor, "Organizational Context and Upward Influence Tactics," *Organizational Behavior and Human Decision Processes* 39 (1987): 39–49.

32. A. Drory and D. Beaty, "Gender Differences in the Perception of Organizational Influence Tactics," *Journal of Organizational Behavior* 12 (1991): 249–258.

33. R. Y. Hirokawa and A. Miyahara, "A Comparison of Influence Strategies Utilized by Managers in American and Japanese Organizations," *Communication Quarterly* 34 (1986): 250–265.

34. K. Kumar and M. S. Thibodeaux, "Organizational Politics and Planned Organizational Change," *Group and Organization Studies* 15 (1990): 354–365.

35. J. J. Gabarro and J. P. Kotter, "Managing Your Boss," *Harvard Business Review* (January-February 1980): 92–100.

36. P. Newman, "How to Manage Your Boss," *Peat, Marwick, Mitchell & Company's Management Focus*, (May-June 1980), 36–37.

37. F. Bertolome, "When You Think the Boss Is Wrong," *Personnel Journal* 69 (1990): 66–73.

38. J. Conger and R. Kanungo, *Charismatic Leadership: The Elusive Factor in Organizational Effectiveness* (New York: Jossey-Bass, 1988).

39. T. Brown, "Fearful of Empowerment," *Industry Week* 239 (1990): 12.

40. P. Block, "How to be the New Kind of Manager," *Working Woman*, July 1990, 51–54.

41. J. T. McKenna, "Smart Scarecrows: The Wizardry of Empowerment," *Industry Week*, 16 July 1990, 8–19.

42. B. Dumaine, "The Bureaucracy Busters," *Fortune*, 17 June 1991, 36–50.

43. J. H. Sheridan, "How Do You Stack Up?" *Industry Week*, 21 February 1994, 53–56.

44. J. P. Kotter, "Power, Dependence, and Effective Management," *Harvard Business Review* 55 (1977): 125–136.

45. J. P. Kotter, *Power and Influence* (New York: Free Press, 1985).

CHAPTER 12
LEADERSHIP AND FOLLOWERSHIP

LEARNING OBJECTIVES

After reading this chapter, you should be able to do the following:

- Define leadership and followership.
- Discuss the differences between leadership and management.
- Distinguish between transformational, transactional, and charismatic leaders.
- Compare autocratic, democratic, and laissez-faire leadership.
- Explain initiating structure and consideration, as well as P-oriented and M-oriented leader behaviors.
- Compare the five leadership styles in the managerial grid.
- Explain Fiedler's contingency theory of leadership.
- Distinguish among three Type IV leadership theories: the path-goal theory, the Vroom-Yetton-Jago theory, and the situational leadership model.
- Discuss the characteristics of effective and dynamic followers.

Leadership in organizations is the process of guiding and directing the behavior of people in the work environment. The first section of the chapter distinguishes leadership from management. Formal leadership occurs when an organization officially bestows upon a leader the power and authority to guide and direct others in the organization. Informal leadership occurs when others in an organization unofficially accord a person the power and influence to guide and direct their behavior. Leadership is among the most researched topics in organizational behavior and one of the least understood social processes in organizations.

Sections two through five examine four types of leadership theories. Section six summarizes guidelines for leadership in organizations. The final section of the chapter focuses on the process of followership. Followership in organizations is the process of being guided and directed by a leader in the work environment. Leaders and followers are companions in these processes.[1] Bob Galvin, former CEO of Motorola, believed that to lead well presumed the ability to follow smartly.

■ LEADERSHIP AND MANAGEMENT

John Kotter suggests that leadership and management are two distinct, yet complementary systems of action in organizations.[2] Specifically, he believes that effective leadership produces useful change in organizations (as exemplified by Lee Iacocca at Chrysler Corporation in the early 1980s) and that good management controls complexity in the organization and its environment (as exemplified by John Scully at Apple Computer). Healthy organizations need both effective leadership and good management. For Kotter, the management process involves (1) planning and budgeting, (2) organizing and staffing, and (3) controlling and problem solving. The management process reduces uncertainty and stabilizes an organization. Alfred P. Sloan's integration and stabilization of General Motors after its early growth years is an example of good management.

In contrast, the leadership process involves (1) setting a direction for the organization; (2) aligning people with that direction through communication; and (3) motivating people to action, partly through empowerment and partly through basic need gratification. The leadership process creates uncertainty and change in an organization. Donald Peterson's championing of a quality revolution at Ford Motor Company exemplified effective leadership. More

currently, General Electric Medical Systems Group (GEMS) uses the Global Leadership Program to train leaders for global operations, focusing on cross-cultural and language skills. Using a personality, as opposed to behavioral, approach, Abraham Zaleznik argues that leaders and managers are fundamentally different types of people.[3] Both make a valuable contribution to an organization, and each one's contribution is different from the other's. Whereas, leaders agitate for change and new approaches, managers advocate stability and the status quo. There is a dynamic tension between leaders and managers that makes it difficult for each to understand the other. Leaders and managers differ along four separate dimensions of personality: attitudes toward goals, conceptions of work, relationships with other people, and sense of self. The differences between these two personality types are summarized in Table 12.1.

This chapter emphasizes leadership and leaders, rather than management and managers. It uses an organization scheme to classify leadership theories according to a two-dimensional scheme.[4] The first dimension divides the theories into those concerned with the leader's traits or personality versus those concerned with the leader's behavior. The second dimension divides the theories into those that may be universal for all leadership situations and those

■ **TABLE 12.1**
Leaders and Managers

PERSONALITY DIMENSION	MANAGER	LEADER
Attitudes toward goals	Has an impersonal, passive, functional attitude; believes goals arise out of necessity and reality	Has a personal and active attitude; believes goals arise from desire and imagination
Conceptions of work	Views work as an enabling process that combines people, ideas, and things; seeks moderate risk through coordination and balance	Looks for fresh approaches to old problems; seeks high-risk positions, especially with high payoffs
Relationships with others	Avoids solitary work activity, preferring to work with others; avoids close, intense relationships; avoids conflict	Is comfortable in solitary work activity; encourages close, intense working relationships; is not conflict averse
Sense of self	Is once born; makes a straightforward life adjustment; accepts life as it is	Is twice born; engages in a struggle for a sense of order in life; questions life

SOURCE: A. Zaleznik, "Managers and Leaders: Are They Different?" *Harvard Business Review 55* (1977): 67–77.

that are situationally specific. The situationally specific theories, are often called contingency theories, and began emerging after 1948.[5] When both dimensions are considered, four types of leadership theories emerge. Type I theories are universal trait theories; Type II are universal behavioral theories; Type III are contingent trait theories; and Type IV are contingent behavior theories. Each type of theory is discussed in a separate section of the chapter.

■ TYPE I THEORIES

Type I theories of leadership were the first attempts at understanding leadership. These theories attempt to identify the traits and/or inherent attributes of leaders, regardless of the leaders' situation or circumstances, as well as the impact of these traits and/or styles on the followers. Early Type I theories focused on a leader's physical attributes, personality, and abilities. Recently, a renewed interest in Type I theories has focused attention on the distinctions between leaders and managers, as well as on charismatic leadership. The implications of Type I theories for organizations involve selection issues rather than training and development issues.

■ Physical Attributes, Personality, and Abilities

The first studies of leadership attempted to identify what physical attributes, personality characteristics, and abilities distinguished leaders from other members of a group.[6] The physical attributes considered have been height, weight, physique, energy, health, appearance, and even age. This line of research yielded some interesting findings. However, very few valid generalizations emerged from this line of inquiry. Therefore, there is insufficient evidence to conclude that leaders can be distinguished from followers on the basis of physical attributes.

Leader personality characteristics that have been examined include originality, adaptability, introversion-extraversion, dominance, self-confidence, integrity, conviction, mood optimism, and emotional control. There is some evidence that leaders may be more adaptable and self-confident than the average group member. With regard to leader abilities, atten-

tion has been devoted to such constructs as social skills, intelligence, scholarship, speech fluency, cooperativeness, and insight. In this area, there is some evidence that leaders are more intelligent, verbal, and cooperative and have a higher level of scholarship than the average group member.

These conclusions suggest traits leaders possess, but the findings are neither strong nor uniform. For each attribute or trait claimed to distinguish leaders from followers, there always were at least one or two studies with contradictory findings. This suggests a limitation in the ability to identify universal, distinguishing attributes of leaders.

■ Transformational and Transactional Leaders

In an in-depth examination of leaders and leadership, James McGregor Burns found a distinction between transactional and transformational leaders.[7] Transactional leaders use formal rewards and punishments to manage followers; they formally or informally engage in deal making and contractual obligations. Transformational leaders inspire and excite followers to high levels of performance. These leaders rely on their personal attributes instead of their official position to manage followers. For example, the late Sam Walton may be considered the transformational leader and the visionary heart of Wal-Mart. Certainly he changed the way the United States did business in retailing. However, as in the case of Wal-Mart, it becomes an organizational challenge to figure out a way to institutionalize a transformational leader's style and vision.[8]

There is some evidence that leaders may learn transformational leadership and benefit from its power to inspire followers to perform beyond expectations.[9] As a young student at Texas A&M University, for example, Henry Cisneros began developing the leadership skills that would later enable him to inspire his diverse followers as mayor of San Antonio; co-chairman of the National Hispanic Leadership Agenda and most recently, President Bill Clinton's Secretary of Housing and Urban Development.[10] Cisneros believes that studying the history and biographies of great leaders can enable a person to develop transformational leadership skills. As U.S. corporations increasingly operate in a global economy, there is a greater demand for leaders who can practice transformational leadership by converting their visions into reality.

A leadership gap may develop in organizations and society if bureaucratic organizations foster the development only of transactional leaders and not transformational leaders.[11] Because leaders challenge established ways of working, they are a source of uncertainty, anxiety, and discomfort to the organization, and they challenge its stability. Leaders want to change the established order to improve the system. While at General Motors, John DeLorean never fully accepted the GM way of doing things; he was a leader who agitated for improvements in the system. DeLorean was less concerned with appearances, which were important at GM, than he was with substance in automotive manufacturing. However, too much agitation led to his early departure from General Motors. The dilemma for an organization is finding out how to draw on the strengths and contributions of each type of personality without alienating either type.

■ Women Leaders

If leaders and managers are different, do women and men lead differently? Historical stereotypes persist and people characterize successful managers as having more male-oriented attributes than female-oriented attributes.[12] Although legitimate gender differences may exist, the same leadership traits may be interpreted differently in a man and a woman because of stereotypes. The real issue should be leader behaviors that are not bound by gender stereotypes.

Women who describe their leadership style in transformational terms may be very successful in traditional or nontraditional organizations.[13] Women leaders are more likely than men to include and energize people, helping them feel important. Women leaders have learned out of necessity to lead without formal authority, so they do not necessarily covet formal authority. Because women have traditionally been excluded from very top-level leadership in corporations, they often go out and build their own organizations. Anita Roddick did exactly that when she built The Body Shop, a large international organization.

■ Charismatic Leadership

Anita Roddick is a charismatic leader who created a vision and sold it to customers and followers alike, motivating her followers to fulfill the vision. Charismatic leadership results when a leader uses the force of personal abilities and talents to have profound and extraordinary effects on followers.[14] Some scholars see transformational leadership and charismatic leadership as very similar, but others believe they are different. Charisma is a Greek word meaning "gift;" the charismatic leader's unique and powerful gifts are the source of their great influence with followers.[15] In fact, followers often view the charismatic leader as one who possesses superhuman, or even mystical, qualities. Charismatic leaders rely heavily on referent power, discussed in Chapter 11. Followers often accept unconditionally the mission and directions of the leader, suspending their own discriminatory judgment. Hence, charismatic leadership carries with it not only great potential for high levels of achievement and performance on the part of followers but also shadowy risks of destructive courses of action that might harm followers or other people.

Charismatic leadership falls to those who are chosen (are born with the "gift" of charisma) or who cultivate that gift. Some say charismatic leaders are born, and others say they are taught.

Recent efforts have attempted to demystify charismatic leadership and distinguish its two faces.[16] The ugly face of charisma is revealed in the personalized power motivations of Adolf Hitler in Nazi Germany and Jim Jones in the Jamestown Colony. Both men led their followers into struggle, conflict, and death. The brighter face of charisma is revealed in the socialized power motivations of U.S. President Franklin D. Roosevelt and of Cable News Network (CNN) entrepreneur Ted Turner, who has built a large business empire. Peter Drucker has thoughtfully described the styles of President Roosevelt and other leaders from first-hand experience. Whereas charismatic leaders with socialized power motivation are concerned about the collective well-being of their followers, charismatic leaders with a personalized power motivation are driven by the need for personal gain and glorification. The former is a constructive force for organizational improvement, whereas the latter is destructive.

Charismatic leadership, like other Type I theories, does not address attributes of the situation that may create contingencies for the exercise of leadership. Whereas the early Type I theories focused on a leader's physical attributes, personality, and abilities, subsequent Type I theories examined leaders from psychodynamic and power motivation perspectives. All Type I theories are concerned with inherent attributes of leaders. Type II theories of leadership shift the focus from traits and attributes to actions and behaviors.

■ TYPE II THEORIES

Type II theories of leadership are concerned with describing leaders' actions and behaviors, often from the perspective of the followers. Like Type I theories, Type II theories exclusively emphasize the leader, as opposed to situational characteristics. Although Type II theories depend in some cases on the descriptions by followers of their leaders, these theories do not consider characteristics of the followers themselves or of the leadership situation in understanding the leadership process. The first Type II theory classified leaders according to one of three basic leadership styles, whereas subsequent Type II theories examined common behavioral dimensions of all leaders. Type II theories help organizations train and develop leaders rather than select them.

■ Leadership Style and Emotional Climate at Work

The earliest research on leadership style, conducted by Kurt Lewin and his students, identified three basic styles: autocratic, democratic, and laissez-faire.[17] Each leader uses one of these three basic styles when approaching a group of followers in a leadership situation. The specific situation is not an important consideration, because the leader's style does not vary with the situation. Rather, the leader's style is a universal trait taken into all situations. The autocratic style is directive, strong, and controlling in relationships. Leaders with an autocratic style use rules and regulations to run the work environment. Followers have little discretionary influence over the nature of the work, its accomplishment, or other aspects of the work environment. The leader with a democratic style is collaborative, responsive, and interactive in relationships and emphasizes rules and regulations less than the autocratic leader. Followers have a high degree of discretionary influence, although the leader has ultimate authority and responsibility. The leader with a laissez-faire style leads through nonleadership. A laissez-faire leader abdicates the authority and responsibility of the position.

Subsequent leadership research has used somewhat different terminology for the same leadership styles: an autocratic style has been labeled boss-centered, job centered, authoritarian, and even dictatorial. All these labels refer to the same basic traits of autocratic leadership. Likewise, a democratic style has been labeled subordinate-centered, employee-centered, and participative. All these labels refer to the same basic traits of democratic leadership. The laissez-faire style of leadership has not had a comparable alternative set of labels. It is uniformly referred to as laissez-faire leadership.

This approach to the study of leadership, developed at the University of Michigan, suggests that the leader's style has very important implications for the emotional atmosphere of the work environment and, therefore, for the followers who work under leaders of each style. Comparing the work environments under autocratic and democratic leadership is easier than attempting to compare either with the work environment under laissez-faire leadership. The most pronounced consequence of laissez-faire leadership tends to be chaos in the work environment, although there are exceptions.

An autocratic leadership style leads to a work environment characterized by constant influence attempts on the part of the leader, either through direct, close supervision or through the use of many written and unwritten rules and regulations for behavior. The resulting restrictive work environment can create high levels of tension for followers. High tension may affect followers in one of two ways in the work environment. Either the followers strongly inhibit their tension and suppress any conflict at work (which leads to a superficially calm atmosphere), or they express their tension (which results in periodic outbursts of intense conflict and aggression). The pathway the followers choose is in part determined by the strength of the leader. In either case, the autocratic style leads to a restriction of the physical and psychological discretion that followers feel. Finally, leader-follower relationships are often rigid in authoritarian environments. When not taken to an extreme, autocratic leadership can provide structure in the work environment and direction for followers who need clear, explicit guidelines for action.

In comparison with an autocratic leadership style, a democratic leadership style leads to a work environment characterized by fewer influence attempts by the leader. The leader exhibits less direct or less close supervision and establishes fewer written or unwritten rules and regulations for behavior. This pattern of influence leads to lower levels of tension among followers. Nonetheless, tension may still exist and be manifested in expressed conflict, usually over ideas and issues. The conflict tends not to be personalized. Followers in a democratic work environment are less inhibited and experience a much greater sense of physical and psychological freedom than are followers in an autocratic work environment. Finally, there is flexibility and spontaneity in the relationships between the leader and followers in the democratic work environment. For those who need more structure, however, a democratic work environment may elicit uncertainty and anxiety.

■ Leadership Behaviors

The leadership research program at Ohio State University measured several specific leader behaviors as an alternative to a generalized leader style, such as autocratic, as was done at Michigan. The initial Ohio State research studied aircrews and pilots.[18] The aircrew members, as followers, were asked a wide range of questions about their lead pilots using the Leader Behavior Description Questionnaire (LBDQ). The results using the LBDQ suggested that there were two important underlying dimensions of leader behaviors.[19] These were labeled initiating structure and consideration.

Initiating structure is leader behavior aimed at defining and organizing work relationships and roles, as well as establishing clear patterns of organization, communication, and ways of getting things done. Consideration is leader behavior aimed at nurturing friendly, warm working relationships, as well as encouraging mutual trust and interpersonal respect within the work unit. These two leader behaviors are independent of each other. That is, a leader may be high in both, low in both, or high in one while low in the other. The Ohio State studies were intended to describe leader behavior, not to evaluate or judge behavior.

The Ohio State approach to the study of leadership suggested that leader behavior was open to change and modification, because it was not an enduring trait or attribute. In a study at International Harvester Company, Edwin Fleishman found that consideration behaviors could be improved through a training program for the company's supervisors.[20] Although the training resulted in changes in both initiating structure and consideration, the changes in either attitude or behavior were not permanent. When back in the work environment, the supervisors tended toward increased initiating structure behavior and less consideration. The conclusion was that the leadership climate at the company was a more important determinant of leader behaviors than was the training. Therefore, upper management's influence on the behaviors of middle managers and supervisors is important. This logic has recently led some corporations (for example, General Electric) to establish desired leader behaviors directly at the top of the organization.[21]

■ Leadership Studies in Japan

Shortly after World War II, a program of research was begun in Japan to examine the generalizability of U.S. leadership approaches to Japanese organizations. This 30-year program of research resulted in the Performance-Maintenance (PM) Theory of Leadership.[22] A P-oriented leader behavior is similar to initiating structure, and M-oriented leader behavior is similar to consideration. According to the Japanese researchers, autocratic leaders emphasize P-oriented behavior to the exclusion of M-oriented behavior, whereas democratic leaders emphasize M-oriented behavior, although not necessarily to the exclusion of P-oriented behavior. Laissez-faire leaders exhibit neither P-oriented or M-oriented behaviors. The Japanese researchers studied leadership in a wide variety of organizations and found that the

■ FIGURE 12.1
The Managerial Grid

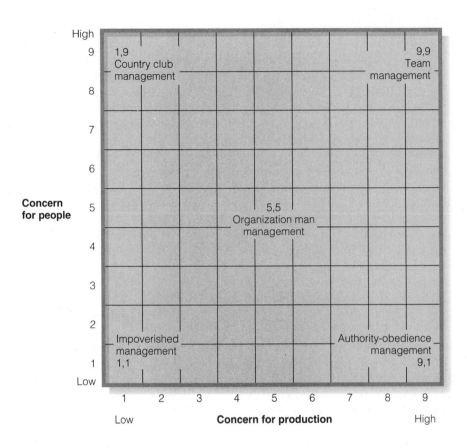

leadership styles of lower and middle level managers affect employee performance in Japan more than in the United States. In addition, autocratic leadership may be less successful in Japanese companies than in some U.S. companies.

■ The Managerial Grid

The Ohio State leadership studies and the subsequent Japanese leadership approaches were behavioral formulations. An attitudinal formulation called the Managerial Grid was developed by Robert Blake and Jane Mouton.[23] The two underlying dimensions of the Grid are labeled Concern for Production and Concern for People. These two attitudinal dimensions are coupled through an interaction process. The five distinct managerial styles shown in Figure 12.1 parallel five orientations to interpersonal relationships of fight (9,1), flight (1,1), depending (1,9), pairing (5,5), and work (9,9) observed in previous clinical practice by Bion.

The organization man manager (5,5) works for adequate organizational performance by creating a balance between getting work done and maintaining morale. This manager goes along to get along, conforming to and maintaining the status quo. The authority-obedience manager (9,1) emphasizes production and works to achieve high levels of efficiency in operations by minimizing any interference from the human element. Production maximization is the hallmark of this manager. The country club manager (1,9) gives thoughtful attention to the needs of people and their relationships so as to create a comfortable working environment. Good feelings are the hallmark of this manager. The team manager (9,9) emphasizes high levels of work accomplishment through committed, trustworthy people; there is no trade-off between people and production. Finally, the impoverished manager (1,1) exerts the minimum effort to get essential work done while maintaining organizational membership. This style of management is similar to the laissez-faire style and is a form of abdication of responsibility.

The Managerial Grid is distinguished from the original Ohio State research in two important ways. First, it has attitudinal overtones that are not present in the original research. Whereas the LBDQ aims to describe behavior, the grid addresses both the behavior and the attitude of the leader. Second, the Ohio State approach is fundamentally descriptive and nonevaluative, whereas the grid is normative and prescriptive. Specifically, the grid evaluates the team manager (9,9) as the very best style of managerial behavior. This is the basis on which the grid has been used for team building and leadership training in organizational development, which are discussed in Chapter 17. As an organizational development method, the grid aims to transform the leadership structure of the organization and the manner in which teams throughout the organization are led and managed.

■ TYPE III THEORIES

Type III theories of leadership are concerned with identifying the situationally specific conditions in which leaders with particular traits are effective. Type III theories classify leaders according to particular traits or attributes, as do Type I theories. However, Type III theories are contingency theories, as opposed to universal theories. They have a dual focus: the leader and the situation in which the leader works. The central concern of Type III theories is how the leader's traits interact with situational factors in determining team effectiveness in task performance. Fiedler's contingency theory is the one Type III leadership theory developed to date. Its implications for organizations concern how to select the right leader for the situation.

■ Fiedler's Contingency Theory

Fiedler's contingency theory of leadership proposes that the fit between the leader's need structure and the favorableness of the leader's situation determine the team's effectiveness in work accomplishment. This theory assumes that leaders are task-oriented or relationship-oriented, depending upon how the leaders obtain their primary need gratification.[24] Task-oriented leaders are primarily gratified by ac-

complishing tasks and getting work done. Relationship-oriented leaders are primarily gratified by developing good, comfortable interpersonal relationships. Accordingly, the effectiveness of both types of leaders depends on the favorableness of their situation. The theory classifies the favorableness of the leader's situation according to the leader's position power, the structure of the team's task, and the quality of the leader-follower relationships.

The Least-Preferred Co-Worker. Fiedler classifies leaders using the Least Preferred Co-worker (LPC) Scale.[25] The LPC Scale is a projective technique through which a leader is asked to think about the person with whom he or she can work least well (the least preferred co-worker, or LPC). This is not necessarily the person the leader likes least; rather, it is the person with whom the leader had the most difficulty getting the job done.

The leader is asked to describe this least preferred co-worker using sixteen eight-point bipolar adjective sets. Three of these follow (the leader marks the blank most descriptive of the least preferred co-worker):

Pleasant	:	:	:	:	:	:	:	: Unpleasant
Efficient	:	:	:	:	:	:	:	: Inefficient
Gloomy	:	:	:	:	:	:	:	: Cheerful

Leaders who describe their least preferred co-worker in positive terms (that is, pleasant, efficient, cheerful, and so on) are classified as high LPC, or relationship-oriented, leaders. Those who describe their least preferred co-workers in negative terms (that is, unpleasant, inefficient, gloomy, and so on) are classified as low LPC, or task-oriented, leaders.

The LPC score is a controversial element in contingency theory. It has been criticized conceptually and methodologically, because it is a projective technique with lower measurement reliability, along with situational favorableness.[26]

Situational Favorableness. The leader's situation has three dimensions: task structure, position power, and leader-member relations. Based on these three dimensions, the situation is either favorable or unfavorable for the leader. Task structure refers to the

■ **FIGURE 12.2**
Leadership Effectiveness in the Contingency Theory

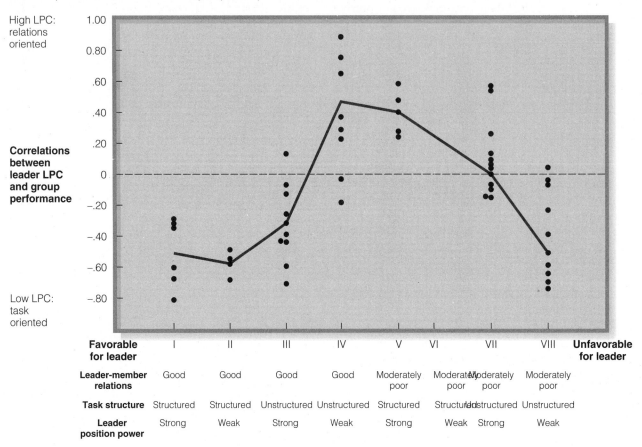

	I	II	III	IV	V	VI	VII	VIII	
Favorable for leader									**Unfavorable for leader**
Leader-member relations	Good	Good	Good	Good	Moderately poor	Moderately poor	Moderately poor	Moderately poor	
Task structure	Structured	Structured	Unstructured	Unstructured	Structured	Structured	Unstructured	Unstructured	
Leader position power	Strong	Weak	Strong	Weak	Strong	Weak	Strong	Weak	

number and clarity of rules, regulations, and procedures for getting the work done. Position power refers to the leader's legitimate authority to evaluate and reward performance, punish errors, and demote group members.

The quality of leader-member relations is measured by the Group-Atmosphere Scale, composed of nine eight-point bipolar adjective sets, such as friendly versus unfriendly, accepting versus rejecting, and warm versus cold.

A favorable leadership situation is one with a structured task for the work group, strong position power for the leader, and good leader-member relations. In contrast, an unfavorable leadership situation is one with an unstructured task, weak position power for the leader, and moderately poor leader-member relations. Between these two extremes, the leadership situation has varying degrees of moderate favorableness for the leader.

■ **Leadership Effectiveness**

The contingency theory suggests that low and high LPC leaders are each effective if placed in the right situation. Specifically, low LPC (task-oriented) leaders are most effective in either very favorable or very unfavorable leadership situations because in both extremes the situation is well and clearly defined. In contrast, high LPC (relationship-oriented) leaders are most effective in situations of intermediate favorableness because these situations are not as well nor clearly defined. Figure 12.2 shows the nature of these relationships and suggests that leadership effectiveness is determined by the degree of fit between the leader and the situation.

What, then, is to be done if there is a misfit? That is, what happens when a low LPC leader is in a moderately favorable situation or when a high LPC leader is in a highly favorable or highly unfavorable situation? It is unlikely that the leader can be changed, according to the theory, because the leader's need structure is an enduring trait requiring intense psychological intervention to alter. This leaves the situation as the preferred point of intervention. Specifically, Fiedler recommends that the leader's situation be reengineered to fit the leader's basic predisposition.[27] Hence, a moderately favorable situation would be reengineered to be more favorable and therefore more suitable for the low LPC leader. The highly favorable or highly unfavorable situation would be changed to one that is moderately favorable, and therefore more suitable for the high LPC leader.

Fiedler's contingency theory is a Type III theory because he considers the leaders' inherent traits, not their behaviors, in considering a fit with the leadership situation. His theory makes an important contribution in drawing our attention to the leader's situation.

TYPE IV THEORIES

Type IV theories of leadership are concerned with identifying the specific leader behaviors that are most effective in specific leadership situations. A number of leader behaviors are considered important by different Type IV theories. Like Type III theories, Type IV theories are considered contingency theories, as opposed to universal theories. The central concern in the Type IV theories is the behavioral contingencies of the leader that yield the most effective performance by the followers. This section considers three specific Type IV theories. They are Robert House's path-goal theory, the Vroom-Yetton-Jago normative decision theory, and the situational leadership model developed by Paul Hersey and Kenneth Blanchard. As with Type II theories, the implications for organizations of Type IV theories concern how to train and develop leaders rather than how to select them.

The Path-Goal Theory

Robert House advocates a path-goal theory of leader effectiveness based on an expectancy theory of motivation.[28] From the perspective of path-goal theory, the basic role of the leader is to enhance follower motivation so that the followers are able to experience need gratification. The leader uses the most appropriate of four leader behavior styles to help followers clarify the paths that lead them to work and personal goals. The key concepts in the theory are shown in Figure 12.3.

The path-goal theory is based on the following two propositions:

- Proposition 1. Leader behavior is acceptable and satisfying to followers to the extent that they see it as an immediate source of satisfaction or as instrumental to future satisfaction.
- Proposition 2. Leader behavior is motivational to the extent that (1) it makes followers' need satisfaction contingent on effective performance and (2) it complements the followers' environment by providing the coaching, guidance, support, and rewards necessary for effective performance—rewards not otherwise available.

A leader selects from the four leader behavior styles, shown in Figure 12.3, the one that is most helpful to followers at a given time. The directive style is used when the leader must give specific guidance about work tasks, schedule the tasks, maintain performance standards, and let followers know what is expected. The supportive style is used when the leader needs to express concern for followers' well-being and social status. The participative style is used when the leader must engage in problem solving and mutual decision-making activities with followers. The achievement-oriented style is used when the leader must set challenging goals for followers, expect very high levels of performance, and show strong confidence in the followers.

In selecting the appropriate leader behavior style, the leader must consider characteristics of the followers and the work environment. A few characteristics are included in Figure 12.3. Let us look at four examples. In Example 1, the followers are inexperienced and working on an ambiguous, unstructured task. The leader in this situation might best use a directive style. In Example 2, the task is structured,

■ **FIGURE 12.3**
The Path-Goal Theory of Leadership

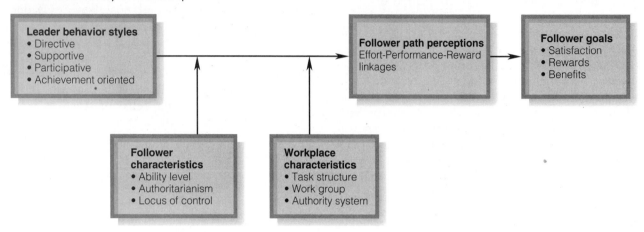

and the followers are experienced and able. Here the leader might better use a supportive style. In Example 3, the followers are experienced and able, yet the task is confusing and unstructured. The leader in this situation may be most helpful in using a participative style. In Example 4, the followers are highly trained professionals, and the task is a difficult yet achievable one. The leader in this situation might best use an achievement-oriented style. The leader always chooses the leader behavior style that helps followers achieve their goals.

The path-goal theory assumes that leaders adapt their behavior and style to fit the characteristics of the followers and the environment in which they work. Actual tests of the path-goal theory and its propositions provide conflicting evidence. Hence, it is premature either to fully accept or fully reject the theory at this point. The path-goal theory does have intuitive appeal and offers a number of constructive ideas for leaders who lead a variety of followers in a variety of work environments.

■ **Vroom-Yetton-Jago Normative Decision Theory**

The Vroom-Yetton-Jago normative decision theory was discussed in Chapter 10, "Decision Making by Individuals and Groups," because a core element of the theory proposes five alternative decision-making

processes. These five processes and the decision process flowchart, or decision tree, are contained in Chapter 10. From a leadership perspective, the Vroom-Yetton-Jago Theory recognizes the potential benefits of authoritarian, as well as democratic, styles of leader behavior.[29] The key situational determinants of the appropriate leader behavior within the theory are the quality of the decision to be made, the acceptance of that decision by employees, the time available for the decision, and the information available to the manager.

The utility of the theory is limited to the leader decision situation. One test supported the theory based on leader perceptions of a recent decision process but failed to support the theory based on follower perceptions of the same process.[30] Vroom and Jago's new model substantially improves the original by adding a number of objectives that leaders may choose to seek, such as cost reduction.[31]

■ **The Situational Leadership Model**

The situational leadership model, developed by Paul Hersey and Kenneth Blanchard, suggests that the leader's behavior should be adjusted to the maturity level of the followers.[32] The model employs two dimensions of leader behavior as used in the Ohio State studies; one dimension is task- or production-oriented, and the other is relationship- or people-oriented. Follower maturity is categorized into four levels, from most mature (willing and able to be responsible) to most immature (unwilling and unable to be responsible). Follower maturity is determined by the ability and willingness of the followers to accept responsibility for completing their work. Followers who are unable and unwilling are the least mature, and those who are both able and willing are the most mature. According to the situational leadership model, a leader should use a telling style of leadership with immature followers who are unable and unwilling to take responsibility for completing their work. This style is characterized by high concern with the task and strong initiating structure behavior, coupled with low concern with relationships and little consideration behavior. As followers mature to the second level, the leader should use a selling style, in which there is high concern with both the task and relationships. The able but unwilling followers are the next most mature and require a participating style from the leader. This style is characterized by high concern with relationships and low concern with the task. Finally, the most mature followers are ones who are both able and willing, thus requiring a delegating style of leadership. The leader employing this style of leadership shows low concern with the task and relationships, because the followers accept responsibility.

One key limitation of the situational leadership model is the absence of central hypotheses that could be tested, which would make it a more valid, reliable theory of leadership. However, the theory has intuitive appeal and is widely used for training and development in corporations. In addition, the theory focuses attention on followers as important participants, if not determinants, of the leadership process.

■ GUIDELINES FOR LEADERSHIP

Leadership is an important topic in organizational behavior and an important contributor to organizational effectiveness. When artifacts are eliminated, studies of leadership succession show a moderately strong leader influence on organizational performance.[33] With this said, it is important to recognize that other factors also influence organizational performance. These include environmental factors (such as general economic conditions) and technological factors (such as efficiency).

Leaders face a paradox of privilege and accountability with their positions.[34] Horton addresses the paradox through various dilemmas involved in decision making, planning, delegation, team building, and ambition. Although no hard or fast leadership rule emerges from either his treatment of these dilemmas or from the extensive research of the past century, five useful guidelines do appear warranted.

First, leaders and organizations should appreciate the unique attributes, predispositions, and talents of each leader. No two leaders are the same, and there is value in this diversity.

Second, although there appears to be no single best style of leadership, there are organizational preferences in terms of style. Leaders should be chosen who challenge the organizational culture, when necessary, without destroying it.

Third, participative, considerate leader behaviors that demonstrate a concern for people appear to enhance the health and well-being of followers in the work environment. This does not imply, however, that a leader must ignore the team's work tasks.

Fourth, different leadership situations call for different leadership talents and behaviors. This may result in different individuals taking the leader role, depending on the specific situation in which the team finds itself.

Fifth, good leaders are likely to be good followers. Although there are distinctions between their social roles, the attributes and behaviors of leaders and followers may not be as distinct as is sometimes thought.

■ FOLLOWERSHIP

In contrast to leadership, the topic of followership has not been extensively researched. Much of the leadership literature suggests that leader and follower roles are highly differentiated. The traditional view casts followers as passive, whereas a more contemporary view casts the follower role as an active one with potential for leadership.[35] The follower role has alternatively been cast as one of self-leadership in which the follower assumes responsibility for influencing his or her own performance. Mike Walsh, CEO of Tenneco, sounds as if he is encouraging self-leadership when exhorting employees to think boldly and set higher goals in a slow-growth economy. Walsh recognizes that this makes leaders more visible and vulnerable, but also more effective. Organizational programs such as empowerment and self-managed work teams may be used to further activate the follower role.[36]

It is increasingly difficult to think of followers as passive agents of willful leaders. One study of leader-follower dynamics over a three-month period actually found leaders responding to follower performance rather than causing or initiating it.[37] Followers are an active component of the leadership process, and we need to expand our core knowledge about followership even further.

This section examines different types of followers and the characteristics of a dynamic subordinate. As we examine the follower role, keep in mind that blind, unquestioning followership may lead to destructive, and even antisocial, behavior.[38]

■ Types of Followers

Contemporary work environments are those in which followers recognize their interdependence with leaders and learn to challenge them while at the same time respecting the leaders' authority.[39] Effective followers are active, responsible, autonomous in their behavior, and critical in their thinking without being insubordinate or disrespectful. Effective followers and four other types of followers are identified based on two dimensions: (1) activity versus passivity and (2) independent, critical thinking versus dependent, uncritical thinking.[40] Figure 12.4 shows these follower types.

Alienated followers are those who think independently and critically, yet are very passive in their behavior. As a result, they become psychologically and emotionally distanced from their leaders. Alienated followers are potentially disruptive and a threat to the health of the organization. Sheep are followers who do not think independently or critically and are passive in their behavior. They simply do as they are told by their leaders. In a sense, they are slaves to the system. Yes people are followers who also do not

■ FIGURE 12.4
Five Types of Followers

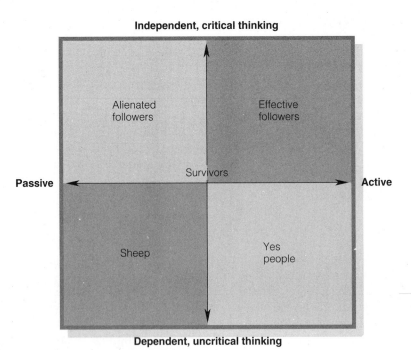

think independently or critically, yet are very active in their behavior. They uncritically reinforce the thinking and ideas of their leaders with enthusiasm, never questioning or challenging the wisdom of the leaders' ideas and proposals. Yes people are the most dangerous to a leader because they are the most likely to give a false positive reaction and give no warning of potential pitfalls. Survivors are followers who are the least disruptive and the lowest-risk followers in an organization. They perpetually sample the wind, and their motto is "Better safe than sorry."

Effective followers are the most valuable to a leader and an organization because of their active contributions. Effective followers share four essential qualities. First, they practice self-management and self-responsibility. A leader can delegate to an effective follower without anxiety about the outcome. Second, they are committed to both the organization and a purpose, principle, or person outside themselves. Effective followers are not self-centered or self-aggrandizing. There is a risk, however, when the follower is committed to a purpose or principle at odds with the organization. Third, effective followers invest in their own competence and professionalism and focus their energy for maximum impact. Effective followers look for challenges and ways in which to add to their talents or abilities. Fourth, they are courageous, honest, and credible.

Effective followers might be thought of as self-leaders who do not require close supervision. The notion of self-leadership, or superleadership, blurs the distinction between leaders and followers. There is a complementary concept of servant leadership that may be most appropriate to address here. Servant leadership casts the leader in the servant role. The leader as servant focuses on followers, caring for their well-being and development, as exemplified by Joseph Grant as CFO at EDS.

■ The Dynamic Follower

The traditional stereotype of the follower or employee is of someone in a powerless and dependent role rather than in a potent, active, significant role. The latter is a more contemporary, healthy role in which the follower is dynamic.[41] The dynamic follower is a responsible steward of his or her job, is effective in managing the relationship with the boss, and practices responsible self-management.

A responsible job steward is one who masters the content of his or her work and possesses or develops the skills required to do a good job. Once prepared, a dynamic follower then does a good job without being led. The dynamic follower is a self-starter.

The dynamic follower becomes a trusted advisor to the boss by keeping the supervisor well informed and building trust and dependability into the relationship. He or she is open to constructive criticism and solicits performance feedback. The dynamic follower shares needs and is responsible.

Self-management requires acquiring self-awareness and control of one's own feelings and behavior. It means being nondefensive and taking risks by challenging the supervisor and the organization.

Dynamic followers are effective in managing the relationship with their bosses along the lines discussed in Chapter 11. John Gabarro and John Kotter aim to achieve the best possible results for the follower, the boss, and the organization.[42] It takes time and patience to nurture a good relationship between a follower and a supervisor. Once this relationship has been developed, it is a valuable resource for both. Therefore, the follower should be selective in the use of the supervisor's time and resources while always keeping the supervisor informed about work.

■ CULTURAL DIFFERENCES IN LEADERSHIP

In Chapter 5 we noted a number of cultural differences in several motivation theories. Parallel differences do not appear to exist in the area of leadership. Earlier in this chapter we noted similar findings when applying American leadership studies in Japan, along with some differences. The People's Republic of China is another country in which American leadership theories have been said to apply.[43] However, some of the groundbreaking research on leadership and culture concluded that ethnic differences were more important than national or industrial ones.[44] For example, David Kearns became convinced that the Japanese copier industry had targeted Xerox Corporation for elimination from that industry. Convinced he was in the battle for Xerox's life, Kearns introduced Leadership-through-Quality to Xerox in the early 1980s after learning from Fuji Xerox that quality improvements would not increase real costs.[45] Kearns' leadership came at the right time to revolutionize Xerox's culture. The situational approaches to leadership would lead to the conclusion that a leader must factor in culture as an important situational variable when exercising influence and authority. Thus, global leaders should expect to be flexible enough to alter their approaches when crossing national boundaries and working with people from foreign cultures.[46]

■ MANAGERIAL IMPLICATIONS: LEADERS AND FOLLOWERS AS PARTNERS

The chapter includes guidelines for leaders and followers, because both affect the quality of work performed and the success, and even survival, of the organization. The actions of national and international competitors and government regulations also affect the success of the organization.

There is no one best leadership theory. Many theories have been proposed, because not one of them works in every situation. One theory may be useful in one manufacturing firm, another is most useful in another firm. The many theories of leadership can be thought of as tools of the trade to be applied selectively by the leader in the most appropriate way. Properly applied, each theory is of some value to the user.

The decade of the 1990s is a period of significant transition for American industries. They must increasingly learn from other countries and cultures about leadership and followership. Some concepts appear to be cross-culturally applicable, whereas others may not be. Leadership within American corporations is changing, too, as more women assume positions of leadership. Women and men may lead differently, and both can benefit from building on their unique strengths and talents.

Followers are equally important partners in the leadership process, for without followers, who would leaders lead? The role of the follower is one deserving greater respect, dignity, and understand-

ing than presently exists. Effective followers keep leaders out of trouble and advance the cause of leaders with vision and imagination.

■ CHAPTER SUMMARY

- Leadership is the process of guiding and directing the behavior of followers in organizations. Followership is the process of being guided and directed by a leader. Leadership and followership involve people, not technology.
- A leader creates meaningful change in organizations, whereas a manager controls complexity. Charismatic leaders have a profound impact on their followers.
- Autocratic leaders create high pressure for followers, whereas democratic leaders create healthier environments for followers.
- Two distinct dimensions of leader behavior are labeled: *initiating structure* and *consideration*. Roughly the same behaviors are labeled P-oriented behavior and M-oriented behavior, respectively, in Japan.
- The five styles in the Managerial Grid are organization man manager (5,5), authority-obedience manager (9,1), country club manager, (1,9), team manager (9,9), and impoverished manager (1,1).
- According to the contingency theory, task-oriented leaders are most effective in highly favorable or highly unfavorable leadership situations, and relationship-oriented leaders are most effective in moderately favorable leadership situations.
- The path-goal theory, Vroom-Yetton-Jago theory, and situational leadership model say that a leader should adjust his or her behavior to the situation and should appreciate diversity among followers.
- Effective, dynamic followers are competent and active in their work, assertive, independent thinkers, sensitive to their bosses' needs and demands, and responsible self-managers.

■ REVIEW QUESTIONS

1. Define leadership and followership. Distinguish between formal leadership and informal leadership.

2. What are the differences between, and the contributions of, leaders and managers in organizations? How do leaders and managers differ? How do charismatic leaders affect their followers?

3. Is it acceptable for a leader to take credit for the work of subordinates who are being supervised?

4. Define initiating structure and consideration as leader behaviors. How do they compare with P-oriented behavior and M-oriented behavior?

5. Describe the organization man manager (5,5), authority-obedience manager (9,1), country club manager (1,9), team manager (9,9), and impoverished manager (1,1).

6. How does the LPC scale measure leadership style? What are the three dimensions of the leader's situation?

7. Is it ethical for leaders to tell followers unilaterally what to do without asking their opinions or getting any input from them?

8. Compare House's path-goal theory of leadership with the situational leadership model.

9. Describe alienated followers, sheep, yes people, survivors, and effective followers.

■ REFERENCES

1. A. S. Phillips and A. G. Bedejan, "Leader-Follower Exchange Quality: The Role of Personal and Interpersonal Attributes," *Academy of Management Journal* 37 (1994): 990–1001.

2. J. P. Kotter, "What Leaders Really Do," *Harvard Business Review* 68 (1990): 103–111.

3. A. Zaleznik, "HBR Classic—Managers and Leaders: Are They Different?" *Harvard Business Review* 70 (1992): 126–135.

4. A. G. Jago, "Leadership: Perspectives in Theory and Research," *Management Science* 28 (1982): 315–336.

5. R. M. Stogdill, *Stogdill's Handbook of Leadership: A Survey of Theory and Research,* rev. B. M. Bass (New York: Free Press, 1981).

6. R. M. Stogdill, "Personal Factors Associated with Leadership: A Survey of the Literature," *Journal of Psychology* 25 (1948): 35–71.

7. J. M. Burns, *Leadership* (New York: Harper & Row, 1978).

8. N. Tichy and M. A. DeVanna, *The Transformational Leader* (New York: Wiley, 1986).

9. B. M. Bass, "From Transactional to Transformational Leadership: Learning to Share the Vision," *Organizational Dynamics* 19 (1990): 19–31; B. M. Bass, *Leadership and Performance Beyond Expectations* (New York: Free Press, 1985).

10. J. R. Joplin, "Developing Effective Leadership: An Interview with Henry Cisneros," *Academy of Management Executive* 7 (1993): 84–92.

11. A. Zaleznik, "The Leadership Gap," *Academy of Management Executive* 4 (1990): 7–22.

12. M. E. Heilman, C. J. Block, R. F. Martell, and M. C. Simon, "Has Anything Changed? Current Characteristics of Men, Women, and Managers," *Journal of Applied Psychology* 74 (1989): 935–942.

13. J. B. Rosener, "Ways Women Lead," *Harvard Business Review* 68 (1990): 119–125.

14. R. J. House and M. L. Baetz, "Leadership: Some Empirical Generalizations and New Research Directions," in B. M. Staw, ed., *Research in Organizational Behavior,* vol. 1 (Greenwood, Conn.: JAI Press, 1979), 399–401.

15. J. A. Conger and R. N. Kanungo, "Toward a Behavioral Theory of Charismatic Leadership in Organizational Settings," *Academy of Management Review* 12 (1987): 637–647.

16. J. M. Howell, "Two Faces of Charisma: Socialized and Personalized Leadership in Organizations," in J. A. Conger, ed., *Charismatic Leadership: Behind the Mystique of Exceptional Leadership* (San Francisco: Jossey-Bass, 1988).

17. K. Lewin, R. Lippitt, and R. K. White, "Patterns of Aggressive Behavior in Experimentally Created 'Social Climates,' " *Journal of Social Psychology* 10 (1939): 271–299.

18. R. M. Stogdill and A. E. Coons, eds., *Leader Behavior: Its Description and Measurement,* research monograph no. 88 (Columbus, Ohio: Bureau of Business Research, The Ohio State University, 1957).

19. A. W. Halpin and J. Winer, "A Factorial Study of the Leader Behavior Description Questionnaire," in R. M. Stogdill, and A. E. Coons, eds., *Leader Behavior: Its Description and Measurement,* research monograph no. 88 (Columbus, Ohio: Bureau of Business Research, The Ohio State University, 1957), 39–51.

20. E. A. Fleishman, "Leadership Climate, Human Relations Training, and Supervisory Behavior," *Personnel Psychology* 6 (1953): 205–222.

21. N. Tichy and R. Charan, "Speed, Simplicity, Self-Confidence: An Interview with Jack Welch," *Harvard Business Review* 67 (1989): 112–121.

22. J. Misumi and M. F. Peterson, "The Performance-Maintenance (PM) Theory of Leadership," *Administrative Science Quarterly* 30 (1985): 198–223.

23. R. R. Blake and J. S. Mouton, *The Managerial Grid III: The Key to Leadership Excellence* (Houston: Gulf, 1985).

24. F. E. Fiedler, *A Theory of Leader Effectiveness* (New York: McGraw-Hill, 1964).

25. F. E. Fiedler, *Personality, Motivational Systems, and Behavior of High and Low LPC Persons,* tech. rep. no. 70–12 (Seattle: University of Washington, 1970).

26. J. T. McMahon, "The Contingency Theory: Logic and Method Revisited," *Personnel Psychology* 25 (1972): 697–710; L. H. Peters, D. D. Hartke, and J. T. Pohlman, "Fiedler's Contingency Theory of Leadership: An Application of the Meta-analysis Procedures of Schmidt and Hunter," *Psychological Bulletin* 97 (1985): 224–285.

27. F. E. Fiedler, "Engineering the Job to Fit the Manager," *Harvard Business Review* 43 (1965): 115–122.

28. R. J. House, "A Path-Goal Theory of Leader Effectiveness," *Administrative Science Quarterly* 16 (1971): 321–338; R. J. House and T. R. Mitchell, "Path-Goal Theory of Leadership," *Journal of Contemporary Business* 3 (1974): 81–97.

29. V. H. Vroom and P. W. Yetton, *Leadership and Decision Making* (Pittsburgh: University of Pittsburgh, 1973).

30. R. H. G. Field and R. J. House, "A Test of the Vroom-Yetton Model Using Manager and Subordinate Reports," *Journal of Applied Psychology* 75 (1990): 362–366.

31. V. H. Vroom and A. G. Jago, *The New Leadership: Managing Participation in Organizations* (Englewood Cliffs, N.J.: Prentice-Hall, 1988).

32. P. Hersey and K. H. Blanchard, "Life Cycle Theory of Leadership," *Training and Development Journal* 23 (1969): 26–34; P. Hersey and K. H. Blanchard, *Management of Organizational Behavior: Utilizing Human Resources,* 3d ed. (Englewood Cliffs, N.J.: Prentice-Hall, 1977).

33. G. A. Yukl, *Leadership in Organizations,* 2d ed. (Englewood Cliffs, N.J.: Prentice-Hall, 1989).

34. T. R. Horton, *The CEO Paradox: The Privilege and Accountability of Leadership* (New York: American Management Association, 1992).

35. E. P. Hollander and L. R. Offerman, "Power and Leadership in Organizations: Relationships in Transition," *American Psychologist* 45 (1990): 179–189.

36. C. C. Manz and H. P. Sims, "Leading Workers to Lead Themselves: The External Leadership of Self-managing Work Teams," *Administrative Science Quarterly* 32 (1987): 106–128.

37. C. N. Greene, "The Reciprocal Nature of Influence between Leader and Subordinate," *Journal of Applied Psychology* 60 (1975): 187–193.

38. H. S. Schwartz, "Antisocial Actions of Committed Organizational Participants," in *Narcissistic Process and Corporate Decay* (New York: NYU Press, 1990): 31–45.

39. L. Hirschhorn, "Leaders and Followers in a Postindustrial Age: A Psychodynamic View," *Journal of Applied Behavioral Science* 26 (1990): 529–542.

40. R. E. Kelley, "In Praise of Followers," *Harvard Business Review* 66 (1988): 142–148.

41. W. J. Crockett, "Dynamic Subordinancy," *Training and Development Journal* (May 1981): 155–164.

42. J. J. Gabarro and J. P. Kotter, "HBR Classic: Managing Your Boss," *Harvard Business Review* 71 (1993): 150–157.

43. T. K. Oh, "Theory Y in the People's Republic of China," *California Management Review* 19 (1976): 77–84.

44. M. Haire, E. E. Ghiselli, and L. W. Porter, "Cultural Patterns in the Role of the Manager," *Industrial Relations* 2 (1963): 95–117.

45. D. T. Kearns and D. A. Nadler, *Prophets in the Dark: How Xerox Reinvented Itself and Beat Back the Japanese* (New York: Harper Business, 1992); D. T. Kearns, "Leadership through Quality," *Academy of Management Executive* 4 (1990): 86–89.

46. N. J. Adler, *International Dimensions in Organizational Behavior* (Boston: PWS-KENT, 1991).

CHAPTER 13
CONFLICT AT WORK

LEARNING OBJECTIVES

After reading this chapter, you should be able to do the following:

- Diagnose functional versus dysfunctional conflict, and identify the different forms of conflict.
- Identify the causes of conflict in organizations.
- Understand the defense mechanisms that individuals exhibit when they engage in interpersonal conflict.
- Conduct an effective role analysis.
- Describe effective and ineffective techniques for managing conflict.
- Understand five styles of conflict management, and diagnose your own preferred style.

■ THE NATURE OF CONFLICTS IN ORGANIZATIONS

All of us have experienced conflict of various types, yet we probably fail to recognize the variety of conflicts that occur in organizations. Conflict is defined as any situation in which incompatible goals, attitudes, emotions, or behaviors lead to disagreement or opposition between two or more parties.[1]

Today's organizations may face greater potential for conflict than ever before in history. The marketplace, with its increasing competition and globalization, magnifies differences among people in terms of personality, values, attitudes, perceptions, languages, cultures, and national backgrounds. With the increasing diversity of the work force, furthermore, comes potential incompatibility and conflict.

■ Importance of Conflict Management Skills for the Manager

Estimates show that managers spend about 21 percent of their time dealing with conflict.[2,3] That is the equivalent of one day every week. And conflict management skills constitute a major predictor of managerial success.[4] All conflicts require skills on the part of the manager.

■ Functional Versus Dysfunctional Conflict

Not all conflict is bad. In fact, some types of conflict encourage new solutions to problems and enhance the creativity in the organization. In these cases, managers will want to encourage the conflicts. Therefore, managers should stimulate functional conflict and prevent or resolve dysfunctional conflict. This is the key to conflict management. However, using the key is not as simple as it may seem. The difficulty lies in trying to tell the difference between dysfunctional and functional conflicts. The consequences of conflict can be positive or negative, as shown in Table 13.1.

Functional conflict is a healthy, constructive disagreement between two or more people. A recent study of twenty corporations revealed that few managers understand the ways in which conflict can benefit an organization.[5] Functional conflict can produce new ideas, learning, and growth among individuals. When individuals engage in constructive conflict, they develop a better awareness of themselves and others. In addition, functional conflict can improve working relationships, because when two parties work through their disagreements, they feel they have accomplished something together. As they release tensions and solve problems in working together, morale is improved. Functional conflict can lead to innovation and positive change for the organization.[6] Because it tends to encourage creativity among individuals, this positive form of conflict can translate into increased productivity.[7] A key for recognizing functional conflict is that it is often cognitive in origin; that is, it arises from someone challenging old policies or thinking of new ways to approach problems.

Dysfunctional conflict is an unhealthy, destructive disagreement between two or more people. Its danger is that it takes the focus away from the work to be done and places the focus on the conflict itself and the parties involved. Excessive conflict drains energy that could be used more productively. A key for recognizing a dysfunctional conflict is that its origin is often emotional or behavioral. Individuals involved in dysfunctional conflict tend to act before thinking, and they often rely on threats, deception, and verbal abuse to communicate. In dysfunctional conflict, the losses to both parties may exceed any potential gain from the conflict.

Diagnosing conflict as good or bad is not easy. The manager must look at the issue, the context of the conflict, and the parties involved. The following questions can be used to diagnose the nature of the conflict a manager faces:

- Are the parties approaching the conflict from a hostile standpoint?
- Is the outcome likely to be a negative one for the organization?
- Do the potential losses of the parties exceed any potential gains?
- Is energy being diverted from goal accomplishment?

If the majority of the answers to these questions are yes, then the conflict is probably dysfunctional. Once the manager has diagnosed the type of conflict, he or she can either work to resolve it (if it is dysfunctional) or to stimulate it (if it is functional).

One occasion in which managers should work to stimulate conflict is when they suspect their group is suffering from groupthink, discussed in Chapter 10. When a group fails to consider alternative solutions and becomes stagnant in its thinking, it might ben-

■ TABLE 13.1
Consequences of Conflict

POSITIVE CONSEQUENCES	NEGATIVE CONSEQUENCES
■ Leads to new ideas	■ Diverts energy from work
■ Stimulates creativity	■ Threatens psychological well-being
■ Motivates change	■ Wastes resources
■ Promotes organizational vitality	■ Creates a negative climate
■ Helps individuals and groups establish identities	■ Breaks down group cohesion
■ Serves as a safety valve to indicate problems	■ Can increase hostility and aggressive behaviors

efit from healthy disagreements. Teams exhibiting symptoms of groupthink should be encouraged to consider creative problem solving and should appoint a devil's advocate to point out opposing perspectives. These actions can help stimulate constructive conflict in a group that might otherwise fall prey to groupthink.

■ CAUSES OF CONFLICT IN ORGANIZATIONS

Conflict is pervasive in organizations. To manage it effectively, managers should understand the many sources of conflict. They can be classified into two broad categories: structural factors, which stem from the nature of the organization and the way in which work is organized, and personal factors, which arise from differences among individuals. Figure 13.1 summarizes the causes of conflict within each category.

■ Structural Factors

Causes of conflict related to the organization's structure include specialization, interdependence, common resources, goal differences, authority relationships, status inconsistencies, and jurisdictional ambiguities.

Specialization. When jobs are highly specialized, employees become experts at certain tasks. For example, at one software company, there is one specialist for data bases, one for statistical packages, and another for expert systems. Highly specialized jobs

can lead to conflict, because people have little awareness of the tasks that others perform.

A classic conflict of specialization is one between salespeople and engineers. Engineers are technical specialists responsible for product design and quality. Salespeople are marketing experts and liaisons with customers. Salespeople are often accused of making delivery promises that engineers cannot keep because the sales force lacks the technical knowledge necessary to develop realistic delivery deadlines.

Interdependence. Work that is interdependent requires groups or individuals to depend on one another to accomplish goals.[8] Depending on other people to get work done is fine when the process works smoothly. However, when there is a problem, it becomes very easy to blame the other party, and conflict escalates. In a garment manufacturing plant, for example, when the fabric cutters get behind in their work, the workers who sew the garments are delayed as well. Considerable frustration may result when the workers at the sewing machines feel their efforts are being blocked by the cutters' slow pace.

Common Resources. Any time multiple parties must share resources, there is potential for conflict. This potential is enhanced when the shared resources become scarce. One resource often shared by managers is secretarial support. It is not uncommon for a secretary to support ten or more managers, each of whom believes his or her work is most important. This puts pressure on the secretaries and leads to potential conflicts in prioritizing and scheduling work.

■ FIGURE 13.1
Causes of Conflict in Organizations

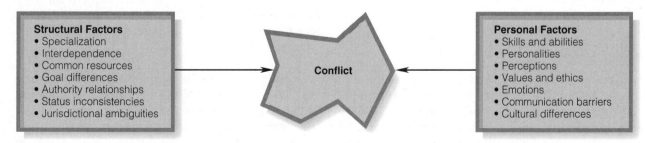

Goal Differences.   When work groups have different goals, these goals may be incompatible. For example, in one cable television company, the salesperson's goal was to sell as many new installations as possible. This created problems for the service department, because its goal was timely installations. With increasing sales, the service department's work load became backed up, and orders delayed. Often these types of conflicts occur because individuals do not have knowledge of another department's objectives.

Goal differences can also create conflicts between managers and employees. A recent study of 313 professionals indicated that goal conflict was the most frequently mentioned form of conflict.[9] Managers must be skilled at clarifying goals and ensuring that employees' perceptions match the managers' understanding of the goals.

Authority Relationships.   The nature of a traditional boss-employee relationship brings to mind a vision of a hierarchy or of a boss who is superior to the employee. For many employees, this relationship is not a comfortable one, because another individual has the right to tell them what to do. Some people resent authority more than others, and obviously this creates conflicts. In addition, some bosses are more autocratic than others; this compounds the potential for conflict in the relationship. As organizations move toward the team approach and empowerment, there should be less potential for conflict from authority relationships.

Status Inconsistencies.   Some organizations have a strong status difference between management and nonmanagement workers. Managers may enjoy privileges—such as flexible schedules, personal telephone calls at work, and longer lunch hours—that are not available to nonmanagement employees. This may result in resentment and conflict.

Jurisdictional Ambiguities.   Have you ever telephoned a company with a problem and had your call transferred through several different people and departments? This situation illustrates jurisdictional ambiguity—that is, unclear lines of responsibility within an organization.[10] When a problem occurs for which there is no definite source of responsibility, workers tend to "pass the buck," or avoid dealing with the problem. Conflicts emerge over responsibility for the problem.

The factors just discussed are structural in that they arise from the ways in which work is organized. Other conflicts come from differences among individuals.

■ **Personal Factors**

The causes of conflict that arise from individual differences include skills and abilities, personalities, perceptions, values and ethics, emotions and communication barriers.

Skills and Abilities.   The work force is composed of individuals with varying levels of skills and ability. Diversity in skills and abilities may be positive for the organization, but it also holds potential for conflict, especially when jobs are interdependent. Experienced, competent workers may find it difficult to work alongside new and unskilled recruits. Workers can become resentful when their new boss, fresh from college, knows a lot about managing people but is unfamiliar with the technology with which they are working.

Personalities.   Individuals do not leave their personalities at the doorstep when they enter the workplace. Personality conflicts are realities in organizations. To expect that you will like all of your co-workers may be a naive expectation, as would be the expectation that they will all like you.

One personality trait that many people find difficult to deal with is abrasiveness.[11] An abrasive person is one who ignores the interpersonal aspects of work and the feelings of colleagues. Abrasive individuals are often achievement-oriented and hardworking, but their perfectionist, critical style often leaves others feeling unimportant. This style creates stress and strain for those around the abrasive person.

Perceptions.   Differences in perception can also lead to conflict. One area in which perceptions can differ is the perception of what motivates employees. If managers and workers do not have a shared perception of what motivates people, the reward system can create conflicts. Managers often provide what they think employees want rather than what employees really want.

Values and Ethics. Differences in values and ethics can be sources of disagreement. Older workers, for example, value company loyalty and probably would not take a sick day when they were not really ill. Younger workers, valuing mobility, like the concept of "mental health days," or calling in sick to get away from work. This may not be true for all workers, but it illustrates that differences in values can lead to conflict.

Most people have their own sets of values and ethics. The extent to which they apply these ethics in the workplace varies. Some people have strong desires for approval from others and will work to meet others' ethical standards. Some people are relatively unconcerned with approval from others and strongly apply their own ethical standards. Still others operate seemingly without regard to ethics or values.[12] When conflicts over values or ethics do arise, heated disagreement is common because of the personal nature of the differences.

Emotions. The moods of others can be a source of conflict in the workplace. Problems at home often spill over into the work arena, and the related moods can be hard for others to deal with.

Communication Barriers. Communication barriers such as physical separation and language can create distortions in messages, and these can lead to conflict. Another communication barrier is value judgment, in which a listener assigns worth to a message before it is received. For example, suppose a team member is a chronic complainer. When this individual enters the manager's office, the manager is likely to devalue the message before it is even delivered. Conflict can then emerge. Many other communication barriers can lead to conflict. These were discussed in Chapter 8.

■ GLOBALIZATION AND CONFLICT

Large transnational corporations employ many different ethnic and cultural groups. In these multiethnic corporations, the widely differing cultures represent vast differences among individuals, so the potential for conflict increases.[13] As indicated in Chapter 2, Hofstede has identified five dimensions along which cultural differences may emerge: individualism/collectivism, power distance, uncertainty avoidance, masculinity/femininity, and long-term/short-term orientation.[14] These cultural differences have many implications for conflict management in organizations.

Individualism means that people believe that their individual interests take priority over society's interests. Collectivism, in contrast, means that people put the good of the group first. For example, the United States is a highly individualistic culture, whereas Japan is a very collectivist culture. The individualism/collectivism dimension of cultural differences strongly influences conflict management behavior. Persons from collectivist cultures use more cooperative approaches in resolving conflicts.

Hofstede's second dimension of cultural differences is power distance. In cultures with high power distance, individuals accept that people in organizations have varying levels of power. In contrast, in cultures with low power distance, individuals do not automatically respect those in positions of authority. For example, the U.S. is a country of low power distance, whereas Brazil is a country with a high power distance. Differences in power distance can lead to conflict. Imagine a U.S. employee managed by a Brazilian supervisor who expects deferential behavior. The supervisor would expect automatic respect based on legitimate power. Without this respect, conflict would arise.

Uncertainty avoidance also varies by culture. In the U.S., employees can tolerate high levels of uncertainty. However, employees in Israel tend to prefer certainty in their work settings. A U.S.-based multinational firm might run into conflicts operating in Israel. Suppose such a firm were installing a new technology. Its expatriate workers from the U.S. would tolerate the uncertainty of the technological transition better than would their Israeli co-workers, and this might lead to conflicts among the employees.

Masculinity versus femininity illustrates the contrast between preferences for assertiveness and material goods versus preferences for human capital and quality of life. The U.S. is a masculine society, whereas Sweden is considered a feminine society.

Adjustment to the assertive interpersonal style of U.S. workers may be difficult for Swedish co-workers.

Conflicts can also arise between cultures that vary in their time orientation of values. China, for example, has a long-term orientation; the Chinese prefer values that focus on the future, such as saving and persistence. The U.S. and Russia, in contrast, have short-term orientations. These cultures emphasize values in the past and present, such as respect for tradition and fulfillment of social obligations. Conflicts can arise when managers fail to understand the nature of differences in values.

An organization whose work force consists of multiple ethnic groups and cultures holds potential for many types of conflict because of the sheer volume of individual differences among workers. The key to managing conflict in a multicultural work force is understanding cultural differences and appreciating their value.

■ FORMS OF CONFLICT IN ORGANIZATIONS

Conflict can take on any of several different forms in an organization, including interorganizational, intergroup, interpersonal, and intrapersonal conflicts. It is important to note that the prefix *inter* means "between," whereas the prefix *intra* means "within."

■ Interorganizational Conflict

Conflict that occurs between two or more organizations is called interorganizational conflict. Examples of interorganizational conflict are corporate takeover attempts, such as AT & T's struggle to gain control of NCR. Although the takeover was finally accomplished, it proved to be a tough one for AT & T, because in one meeting AT & T could not gather enough shareholder votes to oust the majority of NCR's board.[15] Competition among organizations also can spur interorganizational conflict, as seen in the ongoing rivalries between the U.S. and Japanese automakers.

Conflicts between a company and a union may constitute interorganizational conflict. In Germany during February 1992, the powerful IG Metall union of steelworkers endorsed a strike over higher wages. The strike especially threatened Volkswagen and Daimler-Benz, which alerted workers that production standstills might be forthcoming because of lack of steel reserves.[16]

■ Intergroup Conflict

When conflict occurs between groups or teams, it is known as intergroup conflict. Conflict between groups can have predictable effects within each group, such as increased group cohesiveness, more intense focus on tasks, and greater loyalty to the group. In addition, groups in conflict tend to develop an "us against them" mentality whereby each sees the other team as the enemy, becomes more hostile, and decreases its communication with the other group.

Competition between groups must be managed carefully so that it does not escalate into dysfunctional conflict. Research has shown that when groups compete for a goal that only one group can achieve, negative consequences like territoriality, aggression, and prejudice toward the other group can result.[17]

■ Interpersonal Conflict

Conflict between two or more people is interpersonal conflict. Many individual differences lead to conflict between people, including personalities, attitudes, values, perceptions, and the other differences we discussed in Chapters 3 and 4. Later in this chapter, we look at defense mechanisms that individuals exhibit in interpersonal conflict and at ways to cope with difficult people.

■ Intrapersonal Conflict

When conflict occurs within an individual, it is called intrapersonal conflict. There are several types of intrapersonal conflict, including interrole, intrarole, and person-role conflicts. A role is a set of expectations placed on an individual by others.[18] The person occupying the focal role is the role incumbent, and the individuals who place expectations on the person are role senders. Figure 13.2 depicts a set of role relationships.

■ **FIGURE 13.2**

An Organization Member's Role Set

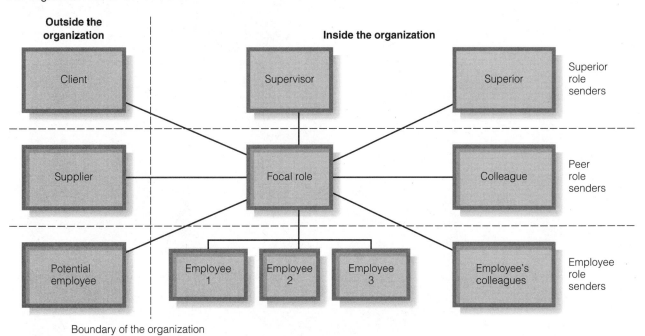

Source: J. C. Quick and J. D. Quick, *Organizational Stress and Preventive Management* (New York:McGraw-Hill,1984):205. Reproduced with permission of McGraw-Hill, Inc.

Interrole conflict occurs when a person experiences conflict among the multiple roles in his or her life. One interrole conflict that many employees experience is work/home conflict, in which their role as worker clashes with their role as spouse or parent.[19] For example, when a child gets sick at school, the parent often must leave work to care for the child.

Intrarole conflict is conflict within a single role. It often arises when a person receives conflicting messages from role senders about how to perform a certain role. Suppose a manager receives counsel from her department head that she needs to socialize less with the nonmanagement employees. She also is told by her project manager that she needs to be a better team member, and that she can accomplish this by socializing more with the other nonmanagement team members. This situation is one of intrarole conflict.

Person-role conflict occurs when an individual in a particular role is expected to perform behaviors that clash with his or her values.[20] Salespeople, for example, may be required to offer the most expensive item in the sales line first to the customer, even when it is apparent that the customer does not want or cannot afford the item. A computer salesman may be required to offer a large, elaborate system to a student he knows is on a tight budget. This may conflict with the salesman's values, and he may experience person-role conflict.

All these forms of conflict can be managed. An understanding of the many forms is a first step. The next section focuses more extensively on interpersonal conflict, due to the pervasiveness of this type in organizations.

■ **INTERPERSONAL CONFLICT**

When a conflict occurs between two or more people, it is known as interpersonal conflict. To manage interpersonal conflict, it is helpful to understand

■ **FIGURE 13.3**
Power Relationships in
Organizations

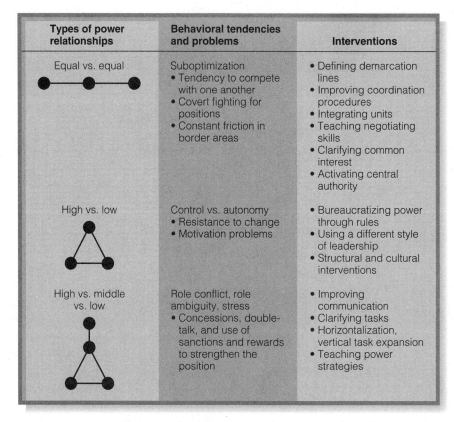

Types of power relationships	Behavioral tendencies and problems	Interventions
Equal vs. equal	Suboptimization • Tendency to compete with one another • Covert fighting for positions • Constant friction in border areas	• Defining demarcation lines • Improving coordination procedures • Integrating units • Teaching negotiating skills • Clarifying common interest • Activating central authority
High vs. low	Control vs. autonomy • Resistance to change • Motivation problems	• Bureaucratizing power through rules • Using a different style of leadership • Structural and cultural interventions
High vs. middle vs. low	Role conflict, role ambiguity, stress • Concessions, double-talk, and use of sanctions and rewards to strengthen the position	• Improving communication • Clarifying tasks • Horizontalization, vertical task expansion • Teaching power strategies

SOURCE: W. F. G. Mastenbroek, *Conflict Management and Organizational Development.* Copyright © 1987, John Wiley and Sons, Ltd. Reprinted by permission of John Wiley and Sons, Ltd.

power networks in organizations, defense mechanisms exhibited by individuals, and ways to cope with difficult people.

■ **Power Networks**

According to Mastenbroek, individuals in organizations are organized in three basic types of power networks.[21] Based on these power relationships, certain kinds of conflict tend to emerge. Figure 13.3 illustrates three basic kinds of power relationships in organizations.

The first relationship is equal versus equal, in which there is a horizontal balance of power among the parties. An example of this type of relationship would be a conflict between individuals from two different project teams. The behavioral tendency is toward suboptimization; that is, the focus is on a win-lose approach to problems, and each party tries

to maximize its power at the expense of the other party. Interventions like improving coordination between the parties and working toward common interests can help manage these conflicts.

The second type of power network is high versus low, or a powerful versus a less powerful relationship. Conflicts that emerge here take the basic form of the powerful individuals trying to control others, with the less powerful people trying to become more autonomous. Organizations typically respond to these conflicts by tightening the rules. However, the more successful ways of managing these conflicts are to try a different style of leadership, such as a coaching and counseling style, or to change the structure to a more decentralized one.

The third type of power network is high versus middle versus low. This power network illustrates the classic conflicts felt by middle managers. Two particular conflicts are evident: role conflict, in

■ **TABLE 13.2**
Common Defense Mechanisms

DEFENSE MECHANISM	PSYCHOLOGICAL PROCESS
Aggessive Mechanisms	
Fixation	Person maintains a persistent, nonadjustive reaction even though all the cues indicate the behavior will not cope with the problem.
Displacement	Individual redirects pent-up emotions toward persons, ideas, or objects other than the primary source of the emotion.
Negativism	Person uses active or passive resistance, operating unconsciously.
Compromise Mechanisms	
Compensation	Individual devotes himself or herself to a pursuit with increased vigor to make up for some feeling or real or imagined inadequacy.
Identification	Individual enhances own self-esteem by patterning behavior after another's, frequently also internalizing the values and beliefs of the other person; also vicariously shares the glories or suffers the disappointments of other individuals or groups.
Rationalization	Person justifies inconsistent or undesirable behavior, beliefs, statements, and motivations by providing acceptable explanations for them.
Withdrawal Mechanisms	
Flight or withdrawal	Person leaves the field in which frustration, anxiety, or conflict is experienced, either physically or psychologically.
Conversion	Emotional conflicts are expressed in muscular, sensory, or bodily symptoms of disability, malfunctioning, or pain.
Fantasy	Person daydreams or uses other forms of imaginative activity to obtain an escape from reality and obtain imagined satisfactions.

SOURCE: Adapted from Timothy W. Costello and Sheldon S. Zalkind, "Psychology in Administration: A Research Orientation."(First appeared in *Journal of Conflict Resolution*, III, 1959, pp.148-149.) Reprinted by permission of Sage Publications, Inc.

which conflicting expectations are placed on the manager from bosses and employees, and role ambiguity, in which the expectations of the boss are unclear. Improved communication among all parties can reduce role conflict and ambiguity. In addition, middle managers can benefit from education in positive ways to influence others.

Knowing the typical kinds of conflicts that arise in various kinds of relationships can help a manager diagnose conflicts and devise appropriate ways to manage them.

■ Defense Mechanisms

When an individual is involved in conflict with another human being, frustration often results. Con-

flicts can often arise within the context of a performance appraisal session. Most people do not react well to negative feedback, as was illustrated in a classic study.[22] In this study, when employees were given criticism about their work, over 50 percent of their responses were defensive.

When individuals are frustrated, as they often are in interpersonal conflict, they respond by exhibiting defense mechanisms.[23] Defense mechanisms are common reactions to the frustration that accompanies conflict. Table 13.2 illustrates several defense mechanisms seen in organizations.

Aggressive mechanisms are aimed at attacking the source of the conflict. Some of these are fixation, displacement, and negativism. In fixation, an individual fixates on the conflict, or keeps up a dysfunctional behavior that obviously will not solve the conflict. An example of fixation occurred in a university, where a faculty member became embroiled in a battle with the dean because the faculty member felt he had not received a large enough salary increase. He persisted in writing angry letters to the dean, whose hands were tied because of a low budget allocation to the college.

Displacement means directing anger toward someone who is not the source of the conflict. For example, a manager may respond harshly to an employee after a telephone confrontation with an angry customer. Another aggressive defense mechanism is negativism, which is active or passive resistance. Negativism is illustrated by a manager who, when appointed to a committee on which she did not want to serve, made negative comments throughout the meeting.

Compromise mechanisms are used by individuals to make the best of a conflict situation. Three compromise mechanisms include compensation, identification, and rationalization. Compensation occurs when an individual tries to make up for an inadequacy by putting increased energy into another activity. Compensation can be seen when a person makes up for a bad relationship at home by spending more time at the office. Identification occurs when one individual patterns his or her behavior after another's. One supervisor at a construction firm, not wanting to acknowledge consciously that she was not likely to be promoted, mimicked the behavior of her boss, even going so far as to buy a car just like the boss's. Rationalization is trying to justify one's behavior by constructing bogus reasons for it. Employees may rationalize unethical behavior like padding their expense accounts because "everyone else does it."

Withdrawal mechanisms are exhibited when frustrated individuals try to flee from a conflict using either physical or psychological means. Flight, conversion, and fantasy are examples of withdrawal mechanisms. Physically escaping a conflict is flight. An employee who takes a day off after a blowup with the boss is an example.

Conversion is a process whereby emotional conflicts become expressed in physical symptoms. Most of us have experienced the conversion reaction of a headache following an emotional exchange with another person. Fantasy is an escape by daydreaming. An excellent example of fantasy was shown in the movie 9 to 5, in which Dolly Parton, Lily Tomlin, and Jane Fonda played characters who fantasized about torturing their boss because he was such a tyrant.

Knowledge of these defense mechanisms can be extremely beneficial to a manager. By understanding the ways in which people typically react to interpersonal conflict, managers can be prepared for employees' reactions and help them uncover their feelings about a conflict.

■ INTRAPERSONAL CONFLICT

Intrapersonal conflict, or conflict within an individual related to social roles, can be managed with careful self-analysis and diagnosis of the situation. Two actions in particular can help prevent or resolve intrapersonal conflicts.

First, when seeking a new job, applicants should find out as much as possible about the values of the organization.[24] Many person-role conflicts center around differences between the organization's values and the individual's values. Research has shown that when there is a good fit between the values of the individual and the organization, the individual is more satisfied and committed and is less likely to leave the organization.[25]

Second, to manage intrarole or interrole conflicts, role analysis is a good tool. In role analysis, the individual asks the various role senders what they expect of him or her. The outcomes are clearer work roles and the reduction of conflict and ambiguity.[26]

■ CONFLICT MANAGEMENT STRATEGIES AND TECHNIQUES

Several strategies can be used to manage conflict in organizations. We examine both effective and ineffective ways of managing conflict.

One way to evaluate conflict management strategies is to examine the win-or-lose potential for the parties involved, as well as for the organization. To do so, we can use the framework of competitive versus cooperative strategies. Table 13.3 depicts the

■ **TABLE 13.3**
Win-Lose versus Win-Win Strategies

STRATEGY	DEPARTMENT A	DEPARTMENT B	ORGANIZATION
Competitive	Lose	Lose	Lose
	Lose	Win	Lose
	Win	Lose	Lose
Cooperative	Win	Win	Win

two strategies and four different conflict scenarios. The competitive strategy is founded on assumptions of win-lose and entails less-than-honest communication, distrust, and a rigid position on the part of both parties.[27] The cooperative strategy is founded on different assumptions: the potential for win-win outcomes, honest communication, trust, openness to risk and vulnerability, and the notion that the whole may be greater than the sum of the parts.

Suppose there is a conflict in a telephone company between service representatives (who deal with customers calling in with problems) and installers (who go to customers' homes to put in telephones). The service representatives (Department A) feel that the installers are not doing quality work and that this lack of quality increases the customer complaints that the service reps must handle. The installers (Department B) feel that the service representatives make unreasonable promises to customers about scheduling their telephone installations.

If no action is taken, both departments and the company as a whole are in a losing mode. Customer complaints will continue to increase, and hostilities between the departments will continue. This is a lose-lose approach.

If the installers demand that the service reps adhere strictly to a reasonable schedule for taking customer orders, it will eliminate part of the conflict. Or, if the service reps insist that the installers begin a service quality program, part of the conflict will be handled. Both of these scenarios, however, are win-lose approaches that do not completely solve the conflict. One group gets its demands satisfied, whereas the other group does not; therefore, the company ends up in a losing posture regarding the conflict.

To construct a win-win solution, the groups must cooperate. The service representatives could adhere to a reasonable schedule, consulting the installers when exceptional cases arise. The installers could institute a service quality program, which would help reduce the complaint calls fielded by the service representatives. This represents a win-win solution whereby the company is in a winning position following the conflict. Both parties have conceded something (note the "win-" in Table 13.3), but the conflict has been resolved with a positive outcome.

■ **Ineffective Techniques**

There are many techniques for dealing with conflict. Before turning to techniques that work, it should be recognized that some actions commonly taken in organizations to deal with conflict are not effective.[28]

Nonaction is doing nothing in hopes that the conflict will disappear. This is not generally a good technique, because most conflicts do not go away, and the individuals involved in the conflict react with frustration.

Secrecy, or trying to keep a conflict out of view of most people, only creates suspicion. An example is an organizational policy of pay secrecy. In some organizations, discussion of salary is grounds for dismissal. When this is the case, employees suspect that the company has something to hide.

Administrative orbiting is delaying action on a conflict by buying time, usually by telling the individuals involved that the problem is being worked on or that the boss is still thinking about the issue. Like nonaction, this technique leads to frustration and resentment.

Due process nonaction is a procedure set up to address conflicts, but it is so costly, time-consuming, or personally risky that no one will use it. Some companies' sexual harassment policies are examples of this technique. To file a sexual harassment complaint, detailed paperwork is required, the accuser must go through appropriate channels, and the accuser risks being branded a troublemaker. Thus, the company has a procedure for handling complaints (due process), but no one uses it (nonaction).

Character assassination is an attempt to label or discredit an opponent. In the confirmation hearings of Supreme Court Justice Clarence Thomas, for example, attempts at character assassination were made upon Anita Hill by referring to her as a spurned woman and by saying she lived in fantasy. Justice Thomas was also a victim of character assassination; he was portrayed as a womanizer and a perpetrator of sexual harassment. Character assassination can backfire and make the individual who uses it appear dishonest and cruel.

▨ Effective Techniques

Fortunately, there are effective conflict management techniques. These include appealing to superordinate goals, expanding resources, changing personnel, changing structure, and confronting and negotiating.

Superordinate Goals.   An organizational goal that is more important to both parties in a conflict than their individual or group goals is a superordinate goal.[29] Superordinate goals cannot be achieved by an individual or by one group alone. The achievement of these goals requires cooperation by both parties.

One effective technique for resolving conflict is to appeal to a superordinate goal—in effect, to focus the parties on a larger issue on which they both agree. This helps them realize their similarities rather than their differences.

In the conflict between service representatives and telephone installers that was discussed earlier, appealing to a superordinate goal would be an effective technique for resolving the conflict. Both departments can agree that superior customer service is a goal worthy of pursuit and that this goal cannot be achieved unless telephones are installed properly and in a timely manner, and customer complaints are handled effectively. Quality service requires that both departments cooperate to achieve the goal.

Expanding Resources.   One conflict resolution technique is so simple that it may be overlooked. If the source of the conflict is common or scarce resources, providing more resources may be a solution. Of course, managers working with tight budgets may not have the luxury of obtaining additional resources. Nevertheless, it is a technique to be considered. In the example earlier in this chapter, one solution to the conflict among managers over secretarial support would be to hire more secretaries.

Changing Personnel.   Sometimes a conflict is prolonged and severe, and efforts at resolution fail. In such cases, it may be appropriate to change personnel. Transferring or firing an individual may be the best solution, but only after due process. An especially difficult situation occurs when the individuals involved are in a family business.

Changing Structure.   Another way to resolve a conflict is to change the structure of the organization. One way of accomplishing this is to create an integrator role. An integrator is a liaison between groups with very different interests. In severe conflicts, it may be best that the integrator be a neutral third party.[30] Creating the integrator role is a way of opening dialogue between groups that have difficulty communicating.

Using cross-functional teams is another way of changing the organization's structure to manage conflict. In the old methods of designing new products in organizations, many departments had to contribute, and delays resulted from difficulties in coordinating the activities of the various departments. Using a cross-functional team made up of members from different departments improves coordination and reduces delays by allowing many activities to be performed at the same time rather than sequentially.[31] The team approach allows members from different departments to work together and reduces the potential for conflict.

Confronting And Negotiating.   Some conflicts require confrontation and negotiation between the parties. Both these strategies require skill on the part of the negotiator and careful planning before engaging in negotiations.[32] The process of negotiating involves an open discussion of problem solutions,

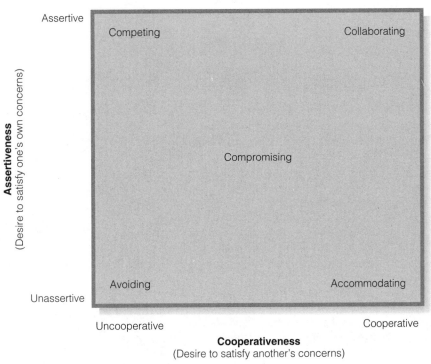

■ FIGURE 13.4
Conflict Management Styles

SOURCE: K. W. Thomas, "Conflict and Conflict Management," in M. D. Dunnette, *Handbook of Industrial and Organizational Psychology*, 900 (Chicago, IL; Rand McNally, 1976). Used with permission of M. D.Dunnette.

and the outcome often is an exchange in which both parties have given up something to reach a mutually beneficial solution.

One tool for helping people engage in open dialogue is called the container. People in a meeting put their fears, hostile thoughts, and feelings into an imaginary container in the middle of the meeting room. The contents of the container are in a safe place for all parties to observe and discuss. Through total openness, the parties can work through barriers that prevent conflict resolution.[33]

■ CONFLICT MANAGEMENT STYLES

Several of the effective techniques for managing conflict require negotiation on the part of the manager. The manager's approach to negotiation depends on a variety of conflict management styles: avoiding, accommodating, competing, compromising, and collaborating. One way of classifying styles

of conflict management is to examine the styles' assertiveness (the extent to which you want your goals met) and cooperativeness (the extent to which you want to see the other party's concerns met).[34] Figure 13.4 graphs the five conflict management styles using these two dimensions. Table 13.4 lists appropriate situations for using each conflict management style.

■ Avoiding

Avoiding is a style low on both assertiveness and cooperativeness. Avoiding is a deliberate decision to take no action on a conflict or to stay out of a conflict situation. One example of an organization that avoided conflict occurred in 1973 and 1974, when Exxon officials quietly withdrew their executives from Argentina because of the increased rate of kidnapping of U.S. executives.[35] In certain situations, it may be appropriate to avoid a conflict. For example, when the parties are angry and need time to

■ **TABLE 13.4**
Uses of Five Styles of Conflict Management

Conflict-Handling Style	Appropriate Situation
Competing	1. When quick, decisive action is vital (e.g., emergencies). 2. On important issues where unpopular actions need implementing (e.g., cost cutting, enforcing unpopular rules, discipline). 3. On issues vital to company welfare when you know you are right. 4. Against people who take advantage of noncompetitive behavior.
Collaborating	1. To find an integrative solution when both sets of concerns are too important to be compromised. 2. When your objective is to learn. 3. To merge insights from people with different perspectives. 4. To gain commitment by incorporating concerns into a consensus. 5. To work through feelings that have interfered with a relationship.
Compromising	1. When goals are important, but not worth the effort or potential disruption of more assertive modes. 2. When opponents with equal power are committed to mutually exclusive goals. 3. To achieve temporary settlements to complex issues. 4. To arrive at expedient solutions under time pressure. 5. As a backup when collaboration or competition is unsuccessful.
Avoiding	1. When an issue is trivial, or more important issues are pressing. 2. When you perceive no chance of satisfying your concerns. 3. When potential disruption outweighs the benefits of resolution. 4. To let people cool down and regain perspective. 5. When gathering information supersedes immediate decision. 6. When others can resolve the conflict more effectively. 7. When issues seem tangential or symptomatic of other issues.
Accommodating	1. When you find you are wrong—to allow a better position to be heard, to learn, and to show your reasonableness. 2. When issues are more important to others than to yourself—to satisfy others and maintain cooperation. 3. To build social credits for later issues. 4. To minimize loss when you are outmatched and losing. 5. When harmony and stability are especially important. 6. To allow employees to develop by learning from mistakes.

SOURCE: K. W. Thomas,"Toward Multi-Dimensional Values in Teaching: The Example of Conflict Behaviors,"*Academy of Management Review* 2 (1977): 484-490.

cool down, it may be best to use avoidance. There is a potential danger in using an avoiding style too often, however. Research shows that overuse of this style results in negative evaluations from others in the workplace.[36]

■ **Accommodating**

A style in which you are concerned that the other party's goals be met but relatively unconcerned with getting your own way is called accommodating. It is cooperative but unassertive. Appropriate situations for accommodating include times when you find you are wrong, when you want to let the other party have his or her way in order to remind the individual that he or she owes you similar treatment later, or when the relationship is important. Overreliance on accommodating has its dangers. If managers constantly defer to others, others may lose respect for them. In addition, accommodating managers may become frustrated because their own needs are never met, and they may lose self-esteem.[37]

■ Competing

Competing is a style that is very assertive and uncooperative. You want to satisfy your own interests and are willing to do so at the other party's expense. In an emergency or in situations where you know you are right, it may be appropriate to put your foot down. For example, environmentalists forced Shell Oil Company to scrap its plans to build a refinery in Delaware after a bitter "To Hell With Shell" campaign.[38] Relying solely on competing strategies is dangerous. Managers who do so may become reluctant to admit when they are wrong and may find themselves surrounded by people who are afraid to disagree with them.

■ Compromising

The compromising style is intermediate in both assertiveness and cooperativeness, because each party must give up something to reach a solution to the conflict. Compromises are often made in the final hours of union-management negotiations, when time is of the essence. Compromise is also an effective backup style when efforts toward collaboration are not successful.[39]

■ Collaborating

A win-win style that is high on both assertiveness and cooperativeness is known as collaborating. Working toward collaborating involves an open and thorough discussion of the conflict and arriving at a solution that is satisfactory to both parties. Situations where collaboration may be effective include times when both parties need to be committed to a final solution or when a combination of different perspectives can be formed into a solution.

Research on the five styles of conflict management indicates that although most managers favor a certain style, they have the capacity to change styles as the situation demands.[40] A study of project managers found that managers who used a combination of competing and avoiding styles were seen as ineffective by the engineers who worked on their project teams.[41] In another study of conflicts between R & D project man-

agers and technical staff, competing and avoiding styles resulted in more frequent conflict and lower performance, whereas the collaborating style resulted in less frequent conflict and better performance.[42]

Cultural differences also influence the use of different styles of conflict management, as was seen in the Scientific Foundation earlier in the chapter. In another study, Turkish and Jordanian managers were compared with U.S. managers. All three groups preferred the collaborating style. Turkish managers also reported frequent use of the competing style, whereas Jordanian and U.S. managers reported that it was one of their least used styles.[43]

It is important to remember that preventing and resolving dysfunctional conflict is only half the task of effective conflict management. Stimulating functional conflict is the other half.

■ MANAGERIAL IMPLICATIONS: CREATING A CONFLICT POSTITIVE ORGANIZATION

Dean Tjosvold argues that well-managed conflict adds to an organization's innovation and productivity.[44] He discusses procedures for making conflict positive. Too many organizations take a win-lose, competitive approach to conflict or avoid conflict altogether. These two approaches view conflict as negative. A positive view of conflict, in contrast, leads to win-win solutions. Figure 13.5 illustrates these three approaches to conflict management.

Four interrelated steps are involved in creating a conflict-positive organization:

1. Value diversity and confront differences. Differences should be seen as opportunities for innovation, and diversity should be celebrated. Open and honest confrontations bring out differences, and diversity is essential for positive conflict.

2. Seek mutual benefits, and unite behind cooperative goals. People must manage conflicts together. Through conflict, individuals learn how much they depend on one another. Even when employees share goals, they may differ on how to accomplish the goals. The important point is that they are moving toward the same objectives. Joint rewards should be given to the whole team for cooperative behavior.

■ FIGURE 13.5
Three Organizational Views of Conflict

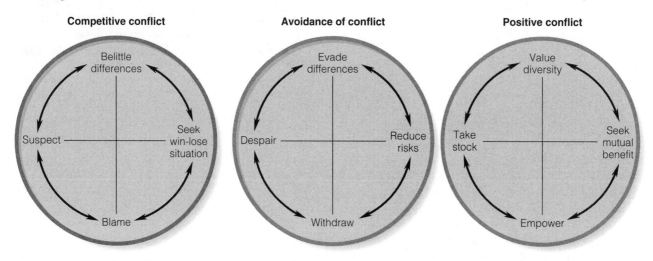

SOURCE: D. Tjosvold, *The Conflict-Positive Organization,* Copyright©1991 by Addison-Wesley Publishing Company, Inc. Reprinted with permission of the publisher.

3. Empower employees to feel confident and skillful. People must be made to feel that they control their conflicts and that they can deal with their differences productively. When they do so, they should be recognized.

4. Take stock to reward success and learn from mistakes. Employees should be encouraged to appreciate one another's strengths and weaknesses and to talk directly about them. They should celebrate their conflict management successes and work out plans for ways they can improve in the future.

Tjosvold believes that a conflict-positive organization has competitive advantages for the future.

■ CHAPTER SUMMARY

■ Conflict management skills are keys to management success. The manager's task is to stimulate functional conflict and prevent or resolve dysfunctional conflict.

■ Structural causes of conflict include specialization, interdependence, common resources, goal differences, authority relationships, status inconsistencies, and jurisdictional ambiguities.

■ Personal factors that lead to conflict include differences in skills and abilities, personalities, perceptions, or values and ethics; emotions; communication barriers; and cultural differences. The increasing diversity of the work force and globalization of business have potential to increase conflict arising from these differences.

■ The levels of conflict include interorganizational, intergroup, interpersonal, and intrapersonal.

■ Individuals engaged in interpersonal conflict often display aggressive, compromise, or withdrawal defense mechanisms.

■ In coping with a difficult person, it is important to identify the reasons the person is perceived as difficult and to analyze the response to the difficult person.

■ Ineffective techniques for managing conflict include nonaction, secrecy, administrative orbiting, due process nonaction, and character assassination.

■ Effective techniques for managing conflict include appealing to superordinate goals, expanding resources, changing personnel, changing structure, and confronting and negotiating.

■ In negotiating, managers can use a variety of conflict management styles, including avoiding, accommodating, competing, compromising, and collaborating.

- Managers should strive to create a conflict-positive organization—one that values diversity, empowers employees, and seeks win-win solutions to conflicts.

■ REVIEW QUESTIONS

1. Discuss the differences between functional and dysfunctional conflict. Why should a manager understand conflict?
2. Identify the structural and personal factors that contribute to conflict.
3. Discuss the four major forms of conflict in organizations.
4. What defense mechanisms do people use in interpersonal conflict?
5. What are the most effective techniques for managing conflict at work? What are some ineffective techniques?
6. Identify and discuss five styles of conflict management.
7. How can you stimulate conflict in an ethical manner?
8. In what situations is the competing style of conflict management appropriate? What unethical behaviors might be associated with this style? How can these behaviors be avoided?

■ REFERENCES

1. Definition adapted from D. Hellriegel, J. W. Slocum, Jr., and R. W. Woodman, *Organizational Behavior*, 6th ed. (St. Paul: West, 1992), and from R. D. Middlemist and M. A. Hitt, *Organizational Behavior* (St. Paul: West, 1988).
2. K. Thomas and W. Schmidt, "A Survey of Managerial Interests with Respect to Conflict," *Academy of Management Journal* 19 (1976): 315-318.
3. G. L. Lippit, "Managing Conflict in Today's Organizations," *Training and Development Journal* 36 (1982): 368-376.
4. M. Rajim, "A Measure of Styles of Handling Interpersonal Conflict," *Academy of Management Journal* 26 (1983): 368-376.
5. C. Morrill, "Learning from Managerial Conflict," *New Management* 3 (1988): 45-49.
6. R. A. Cosier and D. R. Dalton, "Positive Effects of Conflict: A Field Experiment," *International Journal of Conflict Management* 1 (1990): 81-92.
7. D. Tjosvold, "Making Conflict Productive," *Personnel Administrator* 29 (1984): 121-130.
8. J. D. Thompson, *Organizations in Action* (New York: McGraw-Hill, 1967).
9. T. J. Bergmann and R. J. Volkema, "Issues, Behavioral Responses, and Consequences in Interpersonal Conflicts," *Journal of Organizational Behavior* 15 (1994): 467-471.
10. R. Miles, Macro Organizational Behavior (Glenview, Ill.: Scott, Foresman, 1980).
11. H. Levinson, "The Abrasive Personality," *Harvard Business Review* 56 (1978): 86-94.
12. F. N. Brady, "Aesthetic Components of Management Ethics," *Academy of Management Review* 11 (1986): 337-344.
13. T. Cox, Jr., "The Multicultural Organization," *Academy of Management Executive* 5 (1991): 34-47.
14. G. Hofstede, "Cultural Constraints in Management Theories," *Academy of Management Executive* 7 (1993): 81-94.
15. "AT&T's Bid for NCR: Round Thirteen," *Economist*, 20 April 1991, 68-69.
16. A. Choi, "Steelworkers of Germany Endorse Strike," *Wall Street Journal*, 3 February 1992, A6.
17. M. Sherif and C. W. Sherif, *Social Psychology* (New York: Harper & Row, 1969).
18. D. Katz and R. Kahn, *The Social Psychology of Organizations*, 2d ed. (New York: Wiley, 1978).
19. D. L. Nelson and M. A. Hitt, "Employed Women and Stress: Implications for Enhancing Women's Mental Health in the Workplace," in J. C. Quick, J. Hurrell, and L. A. Murphy, eds., *Stress and Well-being at Work: Assessments and Interventions for Occupational Mental Health* (Washington, D.C.: American Psychological Association, 1992).
20. R. L. Kahn et al., *Organizational Stress: Studies in Role Conflict and Ambiguity* (New York: Wiley, 1964).
21. W. F. G. Mastenbroek, *Conflict Management and Organization Development* (Chichester, England: Wiley, 1987).
22. H. H. Meyer, E. Kay, and J. R. P. French, "Split Roles in Performance Appraisal," *Harvard Business Review* 43 (1965): 123-129.
23. T. W. Costello and S. S. Zalkind, *Psychology in Administration: A Research Orientation* (Englewood Cliffs, N.J.: Prentice-Hall, 1963).
24. B. Schneider, "The People Make the Place," *Personnel Psychology* 40 (1987): 437-453.
25. C. A. O'Reilly, J. Chatman, and D. F. Caldwell, "People and Organizational Culture: A Profile Comparison Approach to Assessing Person-Organization Fit," *Academy of Management Journal* 34 (1991): 487-516.
26. R. H. Miles, "Role Requirements as Sources of Organizational Stress," *Journal of Applied Psychology* 61 (1976): 172-179.
27. H. S. Baum, "Organizational Politics against Organizational Culture: A Psychoanalytic Perspective, *Human Resource Management* 28 (1989): 191-200.
28. R. Steers, *Introduction to Organizational Behavior*, 4th ed. (Glenview, Ill.: HarperCollins, 1991).
29. R. M. Kramer, "Intergroup Relations and Organizational Dilemmas: The Role of Categorization Processes," in B. Staw

and L. Cummings, eds., *Research in Organizational Behavior* 13 (Greenwich, Conn.: JAI Press, 1991), 191-228.

30. R. Blake and J. Mouton, "Overcoming Group Warfare," *Harvard Business Review* 64 (1984): 98-108.

31. D. G. Ancona and D. Caldwell, "Improving the Performance of New Product Teams," *Research Technology Management* 33 (1990): 25-29.

32. R. J. Lewicki and J. R. Litterer, *Negotiation* (Homewood, Ill.: Irwin, 1985).

33. B. Dumaine, "Mr. Learning Organizations," *Fortune*, 17 October 1994, 147-157.

34. K. W. Thomas, "Conflict and Conflict Management," in M. D. Dunnette, ed., *Handbook of Industrial and Organizational Psychology* (Chicago: Rand McNally, 1976), 900.

35. T. N. Gladwin and I. Walter, "How Multinationals Can Manage Social and Political Forces," *Journal of Business Strategy* 1 (1980): 54-68.

36. R. A. Baron, S. P. Fortin, R. L. Frei, L. A. Hauver, and M. L. Shack, "Reducing Organizational Conflict: The Role of Socially Induced Positive Affect," *International Journal of Conflict Management* 1 (1990): 133-152.

37. S. L. Phillips and R. L. Elledge, *The Team Building Source Book* (San Diego: University Associates, 1989).

38. Gladwin and Walter, "How Multinationals Can Manage," 228.

39. K. L. Thomas, "Toward Multidimensional Values in Teaching: The Example of Conflict Behaviors," *Academy of Management Review* 2 (1977): 484-490.

40. W. King and E. Miles, "What We Know and Don't Know about Measuring Conflict," *Management Communication Quarterly* 4 (1990): 222-243.

41. J. Barker, D. Tjosvold, and I. R. Andrews, "Conflict Approaches of Effective and Ineffective Project Managers: A Field Study in a Matrix Organization," *Journal of Management Studies* 25 (1988): 167-178.

42. M. Chan, "Intergroup Conflict and Conflict Management in the R & D Divisions of Four Aerospace Companies," *IEEE Transactions on Engineering Management* 36 (1989): 95-104.

43. M K. Kozan, "Cultural Influences on Styles of Handling Interpersonal Conflicts: Comparisons among Jordanian, Turkish, and U.S. Managers," *Human Relations* 42 (1989): 787-799.

44. D. Tjosvold, *The Conflict-Positive Organization* (Reading, Mass.: Addison-Wesley, 1991).

PART IV
ORGANIZATIONAL
PROCESSES AND
STRUCTURE

CHAPTER 14
JOBS AND THE DESIGN OF WORK

LEARNING OBJECTIVES

After reading this chapter, you should be able to do the following:

- Define the term *job,* and identify six patterns of defining work.
- Discuss the four traditional approaches to job design.
- Describe the job characteristics model.
- Compare the social information-processing (SIP) model with traditional job design approaches.
- Explain the interdisciplinary approach to job design.
- Compare Japanese, German, and Scandinavian approaches to work.
- Explain how job control, uncertainty, and conflict can be managed for employee well-being.
- Discuss five emerging issues in the design of work.

Several years ago, "Quality is Job 1!" became the motto of Ford Motor Company. Job 1 has a specific meaning in the context of the automotive industry. What does job mean in general? A job is defined as an employee's specific work and task activities in an organization. A job is not the same as an organizational position or a career. Organizational position identifies a job in relation to other parts of the organization; career refers to a sequence of job experiences over time.

This chapter focuses on jobs and the design of work as elements of the organization's structure. Jobs help people define their work and become integrated into the organization. The first section in the chapter examines the meaning of work in organizations. The second major section addresses four traditional approaches to job design developed between the late nineteenth century and the 1970s. The third major section examines four alternative approaches to job design developed over the past couple of decades. The final section addresses emerging issues in job design.

■ WORK IN ORGANIZATIONS

Work is effortful, productive activity resulting in a product or a service. Work is one important reason why organizations exist. A job is composed of a set of specific tasks, each of which is an assigned piece of work to be done in a specific time period. Work is an especially important human endeavor, because it can have a powerful effect, defining a person's life and binding the person to the reality of a human community.

Work has different meanings for different people. For all people in an organization, work is organized into jobs, and jobs fit into the larger structure of an organization. The structure of jobs is the concern of this chapter, and the structure of the organization is the concern of the next chapter. Both chapters emphasize organizations as sets of task and authority relationships through which people get work done.

■ Cultural Differences

The meaning of work differs from person to person and from culture to culture. One recent study found six patterns people follow in defining work, and these help explain the cultural differences in people's motivation to work.[1] Pattern A people define work as an activity in which value comes from performance and for which a person is accountable. It is generally self-directed and devoid of negative affect. Pattern B people define work as an activity that provides a person with positive personal affect and identity. Work contributes to society and is not unpleasant. Pattern C people define work as an activity from which profit accrues to others by its performance and that may be done in various settings other than a working place. Work is usually physically strenuous and somewhat compulsive. Pattern D people define work as primarily a physical activity a person must do that is directed by others and generally performed in a working place. Work is usually devoid of positive affect and is unpleasantly connected to performance. Pattern E people define work as a physically and mentally strenuous activ-

ity. It is generally unpleasant and devoid of positive affect. Pattern F people define work as an activity constrained to specific time periods that does not bring positive affect through its performance.

These six patterns were studied in six different countries: Belgium, the Federal Republic of Germany, Israel, Japan, the Netherlands, and the United States. There are significant differences among countries in how work is defined. In the Netherlands, work is defined most positively and with the most balanced personal and collective reasons for doing it. Work is defined least positively and with the most collective reason for doing it in Germany and Japan. Belgium, Israel, and the United States represent a middle position between these two. Future international studies should include Arab countries, India, Central and South American countries, and other Far Eastern countries to better represent the world's cultures.

Another international study of 5,550 people across ten occupational groups in 20 different countries completed the Work Value Scales (WVS).[2] The WVS is composed of thirteen items measuring various aspects of the work environment, such as responsibility and job security. The study found two common basic work dimensions across cultures. Work content is one dimension, measured by items such as "the amount of responsibility on the job." Job context is the other dimension, measured by items such as "the policies of my company." This finding suggests that people in many cultures distinguish between the nature of the work itself and elements of the context in which work is done. This supports Herzberg's two-factor theory of motivation (see Chapter 5) and his job enrichment method discussed later in this chapter. Thus, although differences in the meaning of work exist among countries, similarities exist across countries in understanding the structure in which work is done.

■ Jobs in Organizations

Task and authority relationships define an organization's structure. Jobs are the basic building blocks of this task-authority structure and are considered the micro-structural element to which employees most directly relate. Jobs are usually designed to complement and support other jobs in the organization.

Isolated jobs are rare. However, one such isolated job was identified at Coastal Corporation during the early 1970s. Shortly after Oscar Wyatt moved the company from Corpus Christi, Texas, to Houston, Coastal developed organizational charts and job descriptions because the company had grown so large. In the process of charting the organization's structure, it was discovered that the beloved corporate economist reported to no one. Everyone assumed he worked for someone else. Such peculiarities are rare.

Jobs in organizations are interdependent and designed to make a contribution to the organization's overall mission and goals. For salespeople to be successful, the production people must be effective. For production people to be effective, the material department must be effective. These interdependencies require careful planning and design so that all of the "pieces of work" fit together into a whole. For example, if an envelope salesperson takes an order for 1 million envelopes from John Hancock Life Insurance Company and promises a two-week delivery date without knowing that the production department cannot meet that deadline, the salesperson dooms the company to failure in meeting John Hancock's expectations. The central concerns of this chapter are designing work and structuring jobs to prevent such problems and to ensure employee well-being.

Chapter 15 addresses the larger issues in the design of organizations. In particular, it examines the competing processes of differentiation and integration in organizations. Differentiation is the process of subdividing and departmentalizing the work of an organization. Jobs result from differentiation, which is necessary because no one can do it all (contrary to the famous statement made by Harold Geneen, former chairman of ITT: "If I had enough arms and legs and time, I'd do it all myself"). Even small organizations must divide work so that each person is able to accomplish a manageable piece of the whole. At the same time the organization divides up the work, it must also integrate those pieces back into a whole. Integration is the process of connecting jobs and departments into a coordinated, cohesive whole. For example, if the envelope salesperson had coordinated with the production manager before finalizing the order with John Hancock, the company could have met the customer's expectations, and integration would have occurred.

■ TRADITIONAL APPROACHES TO JOB DESIGN

Failure to differentiate, integrate, or do both, may result in badly designed jobs, which in turn cause a variety of performance problems in organizations. Good job design helps avoid these problems, improve productivity, and enhance employee well-being. Four approaches to job design developed during this century are scientific management, job enlargement/job rotation, job enrichment, and the job characteristics theory. Each approach offers unique benefits to the organization, the employee, or both. Each approach also has limitations and drawbacks. The later job design approaches were developed to overcome the limitations of earlier approaches. For example, job enlargement is intended to overcome the problem of boredom associated with scientific management's narrowly defined approach to jobs.

■ Scientific Management

Scientific management, an approach to work design advocated by Frederick Taylor from the late nineteenth century through 1915, emphasized work simplification. Work simplification is the standardization and the narrow, explicit specification of task activities for workers.[3] Jobs designed through scientific management have a limited number of tasks, and each task is scientifically specified so the worker is not required to think or deliberate. According to Taylor, the role of management and the industrial engineer is to calibrate and define each task carefully. The role of the worker is execution and task accomplishment. The elements of scientific management, such as time and motion studies, differential piece rate systems of pay, and the scientific selection of workers, all focus on the efficient use of labor for the economic benefit of both the worker and the corporation. Some employees like scientifically designed jobs, and one study found employees satisfied with various aspects of repetitive work.[4]

Two arguments supported the efficient and standardized job design approach of scientific management in the early days of the American industrial revolution. The first argument was that work simplification allowed workers of diverse ethnic and skill backgrounds to work together in a systematic way.

Large industrial organizations had to design ways to blend the large waves of European immigrants of the late nineteenth century into a productive work force. Work simplification avoided having workers engage in problem-solving or decision-making activities, which would have been difficult, because no one language united all immigrants. Germans, Scots, Hungarians, and Poles might have a difficult time in a quality circle without a common language.[5] Taylor's unique approach to work standardization allowed immigrants of various linguistic and ethnic descents to be blended into a functional work force.

The second argument for scientific management was that work simplification led to production efficiency in the organization and, therefore, to higher profits. This economic argument for work simplification tended to treat labor as a means of production and dehumanized it.

A fundamental limitation of scientific management is that it undervalues the human capacity for thought and ingenuity. Jobs designed through scientific management use only a portion of a person's capabilities. This underutilization makes work boring, monotonous, and understimulating. The failure to utilize fully the workers' capacity in a constructive fashion may cause a variety of work problems. A contemporary example of a work problem resulting from underutilization and boredom might be the intentional placement of a Coke bottle in a car door or even a golf ball in a hubcap on an automobile assembly line as a "joke."

■ Job Enlargement/Job Rotation

Job enlargement proposes to overcome the limitations of overspecialized work, such as boredom. Job enlargement is a method of job design that increases the number of tasks in a job. Job rotation is a variation of job enlargement and exposes a worker to a variety of specialized job tasks over time. The reasoning for these approaches to the problems of overspecialization is as follows. First, the core problem with overspecialized work was believed to be lack of variety. That is, jobs designed by scientific management were too narrow and limited in the number of tasks and activities assigned to each worker. Second, a lack of variety led to understimulation and underutilization of the worker. Third, the worker would be more stimulated and better uti-

lized by increasing the variety in the job. Variety could be increased by increasing the number of activities or by rotating the worker through different jobs. For example, job enlargement for a lathe operator in a steel plant might include selecting the steel pieces to be turned and performing all of the maintenance work on the lathe. An example of job rotation might occur in a small bank where an employee might take new accounts one day, serve as a cashier another day, and process loan applications on a third day.

One of the first studies of the problem of repetitive work was done at IBM after World War II. The company implemented a job enlargement program during the war and evaluated the effort after six years.[6] The two most important results were a significant increase in product quality and a reduction in idle time, both for people and for machines. Less obvious and measurable are the benefits of job enlargement to IBM through enhanced worker status and improved manager-worker communication. Therefore, job enlargement does counter the problems of work specialization.

A later study examined the effects of mass production jobs on assembly line workers in the automotive industry.[7] Mass production jobs are characterized by: (1) mechanical work pace, (2) repetitiveness, (3) minimum skill requirements, (4) predetermined tools and techniques, (5) minute division of the production process, and (6) little requirement for mental attention. The researchers conducted 180 private interviews with assembly line workers and found generally positive attitudes toward pay, security, and supervision. They concluded that job enlargement and job rotation would improve other job aspects, such as repetition and a mechanical work pace.

Job rotation and cross-training programs are variations of job enlargement. A recent study of job rotation among 255 pharmaceutical employees found career antecedents and career outcomes of job rotation.[8] Michael Campion and his colleagues concluded that job rotation may be a proactive way to enhance the career development value of work assignments. In cross-training, workers are trained in different specialized tasks or activities. All three kinds of programs horizontally enlarge jobs; that is, the number and variety of an employee's tasks and activities are increased. Graphics Controls Corporation developed a flexible work force through the Designated Trainee Program, a cross-training program for 300 to 400 highly skilled employees. The program produced savings in time and money.

Job Enrichment

Whereas job enlargement increases the number of job activities through horizontal loading, job enrichment increases the amount of job responsibility through vertical loading. Job enrichment is a job design or redesign method aimed at increasing the motivational factors in a job. Job enrichment builds on Herzberg's two-factor theory of motivation, which distinguished between motivational and hygienic factors for people at work. Whereas job enlargement recommends increasing and varying the number of activities a person does, job enrichment recommends increasing the recognition, responsibility, and opportunity for achievement. For example, enlarging the lathe operator's job means adding maintenance activities, and enriching the job means having the operator meet with customers who buy the products.

Herzberg believes that only certain jobs should be enriched, and the first step is to select the jobs appropriate for job enrichment.[9] He recognizes that some people prefer simple jobs. Once jobs are selected for enrichment, management should brainstorm about possible changes, revise the list to include only specific changes related to motivational factors, and screen out generalities and suggestions related to simply increasing activities or numbers of tasks. Those whose jobs are to be enriched should not participate in this process because of a conflict of interest. Two key problems can arise in the implementation of job enrichment. First, an initial drop in performance can be expected as workers accommodate to the change. Second, first-line supervisors may experience some anxiety or hostility as a result of employees' increased responsibility.

A seven-year implementation study of job enrichment at AT & T found the approach beneficial.[10] Job enrichment required a big change in management style, and AT & T found that it could not ignore hygienic factors in the work environment just because it was enriching existing jobs. Whereas the AT & T experience with job enrichment was positive, a criti-

cal review of job enrichment did not find that to be the case generally.[11] One problem with job enrichment as a strategy for work design is that it is based on an oversimplified motivational theory. Another problem is the lack of consideration for individual differences among employees. Job enrichment, like scientific management's work specialization and job enlargement/job rotation, is a universal approach to the design of work and thus does not differentiate among individuals.

Job Characteristics Theory

The job characteristics theory is a traditional approach to the design of work. Initiated during the mid-1960s, it makes a significant departure from the three earlier approaches. It emphasizes the interaction between the individual and specific attributes of the job; therefore, it is a person-job fit model rather than a universal job design model. Its earliest origins were in a research study of 470 workers in 47 different jobs across 11 industries.[12] The study measured and classified relevant task characteristics for these 47 jobs and found four core job characteristics: job variety, autonomy, responsibility, and interpersonal interaction. The study also found that core job characteristics did not affect all workers in the same way. A worker's values, religious beliefs, and ethnic background influenced the way the worker responded to the job. Specifically, workers with rural values and strong religious beliefs preferred jobs high in core characteristics, and workers with urban values and weaker religious beliefs preferred jobs low in core characteristics.

Richard Hackman and his colleagues modified the original model by including three critical psychological states of the individual and refining the measurement of core job characteristics. The result is the Job Characteristics Model shown in Figure 14.1.[13] The Job Diagnostic Survey (JDS) was developed to diagnose jobs by measuring the five core job characteristics and three critical psychological states shown in the model. The core job characteristics stimulate the critical psychological states in the manner shown in Figure 14.1. This results in varying personal and work outcomes, as identified in the figure.

The five core job characteristics are defined as follows:

■ **FIGURE 14.1**
The Job Characteristics Model

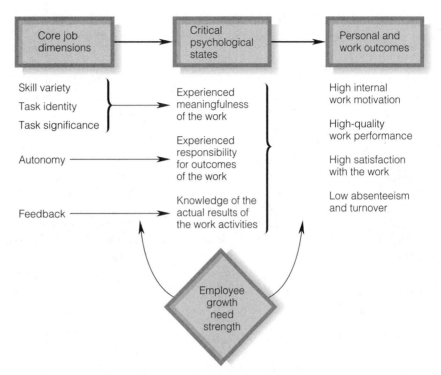

SOURCE: J. R. Hackman and G. R. Oldham, "The Relationship Among Core Job Dimensions, the Critical Psychological States, and On-the Job Outcomes," The Job Diagnostic Survey: An Instrument for the Diagnosis of Jobs and the Evaluation of Job Redesign Projects, Yale University, (1974), 3. Used with permission.

1. **Skill variety.** The degree to which a job includes different activities and involves the use of multiple skills and talents of the employee.
2. **Task identity.** The degree to which the job requires completion of a whole and identifiable piece of work—that is, doing a job from beginning to end with a tangible outcome.
3. **Task significance.** The degree to which the job has a substantial impact on the lives or work of other people, whether in the immediate organization or in the external environment.
4. **Autonomy.** The degree to which the job provides substantial freedom, independence, and discretion of the employee in scheduling the work and in determining the procedures to be used in carrying it out.
5. **Feedback from the job itself.** The degree to which carrying out the work activities results in the employee's obtaining direct and clear information about the effectiveness of his or her performance.

Hackman and his colleagues say that the five core job characteristics interact to determine an overall Motivating Potential Score (MPS) for a specific job. The MPS indicates a job's potential for motivating incumbents. An individual's MPS is determined by the following equation:

$$\text{MPS} = \frac{\left[\begin{array}{c}\text{Skill}\\\text{variety}\end{array}\right] + \left[\begin{array}{c}\text{Task}\\\text{identity}\end{array}\right] + \left[\begin{array}{c}\text{Task}\\\text{significance}\end{array}\right]}{3}$$
$$\times\ [\text{Autonomy}] \times [\text{Feedback}]$$

The Job Characteristics Model includes growth need strength (the desire to grow and fully develop one's abilities) as a moderator. People with a high growth need strength respond favorably to jobs with high MPSs, and individuals with low growth need strength respond less favorably to such jobs. The job characteristics theory further suggests that core job dimensions stimulate three critical psychological states according to the relationships specified in the model. These critical psychological states are defined as follows:

1. Experienced meaningfulness of the work, or the degree to which the employee experiences the job as one that is generally meaningful, valuable, and worthwhile.
2. Experienced responsibility for work outcomes, or the degree to which the employee feels personally accountable and responsible for the results of the work he or she does.
3. Knowledge of results, or the degree to which the employee knows and understands, on a continuous basis, how effectively he or she is performing the job.

In one early study, Hackman and Oldham administered the JDS to 658 employees working on 62 different jobs in seven business organizations.[14] The JDS was useful for job redesign efforts through one or more of five implementing concepts: (1) the combining of tasks into larger jobs, (2) forming natural work teams to increase task identity and task significance, (3) establishing relationships with customers, (4) loading jobs vertically with more responsibility, and/or (5) opening feedback channels for the job incumbent. For example, if an automotive mechanic received little feedback on the quality of repair work performed, one redesign strategy would be to solicit customer feedback one month after each repair.

In an international study, the Job Characteristics Model was tested in a sample of 57 jobs from 37 organizations in Hong Kong.[15] Job incumbents each completed the JDS, and their supervisors completed the Job Rating Form (JRF). The JRF is a supervisory version of the JDS and asks the supervisor to rate the employee's job. The study supported the model in general. However, task significance was not a reliable core job dimension in this study, which suggests either national differences in the measurement of important job dimensions or cultural biases about work. This result may also suggest value differences between American and Asian people with regard to jobs.

An alternative to the Job Characteristics Model is the Job Characteristics Inventory (JCI) developed by Henry Sims and Andrew Szilagyi.[16] The JCI prima-rily measures core job characteristics. It is not as comprehensive as the JDS, because it does not incorporate critical psychological states, personal and work outcomes, or employee needs. The JCI does give some consideration to structural and individual variables that affect the relationship between core job characteristics and the individual. One comparative analysis of the two models found similarities in the measures and in the models' predictions.[17] The comparative analysis also found two differences. First, the variety scales in the two models appear to have different effects on performance. Second, the autonomy scales in the two models appear to have different effects on employee satisfaction. Overall, the two models together support the usefulness of a person-job fit approach to the design of work over the earlier, universal theories.

■ ALTERNATIVE APPROACHES TO JOB DESIGN

Because each of the traditional job design approaches has limitations, several alternative approaches to job design have emerged over the past couple of decades. This section examines four of these alternatives. First, it examines the social information-processing model. Second, it reviews the interdisciplinary approach of Michael Campion and Paul Thayer. Their approach builds on the traditional job design approaches. Third, this section examines the international perspectives of the Japanese, the Germans, and the Scandinavians. Finally, it focuses on the health and well-being aspects of work design. An emerging fifth approach to the design of work through teams and autonomous work groups was addressed in Chapter 9. Jobs in today's workplace must be designed for a world that has moved beyond the industrial age of mass production.

■ Social Information Processing

The traditional approaches to the design of work emphasize objective core job characteristics. In contrast, the social information-processing (SIP) model emphasizes the interpersonal aspects of work design. Specifically, the SIP model says that what others tell us about our jobs is important.[18] The SIP model has four basic premises about the work environment.[19] First, other people provide cues we use to understand the work environment. Second, other people help us judge what is important in our jobs. Third, other people tell us how they see our jobs. Fourth, other people's positive and negative feedback helps us understand our feelings about our jobs.

People's perceptions and reactions to their jobs are shaped by information from other people in the work environment.[20] In other words, what others believe about a person's job may be important to understanding the person's perceptions of, and reactions to, the job. This does not mean that objective job characteristics are unimportant; rather, it means that others can modify the way these characteristics affect us. For example, one study of task complexity found that the objective complexity of a task must be distinguished from the subjective task complexity experienced by the employee.[21] While objective task complexity may be a motivator, the presence of others in the work environment, social interaction, or even daydreaming may be important additional sources of motivation. The SIP model makes an important contribution to the design of work by emphasizing the importance of other people and the social context of work. In some cases, these aspects of the work environment may be more important than objective core job characteristics. For example, the subjective feedback of other people about how difficult a particular task is may be more important to a person's motivation to perform than an objective probability estimate of the task's difficulty.

■ Interdisciplinary Approach

The interdisciplinary approach to job design of Michael Campion and Paul Thayer builds on the traditional job design approaches and does not emphasize the social aspects of the work environment. Four approaches—the mechanistic, motivational, biological, and perceptual/motor approaches—are necessary, they say, because no one approach can solve all performance problems caused by poorly designed jobs. Each approach has its benefits, as well as its limitations.

The interdisciplinary approach allows the job designer or manager to consider trade-offs and alternatives among the approaches based on desired outcomes. If a manager finds poor performance a problem, for example, the manager should analyze the job to ensure a design aimed at improving performance. The interdisciplinary approach is important because badly designed jobs cause far more performance problems than managers realize.[22]

Table 14.1 summarizes the positive and negative outcomes of each job design approach. The mechanistic and motivational approaches to job design are very similar to scientific management's work simplification and to the Job Characteristics Model, respectively. Because these were discussed earlier in the chapter, they are not further elaborated here.

The biological approach to job design emphasizes the person's interaction with physical aspects of the work environment and is concerned with the amount of physical exertion, such as lifting and muscular effort, required by the position. For example, an analysis of medical claims at Chaparral Steel Company identified lower back problems as the most common physical problem experienced by steel makers and managers alike. As a result, the company instituted an education and exercise program under expert guidance to improve care of the lower back. Program graduates received back cushions for their chairs with "Chaparral Steel Company" embossed on them. Lower back problems associated with improper lifting may be costly, but they are not fatal. Campion describes a more catastrophic problem in the case of Three Mile Island, when nuclear materials contaminated the surrounding area and threatened disaster. Campion concluded that poor design of the control room operator's job caused the disaster.

The perceptual/motor approach to job design also emphasizes the person's interaction with physical aspects of the work environment and is based on engineering that considers human factors such as strength or coordination, ergonomics, and experimental psychology. This approach addresses the way people mentally process information acquired from the physical work environment through perceptual and motor skills. The approach emphasizes perception and fine motor skills, as opposed to the gross motor skills and muscle strength emphasized in the mechanistic approach. The perceptual/motor approach is more likely to be relevant to operational

■ **TABLE 14.1**
Summary of Outcomes from Various Job Design Approaches

JOB-DESIGN APPROACH (Discipline)	POSITIVE OUTCOMES	NEGATIVE OUTCOMES
Mechanistic Approach (mechanical engineering)	Decreased training time Higher personnnel utilization levels Lower likelihood of error Less chance of mental overload Lower stress levels	Lower job satisfaction Lower motivation Higher absenteesim
Motivational Approach (industrial psychology)	Higher job satisfaction Higher motivation Greater job involvement Higher job perfromance Lower absenteeism	Increased training time Lower personnel utilization levels Greater chance of errors Greater chance of mental overload and stress
Biological Approach (biology)	Less physical effort Less physicial fatigue Fewer health complaints Fewer medical incidents Lower absenteeism Higher job satisfaction	Higher financial costs because of changes in equipment or job environment
Perceptual/Motor Approach (experimental psychology)	Lower likelihood of error Lower likelihood of accidents Less chance of mental stress Lower training time Higher personnel utilization levels	Lower job satisfaction Lower motivation

SOURCE: Reprinted with permission of publisher, from *Organizational Dynamics,* Winter/1987 © 1987. American Management Association, New York. All rights reserved.

and technical work, which may tax a person's concentration and attention, than to managerial, administrative, and custodial jobs, which are less likely to strain concentration and attention. For example, this approach may be very applicable in keyboard operations and data entry jobs.

One study using the interdisciplinary approach to improve jobs evaluated 377 clerical, 80 managerial and 90 analytical positions.[23] The jobs were improved by combining tasks and adding ancillary duties. The improved jobs provided greater motivation for the incumbents and were better from a perceptual/motor standpoint. However, the jobs were poorly designed from a mechanical engineering viewpoint, and they were unaffected from a biological perspective. Again, the interdisciplinary approach considers trade-offs and alternatives when evaluating job redesign efforts.

■ **Japanese, German, and Scandinavian Perspectives**

Each nation or ethnic group has a unique way of understanding and designing work.[24] As organizations become more global and international, an appreciation of the perspectives of other nations is increasingly important. The Japanese, Germans, and Scandinavians in particular have distinctive perspectives on the designing and organizing of work. Each country's perspective is forged within its unique cultural and economic system.

The Japanese began harnessing their productive energies during the 1950s by drawing on the product quality ideas of W. Edwards Deming.[25] In addition, the central government became actively involved in the economic resurgence of Japan, and it encouraged companies to conquer industries rather

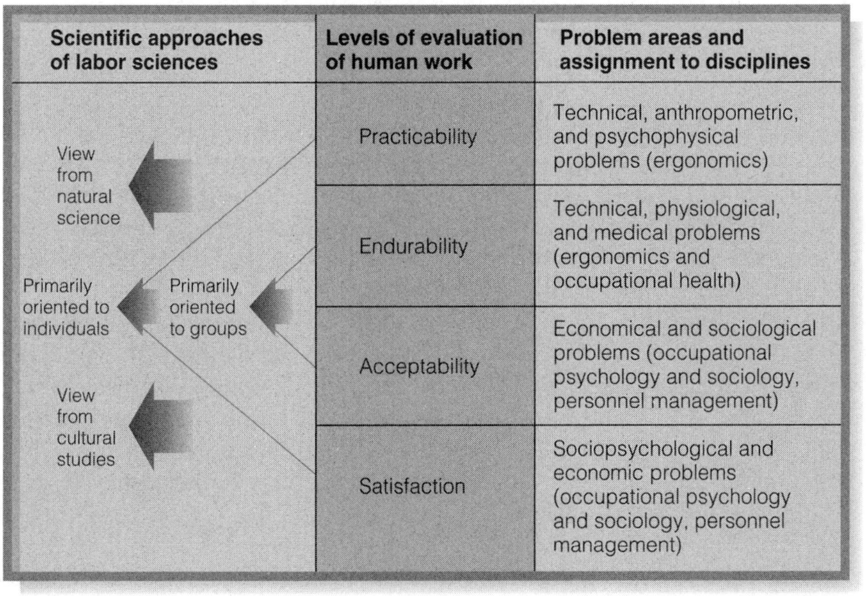

Scientific approaches of labor sciences	Levels of evaluation of human work	Problem areas and assignment to disciplines
View from natural science / Primarily oriented to individuals / Primarily oriented to groups / View from cultural studies	Practicability	Technical, anthropometric, and psychophysical problems (ergonomics)
	Endurability	Technical, physiological, and medical problems (ergonomics and occupational health)
	Acceptability	Economical and sociological problems (occupational psychology and sociology, personnel management)
	Satisfaction	Sociopsychological and economic problems (occupational psychology and sociology, personnel management)

■ **FIGURE 14.2**

Hierarchical Model of Criteria for the Evaluation of Human Work

SOURCE: H. Luczak, " 'Good Work' Design: An Ergonomic, Industrial Engineering Perspective," in J. C. Quick, L. R. Murphy and J.J. Hurrell, eds., *Stress and Well-Being at Work* (Washington, D.C.): American Psychological Association. Reprinted by permission.

than to maximize profits.[26] Such an industrial policy built on the Japanese cultural ethic of collectivism has implications for the way work is done. The Japanese work system emphasizes the strategic level and encourages collective and cooperative working arrangements.[27] The Japanese emphasize performance, accountability, and other- or self-directedness in defining work.

The German approach to work has been shaped by Germany's unique educational system, cultural values, and economic system. The Germans are a highly educated and well-organized people. For example, their educational system has a multitrack design with technical school and university alternatives. The German economic system has a strong emphasis on free enterprise, private property rights, and management-labor cooperation. A comparison of voluntary and mandated management-labor cooperation in Germany found productivity superior in the former type of cooperation.[28] The Germans value hierarchy and authority relationships and, as a result, are generally disciplined.[29] Germany's workers are highly unionized, and their discipline and efficiency have enabled Germany to be highly pro-

ductive while its workers labor substantially fewer hours than do Americans.

The traditional German approach to work design was technocentric, placing technology and engineering at the center of job design decisions. Recently, German industrial engineers have moved to a more anthropocentric approach, moving human considerations to the center of job design decisions. This latter approach relies on a more humanistic process, as shown in Figure 14.2.[30] In the anthropocentric approach, work is evaluated using the criteria of practicability and worker satisfaction at the individual level and the criteria of endurability and acceptability at the group level. Figure 14.2 also identifies problem areas and disciplines concerned with each aspect of the work design.

The Scandinavian cultural values and economic system stand in contrast to the German system. The social democratic tradition in Scandinavia during this century has emphasized social concern rather than industrial efficiency. The Scandinavians place great emphasis on a work design model that encourages high degrees of worker control and good social support systems for workers.[31] Lennart Levi believes that circumstantial, inferential scientific evidence is sufficient as a basis for legislative and policy action for work redesign to enhance worker well-being. An example of such action for promoting good working environments and occupational health, Swedish Government Bill 1976/77:149, states "Work should be safe both physically and mentally, but also provide opportunities for involvement, job satisfaction, and personal development." More recently, the Swedish Working Life Fund was set up by a 1991 decree from the Swedish Parliament to fund research, intervention programs, and demonstration projects in work design. For example, a study of Stockholm police on shift schedules going from a counterclockwise to a clockwise daily rotation, which was more compatible with human biology, resulted in improved sleep, less fatigue, lower systolic blood pressure, and lower blood levels of triglycerides and glucose.[32] Hence, the work redesign improved the police officers' health.

■ Work Design and Well-Being

American social scientists have had concerns like those of the Scandinavians with regard to the effects of work and job design on health and well-being. This issue was discussed briefly in Chapter 7. Economic and industry-specific upheavals in the United States during the past two decades led to job loss and unemployment, and the adverse health impact of these factors has received attention.[33] Attention also has been devoted to the effects of specific work design parameters on psychological health.[34] Organizations should work to redesign jobs to increase worker control and reduce worker uncertainty, while at the same time managing conflict and task/ job demands. These objectives can be achieved in several ways.

Control in work organizations can be increased by (1) giving workers the opportunity to control several aspects of the work and the workplace; (2) designing machines and tasks with optimal response times and/or ranges; and (3) implementing performance-monitoring systems as a source of relevant feedback to workers. Uncertainty can be reduced by (1) providing employees with timely and complete information needed for their work; (2) making clear and unambiguous work assignments; (3) improving

communication at shift change time, and (4) increasing employee access to information sources. Conflict at work can be managed through (1) participative decision making to reduce conflict; (2) the use of supportive supervisory styles to resolve conflict; and (3) sufficient resource availability to meet work demands, thus preventing conflict. Task/job design can be improved by enhancing core job characteristics and not patterning service work after assembly line work.

Task uncertainty was shown to have an adverse effect on morale in a study of 629 employment security work units in California and Wisconsin.[35] More important, the study showed that morale was better predicted by considering both the overall design of the work unit and the task uncertainty. This study suggests that if one work design parameter, such as task uncertainty, is a problem in a job, its adverse effects on people may be mitigated by other work design parameters. For example, higher pay may offset an employee's frustration with a difficult co-worker, or a friendly, supportive working environment may offset frustration with low pay.

■ EMERGING ISSUES IN THE DESIGN OF WORK

A number of issues related to specific aspects of the design of work have emerged over the past several years. Rather than being comprehensive ways to address job design or worker well-being, these issues address one or another aspect of a job. They are not interrelated. The emerging issues addressed are task revision, telecommuting, alternative work patterns, technostress, and skill development.

■ Task Revision

A new concept in the design of work is task revision.[36] This is an innovative way to modify an incorrectly specified role or job. Task revision assumes that organizational roles and job expectations may be correctly or incorrectly defined. Furthermore, a person's behavior in a work role has very different performance consequences depending upon whether the role is correctly or incorrectly defined. Standard role behavior leads to good performance if the role is correctly defined, and it leads to poor performance if the role is incorrectly defined. These performances go to the extreme when incumbents exhibit extreme behavior in their jobs. Going to extremes leads one to exceed expectations and display extraordinary behavior (extra-role behavior); this results in either excellent performance or very poor performance, depending on the accuracy of the role definition.

Counter-role behavior occurs when the incumbent acts contrary to the expectations of the role or exhibits deviant behavior. This is a problem if the role is correctly defined. For example, poor performance occurred on a hospital ward when the nursing supervisor failed to check the administration of all medications for the nurses she was supervising, resulting in one near fatality because a patient was not given required medication by a charge nurse. The nursing supervisor exhibited counter-role behavior in believing she could simply trust the nurses and did not have to double-check their actions. The omission was caught on the next shift. When a role or task is correctly defined (for example, double-checking medication administration), counter-role behavior leads to poor performance.

Task revision is counter-role behavior in an incorrectly specified role and is a useful way to correct for the problem in the role specification. It is a form of role innovation that modifies the job to achieve a better performance. Task revision is the basis for long-term adaptation when the current specifications of a job are no longer applicable.[37] For example, the traditional role for a surgeon is to complete surgical procedures in an accurate and efficient manner. Based on this definition, socio-emotional caregiving is counter-role behavior on the part of the surgeon. However, if the traditional role were to be labeled incorrect, the surgeon's task revision through socio-emotional caregiving would be viewed as leading to much better medical care for patients.

■ Telecommuting

Telecommuting, as noted in Chapter 2, occurs when employees work at home or in other locations geographically separate from their company's main location. Telecommuting may entail working in a combination of home, satellite office, and main office locations. This flexible arrangement is designed to achieve a better fit between the needs of the individual employee and the organization's task demands.

Executives have practiced forms of telecommuting for years. For example, Jonathan Fielding, a professor of public health at UCLA and Johnson & Johnson employee, telecommutes between offices at UCLA, Johnson & Johnson in New Jersey, and other locations throughout the country and the world. A number of companies, such as AT & T in Phoenix and Bell Atlantic, started pilot programs in telecommuting for a wide range of employees. These flexible arrangements help some companies respond to changing demographics and a shrinking labor pool. The Travelers Companies was one of the first businesses to try the idea, and is considered an industry leader in telecommuting. Even though Travelers' policy is informal, some managers have found improvements in communication *and* quality of work.

Pacific Bell has tried telecommuting on a large scale.[38] In 1990, Pacific Bell had 1,500 managers who telecommuted. For example, an employee might work at home four days a week as an information systems designer and spend one day a week at the main office location in meetings, work exchanges, and coordination with others. Of 3,000 Pacific Bell managers responding to a mail survey, 87 percent said telecommuting would reduce employee stress, 70 percent said it would increase job satisfaction while reducing absenteeism, and 64 percent said it would increase productivity.

Telecommuting is neither a cure-all nor a universally feasible alternative. Many telecommuters feel a sense of social isolation. Furthermore, not all forms of work are amenable to telecommuting. For example, firefighters and police officers must be at their duty stations to be successful in their work. Employees for whom telecommuting is not a viable option within a company may feel jealous of those able to telecommute. In addition, it may have the potential to create the sweatshops of the twenty-first century. Telecommuting is a novel, emerging issue.

■ Alternative Work Patterns

Job sharing is an alternative work pattern in which there is more than one person occupying a single job. Job sharing may be an alternative to telecommuting for addressing demographic and labor pool concerns. Job sharing is found throughout a wide range of managerial and professional jobs, as well as in production and service jobs. It is not common among senior executives.

The four-day workweek is a second type of alternative work schedule. Information systems personnel at the United Services Automobile Association (USAA) in San Antonio, Texas, work four 10-hour days and enjoy a three-day weekend. This arrangement provides the benefit of more time for those who want to balance work and family life through weekend travel. However, the longer workdays may be a drawback for employees with many family or social activities on weekday evenings. Hence, the four-day workweek has both benefits and limitations.

Flextime is a third alternative work pattern. Flextime, in which employees can set their own daily work schedules, has been applied in numerous ways in work organizations. For example, many companies in highly concentrated urban areas, like Houston, Los Angeles, and New York City, allow employees to set their own daily work schedules as long as they start their eight hours at any 30-minute interval from 6:00 a.m. to 9:00 a.m. This arrangement is designed to ease traffic and commuting pressures. It also is somewhat responsive to individual biorhythms, allowing early risers to go to work early and nighthawks to work late. Typically, 9:00 a.m. to 3:00 p.m. is the required core working time for everyone in the company. Flextime options take many forms in organizations, depending on the nature of the work and the coordination requirements in various jobs. Even in companies without formal flextime programs, flextime may be an individual option arranged between supervisor and subordinate. For example, a first-line supervisor who wants to complete a college degree may negotiate a work schedule accommodating both job requirements and course schedules at the university.

■ Technostress

Technostress is stress caused by new and advancing technologies in the workplace, most often information technologies.[39] For example, the widespread use of electronic bulletin boards as a forum for rumors of layoffs may cause feelings of uncertainty and anxiety (technostress). However, the same electronic bulletin boards can be an important source of information and uncertainty reduction for workers.

New information technologies enable organizations to monitor employee work performance, even if the employee is not aware of the monitoring.[40] These new technologies also allow organizations to tie pay to performance as it is electronically monitored.[41] The Office of Technology Assessment suggests three guidelines for making electronic workplace monitoring, especially of performance, less distressful.[42] First, workers should participate in the introduction of the monitoring system. Second, performance standards should be seen as fair. Third, performance records should be used to improve performance, not to punish the performer. New technologies at work are a double-edged sword that can be used to improve job performance or to create technostress.

■ Skill Development

Problems in work system design are often seen as the source of frustration for those dealing with technostress.[43] However, system and technical problems are not the only sources of technostress in new information technologies. Some experts see a growing gap between the skills demanded by new technologies and the skills possessed by employees in jobs using these technologies.[44] Although technical skills are important and are emphasized in many training programs, the largest sector of the economy is actually service-oriented, and service jobs require interpersonal skills. Managers also use a wide range of nontechnical skills to be effective in their work.[45] Therefore, any discussion of jobs and the design of work must recognize the importance of incumbent skills and abilities to meet the demands of the work. Organizations must consider the talents and skills of their employees when they engage in job design efforts. The two issues of employee skill development and job design are interrelated. The knowledge and information requirements for jobs of the future are especially high.

■ MANAGERIAL IMPLICATIONS: THE CHANGING NATURE OF WORK

Work is an important aspect of a healthy life. The two central needs in human nature are to engage in productive work and to form healthy relationships with others. Work means different things to different ethnic and national groups. Therefore, job design efforts must be sensitive to cultural values and beliefs.

In crafting work tasks and assignments, managers should make an effort to fit the jobs to the people who are doing them. There are no universally accepted ways to design work, and early efforts to find them have been replaced by a number of alternatives. Early approaches to job design were valuable for manufacturing and administrative jobs of the mid-twentieth century. However, the changing nature of work in the United States challenges managers to find new ways to define work and design jobs.

The distinguishing feature of job design in the foreseeable future is flexibility. Dramatic global, economic, and organizational change dictates that managers be flexible in the design of work in their organizations. Jobs must be designed to fit the larger organizational structures discussed in Chapter 15. Organizations must ask, does the job support the organization's mission? Employees must ask, does the job meet my short- and long-term needs?

Technology is one of the distinguishing features of the modern workplace. Advances in information, mechanical; and computer technology are transforming work into a highly scientific endeavor demanding employees who are highly educated, knowledgeable workers. American workers can expect these technological advances to continue during their lifetimes and should expect to meet the challenge through continuous skill development and enhancement.

■ CHAPTER SUMMARY

■ Different countries have different preferences for one or more of six distinct patterns of defining work.

■ Scientific management, job enlargement/job rotation, job enrichment, and the job characteristics theory are traditional American approaches to the design of work and the management of work force diversity.

■ The social information processing (SIP) model suggests that information from others and the social context are important in a job.

■ The interdisciplinary approach draws on mechanical engineering, industrial psychology, experimental psychology, and biology in considering the advantages and disadvantages of job design efforts.

■ The cultural values and social organizations in Japan, Germany, and Scandinavia lead to unique approaches to the design of work.

■ Control, uncertainty, conflict, and job/task demands are important job design parameters to consider when designing work for the well-being of the workers.

■ Task revision, telecommuting, alternative work patterns, technostress, and skill development are emerging issues in the design of work and the use of information technology.

■ REVIEW QUESTIONS

1. Describe six patterns of working that have been studied in different countries.
2. Describe four traditional approaches to the design of work in America.
3. Identify and define the five core job dimensions and the three critical psychological states in the Job Characteristics Model.
4. What are the salient features of the social information-processing (SIP) model of job design?
5. List the positive and negative outcomes of the four job design approaches considered by the interdisciplinary model.
6. How do the Japanese, German, and Scandinavian approaches to work differ from one another and from the American approach?
7. Describe the key job design parameters considered when examining the effects of work design on health and well-being.

8. What are five emerging issues in jobs and the design of work?

9. Assume that a company has many older, mature workers. Rather than retrain them in new technologies, the company wants to replace the older workers with younger ones. Should this be allowed?

■ REFERENCES

1. G. W. England and I. Harpaz, "How Working Is Defined: National Contexts and Demographic and Organizational Role Influences," *Journal of Organizational Behavior* 11 (1990): 253–266.

2. L. R. Gomez-Mejia, "The Cross-cultural Structure of Task-related and Contextual Constructs," *Journal of Psychology* 120 (1986): 5–19.

3. F. W. Taylor, *The Principles of Scientific Management* (New York: Norton, 1911).

4. A. N. Turner and A. L. Miclette, "Sources of Satisfaction in Repetitive Work," *Occupational Psychology* 36 (1962): 215–231.

5. T. Bell, *Out of This Furnace* (Pittsburgh: University of Pittsburgh Press, 1941).

6. C. R. Walker, "The Problem of the Repetitive Job," *Harvard Business Review* 28 (1950): 54–58.

7. C. R. Walker and R. H. Guest, *The Man on the Assembly Line* (Cambridge, Mass.: Harvard University Press, 1952).

8. Campion, M. A., Cheraskin, Hi & Stevens, M. J. 1994. "Career-related Antecedents and Outcomes of Job Rotation," *Academy of Management Journal* 37: 1518–1542.

9. F. Herzberg, "One More Time: How Do You Motivate Employees?" *Harvard Business Review* 46 (1968): 53–62.

10. R. N. Ford, "Job Enrichment Lessons from AT & T," *Harvard Business Review* 51 (1973): 96–106.

11. R. J. House and L. A. Wigdor, "Herzberg's Dual-Factor Theory of Job Satisfaction and Motivation: A Review of the Evidence and a Criticism," *Personnel Psychology* 20 (1967): 369–389.

12. A. N. Turner and P. R. Lawrence, *Industrial Jobs and the Worker* (Cambridge, Mass.: Harvard University Press, 1965).

13. J. R. Hackman and G. R. Oldham, "The Job Diagnostic Survey: An Instrument for the Diagnosis of Jobs and the Evaluation of Job Redesign Projects," Technical Report No. 4 (New Haven, Conn.: Department of Administrative Sciences, Yale University, 1974).

14. J. R. Hackman and G. R. Oldham, "Development of the Job Diagnostic Survey," *Journal of Applied Psychology* 60 (1975): 159–170.

15. P. H. Birnbaum, J.-L. Farh, and G. Y. Y. Wong, "The Job Characteristics Model in Hong Kong," *Journal of Applied Psychology* 71 (1986): 598–605.

16. H. P. Sims, A. D. Szilagyi, and R. T. Keller, "The Measurement of Job Characteristics," *Academy of Management Journal* 19 (1976): 195–212; H. P. Sims and A. D. Szilagyi, "Job Characteristic Relationships: Individual and Structural Moderators," *Organizational Behavior and Human Performance* 17 (1976): 211–230.

17. Y. Fried, "Meta-Analytic Comparison of the Job Diagnostic Survey and Job Characteristic Inventory as Correlates of Work Satisfaction and Performance," *Journal of Applied Psychology* 76 (1991): 690–698.

18. G. R. Salancik and J. Pfeffer, "A Social Information Processing Approach to Job Attitudes and Task Design," *Administrative Science Quarterly* 23 (1978): 224–253.

19. J. Pfeffer, "Management as Symbolic Action: The Creation and Maintenance of Organizational Paradigms," in L. L. Cummings and B. M. Staw, eds., *Research in Organizational Behavior*, Vol. 3 (Greenwich, Conn.: JAI Press, 1981), 1–52.

20. J. Thomas and R. Griffin, "The Social Information Processing Model of Task Design: A Review of the Literature," *Academy of Management Review* 8 (1983): 672–682.

21. D. J. Campbell, "Task Complexity: A Review and Analysis," *Academy of Management Review* 13 (1988): 40–52.

22. M. A. Campion and P. W. Thayer, "Job Design: Approaches, Outcomes, and Trade-offs," *Organizational Dynamics* 16 (1987): 66–79.

23. M. A. Campion and C. L. McClelland, "Interdisciplinary Examination of the Costs and Benefits of Enlarged Jobs: A Job Design Quasi-Experiment," *Journal of Applied Psychology* 76 (1991): 186–199.

24. B. Kohut, *Country Competitiveness: Organizing of Work* (New York: Oxford University Press, 1993).

25. W. E. Deming, *Out of the Crisis* (Cambridge, Mass.: MIT Press, 1986).

26. L. Thurow, *Head to Head: The Coming Economic Battle Among Japan, Europe, and America* (New York: Morrow, 1992).

27. M. A. Fruin, *The Japanese Enterprise System—Competitive Strategies and Cooperative Structures* (New York: Oxford University Press, 1992).

28. E. Furubotn, "Codetermination and the Modern Theory of the Firm: A Property-Rights Analysis," *Journal of Business* 61 (1988): 165–181.

29. H. Levinson, *Executive: The Guide to Responsive Management* (Cambridge, Mass.: Harvard University Press, 1981).

30. H. Luczak, " 'Good Work' Design: An Ergonomic, Industrial Engineering Perspective," in J. C. Quick, L. R. Murphy and J. J. Hurrell, eds., *Stress and Well-being at Work* (Washington, D.C.: American Psychological Association, 1992), 96–112.

31. B. Gardell, "Scandinavian Research on Stress in Working Life" (Paper presented at the IRRA Symposium on Stress in Working Life, Denver, September 1980).

32. L. Levi, "Psychosocial, Occupational, Environmental, and Health Concepts; Research Results; and Applications," in G. P. Keita and S. L. Sauter, eds., *Work and Well-being: An Agenda for the 1990s* (Washington, D.C.: American Psychological Association, 1992), 199–211.

33. R. L. Kahn, *Work and Health* (New York: Wiley, 1981).

34. F. J. Landy, "Work Design and Stress," in G. P. Keita and S. L. Sauter, eds., *Work and Well-being: An Agenda for the 1990s* (Washington, D.C.: American Psychological Association, 1992), 119–158.

35. C. Gresov, R. Drazin, and A. H. Van de Ven, "Work-Unit Task Uncertainty, Design, and Morale," *Organizational Studies* 10 (1989): 45–62.

36. B. M. Staw and R. D. Boettger, "Task Revision: A Neglected Form of Work Performance," *Academy of Management Journal* 33 (1990): 534–559.

37. C. J. Nemeth and B. M. Staw, "The Tradeoffs of Social Control and Innovation in Groups and Organizations," in L. Berkowitz, ed., *Advances in Experimental Social Psychology*, Vol. 22 (New York: Academic Press, 1989), 175–210.

38. D. S. Bailey and J. Foley, "Pacific Bell Works Long Distance," *HRMagazine*, August 1990, 50–52.

39. S. Zuboff, *In the Age of the Smart Machine: The Future of Work and Power* (New York: Basic Books, 1988).

40. B. A. Gutek and S. J. Winter, "Computer Use, Control over Computers, and Job Satisfaction," in S. Oskamp and S. Spacapan, eds., *People's Reactions to Technology in Factories, Offices, and Aerospace: The Claremont Symposium on Applied Social Psychology* (Newbury Park, Calif.: Sage, 1990), 121–144.

41. L. M. Schleifer and B. C. Amick III, "System Response Time and Method of Pay: Stress Effects in Computer-based Tasks," *International Journal of Human-Computer Interaction* 1 (1989): 23–39.

42. M. J. Smith and P. C. Carayon, "Electronic Monitoring of Worker Performance: A Review of the Potential Effects on Job Design and Stress" (Working paper developed for U.S. Congress, Office of Technology Assessment, Washington, D. C., 1990).

43. M. J. Smith and G. Salvendy, *Work with Computers: Organizational, Management, Stress, and Health Aspects* (New York: Elsevier Press, 1989).

44. D. M. Herold, "Using Technology to Improve our Management of Labor Market Trends," in M. Greller, ed., "Managing Careers with a Changing Workforce," *Journal of Organizational Change Management* 3 (1990): 44–57.

45. D. A. Whetten and K. S. Camerson, *Developing Management Skills*, 3d ed. (New York: HarperCollins, 1995).

CHAPTER 15
ORGANIZATIONAL DESIGN AND STRUCTURE

LEARNING OJBECTIVES

After reading this chapter, you should be able to do the following:

- Define the organizational design processes of differentiation and integration.
- Discuss six basic design dimensions of an organization.
- Briefly describe five structural configurations for organizations.
- Describe four contextual variables for an organization.
- Explain the four forces reshaping organizations.
- Discuss emerging organizational structures.
- Identify the two cautions about the effect of organizational structures on people.

Organizational design is the process of constructing and adjusting an organization's structure to achieve its goals. The design process begins with the organization's goals, which are broken into tasks as the basis for jobs, as discussed in Chapter 14. Jobs are grouped into departments, and departments are linked to form the organizational structure.

The first section of the chapter examines the design processes of differentiation and integration. The second section addresses the six basic design dimensions of an organization's structure. The orga-

nization's structure gives it the form to fulfill its function in the environment. As Louis Sullivan, the father of the skyscraper, said, "Form ever follows function." The third section of the chapter presents five structural configurations for organizations. Based on its mission and purpose, an organization determines the best structural configuration for its unique situation. The fourth section examines size, technology, environment, and the combination of strategy and goals as contextual variables influencing organizational design. When the organization's contextual variables change, the organization must redesign itself to meet new demands and functions. The fifth section examines five forces shaping organizations today. The final section notes several areas about which managers should be cautious with regard to structural weaknesses and dysfunctional structural constellations.

■ KEY ORGANIZATIONAL DESIGN PROCESSES

Differentiation is the design process of breaking the organizational goals into tasks. Integration is the design process of linking the tasks together to form a structure that supports goal accomplishment. These two processes are the keys to successful organizational design. The organizational structure is designed to prevent chaos through an orderly set of reporting relationships and communication channels. Understanding the key design processes and organizational structure helps a person understand the larger working environment and may prevent confusion in the organization.

The organization chart is the most visible representation of the organization's structure and underlying components. Most organizations have a series of organization charts showing reporting relationships throughout the system. The underlying components are (1) formal lines of authority and responsibility (the organizational structure designates reporting relationships by the way jobs and departments are grouped) and (2) formal systems of communication, coordination, and integration (the organizational structure designates the expected patterns of formal interaction among employees).[1]

■ Differentiation

Differentiation is the process of deciding how to divide the work in an organization.[2] Differentiation ensures that all essential organizational tasks are assigned to one or more jobs and that the tasks receive the attention they need. Many dimensions of differentiation have been considered in organizations. Lawrence and Lorsch found four dimensions of differentiation in one study: (1) manager's goal orientation, (2) time orientation, (3) interpersonal orientation, and (4) formality of structure.[3] For example, while a marketing department might have a "sales volume" goal orientation, be interpersonally "people-oriented," and have a less formal structure, an engineering department may have a "design" goal orientation, be interpersonally "task-oriented," and have a more formal structure. Three different forms of differentiation are horizontal, vertical, and spatial.

Horizontal differentiation is the degree of differentiation between organizational subunits and is based on employees' specialized knowledge, education, or training. For example, two university professors who teach specialized subjects in different academic departments are subject to horizontal differentiation. Horizontal differentiation increases with specialization and departmentation.

Specialization refers to the particular grouping of activities performed by an individual.[4] The degree of specialization or the division of labor in the organization gives an indication of how much training is needed, what the scope of a job is, and what individual characteristics are needed for job holders. Specialization can also lead to the development of a specialized vocabulary, as well as other behavioral norms. As the two college professors specialize in their subjects, abbreviations or acronyms take on unique meanings. For example, OB means "organizational behavior" to a professor of management, and it means "obstetrics" to a professor of medicine.

Usually, the more specialized the jobs within an organization, the more departments are differentiated within that organization (the greater the departmentation). Departmentation can be by function, product, service, client, geography, process, or some combination of these. A large organization may departmentalize its structure using all or most of these methods at different levels of the organization.

Vertical differentiation is the difference in authority and responsibility in the organizational hierarchy. Vertical differentiation occurs, for example, between a chief executive and a maintenance supervisor. Tall, narrow organizations have greater vertical differentiation, and flat, wide organizations have less vertical differentiation. The height of the organization is also influenced by level of horizontal differentiation and span of control. The span of control defines the number of subordinates a manager can and should supervise.[5]

Tall structures—those with narrow spans of control—tend to be characterized by closer supervision and tighter controls. In addition, the communication becomes more burdensome, since directives and information must be passed through more layers. The banking industry has often had tall structures. Flat structures—those with wider spans of control—have simpler communication chains and reduced promotion opportunities due to fewer levels of management. Sears is an organization that has gone to a flat structure. With the loss of over a million middle management positions in organizations during the 1980s, many organizations are now flatter. The degree of vertical differentiation affects organizational effectiveness, but there is no consistent finding that flatter or taller organizations are better.[6] Organizational size, type of jobs, skills and personal characteristics of employees, and degree of freedom must all be considered in determining organizational effectiveness.[7]

Spatial differentiation is the geographic dispersion of an organization's offices, plants, and personnel. A Boise-Cascade salesperson in New York and one in Portland experience spatial differentiation. An increase in the number of locations increases the difficulty in organizational design but may be necessary for organizational goal achievement or organizational protection. For example, if an organization wants to expand into a different country, it may be in its best interest to form a separate subsidiary that is partially owned and managed by citizens of that country. Few U.S. citizens think of Shell Oil Company as being a subsidiary of Royal Dutch Shell, a company whose international headquarters is in the Netherlands.

Spatial differentiation may give an organization political and legal advantages in a country because the company is identified as local. Distance is as important as political and legal issues in making spatial differentiation decisions. For example, a salesperson in Lubbock, Texas, would have a hard time servicing accounts in Beaumont, Texas (over 500 miles away), whereas a salesperson in Delaware might be able to cover all of that state, as well as parts of one or two others.

Horizontal, vertical, and spatial differentiation indicate the amount of width, height, and breadth an organizational structure needs. Just because an organization is highly differentiated along one of these dimensions does not mean it must be highly differentiated along all three. The university environment, for example, is generally characterized by great horizontal differentiation but relatively little vertical and spatial differentiation. A company such as Coca-Cola is characterized by a great deal of all three types of differentiation. The more structurally differentiated an organization is, the more complex it is.[8]

Complexity refers to the number of activities, subunits, or subsystems within the organization. Lawrence and Lorsch suggest that an organization's complexity should mirror the complexity of its environment. As the complexity of an organization increases, its need for mechanisms to link and coordinate the differentiated parts also increases. If these links do not exist, the departments or differentiated parts of the organization can lose sight of the organization's larger mission, and the organization runs the risk of chaos. Designing and building linkage and coordination mechanisms is known as integration.

◼ Integration

Integration is the process of coordinating the different parts of an organization. Integration mechanisms are designed to achieve unity among individuals and groups in various jobs, departments, and divisions in the accomplishment of organizational goals and tasks.[9] Integration helps keep the organization in a state of dynamic equilibrium, a condition in which all the parts of the organization are interrelated and balanced.

Vertical linkages are used to integrate activities up and down the organizational chain of command. A variety of structural devices can be used to achieve vertical linkage. These include hierarchical referral, rules and procedures, plans and schedules, positions added to the structure of the organization, and management information systems.[10]

The vertical lines on an organization chart indicate the lines of hierarchical referral up and down the organization. When there is a problem that employees do not know how to solve, it can be referred up the organization for consideration and resolution. Work that needs to be assigned is usually delegated down the chain of command as indicated by the vertical lines.

Rules and procedures, as well as plans and schedules, provide standing information for employees without direct communication. These vertical integrators, for example an employee handbook, communicate to employees standard information or information that they can understand on their own. These integrators allow managers to have wider spans of control, because the managers do not have to inform each employee of what is expected and when. These vertical integrators encourage managers to use management by exception—to make decisions when employees bring problems up the hierarchy. Military organizations depend heavily on vertical linkages. The army, for example, has a well-defined chain of command. Certain duties are expected to be carried out, and proper paperwork is to be in place. However, in times of crisis, much more information is processed, and the proper paperwork becomes secondary to "getting the job done." Vertical linkages help individuals understand their roles in the organization, especially in times of crisis.

Adding positions to the hierarchy is used as a vertical integrator when a manager becomes overloaded by hierarchical referral or problems arise in the chain of command. Positions may be added, such as "assistant to," or another level may be added. Adding levels to the hierarchy often reflects growth and increasing complexity. This action tends to reduce the span of control, thus allowing more communication and closer supervision.

Management information systems that are designed to process information up and down the organization also serve as a vertical linkage mechanism. With the advent of computers and network technology, it has become easier for managers and employees to communicate through written reports that are entered into a network and then electronically compiled for managers in the hierarchy. Electronic mail systems allow managers and employees greater access to one another without having to be in the same place at the same time or even attached by telephone. These types of systems make information processing up and down the organization more efficient.

Generally, the taller the organization, the more vertical integration mechanisms are needed. This is because the chains of command and communication are longer. Additional length requires more linkages to minimize the potential for misunderstandings and miscommunications.

Horizontal integration mechanisms provide the communication and coordination that is necessary for links across jobs and departments in the organization. The need for horizontal integration mechanisms increases as the complexity of the organization increases. Within the design of the organization, the horizontal linkages are built with the inclusion of liaison roles, task forces, integrator positions, and teams.

A liaison role is created when a person in one department or area of the organization has the responsibility for coordinating with another department (for example, a liaison between the engineering and production departments). Task forces are temporary committees composed of representatives from multiple departments who assemble to address a specific problem affecting these departments.[11]

A stronger device for integration is to develop a person or department designed to be an integrator. In most organizations, the integrator has a good deal of responsibility, but not much authority. Such an individual must have the ability to get people together to resolve differences within the perspective of organizational goals.[12]

The strongest method of horizontal integration is through teams. Horizontal teams cut across existing lines of organizational structure to create new entities that make organizational decisions. An example of this is in product development. A team may be formed that includes marketing, research, design, and production personnel. Ford used such a cross-functional team, discussed in detail in Chapter 9, to develop the Taurus automobile, which was designed to regain market share in the United States. The information exchanged by such a product development team should lead to a product that is acceptable to a wider range of organizational groups, as well as to customers.[13]

The use of these linkage mechanisms varies from organization to organization, as well as within areas of the same organization. In general, the flatter the organization, the more necessary horizontal integration mechanisms are.

■ BASIC DESIGN DIMENSIONS

Differentiation, then, is the process of dividing work in the organization, and integration is the process of coordinating work in the organization. From a structural perspective, every manager and organization looks for the best combination of differentiation and integration to accomplish the goals of the organization. There are many ways to approach this process. One way is to establish a desired level of each structural dimension on a high-to-low continuum and then develop a structure that meets the desired configuration. These structural dimensions include the following:[14]

1. Formalization: the degree to which an employee's role is defined by formal documentation (procedures, job descriptions, manuals, and regulations).
2. Centralization: the extent to which decision-making authority has been delegated to lower levels of an organization. An organization is centralized if the decisions are made at the top of the organization and decentralized if decision making is pushed down to lower levels in the organization.
3. Specialization: the degree to which organizational tasks are subdivided into separate jobs. The division of labor and the degree to which formal job descriptions spell out job requirements indicate the level of specialization in the organization.
4. Standardization: the extent to which work activities are described and performed routinely in the same way. Highly standardized organizations have little variation in the definition of jobs.
5. Complexity: the number of activities within the organization and how much differentiation is needed within the organization.
6. Hierarchy of authority: the degree of vertical differentiation through reporting relationships and the span of control within the structure of the organization.

An organization that is high in formalization, centralization, specialization, standardization, and complexity and has a tall hierarchy of authority is said to be highly bureaucratic. Bureaucracies are not in and of themselves bad; however, they are often tainted by abuse and red tape. The Internal Revenue Service is often described as bureaucratic. An organization that is on the opposite end of each of these continua is very flexible and loose. Control is very hard to implement and maintain in such an organization, but at certain times such an organization is appropriate. The research and development departments in many organizations are often more flexible than other departments in order to stimulate creativity.

Another approach to the process of accomplishing organizational goals is to describe what is and is not important to the success of the organization rather than worry about specific characteristics. Henry Mintzberg feels that the following questions can guide managers in designing formal structures that fit each organization's unique set of circumstances:[15]

1. How many tasks should a given position in the organization contain, and how specialized should each task be?
2. How standardized should the work content of each position be?
3. What skills, abilities, knowledge, and training should be required for each position?
4. What should be the basis for the grouping of positions within the organization into units, departments, divisions, and so on?
5. How large should each unit be, and what should the span of control be (that is, how many individuals should report to each manager)?
6. How much standardization should be required in the output of each position?
7. What mechanisms should be established to help individuals in different positions and units to adjust to the needs of other individuals?
8. How centralized or decentralized should decision-making power be in the chain of authority? Should most of the decisions be made at the top of the organization (centralized) or be made down in the chain of authority (decentralized)?

The manager who can answer these questions has a good understanding of how the organization should

■ **TABLE 15.1**
Five Structural Configurations of Organization

STRUCTURAL CONFIGURATION	PRIME COORDINATING MECHANISM	KEY PART OF ORGANIZATION	TYPE OF DECENTRALIZATION
Simple structure	Direct supervision	Upper echelon	Centralization
Machine bureaucracy	Standardization of work processes	Technical staff	Limited horizontal decentralization
Professional bureaucracy	Standardization of skills	Operating level	Vertical and horizontal decentralization
Divisionalized form	Standardization of outputs	Middle level	Limited vertical decentralization
Adhocracy	Mutual adjustment	Support staff	Selective decentralization

SOURCE: H. Mintzberg, *The Structuring of Organizations* (Englewood Cliffs, N.J.: Prentice-Hall, 1979), 301.

implement the basic structural dimensions. These basic design dimensions act in combination with one another and are not entirely independent characteristics of an organization.

■ FIVE STRUCTURAL CONFIGURATIONS

Differentiation, integration, and the basic design dimensions combine to yield various structural configurations. Mintzberg proposes five structural configurations: the simple structure, the machine bureaucracy, the professional bureaucracy, the divisionalized form, and the adhocracy.[16] Table 15.1 summarizes the prime coordinating mechanism, the key part of the organization, and the type of decentralization for each of these structural configurations. The five fundamental elements of the organization, for Mintzberg, are the upper echelon; the middle level; the operating core, where work is accomplished; the technical staff; and the support staff. Each configuration affects people in the organization somewhat differently.

■ Simple Structure

The simple structure is an organization with little technical and support staff, strong centralization of decision making in the upper echelon, and a minimal middle level. This structure has *a* minimum of vertical differentiation of authority and minimum formalization. It achieves coordination through direct supervision, often by the chief executive in the

upper echelon. An example of a simple structure is a small, independent landscape practice in which one or two landscape architects supervise the vast majority of work with no middle-level managers. Even an organization with as few as 30 people can become dysfunctional as a simple structure after an extended period.

■ Machine Bureaucracy

The machine bureaucracy is an organization with a well-defined technical and support staff differentiated from the line operations of the organization, limited horizontal decentralization of decision making, and a well-defined hierarchy of authority. The technical staff is powerful in a machine bureaucracy. There is strong formalization through policies, procedures, rules, and regulations. Coordination is achieved through the standardization of work processes. An example of a machine bureaucracy is an automobile assembly plant, with routinized operating tasks. The strength of the machine bureaucracy is efficiency of operation in stable, unchanging environments. The weakness of the machine bureaucracy is its slow responsiveness to external changes and to individual employee preferences and ideas.

■ Professional Bureaucracy

The professional bureaucracy emphasizes the expertise of the professionals in the operating core of the organization. The technical and support staffs serve the professionals. There is both vertical and horizontal differentiation in this type of bureaucracy. Coordination is achieved through the standardization of the professionals' skills. Examples of professional bureaucracies are hospitals and universities. The doctors, nurses, and professors are given wide latitude to pursue their work based on professional training and indoctrination through training programs. Large accounting firms may fall into the category of professional bureaucracies.

■ Divisionalized Form

The divisionalized form is a loosely coupled, composite structural configuration.[17] It is a configuration composed of divisions, each of which may have its own structural configuration. Each division is designed to respond to the market in which it operates. There is vertical decentralization from the upper echelon to the middle of the organization, and the middle level of management is the key part of the organization. This form of organization may have one division that is a machine bureaucracy, one that is an adhocracy, and one that is a simple structure. An example of this form of organization is Valero Energy Corporation, which produces natural gas and owns an oil refinery in south Texas. The divisionalized organization uses standardization of outputs as its coordinating mechanism.

■ Adhocracy

The adhocracy is a highly organic, rather than mechanistic, configuration with minimal formalization and order. It is designed to fuse interdisciplinary experts into smoothly functioning ad hoc project teams. Liaison devices are the primary mechanism for integrating the project teams in an adhocracy through a process of mutual adjustment. There is a high degree of horizontal specialization based on formal training and expertise. Selective decentralization of the project teams occurs within the adhocracy. An example of this form of organization is the National Aeronautics and Space Administration (NASA), composed of many talented experts who work in small teams on a wide range of projects related to America's space agenda.

■ CONTEXTUAL VARIABLES

The basic design dimensions and the resulting structural configurations play out in the context of the organization's internal and external environments. Four contextual variables influence the success of an organization's design: size, technology, environment, and strategy and goals. These variables provide a manager with challenges in considering an organizational design, although they are not necessarily determinants of structure. As the content of the organization changes, so should the structural design. Also, the amount of change in the contextual variables throughout the life of the organization influences the amount of change needed in the basic dimensions of the organization's structure.[18]

■ Size

The total number of employees is the appropriate definition of size when discussing the design of organizational structure. This is logical, because people and their interactions are the building blocks of structure. Other measures, such as net assets, production rates, and total sales, are usually highly correlated with the total number of employees but may not reflect the actual number of interpersonal relationships that are necessary to structure an organization effectively. EDS has found that large size and customer responsiveness can coexist. In 1991, EDS was a business of $7 billion a year and was growing at 10 percent per year. With nearly 70,000 employees in over 28 countries and over 7,000 customers, EDS was a large organization. Yet, with a strategic business unit (SBU) and strategic support unit (SSU) design, EDS found it could focus to be responsive to its customers.

Although there is some argument over the degree of influence that size has on organizational structure, there is no argument that it does influence design options. In one study, Meyer found size of the organization to be the most important of all variables considered in influencing the organization's structure and design.[19] Other researchers argue that the decision to expand the organization's business causes an increase in size as the structure is adjusted to accommodate the planned growth.[20] Finally, one study found size and CEO need for achievement both affected organization structure, with high- need-for-achievement CEOs preferring centralized, highly structured, and well-integrated organizations.[21]

How much influence size exerts on the organization's structure is not as important as the relationship between size and the design dimensions of structure. In other words, when exploring structural alternatives, what should the manager know about designing structures for large and small organizations? Formalization, specialization, and standardization all tend to be greater in larger organizations, because they are necessary to control activities within the organization. For example, documentation, rules, written policies and procedures, and detailed job descriptions are more likely to be used in larger organizations than is reliance on personal observation by the manager. The more relationships have to be managed by the structure, the more formalized and standardized the processes need to be. McDonald's publishes several volumes that describe how to make all its products, how to greet customers, how to maintain the facilities, and so on. This level of standardization, formalization, and specialization helps McDonald's maintain the same quality of product no matter where a restaurant is located. In contrast, at a small, locally owned cafe, your hamburger and french fries may taste a little different every time you visit. This is evidence of a lack of standardization.

Formalization and specialization also help a large organization decentralize decision making. Because of the complexity and number of decisions in a large organization, formalization and specialization are used to set parameters for decision making at lower levels. Can you imagine the chaos if Robert Crandall, CEO of American Airlines, had to make every decision about flights, food, or ticketing procedures for the airline? By decentralizing decision making, the larger organization adds horizontal and vertical complexity, but not necessarily spatial complexity. However, it is more common for a large organization to have more geographic dispersion.

Another dimension of design, hierarchy of authority, is related to complexity. As size increases, complexity increases; thus, more levels are added to the hierarchy of authority. This keeps the span of

control from getting too large. However, there is a balancing force, because formalization and specialization are added. The more formalized, standardized, and specialized the roles within the organization, the wider the span of control can be.

Balancing the design dimensions relative to size is a perplexing problem with few simple answers. This balancing becomes even more difficult when other contextual variables are taken into account.

■ Technology

An organization's technology is an important contextual variable in determining the organization's structure, as noted in Chapter 2. Technology is defined as the tools, techniques, and actions used by an organization to transform inputs into outputs.[22] The inputs of the organization include human resources, machines, materials, information, and money. The outputs are the products and services that the organization offers to the external environment. Determining the relationship between technology and structure is very complicated, because different departments may employ very different technologies. As organizations become larger, there is greater variation in technologies across units in the organization. Joan Woodward, Charles Perrow, and James Thompson have developed ways to understand traditional organizational technologies. More work is needed to understand better the contemporary engineering, research and development, and knowledge-based technologies of the information age.

Woodward introduced one of the best-known classification schemes for technology, identifying three types: unit, mass, or process production.[23] Unit technology is small-batch manufacturing technology and, sometimes, made-to-order production. Examples include Smith and Wesson's arms manufacture or the manufacture of fine furniture. Mass technology is large-batch manufacturing technology. Examples include American automotive assembly lines or latex glove production. Process production is continuous-production processes. Examples include oil refining and beer making. Woodward classified unit technology as the least complex, mass technology as more complex, and process technology as the

■ **FIGURE 15.1**

Summary of Perrow's Findings about the Relationship between Technology and Basic Design Dimensions

Task Variability

	Few Exceptions	Many Exceptions
Ill-defined and Unanalyzable	Craft 1. Moderate 2. Moderate 3. Moderate 4. Low-moderate 5. High 6. Low	Nonroutine 1. Low 2. Low 3. Low 4. Low 5. High 6. Low
Well-defined and Analyzable	Routine 1. High 2. High 3. Moderate 4. High 5. Low 6. High	Engineering 1. Moderate 2. Moderate 3. High 4. Moderate 5. Moderate 6. Moderate

Problem Analyzability (vertical axis label)

Key:
1. Formalization   4. Standardization
2. Centralization   5. Complexity
3. Specialization   6. Hierarchy of authority

SOURCE: Built from C. Perrow, "A Framework for the Comparative Analysis of Organizations," *American Sociological Review,* April 1967, 194-208.

most complex. The more complex the organization's technology, the more complex the administrative component or structure of the organization needs to be.

Perrow proposed an alternative to Woodward's scheme based on two variables: task variability and problem analyzability. Task variability considers the number of exceptions encountered in doing the tasks within a job. Problem analyzability examines the types of search procedures followed to find ways to respond to task exceptions. For example, for some exceptions encountered while doing a task, the appropriate response is easy to find. If you are driving down a street and see a sign that says, "Detour—Bridge Out," it is very easy to respond to the task variability. However, when Thomas Edison was designing the first electric light bulb, the problem analyzability was very high for his task.

Perrow went on further to identify the key aspects of structure that could be modified to the technology. These four structural elements are (1) the amount of discretion that an individual can exercise

to complete a task, (2) the power of groups to control the unit's goals and strategies, (3) the level of interdependence among groups, and (4) the extent to which organizational units coordinate work using either feedback or planning. Figure 15.1 summarizes Perrow's findings about types of technology and basic design dimensions.[24]

Thompson offered yet another view of technology and its relationship to organizational design. This view is based on the concept of technological interdependence (i.e., the degree of interrelatedness of the organization's various technological elements) and the pattern of an organization's work flows. Thompson's research suggests that greater technological interdependence leads to greater organizational complexity and that the problems of this greater complexity may be offset by decentralized decision making.[25]

The research of these three early scholars on the influence of technology on organizational design can be combined into one integrating concept—

routineness in the process of changing inputs into outputs in an organization. This routineness has a very strong relationship with organizational structure. The more routine and repetitive the tasks of the organization, the higher the degree of formalization that is possible; the more centralized, specialized, and standardized the organization can be; and the more hierarchical levels with wider spans of control that are possible.

However, an important caveat to the discussion of technology has emerged since the work of Woodward, Perrow, and Thompson: the advancement of information technology has influenced how organizations transform inputs into outputs. The introduction of computer-integrated networks, CAD/CAM systems, and computer-integrated manufacturing has broadened the span of control, flattened the organizational hierarchy, decentralized decision making, and lowered the amount of specialization and standardization.[26]

■ Environment

The third contextual variable for organizational design is environment. The environment of an organization is most easily defined as anything outside the boundaries of that organization. Different aspects of the environment have varying degrees of influence on the organization's structure. The general environment includes all conditions that may have an impact on the organization. These conditions could include economic factors, political considerations, ecological changes, sociocultural demands, and governmental regulation.

When aspects of the general environment become more focused in areas of direct interest to the organization, those aspects become part of the task environment, or specific environment. This is that part of the environment that is directly relevant to the organization. Typically, this level of environment includes stakeholders such as unions, customers, suppliers, competitors, government regulatory agencies, and trade associations.

The domain of the organization refers to the area the organization claims for itself with respect to how it fits into its relevant environments. The domain is particularly important because it is defined by the organization, and it influences how

the organization perceives and acts within its environments.[27] For example, Wal-Mart and Neiman-Marcus both sell clothing apparel, but their domains are very different.

The organization's perceptions of its environment and the actual environment may not be the same. The environment that the manager perceives is the environment that the organization responds to and organizes for.[28] Therefore, two organizations may be in relatively the same environment from an objective standpoint, but if the managers perceive differences, the organizations may enact very different structures to deal with this same environment.

The perception of environmental uncertainty or the perception of the lack of environmental uncertainty is how the contextual variable of environment most influences organizational design. Some organizations have relatively static environments with little uncertainty, whereas others are so dynamic that no one is sure what tomorrow may bring. Binney and Smith, for example, has made relatively the same product for over 50 years with very few changes in the product design or packaging. The environment for its Crayola products is relatively static. In fact, customers rebelled when the company tried to get rid of some old colors and add new ones. In contrast, in the last ten years, those who compete in the airline industry have encountered deregulation, mergers, bankruptcies, safety changes, changes in cost and price structures, changes in customer and employee demographics, and changes in global competition. The uncertainty of the environment of the major airlines has been relatively high during this last decade.

The amount of uncertainty in the environment influences the structural dimensions. Burns and Stalker labeled two structural extremes that are appropriate for the extremes of environmental uncertainty—mechanistic structure and organic structure.[29] Table 15.2 compares the structural dimensions of these two extremes. The mechanistic and organic structures are opposite ends of a continuum of organizational design possibilities. Although the general premise of environmental uncertainty and structural dimensions has been upheld by research, the organization must make adjustments for the realities of its perceived environment when designing its structure.[30]

■ **TABLE 15.2**
Mechanistic and Organic Organizational Forms

BASIC DESIGN DIMENSIONS	MECHANISTIC	ORGANIC
Formalization	High	Low
Centralization	High	Low
Specialization	High	Low
Standardization	High	Low
Complexity	Low	High
Hierarchy of authority	Strong, tall	Weak, flat

■ **TABLE 15.3**
Miller's Integrative Framework of Structural and Strategic Dimensions

STRATEGIC DIMENSION	PREDICTED STRUCTURAL CHARACTERISTICS
Innovation—to understand and manage new processes and technologies	Low formalization Decentralization Flat hierarchy
Market differentiation—to specialize in customer preferences	Moderate to high complexity Moderate to high formalization Moderate centralization
Cost control—to produce standardized products efficiently	High formalization High centralization High standardization Low complexity

SOURCE: D. Miller, "The Structural and Environmental Correlates of Business Strategy," *Strategic Management Journal* 8 (1987): 55–76.

The question for those trying to design organizational structures is how to determine environmental uncertainty. Dess and Beard defined three dimensions of environment that should be measured in assessing the degree of uncertainty: capacity, volatility, and complexity.[31] The capacity of the environment reflects the abundance or scarcity of resources. If resources abound, the environment supports expansion, mistakes, or both. In contrast, in times of scarcity, the environment demands survival of the fittest. Volatility is the degree of instability. The airline industry, as described above, is in a volatile environment. This makes it difficult for managers to know what needs to be done. The complexity of the environment refers to the differences and variability among environmental elements.

If the organization's environment is uncertain, dynamic, and complex, and resources are scarce, the manager needs an organic structure that is better able to adapt to its environment. Such a structure allows the manager to monitor the environment from a number of internal perspectives, thus helping the organization maintain flexibility in responding to environmental changes.[32]

■ **Strategy and Goals**

The fourth contextual variable that influences the way the design dimensions of structure should be enacted is the organization's combination of strategies and goals. Strategies and goals provide legitimacy to the organization, as well as employee direction, decision guidelines, and criteria for performance.[33] In addition, strategies and goals help the organization fit into its environment.

In recent years, more understanding about the contextual influence of strategies and goals has been developed. This has led to the definition of several strategic dimensions that influence structure. One of the most recent of these definitions was put forth by Danny Miller.[34] The dimensions of strategy and its implications on organizational structure are shown in Table 15.3.

For example, when Apple Computer introduced personal computers to the market, it was very innovative in its strategies. The structure of the organization was relatively flat and very informal. Apple had Friday afternoon beer and popcorn discussion sessions, and eccentric behavior was easily accepted. However, as the personal computer market has become more competitive, the structure of Apple has changed to help it differentiate its products and to help control costs. Steve Jobs, one of Apple's founders, had a set of innovative strategies and structures that were no longer appropriate. The board of directors recruited John Scully, a marketing expert from PepsiCo, to help Apple better compete in the market it had created.

Limitations exist, however, on how much strategies and goals influence structure. Because the structure of the organization includes the formal information-processing channels in the organization, it stands to reason that the need to change strategies may not be communicated throughout the organization. In such a case, the organization's structure influences its strategic choice.

The inefficiency of the structure to perceive environmental changes may even lead to organizational failure. In the airline industry, several carriers failed to adjust quickly enough to deregulation and the highly competitive marketplace. Only those airlines that were generally viewed as lean structures with good information-processing systems have flourished in the last ten turbulent years.

The four contextual variables—size, technology, environment, and strategy and goals—combine to influence the design process. However, the existing structure of the organization influences how the organization interprets and reacts to information about each of the variables. Each of the contextual variables is represented by management researchers who claim that it is the most important variable in determining the best structural design. Because of the difficulty in studying the interactions of the four contextual dimensions and the complexity of organizational structures, the argument about which variable is most important continues.

What is apparent is that there must be some level of fit between the structure and the contextual dimensions of the organization. The better the fit, the more likely that the organization will achieve its short-run goals. In addition, the better the fit, the more likely that the organization will process information and design appropriate organizational roles for long-term prosperity, as indicated in Figure 15.2.

■ FORCES RESHAPING ORGANIZATIONS

Managers and researchers traditionally examine organizational design and structure within the framework of basic design dimensions and contextual variables. Several forces reshaping organizations are causing managers to go beyond the traditional

■ **FIGURE 15.2**

The Relationships among Key Organizational Design Elements

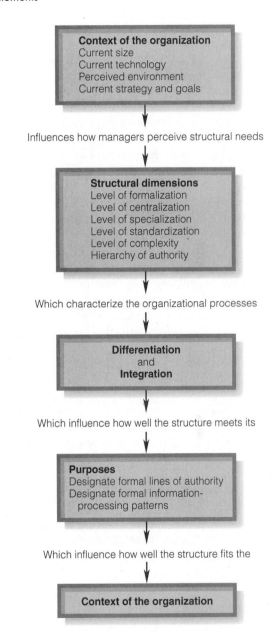

frameworks and to examine ways to make organizations more responsive to customer needs. Some of these forces include shorter life cycles within the organization, globalization, and rapid changes in information technology. These forces together increase the demands on process capabilities within the organization and on emerging organizational structures.[35]

Life Cycles in Organizations

Organizations are dynamic entities. As such, they ebb and flow through different stages. Usually, researchers think of these stages as organizational life cycles. The total organization has a life cycle that begins at birth, moves through growth and maturity to decline, and possibly experiences revival.[36]

Organizational subunits may have very similar life cycles. Because of changes in technology and product design, many organizational subunits are experiencing shorter life cycles, especially those that are product-based. Hence, the subunits that compose the organization will change more rapidly than in the past. These shorter life cycles enable the organization to respond quickly to external demands and changes.

As a new organization or subunit is born, the structure is very organic and informal. If the organization or subunit is successful, it grows and matures. This usually leads to formalization, specialization, standardization, complexity, and a more mechanistic structure. However, if the environment changes, the organization must be able to respond. A mechanistic structure is not able to respond to a dynamic environment as well as an organic one. If the organization or subunit does respond, it becomes more organic and revives; if not, it declines and possibly dies.

Shorter life cycles put more pressure on the organization to be both flexible and efficient at the same time. At each stage the organization differs in its strategies and goals, as well as in its structural emphasis. The effective manager is able to use the redesign process to keep abreast of the needs for structural change.

Globalization

Another force that is reshaping organizations is the globalization of organizations and markets. In other words, organizations operate worldwide rather than in just one country or region. Such globalization makes spatial differentiation even more of a reality for organizations. Besides the obvious geographic

differences, there may be deep cultural and value system differences. This adds another type of complexity to the structural design process and necessitates the creation of integrating mechanisms for people to be able to understand and interpret one another, as well as coordinate with one another.

The choice of structure for managing an international business is generally based on choices concerning the following three factors:

1. The level of vertical differentiation. A hierarchy of authority must be created that clarifies the responsibilities of both domestic and foreign managers.
2. The level of horizontal differentiation. Foreign and domestic operations should be grouped in such a way that the company effectively serves the needs of all customers.
3. The degree of formalization, specialization, standardization, and centralization. The global structure must allow decisions to be made in the most appropriate area of the organization. However, controls must reflect the strategies and goals of the parent firm.[37]

Changes in Information-Processing Technologies

Many of the changes in information-processing technologies have allowed organizations to move into new product and market areas more quickly. However, just as shorter life cycles and globalization have caused new concerns for designing organizational structures, so has the increased availability of advanced information-processing technologies.

Historically, as new capabilities in information processing have emerged, new forms of organizational structures also have emerged.[38] The impact of advanced information-processing technologies on the structure of organizations is already being felt. More integration and coordination is evident, because managers worldwide can be connected through computerized networks. The basic design dimensions also have been affected as follows:

1. The hierarchy of authority has been flattened.
2. The basis of centralization has been changed. Now managers can use technology to acquire

more information and make more decisions, or they can use technology to push information and decision making lower in the hierarchy and thus decrease centralization.

3. Less specialization and standardization are needed, because people using advanced information-processing technologies have more sophisticated jobs that require a broader understanding of the way the organization gets work done.[39]

■ Demands on Organizational Processes

Because of the forces reshaping organizations, managers find themselves trying to meet what seem to be conflicting goals: an efficiency orientation that results in on-time delivery and a quality orientation that results in customized, high-quality goods or services.[40] Efficiency and customization traditionally have been seen by managers as conflicting demands.

To meet them, organizations need to become "dynamically stable."[41] To do so, an organization must have managers who see themselves as architects who clearly understand the "how" of the organizing process. Managers must combine long-term thinking with flexible and quick responses that help improve process and know-how. The organizational structure must help define, at least to some degree, roles for managers who hope to address successfully the conflicting demands of dynamic stability.

■ Emerging Organizational Structures

The demands on managers and on process capabilities place demands on structures. The emphasis in tomorrow's organizations will be on organizing around processes, a key tenet of total quality management (TQM). This process orientation emerges from the combination of three streams of applied organizational design: high-performance, self-managed teams; managing processes rather than functions; and the evolution of information technology.

The horizontal company is an emerging organizational structure. Frank Ostroff and Doug Smith of McKinsey and Company developed a ten-step blueprint for a horizontal company.[42] The steps are as follows: (1) organize primarily around process, not task; (2) flatten the hierarchy by minimizing subdivision of processes and arranging teams in parallel; (3) make senior managers responsible for processes and process performance; (4) use customer satisfaction as the basic link to performance objectives and evaluation; (5) make teams the focus of organizational performance and design; (6) break down vertical barriers in the organization; (7) encourage employees to develop multiple competencies; (8) inform and train people on a just-in-time, need-to-perform basis; (9) maximize contacts for everyone in the organization with suppliers and customers; and (10) reward both individual skills and team performance.

The modular corporation is an alternative to the vertically integrated company. Dell Computer is an example of a modular corporation which has achieved success through the process of outsourcing (i.e., allowing suppliers to provide specified inputs to the organization) as an alternative to vertical integration and a vehicle for greater profits.[43] By defining its core competencies, Dell has been able to maximize its resource utilization through outsourcing.

■ CAUTIONARY NOTES ABOUT STRUCTURE

This chapter has identified the purposes of structure, the processes of organizational design, and the dimensions and contexts that must be considered in structure. In addition, it has looked at forces and trends in organizational design. Two cautionary notes are important for the student of organizational behavior. First, an organizational structure may be weak or deficient. In general, if the structure is out of alignment with its contextual variables, one or more of the following four symptoms appears.[44] First, decision making is delayed because the hierarchy is overloaded and too much information is being funneled through one or two channels. Second, decision making lacks quality, because information linkages are not providing the correct information to the right person in the right format. Third, the organization does not respond innovatively to a changing environment, especially when coordinated effort is lacking across departments. Fourth, a great deal of conflict is evident when departments are working against one another rather than working for the strategies and goals of the organization as a whole; the structure is often at fault.

The second caution is that the personality of the chief executive may adversely affect the structure of the organization. Five dysfunctional combinations of personality and organization have been identified: the paranoid, the depressive, the dramatic, the compulsive, and the schizoid.[45] Each of these personality-organization constellations can create problems for the people who work in the organization. For example, in a paranoid constellation, people are suspicious of each other, and distrust in working relationships may interfere with effective communication and task accomplishment. For another example, in a depressive constellation, people feel depressed and inhibited in their work activities which can lead to low levels of productivity and task accomplishment.

■ MANAGERIAL IMPLICATIONS: FITTING PEOPLE AND STRUCTURES TOGETHER

Organizations are complex social systems made of numerous interrelated components. They can be complicated to understand. Managers who design, develop, and improve organizations must have a mastery of the basic concepts related to the anatomy and processes of organizational functioning. It is essential for executives at the top to have a clear concept of how the organization can be differentiated and then integrated into a cohesive whole.

People can work better in organizations if they understand how their jobs and departments relate to other jobs and teams in the organization. An understanding of the whole organization enables people to better relate their contribution to the overall mission of the organization and to compensate for structural deficiencies that may exist.

Different structural configurations place unique demands on the people who work within them. The diversity of people in work organizations suggests that some people are better suited for a simple structure, others are better suited to a professional bureaucracy, and still others are most productive in

an adhocracy. Organizational structures are not independent of the people who work within them. This is especially true as organizations become more global in their orientation.

Managers must pay attention to the technology of the organization's work, the amount of change occurring in the organization's environment, and the regulatory pressures created by governmental agencies as the managers design effective organizations and subunits to meet emerging international demands and a diverse, multicultural work force.

■ CHAPTER SUMMARY

- Three basic types of differentiation occur in organizations: horizontal, vertical, and spatial.
- The greater the complexity of an organization because of its degree of differentiation, the greater the need for integration.
- Formalization, centralization, specialization, standardization, complexity, and hierarchy of authority are the six basic design dimensions in an organization.
- Simple structure, machine bureaucracy, professional bureaucracy, divisionalized form, and adhocracy are five structural configurations of an organization.
- The contextual variables important to organizational design are size, technology, environment, and strategy and goals.
- Life cycles, globalization, changes in information-processing technologies, and demands on process capabilities are forces reshaping organizations today.
- New, emerging organizational structures differ from the traditional ones.
- Organizational structures may be inherently weak or chief executives may create personality-organization constellations that adversely affect employees.

■ REVIEW QUESTIONS

1. Define the processes of differentiation and integration.
2. Describe the six basic dimensions of organizational design.

3. Discuss five structural configurations from the chapter.

4. Should legal limits be set to prevent large companies from engaging in very competitive behavior to drive small companies out of business?

5. Discuss the effects of the four contextual variables on the basic design dimensions.

6. Identify four forces that are reshaping organizations today.

7. Discuss the nature of emerging organizational structures.

8. List four symptoms of structural weakness and five unhealthy personality-organization combinations.

9. Suppose an employee complains about organizational design problems and suggests a solution. The organization is redesigned accordingly, but that employee's department is eliminated. Is it ethical for the company to terminate the employee? Should the company always make room for a person who has a beneficial idea for the organization?

■ REFERENCES

1. J. Child, *Organization* (New York: Harper & Row, 1984).

2. P. Lawrence and J. Lorsch, "Differentiation and Integration in Complex Organizations," *Administrative Science Quarterly* (June 1967): 1-47.

3. P. Lawrence and J. Lorsch, *Organization and Environment: Managing Differentiation and Integration* (Boston, Mass.: Harvard University Press, 1967).

4. J. Hage, "An Axiomatic Theory of Organizations," *Administrative Science Quarterly* (December 1965): 289-320.

5. W. Ouchi and J. Dowling, "Defining the Span of Control," *Administrative Science Quarterly* (September 1974): 357-365.

6. L. Porter and E. Lawler III, "Properties of Organization Structure in Relation to Job Attitudes and Job Behavior," *Psychological Bulletin* (July 1965): 23-51.

7. J. Ivancevich and J. Donnelly, Jr., "Relation of Organization and Structure to Job Satisfaction, Anxiety-Stress, and Performance," *Administrative Science Quarterly* 20 (1975): 272-280.

8. R. Dewar and J. Hage, "Size, Technology, Complexity, and Structural Differentiation: Toward a Theoretical Synthesis," *Administrative Science Quarterly* 23 (1978): 111-136.

9. Lawrence and Lorsch, "Organization and Environment," 1-47.

10. J. Galbraith, *Designing Complex Organizations* (Reading, Mass.: Addison-Wesley, 1973).

11. W. Altier, "Task Forces: An Effective Management Tool," *Management Review* (February 1987): 26-32.

12. P. Lawrence and J. Lorsch, "New Managerial Job: The Integrator," *Harvard Business Review* 45 (1967): 142-151.

13. J. Lorsch and P. Lawrence, "Organizing for Product Innovation," *Harvard Business Review* 43 (1965): 110-111.

14. D. Pugh, D. Hickson, C. Hinnings, and C. Turner, "Dimensions of Organization Structure," *Administrative Science Quarterly* (1968): 65-91; R. Daft, *Organization Theory and Design*, 4th ed. (St. Paul, MN: West Publishing Company, 1992); B. Reimann, "Dimensions of Structure in Effective Organizations: Some Empirical Evidence," *Academy of Management Journal* (1974): 693-708; S. Robbins, *Organization Theory: The Structure and Design of Organizations*, 3d ed. (Englewood Cliffs, NJ: Prentice-Hall, 1990).

15. H. Mintzberg, *The Structuring of Organizations* (Englewood Cliffs, NJ: Prentice-Hall, 1979).

16. H. Mintzberg, *The Structuring of Organizations*.

17. K. Weick, "Educational Institutions as Loosely Coupled Systems," *Administrative Science Quarterly* (1976): 1-19.

18. D. Miller and C. Droge, "Psychological and Traditional Determinants of Structure," *Administrative Science Quarterly* (1986): 540; H. Tosi, Jr. and J. Slocum, Jr., "Contingency Theory: Some Suggested Directions," *Journal of Management* (Spring 1984): 9-26.

19. M. Meyer, "Size and the Structure of Organizations: A Causal Analysis," *American Sociological Review* (August 1972): 434-441.

20. J. Beyer and H. Trice, "A Reexamination of the Relations between Size and Various Components of Organizational Complexity," *Administrative Science Quarterly* 24 (1979): 48-64; B. Mayhew, R. Levinger, J. McPherson, and T. James, "Systems Size and Structural Differentiation in Formal Organizations: A Baseline Generator for Two Major Theoretical Propositions," *American Sociological Review* (October 1972): 26-43.

21. D. Miller and C. Droge, "Psychological and Traditional Determinants of Structure," *Administrative Science Quarterly* 31 (1986): 539-560.

22. C. Perrow, "A Framework for the Comparative Analysis of Organizations," *American Sociological Review* (April 1967): 194-208; D. Rosseau, "Assessment of Technology in Organizations: Closed versus Open Systems Approaches," *Academy of Management Review* 4 (1979): 531-542.

23. J. Woodward, *Industrial Organization: Theory and Practices* (London: Oxford University Press, 1965).

24. Perrow, "A Framework for the Comparative Analysis of Organizations," 194-208.

25. J. D. Thompson, *Organizations in Action* (New York: McGraw-Hill, 1967).

26. P. Nemetz and L. Fry, "Flexible Manufacturing Organizations: Implication for Strategy Formulation and Organization Design," *Academy of Management Review* 13 (1988): 627-638; G. Huber, "The Nature and Design of Post-industrial Organizations," *Management Science* 30 (1984): 934.

27. Thompson, *Organizations in Action*.

28. H. Downey, D. Hellriegel, and J. Slocum, Jr., "Environmental Uncertainty: The Construct and Its Application," *Administrative Science Quarterly* 20 (1975): 613-629.

29. T. Burns and G. Stalker, *The Management of Innovation* (London: Tavistock, 1961); Mintzberg, *Structuring of Organizations*.

30. M. Chandler and L. Sayles, *Managing Large Systems* (New York: Harper & Row, 1971).

31. G. Dess and D. Beard, "Dimensions of Organizational Task Environments," *Administrative Science Quarterly* 29 (1984): 52-73.

32. J. Courtright, G. Fairhurst, and L. Rogers, "Interaction Patterns in Organic and Mechanistic Systems," *Academy of Management Journal* 32 (1989): 773-802.

33. Daft, *Organization Theory and Design*.

34. D. Miller, "The Structural and Environmental Correlates of Business Strategy," *Strategic Management Journal* 8 (1987): 55-76.

35. A. Boynton and B. Victor, "Beyond Flexibility: Building and Managing a Dynamically Stable Organization," *California Management Review* 8 (Fall 1991): 53-66.

36. D. Miller and P. Friesen, "A Longitudinal Study of the Corporate Life Cycle," *Management Science* 30 (1984): 1161-1183.

37. C. Hill and G. Jones, *Strategic Management Theory*, 2d ed. (Boston: Houghton Mifflin, 1992).

38. A. Chandler, *The Visible Hand: The Managerial Revolution in American Business* (Cambridge, Mass.: Harvard University Press, 1977).

39. Daft, *Organization Theory and Design*.

40. S. Davis, *Future Perfect* (Reading, Mass.: Addison-Wesley, 1987).

41. Boynton and Victor, "Beyond Flexibility," 53-66.

42. T. Stewart, "The Search for the Organization of Tomorrow," *Fortune*, 18 May 1992, 92-98.

43. S. Tully, "The Modular Corporation," *Fortune* (8 February 1993): 106-115; and R. L. Bruning and R.S. Althisar, "Modules: A Team Module for Manufacturing," *Personnel Journal* (1990): 90-96.

44. Child, *Organization*.

45. M. F. R. Kets de Vries and D. Miller, "Personality, Culture, and Organization," *Academy of Management Review* 11 (1986): 266-279.

Chapter 16
Organizational Culture

LEARNING OBJECTIVES

After reading this chapter, you should be able to do the following:

- Define organizational culture and explain its three levels.
- Identify the four functions of culture within an organization.
- Explain the relationship between organizational culture and performance.
- Contrast the characteristics of adaptive and nonadaptive cultures.
- Describe five ways leaders reinforce organizational culture.
- Describe the three stages of organizational socialization and the ways culture is communicated in each step.
- Identify ways of assessing organizational culture.
- Explain actions managers can take to change organizational culture.

■ THE KEY ROLE OF ORGANIZATIONAL CULTURE

The concept of organizational culture has its roots in cultural anthropology. Just as there are cultures in larger human society, there seem to be cultures within organizations. These cultures are similar to societal cultures. They are shared, communicated through symbols, and passed down from generation to generation of employees.

The concept of cultures in organizations was alluded to as early as the Hawthorne Studies, which described work group culture. However, the topic came into its own during the early 1970s, when managers and researchers alike began to search for keys to survival for organizations in a competitive and turbulent environment. Then, in the early 1980s, several books on corporate culture emerged, including Deal and Kennedy's *Corporate Cultures*,[1] Ouchi's *Theory Z*,[2] and Peters and Waterman's *In Search of Excellence*.[3] These books found wide audiences, and research began in earnest on the elusive topic of organizational cultures. Executives echoed the belief that cultures were real and could be managed.

■ Culture and Its Levels

Many definitions of organizational culture have been proposed. Most of them agree that there are several levels of culture and that these levels differ in terms of their visibility and their ability to change. The definition adopted in this chapter is that organizational (corporate) culture is a pattern of basic assumptions that are considered valid and are taught to new members as the way to perceive, think, and feel in the organization.[4]

Edgar Schein, in his comprehensive book on organizational culture and leadership, suggests that organizational culture has three levels. His view of culture is presented in Figure 16.1. The levels range from visible artifacts and creations to testable values to invisible and even preconscious basic assumptions. To achieve a complete understanding of an organization's culture, all three levels must be studied.

■ Artifacts

Symbols of culture in the physical and social work environment are called artifacts. They are the most visible and accessible level of culture. The key to understanding culture through artifacts lies in figuring out what they mean. Artifacts are also the most frequently studied manifestation of organizational culture, perhaps because of their accessibility. Among the artifacts of culture are personal enactment, ceremonies and rites, stories, rituals, and symbols.[5]

Personal Enactment.   Culture may be understood, in part, through an examination of the behavior of organization members. Personal enactment is behavior that reflects the organization's values. In particular, personal enactment by the top managers lends insight into these values. If, for example, customer service is highly valued, then the CEO may be seen going the extra mile for the customer, as did the late Sam Walton of Wal-Mart. He reinforced quality service by visiting stores often and recognizing individual employees. The CEO transmits values to others in the organization by modeling appropriate behavior.

Boone Pickens, CEO of Mesa Petroleum, values physical fitness for its psychological and spiritual benefits and believes a physically fit work force leads to economic benefits for the company. He established a fitness center for employees and is a regular participant at the center. His presence has resulted in fitness participation by three-quarters of Mesa's employees—and cost savings for the company.[6]

Modeled behavior is a powerful learning tool for employees, as Bandura's social learning theory demonstrated. As we saw in Chapter 5, individuals learn vicariously by observing others' behavior and patterning their own behavior similarly. The values reflected in that behavior can permeate the entire employee population.

Ceremonies and Rites.   Relatively elaborate sets of activities that are enacted time and again on impor-

■ FIGURE 16.1

Levels of Organizational Culture

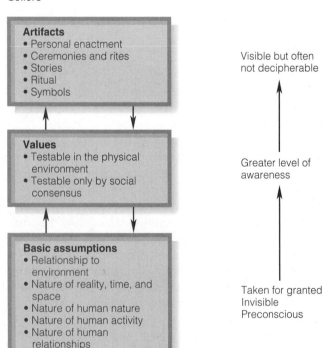

SOURCE: Schein, Edgar H. *Organizational Culture and Leadership: A Dynamic View,* Fig. 1, p. 14. Copyright 1985 by Jossey-Bass, Inc., Publishers. ISBN 0-87589-639-1.

tant occasions are known as organizational ceremonies and rites. These occasions provide opportunities to reward and recognize employees whose behavior is congruent with the values of the company. Ceremonies and rites send a message that individuals who both espouse and exhibit corporate values are heroes to be admired.

The ceremonies also bond organization members together. Southwestern Bell emphasizes the importance of management training to the company. Training classes are kicked off by a high-ranking executive (a rite of renewal), and completion of the classes is signaled by a graduation ceremony (a rite of passage). Six kinds of rites in organizations have been identified:[7]

1. Rites of passage show that an individual's status has changed. Retirement dinners are an example.
2. Rites of enhancement reinforce the achievements of individuals. An example is the awarding of certificates to sales contest winners.
3. Rites of renewal emphasize change in the organization and commitment to learning and growth. An example is the opening of a new corporate training center.
4. Rites of integration unite diverse groups or teams within the organization and renew commitment to the larger organization. Company functions such as annual picnics fall into this category.
5. Rites of conflict reduction focus on dealing with conflicts or disagreements that arise naturally in organizations. Examples are grievance hearings and the negotiation of union contracts.
6. Rites of degradation are used by some organizations to punish persons visibly when they fail to adhere to values and norms of behavior. Some CEOs, for example, are replaced quite publicly for unethical conduct or for failure to achieve organizational goals. Japanese employees who perform poorly in some organizations are given ribbons of shame as punishment.

Mary Kay Cosmetics holds extravagant annual seminars that exemplify several of these rites. Mary Kay Ash, founder of the company, has described these ceremonies as "a combination of the Academy Awards, the Miss America pageant, and a Broadway opening."[8] Each seminar has an elaborate script and a theme expressing a particular corporate value. Several nights of awards ceremonies are held, culminating in the crowning of the director and consultant queens, who receive mink coats and diamonds. The message sent out by these ceremonies is a clear one. Mary Kay Cosmetics' goals are sales performance, personal attention to both organization members and customers, and creating opportunities for every employee with the ability to excel.

Stories. One way to reinforce organizational values is through stories. Stories give meaning and identity to organizations as they are told and retold, especially in orienting new employees. Part of the strength of organizational stories is that the listeners are left to draw their own conclusions—a powerful communication tool.[9]

Often, the stories told are about the CEO's behavior. One story passed down at Monsanto is about Jack Hanley, who, upon taking over the reins of the company, wanted to make it more professional. He went so far as to remove a toothpick dispenser from the company cafeteria because he thought it was not in keeping with a professional image.

Other stories reinforce such values as customer service. IBM once had a client company whose machine went down one afternoon in the midst of payroll processing. Paychecks were to be distributed the following day. As the story goes, IBM flew in another machine and personnel, who worked all night to ensure that the client's payroll was distributed on time.

Research by Joanne Martin and her colleagues has indicated that certain themes appear in stories across different types of organizations:[10]

1. Stories about the boss. These stories may reflect whether or not the boss is "human" or how the boss reacts to mistakes.
2. Stories about getting fired. Events leading to employee firings are recounted.
3. Stories about how the company deals with employees who have to relocate. These stories relate to the company's actions toward employees who have to move—whether or not the company is helpful and takes family and other personal concerns into account.

4. Stories about whether lower-level employees can rise to the top. Often, these stories describe a person who started out at the bottom and eventually became the CEO.
5. Stories about how the company deals with crisis situations. The example of the client crisis at IBM shows how the company overcomes obstacles.
6. Stories about how status considerations work when rules are broken. Tom Watson, Sr., chief executive officer of IBM, was once confronted by a security guard because he was not wearing an ID badge.

These are the themes that can emerge when stories are passed down. The information from these stories serves to guide the behavior of organization members.

Rituals.   Everyday organizational practices that are repeated over and over are rituals. They are usually unwritten, but they send a clear message about "the way we do things around here." While some companies insist that people address each other by their titles (Mr., Mrs., Ms., Miss) and surnames to reinforce a professional image, others prefer that employees operate on a first-name basis—from the top manager on down. Hewlett-Packard values open communication, so its employees address one another by first names only.

The Charles Machine Works, producer of Ditch Witch underground excavation equipment, values informality, teamwork, and a flat organizational structure. One ritual practiced in the company is that a manager's employees are not referred to as subordinates. The idea that one person is lower than others is in opposition to the value placed on teamwork, so the workers are referred to as employees or team members.

As everyday practices, rituals reinforce the organizational culture. Insiders who commonly practice the rituals may be unaware of their subtle influence, but outsiders recognize it easily.

Symbols.   Symbols communicate organizational culture by unspoken messages. Southwest Airlines has used symbols in several ways. During its early years, the airline emphasized its customer service value by using the heart symbol (the "Love" airline) and love bites (peanuts). More recently, the airline has taken on the theme of fun. Flight attendants wear casual sports clothes in corporate colors. Low fares are "fun fares," and weekend getaways are "fun packs." Some aircraft are painted to resemble Shamu the whale, underscoring the fun image.

At Mary Kay Cosmetics, a meaningful symbol is the diamond bumblebee pin awarded to top performers. Engineers have argued that a bumblebee's wings are too small and its body is too heavy for the bee to fly, but the bumblebee flies somehow. The symbol represents success achieved despite great obstacles.

Symbols may be only mental images. At Southwestern Bell, company loyalty is valued. Long-time company employees are referred to as "bleeding blue and gold" (company colors).

Personal enactment, rites and ceremonies, stories, rituals, and symbols serve to reinforce the values that are the next level of culture.

■ Values

Values are the second, and deeper, level of culture. They reflect a person's underlying beliefs of what should be or should not be. Values are often consciously articulated, both in conversation and in a company's mission statement or annual report. However, there may be a difference between a company's espoused values (what the members say they value) and its enacted values (values reflected in the way the members actually behave).[11] Values also may be reflected in the behavior of individuals, which is an artifact of culture.

One company that emphasizes values is Levi Strauss. Its values are espoused in a formal aspirations statement and are enacted by its employees from the CEO down. As guides for behavior, values are reinforced in the aspirations statement and in the reward system of the organization. Work force diversity is valued at Levi Strauss. A former strong supporter of the Boy Scouts of America, the company discontinued its funding after the Scouts were shown to discriminate on the basis of sexual orientation. Mary Gross, a Levi Strauss spokesperson, expressed the company's position on valuing diversity: "One of the family values of this company is treating people who are different from you the same as you'd like to be treated. Tolerance is a pretty important family value."[12]

Assumptions

Assumptions are the deeply held beliefs that guide behavior and tell members of an organization how to perceive and think about things. As the deepest and most fundamental level of an organization's culture, according to Schein, they are the essence of culture. They are so strongly held that a member behaving in any fashion that would violate them would be unthinkable. Another characteristic of assumptions is that they are often unconscious. Organization members may not be aware of their assumptions and may be reluctant or unable to discuss them or change them.

Chaparral Steel's values reflect three basic assumptions. The first is that people are basically good; this assumption is reflected in the company's emphasis on trust. The second assumption is that people want opportunities to learn and grow, as is seen in the value placed on education and training. The third assumption is that people are motivated by opportunities to learn and by work that is challenging and enjoyable, as reflected in Chaparral's goal-setting program.

To decipher an organization's culture fully, one must examine all three levels: artifacts, values, and assumptions.

FUNCTIONS AND EFFECTS OF ORGANIZATIONAL CULTURE

In an organization, culture serves four basic functions. First, culture provides a sense of identity to members and increases their commitment to the organization.[13] When employees internalize the values of the company, they find their work intrinsically rewarding and identify with their fellow workers. Motivation is enhanced, and employees are more committed.

Second, culture is a sense-making device for organization members. It provides a way for employees to interpret the meaning of organizational events.[14]

Third, culture reinforces the values in the organization. Trust is a key value at Johnson & Johnson. Decision-making is decentralized, and employees are encouraged to operate with independence and autonomy.[15]

Finally, culture serves as a control mechanism for shaping behavior. Norms that guide behavior are part of culture. At Westinghouse's Commercial Nuclear Fuels Division, employee suggestions increased fivefold following the company's emphasis on total quality. It became a norm to think of ways to improve processes at the division. These norms helped the company win the 1988 Baldrige National Quality Award.[16]

The effects of organizational culture are hotly debated by organizational behaviorists and researchers. It seems that managers attest strongly to the positive effects of culture in organizations, but it is difficult to quantify these effects. Recently, John Kotter and James Heskett reviewed three theories about the relationship between organizational culture and performance and the evidence that either supports or refutes these theories.[17] The three are the strong culture perspective, the fit perspective, and the adaptation perspective.

The Strong Culture Perspective

The strong culture perspective states that organizations with "strong" cultures perform better than other organizations. A strong culture is an organizational culture with a consensus on the values that drive the company and with an intensity that is recognizable even to outsiders. Thus, a strong culture is deeply held and widely shared. It also is highly resistant to change. One example of a strong culture is IBM's. Its culture is one we are all familiar with: conservative, with a loyal work force and an emphasis on customer service. Nordstorm, the large retail chain, has a strong customer-oriented culture. Its employee manual consists of a card that reads "Use your good judgment in all situations."[18]

Strong cultures are thought to facilitate performance for three reasons. First, these cultures are characterized by goal alignment; that is, all employees share common goals. Second, strong cultures create a high level of motivation because of the values shared by the members. Third, strong cultures provide control without the oppressive effects of a bureaucracy.

To test the strong culture hypothesis, Kotter and Heskett selected 207 firms from a wide variety of industries. They used a questionnaire to calculate a culture strength index for each firm, and they correlated that index with the firm's economic performance over a twelve-year period. They concluded that strong cultures were associated with positive long-term economic performance, but only modestly.

There are also two perplexing questions about the strong culture perspectives. First, what can be said about evidence showing that strong economic performance can create strong cultures, rather than the reverse? Second, what if the strong culture leads the firm down the wrong path? Sears, for example, is an organization with a strong culture. In recent years, however, it has focused inward, ignoring competition and consumer preferences and damaging its performance.

■ The Fit Perspective

The "fit" perspective argues that a culture is good only if it fits the industry's or the firm's strategy. For example, a culture that values a traditional hierarchical structure and stability would not work well in the computer manufacturing industry, which demands fast response and a lean, flat organization. Three particular characteristics of an industry may affect culture: the competitive environment, customer requirements, and societal expectations.[19] In the computer industry, firms face a highly competitive environment, customers who require highly reliable products, and a society that expects state-of-the-art technology and high-quality service. These characteristics affect the culture in computer manufacturing companies.

A study of twelve large U.S. firms indicated that cultures consistent with industry conditions help managers make better decisions. It also indicated that cultures need not change as long as the industry doesn't change. However, if the industry does change, many cultures change too slowly to avoid negative effects on firms' performance.

The fit perspective is useful in explaining short-term performance but not long-term performance. It also indicates that it is difficult to change culture quickly, especially if the culture is widely shared and deeply held. But it doesn't explain how firms can adapt to environmental change.

■ The Adaptation Perspective

The third theory about culture and performance is the adaptation perspective. Its theme is that only cultures that help organizations adapt to environmental change are associated with excellent performance. An adaptive culture is a culture that encourages confidence and risk taking among employees, has leadership that produces change, and focuses on the changing needs of customers.[20] 3M is a company with an adaptive culture, in that it encourages new product ideas from all levels within the company.

To test the adaptation perspective, Kotter and Heskett interviewed industry analysts about the cultures of twenty-two firms. The contrast between adaptive cultures and nonadaptive cultures was striking. The results of the study are summarized in Table 16.1.

Adaptive cultures facilitate change to meet the needs of three groups of constituents: stockholders, customers, and employees. Nonadaptive cultures are characterized by cautious management that tries to protect its own interests. Adaptive firms showed significantly better long-term economic performance in Kotter and Heskett's study. One contrast that can be made is between Hewlett-Packard, a high performer, and Xerox, a lower performer. Hewlett-Packard was viewed by the industry analysts as valuing excellent leadership more than Xerox did and as valuing all three key constituencies more than Xerox did. Economic performance from 1977 through 1988 showed this difference: HP's index of annual net income growth was 40.2, as compared to Xerox's 13.1. Kotter and Heskett concluded that the cultures that promote long-term performance are those that are most adaptive.

Given that high-performing cultures are adaptive ones, it is important to know how managers can develop adaptive cultures. In the next section, we will examine the leader's role in managing organizational culture.

■ **TABLE 16.1**
Adaptive versus Nonadaptive Organizational Cultures

	ADAPTIVE ORGANIZATIONAL CULTURES	NONADAPTIVE ORGANIZATIONAL CULTURES
Core Values	Most managers care deeply about customers, stockholders, and employees. They also strongly value people and processes that can create useful change (e.g., leadership up and down the management hiearchy).	Most managers care mainly about themselves, their immediate work group, or some product (or technology) associated with that work group. They value the orderly and risk-reducing management process much more highly than leadership initiatives.
Common Behavior	Managers pay close attention to all their constituencies, especially customers, and initiate change when needed to serve their legitimate interests, even if that entails taking some risks.	Managers tend to behave somewhat insularly, politically, and bureaucratically. As a result, they do not change their strategies quickly to adjust to or take advantage of changes in their business environments.

SOURCE: Reprinted with the permission of the Free Press, a Division of MacMillan, Inc. From *Corporate Culture and Performance* by John P. Kotter and James L. Heskett. Copyright © 1992 by Kotter Associates, Inc. and James L. Heskett.

■ THE LEADER'S ROLE IN SHAPING AND REINFORCING CULTURE

According to Edgar Schein, leaders play crucial roles in shaping and reinforcing culture. The five most important elements in managing culture are these: (1) what leaders pay attention to; (2) how leaders react to crises; (3) how leaders behave; (4) how leaders allocate rewards; and (5) how leaders hire and fire individuals.

■ What Leaders Pay Attention To

Leaders in an organization communicate their priorities, values, and beliefs through the themes that consistently emerge from what they focus on. These themes are reflected in what they notice, comment on, measure, and control. The late Ray Kroc, founder of McDonald's, paid attention to detail. He built the company on the basis of a vision of providing identical, high-quality hamburgers at low cost.[21] Through careful training, quality control, and even special measuring cups, he honed his company's expertise so that the Big Mac in Miami would be the same as the Big Mac in Moscow.

If leaders are consistent in what they pay attention to, measure, and control, employees receive clear signals about what is important in the organization. If, however, leaders are inconsistent, employees spend a lot of time trying to decipher and find meaning in the inconsistent signals.

■ How Leaders React to Crises

The way leaders deal with crises communicates a powerful message about culture. Emotions are heightened during a crisis, and learning is intense. In Lee Iacocca's effort to turn Chrysler around, the company perceived itself to be in crisis. Iacocca appealed for a government bailout, framing his argument so that the government's refusal would be seen as a lack of commitment to businesses and to America's competitive position.[22] Iacocca had articulated Chrysler's mission as protecting America's jobs, and his reaction to the crisis underscored Chrysler's value that the free enterprise system should be protected.

Difficult economic times present crises for many companies and illustrate their different values. Some organizations do everything possible to prevent laying off workers. Others may claim that employees are important but quickly institute major layoffs at the first signal of an economic downturn. Employees may perceive that the company shows its true colors in a crisis and thus may pay careful attention to the reactions of their leaders.

■ How Leaders Behave

Through role modeling, teaching, and coaching, leaders reinforce the values that support the organizational culture. Employees often emulate leaders' behavior and look to the leaders for cues to appropriate behavior. Ebby Halliday, founder and president of Ebby Halliday Realtors, based in Dallas, believes strongly in giving back to the community. This belief, along with behavior that backs it up, has been a key contributor to her success. Halliday is heavily invested in community activities, including beautification, education, and other efforts to help improve the lives of people in Dallas. She also encourages and supports community involvement on the part of all of her employees.

■ How Leaders Allocate Rewards

To ensure that values are accepted, leaders should reward behavior that is consistent with the values. Some companies, for example, may claim that they use a pay-for-performance system that distributes rewards on the basis of performance. When the time comes for raises, however, the increases are awarded according to length of service with the company. Imagine the feelings of a high-performing newcomer who has heard leaders espouse the value of rewarding individual performance and then receives only a tiny raise.

Some companies may value teamwork. They form cross-functional teams and empower these teams to make important decisions. However, when performance is appraised, the criteria for rating employees focus on individual performance. This sends a confusing signal to employees about the company's culture: Is individual performance valued, or is teamwork the key?

■ How Leaders Hire and Fire Individuals

A powerful way leaders reinforce culture lies in the selection of newcomers to the organization. Leaders often unconsciously look for individuals who are similar to current organizational members in terms of values and assumptions. Some companies hire individuals on the recommendation of a current employee; this tends to perpetuate the culture because the new employees typically hold similar values. Promotion-from-within policies also serve to reinforce organizational culture.

The way a company fires an employee and the rationale behind the firing also communicates the culture. Some companies deal with poor performers by trying to find them a place within the organization where they can perform better and make a contribution. Other companies seem to operate under the philosophy that those who cannot perform are out quickly.

The reasons for terminations may not be directly communicated to other employees, but curiosity leads to speculation. An employee who displays unethical behavior and is caught may simply be reprimanded even though such behavior is clearly against the organization's values. This may be viewed by other employees as a failure to reinforce the values within the organization.

All of these elements are ways leaders act to shape the culture within the organization. One leader who has shaped a distinctive organizational culture is Herb Kelleher of Southwest Airlines. Kelleher has appeared at company parties as Elvis Presley and Roy Orbison, singing "Jailhouse Rock" and "Pretty Woman." When Robert Crandall, CEO of American Airlines (and a Rhode Island native), asked him what he was going to do with the whale droppings from Southwest's freshly painted Shamu airplane, Kelleher's response was, "I am going to turn it into chocolate mousse and feed it to Yankees from Rhode Island." To follow up, he sent a tub of chocolate mousse to Crandall's office, along with a king-size Shamu spoon. His leadership has made humor and altruism two key values at Southwest Airlines.[23]

Kelleher's leadership has established a unique culture at Southwest Airlines. Southwest's costs are the lowest of any major airline, its people are the best paid,

Stages of socialization

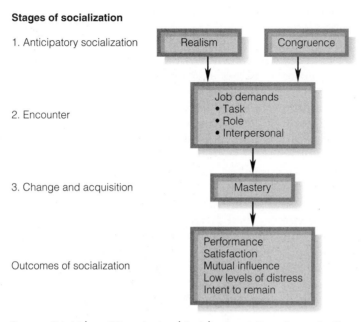

1. Anticipatory socialization

2. Encounter

3. Change and acquisition

Outcomes of socialization

■ FIGURE 16.2
The Organizational
Socialization Process: Stages
and Outcomes

SOURCE: D.L. Nelson, "Organizational Socialization: A Stress Perspective," *Journal of Occupational Behavior 8* (1987): 311-324.

and the annual turnover is the industry's lowest. In a turbulent industry, Southwest is a major player.

■ ORGANIZATIONAL SOCIALIZATION

We have seen that leaders play key roles in shaping an organization's culture. Another process that perpetuates culture is the way it is handed down from generation to generation of employees. Newcomers learn the culture through organizational socialization—the process by which newcomers are transformed from outsiders to participating, effective members of the organization.[24] The process is also a vehicle for bringing newcomers into the organizational culture. As we saw earlier, cultural socialization begins with the careful selection of newcomers who are likely to reinforce the organizational culture.[25] Once selected, newcomers pass through the socialization process.

■ The Stages of the Socialization Process

The organizational socialization process is generally described as having three stages: anticipatory social-

ization, encounter, and change and acquisition. Figure 16.2 presents a model of the process and the key concerns at each stage of it.[26] It also describes the outcomes of the process, which will be discussed in the next section of the chapter.

Anticipatory Socialization. Anticipatory socialization, the first stage, encompasses all of the learning that takes place prior to the newcomer's first day on the job. It includes the newcomer's expectations. The two key concerns at this stage are realism and congruence.

Realism is the degree to which a newcomer holds realistic expectations about the job and about the organization. One thing newcomers should receive information about during entry into the organization is the culture. Information about values at this stage can help newcomers begin to construct a scheme for interpreting their organizational experiences. A deeper understanding of the organization's culture will be possible through time and experience in the organization.

There are two types of congruence between an individual and an organization. The first is between the individual's abilities and the demands of the job. The second is the fit between the organization's values and the individual's values. Value congruence is particularly important for organizational culture. It has even been suggested that employees should be hired to fit the culture of the organization, not just the requirements of the job. This is practiced extensively in Korean chaebols, which are conglomerate groups. Each chaebol has a unique culture and selects newcomers in part on the basis of personality criteria. The Hanjin group, for example, looks for newcomers who possess patriotism and serviceship. Korean Airlines (KAL) is a member of the Hanjin group, which also has other transportation subsidiaries. At KAL, employees are expected to act as civilian diplomats; they are required to master a foreign language and to go abroad at least once. Polished manners and refined language are required, and female employees are forbidden to wear jeans even off duty.[27]

Encounter.   The second stage of socialization, encounter, is when newcomers learn the tasks associated with the job, clarify their roles, and establish new relationships at work. This stage commences on the first day at work and is thought to encompass the first six to nine months on the new job. Newcomers face task demands, role demands, and interpersonal demands during this period.

Task demands involve the actual work performed. Learning to perform tasks is related to the organization's culture. In some organizations, considerable latitude is given to newcomers to experiment with new ways to do the job, and value is placed on creativity. In others, newcomers are expected to learn their tasks using established procedures. Newcomers may also need guidance from the culture about work hours. Is there a value placed on putting in long hours, or is leaving work at 5:00 to spend time with family more the norm?

Role demands involve the expectations placed on newcomers. Newcomers may not know exactly what is expected of them (role ambiguity) or may receive conflicting expectations from other individuals (role conflict). The way newcomers approach these demands is dependent in part on the culture of the organization. Are newcomers expected to operate with considerable uncertainty, or is the manager expected to clarify the newcomers' roles so they are

straightforward? Some cultures even put newcomers through considerable stress in the socialization process, including humility-inducing experiences, so newcomers will be more open to accepting the firm's values and norms. Long hours, tiring travel schedules, and an overload of work are part of some socialization practices.

Interpersonal demands arise from relationships at work. Politics, leadership style, and group pressure are interpersonal demands. All of them reflect the values and assumptions that operate within the organization. Most organizations have basic assumptions about the nature of human relationships. The Korean chaebol Lucky-Goldstar strongly values harmony in relationships and in society, and its decision-making policy emphasizes unanimity.

In the encounter stage, the expectations formed in anticipatory socialization may clash with the realities of the job. It is a time of facing the task, role, and interpersonal demands of the new job.

Change and Acquisition.   In the third and final stage of socialization, change and acquisition, newcomers begin to master the demands of the job. They become proficient at managing their tasks, clarifying and negotiating their roles, and engaging in relationships at work. The completion of the socialization process varies widely, depending on the individual, the job, and the organization. Its end is signaled by newcomers being considered by themselves and others as organizational insiders.

■ Outcomes of Socialization

Newcomers who are successfully socialized should exhibit good performance, high job satisfaction, and the intention to stay with the organization. In addition, they should exhibit low levels of distress symptoms and high levels of organizational commitment.[28] This commitment is facilitated throughout the socialization process when newcomers buy into the values the organization communicates. Successful socialization is also signaled by mutual influence; that is, the newcomers have made adjustments in the job and organization to accommodate their knowledge and personalities. Newcomers are expected to leave their marks on the organization and not to conform in all things.

This is something of a paradox for organizations socializing individuals into their cultures. Organizations desire strong cultures but also want to allow the unique qualities of newcomers to affect the work situation. This can be accomplished by creating a culture that values empowerment and that encourages newcomers to apply their creative potential to the new job.[29]

■ Socialization as Cultural Communication

Socialization is a powerful cultural communication tool. While the transmission of information about cultural artifacts is relatively easy, the transmission of values is more difficult. The communication of organizational assumptions is almost impossible, since organization members themselves may not be consciously aware of them.

The primary purpose of socialization is the transmission of core values to new organization members.[30] Newcomers are exposed to these values through the role models they interact with, the training they receive, and the behavior they observe being rewarded and punished. Newcomers are vigilant observers, seeking out clues to the organization's culture and consistency in the cultural messages they receive. If they are expected to adopt these values, it is essential that the message reflect the underlying values of the organization.

One company known for its culture is the Walt Disney Company. Disney transmits its culture to employees through careful selection, socialization, and training. New employees at Disneyland and Disney World go through a careful socialization process to ensure that they understand the corporate culture and its emphasis on keeping guests happy.

Companies such as Disney use the socialization process to communicate messages about organizational culture. Both individuals and organizations can take certain actions to ensure the success of the socialization process. Socialization is explored further in the following chapter, on career management.

■ ASSESSING ORGANIZATIONAL CULTURE

While some organizational scientists would argue for assessing organizational culture with quantitative methods, others would say that organizational culture must be assessed with qualitative methods.[31] Quantitative methods, such as questionnaires, are valuable because of their precision, comparability, and objectivity. Qualitative methods, such as interviews and observations, are valuable because of their detail, descriptiveness, and uniqueness.

Two widely used quantitative assessment instruments are the Organizational Culture Inventory (OCI) and the Kilmann-Saxton Culture-Gap Survey. Both assess the behavioral norms of organizational cultures, as opposed to the artifacts, values, or assumptions of the organization.

■ Organizational Culture Inventory

The OCI focuses on behaviors that help employees fit into the organization and meet the expectations of co-workers. Using Maslow's motivational need hierarchy as its basis, it measures twelve cultural styles. The two underlying dimensions of the OCI are task/people and security/satisfaction. There are four satisfaction cultural styles and eight security cultural styles.

A self-report instrument, the OCI contains 120 questions. It provides an individual assessment of culture and may be aggregated to the work group and to the organizational level.[32] It has been used in firms throughout North America, Western Europe, New Zealand, and Thailand, as well as in U.S. military units, the Federal Aviation Administration, and nonprofit organizations.

■ Kilmann-Saxton Culture-Gap Survey

The Kilmann-Saxton Culture-Gap Survey focuses on what actually happens and on the expectations of others in the organization.[33] Its two underlying dimensions are technical/human, and time (the short term versus the long term). With these two dimensions, the actual operating norms and the ideal norms in four areas are assessed. The areas are task support (short-term technical norms), task innovation (long-term technical norms), social relationships (short-term human orientation norms), and personal freedom (long-term human orientation norms). Significant gaps in any of the four areas are used as points of departure for cultural change to improve performance, job satisfaction, and morale.

A self-report instrument, the Gap Survey provides an individual assessment of culture and may be aggregated to the work group. It has been used in firms throughout the United States and in nonprofit organizations.

■ Triangulation

A study of a rehabilitation center in a 400-bed hospital incorporated triangulation (the use of multiple methods to measure organizational culture) to improve inclusiveness and accuracy in measuring the organizational culture.[34] Triangulation has been used by anthropologists, sociologists, and other behavioral scientists to study organizational culture. Its name comes from the navigational technique of using multiple reference points to locate an object. In the rehabilitation center study, the three methods used to triangulate on the culture were (1) observations by eight trained observers, which provided an outsider perspective; (2) self-administered questionnaires, which provided quantitative insider information; and (3) personal interviews with the center's staff, which provided qualitative contextual information.

The study showed that each of the three methods made unique contributions toward the discovery of the rehabilitation center's culture. The complete picture could not have been drawn with just a single technique. Triangulation can lead to a better understanding of the phenomenon of culture and is the best approach to assessing organizational culture.

■ CHANGING ORGANIZATIONAL CULTURE

Changing situations may require changes in the existing culture of an organization. With rapid environmental changes such as globalization, work force diversity, and technological innovation, the fundamental assumptions and basic values that drive the organization may need to be altered. One particular situation that may require cultural change is a merger or acquisition. The blending of two distinct organizational cultures may prove difficult.

Another situation that may require alterations in culture is an organization's employment of people from different countries. Research indicates that some organizational cultures actually enhance differences in national cultures. One study compared foreign employees working in a multinational organization to employees working in different organizations within their own countries. The assumption was that employees from the various countries working for the same multinational organization would be more similar than employees working in diverse organizations in their native countries. The results were surprising, in that there were significantly greater differences between the employees of the multinational than there were between managers working for different companies within their native countries. In the multinational, Swedes became more Swedish, Americans became more American, and so forth. It appears that employees enhance their national culture traditions even when working within a single organizational culture.[35]

Changing an organization's culture is feasible but difficult.[36] One reason for the difficulty is that assumptions—the deepest level of culture—are often unconscious. As such, they are often nonconfrontable and nondebatable. Another reason for the difficulty is that culture is deeply ingrained and behavioral norms and rewards are well learned. In a sense, employees must unlearn the old norms before they can learn new ones. Managers who want to change the culture should look first to the ways culture is maintained.

A cultural change model that summarizes the interventions managers can use is presented in Figure 16.3. In this model, the numbers represent the actions managers can take. There are two basic approaches to changing the existing culture: (1) helping current members buy into a new set of values (actions 1, 2, and 3); or (2) adding newcomers and socializing them into the organization and removing current members as appropriate (actions 4 and 5).[37]

The first action is to change behavior in the organization. However, even if behavior does change, this change is not sufficient for cultural change to occur. Behavior is an artifact (level 1) of culture. Individuals may change their behavior but not the values that drive it. They may rationalize, "I'm only doing this because my manager wants me to."

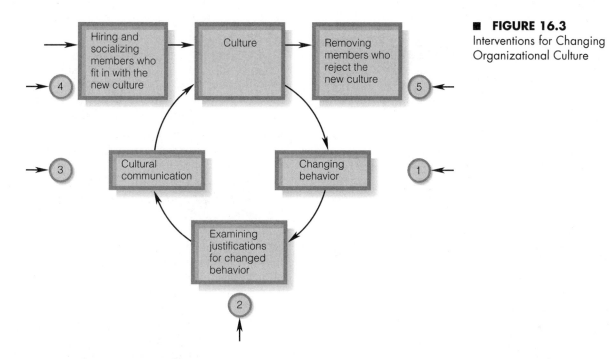

➤ Managers seeking to create cultural change must intervene at these points.

SOURCE: Sathe, Vijay. "How to Decipher and Change Corporate Culture," in R. H. Kilmann, M.J.
Saxton, R. Serpa, and Associates, *Gaining Control of the Corporate Culture*, Fig. 1, p. 245.
Copyright 1985 by Jossey-Bass, Inc., Publishers. ISBN 0-87584-666-9.

Therefore, managers must use action 2, which is to examine the justifications for the changed behavior. Are employees buying into the new set of values, or are they just complying?

The third action, cultural communication, is extremely important. All of the artifacts (personal enactment, stories, rites and ceremonies, rituals, and symbols) must send a consistent message about the new values and beliefs. It is crucial that the communication be credible; that is, managers must live the new values rather than just talking about them. The communication must also be persuasive. Individuals may resist cultural change and may have to be persuaded to try the new behavior by someone they respect and can identify with.

The two remaining actions (4 and 5) involve shaping the work force to fit the intended culture. First, organizations can revise their selection strategies to more accurately reflect the new culture. Second, the organization can identify individuals who resist the cultural change or who are no longer

comfortable with the values in the organization. This is not intended to be a ruthless pursuit; it should be a gradual and subtle change that takes considerable time. Changing personnel in the organization is a lengthy process; it cannot be done effectively in a short period of time without considerable problems.

Evaluating the success of cultural change may be best done by looking at behavior. Culture change can be assumed to be successful if the behavior is intrinsically motivated—on "automatic pilot." If the new behavior would persist even if rewards were not present, and if the employees have internalized the new value system, then the behavior is probably intrinsically motivated. If employees automatically respond to a crisis in ways consistent with the corporate culture, then the cultural change effort can be deemed successful.

One organization that has changed its culture is AT&T. In 1984, the courts ordered the breakup of AT&T. Prior to the breakup, the company operated in a stable environment with low levels of uncertainty. The organization was a highly structured bureaucracy. The culture emphasized lifetime employment, promotion from within, and loyalty. AT&T faced minimal competition, and it offered individual security. When the courts ordered AT&T to divest its Bell operating companies, the old culture was no longer effective. The company had to move toward a culture that holds individuals accountable for their performance. Change at AT&T was painful and slow, but it was necessary for the company to be able to operate in the new competitive environment.[38]

Given the current business environment, managers may want to focus on three particular cultural modifications. They are (1) support for a global view of business, (2) reinforcement of ethical behavior, and (3) empowerment of employees to excel in product and service quality.

■ Developing a Global Organizational Culture

The values that drive the organizational culture should support a global view of the company and its efforts. To do so, the values should be clear to everyone involved, so everyone understands them. The values should also be strongly supported at the top. Management should embody the shared values and reward employees who support the global view. Finally, the values should be consistent over time. Consistent values give an organization a unifying theme that competitors may be unable to emulate.[39]

Global corporations suffer from the conflicting pressures of centralization and decentralization. When subsidiaries are decentralized around the world, an overarching corporate culture that integrates them can be an asset in the increasingly competitive global marketplace.

Following are six specific guidelines for managers who want to create a global culture:[40]

1. Create a clear and simple mission statement. A shared mission can unite individuals from diverse cultural backgrounds.
2. Create systems that ensure an effective flow of information. Coordination councils and global task forces can be used to ensure that flows of

information throughout the geographically dispersed organization are consistent.
3. Create "matrix minds" among managers; that is, broaden managers' minds to allow them to think globally. IBM does this through temporary overseas assignments. Managers with international experience share that experience when they return to the home organization.
4. Develop global career paths. This means ensuring not only that home country executives go overseas but also that executives from other countries rotate into service in the home office.
5. Use cultural differences as a major asset. Digital Equipment Corporation, for example, has transferred its research and development functions to Italy to take advantage of the free-flowing Italian management style that encourages creativity. Its manufacturing operations go to Germany, which offers a more systematic management style.
6. Implement worldwide management education and team development programs. Unified training efforts that emphasize corporate values can help establish a shared identity among employees.

These guidelines are specifically aimed toward multinational organizations that want to create a global corporate culture. Other organizations can also benefit from them. Companies that want to broaden employees' views or to use the diversity of the work force as a resource will find several of these recommendations advantageous.

■ Developing an Ethical Organizational Culture

The organizational culture can have profound effects on the ethical behavior of organization members.[41] When a company's culture promotes ethical norms, individuals behave accordingly. The integration of ethics into the culture is usually achieved by codes of conduct, as we discussed in chapter 2, and by ethics training. Most ethics training courses include three elements: messages from the CEO touting ethical business practices, discussion of the company's code of ethics, and procedures for reporting unethical behavior.[42]

Managers can encourage ethical behavior by being good role models for employees. They can institute the philosophy that ethical behavior makes good business sense. Managers can also communicate that rationalizations for unethical behavior are not tolerated. For example, some salespersons justify padding their expense accounts because everyone else does it. Declaring these justifications illegitimate sends a clear message about the lack of tolerance for such behavior. Communication is a key ingredient in an ethical organizational culture. Disseminating the code of ethics, keeping employees informed of ethical issues, and involving employees of all levels in solving ethical dilemmas can keep ethics at the forefront of culture.

Trust is another key to effectively managing ethical behavior, especially in cultures that encourage whistle-blowing (as we saw in Chapter 2). Employees must trust that whistle-blowers will be protected, that procedures used to investigate ethical problems will be fair, and that management will take action to solve problems that are uncovered.

Managers can reward ethical behavior on the part of the employees and punish individuals who behave unethically. Ethical decision making can also be integrated into the performance appraisal system.

The reasons most often cited for unethical corporate conduct are interesting.[43] They include the belief that a behavior is not really unethical, that it is in the organization's best interest, that it will not be discovered, and that the organization will support it because it offers a good outcome for the organization.

An ethical corporate culture can eliminate the viability of these excuses through clear communication of the boundaries of ethical conduct, the selection of employees who support the ethical culture, the rewarding of ethical behavior on the part of the organization members, and the conspicuous punishment of members who engage in unethical behavior.

■ Developing a Culture of Empowerment and Quality

Throughout this book, we have seen that successful organizations promote a culture that empowers employees and excels in product and service quality. Motorola and Federal Express are prime examples. Empowerment serves to unleash employees' creativity and productivity. It requires eliminating traditional hierarchical notions of power.

General Motors' Cadillac Division experienced a massive cultural change over a short period of time. In 1985, the company installed state-of-the-art robotics technology at its Hamtramck Assembly Center.[44] The idea was to use tomorrow's technology to build the Cadillac of the future. The plant, intended to be a technology showcase, turned into a technology disaster. Robots went haywire, spray-painting one another, smashing windshields, and destroying cars. Computer systems had bugs that led to body parts being installed on the wrong cars.

The new technology was considered a total failure, and the reason cited for the failure was that "people issues" were not addressed. The technology was yanked. The plant was redesigned to develop a balance between technology and people. Extensive employee involvement and a teamwork approach to design were used to empower employees throughout the Cadillac division.

Managers decided to incorporate input from assemblers in the product design process.[45] Designers, product development engineers, and assembly workers came together in teams to design the new car models. Once the cars were designed, the rest of the assembly workers were consulted a year and a half prior to the scheduled date of production. The designs were then revised to improve the cars' quality. On the Seville and El Dorado models alone, over 300 modifications were made.

Teams were also used to improve quality once a model went into production. A team made up of engineers, assemblers, and supervisors worked on a continuous quality improvement process that targeted electrical system problems. The team effort reduced defects by 90 percent. Employee involvement was the key to the turnaround of Cadillac's culture. The original culture, emphasizing technology as the means for success, was replaced with a culture that emphasizes empowerment and product quality. One of the results was the 1990 Malcolm Baldrige National Quality Award.

Managers can learn from the experience of Cadillac that employee empowerment is a key to achieving quality. Involving employees in decision making, removing obstacles to their performance, and communicating the value of product and service quality reinforces the values of empowerment and quality in the organizational culture.

■ MANAGERIAL IMPLICATIONS: THE ORGANIZATIONAL CULTURE CHALLENGE

Managing organizational culture is a key challenge for leaders in today's organizations. With the trend toward downsizing and restructuring, maintaining an organizational culture in the face of change is difficult. In addition, such challenges as globalization, work force diversity, technology, and managing ethical behavior often require that an organization change its culture. Adaptive cultures that can respond to changes in the environment can lead the way in terms of organizational performance.

Managers have at their disposal many techniques for managing organizational culture. These range from manipulating the artifacts of culture, such as ceremonies and symbols, to communicating the values that guide the organization. Socialization is a powerful cultural communication process. Managers are models who communicate the organizational culture to employees through personal enactment. Their modeled behavior sets the norms for the other employees to follow. Their leadership is essential for developing a culture that values diversity, supports empowerment, fosters innovations in product and service quality, and promotes ethical behavior.

■ CHAPTER SUMMARY

- Organizational (corporate) culture is a pattern of basic assumptions that are considered valid and that are taught to new members as the way to perceive, think, and feel in the organization.
- The most visible and accessible level of culture is that of artifacts, which include personal enactment, ceremonies and rites, stories, rituals, and symbols.
- Organizational culture has four functions: giving members a sense of identity and increasing their commitment; serving as a sense-making device for members; reinforcing organizational values, and serving as a control mechanism for shaping behavior.

- Three theories about the relationship between culture and performance are the strong culture perspective, the fit perspective, and the adaptation perspective.
- Leaders shape and reinforce culture by what they pay attention to, how they react to crises, how they behave, how they allocate rewards, and how they hire and fire individuals.
- Organizational socialization is the process by which newcomers become participating, effective members of the organization. Its three stages are anticipatory socialization; encounter; and change and acquisition. Each stage plays a unique role in communicating organizational culture.
- The Organizational Culture Inventory and Kilmann-Saxton Culture-Gap Survey are two quantitative instruments for assessing organizational culture. Triangulation, using multiple methods for assessing culture, is an effective measurement strategy.
- It is difficult but not impossible to change organizational culture. Managers can do so by helping current members buy into a new set of values and by adding newcomers, socializing them into the organization, and removing current members as appropriate.

■ REVIEW QUESTIONS

1. Explain the three levels of organizational culture. How can each level of culture be measured?
2. Describe five artifacts of culture, and give an example of each.
3. Explain three theories about the relationship between organizational culture and performance. What does the research evidence say about each one?
4. Contrast adaptive and nonadaptive cultures.
5. How can leaders shape organizational culture?
6. Describe the three stages of organizational socialization. How is culture communicated in each stage?
7. How can managers assess the organizational culture? What actions can they take to change it?
8. How can leaders use organizational culture as a vehicle for encouraging ethical behavior?

■ REFERENCES

1. T. E. Deal and A. A. Kennedy, *Corporate Cultures* (Reading, Mass.: Addison-Wesley, 1982).

2. W. Ouchi, *Theory Z* (Reading, Mass.: Addison-Wesley, 1981).

3. T. J. Peters and R. H. Waterman, *In Search of Excellence* (New York: Harper & Row, 1982).

4. Definition adapted from E. H. Schein, *Organizational Culture and Leadership* (San Francisco: Jossey-Bass, 1985), 9.

5. C. D. Sutton and D. L. Nelson, "Elements of the Cultural Network: The Communicators of Corporate Values," *Leadership and Organization Development* 11 (1990): 3–10.

6. B. Pickens, *Boone* (Boston: Houghton Mifflin, 1987).

7. H. M. Trice and J. M. Beyer, "Studying Organizational Cultures through Rites and Ceremonials," *Academy of Management Review* 9 (1984): 653–669.

8. M. K. Ash, *Mary Kay* (New York: Harper & Row, 1981).

9. V. Sathe, "Implications of Corporate Culture: A Manager's Guide to Action," *Organizational Dynamics* 12 (1987): 5–23.

10. J. Martin, M. S. Feldman, M. J. Hatch, and S. B. Sitkin, "The Uniqueness Paradox in Organizational Stories," *Administrative Science Quarterly* 28 (1983): 438–453.

11. C. Argyris and D. A. Schon, *Organizational Learning* (Reading, Mass.: Addison-Wesley, 1978).

12. "Sounds Like a New Woman," *New Woman,* February 1993, 144.

13. L. Smircich, "Concepts of Culture and Organizational Analysis," *Administrative Science Quarterly* (1983): 339–358.

14. M. R. Louis, "Surprise and Sense Making: What Newcomers Experience in Entering Unfamiliar Organizational Settings," *Administrative Science Quarterly* 25 (1980): 209–264.

15. B. O'Reilly, "J & J is on a Roll," *Fortune,* 26 December 1994, 178–192.

16. E. Segalla, "All for Quality and Quality for All," *Training and Development Journal* (September 1989): 36–45.

17. J. P. Kotter and J. L. Heskett, *Corporate Culture and Performance* (New York: Free Press, 1992).

18. J. C. Collins and J. Porras, *Built to Last* (New York: Harper Business, 1994).

19. G. G. Gordon, "Industry Determinants of Organizational Culture," *Academy of Management Review* 16 (1991): 396–415.

20. J. P. Kotter, *A Force for Change: How Leadership Differs from Management* (New York: Free Press, 1990).

21. W. A. Cohen, *The Art of the Leader* (Englewood Cliffs, N.J.: Prentice-Hall, 1990).

22. J. Conger, "Inspiring Others: The Language of Leadership," *Academy of Management Executive* 5 (1991): 31–45.

23. J. C. Quick, "Crafting an Organizational Culture: Herb's Hand at Southwest Airlines," *Organizational Dynamics* (Autumn 1992): 45–56.

24. D. C. Feldman, "The Multiple Socialization of Organization Members," *Academy of Management Review* 6 (1981): 309–318.

25. R. Pascale, "The Paradox of Corporate Culture: Reconciling Ourselves to Socialization," *California Management Review* 27 (1985): 26–41.

26. D. L. Nelson, "Organizational Socialization: A Stress Perspective," *Journal of Occupational Behavior* 8 (1987): 311–324.

27. S. M. Lee, S. Yoo, and T. M. Lee, "Korean Chaebols: Corporate Values and Strategies," *Organizational Dynamics* 19 (1991): 36–50.

28. D. L. Nelson, J. C. Quick, and M. E. Eakin, "A Longitudinal Study of Newcomer Role Adjustment in U.S. Organizations," *Work and Stress* 2 (1988): 239–253.

29. D. E. Bowen, G. E. Ledford, Jr., and B. R. Nathan, "Hiring for the Organization, Not the Job," *Academy of Management Executive* 5 (1991): 35–51.

30. Y. Weiner, "Forms of Value Systems: A Focus on Organizational Effectiveness and Cultural Change and Maintenance," *Academy of Management Review* 13 (1988): 534–545.

31. D. M. Rousseau, "Assessing Organizational Culture: The Case for Multiple Methods," in B. Schneider, ed., *Organizational Climate and Culture* (San Francisco: Jossey-Bass, 1990).

32. R. A. Cooke and D. M. Rousseau, "Behavioral Norms and Expectations: A Quantitative Approach to the Assessment of Organizational Culture," *Group and Organizational Studies* 12 (1988): 245–273.

33. R. H. Kilmann and M. J. Saxton, *Kilmann-Saxton Culture-Gap Survey* (Pittsburgh: Organizational Design Consultants, 1983).

34. W. J. Duncan, "Organizational Culture: 'Getting a Fix' on an Elusive Concept," *Academy of Management Executive* 3 (1989): 229–236.

35. A. Laurent, "The Cultural Diversity of Western Conceptions of Management," *International Studies of Management and Organization* 13 (1983): 75–96.

36. P. Bate, "Using the Culture Concept in an Organization Development Setting," *Journal of Applied Behavior Science* 26 (1990): 83–106.

37. V. Sathe, "How to Decipher and Change Organizational Culture," in R. H. Kilman et al., *Managing Corporate Cultures* (San Francisco: Jossey-Bass, 1985).

38. J. B. Shaw, C. D. Fisher, and W. A. Randolph, "From Maternalism to Accountability: The Changing Cultures of Ma Bell and Mother Russia," *Academy of Management Executive* 5 (1991): 7–20.

39. D. Lei, J. W. Slocum, Jr., and R. W. Slater, "Global Strategy and Reward Systems: The Key Roles of Management Development and Corporate Culture," *Organizational Dynamics* 19 (1990): 27–41.

40. S. H. Rhinesmith, "Going Global from the Inside Out," *Training and Development Journal* 45 (1991): 42–47.

41. L. K. Trevino, "A Cultural Perspective on Changing and Developing Organizational Ethics," in W. A. Pasmore and

R. W. Woodman, eds., *Research in Organizational Change and Development*, vol. 4 (Greenwich, Conn.: JAI Press, 1990).

42. S. J. Harrington, "What Corporate America Is Teaching about Ethics," *Academy of Management Executive* 5 (1991): 21–30.

43. S. W. Gellerman, "Why Good Managers Make Bad Ethical Choices," *Harvard Business Review* 64 (1986): 85–90.

44. J. Teresko, "Best Plants: Cadillac," *Industry Week*, 21 October 1991, 29–32.

45. M. Krebs, "Cadillac Starts Down a New Road," *Industry Week*, 5 August 1991, 18–23.

CHAPTER 17
CAREER MANAGEMENT

LEARNING OBJECTIVES

After reading this chapter, you should be able to do the following:

- Define career and career management.
- Explain occupational and organizational choice decisions.
- Describe the four stages of the career model.
- Explain the psychological contract.
- Describe how mentors help organizational newcomers.
- Describe ways to manage conflicts between work and home.
- Explain how career anchors help form a career identity.

■ CAREERS AS JOINT RESPONSIBILITIES

Career management is an integral activity in our lives. There are three reasons why it is important to understand careers. First, if we know what to look forward to over the course of our careers, we can take a proactive approach to planning and managing them. Second, as managers, we need to understand the experiences of our employees and colleagues as they pass through the various stages of careers over their life spans. Third, career management is good business. It makes good financial sense to have highly trained employees keep up with their fields

so that organizations can protect valuable investments in human resources.

A career is a pattern of work-related experiences that span the course of a person's life.[1] There are two elements in a career: the objective element and the subjective element.[2] The objective element of the career is the observable, concrete environment. For example, you can manage a career by getting training to improve your skills. In contrast, the subjective element involves your perception of the situation. Rather than getting training (an objective element), you might change your aspirations (a subjective element). Thus, both objective events and the individual's perception of those events are important in defining a career.

Career management is a lifelong process of learning about self, jobs, and organizations; setting personal career goals; developing strategies for achieving the goals; and revising the goals based on work and life experiences. Whose responsibility is career management? It is tempting to place the responsibility on individuals, and it is appropriate. However, it is also the organization's duty to form partnerships with individuals in managing their careers. Careers are made up of exchanges between individuals and organizations. Inherent in these exchanges is the idea of reciprocity, or give and take.

■ The Notion of Reciprocity

Reciprocity between individuals and organizations is an idea derived from the Barnard and Simon inducement-contribution model. The basic idea behind the model is: both the contributions individuals make to organizations and the inducements organizations provide to individuals should be satisfactory for an effective association to continue.[3] If these inducements and contributions are not satisfactory to one or both parties, negative consequences can result.

Let us look at an example from the individual's perspective. One inducement that organizations provide for individuals is challenging work. Suppose that the organization increases its control over the way work is performed, and an individual perceives the job as no longer offering enough challenge. Boredom will be a likely result, and the individual might leave the organization.[4] Now we can turn the example around to look at the issue from the organization's point of view. One contribution that individuals provide to organizations is creativity. Suppose the individual's creativity in the job diminishes to the point where the organization perceives the person to be stagnating. Productivity may be affected, and the organization may elect to replace the employee with a more creative worker.

Individual-organization reciprocity is important to career management. The ongoing exchange relationship forms the basis for careers, so it is natural that career management be a joint responsibility between individuals and organizations. Throughout this chap-

ter, you see the theme of reciprocity. We will discuss both individual and organizational actions that can contribute to successful career management and to positive outcomes for both individuals and organizations.

Before turning to the stages of an individual's career, we will examine the process of preparation for the world of work. Prior to beginning a career, individuals must make several important decisions.

■ PREPARING FOR THE WORLD OF WORK

From one perspective, you might say that we spend our youth preparing for the world of work. Educational experiences and personal life experiences help an individual develop the skills and maturity needed to enter a career. Preparation for work is a developmental process that gradually unfolds over time. As the time approaches for beginning a career, individuals face two difficult decisions: the choice of occupation and the choice of organization.

■ Occupational Choice

In choosing an occupation, individuals assess their needs, values, abilities, and preferences and attempt to match them with an occupation that provides a fit. Personality plays a role in the selection of occupation. John Holland's theory of occupational choice contends that there are six types of personalities and that each is characterized by a set of interests and values.[5] Holland's six types are as follows:

1. Realistic: stable, persistent, and materialistic.
2. Artistic: imaginative, emotional, and impulsive.
3. Investigative: curious, analytical, and independent.
4. Enterprising: ambitious, energetic, and adventurous.
5. Social: generous, cooperative, and sociable.
6. Conventional: efficient, practical, and obedient.

Holland also shows how occupations can be classified using this typology. For example, realistic occupations include mechanic, restaurant server, and mechanical engineer. Artistic occupations in-

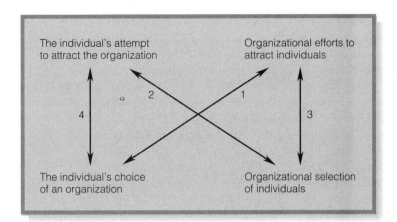

Source: L.W. Porter, E. E. Lawler III, and J.R. Hackman, *Behavior in Organizations* (New York: McGraw-Hill, Inc., 1975): 134. Reproduced with permission of McGraw-Hill, Inc.

■ FIGURE 17.1
Conflicts during Organizational Entry

clude architect, voice coach, and interior designer. Investigative occupations include physicist, surgeon, and economist. Real estate agent, human resource manager, and lawyer are enterprising occupations. The social occupations include counselor, social worker, and member of the clergy. Conventional occupations include word processor, accountant, and data entry operator.

An assumption that drives Holland's theory is that people choose occupations that match their own personalities. A mismatch occurs when, for example, an artistic personality ends up working in real estate sales, an enterprising occupation. The artistic individual would become dissatisfied and move toward an occupation more likely to satisfy his or her needs, such as interior designer.

Although personality is a major influence on occupational choice, it is not the only influence. Other influences include social class, parents' occupations, economic conditions, and geography. Once a choice of occupation has been made, another major decision is the choice of organizations.

■ Organizational Choice and Entry

Several theories on the ways individuals choose organizations exist, from those that postulate very logical and rational choice processes to those that offer seemingly irrational processes. Expectancy theory, which we discussed in Chapter 5, can be applied to organizational choice. According to expectancy theory, individuals choose organizations that maximize positive outcomes and avoid negative outcomes. Job candidates calculate the probability that an organization will provide a certain outcome and then compare the probabilities across organizations.

Other theories propose that people select organizations in a much less rational fashion. Job candidates may satisfice, that is, select the first organization that meets one or two important criteria and then justify their choice by distorting their perceptions.

The method of selecting an organization varies greatly among individuals. It may reflect a combination of the expectancy theory and theories that postulate less rational approaches. Entry into an organization is further complicated by the conflicts that occur between individuals and organizations during the process. Figure 17.1 illustrates these potential conflicts. The arrows in the figure illustrate four types of conflicts that can occur as individuals choose organizations and vice versa. The first two conflicts (1 and 2) occur between individuals and organizations. The first is between the organization's effort to attract candidates and the individual's choice of an organization. The individual needs complete and accurate information to make a good choice, but the organization may not provide it. The organization is trying to attract a large number of qualified candidates, so it presents itself in an overly attractive way.

The second conflict is between the individual's attempt to attract several organizations and the organization's need to select the best candidate. Individuals want good offers, so they do not disclose their faults. They describe their preferred job in terms of the organization's opening instead of describing a job they would really prefer.

Conflicts 3 and 4 are internal to the two parties. The third is between the organization's desire to recruit a large pool of qualified applicants and the organization's need to select and retain the best candidate. In recruiting, organizations tend to give only positive information, and this results in mismatches between the individual and the organization. The fourth conflict is internal to the individual; it is between the individual's desire for several job offers and the need to make a good choice. When individuals present themselves as overly attractive, they risk being offered positions that are poor fits in terms of their skills and career goals.[6]

The organizational choice and entry process is very complex due to the nature of these conflicts. Partial responsibility for preventing these conflicts rests with the individual. Individuals should conduct thorough research of the organization through published reports and industry analyses. Individuals also should conduct a careful self-analysis and be as honest as possible with organizations to ensure a good match. Partial responsibility for good matches also rests with the organization. One way of avoiding the conflicts and mismatches is to utilize a realistic job preview.

■ Realistic Job Previews

The conflicts just discussed may result in unrealistic expectations on the part of the candidate. People entering the world of work may expect, for example, that they will receive explicit directions from their bosses, only to find that they are left with ambiguity about how to do the job. They may expect that promotions will be based on performance and find that promotions are based mainly on political considerations. A recent study illustrated that newly recruited graduates to a British oil company had unrealistic expectations about their jobs in terms of management content. The recruits expected to be given managerial responsibilities right away; how-

ever, this was not the case. They were given managerial responsibility gradually over time.[7]

Giving potential employees a realistic picture of the job they are applying for is known as a realistic job preview (RJP). When candidates are given both positive and negative information, they can make more effective job choices. Traditional recruiting practices produce unrealistically high expectations, which produce low job satisfaction when these unrealistic expectations hit the reality of the job situation. RJPs tend to create expectations that are much closer to reality, and they increase the numbers of candidates who withdraw from further consideration. This occurs because candidates with unrealistic expectations tend to look for employment elsewhere.

RJPs can also be thought of as inoculation against disappointment. If new recruits know what to expect in the new job, they can prepare for the experience. Ultimately, this can result in more effective matches, lower turnover, and higher commitment and satisfaction.[8,9]

Job candidates who receive RJPs view the organization as honest and also have a greater ability to cope with the demands of the job. RJPs perform another important function: uncertainty reduction. Knowing what to expect, both good and bad, gives a newcomer a sense of control that is important to job satisfaction and performance.

In summary, the needs and goals of individuals and organizations can clash during entry into the organization. To avoid potential mismatches, individuals should conduct a careful self-analysis and provide accurate information about themselves to potential employers. Organizations should present realistic job previews to show candidates both the positive and negative aspects of the job, along with the potential career paths available to the employee.

After entry into the organization, individuals embark on their careers. A person's work life can be traced through successive stages, as we see in the career stage model.

■ THE CAREER STAGE MODEL

A common way of understanding careers is viewing them as a series of stages that individuals pass

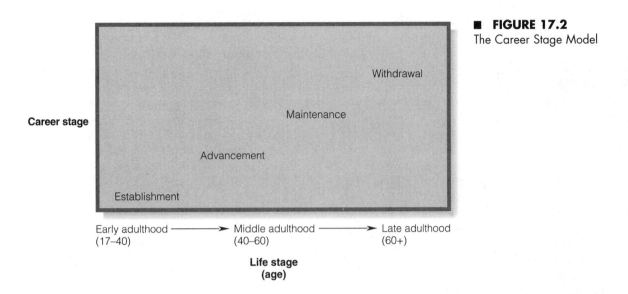

■ FIGURE 17.2
The Career Stage Model

through in their working lives.[10] Figure 17.2 presents the career stage model, which will form the basis for our discussion in the remainder of this chapter.[11] The career stage model shows that individuals pass through four stages in their careers: establishment, advancement, maintenance, and withdrawal. It is important to note that the age ranges shown are approximations; that is, the timing of the career transitions varies greatly between individuals.

Establishment is the first stage of a person's career. The activities that occur in this stage center around learning the job and fitting into the organization and occupation. Advancement is a highly achievement-oriented stage in which people focus on increasing their competence. The maintenance stage finds the individual trying to maintain productivity while evaluating progress toward career goals. The withdrawal stage involves contemplation of retirement or possible career change.

Along the horizontal axis in Figure 17.2 are the corresponding life stages for each career stage. These life stages are based on the pioneering research on adult development conducted by Levinson and his colleagues. Levinson conducted extensive biographical interviews to trace the life stages of men and women. He found through his research that life stages are characterized by alternating patterns of stability and transition.[12] Throughout the discussion of career stages that follows, we weave in the tran-

sitions of Levinson's life stages. Work and personal life are inseparable, and to understand a person's career experiences, we must also examine the unfolding of the person's personal experiences.

You can see that adult development provides unique challenges for the individual and that there may be considerable overlap between the stages. Now let us examine each career stage in detail.

■ THE ESTABLISHMENT STAGE

During the establishment stage, the individual begins a career as a newcomer to the organization. This is a period of great dependence on others, as the individual is learning about the job and the organization. The establishment stage usually occurs during the beginning of the early adulthood years (ages eighteen to twenty-five). During this time, Levinson notes, an important personal life transition into adulthood occurs: the individual begins to separate from his or her parents and becomes less emotionally and financially dependent. Following this period is a fairly stable time of exploring the adult role and settling down. The transition from school to work is a part of the establishment stage. Many graduates find the transition to be a memorable experience. The following description was provided by a newly graduated individual who went to work at a large public utility:

We all tried to one-up each other about jobs we had just accepted ... bragging that we had the highest salary, the best management training program, the most desirable co-workers, the most upward mobility ... and believed we were destined to become future corporate leaders.... Every Friday after work we met for happy hour to visit and relate the events of the week. It is interesting to look at how the mood of those happy hours changed over the first few months ... at first, we jockeyed for position in terms of telling stories about how great these new jobs were, or how weird our bosses were.... Gradually, things quieted down at happy hour. The mood went from "Wow, isn't this great," to "What in the world have we gotten ourselves into?" There began to be general agreement that business wasn't all it was cracked up to be.[13]

Establishment is thus a time of big transitions in both personal and work life. At work, three major tasks face the newcomer: negotiating effective psychological contracts, managing the stress of socialization, and making a transition from organizational outsider to organizational insider.

■ Psychological Contracts

A psychological contract is an implicit agreement between the individual and the organization that specifies what each is expected to give and receive in the relationship.[14] Individuals expect to receive salary, status, advancement opportunities, and challenging work to meet their needs. Organizations expect to receive time, energy, talents, and loyalty in order to meet their goals. Working out the psychological contract with the organization begins with entry, but the contract is modified as the individual proceeds through the career.

Psychological contracts also form and exist between individuals.[15] During the establishment stage, newcomers form attachment relationships with many people in the organization. Working out effective psychological contracts within each relationship is important. Newcomers need social support in many forms and from many sources. Table 17.1 shows the type of psychological contracts, in the form of social support, that newcomers may work out with key insiders in the organization.

One common newcomer concern, for example, is whose behavior to watch for cues to appropriate behavior. Senior colleagues can provide modeling support by displaying behavior that the newcomer can emulate. This is only one of many types of support that newcomers need. Newcomers should contract with others to receive each of the needed types of support so that they can adjust to the new job. Organizations should help newcomers form relationships early and should encourage the psychological contracting process between newcomers and insiders.

■ The Stress of Socialization

In Chapter 16 on organizational culture and socialization, we discussed three phases that newcomers go through in adjusting to a new organization: anticipatory socialization; encounter; and change and acquisition. (You may want to refer to Figure 16.2 for review.) Another way to look at these three phases is to examine the kinds of stress newcomers experience during each stage.[16]

In anticipatory socialization, the newcomer is gathering information from various sources about the job and organization. The likely stressor in this stage is ambiguity, so the provision of accurate information is important. During this stage, the psychological contract is formed. It is essential that both parties go into it with good intentions of keeping up their end of the agreement.

In the encounter phase, the demands of the job in terms of the role, task, interpersonal relationships, and physical setting become apparent to the newcomer. The expectations formed in anticipatory socialization may clash with the realities of organizational life, and reality shock can occur. This very predictable "surprise" reaction may find the new employee thinking, "What have I gotten myself into?" The degree of reality shock depends on the expectations formed in the anticipatory socialization stage. If these expectations are unrealistic or unmet, reality shock may be a problem.

In the change and acquisition phase, the newcomer begins to master the demands of the job. Newcomers need to feel that they have some means of control over job demands.

■ **TABLE 17.1**

Newcomer-Insider Psychological Contracts for Social Support

TYPE OF SUPPORT	FUNCTION OF SUPPORTIVE ATTACH-MENTS	NEWCOMER CONCERN	EXAMPLES OF INSIDER RESPONSE/ACTION
Protection from stressors	Direct assistance in terms of resources, time, labor, or environmental modification	What are the major risks/threats in this environment?	*Supervisor* cues newcomer in to risks/threats.
Informational	Provision of information necessary for managing demands	What do I need to know to get things done?	*Mentor* provides advice on informal political climate in organization.
Evaluative	Feedback on both personal and professional role performances	How am I doing?	*Supervisor* provides day-to-day performance feedback during first week on new job.
Modeling	Evidence of behavioral standards provided through modeled behavior	Who do I follow?	Newcomer is apprenticed to *senior colleague.*
Emotional	Empathy, esteem, caring, or love	Do I matter? Who cares if I'm here or not?	*Other newcomers* empathize with and encourage individual when reality shock sets in.

Source: D. L. Nelson, J. C. Quick, and J. R. Joplin, "Psychological Contracting and Newcomer Socialization: An Attachment Theory Foundation," *Journal of Social Behavior and Personality* 6 (1991): 65.

■ Easing the Transition from Outsider to Insider

Being a newcomer in an organization is stressful. The process of becoming a functioning member of the organization takes time, and the newcomer needs support in making the transition. A successful transition from outsider to insider can be ensured if both the newcomer and the organization work together to smooth the way.

Individual Actions. Newcomers should ask about the negative side of the job if they were not given a realistic job preview. In particular, newcomers should ask about the stressful aspects of the job. Other employees are good sources of this information. Research has shown that newcomers who underestimate the stressfulness of job demands do not adjust well.[17] In addition, newcomers should present honest and accurate information about their own weaknesses. Both actions can promote good matches.

During the encounter phase, newcomers must prepare for reality shock. Realizing that slight depression is natural when adjusting to a new job can help alleviate the distress. Newcomers can also plan ways to cope with job stress ahead of time. If, for example, long assignments away from home are typical, newcomers can plan for these trips in advance. Part of the plan for dealing with reality shock should include ways to seek support from others. Networking with other newcomers who emphathize can help individuals cope with the stress of the new job.

In the change and acquisition stage of adjusting to a new organization, newcomers should set realistic goals and take credit for the successes that occur as they master the job. Newcomers must seek feedback on job performance from their supervisors and co-workers. Organizations also can assist newcomers in their transition from outsiders to insiders.

Organizational Actions. Realistic job previews start the relationship between the newcomer and the organization with integrity and honesty. Careful recruitment and selection of new employees can help ensure good matches.

During the encounter phase, organizations should provide early job assignments that present opportunities for the new recruit to succeed. Newcomers who face early job challenges successfully tend to be higher performers later in their careers.[18] One way of providing early job challenges is job rotation, in which the newcomer moves through a series of specialized jobs. By rotating from job to job, newcomers acquire a variety of skills that can enhance their careers. The benefits of job rotation include increased job satisfaction and commitment, transfer of company culture to the newcomer, and improved coping skills for the newcomer.[19] Providing encouragement and feedback to the newcomer during this stage is crucial. The immediate supervisor, peers, other newcomers, and support staff are important sources of support during encounter.[20]

During the change and acquisition phase, rewards are important. Organizations should tie the newcomers' rewards as explicitly as possible to performance. Feedback is also crucial. Newcomers should receive daily, consistent feedback. This communicates that the organization is concerned about their progress and wants to help them learn the ropes along the way.

The establishment stage marks the beginning of an individual's career. Its noteworthy transitions include the transition from school to work, from dependence on parents to dependence on self, from organizational outsider to organizational insider. Negotiating sound psychological contracts and planning for the stress of adjusting to a new organization can help newcomers start off successfully. Once they have met their need to fit in, individuals move on to the advancement stage of their careers.

THE ADVANCEMENT STAGE

The advancement stage is a period when many individuals strive for achievement. They seek greater responsibility and authority and strive for upward mobility. Usually around age thirty, an important life transition occurs. Individuals reassess their goals and feel the need to make changes in their career dreams. The transition at age thirty is followed by a period of stability during which the individual tries to find a role in adult society and wants to succeed in the career. During this stage, several issues are important: exploring career paths, finding a mentor, working out dual-career partnerships, and managing conflicts between work and personal life.

■ Career Paths and Career Ladders

Career paths are sequences of job experiences along which employees move during their careers. At the advancement stage, individuals examine their career dreams and the paths they must follow to achieve those dreams. For example, suppose a person's dream is to become a top executive in the pharmaceutical industry. She majors in chemistry in undergraduate school and takes a job with a nationally recognized firm. After she has adjusted to her job as a quality control chemist, she reevaluates her plan and decides that further education is necessary. She plans to pursue an MBA degree part-time, hoping to gain expertise in management. From there, she hopes to be promoted to a supervisory position within her current firm. If this does not occur within five years, she will consider moving to a different pharmaceutical company. An alternate route would be to try and transfer to a sales position, from which she might advance into management.

A career ladder is a structured series of job positions through which an individual progresses in an organization. For example, at Southwestern Bell, it is customary to move through a series of alternating line and staff supervisory assignments to advance toward upper management. Supervisors in customer service might be assigned next to the training staff and then rotate back as line supervisors in network services to gain experience in different departments.

Some companies use the traditional concept of career ladders to help employees advance in their careers. Other organizations take a more contemporary approach to career advancement. Sony encourages creativity from its engineers by using nontraditional career paths. At Sony, individuals have the freedom to move on to interesting and challenging job assignments as they wish. Even employees in firms with more traditional career ladders, however, can help themselves move up by finding out what the career ladders are and nominating themselves for opportunities to move up.

Exploring career paths is one important activity in advancement. Another crucial activity during advancement is finding a mentor.

■ Finding a Mentor

A mentor is an individual who provides guidance, coaching, counseling, and friendship to a protege. Mentors are important to career success because they perform both career and psychosocial functions.[21]

The career functions provided by a mentor include sponsorship, facilitating exposure and visibility, coaching, and protection. Sponsorship means active efforts to help the individual get job experiences and promotions. Facilitating exposure and visibility means providing opportunities for the protege to develop relationships with key figures in the organization in order to advance. Coaching involves providing advice in both career and job performance. Protection is provided by shielding the protege from potentially damaging experiences.

The mentor also performs psychosocial functions. Role modeling occurs when the mentor displays behavior for the protege to emulate. This facilitates social learning. The act of acceptance and confirmation is important to both the mentor and protege. When the protege feels accepted by the mentor, it fosters a sense of pride. Likewise, positive regard and appreciation from the junior colleague provide a sense of satisfaction for the mentor. Counseling by a mentor helps the protege explore personal issues that arise and require assistance. Friendship is another psychosocial function, and it benefits both mentor and protege alike.

Some companies have formal mentoring programs in which a junior employee is assigned to a senior employee who serves as mentor. Dow Jones uses a "quad" system that matches a high-level mentor with a group of three employees: a white man, a white or minority woman, and a minority man or woman. If an employee does not have rapport with the mentor in the quad, that employee still may relate to the other two members of the quad. Capitalizing on diversity makes the quad mentoring

system successful.[22] At Bell Labs, a formal mentoring program has benefited all workers and has particularly helped the career progress of minorities and women. Matchups are carefully tailored to the newcomers' career development needs, and minorities and women are assigned to mentors with similar backgrounds who hold positions that the newcomers strive to attain. The formal mentoring program helped Bell Labs to increase the representation of women and minorities in management positions.[23]

The mentoring process, however, presents unique problems, including the availability of mentors, issues of language and acculturation, and cultural sensitivity for minority groups such as Hispanic-Americans. Adding to this challenge is the substantial diversity within the Hispanic-American population in terms of country of origin and country of birth.[24] Companies can make the mentoring process easier for minority workers by creating formal programs that address special needs in the mentoring process and by creating a culture that values diversity, as was discussed in Chapter 16.

Although some companies have formal mentoring programs, junior employees more often are left to negotiate their own mentor relationships. Sometimes an individual hesitates to ask a senior person to be the mentor. Barriers to finding a mentor include lack of access to mentors, fears of initiating a relationship, and fears that supervisors or coworkers might disapprove of mentoring relationships.[25]

Organizations can encourage junior workers to approach mentors by providing opportunities for them to interact with senior colleagues. The immediate supervisor is not always the best mentor for an individual, so exposure to other senior workers is important. Seminars, multilevel teams, and social events can serve as vehicles for bringing together potential mentors and proteges.

Mentoring relationships go through a series of phases: initiation, cultivation, separation, and redefinition. There is no fixed time length for each phase, because each relationship is unique. In the initiation phase, the mentoring relationship begins to take on significance for both the mentor and the protege. In the cultivation phase, the relationship becomes more meaningful, and the protege shows rapid progress because of the career and psychosocial support provided by the mentor.

In the separation phase, the protege feels the need to assert independence and work more autonomously. Separation can be voluntary, or it can result from an involuntary change (the protege or mentor may be promoted or transferred). The separation phase can be difficult if it is resisted, either by the mentor (who is reluctant to let go of the relationship), or by the protege (who resents the mentor's withdrawal of support). Separation can proceed smoothly and naturally or can result from a conflict that disrupts the mentoring relationship.

The redefinition phase occurs if separation has been successful. In this phase, the relationship takes on a new identity as both parties consider themselves colleagues or friends. The mentor feels pride in the protege, and the protege develops a deeper appreciation for the support from the mentor.

Why are mentors so important? Aside from the support they provide, the research shows that mentors are important to the protege's future success. For example, studies have demonstrated that individuals with mentors have higher promotion rates and higher incomes than individuals who do not have mentors.[26-28] Individuals with mentors also tend to be better decision makers.[29]

During the advancement stage, many individuals face another transition: they settle into a relationship with a life partner. This life-style transition requires adjustment in many respects: learning to live with another person, being concerned with someone besides yourself, dealing with an extended family, and many other demands. The partnership can be particularly stressful if both members are career-oriented.

■ Dual-Career Partnerships

The two-career life-style has increased in recent years due to the need for two incomes to maintain a preferred standard of living. Dual-career partnerships are relationships in which both people have important career roles. This type of partnership can be mutually beneficial, but it can also be stressful. Often these stresses center around stereotypical ideas that providing income is a man's responsibility and taking care of the home is the woman's domain.

One stressor in a dual-career partnership is time pressure. When both partners work outside the home, there may be a time crunch in fitting in work, family, and leisure time. Another potential problem is jealousy. When one partner's career blooms before the other's, the partner may feel threatened. Another issue to work out is whose career takes precedence. For example, what happens if one partner gets transferred to another city? Must the other partner make a move that might threaten his or her own career in order to be with the individual who was transferred? Who, if anyone, will stay home and take care of a new baby?

Working out a dual-career partnership takes careful planning and consistent communication between the partners. Each partner must serve as a source of social support for the other. Couples can also turn to other family members, friends, and professionals for support if the need arises.

■ Work-Home Conflicts

An issue related to dual-career partnerships, faced throughout the career cycle but often first encountered in the advancement phase, is the conflict between work and personal life. Experiencing a great deal of work-home conflict negatively affects an individual's overall quality of life. Responsibilities at home can clash with responsibilities at work, and these conflicts must be planned for. For example, suppose a child gets sick at school. Who will pick up the child and stay home with him or her? Couples must work together to resolve these conflicts.

Work-home conflicts are particular problems for working women.[30] Women have been quicker to share the provider role than men have been to share responsibilities at home. When working women experience work-home conflict, their performance declines, and they suffer more strain. Work-home conflicts in Japan are different from those in the United States. In Japan, women are expected to leave the work force at an early age to marry and raise a family. Women who work after having children are looked down upon.[31] This attitude is slowly changing, and Japanese women are turning to temporary employment to balance their work and home responsibilities.

To help individuals deal with work-home conflict, companies can offer flexible work schedules.[32] These programs, such as flextime, which we discussed in Chapter 14, give employees freedom to take care of personal concerns while still getting their work done. Company-sponsored child care is another way to help. Companies with on-site day care centers include Johnson & Johnson, Stride Rite, and Campbell Soup. Whereas large companies may offer corporate day care, small companies can also assist their workers by providing referral services for locating the type of child care the workers need. For smaller organizations, this is a cost-effective alternative. At the very least, companies can be sensitive to work-home conflicts and handle them on a case-by-case basis with flexibility and concern.

An increasingly interesting program that organizations can provide is eldercare. Often workers find themselves part of the sandwich generation: they are expected to care for both their children and their elderly parents. This extremely stressful role is reported more often by women than men.[33] Companies have taken a variety of approaches to assisting employees with eldercare. PepsiCo has in-house seminars to provide information, a resource guide, and a hotline to a university center on aging. Stride-Rite operates a center where employees can bring both children and the elderly for day care.[34]

DuPont is an example of a company concerned about the balance between work and home. DuPont conducted a survey of its employees and found that the need for company change was great. The majority of employees said that they had difficulty finding child care that conformed to their work hours, that they had difficulty attending school activities, and that many of their ten-to thirteen-year-olds were left alone routinely after school. DuPont formed a company-wide committee that made twenty-three recommendations for action, including flexible work arrangements, more benefit options for child care and eldercare, and the incorporation of work and family topics in training sessions. DuPont is currently implementing these recommendations.[35]

The advancement stage is filled with the challenges of finding a mentor, balancing dual-career partnerships, and dealing with work-home conflicts. Developmental changes that occur in either the late advancement stage or the early maintenance stage can prove stressful, too. The mid-life transition, which takes place approximately between ages forty and forty-five, is often a time of crisis. Levinson points out three major changes that contribute to the midlife transition. First, people realize that their lives are half over and that they are mortal. Second, age forty is considered by people in their twenties and thirties to be "over the hill" and not part of the youthful culture. Finally, people reassess their dreams and evaluate how close they have come to achieving those dreams. All these factors make up the midlife transition.

■ THE MAINTENANCE STAGE

Maintenance may be a misnomer for this career stage, because some people continue to grow in their careers, although the growth is usually not at the rate it was earlier. A career crisis at midlife may accompany the midlife transition. A senior product manager at Borden found himself in such a crisis and described it this way: "When I was in college, I had thought in terms of being president of a company. . . . But at Borden I felt used and cornered. Most of the guys in the next two rungs above me had either an MBA or 15 to 20 years of experience in the food business. My long-term plans stalled." [36]

Some individuals who reach a career crisis are burned out, and a month's vacation will help, according to Carolyn Smith Paschal, who owns an executive search firm. She recommends that companies give employees in this stage sabbaticals instead of bonuses. This would help rejuvenate them.

Some individuals reach the maintenance stage with a sense of achievement and contentment, feeling no need to strive for further upward mobility. Whether the maintenance stage is a time of crisis or contentment, however, there are two issues to grapple with: sustaining performance and becoming a mentor.

■ Sustaining Performance

Remaining productive is a key concern for individuals in the maintenance stage. This becomes challenging when one reaches a career plateau, a point where the probability of moving further up the hierarchy is low. Some people handle career plateauing fairly well, but others may become frustrated, bored, and dissatisfied with their jobs.

To keep employees productive, organizations can provide challenges and opportunities for learning. Lateral moves are one option. Another option is to involve the employee in project teams that provide new tasks and skill development. The key is keeping the work stimulating and involving. Individuals at this stage also need continued affirmation of their value to the organization. They need to know that their contributions are significant and appreciated.

Becoming a Mentor

During maintenance, individuals can make a contribution by sharing their wealth of knowledge and experience with others. Opportunities to be mentors to new employees can keep senior workers motivated and involved in the organization. It is important for organizations to reward mentors for the time and energy they expend. Some employees adapt naturally to the mentor role, but others may need training on how to coach and counsel junior workers.

Kathy Kram notes that there are four keys to the success of a formal mentoring program. First, participation should be voluntary. No one should be forced to enter a mentoring relationship, and careful matching of mentors and proteges is important. Second, support from top executives is needed to convey the intent of the program and its role in career development. Third, training should be provided to mentors so they understand the functions of the relationship. Finally, a graceful exit should be provided for mismatches or for people in mentoring relationships that have fulfilled their purpose.[37]

Maintenance is a time of transition, like all career stages. It can be managed by individuals who know what to expect and plan to remain productive, as well as by organizations that focus on maximizing employee involvement in work. According to Levinson, during the latter part of the maintenance stage, another life transition occurs. The age fifty transition is another time of reevaluating the dream and the issue of psychological success in one's life work. This type of success involves not only the career, but also work as a spouse, parent, community member, and self-developer. Individuals evaluate

the balance in their lives and their progress in meeting their goals in many areas of life.[38] Following the age fifty transition is a fairly stable period. During this time, individuals begin to plan seriously for withdrawing from their careers.

THE WITHDRAWAL STAGE

The withdrawal stage usually occurs later in life and signals that a long period of continuous employment will soon come to a close. Older workers may face discrimination and stereotyping. They may be viewed by others as less productive, more resistant to change, and less motivated. However, older workers are among the most undervalued groups in the work force. They can provide continuity in the midst of change and can serve as mentors and role models to younger generations of employees.

Discrimination against older workers is prohibited under the Age Discrimination in Employment Act. Organizations must create a culture that values older workers' contributions. With their level of experience, strong work ethic, and loyalty, these workers have much to contribute. In fact, older workers have lower rates of tardiness and absenteeism, are more safety conscious, and are more satisfied with their jobs than are younger workers.[39]

Retirement is a very individual decision, with some individuals retiring as early as age forty and some never leaving the work force. Some individuals withdraw from work gradually by scaling back their work hours or by working part-time. Some retire and change careers. The key to making transitions at this career stage is careful planning.

Planning for Change

The decision to retire is an individual one, but the need for planning is universal. A retired sales executive from Boise-Cascade said that the best advice is to "plan no unplanned retirement."[40] This means carefully planning not only the transition but also the activities you will be involved in once the transition is made. All options should be open for consideration. One recent trend is the need for temporary top-level executives. Some companies are hiring senior managers from the outside on a temporary basis. The qualities of a good temporary executive include substantial high-level management experience, financial security that allows the executive to choose only assignments that really interest him or her, and a willingness to relocate.[41] Some individuals at the withdrawal stage find this an attractive option.

Planning for retirement should include not only financial planning but also a plan for psychological withdrawal from work. The pursuit of hobbies and travel, volunteer work, or more time with extended family can all be part of the plan. The key is to plan early and carefully, as well as to anticipate the transition with a positive attitude and a full slate of desirable activities.

■ Retirement

The decision to retire can focus on early retirement, traditional retirement at age sixty-five, or postponed retirement. With many organizations downsizing, forced early retirements are increasing. Factors that influence the decision on when to retire include company policy, financial considerations, family support or pressure, health, and opportunities for other productive activities.[42]

During the withdrawal stage, the individual faces a major life transition that Levinson refers to as the late adulthood transition (ages sixty to sixty-five). One's own mortality becomes a major concern and the loss of one's family members and friends becomes more frequent. There is a major psychological development task to be accomplished during this transition. The person works to achieve a sense of integrity in life-that is, the person works to find the encompassing meaning and value in life.

Retirement can be stressful. Besides the fact that it is a major life transition, there are stressors involved, such as dual-career considerations, income uncertainty, declining physical capacity, and spouse's concerns and anxieties. Knowing what to expect can help a retiree cope with these stressors. Careful planning and knowing what to expect can produce a transition into a meaningful and rewarding retirement.

Retirement need not be a complete cessation of work. Many alternative work arrangements can be considered, and many companies offer flexibility in these options. Phased retirement, such as part-time work, consulting, and mentoring, will probably become more common as large numbers of baby boomers near retirement. Not all baby boomers will want to retire, and many organizations will not be able to afford the loss of large numbers of experienced employees at once.

■ CAREER ANCHORS

Much of an individual's self-concept rests upon a career. Over the course of the career, career anchors are developed. Career anchors are self-perceived talents, motives, and values that guide an individual's career decisions.[43] Edgar Schein developed the concept of career anchors based on a twelve-year study of MBA graduates from the Massachusetts Institute of Technology (MIT). Schein found great diversity in the graduates' career histories but great similarities in the way they explained the career decisions they had made. From extensive interviews with the graduates, Schein developed five career anchors:

1. **Technical/functional competence.** Individuals who hold this career anchor want to specialize in a given functional area (for example, finance or marketing) and become competent. The idea of general management does not interest them.
2. **Managerial competence.** Adopting this career anchor means individuals want general management responsibility. They want to see their efforts have an impact on organizational effectiveness.
3. **Autonomy and independence.** Freedom is the key to this career anchor, and often these individuals are uncomfortable working in large organizations. Autonomous careers like writer, professor, or consultant attract these individuals.
4. **Creativity.** Individuals holding this career anchor feel a strong need to create something. They are often entrepreneurs.
5. **Security/stability.** Long-term career stability, whether in a single organization or in a single geographic area, fits people with this career anchor. Some government jobs provide this type of security.

■ **FIGURE 17.3**
The Hottest Job Prospects

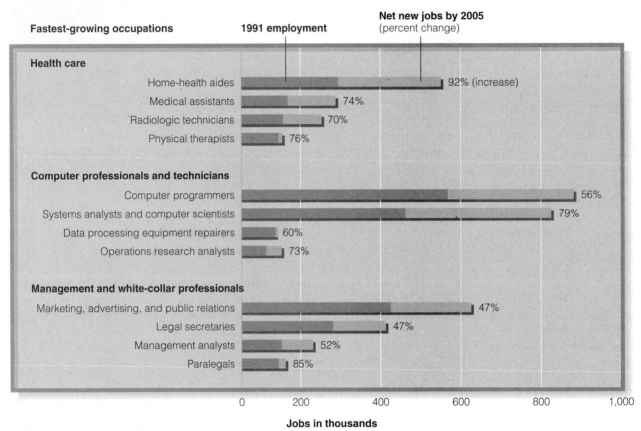

Career anchors emerge over time and may be modified by work or life experiences. The importance of knowing your career anchor is that it can help you find a match between yourself and an organization. For example, individuals with creativity as an anchor may find themselves stifled in bureaucratic organizations. Textbook sales may not be the place for an individual with a security anchor because of the frequent travel and seasonal nature of the business.

■ **MANAGERIAL IMPLICATIONS:
MANAGING YOUR CAREER**

The challenges of globalization, diversity, technology, and ethics have provided unique opportunities and threats for career management. The ongoing restructuring of American organizations with its accompanying downsizing has resulted in a reduction of 25 percent of the jobs held in the Fortune 500 companies, which translates into 3.7 million fewer workers in 1992 than in 1981.[44] The flattening of the organizational hierarchy has resulted in fewer opportunities for promotion. Forty-year careers with one organization, a phenomenon baby boomers saw their parents experience, are becoming less and less the norm. Negotiating the turbulent waters of the U.S. employment market will be a challenge in the foreseeable future.

Many industries are experiencing sinking employment, but there are some bright spots. According to Labor Department projections, the U.S. economy will add approximately 25 million jobs by the year 2005, with most of them in service industries. Figure 17.3 shows where the new jobs will be found.

Managing your career is a challenge that can be met, even in a turbulent economy. Performing a careful self-analysis, making the most of your current job situation, periodically reappraising your career and skills, and targeting new opportunities can lead to successful career management.

■ CHAPTER SUMMARY

- Career management is a joint responsibility of individuals and organizations.
- Good matches between individuals and organizations can be promoted with a realistic job preview (RJP).
- There are four stages in an individual's career: establishment, advancement, maintenance, and withdrawal. Each stage has unique challenges.
- Psychological contracts are implicit agreements between individuals and organizations.
- Mentoring is crucial to both the career success of young workers and the needs of older workers.
- Childcare, eldercare, and flexible work schedules can help employees manage work-home conflicts.
- Career anchors help an individual form a career identity and formulate an effective career plan.

■ REVIEW QUESTIONS

1. Define the terms *career, career management, career path,* and *career ladder.*
2. List and describe Holland's six personality types and name an occupation that fits each type.
3. What psychosocial functions do mentors perform? What are their career functions?
4. What factors keep newcomers from approaching a potential mentor? How can organizations encourage mentoring?
5. What can organizations do to assist dual-career partnerships?
6. What are the major concerns of individuals at each of the four career stages? What major life transitions occur within each stage?

7. Describe career plateaus and career anchors.
8. You are leaving your current job to look for employment elsewhere. Should you tell your current employer? Is it ethical not to reveal your job search to your employer?
9. You are interviewing a job candidate who inquires about the career paths within your organization. A natural next step from the job she is seeking would be middle management, but you know that your company is flattening its hierarchy and that most middle-management jobs will be eliminated. You are afraid that this information will discourage this very talented candidate from taking the job. What should you do?

■ REFERENCES

1. J. H. Greenhaus, *Career Management* (Hinsdale, Ill.: CBS College Press, 1987).
2. D. T. Hall, *Careers in Organizations* (Pacific Palisades, Calif.: Goodyear, 1976).
3. J. G. March and H. A. Simon, *Organizations* (New York: Wiley, 1958).
4. M. B. Arthur and K. E. Kram, "Reciprocity at Work: The Separate Yet Inseparable Possibilities for Individual and Organizational Development," in M. B. Arthur, D. T. Hall, and B. S. Lawrence, eds., *Handbook of Career Theory* (Cambridge: Cambridge University Press, 1989), 292–312.
5. J. L. Holland, *Making Vocational Choices: A Theory of Careers* (Englewood Cliffs, N.J.: Prentice-Hall, 1973).
6. J. P. Wanous, *Organizational Entry: Recruitment, Selection, and Socialization of Newcomers* (Reading, Mass.: Addison-Wesley, 1980).
7. N. Nicholson and J. Arnold, "From Expectation to Experience: Graduates Entering a Large Corporation," *Journal of Organizational Behavior* 12 (1991): 413–429.
8. J. P. Wanous and A. Colella, "Organizational Entry Research: Current Status and Future Directions," in K. R. Rowland and G. R. Ferris, eds., *Research in Personnel and Human Resources Management* (New York: JAI Press, 1989), 59–120.
9. R. J. Vandenberg and V. Scarpello, "The Matching Model: An Examination of the Processes Underlying Realistic Job Previews," *Journal of Applied Psychology* 75 (1990): 60–67.
10. S. Cytrynbaum and J. O. Crites, "The Utility of Adult Development in Understanding Career Adjustment Process," in M. B. Arthur, D. T. Hall, and B. S. Lawrence, eds., *Handbook of Career Theory* (Cambridge: Cambridge University Press, 1989), 66–88.
11. D. E. Super, "A Life-Span, Life-Space Approach to Career Development," *Journal of Vocational Behavior* 16 (1980): 282–298.

12. D. J. Levinson, "A Conception of Adult Development," *American Psychologist* 41 (1986): 3–13.

13. D. L. Nelson, "Adjusting to a New Organization: Easing the Transition from Outsider to Insider," in J. C. Quick, R. E. Hess, J. Hermalin, and J. D. Quick, eds., *Career Stress in Changing Times* (New York: Haworth Press, 1990), 61–86.

14. J. P. Kotter, "The Psychological Contract: Managing the Joining Up Process," *California Management Review* 15 (1973): 91–99.

15. D. M. Rousseau, "New Hire Perceptions of Their Own and Their Employers' Obligations: A Study of Psychological Contracts," *Journal of Organizational Behavior* 11 (1990): 389–400.

16. D. L. Nelson, "Organizational Socialization: A Stress Perspective," *Journal of Occupational Behavior* 8 (1987): 311–324.

17. D. L. Nelson and C. D. Sutton, "The Relationship between Newcomer Expectations of Job Stressors and Adjustment to the New Job," *Work and Stress* 5 (1991): 241–254.

18. G. F. Dreher and R. D. Bretz, Jr., "Cognitive Ability and Career Attainment: Moderating Effects of Early Career Success," *Journal of Applied Psychology* 76 (1991): 392–397.

19. M.A. Campion, L. Cheraskin, and M.J. Stevens, "Career-Related Antecedents and Outcomes of Job Rotation," *Academy of Management Journal* 37 (1994): 1518–1542.

20. D. L. Nelson and J. C. Quick, "Social Support and Newcomer Adjustment in Organizations: Attachment Theory at Work?" *Journal of Organizational Behavior* 12 (1991): 543–554.

21. K. E. Kram, *Mentoring at Work: Developmental Relationships in Organizational Life* (Glenview, Ill.: Scott, Foresman, 1985).

22. M. Granfield, "90s Mentoring: Circles and Quads," *Working Woman*, November 1992, 15.

23. "A Little Help from a Mentor," *Business Month*, August 1989, 15.

24. S. B. Knouse, "The Mentoring Process for Hispanics," in S. B. Knouse, P. Rosenfield, and A. L. Culbertson, eds., *Hispanics in the Workplace* (Newbury Park, Calif.: Sage Publications, 1992), 137–150.

25. B. R. Ragins and J.L. Cotton, "Easier Said Than Done: Gender Differences in Perceived Barriers to Gaining a Mentor," *Academy of Management Journal* 34 (1991): 939–951.

26. W. Whiteley, T. W. Dougherty, and G. F. Dreher, "Relationship of Career Mentoring and Socioeconomic Origin to Managers' and Professionals' Early Career Progress," *Academy of Management Journal* 34 (1991): 331–351.

27. G. F. Dreher and R. A. Ash, "A Comparative Study of Mentoring among Men and Women in Managerial, Professional, and Technical Positions," *Journal of Applied Psychology* 75 (1990): 539–546.

28. T. A. Scandura, "Mentorship and Career Mobility: An Empirical Investigation," *Journal of Organizational Behavior* 13 (1992): 169–174.

29. D. D. Horgan and R. J. Simeon, "Mentoring and Participation: An Application of the Vroom-Yetton Model," *Journal of Business and Psychology* 5 (1990): 63–84.

30. D. L. Nelson, J. C. Quick, M. A. Hitt, and D. Moesel, "Politics, Lack of Career Progress, and Work/Home Conflict: Stress and Strain for Working Women," *Sex Roles* 23 (1990): 169–185.

31. J. E. Rehfeld, "What Working for a Japanese Company Taught Me," *Harvard Business Review* (November-December 1990): 167–172.

32. D. L. Nelson and M. A. Hitt, "Employed Women and Stress: Implications for Enhancing Women's Mental Health in the Workplace," in J. C. Quick, L. R. Murphy, and J. J. Hurrell, eds., *Stress and Well-being at Work: Assessments and Interventions for Occupational Mental Health* (Washington, D.C.: American Psychological Association, 1992), 164–177.

33. J. W. Anastas, J. L. Gibson, and P. J. Larson, "Working Families and Eldercare: A National Perspective in an Aging America," *Social Work* 35 (1990): 405–411.

34. C. Dusell and M. Roman, "The Eldercare Dilemma," *Generations: The Journal of the Western Gerontological Society* 13 (1989): 30–32.

35. D. T. Hall, "Promoting Work/Family Balance: An Organization-Change Approach," *Organizational Dynamics* (Winter 1990): 5–18.

36. J. Kaplan, "Hitting the Wall at Forty," *Business Month*, September 1990, 52–58.

37. K. E. Kram, "Phases of the Mentoring Relationship," *Academy of Management Review* 26 (1983): 608–625.

38. P. H. Mirvis and D. T. Hall, "Psychological Success and the Boundaryless Career," *Journal of Organizational Behavior* 15 (1994): 365–380.

39. J. W. Gilsdorf, "The New Generation: Older Workers," *Training and Development Journal* (March 1992): 77–79.

40. J. F. Quick, "Time to Move On?" in J. C. Quick, R. E. Hess, J. Hermalin, and J. D. Quick, eds., *Career Stress in Changing Times* (New York: Haworth Press, 1990), 239–250.

41. D. Machan, "Rent-an-Exec," *Forbes*, 22 January 1990, 132–133.

42. E. McGoldrick and C. L. Cooper, "Why Retire Early?" in J. C. Quick, R. E. Hess, J. Hermalin, and J. D. Quick, eds., *Career Stress in Changing Times* (New York: Haworth Press, 1990), 219–238.

43. E. Schein, *Career Anchors* (San Diego: University Associates, 1985).

44. B. O'Reilly, "The Job Drought," *Fortune*, 24 August 1992, 62–74.

CHAPTER 18
MANAGING CHANGE

LEARNING OBJECTIVES

After reading this chapter, you should be able to do the following:

- Identify the major external and internal forces for change in organizations.
- Define the terms *incremental change, strategic change, transformational change,* and *change agent.*
- Describe the major reasons individuals resist change, and discuss methods organizations can use to manage resistance.
- Apply force field analysis to a problem.
- Explain Lewin's organizational change model.
- Describe the use of organizational diagnosis and needs analysis as a first step in organizational development.
- Discuss the major organization development interventions.
- Identify the ethical issues that must be considered in organization development efforts.

■ FORCES FOR CHANGE IN ORGANIZATIONS

Change has become the norm in most organizations. Plant closings, business failures, mergers and acquisitions, and downsizing have become experiences common to American companies. Organizations that will succeed in meeting the competitive challenges will need to manage change proactively. In the past, organizations could succeed by claiming excellence in one area—quality, reliability, or cost, for example—but this is not the case today. The current environment demands excellence in all areas, and organizations like Federal Express are taking steps to achieve this goal.

Modern organizations face limited fiscal resources and often turn to layoffs, wage reductions, and other cost containment measures. These organizations also must deal with ethical, environmental, and other social issues. Competition is becoming fierce, and companies can no longer afford to rest on their laurels. At American Airlines, a series of programs has been developed to ensure that the company constantly reevaluates and changes its operating methods to prevent the company from stagnating. GE holds off-site WorkOut sessions with groups of managers and employees whose goal is to make GE a faster, less complex organization that can respond effectively to change. In the WorkOut sessions, employees recommend specific changes, explain why they are needed, and propose ways the changes can be implemented. Top management must make an immediate response: an approval, a disapproval (with an explanation), or a request for more information. The GE WorkOut sessions eliminate the barriers that keep employees from contributing to change.

There are two basic forms of change in organizations. Planned change is change resulting from a deliberate decision to alter the organization. Companies that wish to move from a traditional hierarchical structure to one that facilitates self-managed teams must use a proactive, carefully orchestrated approach. Not all change is planned, however. Unplanned change is imposed on the organization and is often unforeseen. Changes in government regulations and changes in the economy, for example, are often unplanned. Responsiveness to unplanned change requires tremendous flexibility and adaptability on the part of organizations. Managers must be prepared to handle both planned and unplanned forms of change in organizations.

Forces for change can come from many sources. Some of these are external, arising from outside the company, whereas others are internal, arising from sources within the organization.

■ External Forces

The four major managerial challenges we have described throughout the book are major external forces for change. Globalization, work force diversity, technological change, and managing ethical behavior are challenges that precipitate change in organizations.

Globalization. The power players in the global market are the multinational and transnational organizations. Conoco recently formed a joint venture with Arkhangelskgeologia, a Russian firm, to develop a new oil field in Russia. This partnership, named Polar Lights, is the first of its kind. It will explore a geographic area where there is no existing production, and its investment could total $3 billion.[1] Expanding into ventures such as this one requires extreme adaptability and flexibility on the part of both parties to the agreement.

New opportunities are not limited to the former Soviet Union, however, and the United States is but one nation in the drive to open new markets. Japan and Germany are responding to global competition in powerful ways, and the emergence of the European Community as a powerful trading group will have a profound impact on world markets. By joining with their European neighbors, companies in smaller countries will begin to make major progress in world markets, thus increasing the fierce competition that already exists.

Another example of a company taking giant strides in terms of the global marketplace is IBS. As managing director of IBS (a software and services business based in Sweden), Steffan Edberg has expanded his company by acquiring small, well-positioned firms in several European countries. He uses cross-border contracts and a wealth of experience in the industry to stay on top. The acquired firms retain their own management but draw on the capital and experience of other offices. Edberg maintains a low overhead and considers himself headquartered "wherever I happen to be."[2] IBS is just one of many companies that are beginning to look at the world as their marketplace.

All of these changes, along with others, have led companies to rethink the borders of their markets and to encourage their employees to think globally. Jack Welch of GE has called for a boundaryless company, in which there are no mental distinctions between domestic and foreign operations or between managers and employees.[3] The thought that drives the boundaryless company is that barriers that get in the way of people's working together should be removed. Globalizing an organization means rethinking the most efficient ways to use resources, disseminate and gather information, and develop people. It requires not only structural changes but also changes in the minds of employees.

Work Force Diversity. Related to globalization is the challenge of work force diversity. As we have seen throughout this book, work force diversity is a powerful force for change in organizations.

Managers will encounter an increasingly diverse work force in terms of age, gender, and culture. Managing diversity effectively requires that organizations help employees view differences as valuable assets. Monsanto is a leader in managing diversity. The company uses a formal diversity program that evaluates and pays managers based on how effectively they pay and promote women.

Successfully managing work force diversity means enabling all workers, including physically and mentally disabled employees, to reach their potential. Marriott Corporation considers disabled individuals an untapped gold mine and is proud that its turnover rate among disabled employees is only 8 percent.[4] Part of Marriott's success is due to its practice of pairing new disabled workers with managers who serve as coaches for the newcomers.

Technological Change. Rapid technological innovation is another force for change in organizations, and those who fail to keep pace can quickly fall behind. The technological competition between the United States and Japan is heated. There is a widely held perception that the U.S. is closing the quality gap with Japan. However, Japanese manufacturers are said to have moved beyond quality to flexibility as a new strategy. Manufacturing innovations seem to pass through stages from quality (doing it right) to reliability (always doing it right) to flexibility (adding variety and speed). At Toshiba, in Japan, flexibility means making a greater variety of products with the same equipment and employees. In Toshiba's Ome plant, workers assemble nine different word processors on one line and twenty different laptop computers on another.[5] Flexibility gives organizations a competitive edge through the ability to read the market quickly and respond faster than competitors.

Technological innovations bring about profound change because they are not just changes in the way work is performed. The innovation process brings about associated changes in work relationships and organizational structures.[6] The team approach adopted by many organizations, including Levi Strauss, brings about flatter structures, decentralized decision making, and more open communication between leaders and team members.

Managing Ethical Behavior. Recent ethical scandals have brought ethical behavior in organizations to the forefront of public consciousness. Ethical issues, however, are not always public and monumental. Employees face ethical dilemmas in their daily work lives. The need to manage ethical behavior has brought about several changes in organizations. Most center around the idea that an organization must create a culture that encourages ethical behavior.

One organization that made changes to support ethical behavior is Citicorp. It uses a game called "The Work Ethic" to transmit organizational values. In the game, teams wrestle with ethical dilemmas actually experienced at Citicorp. The teams' choices are scored in terms of their appropriateness. If a team disagrees, it can present its rationale to an appeals board of senior Citicorp managers. The game is a successful training tool because it integrates formal and informal culture in a way that is enjoyable to employees.[7]

Society expects organizations to maintain ethical behavior both internally and in relationships with other organizations. Ethical behavior is expected in relationships with customers, the environment, and society. These expectations may be informal, or they may come in the form of increased legal requirements.

These four challenges are forces that place pressures to change on organizations. Other powerful forces for change originate from within the organization.

■ Internal Forces

Pressures for change that originate inside the organization are generally recognizable in the form of signals indicating that something needs to be altered.

Declining effectiveness is a pressure to change. A company that experiences its third quarterly loss within a fiscal year is undoubtedly motivated to do something about it. Some companies react by instituting layoffs and massive cost-cutting programs, whereas others look at the bigger picture, view the loss as symptomatic of an underlying problem, and seek out the cause of the problem.

A crisis also may stimulate change in an organization. Strikes or walkouts may lead management to change the wage structure. The resignation of a key decision maker is one crisis that causes the company to rethink the composition of its management team and its role in the organization. A much-publicized crisis that led to change with Exxon was the oil spill accident with Exxon's Valdez. The accident brought about many changes in Exxon's environmental policies.

Changes in employee expectations also can trigger change in organizations. A company that hires a group of young newcomers may be met with a set of expectations very different from those expressed by older workers. The work force is more educated than ever before. Although this has its advantages, workers with more education demand more of employers. Today's work force is also concerned with career and family balance issues, such as dependent care. The many sources of work force diversity hold potential for a host of differing expectations among employees.

Changes in the work climate at an organization can also stimulate change. A work force that seems lethargic, unmotivated, and dissatisfied is a symptom that must be addressed. This symptom is common in organizations that have experienced layoffs. Workers who have escaped a layoff may grieve for those who have lost their jobs and may find it hard to continue to be productive. They may fear that they will be laid off as well, and many feel insecure in their jobs.

■ CHANGE IS INEVITABLE

We have seen that organizations face substantial pressures to change from both external and internal sources. Change in organizations is inevitable, but change is a process that can be managed. The scope of change can vary from small to quantum.

■ The Scope of Change

Change can be of a relatively small scope, such as a modification in a work procedure (an incremental change). Such changes, in essence, are a fine-tuning of the organization, or the making of small improvements. Change also can be of a larger scale, such as the restructuring of an organization (a strategic change).[8] In strategic change, the organization moves from an old state to a known new state during a controlled period of time. Strategic change usually involves a series of transition steps.

The most massive scope of change is transformational change, in which the organization moves to a radically different, and sometimes unknown, future state. In transformational change, the organization's mission, culture, goals, structure, and leadership may all change dramatically.[9]

Many organizations undertake transformational change in order to meet the competitive challenge of globalization. In 1982, British Airways faced two extreme external pressures. One pressure was the deregulation of international air traffic, with resulting fare wars among airlines. Another pressure was the British government's decision to take British Airways from government to private ownership. British Airways made radical changes in its structure, systems, culture, and mission in order to survive the competitive challenge.[10]

■ The Change Agent's Role

The individual or group who undertakes the task of introducing and managing a change in an organization is known as a change agent. Change agents can be internal, such as managers or employees who are appointed to oversee the change process. In her book *The Change Masters*, Rosabeth Moss Kanter notes that at companies like Hewlett-Packard and Polaroid, managers and employees alike are developing the needed skills to produce change and innovation in the organization.[11] Change agents can also be external, such as outside consultants.

Internal change agents have certain advantages in managing the change process. They know the organization's past history, its political system, and its culture. Because they must live with the results of their change efforts, internal change agents are likely to be very careful about managing change. There are disadvantages, however, to using internal change agents. They may be associated with certain factions within the organization and may easily be accused of favoritism. Furthermore, internal change agents may be too close to the situation to have an objective view of what needs to be done.

External change agents bring an outsider's objective view to the organization. They may be preferred by employees because of their impartiality. External change agents face certain problems, including their limited knowledge of the organization's history. In addition, they may be viewed with suspicion by organization members. External change agents have more power in directing changes if employees perceive the change agents as being trustworthy, possessing important expertise, having a track record that establishes credibility, and being similar to the employees themselves.[12]

THE PROCESS OF CHANGE IN ORGANIZATIONS

Once an organization has made the decision to change, careful planning and analysis must take place. Part of the planning involves the recognition that individuals, when faced with change, often resist. Some individuals are more open to change, in general, than others.

The challenge of managing the change process involves harnessing the energy of diverse individuals who hold a variety of views of change. It is important to recognize that most changes will be met with varying degrees of resistance and to understand the basis of resistance to change.

Resistance to Change

People often resist change in a rational response based on self-interest. However, there are countless other reasons people resist change. Many of these center around the notion of reactance—that is, a negative reaction that occurs when individuals feel that their personal freedom is threatened.[13] Some of the major reasons for resisting change follow.

Fear of the Unknown.   Change often brings with it substantial uncertainty. Employees facing a technological change, such as the introduction of a new computer system, may resist the change simply because it introduces ambiguity into what was once a comfortable situation for them. This is especially a problem when there has been a lack of communication about the change.

Fear of Loss.   When a change is impending, some employees may fear losing their jobs, particularly when an advanced technology like robotics is introduced. Employees also may fear losing their status because of a change. Computer systems experts, for example, may feel threatened when they feel their expertise is eroded by the installation of a more user-friendly networked information system. Another common fear is that changes may diminish the positive qualities the individual enjoys in the job. Computerizing the customer service positions at Southwestern Bell, for example, threatened the autonomy that representatives previously enjoyed.

Fear of Failure.   Some employees fear changes because they fear their own failure. Introducing computers into the workplace often arouses individuals' self-doubts about their ability to interact with the computer.[14] Resistance can also stem from a fear that the change itself will not really take place. In one large library that was undergoing a major automation effort, employees had their doubts as to whether the vendor could really deliver the state-of-the-art system that was promised. In this case, the implementation never became a reality—the employees' fears were well founded.[15]

Disruption of Interpersonal Relationships.   Employees may resist change that threatens to limit meaningful interpersonal relationships on the job. Librarians facing the automation effort described previously feared that once the computerized system was implemented, they would not be able to interact as they did when they had to go to another floor of the library to get help finding a resource. In the new system, with the touch of a few buttons on the computer, they would get their information without consulting another librarian.

Personality Conflicts.   Sometimes there are personality conflicts between change agents and employees. A change agent who appears insensitive to employee concerns and feelings may meet considerable resistance, because employees perceive that their needs are not being taken into account.

Politics.   Organizational change may also shift the existing balance of power in the organization. Individuals or groups who hold power under the current arrangement may be threatened with losing these political advantages in the advent of change.

Cultural Assumptions and Values.   Sometimes cultural assumptions and values can be impediments to change, particularly if the assumptions underlying the change are alien to employees. This form of resistance can be very difficult to overcome, because some cultural assumptions are unconscious. As we discussed in Chapter 2, some cultures tend to avoid uncertainty. In Mexican and Greek cultures, for example, change that creates a great deal of uncertainty may be met with great resistance.

We have described several sources of resistance to change. The reasons for resistance are as diverse as the work force itself and vary with individuals and organizations. The challenge for managers is introducing change in a positive manner and managing employee resistance.

■ MANAGING RESISTANCE TO CHANGE

The traditional view of resistance to change treated it as something to be overcome, and many organizational attempts to reduce the resistance have only served to intensify it. The contemporary view holds that resistance is simply a form of feedback and that this feedback can be used very productively to manage the change process. One key to managing resistance is to plan for it and to be ready with a variety of strategies for using the resistance as feedback and helping employees negotiate the transition. Three key strategies for managing resistance to change are communication; participation; and empathy and support.[16]

Communication about impending change is essential if employees are to adjust effectively. The details of the change should be provided, but equally important is the rationale behind the change. Employees want to know why change is needed. If there is no good reason for it, why should they favor the change? Providing accurate and timely information about the change can help prevent unfounded fears and potentially damaging rumors from developing. It is also beneficial to inform people at all levels about the potential consequences of the change. When employees fail to comprehend a change, they are likely to react with anxiety or apathy. If, on the other hand, employees can integrate the change with their mental images of the organization, they are more likely to support it.[17]

There is substantial research support underscoring the importance of participation in the change process. In a classic study, workers in a garment factory were introduced to change in three different ways. One group was simply told about the new procedure, one group was introduced to the change by a trained worker, and one was allowed to help plan the implementation of the new production. The results were dramatic. The third group, those who participated in the change, adopted the new method more quickly, was more productive, and experienced no turnover.[18] Participation helps employees become involved in the change and establish a feeling of ownership in the process. When employees are allowed to participate, they are more committed to the change.

Flight Time Corporation, a company that arranges passenger charter air transportation, successfully implemented changes in its operations by using a participative approach. After experiencing steady growth for five years, the company was faced with the economic recession and related severe decline in leisure travel. In addition, the Persian Gulf crisis virtually stopped international travel. Flight Time responded to this crisis by gathering all its employees together to brainstorm about ways to save money and secure new business. The employees discussed various options and agreed to postpone vacations, take a 20 percent reduction in pay, and work longer hours. The company set up a nursery for employees' children to compensate for the loss of earnings, and weekly goals were set by managers and employees together. Flight Time made the best of a bad situation. The company asked employees to participate in the plans for change and used the employees' ideas. This helped everyone accept the temporary changes that were necessary. Today, Flight Time's cash flow has significantly improved, and sales have grown over 80 percent in the past three years. Full pay has been restored to all employees, and a sizable contribution was made to the profit-sharing plan. Change efforts can be implemented successfully if care is taken to initiate them properly.[19]

Another strategy for managing resistance is providing empathy and support to employees who have trouble dealing with the change. Active listening, as was discussed in Chapter 8, is an excellent tool for identifying the reasons behind resistance and for uncovering fears. An expression of concerns about the change can provide important feedback that managers can use to improve the change process. Emotional support and encouragement can help an employee deal with the anxiety that is a natural response to change. Employees who experience severe reactions to change can benefit from talking with a counselor. Some companies provide counseling through their employee assistance plans.

Open communication, participation, and emotional support can go a long way toward managing resistance to change. Managers must realize that some resistance is inevitable, however, and should plan ways to deal with resistance early in the change process.

■ Behavioral Reactions to Change

In spite of attempts to minimize the resistance to change in an organization, some reactions to change are inevitable. Negative reactions may be manifested in overt behavior, or change may be resisted more passively. People show four basic, identifiable reactions to change: disengagement, disidentification, disenchantment, and disorientation.[20-22] Managers can use interventions to deal with these reactions, as shown in Table 18.1.

Disengagement is psychological withdrawal from change. The employee may appear to lose initiative and interest in the job. Employees who disengage may fear the change but take on the approach of doing nothing and simply hoping for the best. Disengaged employees are physically present but mentally absent. They lack drive and commitment, and they simply comply without real psychological investment in their work. Disengagement can be recognized by behaviors such as being hard to find or

■ **TABLE 18.1**

Reactions to Change and Managerial Interventions

REACTION	EXPRESSION	MANAGERIAL INTERVENTION
Disengagement	Withdrawal	Confront, identify
Disidentification	Sadness, worry	Explore, transfer
Disenchantment	Anger	Neutralize, acknowledge
Disorientation	Confusion	Explain, plan

SOURCE: Adapted from H. Woodward and S. Buchholz, *Aftershock: Helping People through Corporate Change*, p. 15. Copyright ©1987 John Wiley & Sons, Inc. Reprinted by permission of John Wiley & Sons, Inc.

doing only the basics to get the job done. Typical disengagement statements include "No problem," or "This won't affect me."

The basic managerial strategy for dealing with disengaged individuals is to confront them with their reaction and draw them out so that they can identify the concerns that need to be addressed. Disengaged employees may not be aware of the change in their behavior, and they need to be assured of your intentions. Drawing them out and helping them air their feelings can lead to productive discussions. Disengaged people seldom become cheerleaders for the change, but they can be brought closer to accepting and working with a change by open communication with an empathetic manager who is willing to listen.

Another reaction to change is disidentification. Individuals reacting in this way feel that their identity has been threatened by the change, and they feel very vulnerable. Many times they cling to a past procedure because they had a sense of mastery over it, and it gave them a sense of security. "My job is completely changed," and "I used to . . ." are verbal indications of disidentification. Disidentified employees often display sadness and worry. They may appear to be sulking and dwelling in the past by reminiscing about the old ways of doing things.

Because disidentified employees are so vulnerable, they often feel like victims in the change process. Managers can help them through the transition by encouraging them to explore their feelings and helping them transfer their positive feelings into the new situation. One way to do this is to help them identify what it is they liked in the old situation, as well as to show them how it is possible to have the same positive experience in the new situation. Disidentified employees need to see that work itself and emotion are separable—that is, that they can let go of old ways and experience positive reactions to new ways of performing their jobs.

Disenchantment is also a common reaction to change. It is usually expressed as negativity or anger. Disenchanted employees realize that the past is gone, and they are mad about it. They may try to enlist the support of other employees by forming coalitions. Destructive behaviors like sabotage and backstabbing may result. Typical verbal signs of disenchantment are, "This will never work," and "I'm getting out of this company as soon as I can." The anger of a disenchanted person may be directly expressed in organizational cultures where it is permissible to do so. This behavior tends to get the issues out in the open. More often, however, cultures view the expression of emotion at work as improper and unbusinesslike. In these cultures, the anger is suppressed and emerges in more passive-aggressive ways, such as badmouthing and starting rumors. One of the particular dangers of disenchantment is that it is quite contagious in the workplace.

It is often difficult to reason with disenchanted employees. Thus, the first step in managing this reaction is to bring these employees from their highly negative, emotionally charged state to a more neutral state. To neutralize the reaction does not mean to dismiss it; rather, it means to allow the individuals to let off the necessary steam so that they can come to terms with their anger. The second part of the strategy for dealing with disenchanted employees is to acknowledge that their anger is normal and that you do not hold it against them. Sometimes disenchantment is a mask for one of the other three reactions, and it must be worked through to get to the core of the employee's reaction.

A final reaction to change is disorientation. Disoriented employees are lost and confused, and often they are unsure of their feelings. They waste energy trying to figure out what to do instead of how to do things. Disoriented individuals ask a lot of questions and become very detail-oriented. They

may appear to need a good deal of guidance and may leave their work undone until all of their questions have been answered. "Analysis paralysis" is characteristic of disoriented employees. They feel that they have lost touch with the priorities of the company, and they may want to analyze the change to death before acting on it. Disoriented employees may ask questions like, "Now what do I do?" or "What do I do first?"

Disorientation is a common reaction among people who are used to clear goals and unambiguous directions. When change is introduced, it creates uncertainty and a lack of clarity. The managerial strategy for dealing with this reaction is to explain the change in a way that minimizes the ambiguity that is present. The information about the change needs to be put into a framework or an overall vision so that the disoriented individual can see where he or she fits into the grand scheme of things. Once the disoriented employee sees the broader context of the change, you can plan a series of steps to help this employee adjust. The employee needs a sense of priorities to work on.

Managers need to be able to diagnose these four reactions to change. Because each reaction brings with it significant and different concerns, no single universal strategy can help all employees adjust. By recognizing each reaction and applying the appropriate strategy, it is possible to help even strong resisters work through a transition successfully.

■ LEWIN'S CHANGE MODEL

Kurt Lewin developed a model of the change process that has stood the test of time and continues to influence the way organizations manage planned change. Lewin's model is based on the idea of force field analysis.[23] Figure 18.1 shows a force field analysis of a decision to engage in exercise behavior.

This model contends that a person's behavior is the product of two opposing forces; one force pushes toward preserving the status quo, and another force pushes for change. When the two opposing forces are approximately equal, current behavior is maintained. For behavioral change to occur, the forces maintaining the status quo must be overcome. This can be accomplished by increasing the forces

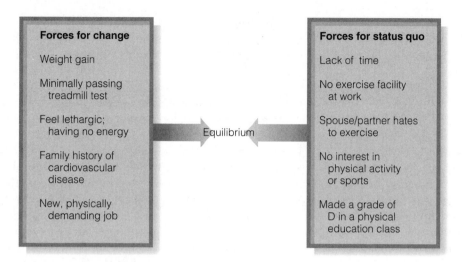

Force Field Analysis of a Decision to Engage in Exercise

for change, by weakening the forces for the status quo, or by a combination of these actions.

Lewin's change model is a three–step process, as shown in Figure 18.2. The process begins with unfreezing, which is a crucial first hurdle in the change process. Unfreezing involves encouraging individuals to discard old behaviors by shaking up the equilibrium state that maintains the status quo. Organizations often accomplish unfreezing by eliminating the rewards for current behavior and showing that current behavior is not valued. Unfreezing on the part of individuals is an acceptance that change needs to occur. In essence, individuals surrender by allowing the boundaries of their status quo to be opened in preparation for change.

The second step in the change process is moving. In the moving stage, new attitudes, values, and behaviors are substituted for old ones. Organizations accomplish moving by initiating new options and explaining the rationale for the change, as well as by providing training to help employees develop the new skills they need. Employees should be presented the overall plan for the change so that they can establish their roles within the new organizational structure and processes.[24]

Refreezing is the final step in the change process. In this step, new attitudes, values, and behaviors are established as the new status quo. The new ways of operating are cemented in and reinforced. Managers should ensure that the organizational culture and formal reward systems encourage the new behaviors and avoid rewarding the old ways of operating. Changes in the reward structure may be needed to ensure that the organization is not rewarding the old behaviors.

Monsanto's approach to increasing opportunities for women within the company is an illustration using the Lewin model effectively. First, Monsanto emphasized unfreezing by helping employees debunk negative stereotypes about women in business. This also helped overcome resistance to change. Second, Monsanto moved employees' attitudes and behaviors by diversity training in which differences were emphasized as positive, and supervisors learned ways of training and developing female employees. Third, Monsanto changed its reward system so that managers were evaluated and paid according to how they coached and promoted women, which helped refreeze the new attitudes and behaviors.[25]

Unfreezing	Moving	Refreezing
Reducing forces for status quo	Developing new attitudes, values, and behaviors	Reinforcing new attitudes, values, and behaviors

■ **FIGURE 18.2**
Lewin's Change Model

Lewin's model proposes that for change efforts to be successful, the three–stage process must be completed. Failures in efforts to change can be traced back to one of the three stages. Successful change thus requires that old behaviors be discarded, new behaviors be introduced, and these new behaviors be institutionalized and rewarded. This is a learning process, and the learning theories discussed in Chapter 6 certainly apply. Skinner's work helps us understand how to encourage new behaviors and extinguish old ones by using reinforcers. Bandura's social learning theory points out the importance of modeling. Managers should model appropriate behavior, because employees look to them and pattern their own behavior after the managers' behavior.

Organizations that wish to change can select from a variety of methods to make a change become reality. Organization development consists of various programs for making organizations more effective.

ORGANIZATION DEVELOPMENT INTERVENTIONS

Organization development (OD) is a systematic approach to organizational improvement that applies behavioral science theory and research in order to increase individual and organizational well-being and effectiveness.[26] This definition implies certain characteristics. First, OD is a systematic approach to planned change. It is a structured cycle of diagnosing organizational problems and opportunities and then applying expertise to them. Second, OD is grounded in solid research and theory. It involves the application of our knowledge of behavioral science to the challenges that organizations face. Third,

OD recognizes the reciprocal relationship between individuals and organizations. It acknowledges that for organizations to change, individuals must change. Finally, OD is goal-oriented. It is a process that seeks to improve both individual and organizational well-being and effectiveness.

Organization development has a rich history. Some of the early work in OD was conducted by Kurt Lewin and his associates during the 1940s. This work was continued by Rensis Likert, who pioneered the use of attitude surveys in OD. During the 1950s, Eric Trist and his colleagues at the Tavistock Institute in London focused on the technical and social aspects of organizations and how they affect the quality of work life. These programs on the quality of work life migrated to the U.S. during the 1960s. During this time, a 200-member OD network was established, and it has grown to over 2,000 members today. As the number of practitioners has increased, so has the number of different OD methods. Organization development is being used internationally. OD has been applied in Canada, Sweden, Norway, Germany, Japan, Australia, Israel, and Mexico, among others. Some OD methods are difficult to implement in other cultures. As OD becomes more internationally widespread, we will increase our knowledge of how culture affects the success of different OD approaches.

Prior to deciding on a method of intervention, managers must carefully diagnose the problem they are attempting to address. Diagnosis and needs analysis is a critical first step in any OD intervention. Following this, an intervention method is chosen and applied. Finally, a thorough follow-up of the OD process is conducted. Figure 18.3 presents the OD cycle, a continuous process of moving the organization and its employees toward effective functioning.

■ **FIGURE 18.3**
The Organization
Development Cycle

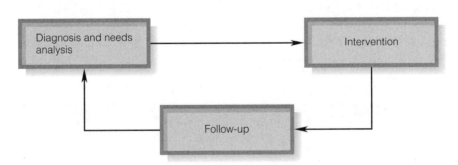

■ Diagnosis and Needs Analysis

Before any intervention is planned, a thorough organizational diagnosis should be conducted. Diagnosis is an essential first step for any organization development intervention.[27] The term diagnosis comes from dia (through) and gnosis (knowledge of). Thus, the diagnosis should pinpoint specific problems and areas in need of improvement. Problems can arise in any part of the organization.

Harry Levinson's diagnostic approach asserts that the process should begin by identifying where the pain (the problem) in the organization is, what it is like, how long it has been happening, and what has already been done about it.[28] Then a four-part, comprehensive diagnosis can begin. The first part of the diagnosis is an understanding of the organization's history. The second part is an analysis of the organization as a whole to obtain data about the structure and processes of the organization. The third part is the gathering of interpretive data about attitudes, relationships, and current organizational functioning. The fourth part of the diagnosis is an analysis of the data and conclusions. The data in each stage of the diagnosis can be gathered using a variety of methods, including observation, interviews, questionnaires, and archival records.

The diagnostic process may yield the conclusion that change is necessary. As part of the diagnosis, it is important to address the following issues:

- What are the forces for change?
- What are the forces preserving the status quo?
- What are the most likely sources of resistance to change?
- What are the goals to be accomplished by the change?

This information constitutes a force field analysis, as discussed earlier in the chapter.

A needs analysis is another crucial step in managing change. This is an analysis of the skills and competencies that employees must have to achieve the goals of the change. A needs analysis is essential because interventions such as training programs must target these skills and competencies.

Hundreds of alternative OD intervention methods exist. One way of classifying these methods is by the target of change. This may be the organization, groups within the organization, or individuals.

■ Organization-and Group-Focused Techniques

Some OD intervention methods emphasize changing the organization itself or changing the work groups within the organization. Intervention methods in this category are survey feedback, management by objectives, product and service quality programs, team building, and process consultation.

Survey Feedback. A widely used intervention method whereby employee attitudes are solicited using a questionnaire is known as survey feedback. Once the data are collected, they are analyzed and fed back to the employees to diagnose problems and plan other interventions. Survey feedback is often used as an exploratory tool and then is combined with some other intervention. The effectiveness of survey feedback in actually improving outcomes (absenteeism or productivity, for example) increases substantially when this method is combined with other interventions.[29]

Some surveys are developed by managers within the organization and tailored to a specific problem or issue. Well-established and widely used surveys also are available for use. Two such surveys are the Survey of Organizations and the Michigan Organizational Assessment Questionnaire, both of which were developed at the University of Michigan's Institute for Social Research.[30] A large body of research indicates that these surveys have good reliability and validity, and they are useful tools for gathering employees' perceptions of their work environments.

For survey feedback to be an effective method, certain guidelines should be used. Employees must be assured that their responses to the questionnaire will be confidential and anonymous. Unless this assurance is given, the responses may not be honest. Feedback should be reported in a group format; that is, no individual responses should be identified. Employees must be able to trust that there will be no negative repercussions from their responses. Employees should be informed of the purpose of the survey. Failing to do this can set up unrealistic expectations about the changes that might come from the surveys.

In addition, management must be prepared to follow up on the survey results. If some things cannot be changed, the rationale (for example, prohibitive cost) must be explained to the employees. Without appropriate follow-through, employees will not take the survey process seriously the next time.

Management by Objectives. As an organization-wide technique, management by objectives (MBO) involves joint goal setting between employees and managers. The MBO process includes the setting of initial objectives, periodic progress reviews, and problem solving to remove any obstacles to goal achievement.[31] All these steps are joint efforts between managers and employees.

MBO is a valuable intervention because it meets three needs. First, it clarifies what is expected of employees. This reduces role conflict and ambiguity. Second, MBO provides knowledge of results, an essential ingredient in effective job performance. Finally, MBO provides an opportunity for coaching and counseling by the manager. The problem-solving approach encourages open communication and discussion of obstacles to goal achievement.

Companies that have used MBO successfully include Tenneco, Mobil Oil, and General Electric. The success of MBO in effecting organizational results hinges on the linking of individual goals to the goals of the organization. There is a caution to be exercised in using MBO programs. An excessive emphasis on goal achievement can result in cut-throat competition among employees, falsification of results, and striving for results at any cost. In addition, top management support is essential if the program aspires to be more than just an exercise in red tape.

Product and Service Quality Programs. Quality programs—programs that embed product and service quality excellence into the organized culture—are assuming key roles in the organization development efforts of many companies. For example, the success or failure of a service company may depend on the quality of customer service it provides.[32] The quality revolution consists of programs that entail two steps. The first step is to raise aspirations about the product and service quality, both within the company and among its customers. If the organization is to improve, employees must be committed to product and service quality excellence, and customers must expect it. The second step is to embed

product and service quality excellence in the organizational culture, using continual improvement tools such as benchmarking to change habits, attitudes, skills, and knowledge. Benchmarking is comparing products and processes with those of other companies in order to imitate and improve on them. Xerox uses benchmarking to improve the product quality of its copiers. Service quality improvement programs can lead to competitive advantage, increased productivity, enhanced employee morale, and word-of-mouth advertising from satisfied customers. One company known for service quality is Gateway 2000, a mail-order computer business based in North Sioux City, South Dakota. The company provides toll-free technical support for the life of the customer's Gateway computer system, and it is reputed to have the best-qualified technical support staff in the industry.

The Ritz-Carlton ® Hotel Company integrates its comprehensive service quality program into marketing and business objectives. The Atlanta-based company manages twenty-eight luxury hotels and won the 1992 Malcolm Baldrige Award for service quality. Key elements of Ritz-Carlton's quality program include participatory executive leadership, thorough information gathering, coordinated execution, and employees who are empowered to "move heaven and earth" to satisfy customers.[33]

At Ritz-Carlton, the company president and thirteen senior executives make up the senior quality management team, which meets weekly to focus on service quality. Quality goals are established at all levels of the company. The crucial product and service requirements of travel consumers are translated into Ritz-Carlton Gold Standards, which include a credo, a motto, three steps of service, and twenty Ritz-Carlton Basics. These standards guide service quality throughout the organization.

Employees are required to act on a customer complaint at once and are empowered to provide "instant pacification," no matter what it takes. Quality teams set action plans at all levels of the company. Each hotel has a quality leader, who serves as a resource to the quality teams. Daily quality production reports provide an early warning system for identifying areas that need quality improvement.

The Ritz-Carlton program has all of the hallmarks of an excellent service quality program: committed leadership, empowered teams and employees, carefully researched standards and goals, and constant monitoring. The company has reaped rewards from its excellent service; it received 121 quality-related awards in 1991, along with best-in-industry rankings from all three major hotel-dranking organizations.

Team Building.   As an organization development intervention, team building can improve the effectiveness of work groups. Team building usually begins with a diagnostic process through which team members identify problems, and it continues with the team's planning actions to take in order to resolve those problems. The OD practitioner in team building serves as a facilitator, and the work itself is completed by team members.[34]

Team building is a very popular OD method. A recent survey of Fortune 500 companies indicated that human resource managers considered team building the most successful OD technique.[35] Four areas in team building are critical to the success of the intervention:

1. Team building should develop communication that facilitates respect for other members' input and the desire to work for the good of the team.
2. Team building should encourage member interaction and mutual interdependence.
3. Team building should emphasize team goals. Team members should learn one another's responsibilities so that the team can deal adaptively with crisis situations.
4. Team building must provide examples of effective and ineffective teamwork, and it should stress flexibility.[36]

One popular technique for team building is the use of outdoor challenges. Participants go through a series of outdoor activities, such as climbing a 14-foot wall. Similar physical challenges require the participants to work as a team and focus on trust, communication, decision making, and leadership. GE and Weyerhaeuser use outdoor challenges at the beginning of their team-building courses, and later in the training, team members apply what they have learned to actual business situations.[37]

Process Consultation.   Pioneered by Edgar Schein, process consultation is an OD method that helps managers and employees improve the processes that are used in organizations.[38] The processes most often targeted are communication, conflict resolution, decision making, group interaction, and leadership.

One of the distinguishing features of the process consultation approach is that an outside consultant is used. The role of the consultant is to help employees help themselves. The consultant guides the organization members in examining the processes in the organization and in refining them. The steps in process consultation are entering the organization, defining the relationship, choosing an approach, gathering data and diagnosing problems, intervening, and gradually leaving the organization. Process consultation is an interactive technique between employees and an outside consultant, so it is seldom used as a sole OD method. Most often, it is used in combination with other OD interventions.

All the preceding OD methods focus on changing the organization or the work group. Other OD methods are aimed at facilitating change within individuals.

■ Individual-Focused Techniques

Organization development efforts that are targeted toward individuals include skills training, sensitivity training, management development training, role negotiation, job redesign, stress management programs, and career planning.

Skills Training.   The key question addressed by skills training is, "What knowledge, skills, and abilities are necessary to do this job effectively?" Skills training is accomplished either in formal classroom settings or on the job. The challenge of integrating skills training into organization development is the rapid change that most organizations face. The job knowledge in most positions requires continual updates to keep pace with rapid change.

Sensitivity Training.   Also called T-group training, sensitivity training is designed to help individuals understand how their behavior affects others. In a typical session, groups of ten to twelve strangers

(T-groups) are formed. Participants from the same organization are placed in different T-groups. The trainer serves as a resource person but does not engage in structuring behaviors. The members are left on their own to work out the interaction in the group, and they are encouraged to concentrate on the "here and now" of the experience and on openness with other group members. It is important that the trainer be well qualified to monitor the group's progress. The trainer intervenes only to help move the group forward.[39]

The outcome of sensitivity training should be an increased sensitivity to others, and in some cases this has been demonstrated. In other cases, however, the new and better ways of dealing with others did not persist on the job. When people returned to their jobs, which rewarded the old behaviors, the new behavior patterns were quickly extinguished. There are also side effects from T-groups. Because they result in emotional exposure, some participants feel vulnerable and react negatively to the extreme personal nature of the interactions.

Sensitivity training is less popular today than it was in the early 1980s. It can still be used, however, to help managers deal with current challenges like cultural, gender, age, and ability diversity. T-groups can help employees understand others better, become aware of their own feelings and perceptions, and improve communication.

Management Development Training.   Management development encompasses a host of techniques designed to enhance a manager's skills on the job. Management development training generally focuses on four types of learning: verbal information, intellectual skills, attitudes, and development.

Development as a manager requires an integration of classroom learning with on-the-job experiences. One way of accomplishing development is through the use of action learning, a technique that was pioneered in Europe.[40] In action learning, managers take on unfamiliar problems or familiar problems in unfamiliar settings. The managers work on the problems and meet weekly in small groups made up of individuals from different organizations. The outcome of action learning is that managers learn about themselves through the challenges of their comrades. Other techniques that provide active learning

for participants are simulation, business games, role-playing, and case studies.

Management development can be conducted in a formal classroom setting or consist of on-the-job training. McDonald's managers attend Hamburger University and receive training similar to a crash MBA program. Once the butt of jokes, Hamburger U. is visited by execs from other companies who want to adopt their management development model. McDonald's managers from 72 countries are trained in TQM, which is simultaneously translated into 20 languages.[41]

Role Negotiation.   Individuals who work together sometimes have differing expectations of one another within the working relationship. Role negotiation is a simple technique whereby individuals meet and clarify their psychological contract. In doing this, the expectations of each party are clarified and negotiated. The outcome of role negotiation is a better understanding between the two parties of what each can be expected to give and receive in the reciprocal relationship. When both parties have a mutual agreement on expectations, there is less ambiguity in the process of working together.

Job Redesign.   As an OD intervention method, job redesign emphasizes the fit between individual skills and the demands of the job. Chapter 14 outlined several approaches to job design. Many of these methods are used as OD techniques for realigning task demands and individual capabilities, or for redesigning jobs to fit new techniques or organization structures better.

One company that has undergone tremendous change is Harley-Davidson. The motorcycle manufacturer was close to financial disaster when it engaged in a radical restructuring effort. The company essentially threw out the old hierarchies and traditional jobs, opted for a leaner organization, and redesigned jobs to allow employees more participation and control. The company credits its renewed success, in part, to its redesign efforts.[42]

Steelcase, the world's leading designer and manufacturer of office furniture, used job redesign as a key component of its comprehensive change from a traditional manufacturing system to a "factory within a factory" design. In the old system, jobs were designed around the principle of task simplicity and specialization. In the new design, operations are arranged by products, with each factory run by a self-managed team. Employees' jobs are now flexible, team oriented, and characterized by high levels of empowerment.

Health Promotion Programs. As organizations have become increasingly concerned with the costs of distress in the workplace, health promotion programs have become a part of larger organization development efforts. In Chapter 7, we examined stress and strain at work. Companies that have successfully integrated health promotion programs into their organizations include AT&T, Caterpillar Tractor, Kimberly-Clark, and Johnson & Johnson.

The components of health promotion and stress management programs vary widely. They can include education about stress and coping, diagnosis of the causes of stress, relaxation training, company-provided exercise programs, and employee assistance programs. These efforts all focus on helping employees manage stress before it becomes a problem.

Career Planning. Matching an individual's career aspirations with the opportunities in the organization is career planning. This proactive approach to career management is often part of an organization's development efforts. Career planning is a joint responsibility of organizations and individuals. Companies like IBM, Travelers Insurance, and 3M have implemented career planning programs.

Career planning activities benefit the organization, as well as its individuals. Through counseling sessions, employees identify their skills and skill deficiencies. The organization then can plan its training and development efforts based on this information. In addition, the process can be used to identify and nurture talented employees for potential promotion.

Managers can choose from a host of organization development techniques to facilitate organizational change. Some of these techniques are aimed toward organizations or groups, and others focus on individuals. Large-scale changes in organizations require the use of multiple techniques. For example, implementing a new technology like robotics may require simultaneous changes in the structure of the

organization, the configuration of work groups, and individual attitudes.

We should recognize at this point that the organization development methods just described are means to an end. Programs do not drive change; business needs do. The OD methods are merely vehicles for moving the organization and its employees in a more effective direction.

ETHICAL CONSIDERATIONS IN ORGANIZATION DEVELOPMENT

Organization development is a process of helping organizations improve. It may involve sensitive issues. Further, the change agent, whether a manager from within the organization or a consultant from outside, is in a position of directing the change. Such a position carries the potential for misuse of power. The ethical concerns surrounding the use of organization development center around four issues.[43]

The first issue is the selection of the OD method to be used. Every change agent has inherent biases about particular methods, but these biases must not enter into the decision process. The OD method used must be carefully chosen in accordance with the problem as diagnosed, the organization's culture, and the employees concerned. All alternatives should be given fair consideration in the choice of a method. In addition, the OD practitioner should never use a method he or she is not skilled in delivering. Using a method you are not an expert in is unethical, because the client assumes you are.

The second ethical issue is voluntary participation. No employee should be forced to participate in any OD intervention.[44] To make an informed decision about participation, employees should be given information about the nature of the intervention and what will be expected of them. They should also be afforded the option to discontinue their participation at any time they so choose.

The third issue of ethical concern is confidentiality. Change agents gather a wealth of information during organizational diagnoses and interventions. Successful change agents develop a trusting relationship with employees. They may receive privileged information, sometimes unknowingly. It is unethical for a change agent to reveal information in order to give some group or individual political advantage or to enhance the change agent's own standing. Consultants should not reveal information about an organization to its competitors. The use of information gathered from OD efforts is a sensitive issue and presents ethical dilemmas.

A final ethical concern in OD is the potential for manipulation by the change agent. Because any change process involves influence, some individuals may feel manipulated. The key to alleviating the potential for manipulation is open communication. Participants should be given complete knowledge of the rationale for change, what they can expect of the change process, and what the intervention will entail.

■ ARE ORGANIZATION DEVELOPMENT EFFORTS EFFECTIVE?

Because organization development is designed to help organizations manage change, it is important to evaluate the effectiveness of these efforts. The success of any OD intervention depends on a host of factors, including the technique used, the competence of the change agent, the organization's readiness for change, and top management commitment. No single method of OD is effective in every instance. Instead, multiple-method OD approaches are recommended, because they allow organizations to capitalize on the benefits of several approaches.

Recent efforts to evaluate OD efforts have focused on outcomes such as productivity. One review of over 200 interventions indicated that worker productivity improved in 87 percent of the cases. Ninety-eight of these interventions revealed impressive productivity increases.[45] We can conclude that when properly applied and managed, organization development programs have positive effects on performance.

■ MANAGERIAL IMPLICATIONS: MANAGING CHANGE

Several guidelines can be used to facilitate the success of management change efforts.[46] First, managers should recognize the forces for change. These forces can come from a combination of sources both internal and external to the organization.

A shared vision of the change should be developed that includes participation by all employees in the planning process. Top management must be committed to the change and should visibly demonstrate support, because employees look to these leaders to model appropriate behavior. A comprehensive diagnosis and needs analysis should be conducted. The company then must ensure that there are adequate resources for carrying out the change. Resistance to change should be planned for and managed. Communication, participation, and empathetic support are ways of helping employees adjust. The reward system within the organization must be carefully evaluated to ensure that new behaviors, rather than old ones, are being reinforced. Participation in the change process should also be recognized and rewarded.

The organization development technique used should be carefully selected to meet the goals of the change. Finally, organization development efforts should be managed in an ethical manner and should preserve employees' privacy and freedom of choice. By using these guidelines, managers can meet the challenges of managing change while enhancing productivity in their organizations.

■ CHAPTER SUMMARY

- Organizations face many pressures to change. Some forces are external, including globalization, work force diversity, technological innovation, and ethics. Other forces are internal, such as declining effectiveness, crises, changing employee expectations, and changing work climate.
- Organizations face both planned and unplanned change. Change can be of an incremental, strategic, or transformational nature. The individual who directs the change, known as a change agent, can be internal or external to the organization.
- Individuals resist change for many reasons, and many of these reasons are rooted in fear. Organizations can help manage resistance by educating workers and openly communicating the change, encouraging worker participation in the change

efforts, and providing empathy and support to those who have difficulty dealing with change.

- Reactions to change may be manifested in behaviors reflecting disengagement, disidentification, disenchantment, and disorientation. Managers can use separate interventions targeted toward each reaction.

- Force field analysis states that when the forces for change are balanced by the forces restraining change, an equilibrium state exists. For change to occur, the forces for change must increase, or the restraining forces must decrease.

- Lewin's change model proposes three stages of change: unfreezing, moving, and refreezing.

- A thorough diagnosis and needs analysis is a critical first step in any organization development (OD) intervention.

- OD interventions targeted toward organizations and groups include survey feedback, management by objectives, product and service quality programs, team building, and process consultation.

- OD interventions that focus on individuals include skills training, sensitivity training, management development training, role negotiation, job redesign, stress management programs, and career planning.

- OD efforts should be managed ethically and should preserve individual freedom of choice and privacy.

- When properly conducted, organization development can have positive effects on performance.

■ REVIEW QUESTIONS

1. What are the major external and internal forces for change in organizations?
2. Contrast incremental, strategic, and transformational change.
3. What is a change agent? Who plays this role?
4. What are the major reasons individuals resist change? How can organizations deal with resistance?
5. Name the four behavioral reactions to change. Describe the behavioral signs of each reaction and an organizational strategy for dealing with each reaction.

6. Describe force field analysis and its relationship to Lewin's change model.
7. What is organization development? Why is it undertaken by organizations?
8. Name six areas to be critically examined in any comprehensive organizational diagnosis.
9. What are the major organization-focused and group-focused OD intervention methods? The major individual-focused methods?
10. What constitutes abuse of a change agent's power? How can organizations prevent this?
11. Is it ethical to coerce individuals in organizations to change?

■ REFERENCES

1. "Conoco Plans to Develop Oil Fields in Russia: Cost of Up to $3 Billion," *Journal Record* 19 (June 1992): 16.
2. J. A. Belasco, *Teaching the Elephant to Dance* (New York: Crown, 1990).
3. L. Hirschhorn and T. Gilmore, "The New Boundaries of the 'Boundaryless' Company," *Harvard Business Review* (May-June 1992): 104–115.
4. N. J. Perry, "The Workers of the Future," *Fortune* 123 (Spring/Summer 1991): 68–72.
5. T. A. Stewart, "Brace for Japan's Hot New Strategy," *Fortune,* 21 September 1992, 63–74.
6. R. M. Kanter, "Improving the Development, Acceptance, and Use of New Technology: Organizational and Interorganizational Challenges," in *People and Technology in the Workplace* (Washington, D. C.: National Academy Press, 1991), 15–56.
7. L. K. Trevino, "A Cultural Perspective on Changing and Developing Organizational Ethics," *Research in Organizational Change and Development* 4 (1990): 195–230.
8. D. Nadler, "Organizational Frame-Bending: Types of Change in the Complex Organization," in R. Kilmann and T. Covin, eds., *Corporate Transformation* (San Francisco: Jossey-Bass, 1988), 66–83.
9. T. D. Jick, *Managing Change* (Homewood, Ill., Irwin, 1993), 3.
10. L. D. Goodstein and W. W. Burke, "Creating Successful Organizational Change," *Organizational Dynamics* (Spring 1991): 4–17.
11. R. M. Kanter, *The Change Masters* (New York: Simon and Schuster, 1983).
12. M. Beer, *Organization Change and Development: A Systems View* (Santa Monica, Calif.: Goodyear, 1980), 78.
13. J. W. Brehm, *A Theory of Psychological Reactance* (New York: Academic Press, 1966).
14. S. Zuboff, "New Worlds of Computer-Mediated Work," *Harvard Business Review* 60 (1982): 142–152.

15. D. L. Nelson and M. A. White, "Management of Technological Innovation: Individual Attitudes, Stress, and Work Group Attributes," *Journal of High Technology Management Research* 1 (1990): 137–148.

16. T. G. Cummings and E. F. Huse, *Organizational Development and Change* (St. Paul: West, 1989).

17. R. K. Reger, J. V. Mullane, L. T. Gustafson, and S. M. De-Marie, "Creating Earthquakes to Change Organizational Mindsets," *Academy of Management Executive* 8 (1994): 31–46.

18. L. Coch and J. P. French, "Overcoming Resistance to Change," *Human Relations* 1 (1948): 512–532.

19. Connecticut Mutual Life Insurance Company and the U.S. Chamber of Commerce, *Strengthening America's Competitiveness: Resource Management Insights for Small Business Success* (New York: Warner Books, 1991), 4–5.

20. J. P. Kotter and L. A. Schlesinger, "Choosing Strategies for Change," *Harvard Business Review* 57 (1979): 109–112.

21. W. Bridges, *Transitions: Making Sense of Life's Changes* (Reading, Mass.: Addison-Wesley, 1980).

22. H. Woodward and S. Buchholz, *Aftershock: Helping People through Corporate Change* (New York: Wiley, 1987).

23. K. Lewin, "Frontiers in Group Dynamics," *Human Relations* 1 (1947): 5–41.

24. M. Beer and E. Walton, "Developing the Competitive Organization: Interventions and Strategies," *American Psychologist* 45 (1990): 154–161.

25. A. B. Fisher, "When Will Women Get to the Top?" *Fortune,* 21 September 1992, 44–56.

26. W. L. French and C. H. Bell, *Organization Development: Behavioral Science Interventions for Organization Improvement,* 4th ed. (Englewood Cliffs, N.J.: Prentice-Hall, 1990).

27. A. O. Manzini, *Organizational Diagnosis* (New York: AMA-COM, 1988).

28. H. Levinson, *Organizational Diagnosis* (Cambridge, Mass.: Harvard University Press, 1972).

29. J. Nicholas, "The Comparative Impact of Organization Development Interventions," *Academy of Management Review* 7 (1982): 531–542.

30. C. Cammann, M. Fichman, G. D. Jenkins, and J. Klesh, "Assessing the Attitudes and Perceptions of Organization Members," in S. Seashore, E. Lawler III, P. Mirvis, and C. Cammann, eds., *Assessing Organizational Change: A Guide to Methods, Measures, and Practices* (New York: Wiley, 1983), 71–138.

31. G. Odiorne, *Management by Objectives* (Marshfield, Mass. Pitman, 1965).

32. L. L. Berry and A. Parasuraman, "Prescriptions for a Service Quality Revolution in America," *Organizational Dynamics* 20 (1992): 5–15.

33. Five Companies Win 1992 Baldrige Quality Awards," *Business America,* 2 November 1992, 7–16.

34. W. G. Dyer, *Team Building: Issues and Alternatives,* 2d ed. (Reading, Mass., Addison-Wesley, 1987).

35. E. Stephan, G. Mills, R. W. Pace, and L. Ralphs, "HRD in the Fortune 500: A Survey," *Training and Development Journal* (January 1988): 26–32.

36. R. Swezey and E. Salas, eds., *Teams: Their Training and Performance* (Norwood, N.J.: Ablex, 1991).

37. M. Whitmire and P. R. Nienstedt, "Lead Leaders into the '90s," *Personnel Journal* (May 1991): 80–85.

38. E. Schein, Its Role in Organization Development, vol. 1 of *Process Consultation* (Reading, Mass:, Addison-Wesley, 1988).

39. J. Campbell and M. Dunnette, "Effectiveness of T-Group Experiences in Managerial Training and Development," *Psychological Bulletin* 70 (1968): 73–103.

40. R. W. Revans, *Action Learning* (London: Blonde and Briggs, 1980).

41. I. O. Goldstein, *Training in Organizations,* 3d ed. (Pacific Grove, Calif., Brooks/Cole, 1993).

42. C. Steinburg, "Taking Charge of Change," *Training and Development* (March 1992): 26–32.

43. P. E. Connor and L. K. Lake, *Managing Organizational Change* (New York: Praeger, 1988).

44. R. L. Lowman, "Ethical Human Resource Practice in Organizational Settings," in D. W. Bray, ed., *Working with Organizations* (New York: Guilford Press, 1991).

45. R. A. Guzzo, R. D. Jette, and R. A. Katzell, "The Effects of Psychologically Based Intervention Programs on Worker Productivity," *Personnel Psychology* 38 (1985): 275–291.

46. T. Covin and R. H. Kilmann, "Participant Perceptions of Positive and Negative Influences on Large-Scale Change," *Group and Organization Studies* 15 (1990): 233–248.

NAME INDEX

SUBJECT INDEX